Autodesk® Revit® 2020 Architecture Fundamentals

ASCENT – Center for Technical Knowledge®

SDC PUBLICATIONS

SDC Publications
P.O. Box 1334
Mission KS 66222
913-262-2664
www.SDCpublications.com
Publisher: Stephen Schroff

ISBN-13: 978-1-63057-277-8
ISBN-10: 1-63057-277-2

Printed and bound in the United States of America.

Contents

Introduction to BIM and Autodesk Revit

Design Development Phase

Construction Documents Phase

Preface

The Autodesk® Revit® software is a powerful Building Information Modeling (BIM) program that works the way architects think. The program streamlines the design process through the use of a central 3D model, where changes made in one view update across all views and on the printable sheets.

The objective of the *Autodesk® Revit® 2020: Fundamentals for Architecture* guide is to enable you to create a full 3D architectural project model including walls, doors, windows, components, floors, ceilings, roofs, stairs, the basic tools that the majority of architectural users need. This includes how to navigate the user interface and use the basic drawing, editing, and viewing tools.The final part of the course focuses on creating construction documents.

Topics Covered

- Understanding the purpose of BIM and how it is applied in the Autodesk Revit software.
- Navigating the Autodesk Revit workspace and interface.
- Working with the basic sketching and modifying tools.
- Linking CAD and Revit files as the basis of a project.
- Creating Levels and Grids as datum elements for the model.
- Creating a 3D building model with walls, curtain walls, windows, and doors.
- Adding component features, such as furniture and equipment.
- Adding floors, ceilings, and roofs to the building model.
- Modeling stairs, railings, and ramps.
- Setting up sheets for plotting with text, dimensions, details, tags, and schedules.
- Creating details.

Prerequisites

- An understanding of architectural terminology is an asset.
- Access to the 2020 version of the software. The practices and files included with this guide might not be compatible with prior versions.

Note on Software Setup

This guide assumes a standard installation of the software using the default preferences during installation. Lectures and practices use the standard software templates and default options for the Content Libraries.

Students and Educators can Access Free Autodesk Software and Resources

Autodesk challenges you to get started with free educational licenses for professional software and creativity apps used by millions of architects, engineers, designers, and hobbyists today. Bring Autodesk software into your classroom, studio, or workshop to learn, teach, and explore real-world design challenges the way professionals do.

Get started today - register at the Autodesk Education Community and download one of the many Autodesk software applications available.

Visit www.autodesk.com/education/home/

Note: Free products are subject to the terms and conditions of the end-user license and services agreement that accompanies the software. The software is for personal use for education purposes and is not intended for classroom or lab use.

Lead Contributor: Martha Hollowell Orcutt

Martha incorporates her passion for building design and education into all her projects, including the training guides she creates on Autodesk Revit for Architecture, MEP, Structure, and landscape design as well as Advance Steel and other related programs. She has worked with Autodesk products since the 1990's and has focused primarily on Autodesk Revit for the last 16 years.

After receiving a B.Sc. in Architecture from the University of Virginia, she worked in architectural offices and consulted with firms setting up and customizing AutoCAD for their companies.

Martha has over 20 years' experience as a trainer and instructional designer. She is skilled in leading individuals and small groups to understand and build on their potential. Martha is trained in Instructional Design and has achieved the Autodesk Certified Professional designation for Revit Architecture.

Martha Hollowell Orcutt has been the Lead Contributor for *Autodesk Revit Fundamentals for Architecture* since its initial release in 2003.

In this Guide

The following images highlight some of the features that can be found in this guide.

Link to the practice files

Practice Files

To download the practice files for this student guide, use the following steps:

1. Type the URL shown below into the address bar of your Internet browser. The URL must be typed **exactly as shown**. If you are using an ASCENT ebook, you can click on the link to download the file.

   Address bar
   http://www.ASCENTed.com/getfile?id=xxxxxxxx
   File Edit View Favorites Tools Help

2. Press <Enter> to download the .ZIP file that contains the Practice Files.
3. Once the download is complete, unzip the file to a local folder. The unzipped file contains an .EXE file.
4. Double-click on the .EXE file and follow the instructions to automatically install the Practice Files on the C:\ drive of your computer.

   Do not change the location in which the Practice Files folder is installed. Doing so can cause errors when completing the practices in this student guide.

http://www.ASCENTed.com/getfile?id=xxxxxxxx

Stay Informed!
Interested in receiving information about upcoming promotional offers, educational events, invitations to complimentary webcasts, and discounts? If so, please visit:
www.ASCENTed.com/updates/

Help us improve our product by completing the following survey:
www.ASCENTed.com/feedback
You can also contact us at: *feedback@ASCENTed.com*

Practice Files

The Practice Files page tells you how to download and install the practice files that are provided with this guide.

Learning Objectives for the chapter

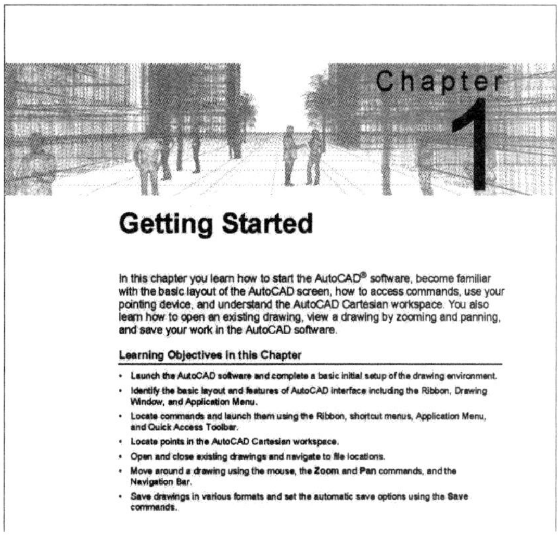

Chapter 1

Getting Started

In this chapter you learn how to start the AutoCAD® software, become familiar with the basic layout of the AutoCAD screen, how to access commands, use your pointing device, and understand the AutoCAD Cartesian workspace. You also learn how to open an existing drawing, view a drawing by zooming and panning, and save your work in the AutoCAD software.

Learning Objectives in this Chapter

- Launch the AutoCAD software and complete a basic initial setup of the drawing environment.
- Identify the basic layout and features of AutoCAD interface including the Ribbon, Drawing Window, and Application Menu.
- Locate commands and launch them using the Ribbon, shortcut menus, Application Menu, and Quick Access Toolbar.
- Locate points in the AutoCAD Cartesian workspace.
- Open and close existing drawings and navigate to file locations.
- Move around a drawing using the mouse, the **Zoom** and **Pan** commands, and the Navigation Bar.
- Save drawings in various formats and set the automatic save options using the **Save** commands.

Chapters

Each chapter begins with a brief introduction and a list of the chapter's Learning Objectives.

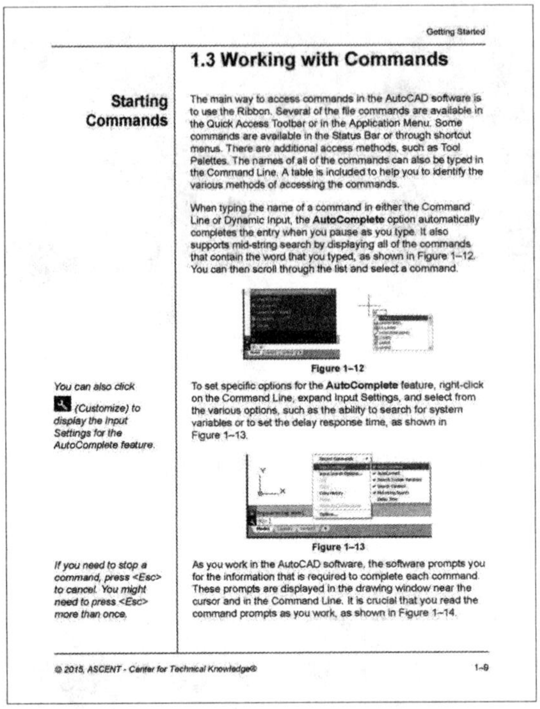

Getting Started

1.3 Working with Commands

Starting Commands

The main way to access commands in the AutoCAD software is to use the Ribbon. Several of the file commands are available in the Quick Access Toolbar or in the Application Menu. Some commands are available in the Status Bar or through shortcut menus. There are additional access methods, such as Tool Palettes. The names of all of the commands can also be typed in the Command Line. A table is included to help you to identify the various methods of accessing the commands.

When typing the name of a command in either the Command Line or Dynamic Input, the **AutoComplete** option automatically completes the entry when you pause as you type. It also supports mid-string search by displaying all of the commands that contain the word that you typed, as shown in Figure 1–12. You can then scroll through the list and select a command.

Figure 1–12

You can also click (Customize) to display the Input Settings for the AutoComplete feature.

To set specific options for the **AutoComplete** feature, right-click on the Command Line, expand Input Settings, and select from the various options, such as the ability to search for system variables or to set the delay response time, as shown in Figure 1–13.

Figure 1–13

If you need to stop a command, press <Esc> to cancel. You might need to press <Esc> more than once.

As you work in the AutoCAD software, the software prompts you for the information that is required to complete each command. These prompts are displayed in the drawing window near the cursor and in the Command Line. It is crucial that you read the command prompts as you work, as shown in Figure 1–14.

© 2015, ASCENT - Center for Technical Knowledge® 1–9

Side notes

Side notes are hints or additional information for the current topic.

Instructional Content

Each chapter is split into a series of sections of instructional content on specific topics. These lectures include the descriptions, step-by-step procedures, figures, hints, and information you need to achieve the chapter's Learning Objectives.

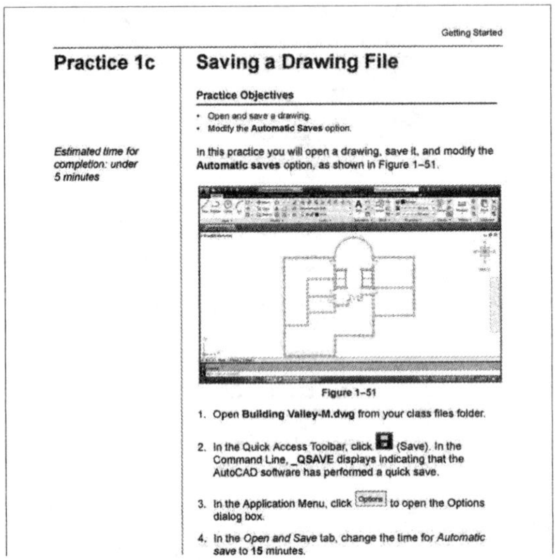

Getting Started

Practice 1c — **Saving a Drawing File**

Practice Objectives

- Open and save a drawing.
- Modify the **Automatic Saves** option.

Estimated time for completion: under 5 minutes

In this practice you will open a drawing, save it, and modify the **Automatic saves** option, as shown in Figure 1–51.

Figure 1–51

1. Open **Building Valley-M.dwg** from your class files folder.
2. In the Quick Access Toolbar, click (Save). In the Command Line, **_QSAVE** displays indicating that the AutoCAD software has performed a quick save.
3. In the Application Menu, click Options to open the Options dialog box.
4. In the *Open and Save* tab, change the time for *Automatic save* to **15** minutes.

Practice Objectives

Practices

Practices enable you to use the software to perform a hands-on review of a topic.

Some practices require you to use prepared practice files, which can be downloaded from the link found on the Practice Files page.

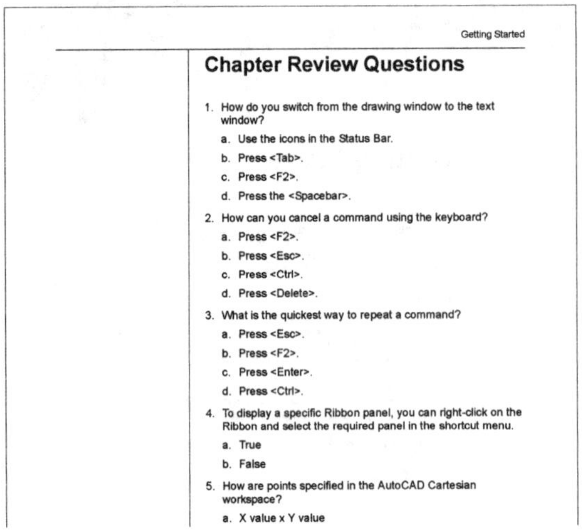

Getting Started

Chapter Review Questions

1. How do you switch from the drawing window to the text window?
   a. Use the icons in the Status Bar.
   b. Press <Tab>.
   c. Press <F2>.
   d. Press the <Spacebar>.
2. How can you cancel a command using the keyboard?
   a. Press <F2>.
   b. Press <Esc>.
   c. Press <Ctrl>.
   d. Press <Delete>.
3. What is the quickest way to repeat a command?
   a. Press <Esc>.
   b. Press <F2>.
   c. Press <Enter>.
   d. Press <Ctrl>.
4. To display a specific Ribbon panel, you can right-click on the Ribbon and select the required panel in the shortcut menu.
   a. True
   b. False
5. How are points specified in the AutoCAD Cartesian workspace?
   a. X value x Y value

Chapter Review Questions

Chapter review questions, located at the end of each chapter, enable you to review the key concepts and learning objectives of the chapter.

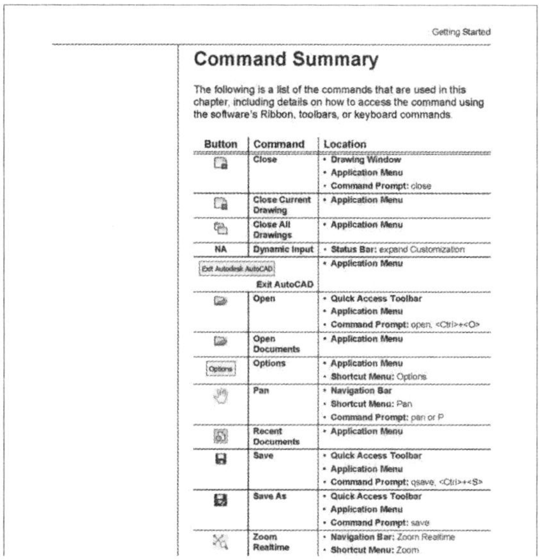

Getting Started

Command Summary

The following is a list of the commands that are used in this chapter, including details on how to access the command using the software's Ribbon, toolbars, or keyboard commands.

Button	Command	Location
	Close	• **Drawing Window** • **Application Menu** • **Command Prompt:** close
	Close Current Drawing	• **Application Menu**
	Close All Drawings	• **Application Menu**
NA	Dynamic Input	• **Status Bar:** expand Customization
Exit Autodesk AutoCAD	Exit AutoCAD	• **Application Menu**
	Open	• **Quick Access Toolbar** • **Application Menu** • **Command Prompt:** open, <Ctrl>+<O>
	Open Documents	• **Application Menu**
Options	Options	• **Application Menu** • **Shortcut Menu:** Options
	Pan	• **Navigation Bar** • **Shortcut Menu:** Pan • **Command Prompt:** pan or P
	Recent Documents	• **Application Menu**
	Save	• **Quick Access Toolbar** • **Application Menu** • **Command Prompt:** qsave, <Ctrl>+<S>
	Save As	• **Quick Access Toolbar** • **Application Menu** • **Command Prompt:** save
	Zoom Realtime	• **Navigation Bar:** Zoom Realtime • **Shortcut Menu:** Zoom

Command Summary

The Command Summary is located at the end of each chapter. It contains a list of the software commands that are used throughout the chapter, and provides information on where the command is found in the software.

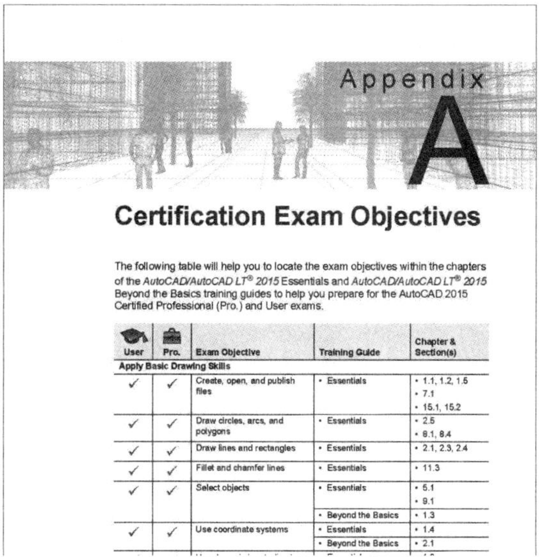

Appendix A

Certification Exam Objectives

The following table will help you to locate the exam objectives within the chapters of the *AutoCAD/AutoCAD LT® 2015* Essentials and *AutoCAD/AutoCAD LT® 2015* Beyond the Basics training guides to help you prepare for the AutoCAD 2015 Certified Professional (Pro.) and User exams.

User	Pro.	Exam Objective	Training Guide	Chapter & Section(s)
Apply Basic Drawing Skills				
✓	✓	Create, open, and publish files	• Essentials	• 1.1, 1.2, 1.5 • 7.1 • 15.1, 15.2
✓	✓	Draw circles, arcs, and polygons	• Essentials	• 2.5 • 8.1, 8.4
✓	✓	Draw lines and rectangles	• Essentials	• 2.1, 2.3, 2.4
✓	✓	Fillet and chamfer lines	• Essentials	• 11.3
✓	✓	Select objects	• Essentials	• 5.1 • 9.1
			• Beyond the Basics	• 1.3
✓	✓	Use coordinate systems	• Essentials	• 1.4
			• Beyond the Basics	• 2.1

Autodesk Certification Exam Appendix

This appendix includes a list of the topics and objectives for the Autodesk Certification exams, and the chapter and section in which the relevant content can be found.

Practice Files

To download the practice files for this guide, use the following steps:

1. Type the URL shown below into the address bar of your Internet browser. The URL must be typed **exactly as shown**.

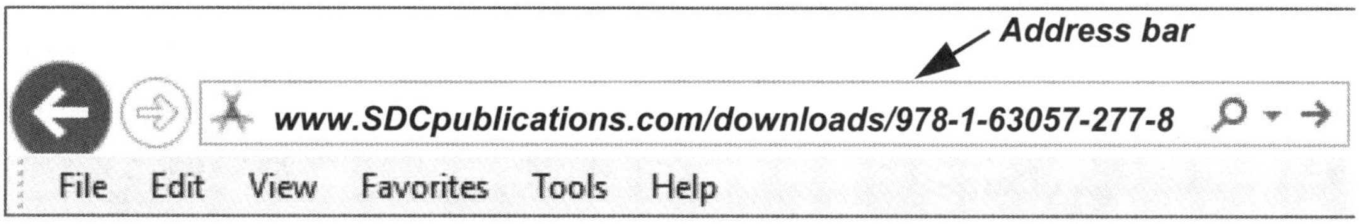

2. Press <Enter> to download the .ZIP file that contains the practice files.
3. Once the download is complete, unzip the file to a local folder. The unzipped file contains an .EXE file.
4. Double-click on the .EXE file and follow the instructions to automatically install the practice files on the C:\ drive of your computer.

   Do not change the location in which the practice files folder is installed. Doing so can cause errors when completing the practices.

   The default practice files folder location is:
   C:\Revit 2020 Fundamentals for Architecture Practice Files

www.SDCpublications.com/downloads/978-1-63057-277-8

Introduction to BIM and Autodesk Revit

This guide is divided into three sections: Introduction to BIM and Autodesk Revit, Design Development, and Construction Documents.

The first section provides an overview of using Building Information Modeling (BIM) with the Autodesk® Revit® software, working with the software interface, how to use the basic drawing and modify tools, and incorporating datum elements.

This section includes the following chapters:

- Chapter 1: Introduction to BIM and Autodesk Revit
- Chapter 2: Basic Sketching and Modify Tools
- Chapter 3: Starting Architectural Projects

Introduction to BIM and Autodesk Revit

Building Information Modeling (BIM) and the Autodesk® Revit® software work hand in hand to help you create smart, 3D models that are useful at all stages in the building process. Understanding the software interface and terminology enhances your ability to create powerful models and move around in the various views of the model.

Learning Objectives in this Chapter

- Describe the concept and workflow of Building Information Modeling in relation to the Autodesk Revit software.
- Navigate the graphic user interface, including the ribbon (where most of the tools are found), the Properties palette (where you make modifications to element information), and the Project Browser (where you can open various views of the model).
- Open existing projects and start new projects using templates.
- Use viewing commands to move around the model in 2D and 3D views.

1.1 BIM and Autodesk Revit

Building Information Modeling (BIM) is an approach to the entire building life cycle, including design, construction, and facilities management. The BIM process supports the ability to coordinate, update, and share design data with team members across disciplines.

The Autodesk Revit software is a true BIM product. It enables you to create complete 3D building models (as shown on the left in Figure 1–1) that provide considerable information reported through construction documents, and enables you to share these models with other programs for more extensive analysis.

The Autodesk® Revit® software includes tools for architectural, mechanical, electrical, plumbing, and structural design.

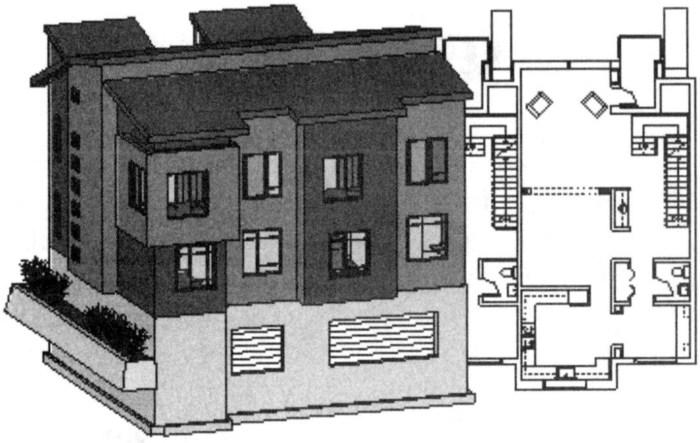

Figure 1–1

The Autodesk Revit software is considered a Parametric Building Modeler:

- *Parametric:* A relationship is established between building elements: when one element changes, other related elements change as well. For example, if you add an element in a plan view, it also displays in all of the other views.
- *Building:* The software is designed for working with buildings and the surrounding landscape, as opposed to gears or highways.
- *Modeler:* A project is built in a single file based on the 3D building model, as shown on the left in Figure 1–1. All views, such as plans (as shown on the right in Figure 1–1), elevations, sections, details, construction documents, and reports are generated based on the model.
- It is important that everyone who is collaborating on a project works in the same version and build of the software.

Workflow and BIM

BIM has changed the process of how a building is planned, budgeted, designed, constructed, and (in some cases) operated and maintained.

In the traditional design process, construction documents are created independently, typically including plans, sections, elevations, details, and notes. Sometimes, a separate 3D model is created in addition to these documents. Changes made in one document, such as the addition of a light fixture in a plan, have to be coordinated with the rest of the documents and schedules in the set, as shown in Figure 1–2.

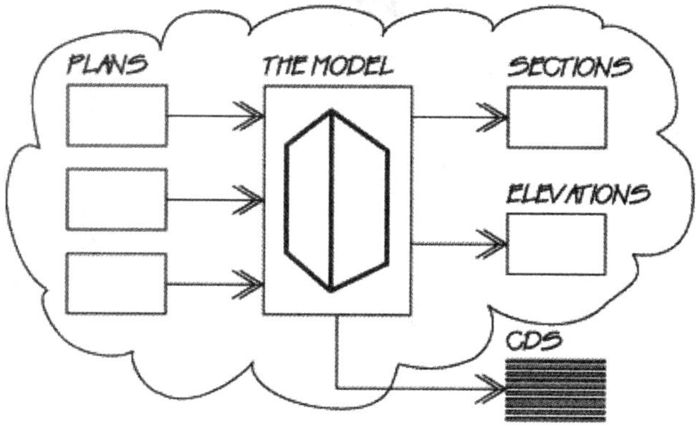

Figure 1–2

In BIM, the design process revolves around the model, as shown in Figure 1–3. Plans, elevations, and sections are simply 2D versions of the 3D model, while and schedules are a report of the information stored in the model. Changes made in one view automatically update in all views and related schedules. Even Construction Documents update automatically with callout tags in sync with the sheet numbers. This is called bidirectional associativity.By creating complete models and associated views of those models, the Autodesk Revit software takes much of the tediousness out of producing a building design.

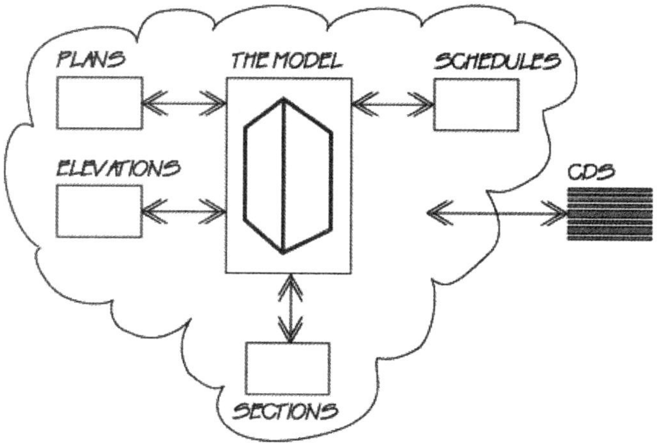

Figure 1–3

Revit Terms

When working in the Autodesk Revit software, it is important to know the typical terms used to describe items. Views and reports display information about the elements that form a project. There are three types of elements: Model, Datum, and View-specific, as shown in Figure 1–4 and described below:

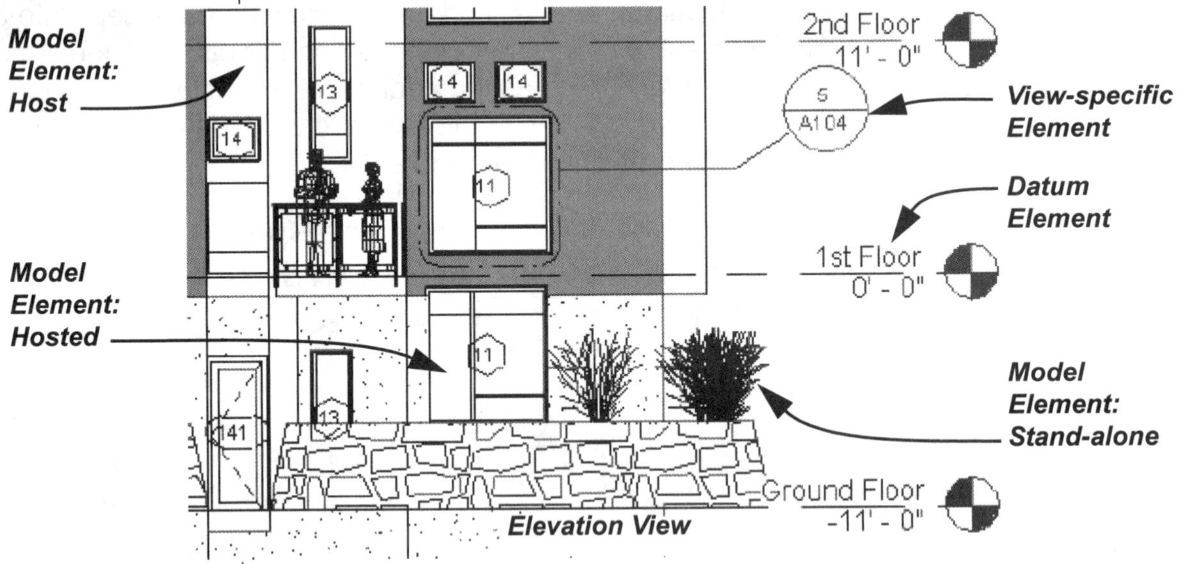

Figure 1–4

Views	Enable you to display and manipulate the model. For example, you can view and work in floor plans, ceiling plans, elevations, sections, schedules, and 3D views. You can change a design from any view. All views are stored in the project.
Reports	Reports, including schedules, gather information from the building model element that can be presented in the construction documents or used for analysis.
Model Elements	Include all parts of a building such as walls, floors, roofs, ceilings, doors, windows, plumbing fixtures, lighting fixtures, mechanical equipment, columns, beams, furniture, plants and many more. • Host elements support other categories of elements. • Hosted elements must be attached to a host element. • Standalone elements do not require hosts.
Datum Elements	Define the project context such as the levels for the floors and other vertical distances, column grids, and reference planes.
View-specific Elements	Only display in the view in which they are placed. The view scale controls their size. These include annotation elements such as dimensions, text, tags, and symbols as well as detail elements such as detail lines, filled regions, and 2D detail components.

- Autodesk Revit elements are "smart": the software recognizes them as walls, columns, plants, ducts, or lighting fixtures. This means that the information stored in their properties automatically updates in schedules, which ensures that views and reports are coordinated across an entire project, and are generated from a single model.

Revit and Construction Documents

In the traditional workflow, the most time-consuming part of the project is the construction documents. With BIM, the base views of those documents (i.e., plans, elevations, sections, and schedules) are produced automatically and update as the model is updated, saving hours of work. The views are then placed on sheets that form the construction document set.

For example, a floor plan is duplicated. Then, in the new view, all but the required categories of elements are hidden or set to halftone and annotations are added. The plan is then placed on a sheet, as shown in Figure 1–5.

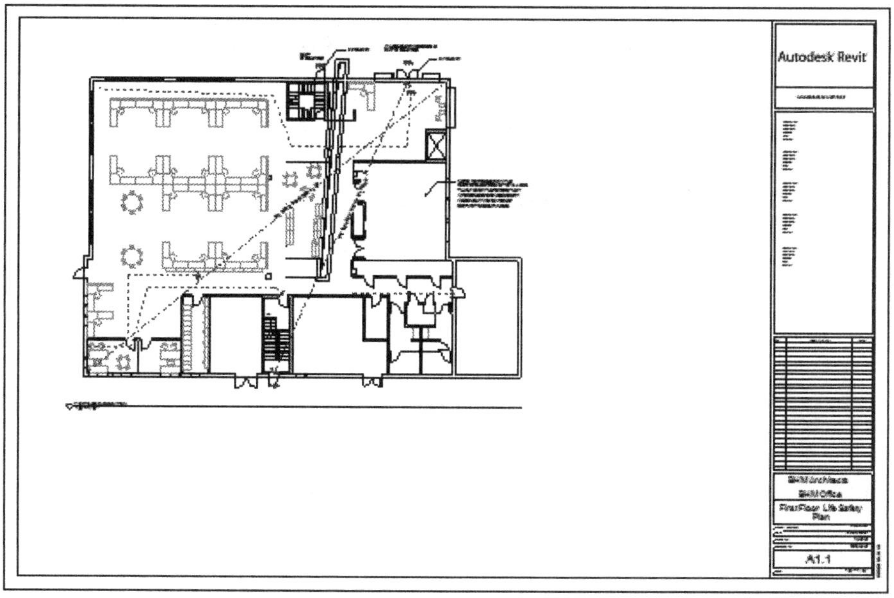

Figure 1–5

- Work can continue on a view and is automatically updated on the sheet.

- Annotating views in the preliminary design phase is often not required. You might be able to wait until you are further along in the project.

1.2 Overview of the Interface

The Autodesk Revit interface is designed for intuitive and efficient access to commands and views. It includes the ribbon, Quick Access Toolbar, Navigation Bar, and Status Bar, which are common to most of the Autodesk® software. It also includes tools that are specific to the Autodesk Revit software, including the Properties Palette, Project Browser, and View Control Bar. The interface is shown in Figure 1–6.

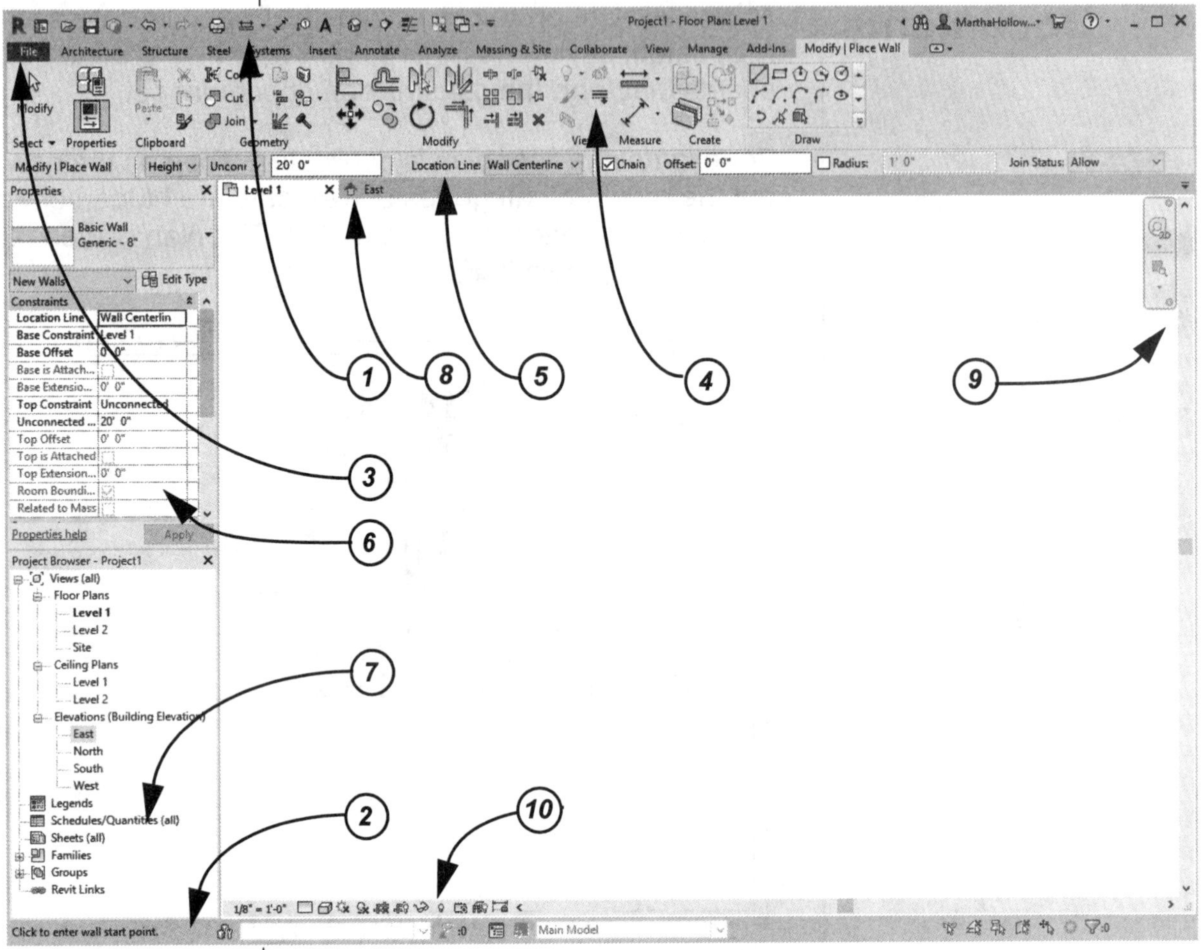

Figure 1–6

1. Quick Access Toolbar	6. Properties Palette
2. Status Bar	7. Project Browser
3. File tab	8. View Tabs
4. Ribbon	9. Navigation Bar
5. Options Bar	10. View Control Bar

The Home Screen

When you first open the Autodesk Revit software, the **Home** screen displays, showing recently used projects and families, as well as links to BIM 360 files, as shown in Figure 1–7.

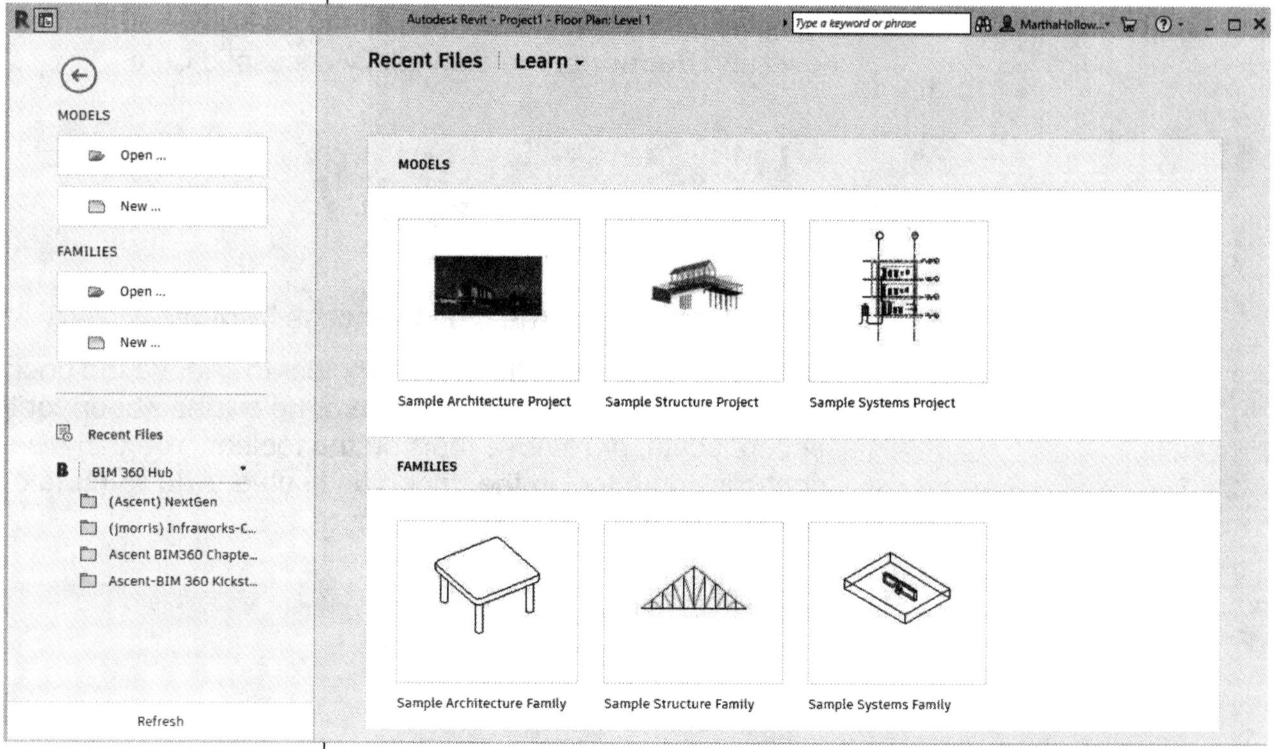

Figure 1–7

- Click on the picture to open a recent project. Hover over the name of the file, to display additional information.
- In the Quick Access Toolbar, click (Home) to return to the screen.
- In the Home screen, click (Back) to return to the active model.
- Press **<Ctrl>+D** to toggle between the Home screen and active model.

1. Quick Access Toolbar

The Quick Access Toolbar (shown in Figure 1–8) includes commonly used commands, such as **Home, Open**, **Save**, **Undo**, **Redo,** and **Print**. It also includes frequently used annotation tools, including Measuring tools, **Aligned Dimension**, **Tag by Category**, and **Text**. Viewing tools, including several different 3D Views and **Sections**, are also easily accessed here.

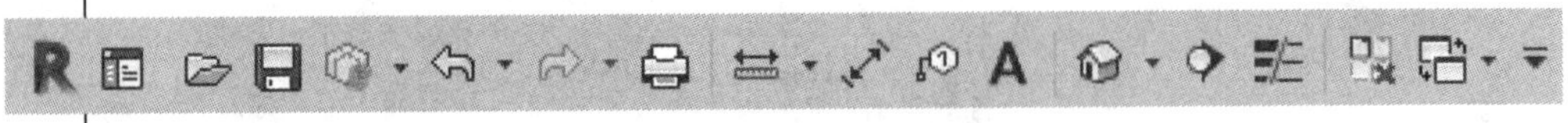

Figure 1–8

Hint: Customizing the Quick Access Toolbar

Right-click on the Quick Access Toolbar to change the docked location of the toolbar to be above or below the ribbon, or to add, relocate, or remove tools on the toolbar. You can also right-click on a tool in the ribbon and select **Add to Quick Access Toolbar**, as shown in Figure 1–9.

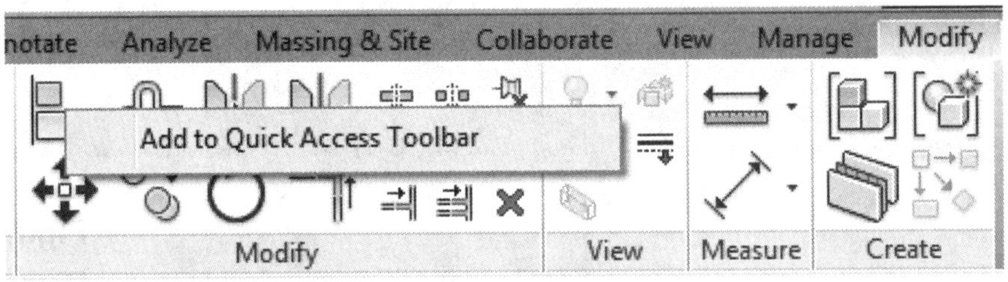

Figure 1–9

The top toolbar also hosts the InfoCenter (as shown in Figure 1–10) which includes the Autodesk A360 sign-in, access to the Autodesk App Store, and Help options. A search field, as shown in Figure 1–11, is also available to find help on the web

Figure 1–10

Click here to expand or collapse the search field.

Figure 1–11

2. Status Bar

The Status Bar provides information about the current process, such as the next step for a command, as shown in Figure 1–12.

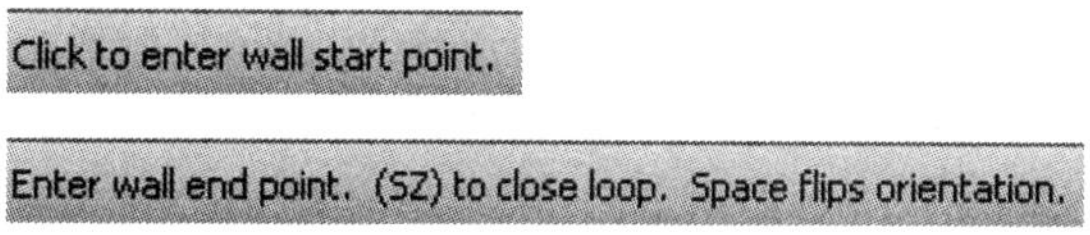

Figure 1–12

Other options in the Status Bar are related to Worksets and Design Options (advanced tools) as well as selection methods and filters.

Hint: Shortcut Menus

Shortcut menus help you to work smoothly and efficiently by enabling you to quickly access required commands. These menus provide access to basic viewing commands, recently used commands, and the available Browsers, as shown in Figure 1–13. Additional options vary depending on the element or command that you are using.

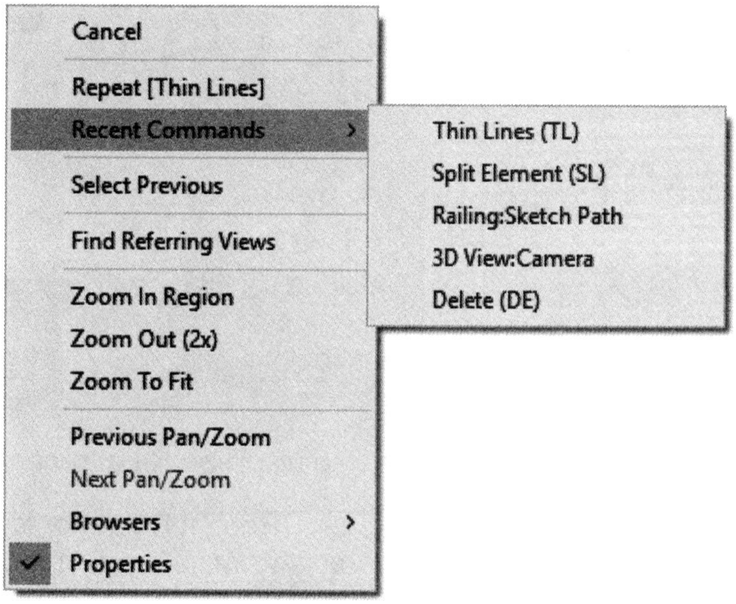

Figure 1–13

3.File Tab

The *File* tab of the ribbon provides access to file commands, settings, and documents, as shown in Figure 1–14. Hover the cursor over a command to display a list of additional tools.

If you click the primary icon, rather than the arrow, it starts the default command.

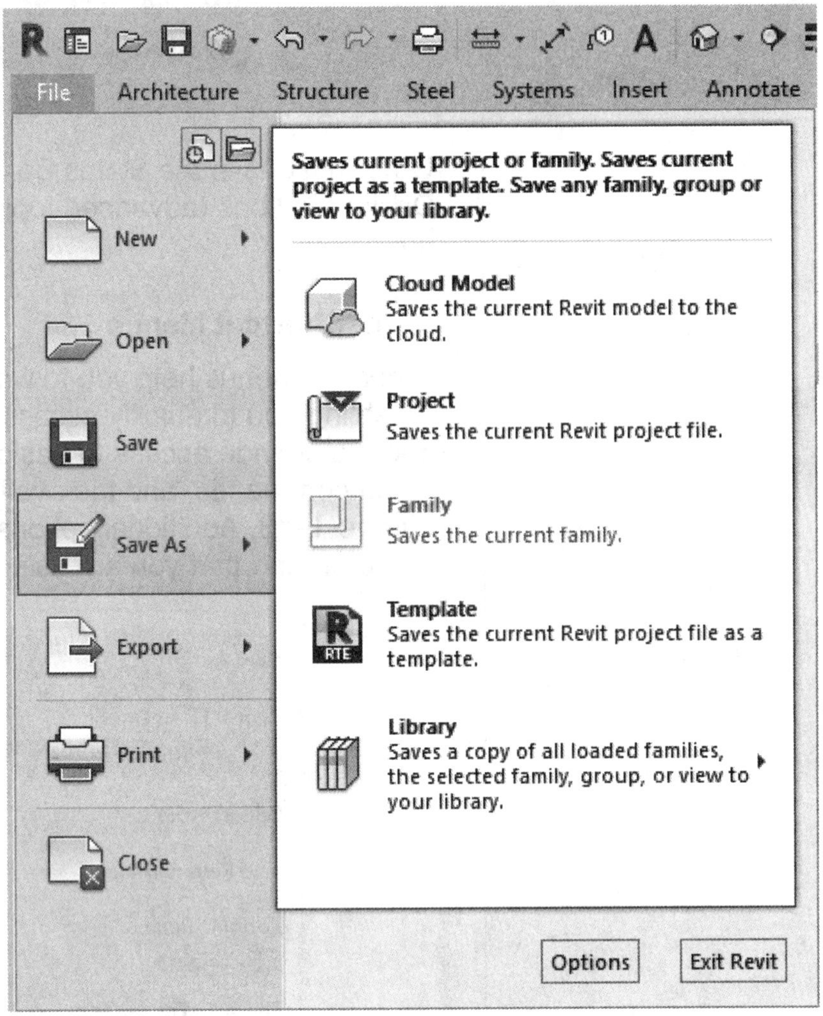

Figure 1–14

- To display a list of recently used documents, click (Recent Documents). The documents can be reordered as shown in Figure 1–15.

Click (Pin) next to a document name to keep it available.

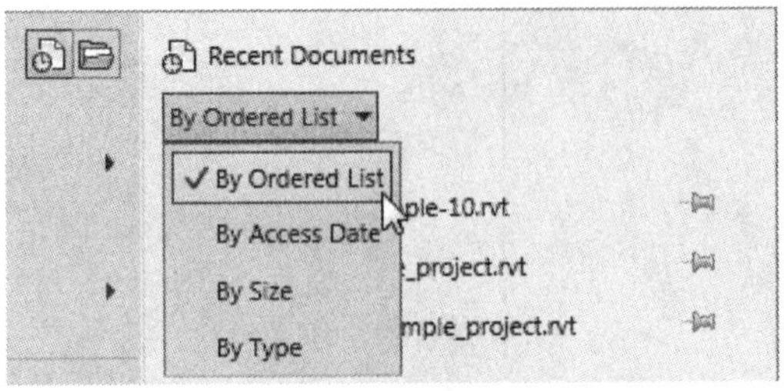

Figure 1–15

You can use the Open Documents list to change between views.

- To display a list of open documents and views, click (Open Documents). The list displays the documents and views that are open, as shown in Figure 1–16.

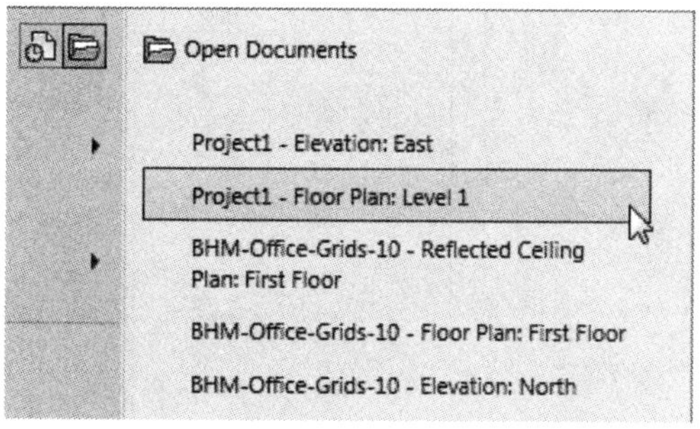

Figure 1–16

- Click (Close) to close the current project.

At the bottom of the menu, click **Options** to open the Options dialog box or click **Exit Revit** to exit the software.

4. Ribbon

The ribbon contains tools in a series of tabs and panels as shown in Figure 1–17. Selecting a tab displays a group of related panels. The panels contain a variety of tools, grouped by task.

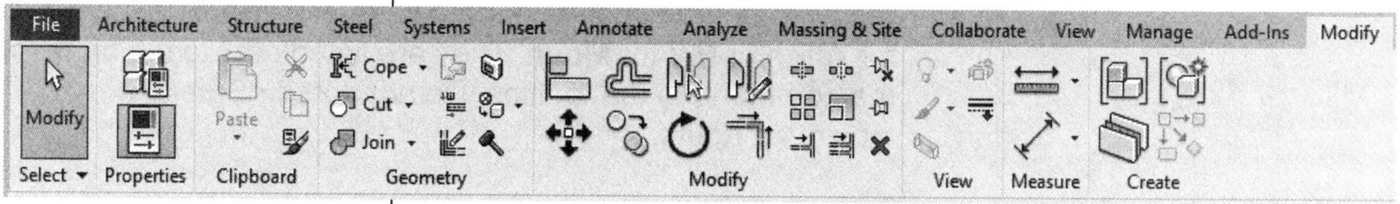

Figure 1–17

When you start a command that creates new elements or you select an element, the ribbon displays the *Modify | contextual* tab. This contains general editing commands and command specific tools, as shown in Figure 1–18.

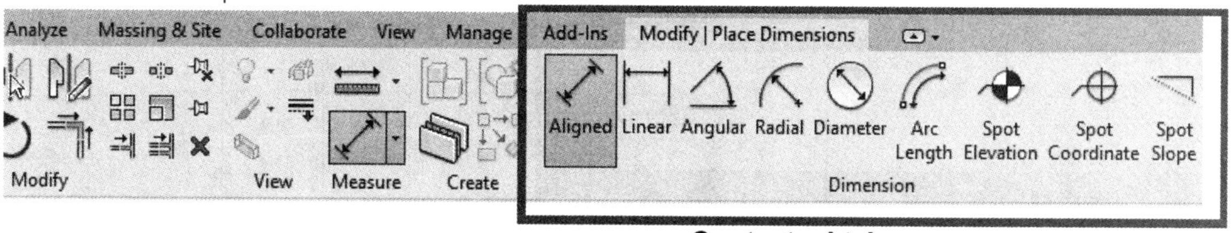

Contextual tab

Figure 1–18

- When you hover over a tool on the ribbon, tooltips display the tool's name and a short description. If you continue hovering over the tool, a graphic displays (and sometimes a video), as shown in Figure 1–19.

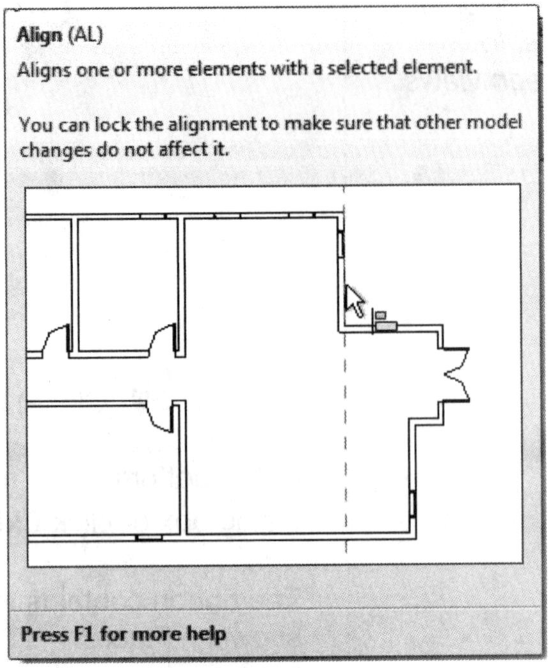

Figure 1–19

- Many commands have shortcut keys. For example, type **AL** for **Align** or **MV** for **Move**. They are listed next to the name of the command in the tooltips. Do not press <Enter> when typing shortcuts.

- To arrange the order in which the ribbon tabs are displayed, select the tab, hold <Ctrl>, and drag it to a new location. The location is remembered when you restart the software.

- Any panel can be dragged by its title into the view window to become a floating panel. Click the **Return Panels to Ribbon** button (as shown in Figure 1–20) to reposition the panel in the ribbon.

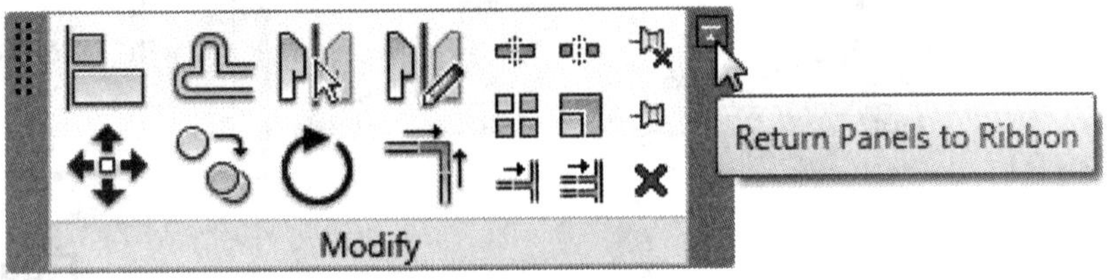

Figure 1–20

Hint: You are always in a command when using the Autodesk Revit software.

When you are finished working with a tool, you typically default back to the **Modify** command. To end a command, use one of the following methods:

- In any tab on the ribbon, click (Modify).
- Press <Esc> once or twice to revert to **Modify**.
- Right-click and select **Cancel...** once or twice.
- Start another command.

5. Options Bar

The Options Bar displays options that are related to the selected command or element. For example, when the **Rotate** command is active it displays options for rotating the selected elements, as shown at the top in Figure 1–21. When the **Place Dimensions** command is active it displays dimension related options, as shown at the bottom in .

Options Bar for Rotate Command

Options Bar for Dimension Command

Figure 1–21

6. Properties Palette

The Properties palette contains several parts, as shown in Figure 1–22. The Type Selector can be found at the top, which enables you to choose the size or style of the element you are adding or modifying. The options available on the palette enable you to make changes to information (parameters). There are two types of properties:

- **Instance Properties** are set for the individual element(s) you are creating or modifying.
- **Type Properties** control options for all elements of the same type. If you modify these parameter values, all elements of the selected type change.

*The Properties palette is usually kept open while working on a project to easily permit changes at any time. If it does not display, in the Modify tab>Properties panel, click (Properties) or type **PP**.*

Some parameters are only available when you are editing an element. They are grayed out when unavailable.

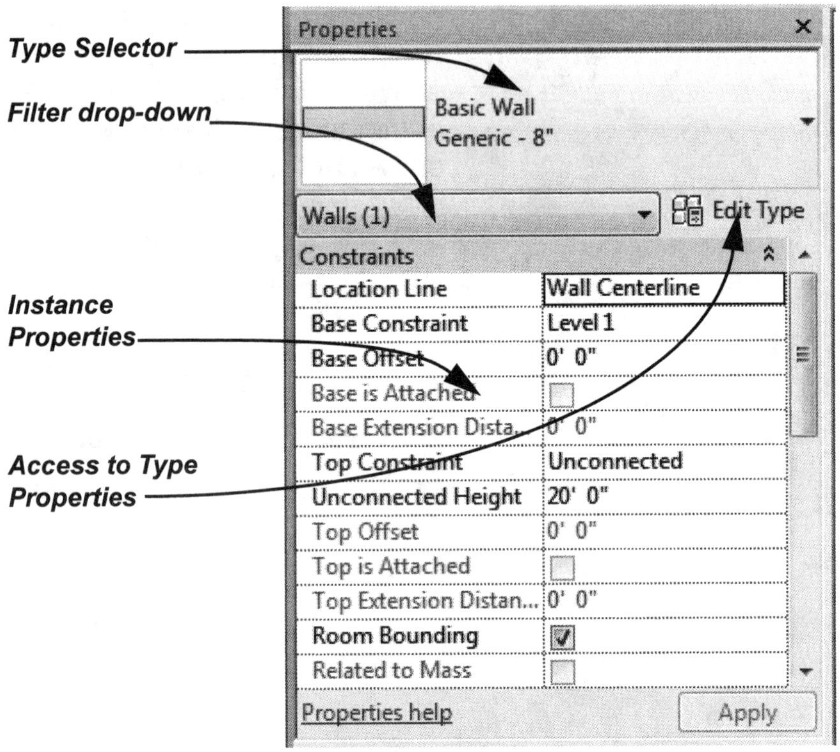

Figure 1–22

- Options for the current view display if the **Modify** command is active, but you have not selected an element.
- If a command or element is selected, the options for the associated element display.
- You can save the changes by either moving the cursor off of the palette, or by pressing <Enter>, or by clicking **Apply**.

- When you start a command or select an element, you can set the element type in the Type Selector, as shown in Figure 1–23.

You can limit what shows in the drop-down list by typing in the search box.

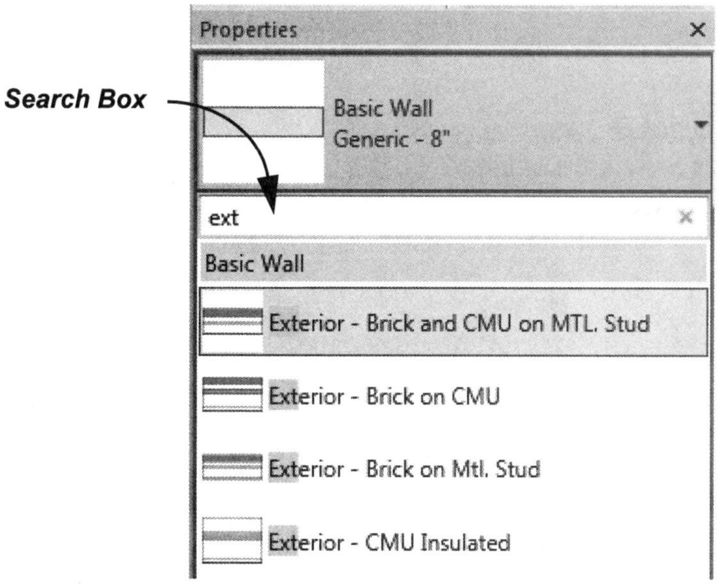

Figure 1–23

- When multiple elements are selected, you can filter the type of elements that display using the drop-down list, as shown in Figure 1–24.

The Properties palette can be placed on a second monitor, or floated, resized, and docked on top of the Project Browser or other dockable palettes, as shown in Figure 1–25. Click the tab to display its associated panel.

7. Project Browser

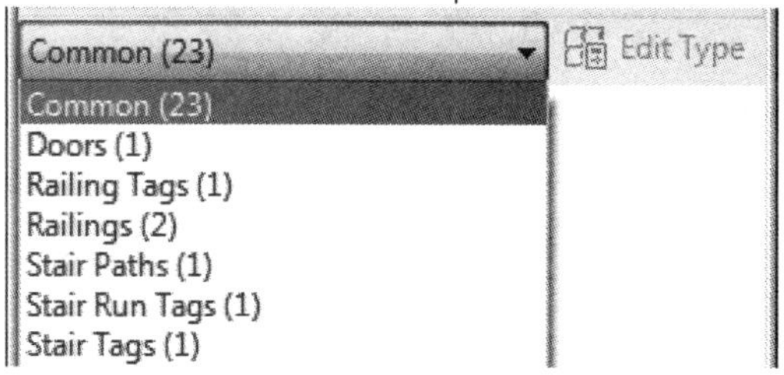

Figure 1–24

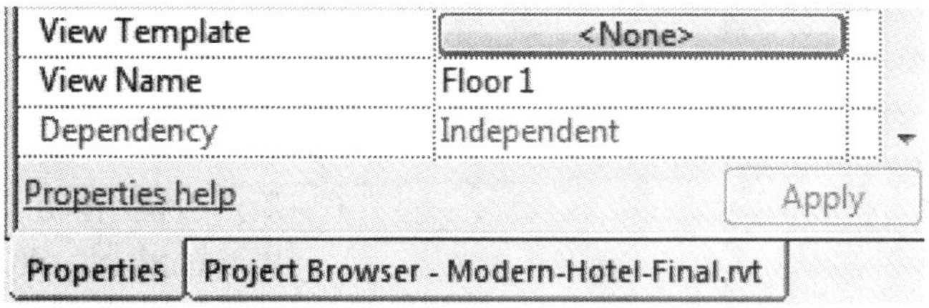

Figure 1–25

The Project Browser displays the name of the active project.

The Project Browser lists all views of the model in which you can work (as shown in Figure 1–26) and any additional views that you create, such as floor plans, ceiling plans, 3D views, elevations, sections, etc. It also includes schedules, legends, sheets (for plotting), lists of families by category, groups, and Autodesk Revit Links.

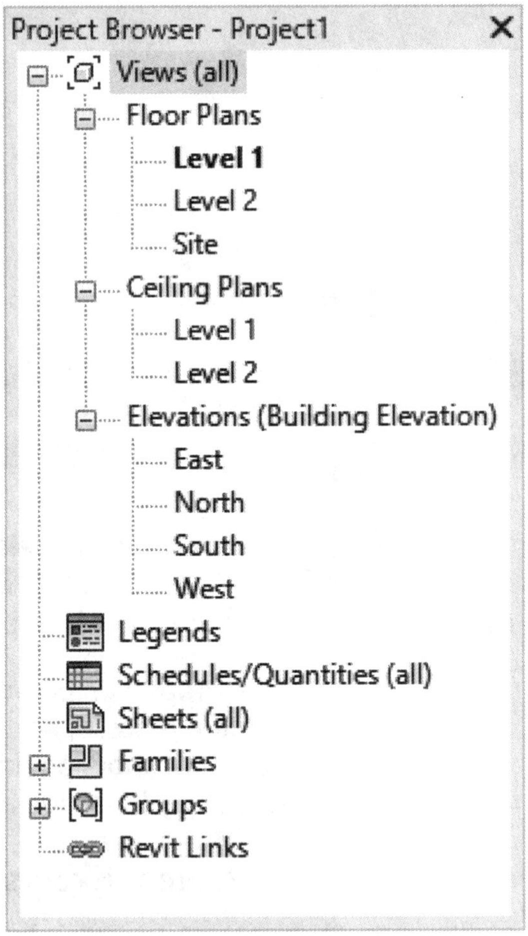

Figure 1–26

- To open a view, double-click on the view name or right-click and select **Open**.
- To rename a view, slowly double-click on the view name and the text highlights as shown in Figure 1–27. You can also right-click on a view name and select **Rename...** or press <F2>.

To display the views associated with a view type, click (Expand) next to the section name. To hide the views in the section, click (Collapse). You can also expand and collapse sets using the shortcut menu, as shown in Figure 1–28.

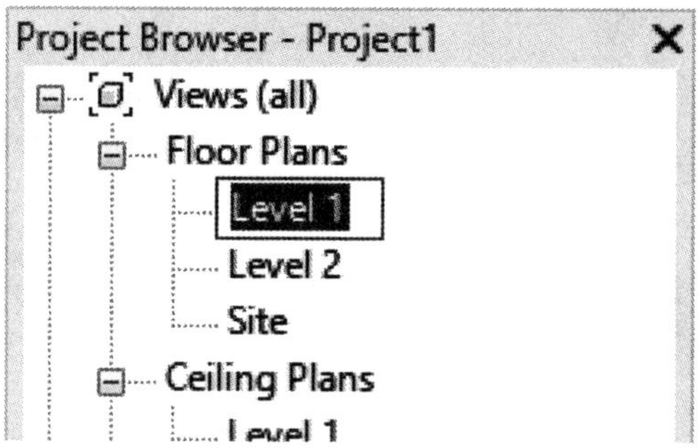

Figure 1–27

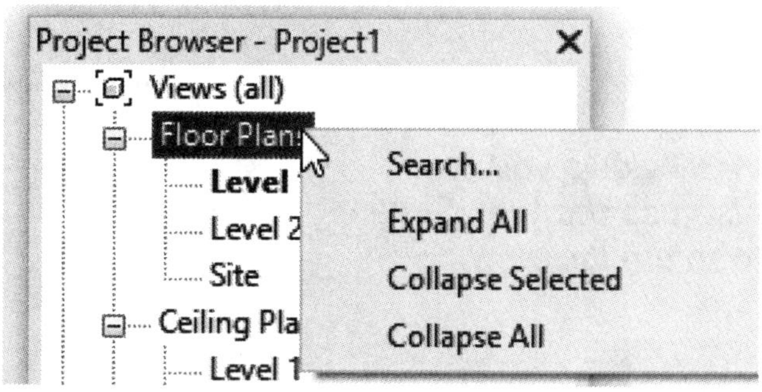

Figure 1–28

- If you no longer require a view, you can remove it. Right-click on its name in the Project Browser and select **Delete**.
- The Project Browser can be floated, resized, docked on top of the Properties palette, and customized.

How To: Search the Project Browser

1. In the Project Browser, right-click on a view type (not a view name) and select **Search...**.
2. In the Search in Project Browser dialog box, type the words that you want to find (as shown in Figure 1–29), and click **Next**.
3. In the Project Browser, the first instance of that search displays, as shown in Figure 1–30.

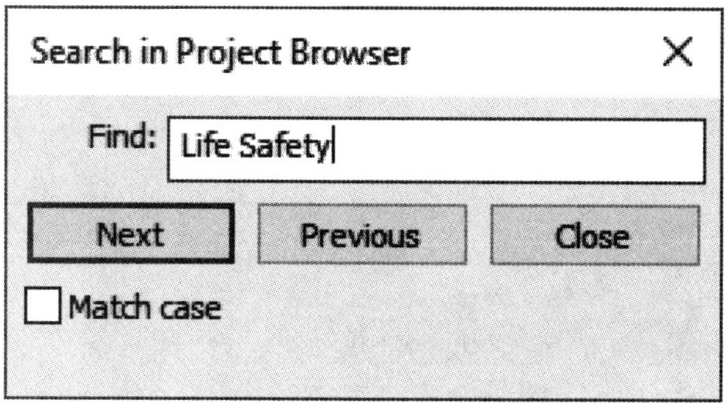

Figure 1–29

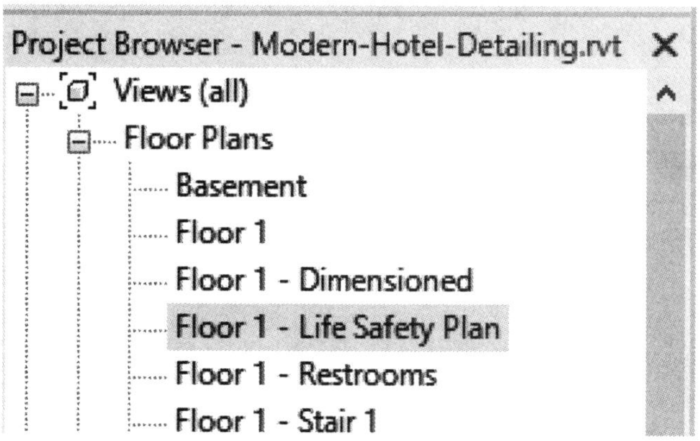

Figure 1–30

4. Continue using **Next** and **Previous** to move through the list.
5. Click **Close** when you are done.

8. View Tabs

Each view of a project opens in its own tab. Each view displays a Navigation Bar (for quick access to viewing tools) and the View Control Bar, as shown in Figure 1–31. You can drag tabs to other monitors.

In 3D views you can also use the ViewCube to rotate the view.

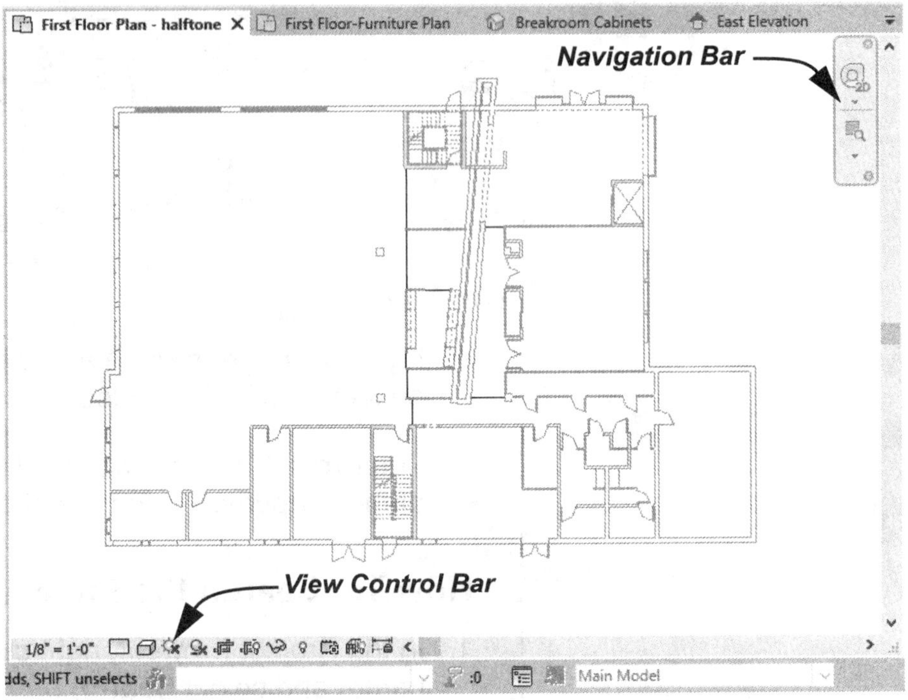

Figure 1–31

- Click on the tab to switch between views. You can also:
  - Press <Ctrl>+<Tab>.
  - Select the view in the Project Browser.
  - In the Quick Access Toolbar or *View* tab>Windows panel, expand  (Switch Windows) and select the view from the list.
  - Expand the drop-down list at the far end of the tabs, as shown in Figure 1–32.

Figure 1–32

- To close a tab, press the **X** that displays when you hover over the tab or the name in the list, as shown in Figure 1–32.

- To close all open views except the current view, in the Quick Access Toolbar or *View* tab>Windows panel, click (Close Inactive Views). If you have multiple projects open, one view of each project remains open.

- You can switch between tabbed and tiled views, as shown in Figure 1–33. In the *View* tab>Windows panel, click (Tab Views) or (Tile Views).

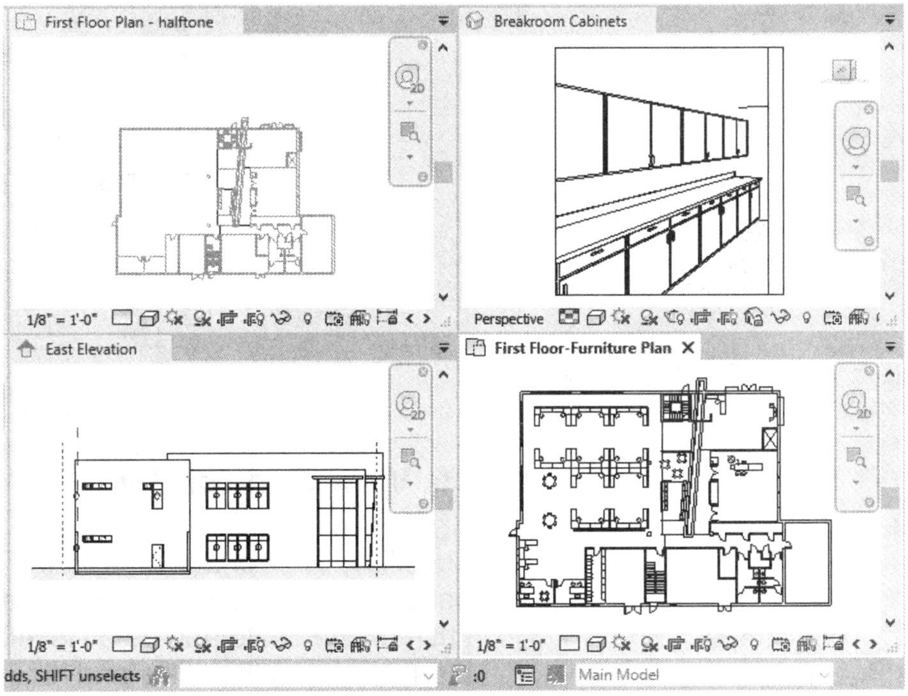

Figure 1–33

Drag the edge of tiled views to resize them. The other views resize to match.

9. Navigation Bar

The Navigation Bar enables you to access various viewing commands, as shown in Figure 1–34.

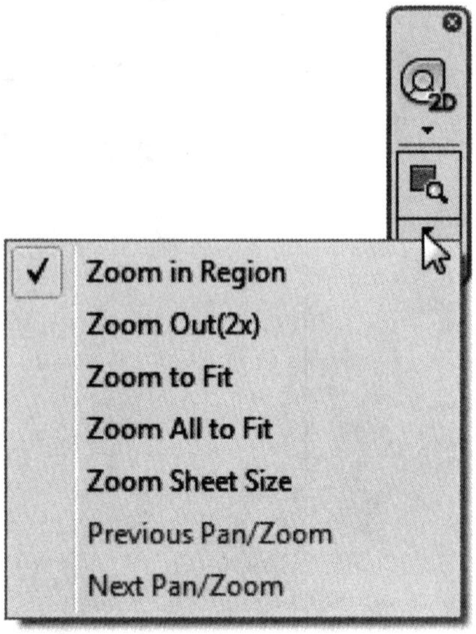

Figure 1–34

10. View Control Bar

The View Control Bar (shown in Figure 1–35), displays at the bottom of each view window. It controls aspects of that view, such as the scale and detail level. It also includes tools that display parts of the view and hide or isolate elements in the view.

Figure 1–35

- The number of options in the View Control Bar change when you are in a 3D view.

1.3 Starting Projects

File operations to open existing files, create new files from a template, and save files in the Autodesk Revit software are found in the *File* tab, as shown in Figure 1–36.

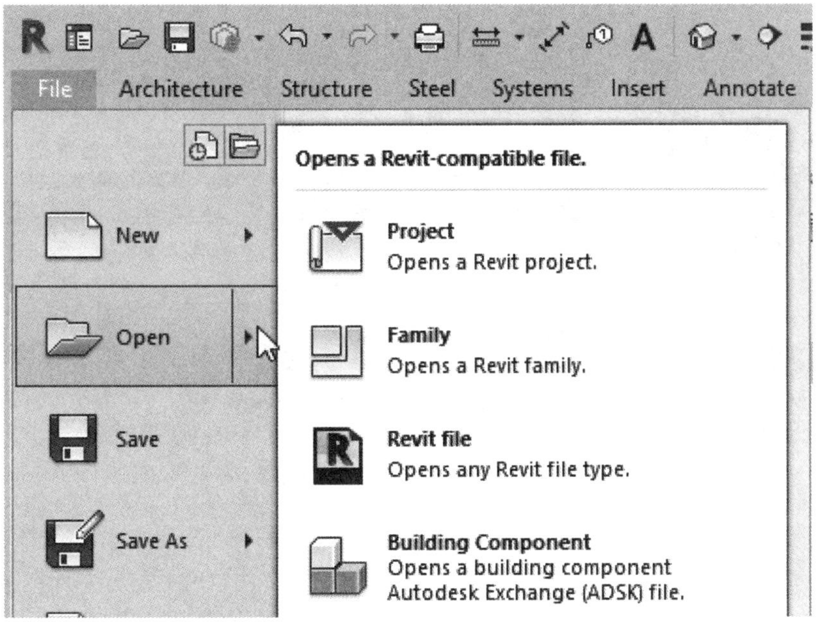

Figure 1–36

There are three main file formats:

- **Project files (.rvt):** These are where you do the majority of your work in the building model by adding elements, creating views, annotating views, and setting up printable sheets. They are initially based on template files.

- **Family files (.rfa):** These are separate components that can be inserted in a project. They include elements that can stand alone (e.g., a table or piece of mechanical equipment) or are items that are hosted in other elements (e.g., a door in a wall or a lighting fixture in a ceiling). Title block and Annotation Symbol files are special types of family files.

- **Template files (.rte and .rft):** These are the base files for any new project or family. Project templates hold standard information and settings for creating new project files. The software includes several templates for various types of projects. You can also create custom templates. Family templates include base information for creating families. Template files are usually saved as a new file.

Opening Projects

To open an existing project, in the Quick Access Toolbar or *File* tab click  (Open), or press <Ctrl>+<O>. The Open dialog box opens (as shown in Figure 1–37), in which you can navigate to the required folder and select a project file.

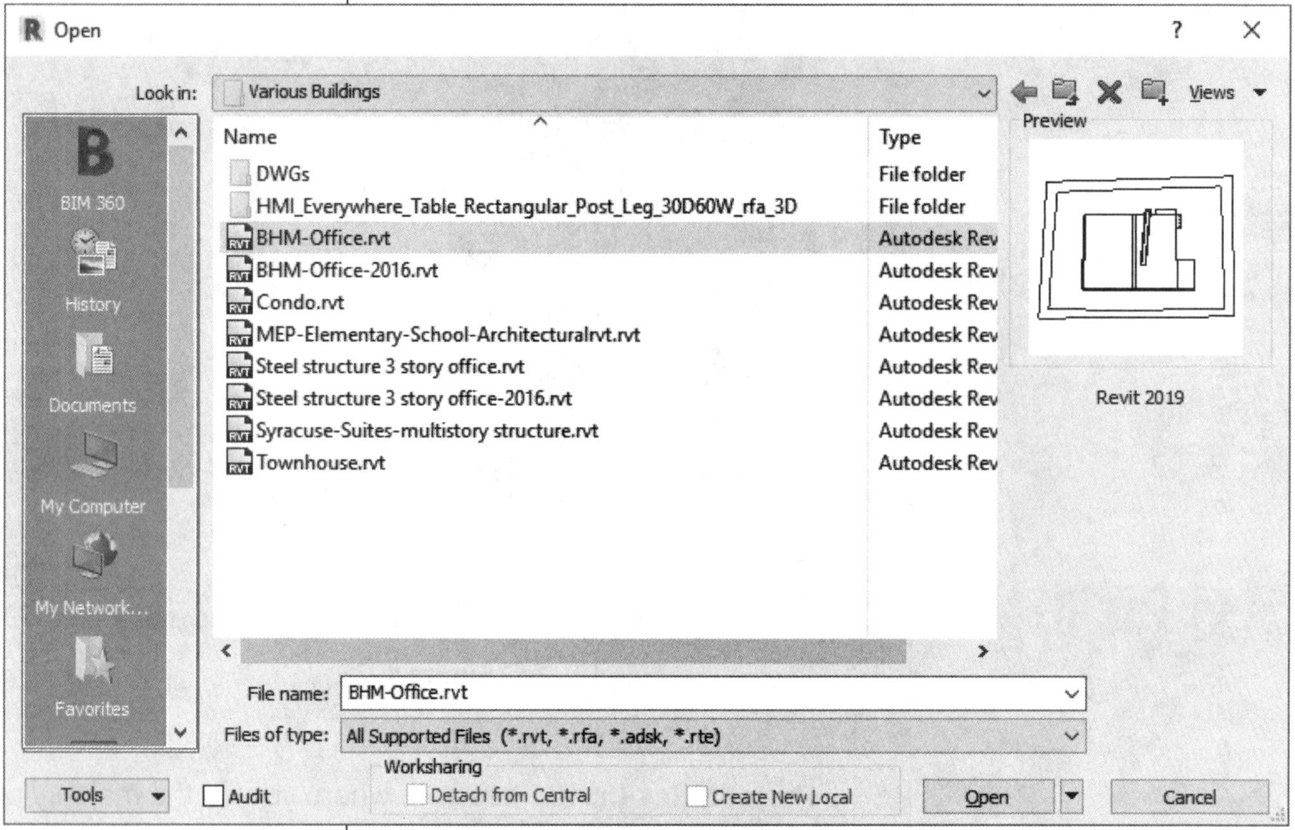

Figure 1–37

- The software release version of the currently selected project displays below the preview. Do not open a drawing that should remain in an earlier version, as you cannot save back to previous versions.

  Note: It is important that everyone working on a project uses the same software version. While your software may be able to open files created in its earlier versions, it will not be able to open files created in versions newer than the one you are using currently.

- When you open a file created in an earlier version, the Model Upgrade dialog box (shown in Figure 1–38) indicates the release of a file and the release to which it will be upgraded. If required, you can cancel the upgrade before it completes.

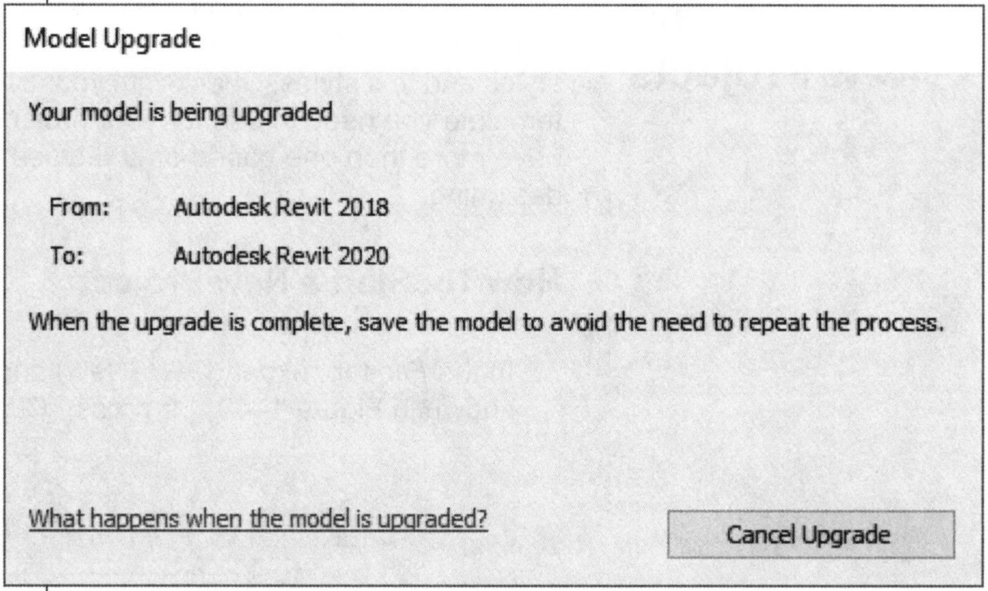

Figure 1–38

Hint: Opening Workset-Related Files

Worksets are used when the project becomes large enough for multiple people to work on it at the same time. At this point, the project manager creates a central file with multiple worksets (such as element interiors, building shell, and site) that are used by the project team members.

When you open a workset related file it creates a new local file on your computer as shown in Figure 1–39. Do not work in the main central file.

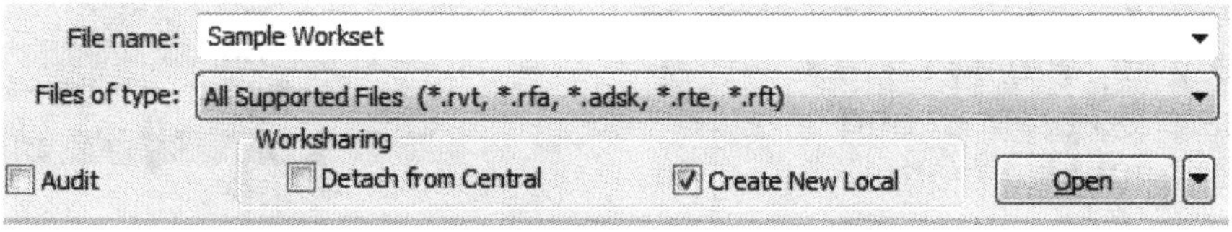

Figure 1–39

- For more information about opening and saving workset-related files, see *Appendix A.1 Introduction to Worksets.*
- When you click on a central model showing in the Home screen, a local copy of the file is created.
- For more information on establishing and using Worksets, refer to the *Autodesk Revit: Collaboration Tools* learning guide.

Starting New Projects

New projects are based on a template file. The template file includes preset levels, views, and some families, such as wall styles and text styles. Check with your BIM Manager about which template you need to use for your projects. Your company might have more than one based on the types of building that you are designing.

How To: Start a New Project

1. In the *File* tab, expand 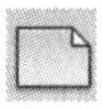 (New) and click  (Project) (as shown in Figure 1–40), or press <Ctrl>+<N>.

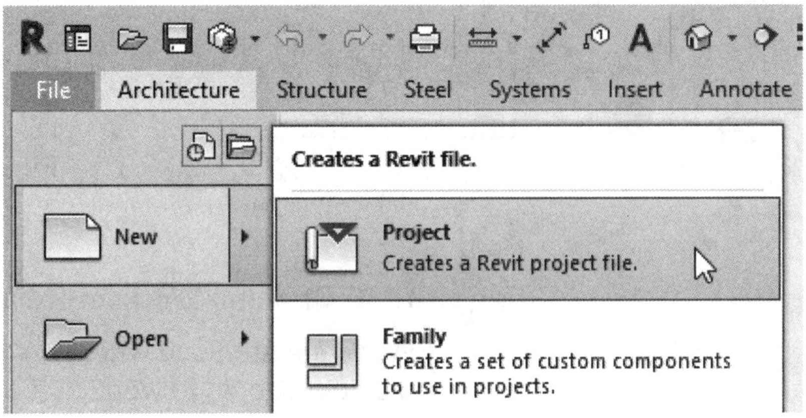

Figure 1–40

2. In the New Project dialog box (shown in Figure 1–41), select the template that you want to use and click **OK**.

The list of Template files is set in the Options dialog box in the File Locations pane. It might vary depending on the installed product and company standards.

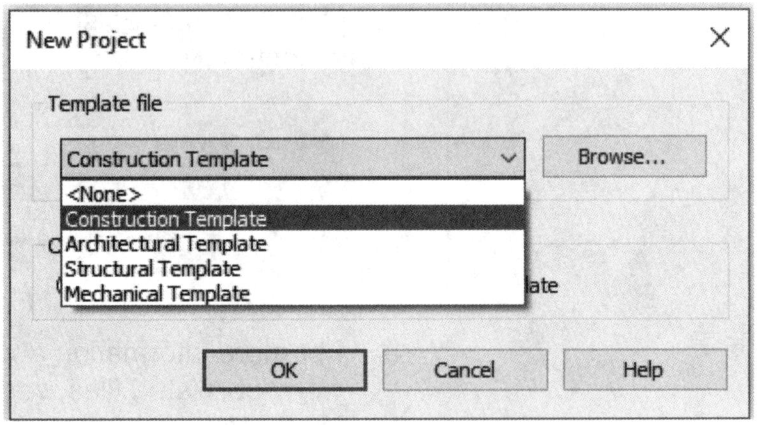

Figure 1–41

- You can select from a list of templates if they have been set up by your BIM Manager.

- You can add (New) to the Quick Access Toolbar. At the end of the Quick Access Toolbar, click (Customize Quick Access Toolbar) and select **New**, as shown in Figure 1–42.

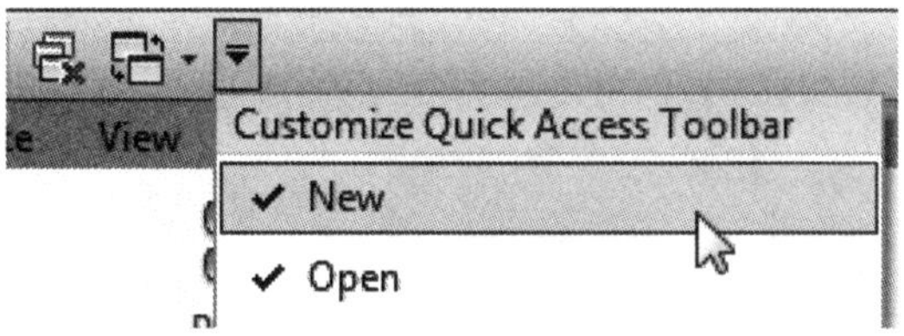

Figure 1–42

Saving Projects

It is important to save your projects frequently. In the Quick Access Toolbar or *File* tab click (Save), or press <Ctrl>+<S> to save your project. If the project has not yet been saved, the Save As dialog box opens, where you can specify a file location and name.

- To save an existing project with a new name, in the *File* tab, expand (Save As) and click (Project).
- If you have not saved in a set amount of time, the software opens the Project Not Saved Recently alert box, as shown in Figure 1–43. Select **Save the project**. If you want to set reminder intervals or not save at this time, select the other options.

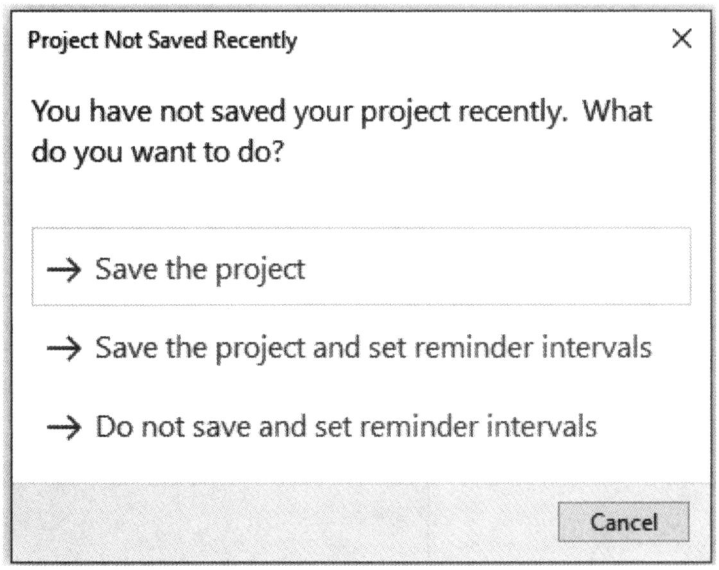

Figure 1–43

- You can set the *Save Reminder interval* to **15** or **30 minutes**, **1**, **2**, or **4 hours**, or to have **No reminders** display. In the *File* tab, click **Options** to open the Options dialog box. In the left pane, select **General** and set the interval as shown in Figure 1–44.

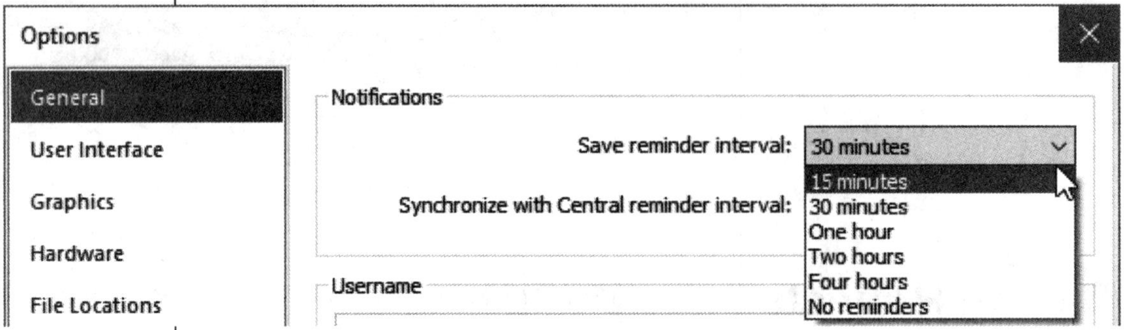

Figure 1–44

Saving Backup Copies

By default, the software saves a backup copy of a project file when you save the project. Backup copies are numbered incrementally (e.g., **My Project.0001.rvt**, **My Project.0002.rvt**, etc.) and are saved in the same folder as the original file. In the Save As dialog box, click **Options...** to control how many backup copies are saved. The default number is three backups. If you exceed this number, the software deletes the oldest backup file.

Hint: Saving Workset-Related Projects

If you use worksets in your project, you need to save the project locally and to the central file. It is recommended to save the local file frequently, just like any other file, and save to the central file every hour or so by synchronizing with the central file.

To synchronize your changes with the main file, in the Quick Access Toolbar expand (Synchronize and Modify Settings) and click (Synchronize Now). After you save to the central file, save the file locally again.

At the end of the day, or when you are finished with the current session, in the Quick Access Toolbar, expand (Synchronize and Modify Settings) and click (Synchronize and Modify Settings) to relinquish the files you have been working on to the central file.

- The maximum number of backups for workset-enabled files is set to 20 by default.

1.4 Viewing Commands

Viewing commands are crucial to working efficiently in most drawing and modeling programs and the Autodesk Revit software is no exception. Once in a view, you can use the Zoom controls to navigate in it. You can zoom in and out and pan in any view. There are also special tools for viewing in 3D.

Zooming and Panning

Using The Mouse to Zoom and Pan

Use the mouse wheel (shown in Figure 1–45) as the main method of moving around the models.

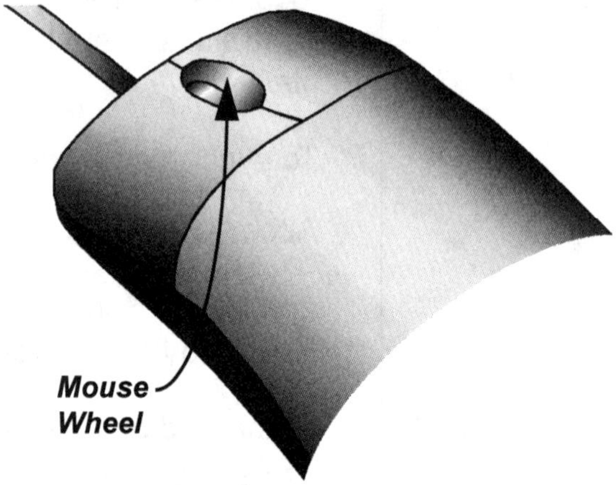

Figure 1–45

- Scroll the wheel on the mouse up to zoom in and down to zoom out.
- Hold the wheel and move the mouse to pan.
- Double-click on the wheel to zoom to the extents of the view.
- In a 3D view, hold <Shift> and the mouse wheel and move the mouse to rotate around the model.

- When you save a model and exit the software, the pan and zoom location of each view is remembered. This is especially important for complex models.

Zoom Controls

A number of additional zoom methods enable you to control the screen display. **Zoom** and **Pan** can be performed at any time while using other commands.

- You can access the **Zoom** commands in the Navigation Bar in the upper right corner of the view (as shown in Figure 1–46). You can also access them from most shortcut menus and by typing the shortcut commands.

 *(2D Wheel) provides cursor-specific access to* ***Zoom*** *and* ***Pan****.*

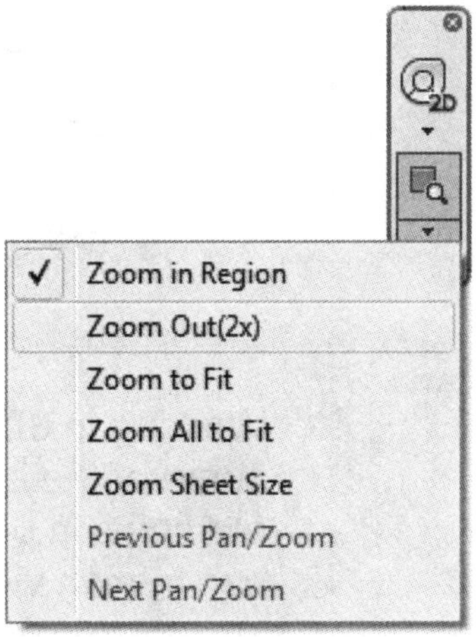

Figure 1–46

Zoom Commands

	**Zoom In Region (ZR)**	Zooms into a region that you define. Drag the cursor or select two points to define the rectangular area you want to zoom into. This is the default command.
	**Zoom Out(2x) (ZO)**	Zooms out to half the current magnification around the center of the elements.
	**Zoom To Fit (ZF or ZE)**	Zooms out so that the entire contents of the project only display on the screen in the current view.
	**Zoom All To Fit (ZA)**	Zooms out so that the entire contents of the project display on the screen in all open views.
	**Zoom Sheet Size (ZS)**	Zooms in or out in relation to the sheet size.
N/A	**Previous Pan/Zoom (ZP)**	Steps back one **Zoom** command.
N/A	**Next Pan/Zoom**	Steps forward one **Zoom** command if you have done a **Previous Pan/Zoom**.

Viewing in 3D

Even if you started a project entirely in plan views, you can quickly create 3D views of the model, as shown in Figure 1–47. There are two types of 3D views: isometric views created by the **Default 3D View** command and perspective views created by the **Camera** command.

Figure 1–47

Working in 3D views helps you visualize the project and position some of the elements correctly. You can create and modify elements in both isometric and perspective 3D views, just as you can in plan views.

- Once you have created a 3D view, you can save it and easily return to it.

How To: Create and Save a 3D Isometric View

You can spin the view to a different angle using the mouse wheel or the middle button of a three-button mouse. Hold <Shift> as you press the wheel or middle button and drag the cursor.

1. In the Quick Access Toolbar or *View* tab>Create panel, click  (Default 3D View). The default 3D Southeast isometric view opens, as shown in Figure 1–48.

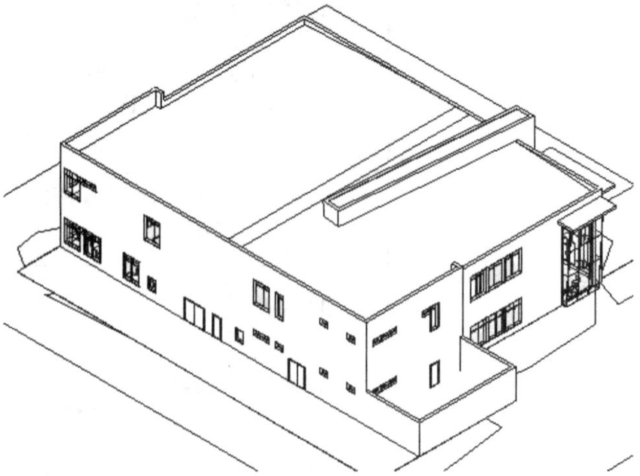

Figure 1–48

2. Modify the view to display the building from other directions.

3. In the Project Browser, double-click slowly or right-click on the {3D} view and select **Rename....**
4. The name is placed in a text box with the original name highlighted, as shown in Figure 1–49. Type a new name in the Rename View dialog box, as shown in Figure 1–50.

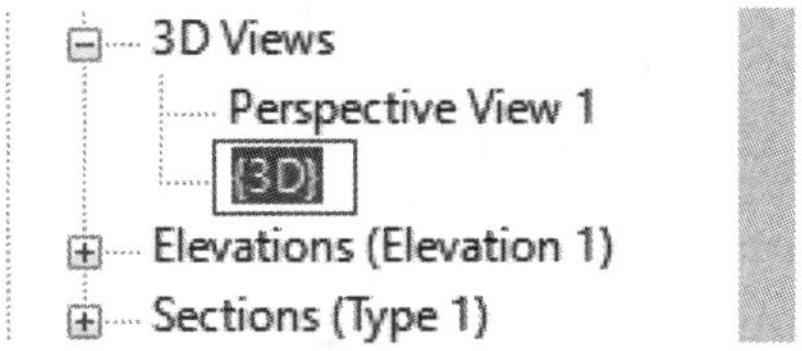

Figure 1–49

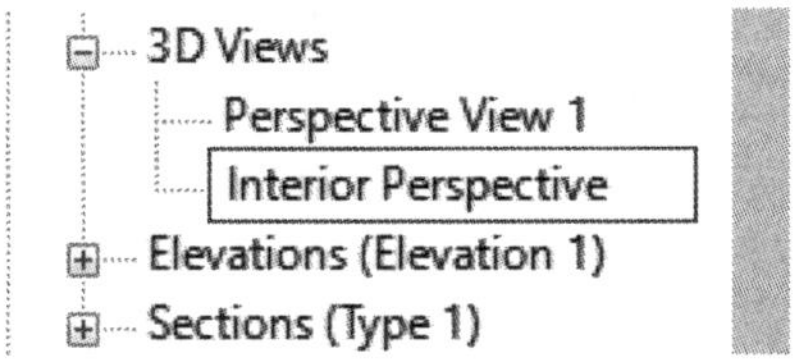

Figure 1–50

All types of views can be renamed.

- When changes to the default 3D view are saved and you start another default 3D view, it displays the Southeast isometric view once again. If you modified the default 3D view but did not save it to a new name, the **Default 3D View** command opens the view in the last orientation you specified.

How To: Create a Perspective View

1. Switch to a Floor Plan view.
2. In the Quick Access Toolbar or *View* tab>Create panel, expand (Default 3D View) and click (Camera).
3. Place the camera on the view.
4. Point the camera in the direction in which you want it to shoot by placing the target on the view, as shown in Figure 1–51.

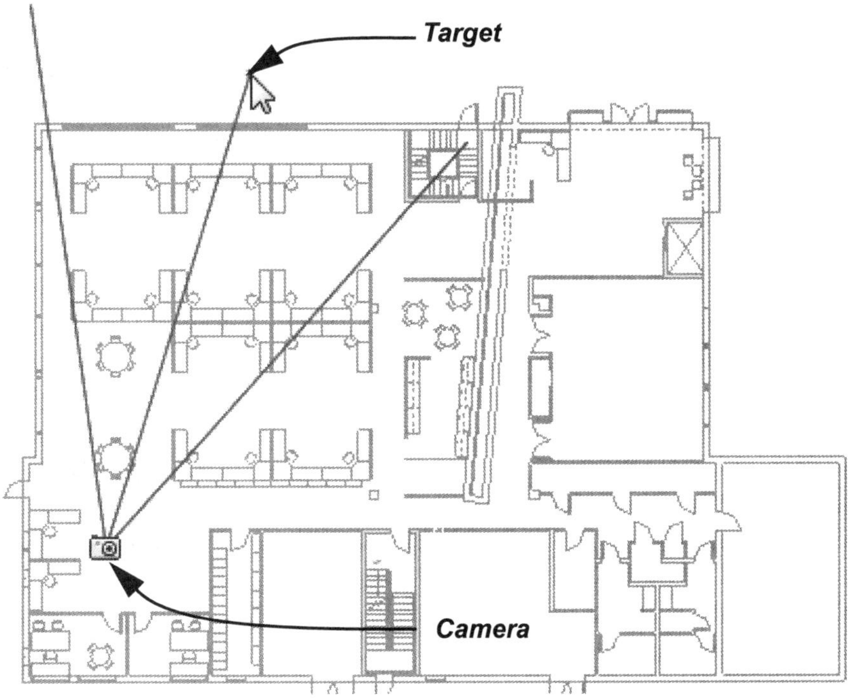

Figure 1–51

Use the round controls to modify the display size of the view and press <Shift> + the mouse wheel to change the view.

A new view is displayed, as shown in Figure 1–52.

Figure 1–52

5. In the Properties palette scroll down and adjust the *Eye Elevation* and *Target Elevation* as required.

- If the view becomes distorted, reset the target so that it is centered in the boundary of the view (called the crop region).

  In the *Modify | Cameras* tab>Camera panel, click (Reset Target).

- You can further modify a view by adding shadows, as shown in Figure 1–53. In the View Control Bar, toggle (Shadows Off) and (Shadows On). Shadows display in any model view, not just in the 3D views. To setup the sun location, expand (Sun Path Off) and select **Sun Settings...**. Select (Sun Path On) to see the visual location of the sun.

Figure 1–53

Hint: Using the ViewCube

The ViewCube provides visual clues as to where you are in a 3D view. It helps you move around the model with quick access to specific views (such as top, front, and right), as well as corner and directional views, as shown in Figure 1–54.

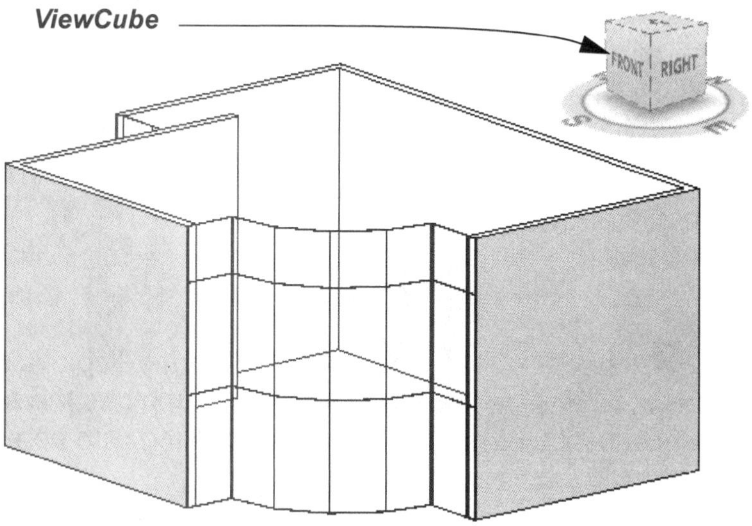

Figure 1–54

Move the cursor over any face of the ViewCube to highlight it. Once a face is highlighted, you can select it to reorient the model. You can also click and drag on the ViewCube to rotate the box, which rotates the model.

-  (Home) displays when you roll the cursor over the ViewCube. Click it to return to the view defined as **Home**. To change the Home view, set the view as you want it, right-click on the ViewCube, and select **Set Current View as Home**.
- The ViewCube is available in isometric and perspective views.
- You can switch between Perspective and Isometric mode by right-clicking on the View Cube and selecting **Perspective** or **Orthographic**.

Visual Styles

Any view can have a visual style applied. The **Visual Style** options found in the View Control Bar (as shown in Figure 1–55), specify the shading of the building model. These options apply to plan, elevation, section, and 3D views.

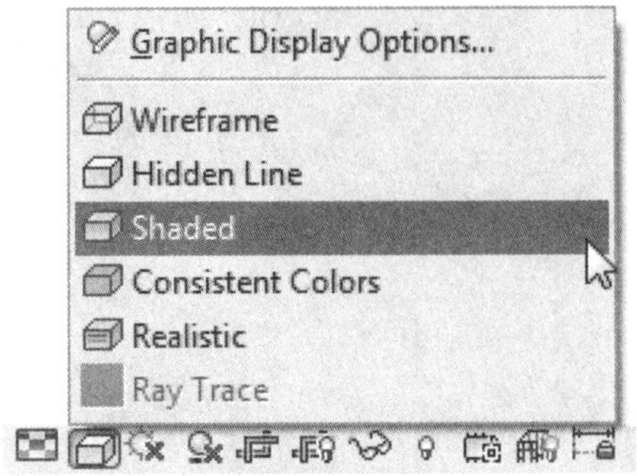

Figure 1–55

- (Wireframe) displays the lines and edges that make up elements, but hides the surfaces. This can be useful when you are dealing with complex intersections.
- (Hidden Line) displays the lines, edges, and surfaces of the elements, but it does not display any colors. This is the most common visual style to use while working on a design.
- (Shaded) and (Consistent Colors) give you a sense of the materials, including transparent glass. An example that uses Consistent Colors is shown in Figure 1–56.

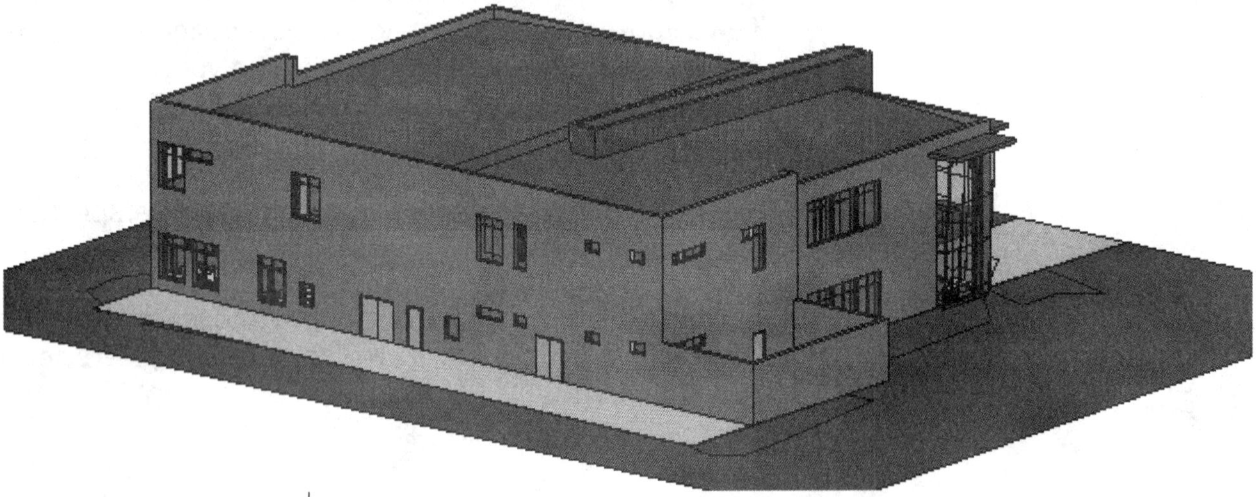

Figure 1–56

- (Realistic) displays what is shown when you render the view, including RPC (Rich Photorealistic Content) components and artificial lights. It takes a lot of computer power to execute this visual style. Therefore, it is better to use the other visual styles most of the time as you are working.

- (Ray Trace) is useful if you have created a 3D view that you want to render. It gradually moves from draft resolution to photorealistic. You can stop the process at any time.

Hint: Rendering

Rendering is a powerful tool which enables you to display a photorealistic view of the model you are working on, such as the example shown in Figure 1–57. This can be used to help clients and designers to understand a building's design in better detail.

Figure 1–57

- In the View Control Bar, click (Show Rendering Dialog) to set up the options. **Show Rendering Dialog** is only available in 3D views.

Practice 1a Open and Review a Project

Practice Objectives

- Navigate the graphic user interface.
- Manipulate 2D and 3D views by zooming and panning.
- Create 3D Isometric and Perspective views.
- Set the Visual Style of a view.

In this practice, you will open a project file and view each of the various areas in the interface. You will investigate elements, commands, and their options. You will also open views through the Project Browser and view the model in 3D, as shown in Figure 1–58.

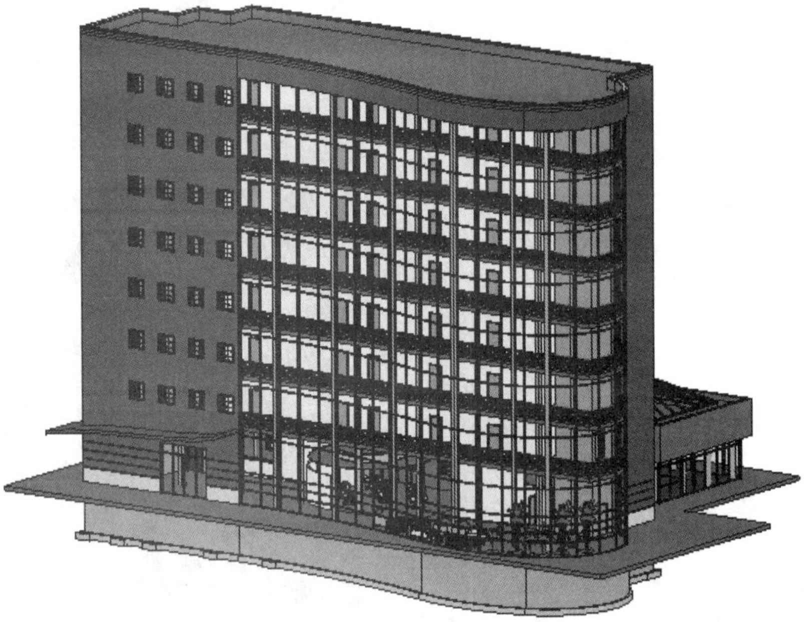

Figure 1–58

- This is a version of the main project you will work on throughout this guide.

Task 1 - Explore the interface.

1. In the *File* tab, expand (Open) and click (Project).
2. In the Open dialog box, navigate to the practice files folder and select **Modern-Hotel-Final.rvt**.
3. Click **Open**. The 3D view of the modern hotel building opens in the view window.

If the Project Browser and Properties palette are docked over each other, use the Project Browser tab at the bottom to display it.

4. In the Project Browser, expand the *Floor Plans* node. Double-click on **Floor 1** to open it. This view is referred to as **Floor Plans: Floor 1**.

5. Take time to review the floor plan to get acquainted with it.

6. Review the various parts of the screen.

7. In the view, hover the cursor over one of the doors. A tooltip displays describing the element, as shown in Figure 1–59.

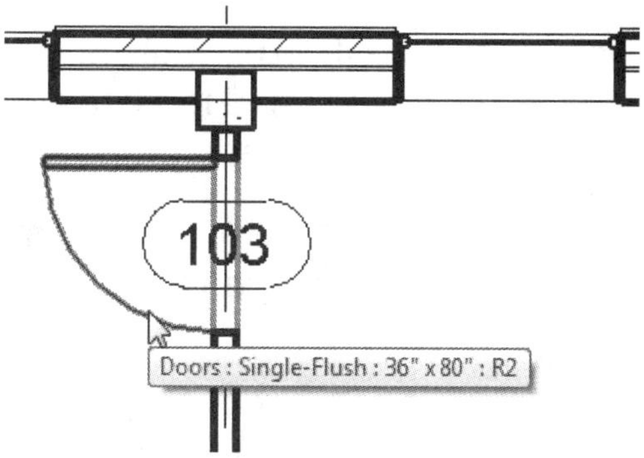

Figure 1–59

8. Hover the cursor over another element to display its description.

9. Select a door. The ribbon changes to the *Modify* | *Doors* tab.

10. Click in an empty space to release the selection.

11. Hold <Ctrl> and select several elements of different types. The ribbon changes to the *Modify* | *Multi-Select* tab.

12. Press <Esc> to clear the selection.

13. In the *Architecture* tab>Build panel, click  (Wall). The ribbon changes to the *Modify* | *Place Wall* tab and at the end of the ribbon, the Draw panel is displayed. It contains tools that enable you to create walls. The rest of the ribbon displays the same tools that are found on the *Modify* tab.

14. In the Select panel, click  (Modify) to return to the main ribbon.

15. In the *Architecture* tab>Build panel, click  (Door). The ribbon changes to the *Modify* | *Place Door* tab and displays the options and tools you can use to create doors.

16. In the Select panel, click  (Modify) to return to the main ribbon.

You might need to widen the Project Browser to display the full names of the views.

Task 2 - Look at views.

1. In the Project Browser, verify that the *Floor Plans* node is open. Double-click on the **Floor 1 - Furniture Plan** view.
2. The basic floor plan displays with the furniture, but without the annotations that were displayed in the **Floor 1** view.
3. Open the **Floor1 - Life Safety Plan** view by double-clicking on it.
4. The walls and furniture display, but the furniture is grayed out and red lines describing important life safety information display.
5. At the top of the views, click each tab to switch between the open views.
6. In the *View* tab>Windows panel, click  (Tile Views). All of the open views are tiled. Type **ZA** (for Zoom All) to zoom out to the extents of each view, as shown in Figure 1–60.

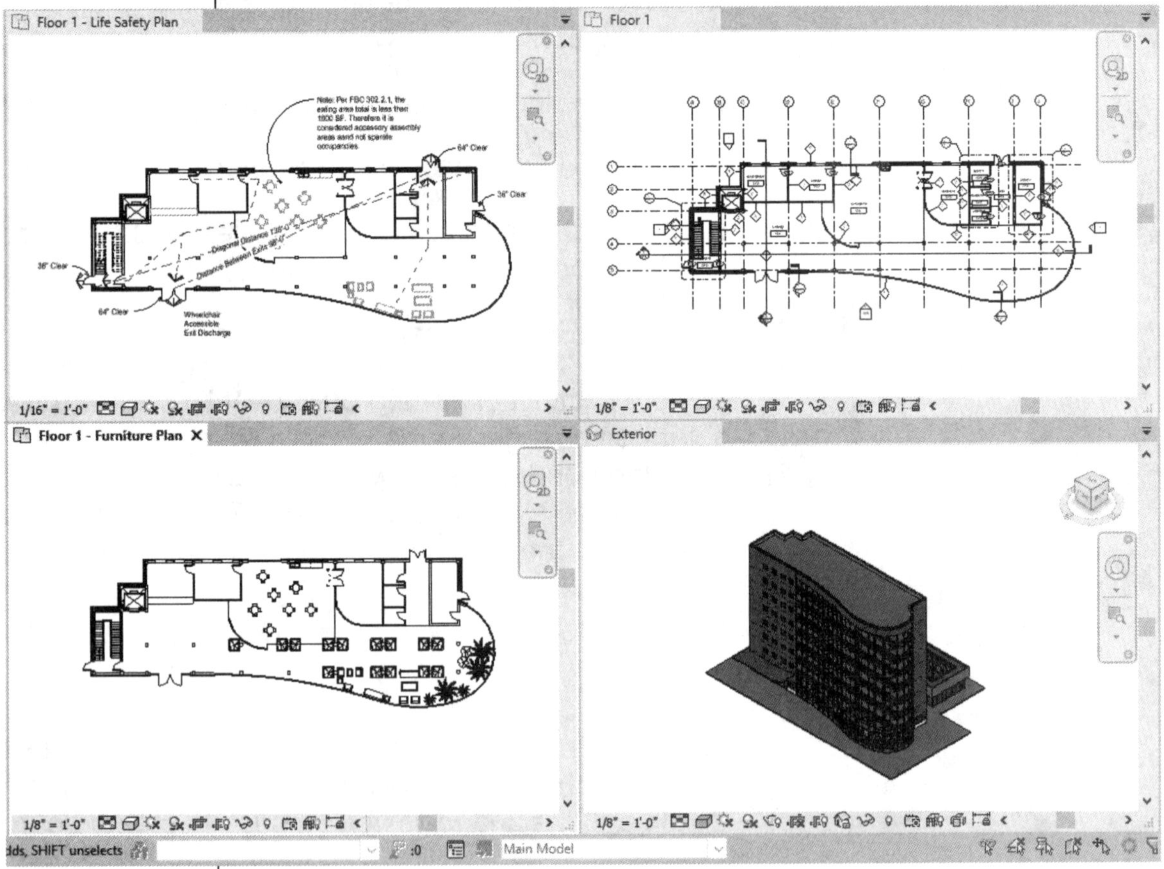

Figure 1–60

7. Click inside the 3D view to make it active.

8. In the *View* tab>Windows panel, click  (Tab Views). The views return to the tabs and the 3D view is first in the group.

*This view is referred to as **Elevations (Building Elevation): East** view.*

9. In the Project Browser, scroll down and expand *Elevations (Building Elevation)*. Double-click on the **East** elevation to open the view.

10. Expand *Sections (Building Section)* and double-click on the **East-West Section** to open it.

11. At the bottom of the view window, in the View Control Bar, click  (Visual Style) and select **Shaded**. The elements in the section are now easier to read.

12. In the Project Browser, scroll down to the *Sheets (all)* node and expand the node.

13. View several of the sheets. Some have views already applied, (e.g., **A2.3 - 2nd-8th Floor Plan (Typical)** as shown in Figure 1–61).

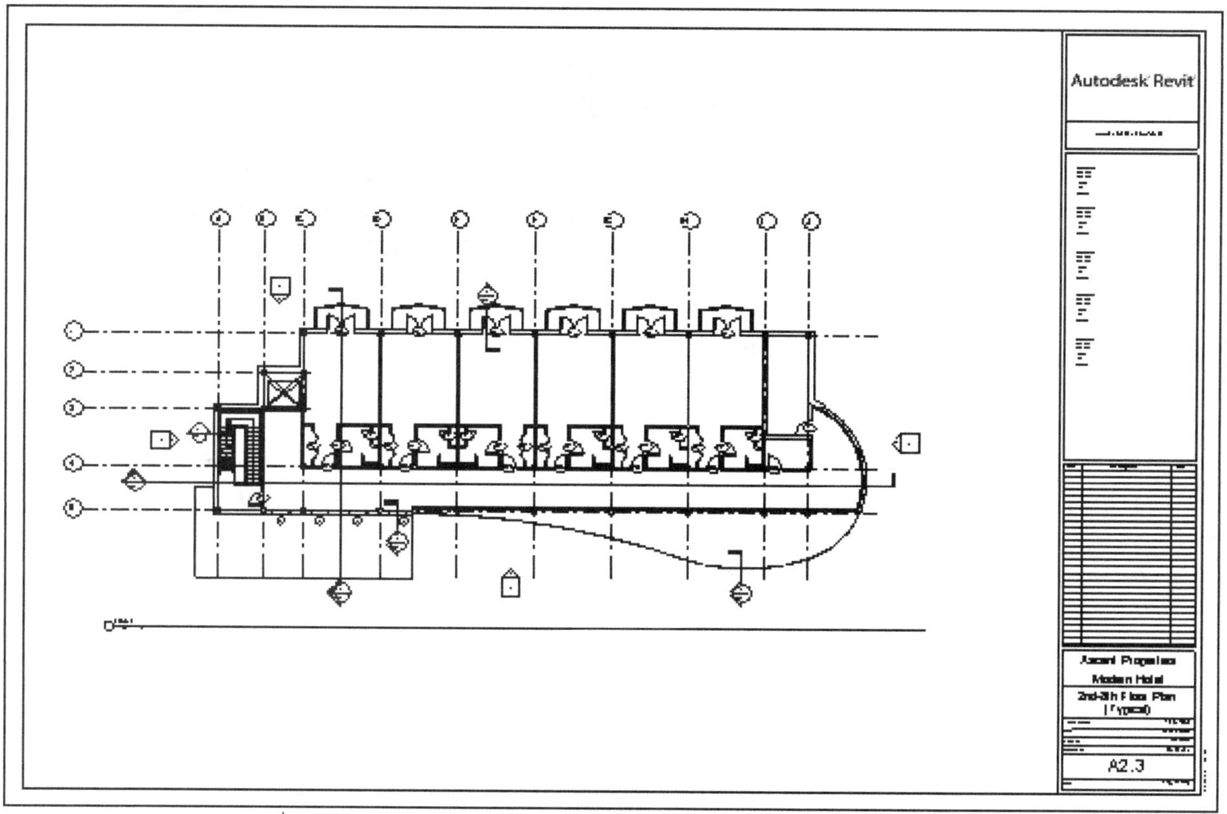

Figure 1–61

14. Which sheet displays the view that you just set to **Shaded**?

Task 3 - Practice viewing tools.

1. At the far right of the view tabs, expand Switch Windows and select **Floor 1**, as shown in Figure 1–62.

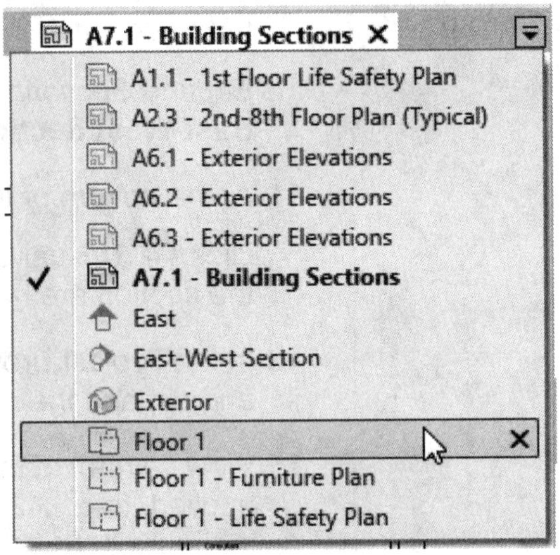

Figure 1–62

2. In the Navigation Bar, click  and select **Zoom In Region** or type **ZR**. Zoom in on one of the stairs.

3. Pan to another part of the building by holding and dragging the middle mouse button or wheel. Alternatively, you can use the 2D Wheel in the Navigation Bar.

4. Double-click on the mouse wheel to zoom out to fit the extents of the view.

5. In the Quick Access Toolbar, click (Default 3D View) to open the default 3D view, as shown in Figure 1–63.

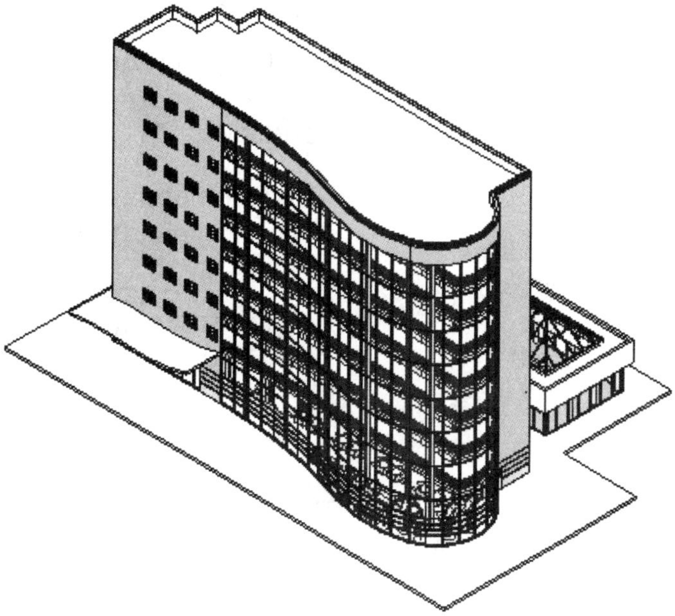

Figure 1–63

6. Hold <Shift> and use the middle mouse button or wheel to rotate the model in the 3D view.

7. In the View Control Bar, change the *Visual Style* to (Shaded). Then try (Consistent Colors). Which one works best when you view the back of the building?

8. Use the ViewCube to find a view that you want to use.

9. In the Project Browser, expand *3D Views* and right-click on the {3D} view and select **Rename....** and type in a new name for the view.

10. Review the other 3D views that have already been created.

11. Press <Ctrl>+<Tab> to cycle through the open views.

12. In the Quick Access Toolbar, expand (Switch Windows) and select the **Modern-Hotel-Final.rvt - Floor Plan: Floor 1** view.

13. In the Quick Access Toolbar, click (Close Inactive Views). This closes all of the other windows except the one in which you are working.

14. In the Quick Access Toolbar, expand (Default 3D View) and click (Camera).

15. Click the first point near the Lobby room name and click the second point (target) outside the building, as shown in Figure 1–64.

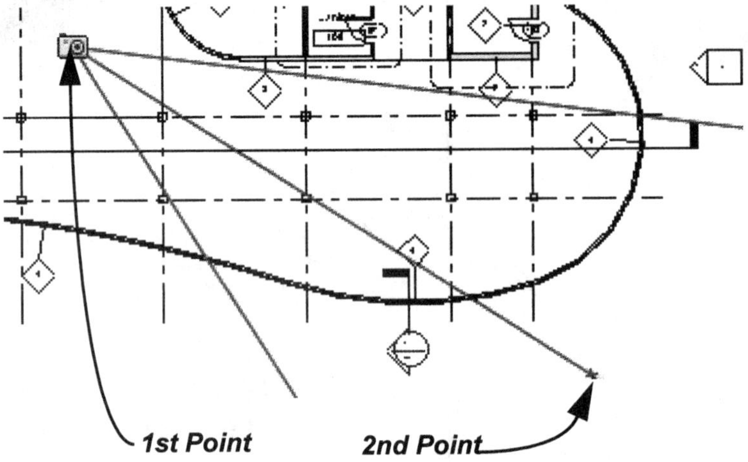

Figure 1–64

16. The furniture and planters display even though they did not display in the floor plan view.

This file is not set up to work with Raytrace.

17. In the View Control Bar, set the *Visual Style* to (Realistic).

18. In the Project Browser, right-click on the new camera view and select **Rename....** Type **Lobby Seating Area**.

19. In the Quick Access Toolbar, click (Save) to save the project.

20. In the *File* tab, click (Close). This closes the entire project.

Chapter Review Questions

1. When you create a project in the Autodesk Revit software, do you work in 3D (as shown on the left in Figure 1–65) or 2D (as shown on the right in Figure 1–65)?

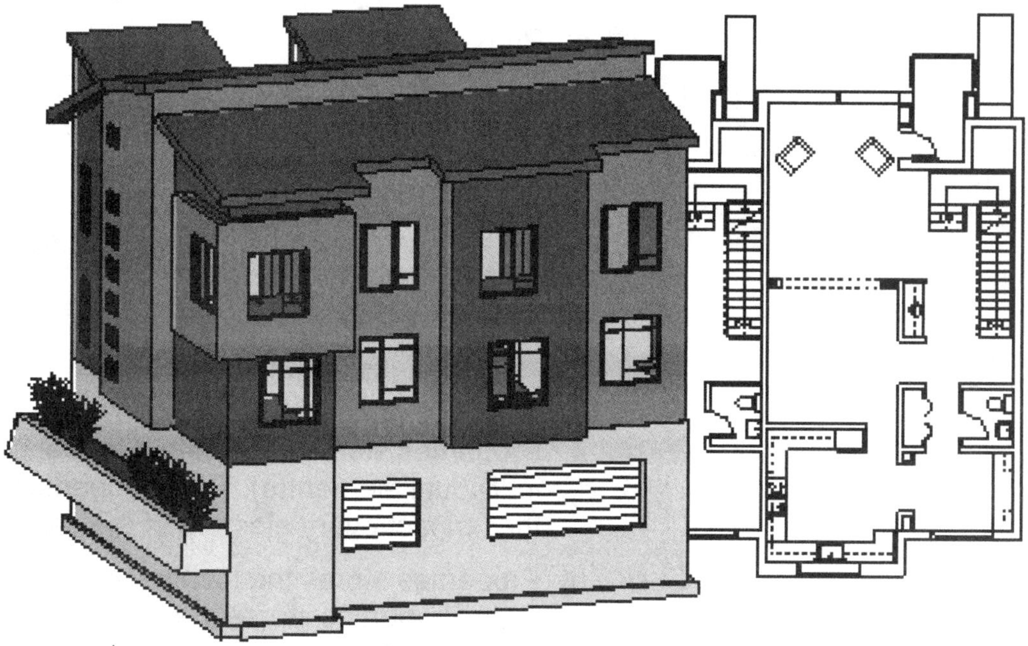

Figure 1–65

   a. You work in 2D in plan views and in 3D in non-plan views.
   b. You work in 3D almost all of the time, even when you are using what looks like a flat view.
   c. You work in 2D or 3D depending on how you toggle the 2D/3D control.
   d. You work in 2D in plan and section views and in 3D in isometric views.

2. What is the purpose of the Project Browser?
   a. It enables you to browse through the building project, similar to a walk through.
   b. It is the interface for managing all of the files that are required to create the complete architectural model of the building.
   c. It manages multiple Autodesk Revit projects as an alternative to using Windows Explorer.
   d. It is used to access and manage the views of the project.

3. Which part(s) of the interface changes when you start a command such as Wall, Beam, or Duct? (Select all that apply.)
   a. Ribbon
   b. View Control Bar
   c. Options Bar
   d. Properties Palette

4. The difference between Type Properties and Properties (the ribbon location is shown in Figure 1–66) is...

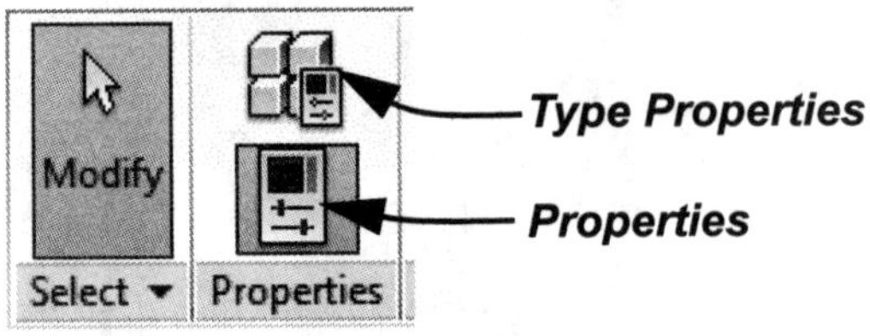

Figure 1–66

   a. Properties stores parameters that apply to the selected individual element(s). Type Properties stores parameters that impact every element of the same type in the project.
   b. Properties stores the location parameters of an element. Type Properties stores the size and identity parameters of an element.
   c. Properties only stores parameters of the view. Type Properties stores parameters of model components.

5. When you start a new project, how do you specify the base information in the new file?
   a. Transfer the base information from an existing project.
   b. Select the right template for the task.
   c. The Autodesk Revit software automatically extracts the base information from imported or linked file(s).

6. What is the main difference between a view made using (Default 3D View) and a view made using (Camera)?
    a. Use Default **3D View** for exterior views and **Camera** for interiors.
    b. **Default 3D View** creates a static image and a **Camera** view is live and always updated.
    c. **Default 3D View** is isometric and a **Camera** view is perspective.
    d. **Default 3D View** is used for the overall building and a **Camera** view is used for looking in tight spaces.

Command Summary

Button	Command	Location
General Tools		
	Home	• Quick Access Toolbar • **Shortcut:** <Ctrl>+<D>
	Modify	• **Ribbon:** All tabs>Select panel • **Shortcut:** MD
	New	• • ***File* tab** • **Shortcut:** <Ctrl>+<N>
	Open	• **Quick Access Toolbar** • ***File* tab** • **Shortcut:** <Ctrl>+<O>
	Open Documents	• ***File* tab**
	Properties	• **Ribbon:** *Modify* tab>Properties panel • **Shortcut:** PP
	Recent Documents	• ***File* tab**
	Save	• **Quick Access Toolbar** • ***File* tab** • **Shortcut:** <Ctrl>+<S>
	Synchronize and Modify Settings	• **Quick Access Toolbar**
	Synchronize Now/	• **Quick Access Toolbar**>expand Synchronize and Modify Settings
	Type Properties	• **Ribbon:** *Modify* tab>Properties panel • **Properties palette**
Viewing Tools		
	Camera	• **Quick Access Toolbar**> Expand Default 3D View • **Ribbon:** *View* tab>Create panel> expand Default 3D View
	Close Inactive Views	• **Quick Access Toolbar** • **Ribbon:** *View* tab> Windows panel
	Default 3D View	• **Quick Access Toolbar** • **Ribbon:** *View* tab>Create panel
	Home	• **ViewCube**
N/A	**Next Pan/Zoom**	• **Navigation Bar** • **Shortcut Menu**

N/A	**Previous Pan/Zoom**	• **Navigation Bar** • **Shortcut Menu** • **Shortcut:** ZP
	Shadows On/Off	• **View Control Bar**
	Show Rendering Dialog/ Render	• **View Control Bar** • **Ribbon:** *View* tab>Graphics panel • **Shortcut:** RR
	Switch Windows	• **Quick Access Toolbar** • **Ribbon:** *View* tab> Windows panel
	Tab Views	• **Ribbon:** *View* tab> Windows panel • **Shortcut: TW**
	Tile Views	• **Ribbon:** *View* tab> Windows panel • **Shortcut: WT**
	Zoom All to Fit	• **Navigation Bar** • **Shortcut:** ZA
	Zoom in Region	• **Navigation Bar** • **Shortcut Menu** • **Shortcut:** ZR
	Zoom Out (2x)	• **Navigation Bar** • **Shortcut Menu** • **Shortcut:** ZO
	Zoom Sheet Size	• **Navigation Bar** • **Shortcut:** ZS
	Zoom to Fit	• **Navigation Bar** • **Shortcut Menu** • **Shortcut:** ZF, ZE
Visual Styles		
	Consistent Colors	• **View Control Bar**:
	Hidden Line	• **View Control Bar** • **Shortcut:** HL
	Ray Trace	• **View Control Bar**:
	Realistic	• **View Control Bar**
	Shaded	• **View Control Bar** • **Shortcut:** SD
	Wireframe	• **View Control Bar** • **Shortcut:** WF

Basic Sketching and Modify Tools

Basic sketching, selecting, and modifying tools are the foundation of working with all types of elements in the Autodesk® Revit® software. Using these tools with drawing aids helps you to place and modify elements to create accurate building models.

Learning Objectives in this Chapter

- Sketch linear elements such as walls, beams, and pipes.
- Ease the placement of elements by incorporating drawing aids, such as alignment lines, temporary dimensions, and snaps.
- Place Reference Planes as temporary guide lines.
- Use techniques to select and filter groups of elements.
- Modify elements using a contextual tab, Properties, temporary dimensions, and controls.
- Move, copy, rotate, and mirror elements and create array copies in linear and radial patterns.
- Align, trim, and extend elements with the edges of other elements.
- Split linear elements anywhere along their length.
- Offset elements to create duplicates a specific distance away from the original.

2.1 Using General Sketching Tools

When you start a command, the contextual tab on the ribbon, the Options Bar, and the Properties palette enable you to set up features for each new element you are placing in the project. As you are working, several features called *drawing aids* display, as shown in Figure 2–1. They help you to create designs quickly and accurately.

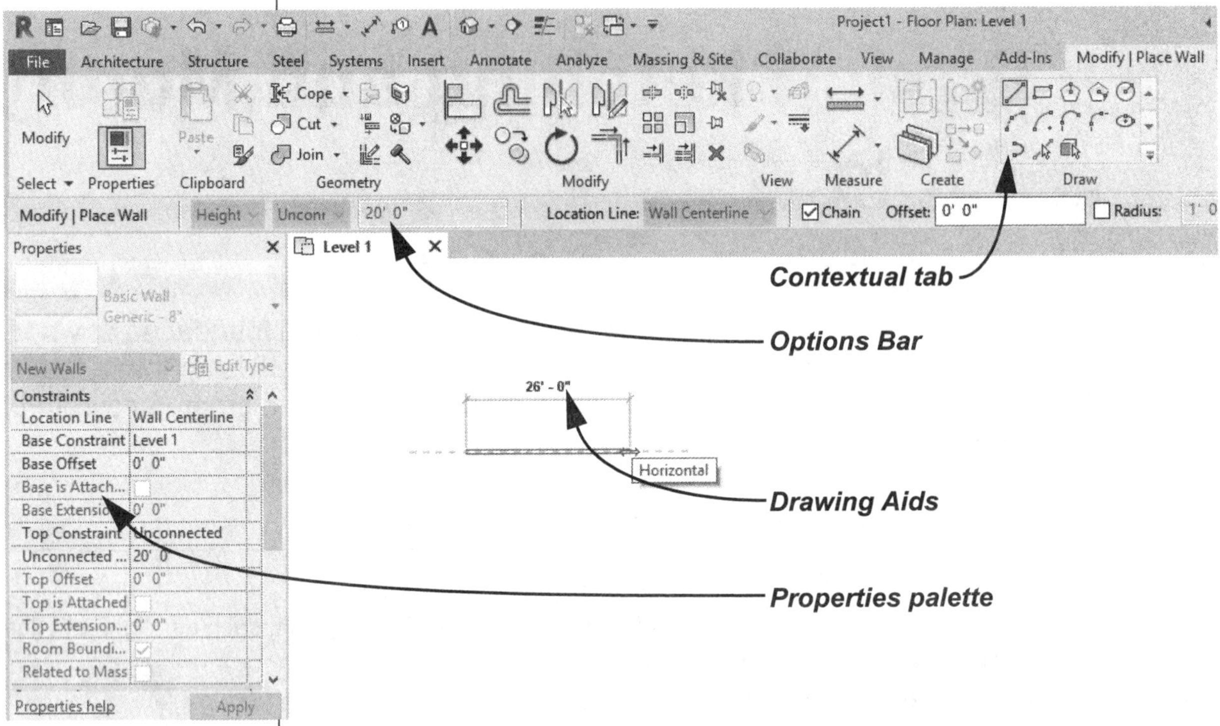

Figure 2–1

- in Autodesk Revit, you are most frequently creating 3D model elements rather than 2D sketches. These tools work with both 3D and 2D elements in the software.

Draw Tools

Many linear elements (such as walls, beams, ducts, pipes, and conduits) are modeled using the tools on the contextual tab on the *Draw* panel, as shown for walls in Figure 2–1. Other elements (such as floors, ceilings, roofs, and slabs) have boundaries that are sketched using many of the same tools. Draw tools are also used when you create details or schematic drawings.

Two methods are available:

The exact tools vary according to the element being modeled.

- *Draw* the element using a geometric form
- *Pick* an existing element (such as a line, face, or wall) as the basis for the new element's geometry and position.

How To: Create Linear Elements

1. Start the command you want to use.
2. In the contextual tab>Draw panel, as shown in Figure 2–2, select a drawing tool.
3. Select points to define the elements.

You can change from one Draw tool shape to another in the middle of a command.

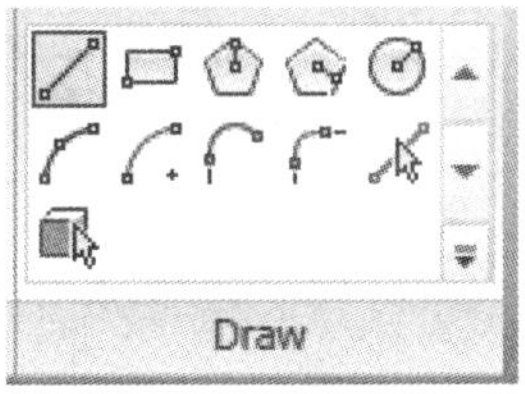

Figure 2–2

4. Finish the command using one of the standard methods:
   - Click  (Modify).
   - Press <Esc> twice.
   - Start another command.

Draw Options

When you are in Drawing mode, several options display in the Options Bar, as shown in Figure 2–3.

Different options display according to the type of element that is selected or the command that is active.

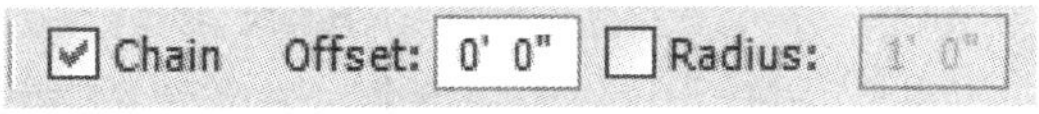

Figure 2–3

- **Chain**: Controls how many segments are created in one process. If this option is not selected, the **Line** and **Arc** tools only create one segment at a time. If it is selected, you can continue adding segments until you press <Esc> or select the command again.
- **Offset**: Enables you to enter values so you can create linear elements at a specified distance from the selected points or element.
- **Radius**: Enables you to enter values when using a radial tool or to add a radius to the corners of linear elements as you sketch them.

Draw Tools

	**Line**	Draws a straight line defined by the first and last points. If Chain is enabled, you can continue selecting end points for multiple segments.
	**Rectangle**	Draws a rectangle defined by two opposing corner points. You can adjust the dimensions after selecting both points.
	**Inscribed Polygon**	Draws a polygon inscribed in a hypothetical circle with the number of sides specified in the Options Bar.
	**Circumscribed Polygon**	Draws a polygon circumscribed around a hypothetical circle with the number of sides specified in the Options Bar.
	**Circle**	Draws a circle defined by a center point and radius.
	**Start-End-Radius Arc**	Draws a curve defined by a start, end, and radius of the arc. The outside dimension shown is the included angle of the arc. The inside dimension is the radius.
	**Center-ends Arc**	Draws a curve defined by a center, radius, and included angle. The selected point of the radius also defines the start point of the arc.
	**Tangent End Arc**	Draws a curve tangent to another element. Select an end point for the first point, but do not select the intersection of two or more elements. Then select a second point based on the included angle of the arc.
	**Fillet Arc**	Draws a curve defined by two other elements and a radius. Because it is difficult to select the correct radius by clicking, this command automatically moves to edit mode. Select the dimension and then modify the radius of the fillet.
	**Spline**	Draws a spline curve based on selected points. The curve does not actually touch the points (Sketches, Model and Detail Lines only).
	**Ellipse**	Draws an ellipse from a primary and secondary axis (Walls, Sketches, Model and Detail Lines only).
	**Partial Ellipse**	Draws only one side of the ellipse, like an arc. A partial ellipse also has a primary and secondary axis (Sketches, Model and Detail Lines only).

Pick Tools

	Pick Lines	Use this option to select existing linear elements in the project. This is useful when you start the project from an imported 2D drawing.
	Pick Face	Use this option to select the face of a 3D massing element (walls and 3D views only).
	Pick Walls	Use this option to select an existing wall in the project to be the basis for a new sketch line (floors, ceilings, etc.).

Drawing Aids

As soon as you start sketching or placing elements, three drawing aids display, as shown in Figure 2–4:

- Alignment lines
- Temporary dimensions
- Snaps

These aids are available with most modeling and many modification commands.

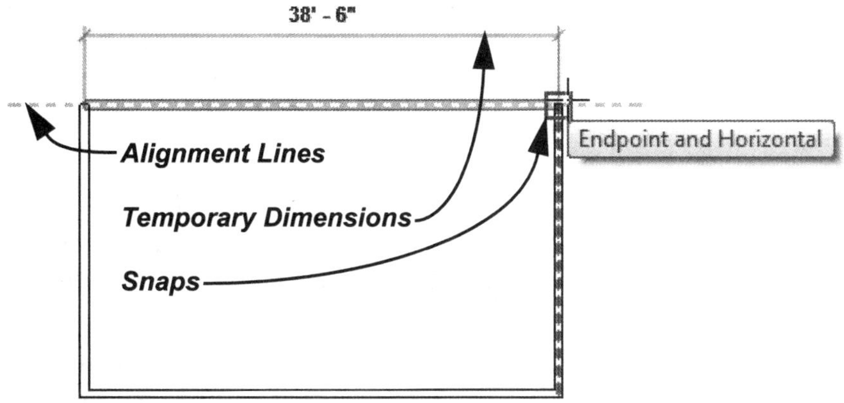

Figure 2–4

Alignment lines display as soon as you select your first point. They help keep lines horizontal, vertical, or at a specified angle. They also line up with the implied intersections of walls and other elements.

- Hold <Shift> to force the alignments to be orthogonal (90 degree angles only).

Temporary dimensions display to help place elements at the correct length, angle and location.

- You can type in a value, or move the cursor until you see the dimension you want, or you can place the element and then modify the value as required.
- The length and angle increments shown vary depending on how far in or out the view is zoomed.
- For Imperial measurements (feet and inches), the software uses a default of feet. For example, when you type **4** and press <Enter>, it assumes 4'-0". For a distance such as 4'-6", you can type any of the following: **4'-6"**, **4'6**, **4-6**, or **4 6** (the numbers separated by a space). To indicate distances less than one foot, type the inch mark (") after the distance, or enter **0**, a space, and then the distance.

Hint: Temporary Dimensions and Permanent Dimensions

Temporary dimensions disappear as soon as you finish adding elements. If you want to make them permanent, select the control shown in Figure 2–5.

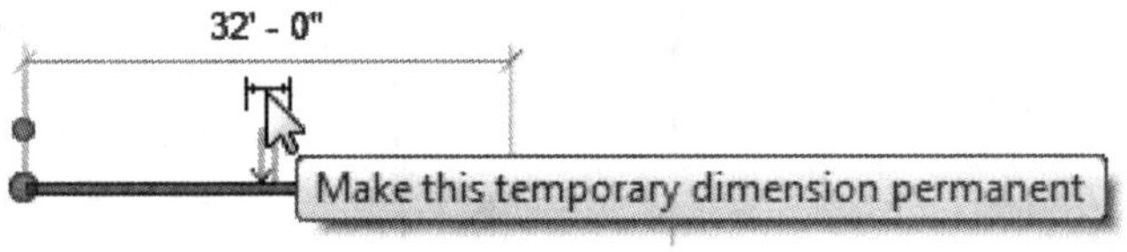

Figure 2–5

Snaps are key points that help you reference existing elements to exact points when modeling, as shown in Figure 2–6.

Figure 2–6

- When you move the cursor over an element, the snap symbol displays. Each snap location type displays with a different symbol.

Hint: Snap Settings and Overrides

In the *Manage* tab>Settings panel, click (Snaps) to open the Snaps dialog box, which is shown in Figure 2–7. The Snaps dialog box enables you to set which snap points are active, and set the dimension increments displayed for temporary dimensions (both linear and angular).

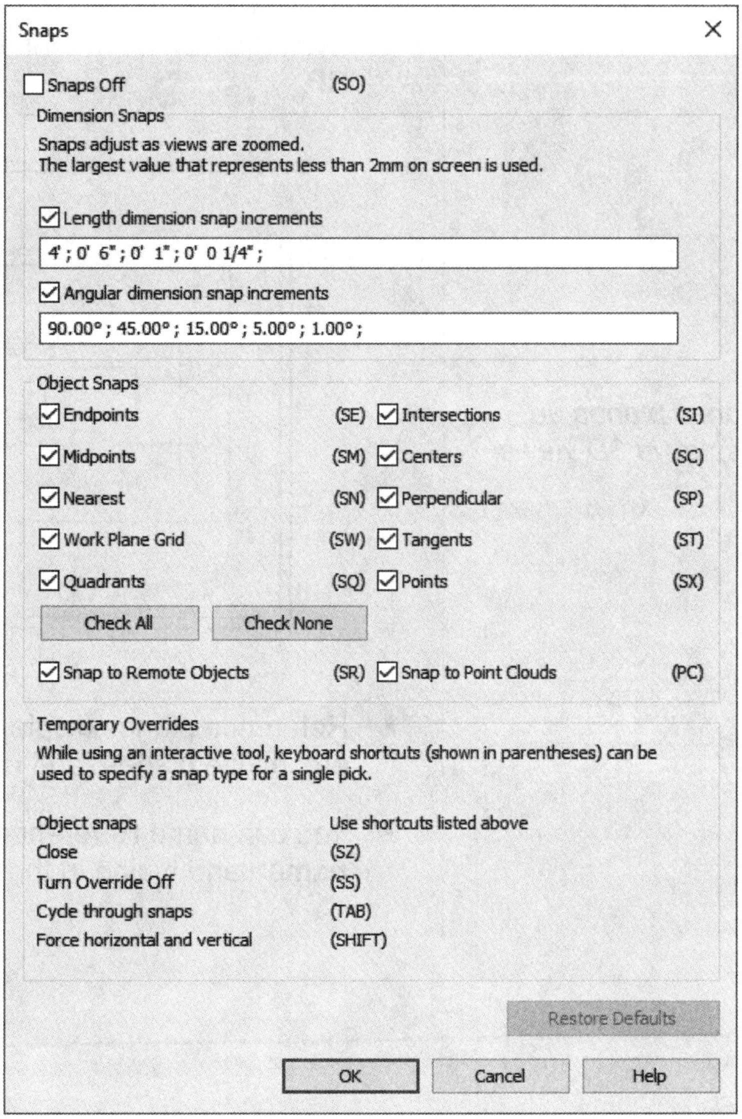

Figure 2–7

- Keyboard shortcuts for each snap can be used to override the automatic snapping.Temporary overrides only affect a single pick, but can be very helpful when there are snaps nearby other than the one you want to use.

Reference Planes

As you develop designs in the Autodesk Revit software, there are times when you need lines to help you define certain locations. You can sketch reference planes (displayed as dashed green lines) and snap to them whenever you need to line up elements. For the example shown in Figure 2–8, the lighting fixtures in the reflected ceiling plan are placed using reference planes.

- To insert a reference plane, in the *Architecture, Structure*, or *Systems* tab>Work Plane panel, click (Ref Plane) or type **RP**.

Reference planes do not display in 3D views.

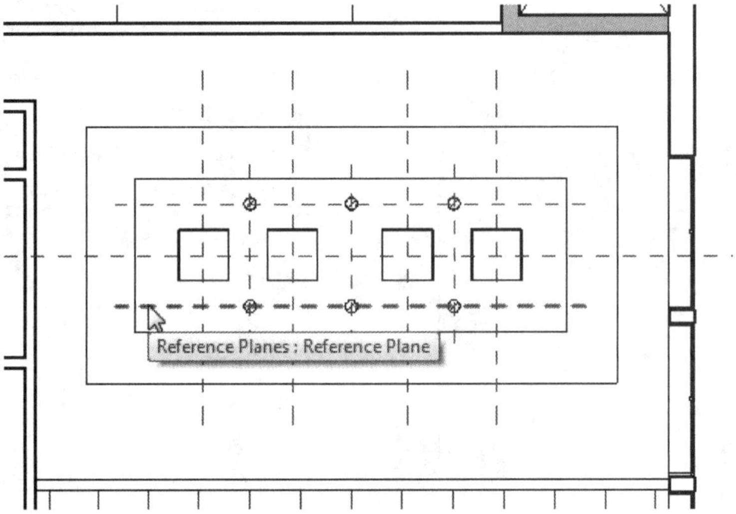

Figure 2–8

- Reference planes display in associated views because they are infinite planes, and not just lines.
- You can name Reference planes by clicking on **<Click to name>** and typing in the text box, as shown in Figure 2–9.

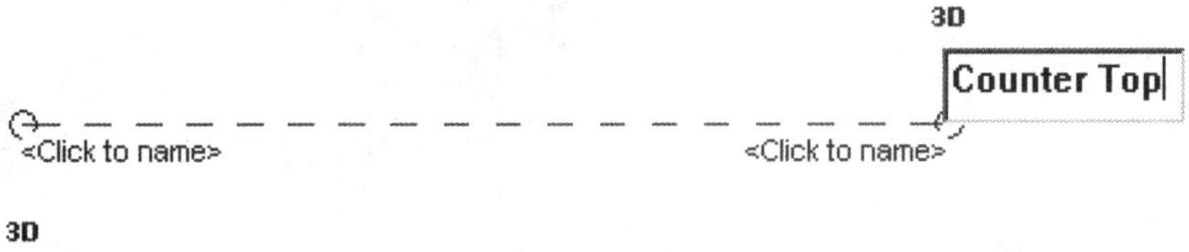

Figure 2–9

- If you sketch a reference pane in Sketch Mode (used with floors and similar elements), it does not display once the sketch is finished.
- Reference planes can have different line styles if they have been defined in the project. In Properties, select a style from the Subcategory list..

Hint: Model Lines vs. Detail Lines

While most of the elements that you create are representations of actual building elements, there are times you may need to add lines to clarify the design intent. These can be either detail lines (as shown in Figure 2–10) or model lines. Detail lines are also useful as references because they are only reflected in the view in which you sketch them.

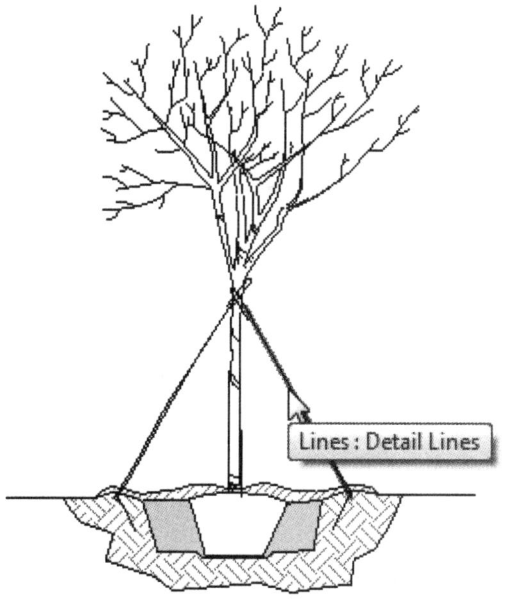

Figure 2–10

- Model Lines (*Architecture* or *Structure* tab>Model panel (Model Line)) function as 3D elements and display in all views.
- Detail Lines (*Annotate* tab>Detail panel> (Detail Lines) are strictly 2D elements that only display in the view in which they are drawn.
- In the *Modify* contextual tab, as shown in Figure 2–11, select a Line Style and then the Draw tool that you want to use to draw the model or detail line.

Figure 2–11

2.2 Editing Elements

Building design projects typically involve extensive changes to the model. The Autodesk Revit software was designed to make such changes quickly and efficiently. You can change an element using the following methods, as shown in Figure 2–12:

- Type Selector enables you to specify a different type. This is frequently used to change the size and/or style of the elements.
- Properties enables you to modify the information (parameters) associated with the selected elements.
- The contextual tab in the ribbon contains the Modify commands and element-specific tools.
- Temporary dimensions enable you to change the element's dimensions or position.
- Controls enable you to drag, flip, lock, and rotate the element.
- Shape handles (not shown) enable you to drag elements to modify their height or length.

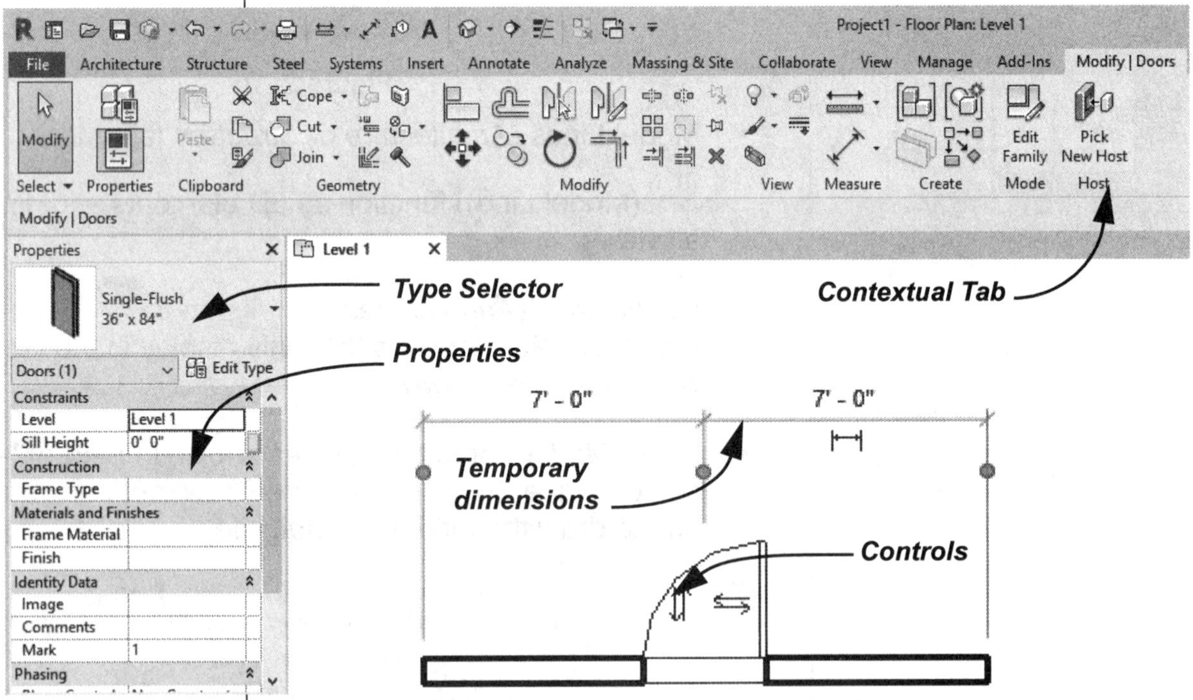

Figure 2–12

- To delete an element, select it and press <Delete>, right-click and select **Delete**, or in the Modify panel, click (Delete).

Working with Controls and Shape Handles

When you select an element, various controls and shape handles display depending on the element and view. For example, in plan view you can use controls to drag the ends of a wall and change its orientation. You can also drag the wall ends in a 3D view, and you can also use the arrow shape handles to change the height of the wall, as shown in Figure 2–13.

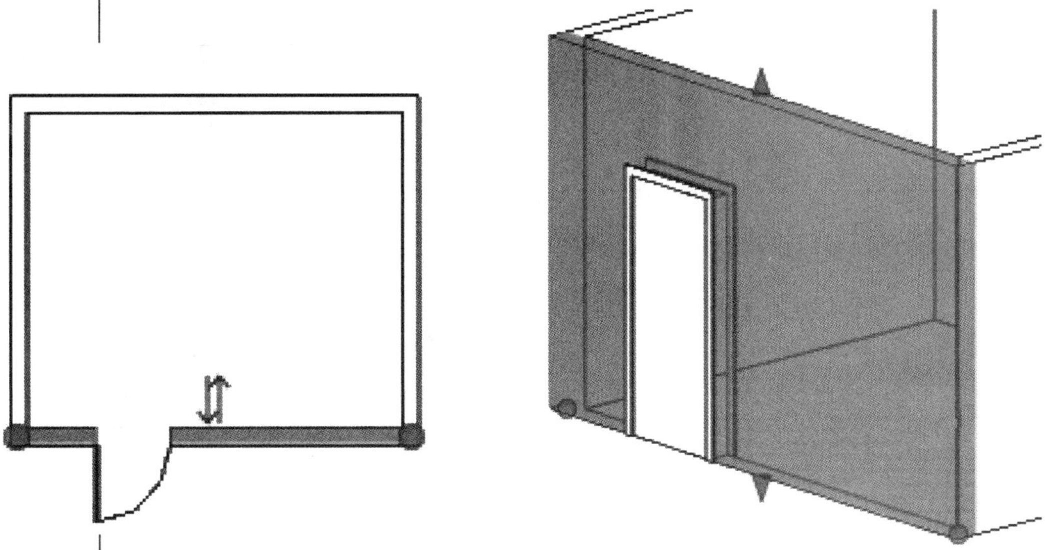

Figure 2–13

- If you hover the cursor over the control or shape handle, a tool tip displays showing its function.

Hint: Editing Temporary Dimensions

Temporary dimensions automatically link to the closest wall. To change this, drag the *Witness Line* control (as shown in Figure 2–14) to connect to a new reference. You can also click on the control to toggle between justifications in the wall.

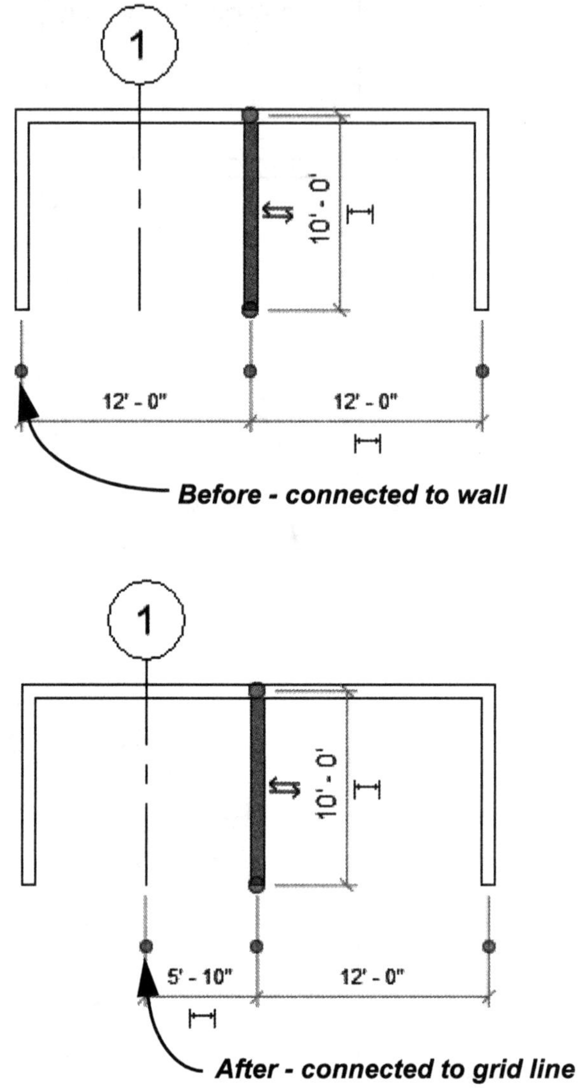

Figure 2–14

- The new location of a temporary dimension for an element is remembered as long as you are in the same session of the software.

Selecting Multiple Elements

- Once you have selected at least one element, hold <Ctrl> and select another item to add it to a selection set.
- To remove an element from a selection set, hold <Shift> and select the element.
- If you click and drag the cursor to *window* around elements, you have two selection options, as shown in Figure 2–15. If you drag from left to right, you only select the elements completely inside the window. If you drag from right to left, you select elements both inside and crossing the window.

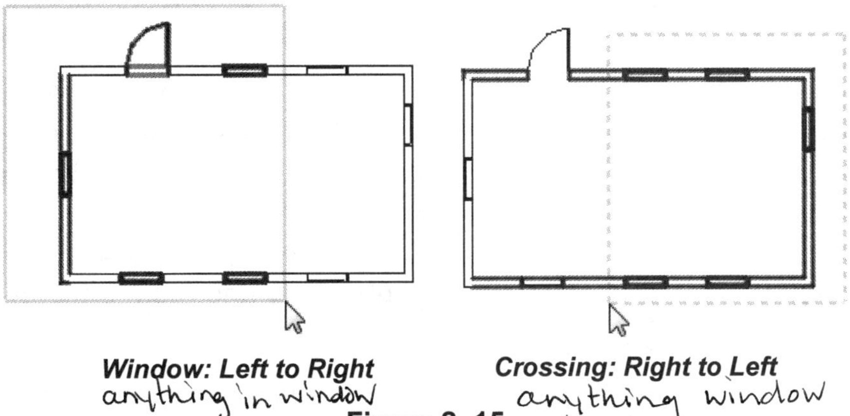

Figure 2–15

- If several elements are on or near each other, press <Tab> to cycle through them before you click. If there are elements that might be linked to each other, such as walls that are connected, pressing <Tab> selects the chain of elements.
- Press <Ctrl>+<Left Arrow> to reselect the previous selection set. You can also right-click in the view window with nothing selected and select **Select Previous**.
- To select all elements of a specific type, right-click on an element and select **Select All Instances>Visible in View** or **In Entire Project**, as shown in Figure 2–16. For example, if you select a column of a specific size and use this command, only the columns of the same size are selected.

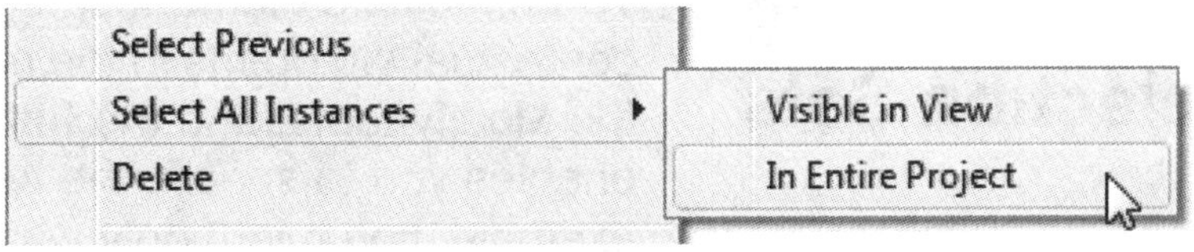

Figure 2–16

- You can save selections and use them again. For more information see *Appendix B.1 Reusing Selection Sets.*

Hint: Measuring Tools

When modifying a model, it is useful to know the distance between elements. This can be done with temporary dimensions, or more frequently, by using the measuring tools found in the Quick Access Toolbar or on the *Modify* tab> Measure panel, as shown in Figure 2–17.

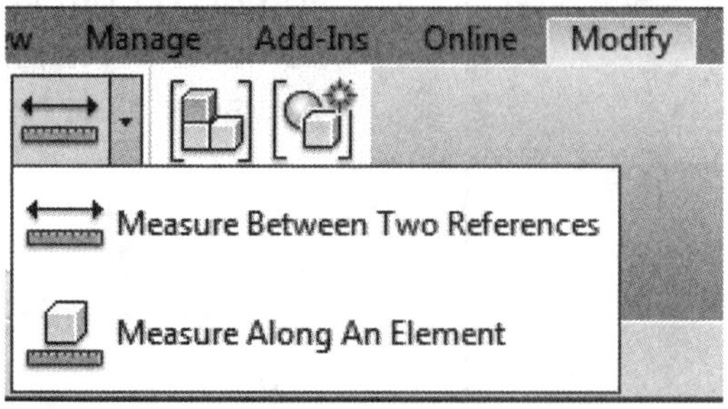

Figure 2–17

- (Measure Between Two References) - Select two elements and the measurement displays.
- (Measure Along An Element) - Select the edge of a linear element and the total length displays. Use <Tab> to select other elements and then click to measure along all of them, as shown in Figure 2–18.

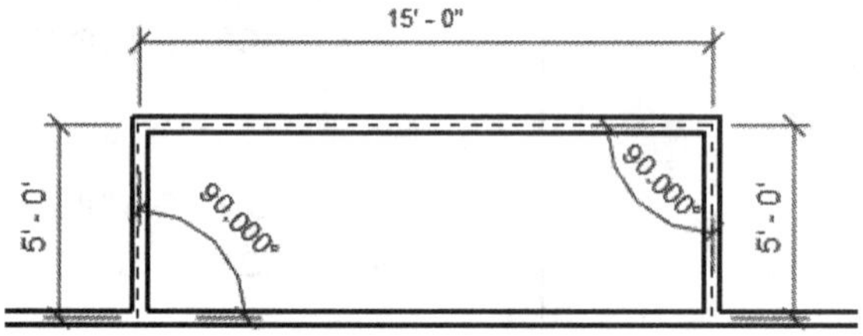

Figure 2–18

- References include any snap point, wall lines, or other parts of elements (such as door center lines).

Filtering Selection Sets

When multiple element categories are selected, the *Multi-Select* contextual tab opens in the ribbon. This gives you access to all of the Modify tools, and the **Filter** command. The **Filter** command enables you to specify the types of elements to select. For example, you might only want to select columns, as shown in Figure 2–19.

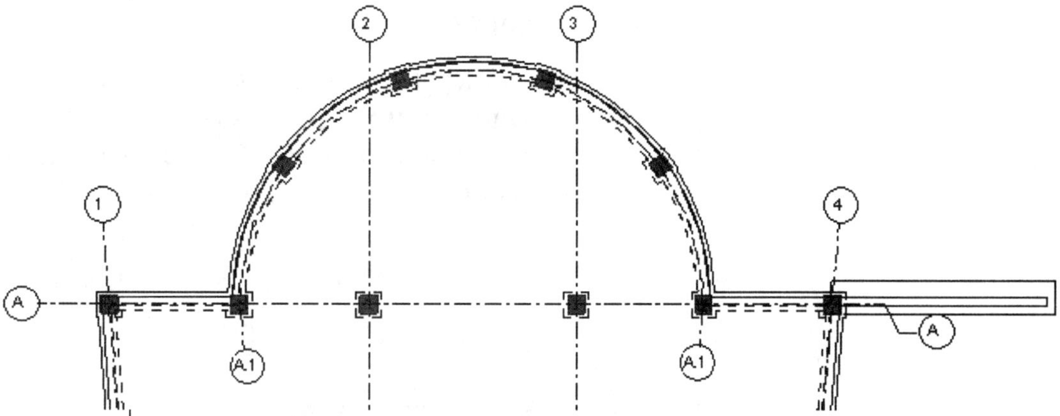

Figure 2–19

How To: Filter a Selection Set

1. Select everything in the required area.
2. in the *Modify* | *Multi-Select* tab>Selection panel, or in the Status Bar, click (Filter). The Filter dialog box opens, as shown in Figure 2–20.

The Filter dialog box displays all types of elements in the original selection.

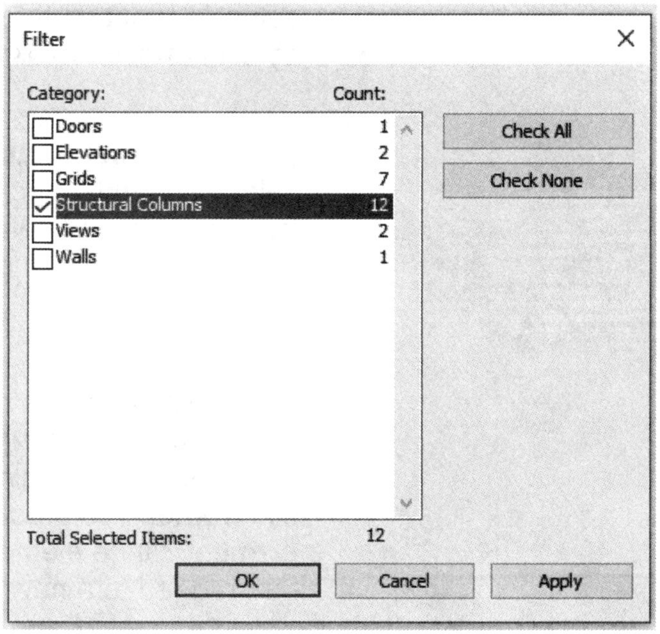

Figure 2–20

3. Click **Check None** to clear all of the options or **Check All** to select all of the options. You can also select or clear individual categories as required.
4. Click **OK**. The selection set is now limited to the elements you specified.

- The number of elements selected displays on the right end of the status bar and in the Properties palette.

Hint: Selection Options

You can control how the software selects specific elements in a project by toggling Selection Options on and off on the Status Bar, as shown in Figure 2–21. Alternatively, in any tab on the ribbon, expand the Select panel's title and select the option.

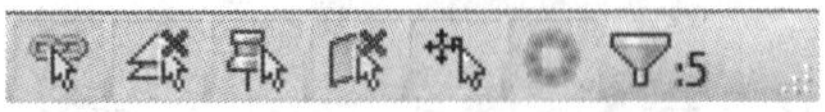

Figure 2–21

-  **Select links:** When toggled on, you can selected linked CAD drawings or Autodesk Revit models. When it is toggled off you cannot select them when using **Modify** or **Move**.

-  **Select underlay elements:** When toggled on, you can select underlay elements. When toggled off, you cannot select them when using **Modify** or **Move**.

-  **Select pinned elements:** When toggled on, you can selected pinned elements. When toggled off, you cannot select them when using **Modify** or **Move**.

-  **Select elements by face:** When toggled on you can select elements (such as the floors or walls in an elevation) by selecting the interior face or selecting an edge. When toggled off, you can only select elements by selecting an edge.

-  **Drag elements on selection:** When toggled on, you can hover over an element, select it, and drag it to a new location. When toggled off, the Crossing or Box select mode starts when you press and drag, even if you are on top of an element. Once elements have been selected they can still be dragged to a new location.

Practice 2a

Sketch and Edit Elements

Practice Objective

- Use sketch tools and drawing aids.

In this practice, you will use the **Wall** command along with sketching tools and drawing aids, such as temporary dimensions and snaps. You will use the **Modify** command and modify the walls using grips, temporary dimensions, the Type Selector, and Properties. You will add a door and modify it using temporary dimensions and controls. The completed model is shown in Figure 2–22.

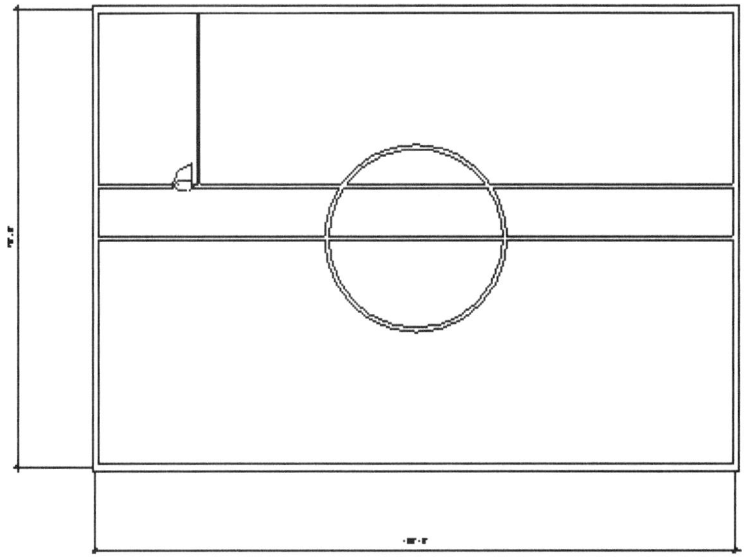

Figure 2–22

Task 1 - Use sketching tools and Temporary Dimensions to model and modify walls.

1. In the *File Tab*, click (New)> (Project).
2. In the New Project dialog box, select **Architectural Template** in the Template file drop-down list, and click **OK**.
3. In the Quick Access Toolbar, click (Save). When prompted, name the project **Simple Building.rvt**.
4. In the *Architecture* tab>Build panel, click (Wall).

5. In the *Modify | Place Wall* tab>Draw panel, click

   (Rectangle) and sketch a rectangle approximately **100' x 70'**. You do not have to be precise because you can change the dimensions later.

6. Note that the dimensions are temporary. Select the vertical dimension text and type **70' 0"**, as shown in Figure 2–23. Press <Enter>.

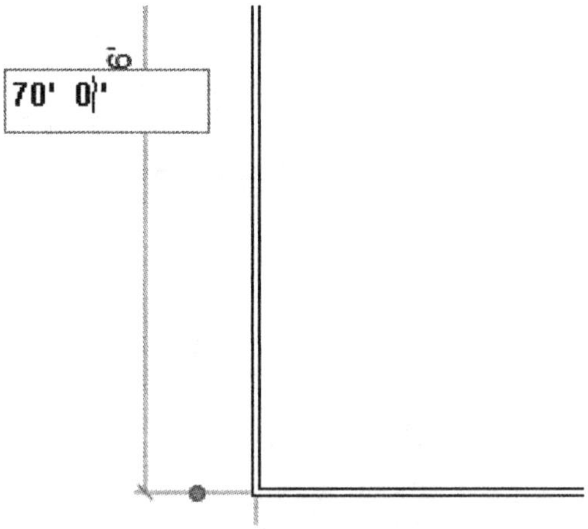

Figure 2–23

7. The dimensions are still displayed as temporary. Click the dimension controls of both the dimensions to make them permanent, as shown in Figure 2–24.

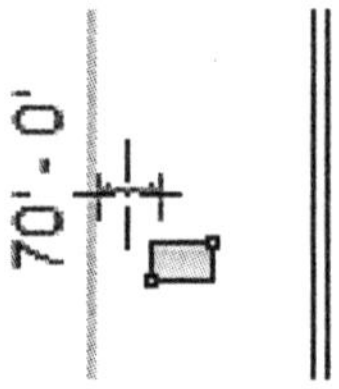

Figure 2–24

   • You will change the horizontal wall dimension using the permanent dimension.

8. In the Select panel, click (Modify). You can also use one of the other methods to switch to **Modify:**

   • Type the shortcut **MD**.
   • Press <Esc> once or twice.

9. Select either vertical wall. The horizontal dimension becomes active (changes to blue). Click the dimension text and type **100' 0"**, as shown in Figure 2–25.

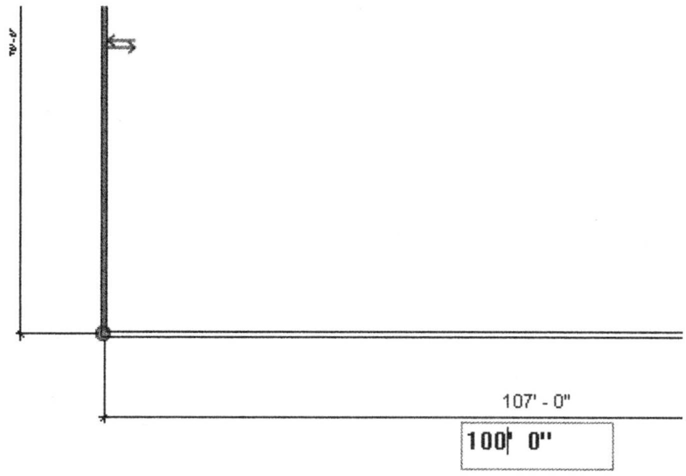

Figure 2–25

10. Click in an empty space to end the selection. You are still in the **Modify** command.

11. In the *Architecture* tab>Build panel, click (Wall). In the Draw panel, verify that (Line) is selected. Sketch a wall horizontally from midpoint to midpoint of the vertical walls.

12. Draw another horizontal wall **8'-0"** above the middle horizontal wall. You can use temporary dimensions or the *Offset* field to do this.

13. Draw a vertical wall exactly **16'-0"** from the left wall, as shown in Figure 2–26.

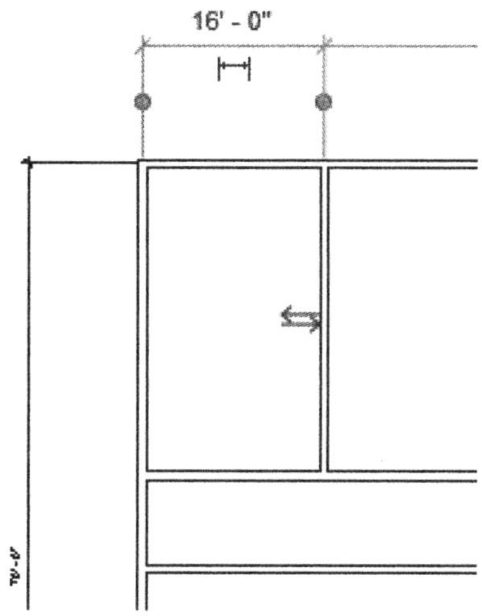

Figure 2–26

14. In the Draw panel, click (Circle) and sketch a **14'-0"** radius circular wall at the midpoint of the lower interior horizontal wall, as shown in Figure 2–27.

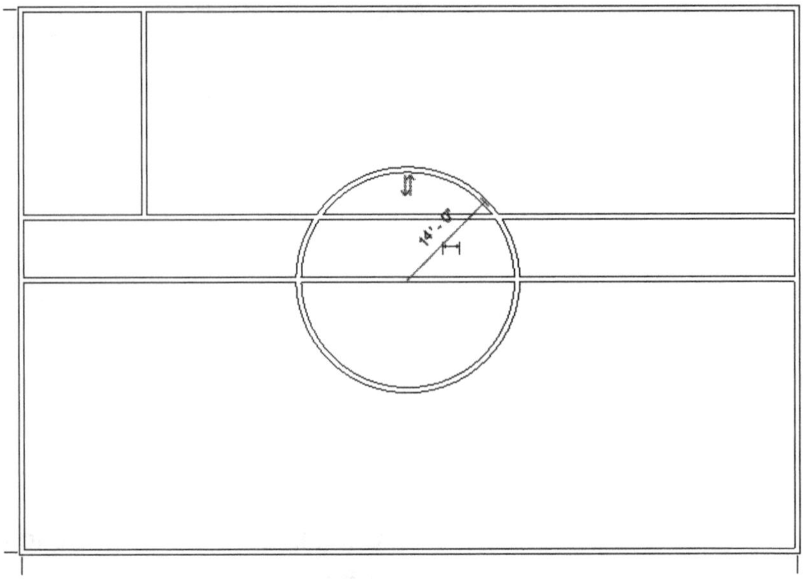

Figure 2–27

15. Click (Modify) to finish the command.

16. Hover the cursor over one of the outside walls, press <Tab> to highlight the chain of outside walls, and click to select the walls.

17. In the Type Selector, select **Basic Wall: Generic-12"**, as shown in Figure 2–28. The thickness of the outside walls change.

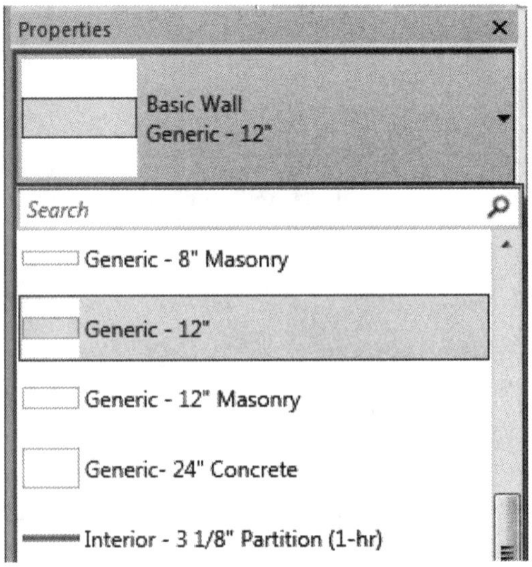

Figure 2–28

18. Click in empty space to release the selection.
19. Select the vertical interior wall. In the Type Selector, change the wall to one of the small interior partition styles.
20. Click in an empty space to release the selection.

Task 2 - Add and modify a door.

1. Zoom in on the room in the upper left corner.
2. In the *Architecture* tab>Build panel, click (Door).
3. In the *Modify | Place Door* tab>Tag panel, click (Tag on Placement) if it is not already selected.
4. Place a door anywhere along the wall in the hallway.
5. Click (Modify) to finish the command.
6. Select the door. Use temporary dimensions to move it so that it is **2'-6"** from the right interior vertical wall. If required, use controls to flip the door so that it swings into the room, as shown in Figure 2–29.

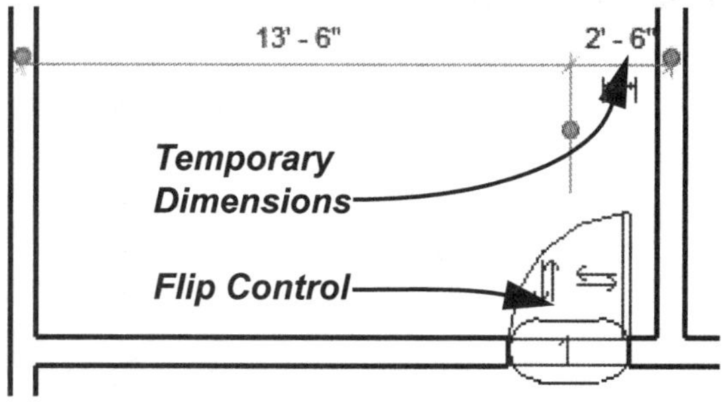

Figure 2–29

7. Type **ZE** to zoom out to the full view.
8. Save the project.

2.3 Working with Basic Modify Tools

The basic modifying tools of **Move**, **Copy**, **Rotate**, **Mirror**, and **Array** can be used with individual elements or any selection of elements. They are found in the Modify panel (as shown in Figure 2–30), in the *Modify* tab, and in contextual tabs.

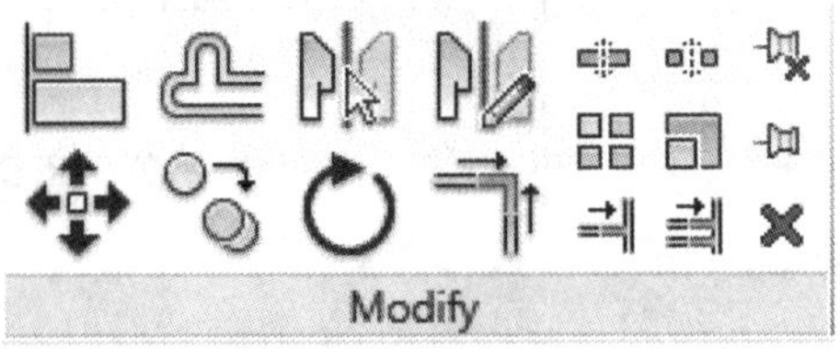

Figure 2–30

- For these modify commands, you can either select the elements and start the command, or start the command, select the elements, and press <Enter> to finish the selection and move to the next step in the command.

Moving and Copying Elements

The **Move** and **Copy** commands enable you to select the element(s) and move or copy them from one place to another. You can use alignment lines, temporary dimensions, and snaps to help place the elements, as shown in Figure 2–31.

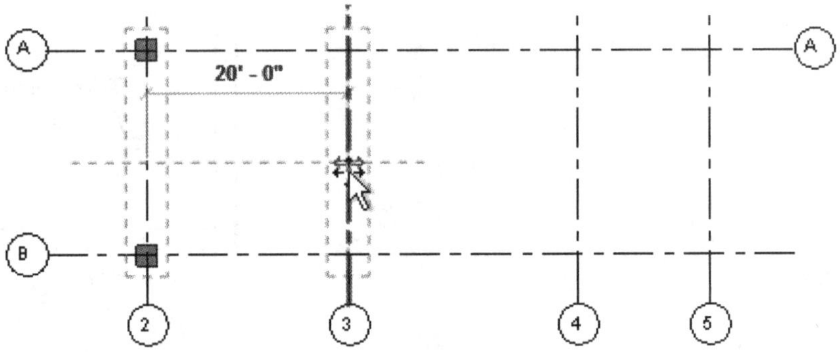

Figure 2–31

How To: Move or Copy Elements

*You can also use the shortcut for **Move, MV** or for **Copy, CO**.*

1. Select the elements you want to move or copy.
2. In the Modify panel, click  (Move) or  (Copy). A boundary box displays around the selected elements.
3. Select a move start point on or near the element.
4. Select a second point. Use alignment lines and temporary dimensions to help place the elements.

5. When you are finished, you can start another modify command using the elements that remain selected, or switch back to **Modify** to end the command.

- You can drag elements to new locations without starting the **Move** command. Holding <Ctrl> and dragging copies the element. This is quick but not very precise.

Move/Copy Elements Options

The **Move** and **Copy** commands have several options that display in the Options Bar, as shown in Figure 2–32.

Figure 2–32

Constrain	Restricts the movement of the cursor to horizontal or vertical, or along the axis of an item that is at an angle. This keeps you from selecting a point at an angle by mistake. **Constrain** is off by default.
Disjoin (Move only)	Breaks any connections between the elements being moved and other elements. If **Disjoin** is on, the elements move separately. If it is off, the connected elements also move or stretch. **Disjoin** is off by default.
Multiple (Copy only)	Enables you to make multiple copies of one selection. **Multiple** is off by default.

- These commands only work in the current view, not between views or projects. To copy between views or projects, In the *Modify* tab>Clipboard panel use (Copy to Clipboard), (Cut to the Clipboard) and (Paste from Clipboard).

Hint: Pinning Elements

If you do not want elements to be moved, you can pin them in place, as shown in Figure 2–33. Select the elements and in the *Modify* tab, in the Modify panel, click (Pin). Pinned elements can be copied, but not moved. If you try to delete a pinned element, a warning dialog displays reminding you that you must unpin the element before the command can be started.

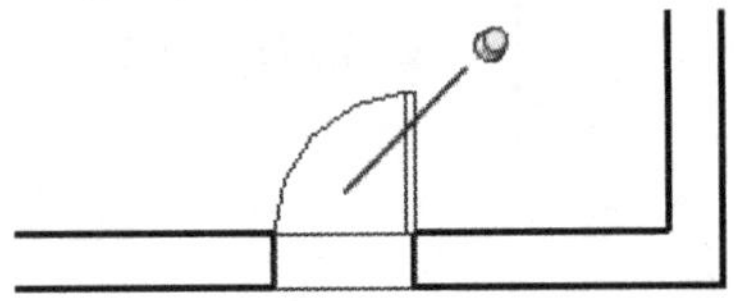

Figure 2–33

Select the element and click (Unpin) or type the shortcut **UP** to free it.

Rotating Elements

The **Rotate** command enables you to rotate selected elements around a center point or origin, as shown in Figure 2–34. You can use alignment lines, temporary dimensions, and snaps to help specify the center of rotation and the angle. You can also create copies of the element as it is being rotated.

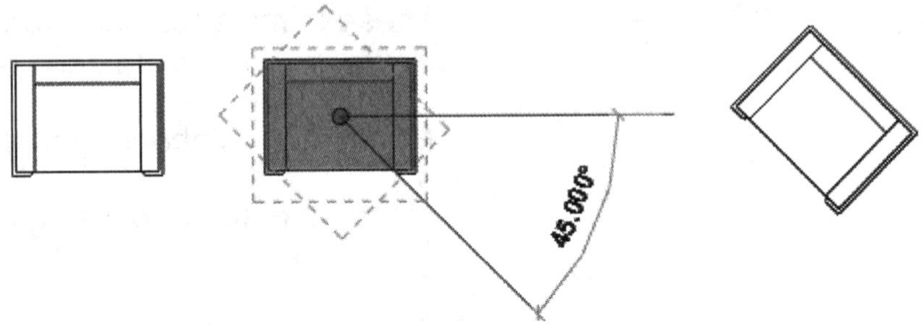

Figure 2–34

How To: Rotate Elements

1. Select the element(s) you want to rotate.
2. In the Modify panel, click (Rotate) or type the shortcut **RO**.

control 2 =undo

*To start the **Rotate** command with a prompt to select the center of rotation, select the elements first and type **R3**.*

3. The center of rotation is automatically set to the center of the element or group of elements, as shown on the left in Figure 2–35. To change the center of rotation, as shown on the right in Figure 2–35, use the following:

   - Drag the (Center of Rotation) control to a new point.
   - In the Options Bar, next to **Center of rotation**, click **Place** and use snaps to move it to a new location.
   - Press <Spacebar> to select the center of rotation and click to move it to a new location.

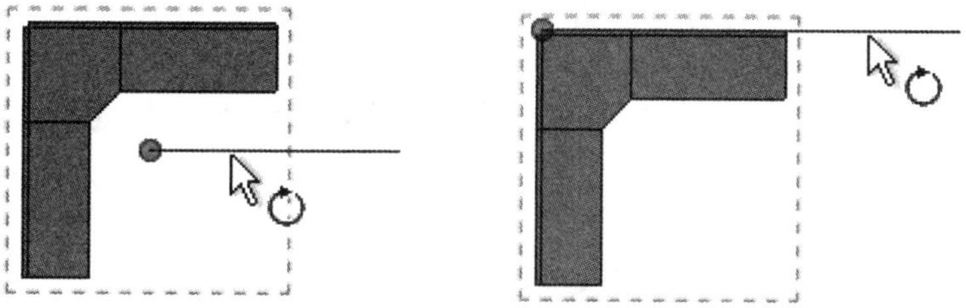

Figure 2–35

4. In the Options Bar, specify if you want to make a Copy (select **Copy**), type an angle in the *Angle* field (as shown in Figure 2–36), and press <Enter>. You can also specify the angle on screen using temporary dimensions.

Figure 2–36

5. The rotated element(s) remain highlighted, enabling you to start another command using the same selection, or click (Modify) to finish.

- The **Disjoin** option breaks any connections between the elements being rotated and other elements. If **Disjoin** is on (selected), the elements rotate separately. If it is off (cleared), the connected elements also move or stretch, as shown in Figure 2–37. **Disjoin** is toggled off by default.

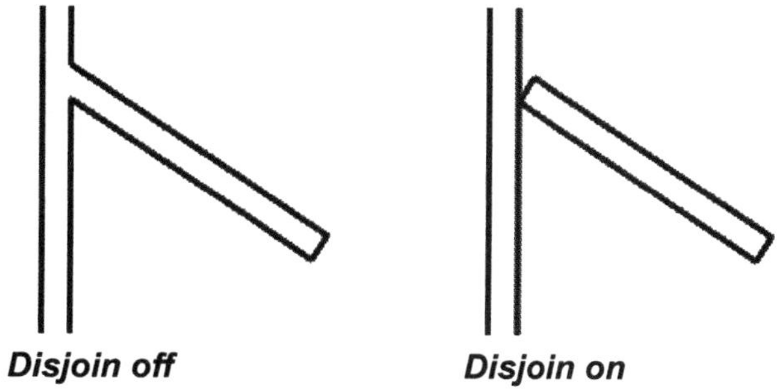

Figure 2–37

Mirroring Elements

The **Mirror** command enables you to mirror elements about an axis defined by a selected element, as shown in Figure 2–38, or by selected points.

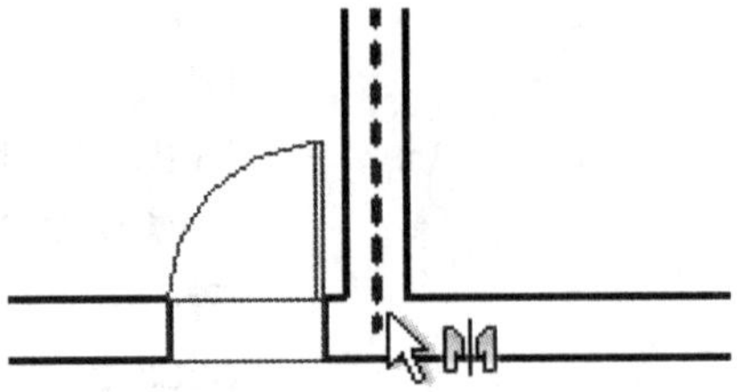

Figure 2–38

How To: Mirror Elements

1. Select the element(s) to mirror.
2. In the Modify panel, select the method you want to use:
   - Click (Mirror - Pick Axis) or type the shortcut **MM**. This prompts you to select an element as the **Axis of Reflection** (mirror line).
   - Click (Mirror - Draw Axis) or type the shortcut **DM**. This prompts you to select two points to define the axis about which the elements mirror.
3. The new mirrored element(s) remain highlighted, enabling you to start another command, or return to **Modify** to finish.

- By default, the original elements that were mirrored remain. To delete the original elements, clear the **Copy** option in the Options Bar.

Hint: Scale

The Autodesk Revit software is designed with full-size elements. Therefore, not much should be scaled. For example, scaling a wall increases its length but does not impact the width, which is set by the wall type. However, you can use (Scale) in reference planes, images, and imported files from other programs.

Creating Linear and Radial Arrays

A linear array creates a straight line pattern of elements, while a radial array creates a circular pattern around a center point.

The **Array** command creates multiple copies of selected elements in a linear or radial pattern, as shown in Figure 2–39. For example, you can array a row of columns to create a row of evenly spaced columns on a grid, or array a row of parking spaces. The arrayed elements can be grouped or placed as separate elements.

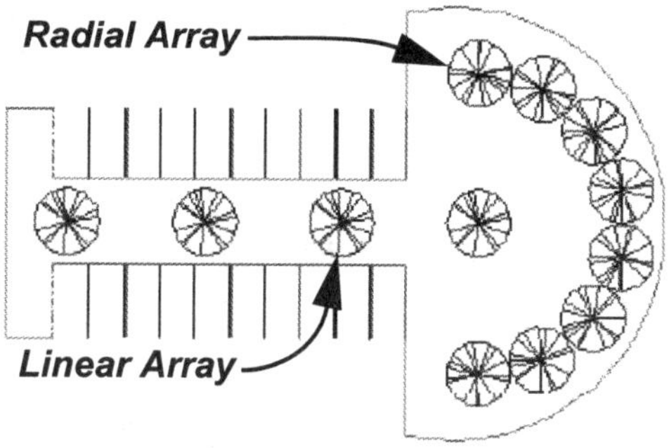

Figure 2–39

How To: Create a Linear Array

1. Select the element(s) to array.
2. In the Modify panel, click  (Array) or type the shortcut **AR**.
3. In the Options Bar, click  (Linear).
4. Specify the other options as required.
5. Select a start point and an end point to set the spacing and direction of the array. The array is displayed.
6. If **Group and Associate** is selected, you are prompted again for the number of items, as shown in Figure 2–40. Type a new number or click on the screen to finish the command.

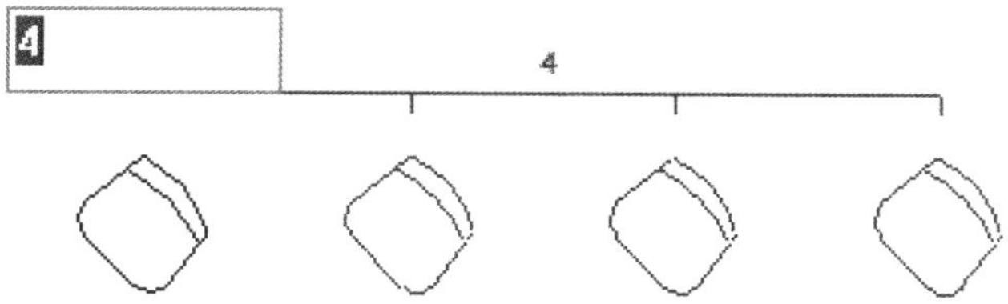

Figure 2–40

- To make a linear array in two directions, you need to array one direction first, select the arrayed elements, and then array them again in the other direction.

Array Options

In the Options Bar, set up the **Array** options for **Linear Array** (top of Figure 2–41) or **Radial Array** (bottom of Figure 2–41).

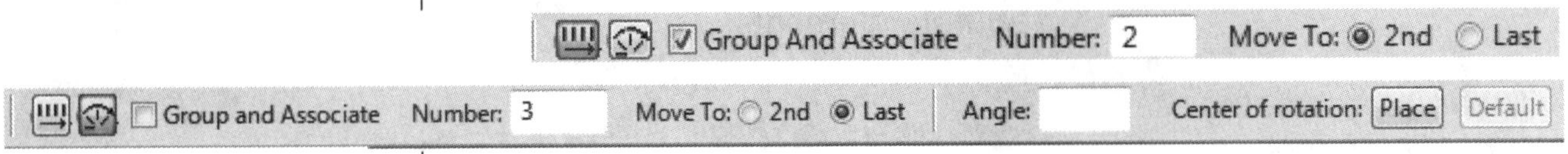

Figure 2–41

Group and Associate	Creates an array group element out of all arrayed elements. Groups can be selected by selecting any elements in the group.
Number	Specifies how many instances you want in the array.
Move To:	**2nd** specifies the distance or angle between the center points of the two elements. **Last** specifies the overall distance or angle of the entire array.
Constrain	Restricts the direction of the array to only vertical or horizontal (Linear only).
Angle	Specifies the angle (Radial only).
Center of rotation	Specifies a location for the origin about which the elements rotate (Radial only).

How To: Create a Radial Array

1. Select the element(s) to array.
2. In the Modify panel, click (Array).
3. In the Options Bar, click (Radial).
4. Drag (Center of Rotation) or use **Place** to the move the center of rotation to the appropriate location, as shown in Figure 2–42.

*Remember to set the **Center of Rotation** control first, because it is easy to forget to move it before specifying the angle.*

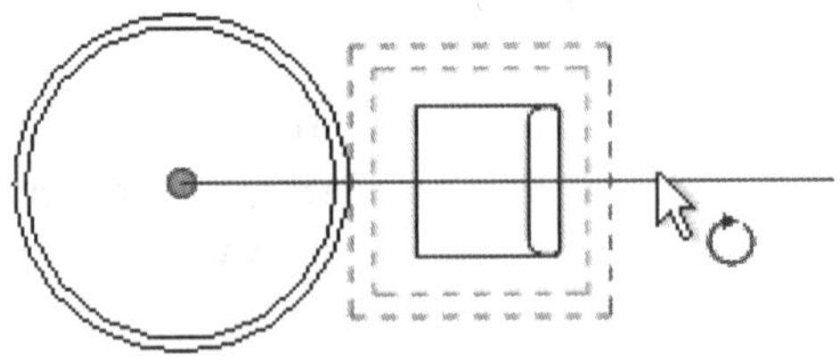

Figure 2–42

5. Specify the other options as required.
6. In the Options Bar, type an angle and press <Enter>, or specify the rotation angle by selecting points on the screen.

Modifying Array Groups

When you select an element in an array that has been grouped, you can change the number of instances in the array, as shown in Figure 2–43. For radial arrays you can also modify the distance to the center.

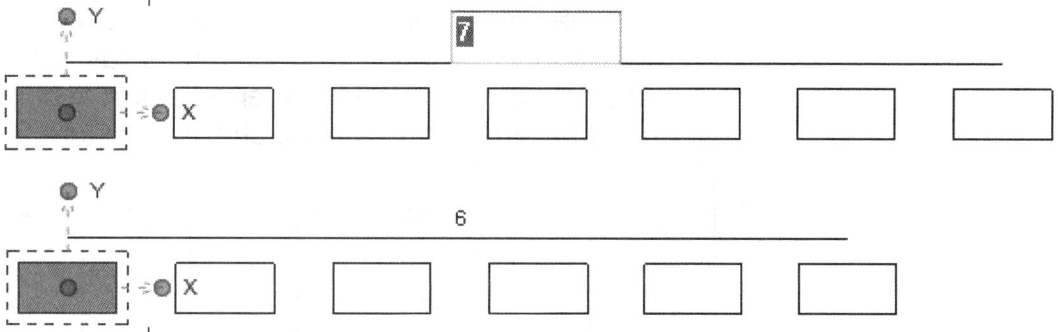

Figure 2–43

- Dashed lines surround the element(s) in a group, and the XY control lets you move the origin point of the group

If you move one of the elements in the array group, the other elements move in response based on the distance and/or angle, as shown in Figure 2–44.

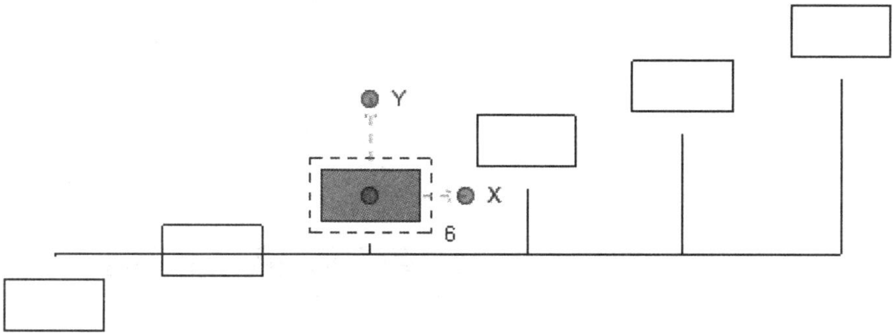

Figure 2–44

- To remove the array constraint on the group, select all of the elements in the array group and, in the *Modify* contextual tab>Group panel, click (Ungroup).
- If you select an individual element in an array and click (Ungroup), the element you selected is removed from the array, while the rest of the elements remain in the array group.
- You can use (Filter) to ensure that you are selecting only **Model Groups**.

Practice 2b Work with Basic Modify Tools

Practice Objective

- Use basic modify tools such as Move, Copy, Rotate, and Array Elements.

In this practice, you will create a series of offices using the Copy and Mirror commands. You will then array desks around a circular wall, then rotate and array a pair of columns across the front of a simple building, as shown in Figure 2–45.

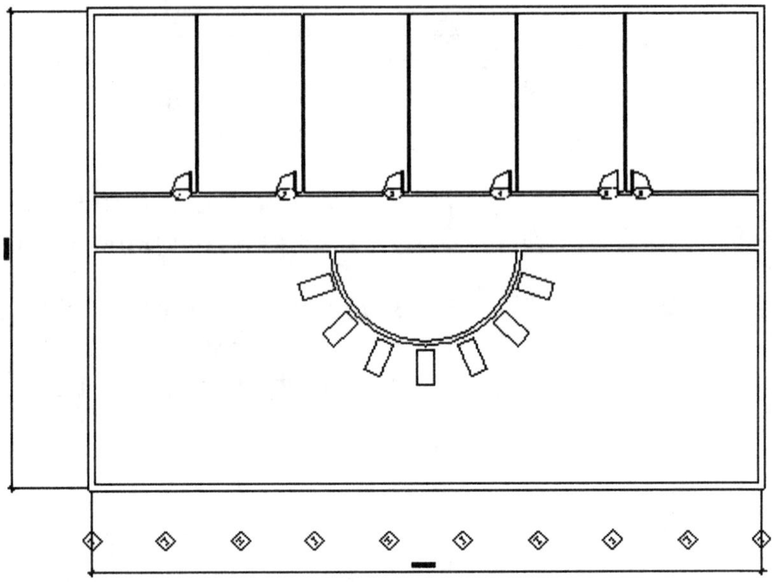

Figure 2–45

Task 1 - Modify walls and doors.

1. Open the project **Simple-Building-1.rvt** from your practice files folder.

2. Select the top arc of the circular wall.

*Remember that you can also press <Delete>, or right-click and select **Delete**.*

3. In the Modify panel, click ✖ (Delete). The walls that the circular wall crossed are automatically cleaned up.

4. Select the vertical interior wall, door, and door tag. Hold <Ctrl> to select more than one element, or use a selection window.

5. In the Modify panel, click (Copy).

6. In the Options Bar, select **Constrain** and **Multiple**. The **Constrain** option forces the cursor to move only horizontally or vertically.

7. Select the start point and the end point, as shown in Figure 2–46. The wall, door, and door tag are copied to the right and the door tag displays **2**.

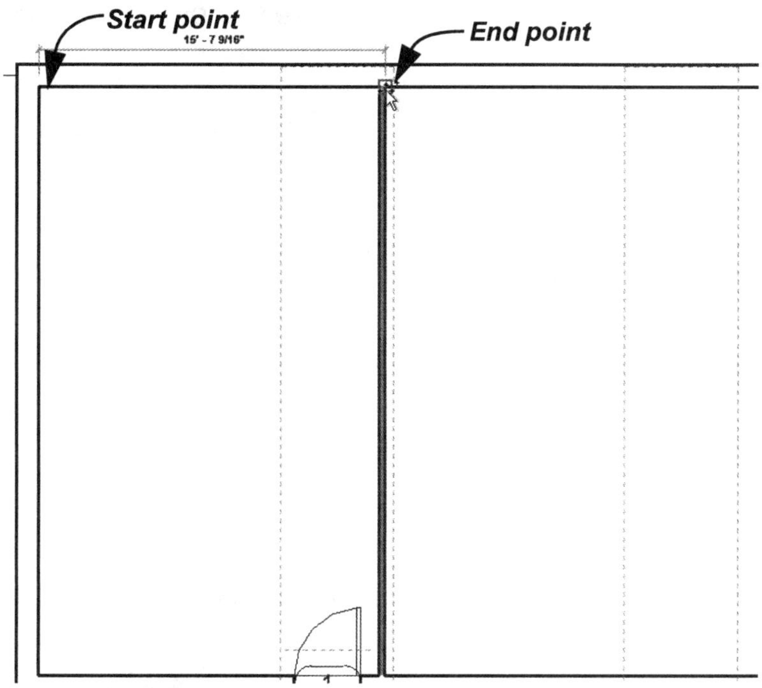

Figure 2–46

8. The new elements are still selected and you can continue to copy them. Use similar start and end points for the additional copies, or type **16** (16'-0") and press <Enter> to set the distance between each copy. The final layout is shown in Figure 2–47.

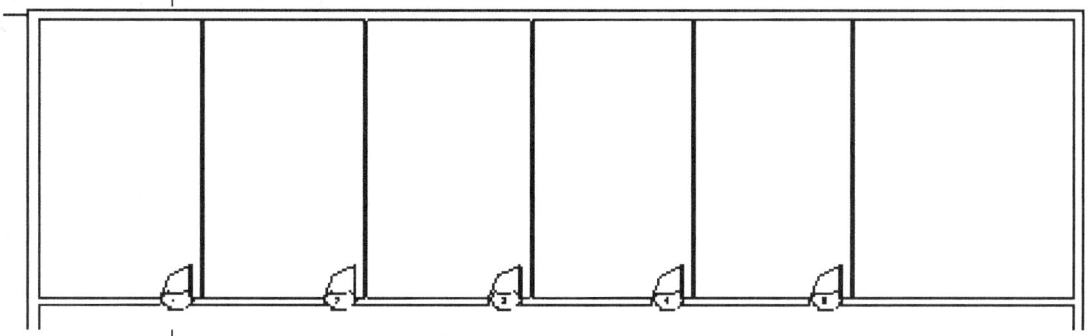

Figure 2–47

9. Click (Modify) to finish the command.

10. Zoom in on the room to the far right.

11. Select door #5 and the associated door tag.

12. In the Modify panel, click (Mirror - Pick Axis). In the Options Bar, ensure that **Copy** is selected.

13. Select the vertical wall between the rooms as the mirror axis. An alignment line displays along the center of the wall. Place the new door, as shown in Figure 2–48.

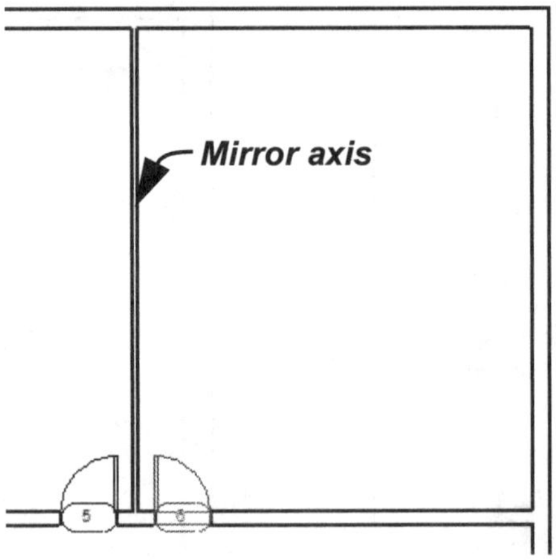

Figure 2–48

14. Click in empty space to release the selection.

Task 2 - Add reference planes and use them to place a component.

1. In the *Architecture* tab>Work plane panel, click (Ref Plane).

2. Draw two reference planes, as shown in Figure 2–49. The vertical one starts at the midpoint of the wall. You can place the horizontal plane anywhere, and then use temporary dimensions to place it more exactly.)

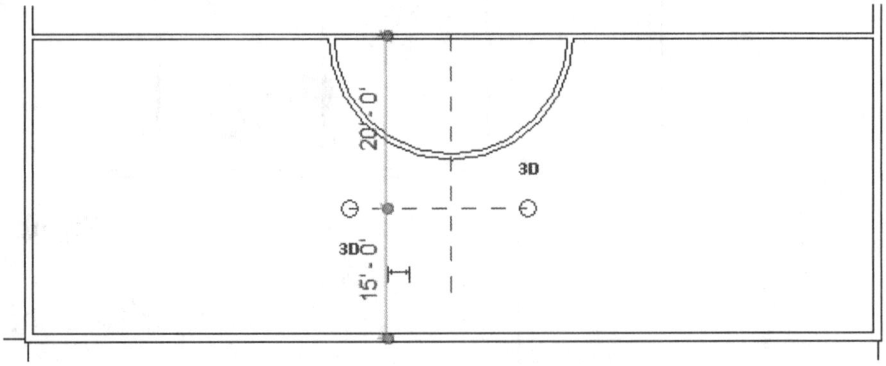

Figure 2–49

3. In the *Architecture* tab>Build panel, click (Component).

4. In the Properties palette, in the Type Selector, verify that **Desk: 60" x 30"** is selected, as shown in Figure 2–50.

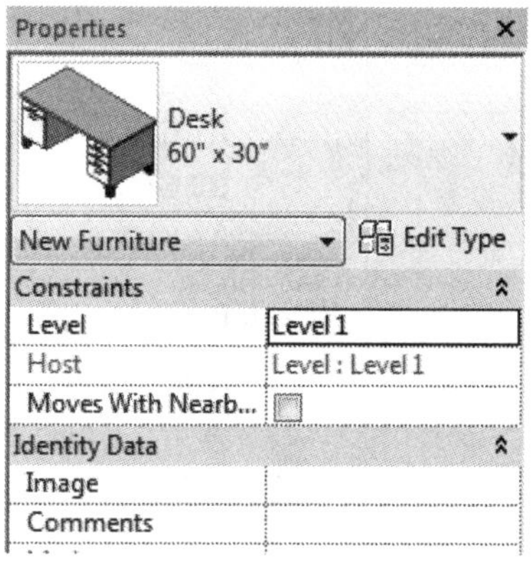

Figure 2–50

5. As you move the cursor you can see that the desk is horizontal. Press <Spacebar> to rotate the desk 90 degrees.

6. Place the desk at the intersection of the two reference planes, as shown in Figure 2–51. Zoom in as required to ensure that you are connected to the reference planes, and not to any other alignment lines.

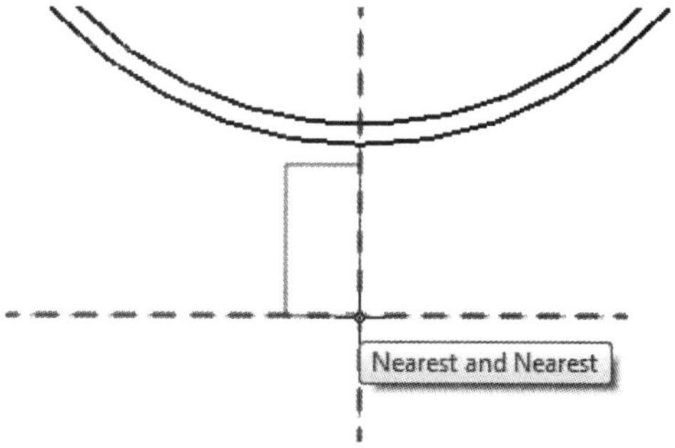

Figure 2–51

7. Click (Modify) and select the desk you just placed.

8. In the Modify panel, click (Move). Select the start point of the move as the vertical alignment line of the desk, and the end point as the vertical reference plane.

9. Save the project.

Task 3 - Create a Radial Array.

1. Select the desk.
2. In the Modify panel, click (Array).
3. In the Options Bar, click (Radial). Clear the **Group and associate** option, set the *Number* field to 15, and set the *Move to:* field to **2nd.**
4. Drag the center of rotation from the center of the desk to the midpoint of the wall, as shown in Figure 2–52.

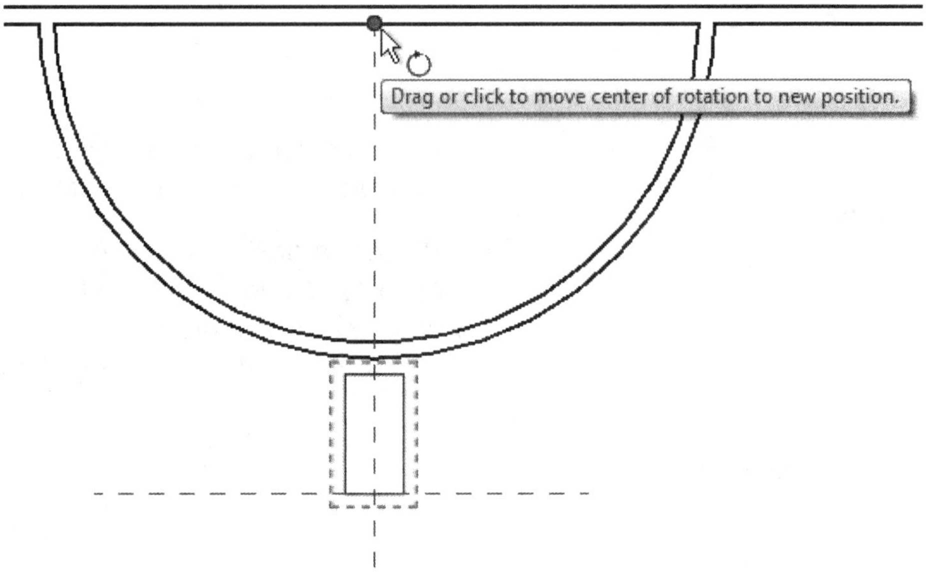

Figure 2–52

5. Return to the Options Bar and set the *Angle* to **360**. Press <Enter>. The array displays as shown in Figure 2–53.

Sometimes it is easier to create more elements then you need, and then delete the ones that are not required, as is done in this example.

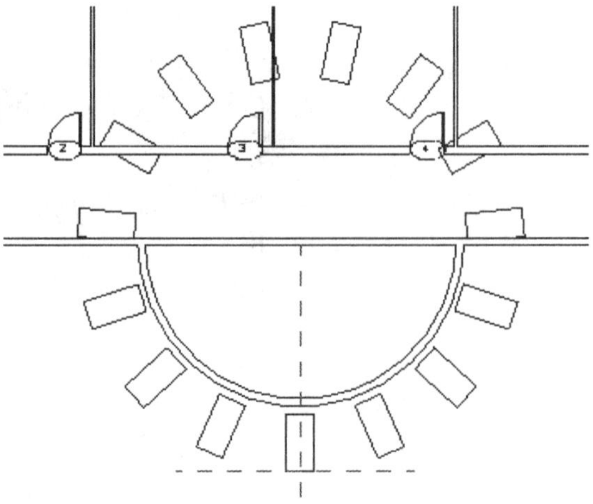

Figure 2–53

6. Delete all of the desks that are outside of the room that has the original desk.

7. Zoom out to display the entire view.

Task 4 - Place columns in appropriate locations.

1. Two columns (one architectural and one structural) have been added to the project. Select the square architectural column and drag it over so that it lines up with the wall, as shown in Figure 2–54. Use the temporary dimension to set the distance off the wall.

2. Place the structural column at the center of the architectural column (as shown in Figure 2–55) using the **Midpoint and Extension** snaps.

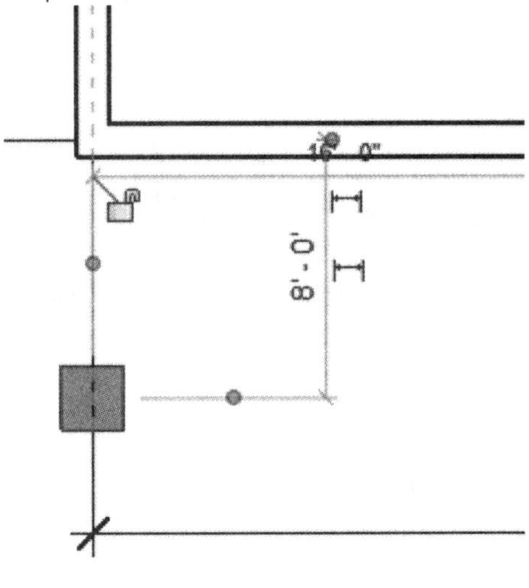

Figure 2–54

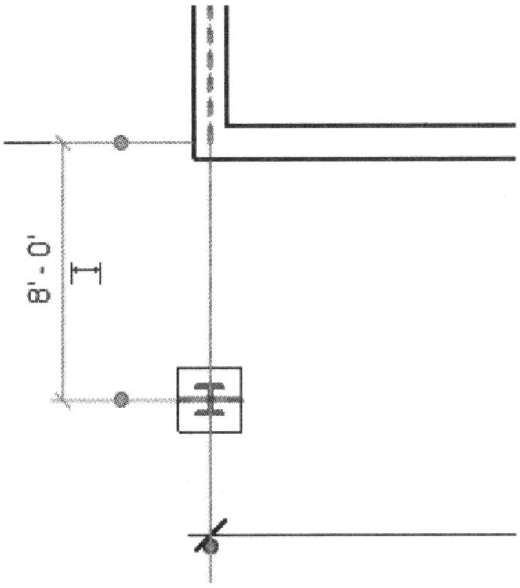

Figure 2–55

3. Save the project.

Task 5 - Rotate and Array the columns.

1. Click (Modify) and select the two columns.

2. In the *Modify | Multi-Select* tab>Modify panel, click (Rotate).

3. For the start ray, click horizontally, as shown in Figure 2–56.

4. Move the ray line until you see the temporary dimension **45.000**, as shown in Figure 2–57.

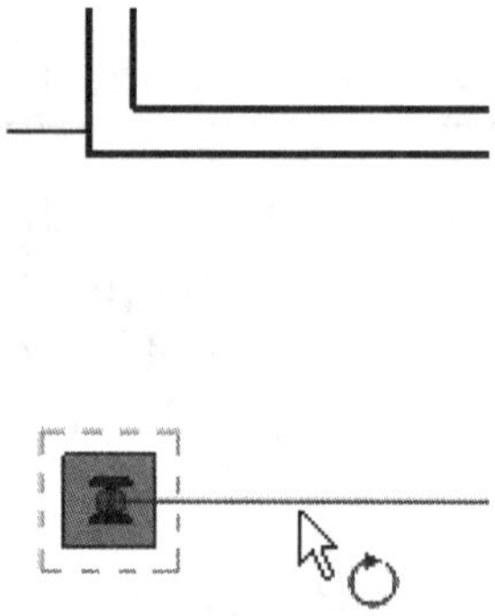

Figure 2–56

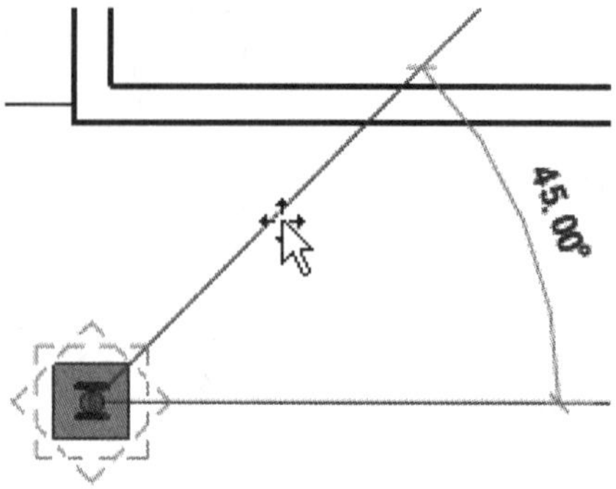

Figure 2–57

5. With the two columns still selected, in the *Modify | Multi-Select* tab>Modify panel, click (Array).

6. In the Options Bar, click (Linear), clear **Group and Associate**, set the *Number* to **10**, and set *Move To:* to **Last**.

7. For the start point, click the midpoint of the columns. For the endpoint of the array, select the **Horizontal and Extension** of the center of the far right wall as shown in Figure 2–58.

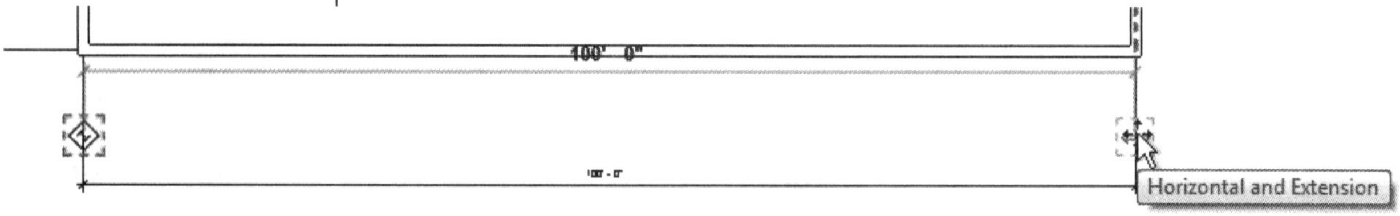

Figure 2–58

8. Zoom out to display the entire building.

9. The columns are arrayed evenly across the front of the building as shown in Figure 2–59.

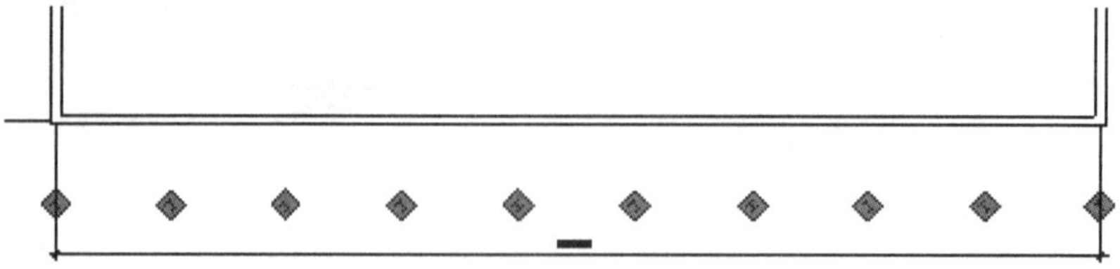

Figure 2–59

10. Save the project.

2.4 Working with Additional Modify Tools

As you work on a project, some additional tools on the *Modify* tab>Modify panel, as shown in Figure 2–60, can help you with placing, modifying, and constraining elements. **Align** can be used with a variety of elements, while **Split Element**, **Trim/Extend**, and **Offset** can only be used with linear elements.

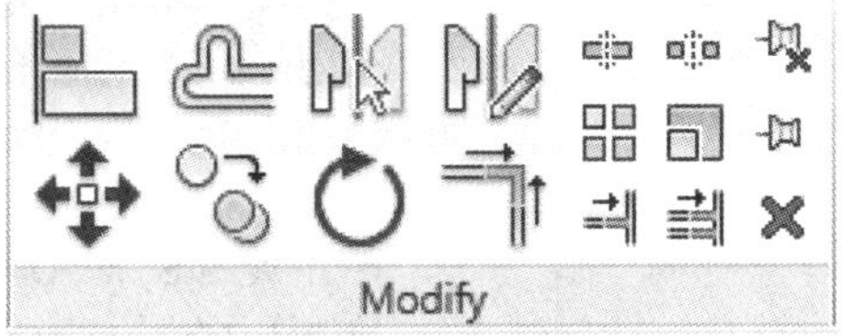

Figure 2–60

Aligning Elements

The **Align** command enables you to line up one element with another, as shown in Figure 2–61. Most Autodesk Revit elements can be aligned. For example, you can line up the tops of windows with the top of a door, or line up furniture with a wall.

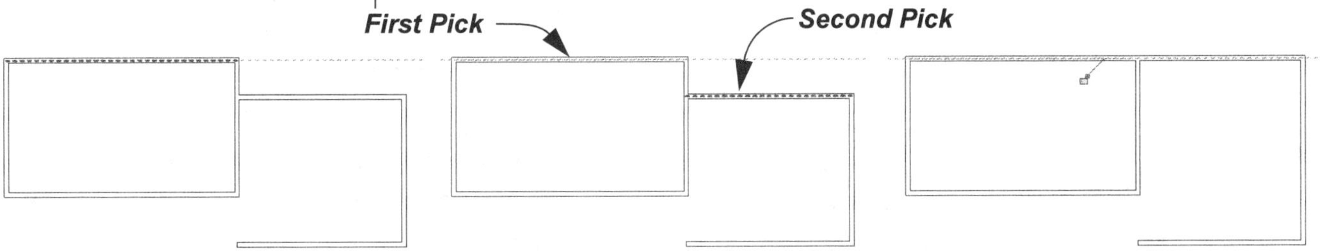

Figure 2–61

How To: Align Elements

1. In the *Modify* tab>Modify panel, click  (Align).
2. Select a line or point on the element that is going to remain stationary. For walls, press <Tab> to select the correct wall face.
3. Select a line or point on the element to be aligned. The second element moves into alignment with the first one.

- The **Align** command works in all model views, including parallel and perspective 3D views.

- You can lock alignments so that the elements move together if either one is moved. Once you have created the alignment, a padlock is displayed. Click on the padlock to lock it, as shown in Figure 2–62.

Locking elements enlarges the size of the project file, so use this option carefully.

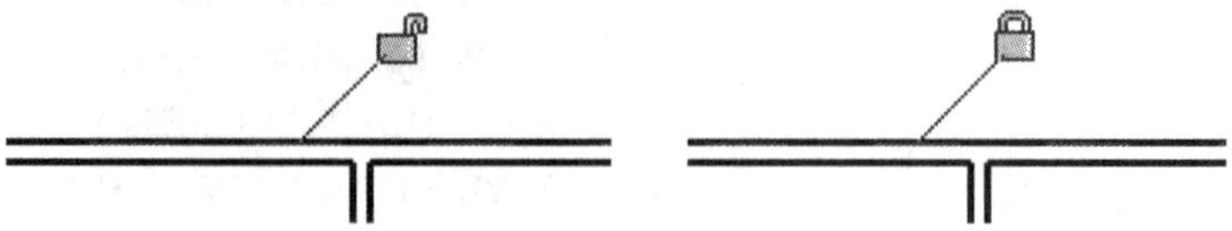

Figure 2–62

- Select **Multiple Alignment** to select multiple elements to align with the first element. You can also hold <Ctrl> to make multiple alignments.

- For walls, you can specify if you want the command to prefer **Wall centerlines**, **Wall faces**, **Center of core**, or **Faces of core**, as shown in Figure 2–63. The core refers to the structural members of a wall as opposed to facing materials, such as sheet rock.

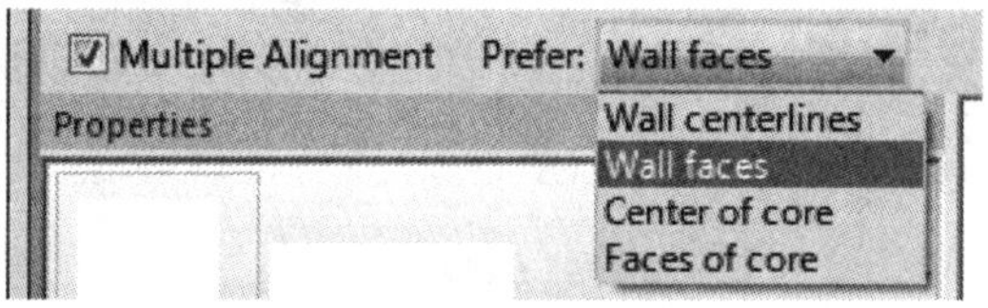

Figure 2–63

Splitting Linear Elements

The **Split** Element command enables you to break a linear element at a specific point. You can use alignment lines, snaps, and temporary dimensions to help place the split point. After you have split the linear element, you can use other editing commands to modify the two parts, or change the type of one part, as shown with walls in Figure 2–64.

You can split walls in plan, elevation or 3D views.

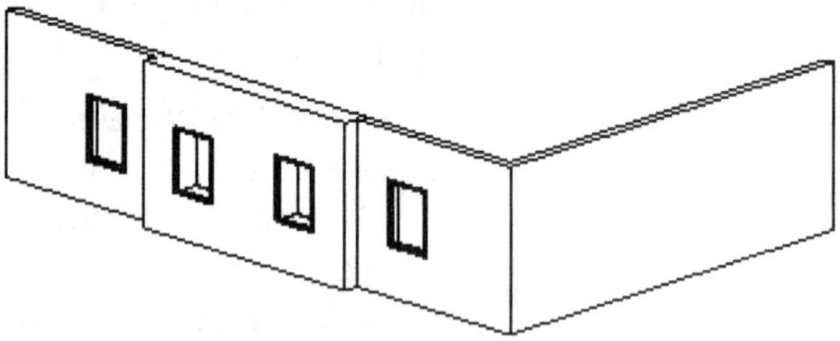

Figure 2–64

How To: Split Linear Elements

1. In the *Modify* tab>Modify panel, click (Split Element) or type the shortcut **SL**.
2. In the Options Bar, select or clear the **Delete Inner Segment** option.
3. Move the cursor to the point you want to split and select the point.
4. Repeat for any additional split locations.
5. Modify the elements that were split, as required.

- The **Delete Inner Segment** option is used when you select two split points along a linear element. When the option is selected, the segment between the two split points is automatically removed.

- An additional option, (Split with Gap), splits the linear element at the point you select (as shown in Figure 2–65), but also creates a *Joint Gap* specified in the Options Bar.

This command is typically used with structural precast slabs.

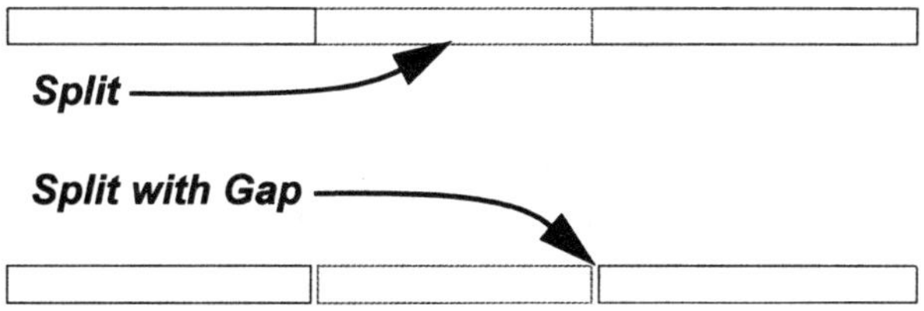

Figure 2–65

Trimming and Extending

* click the sides you * want to * Keep *

There are three trim/extend methods that you can use with linear elements: **Trim/Extend to Corner**, **Trim/Extend Single Element**, and **Trim/Extend Multiple Elements**.

- When selecting elements to trim, click the part of the element that you want to keep. The opposite part of the line is then trimmed.

How To: Trim/Extend to Corner

1. In the *Modify* tab>Modify panel, click (Trim/Extend to Corner) or type the shortcut **TR**.
2. Select the first linear element on the side you want to keep.

3. Select the second linear element on the side you want to keep, as shown in Figure 2–66.

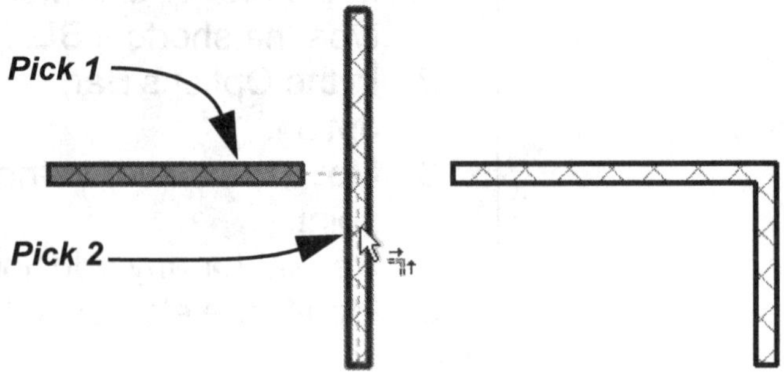

Figure 2–66

How To: Trim/Extend a Single Element

1. In the *Modify* tab>Modify panel, click (Trim/Extend Single Element).
2. Select the cutting or boundary edge.
3. Select the linear element to be trimmed or extended, as shown in Figure 2–67.

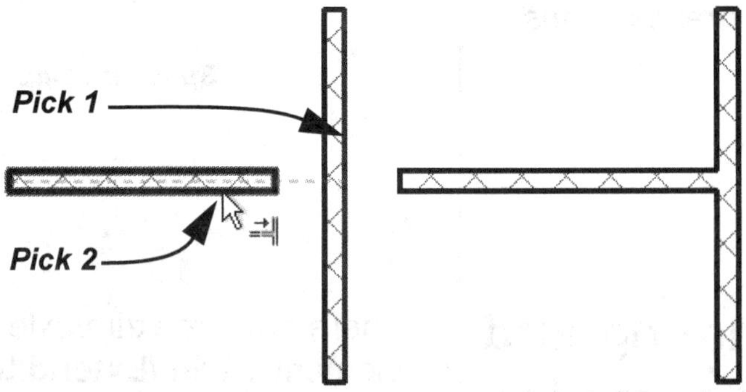

Figure 2–67

How To: Trim/Extend Multiple Elements

1. In the *Modify* tab>Modify panel, click (Trim/Extend Multiple Elements).
2. Select the cutting or boundary edge.

3. Select the linear elements that you want to trim or extend by selecting one at a time, or by using a crossing window, as shown in Figure 2–68. For trimming, select the side you want to keep.

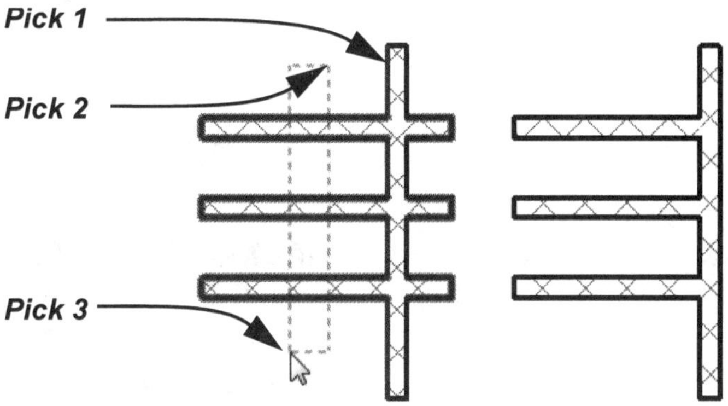

Figure 2–68

- You can click in an empty space to clear the selection and select another cutting edge or boundary.

Offsetting Elements

The **Offset** command is an easy way of creating parallel copies of linear elements at a specified distance, as shown in Figure 2–69. Walls, beams, braces, and lines are among the elements that can be offset.

Figure 2–69

- If you offset a wall that has a door or window embedded in it, the elements are copied with the offset wall.

The offset distance can be set by typing the distance (**Numerical** method shown in Figure 2–70) or by selecting points on the screen (**Graphical** method).

Figure 2–70

How To: Offset using the Numerical Method

*The **Copy** option (which is on by default) makes a copy of the element being offset. If this option is not selected, the **Offset** command moves the element the set offset distance.*

1. In the *Modify* tab>Modify panel, click (Offset) or type the shortcut **OF**.
2. In the Options Bar, select the **Numerical** option.
3. In the Options Bar, type the required distance in the *Offset* field.
4. Move the cursor over the element you want to offset. A dashed line previews the offset location. Move the cursor to flip the sides, as required.
5. Click to create the offset.
6. Repeat Steps 4 and 5 to offset other elements by the same distance, or to change the distance for another offset.

- With the **Numerical** option, you can select multiple connected linear elements for offsetting. Hover the cursor over an element and press <Tab> until the other related elements are highlighted. Select the element to offset all of the elements at the same time.

How To: Offset using the Graphical Method

1. Start the **Offset** command.
2. In the Options Bar, select **Graphical**.
3. Select the linear element to offset.
4. Select two points that define the distance of the offset and which side to apply it. You can type an override in the temporary dimension for the second point.

- Most linear elements connected at a corner automatically trim or extend to meet at the offset distance, as shown in Figure 2–71.

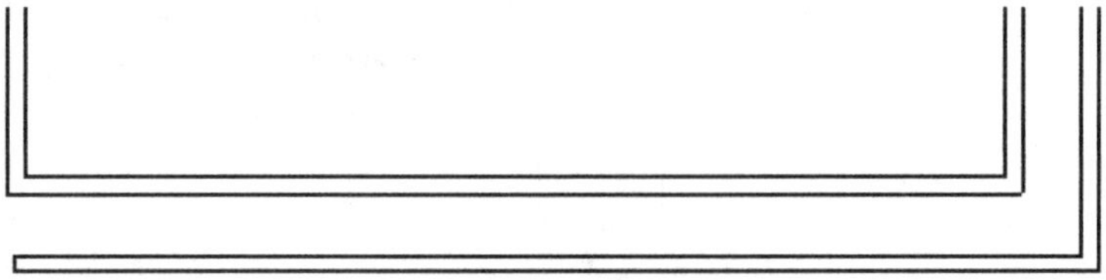

Figure 2–71

Practice 2c Work with Additional Modify Tools

Practice Objective

- Align, Split, Trim/Extend, and Offset elements.

In this practice, you will split a wall into three parts and delete the middle portion. You will offset walls and then trim or extend them to form new rooms. You will then align the new walls to match existing walls.as shown in Figure 2–72.

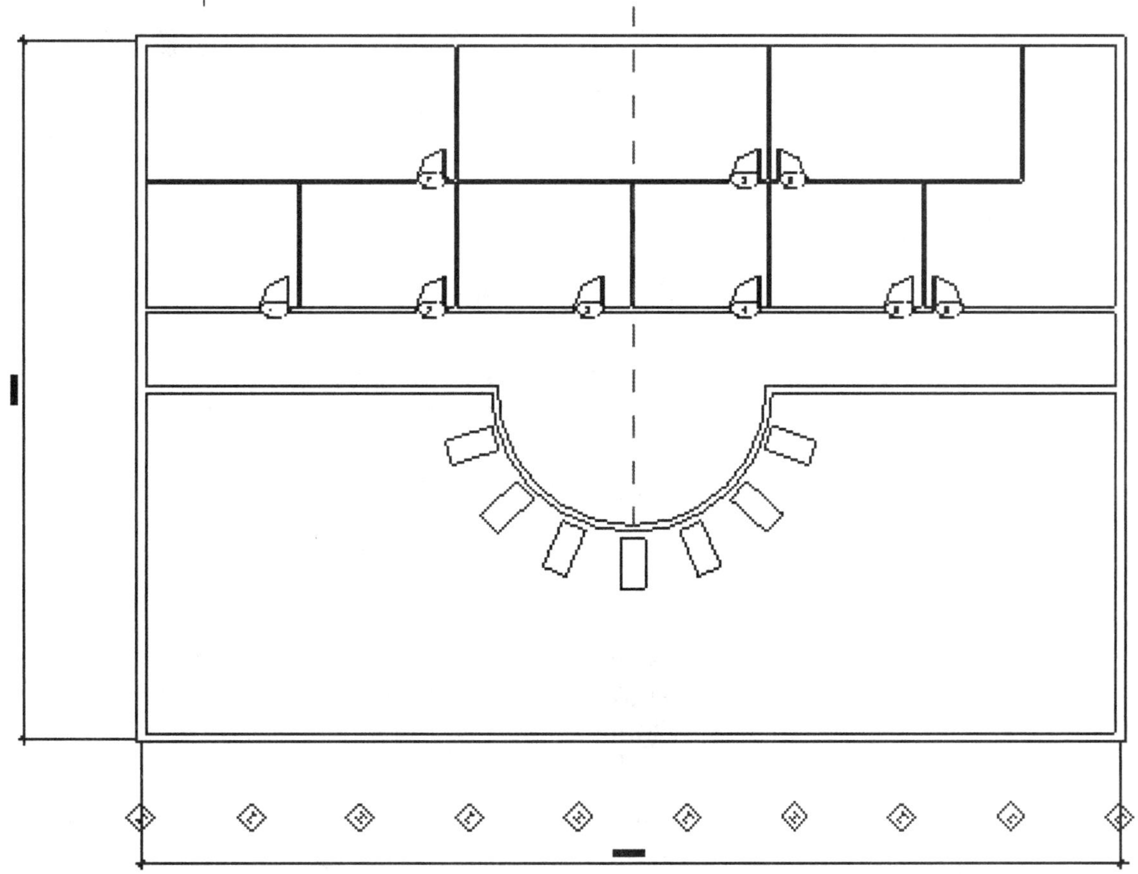

Figure 2–72

Task 1 - Split and Remove Walls

1. Open the project **Simple-Building-2.rvt** from the practice files folder.

2. In the *Modify* tab>Modify panel, click (Split Element).

3. In the Options Bar, select **Delete Inner Segment**.

4. Click on the horizontal wall where it intersects with the curved wall at both ends. The wall segment between these points is removed, as shown in Figure 2–73.

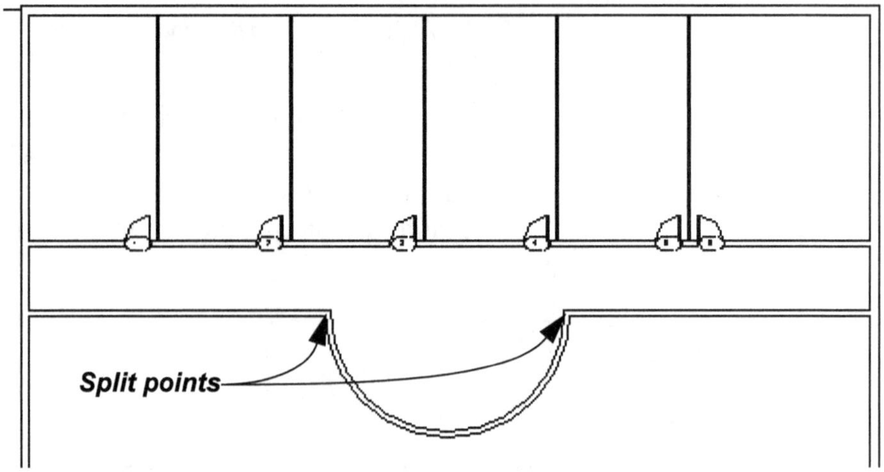

Figure 2–73

5. Click (Modify) to finish.

Task 2 - Offset and Trim Walls

1. In the *Modify* tab>Modify panel, click (Offset).

2. In the Options Bar set the *Offset* to **14'-0"** and ensure that **Copy** is selected.

3. Select the top horizontal wall while ensuring that the dashed alignment line displays inside the building, as shown in Figure 2–74.

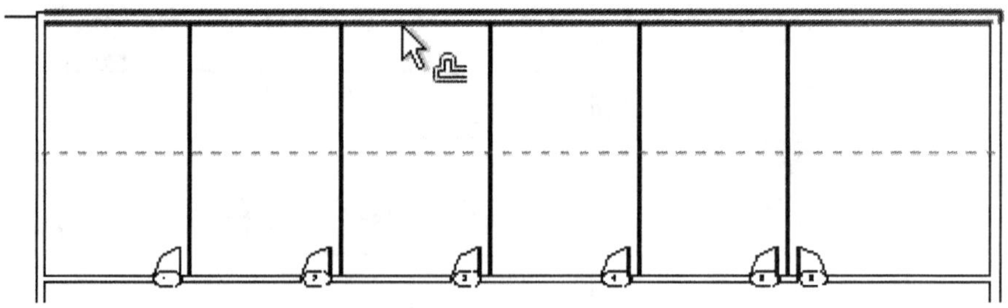

Figure 2–74

4. With **Offset** still active, change the *Offset* to **10'-0"** and offset the last vertical interior wall to the right, as shown in Figure 2–75.

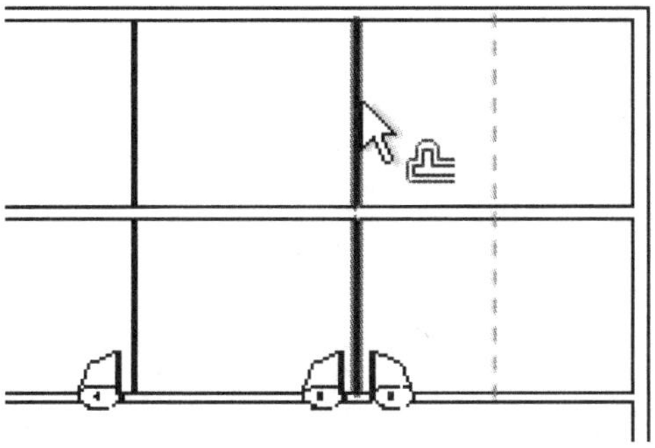

Figure 2–75

5. Click (Modify) and select the new horizontal wall that was created from the exterior wall. Change the wall to **Basic Wall: Interior - 3 1/8" Partition (1-hr).** The layout of the new walls should display as shown in Figure 2–76.

The vertical wall does not need to be changed because it was offset from an interior wall.

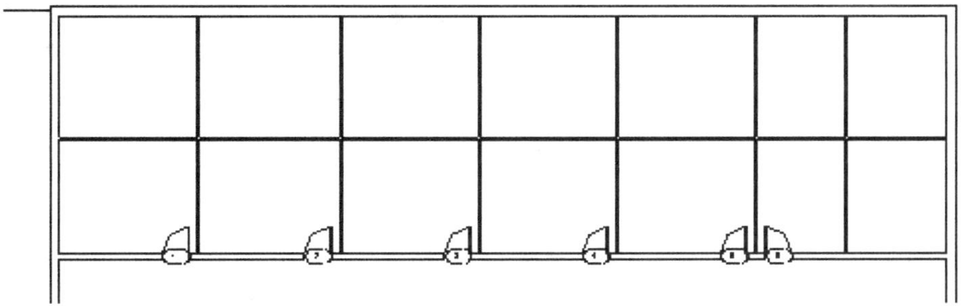

Figure 2–76

6. In the *Modify* tab>Modify panel, click (Trim/Extend Multiple Elements).
7. Select the new horizontal wall as the element to trim against.
8. Select every other wall BELOW the new wall. (Remember, you select the elements that you want to keep.) The walls should display as shown in Figure 2–77.

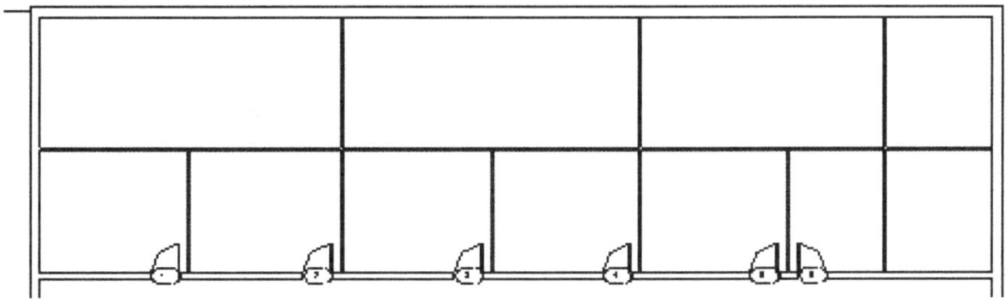

Figure 2–77

9. In the *Modify* tab>Modify panel, click  (Trim/Extend to Corner) and select the two walls to trim as shown in Figure 2–78.

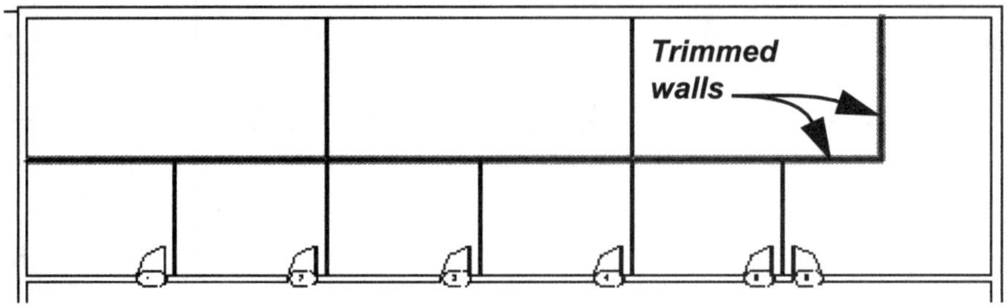

Figure 2–78

10. Add doors into the new rooms.

11. Save the project.

Task 3 - Align Walls.

1. Select the vertical reference plane and use the control to drag the top end so it extends beyond the outer wall, as shown in Figure 2–79.

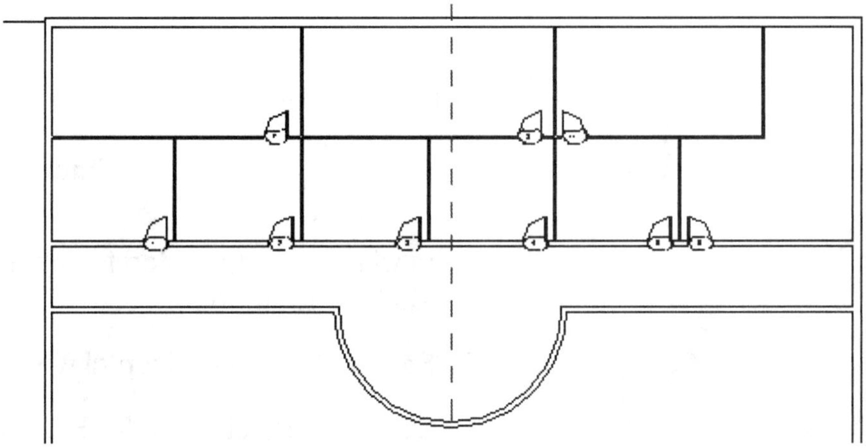

Figure 2–79

2. In the *Modify* tab>Modify panel, click  (Align).

3. Select the reference plane, and then the wall to the left. The wall should line up with the reference plane.

4. Save and close the project.

Chapter Review Questions

1. What is the purpose of an alignment line?
    a. Displays when the new element you are placing or modeling is aligned with the grid system.
    b. Indicates that the new element you are placing or modeling is aligned with an existing element.
    c. Displays when the new element you are placing or modeling is aligned with a selected tracking point.
    d. Indicates that the new element is aligned with true north rather than project north.
2. When you are modeling (not editing) a linear element, how do you edit the temporary dimension, as that shown in Figure 2–80?

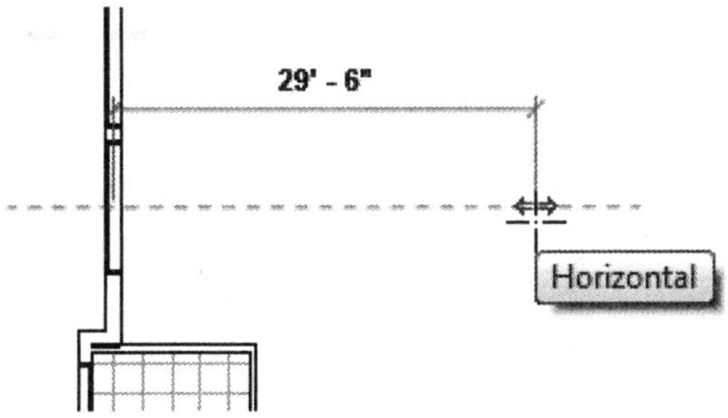

Figure 2–80

    a. Select the temporary dimension and enter a new value.
    b. Type a new value and press <Enter>.
    c. Type a new value in the Distance/Length box in the Options Bar and press <Enter>.
3. How do you select all the doors of various sizes, but no other elements in a view?
    a. In the Project Browser, select the *Door* category.
    b. Select one door, right-click and select **Select All Instances>Visible in View**.
    c. Select all of the elements in the view and use  (Filter) to clear the other categories.
    d. Select one door, and click  (Select Multiple) in the ribbon.

4. What are the two methods for starting commands such as **Move, Copy, Rotate, Mirror,** and **Array**? Start the command from the *Modify* tab and select the elements, or...
   a. Select the elements and then start the command.
   b. Select the elements and then select the command from the Status Bar.
   c. Select the elements, right-click and select the command from the list.
5. Where do you change the wall type for a selected wall, as shown in Figure 2–81?

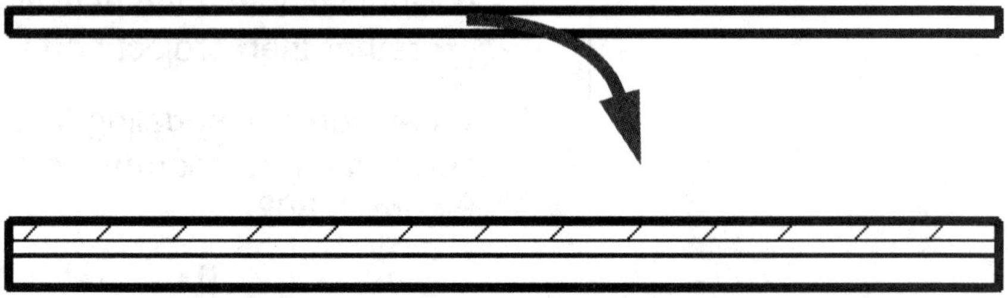

Figure 2–81

   a. In the *Modify | Walls* tab>Properties panel, click  (Type Properties) and select a new wall type in the dialog box.
   b. In the Options Bar, click **Change Element Type**.
   c. Select the dynamic control next to the selected wall and select a new type in the drop-down list.
   d. In Properties, select a new type in the Type Selector drop-down list.

6. Both (Rotate) and (Array) with (Radial) have a center of rotation that defaults to the center of the element or group of elements you have selected. How do you move the center of rotation to another point as shown in Figure 2–82? (Select all that apply.)

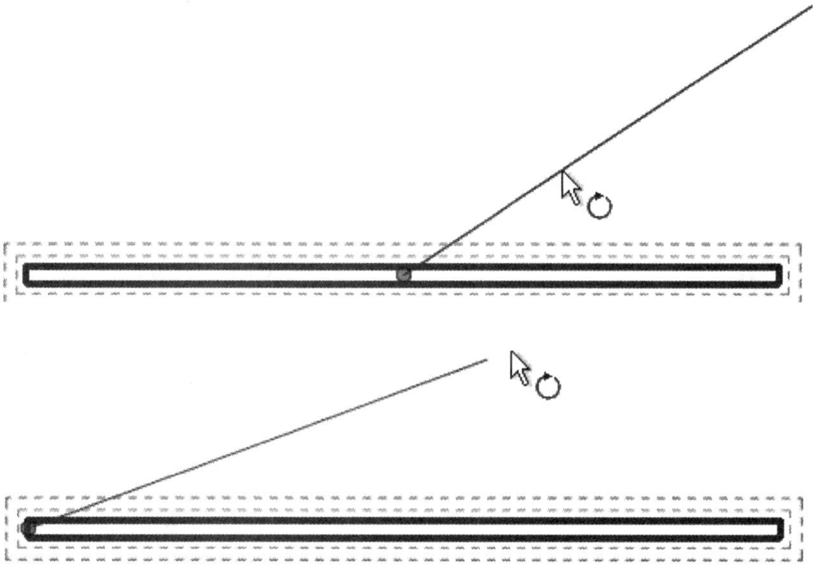

Figure 2–82

   a. Select the center of rotation and drag it to a new location.
   b. In the Options Bar, click **Place** and select the new point.
   c. In the *Modify* tab>Placement panel, click (Center) and select the new point.
   d. Right-click and select **Snap Overrides>Centers** and select the new point.

7. Which command would you use to remove part of a wall?
   a. (Split Element)
   b. (Wall Joins)
   c. (Cut Geometry)
   d. (Demolish)

8. Which of the following are ways in which you can create additional parallel walls, as shown in Figure 2–83? (Select all that apply.)

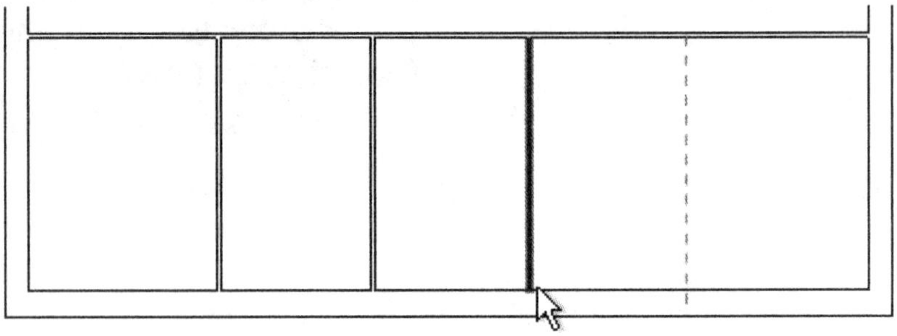

Figure 2–83

   a. Use the **Trim/Extend Multiple Elements** tool.
   b. Use the **Offset** tool in the *Modify* tab.
   c. Select an existing wall, hold <Ctrl> and drag the wall to a new location.
   d. Use the **Align** command with an offset.

9. Which command do you use if you want two walls that are not touching to come together, as shown in Figure 2–84?

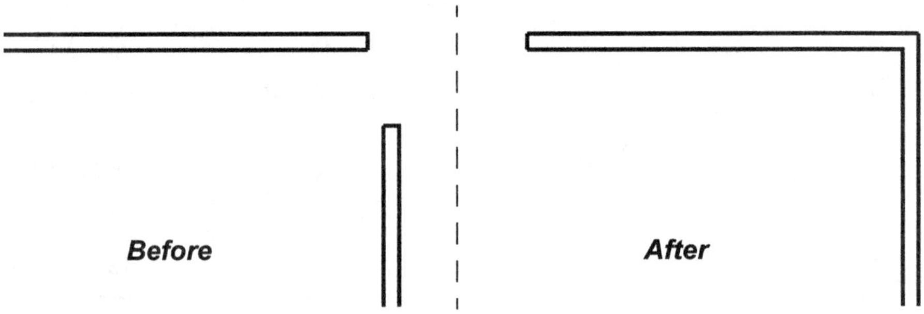

Figure 2–84

   a.  (Edit Wall Joins)
   b.  (Trim/Extend to Corner)
   c.  (Join Geometry)
   d.  (Edit Profile)

Command Summary

Button	Command	Location
Draw Tools		
	**Center-ends Arc**	• **Ribbon:** *Modify* | *(various linear elements)* tab>Draw panel
	**Circle**	• **Ribbon:** *Modify* | *(various linear elements)* tab>Draw panel
	**Circumscribed Polygon**	• **Ribbon:** *Modify* | *(various linear elements)* tab>Draw panel
	**Ellipse**	• **Ribbon:** *Modify* | *Place Lines, Place Detail Lines, and various boundary sketches*>Draw panel
	**Ellipse Arc**	• **Ribbon:** *Modify* | *Place Lines, Place Detail Lines, and various boundary sketches*>Draw panel
	**Fillet Arc**	• **Ribbon:** *Modify* | *(various linear elements)* tab>Draw panel
	**Inscribed Polygon**	• **Ribbon:** *Modify* | *(various linear elements)* tab>Draw panel
	**Line**	• **Ribbon:** *Modify* | *(various linear elements)* tab>Draw panel
	**Pick Faces**	• **Ribbon:** *Modify* | *Place Wall*> Draw panel
	**Pick Lines**	• **Ribbon:** *Modify* | *(various linear elements)* tab>Draw panel
	**Pick Walls**	• **Ribbon:** *Modify* | *(various boundary sketches)*>Draw panel
	**Rectangle**	• **Ribbon:** *Modify* | *(various linear elements)* tab>Draw panel
	**Spline**	• **Ribbon:** *Modify* | *Place Lines, Place Detail Lines, and various boundary sketches*>Draw panel
	**Start-End-Radius Arc**	• **Ribbon:** *Modify* | *(various linear elements)* tab>Draw panel
	**Tangent End Arc**	• **Ribbon:** *Modify* | *(various linear elements)* tab>Draw panel
Modify Tools		
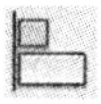	**Align**	• **Ribbon:** *Modify* tab>Modify panel • **Shortcut:** AL
	**Array**	• **Ribbon:** *Modify* tab>Modify panel • **Shortcut:** AR
	**Copy**	• **Ribbon:** *Modify* tab>Modify panel • **Shortcut:** CO

	**Copy to Clipboard**	• **Ribbon:** *Modify* tab>Clipboard panel • **Shortcut:** <Ctrl>+<C>
	**Delete**	• **Ribbon:** *Modify* tab>Modify panel • **Shortcut:** DE
	**Mirror - Draw Axis**	• **Ribbon:** *Modify* tab>Modify panel • **Shortcut:** DM
	**Mirror - Pick Axis**	• **Ribbon:** *Modify* tab>Modify panel • **Shortcut:** MM
	**Move**	• **Ribbon:** *Modify* tab>Modify panel • **Shortcut:** MV
	**Offset**	• **Ribbon:** *Modify* tab>Modify panel • **Shortcut:** OF
	**Paste**	• **Ribbon:** *Modify* tab>Clipboard panel • **Shortcut:** <Ctrl>+<V>
	**Pin**	• **Ribbon:** *Modify* tab>Modify panel • **Shortcut:** PN
	**Rotate**	• **Ribbon:** *Modify* tab>Modify panel • **Shortcut:** RO
	**Scale**	• **Ribbon:** *Modify* tab>Modify panel • **Shortcut:** RE
	**Split Element**	• **Ribbon:** *Modify* tab>Modify panel • **Shortcut:** SL
	**Split with Gap**	• **Ribbon:** *Modify* tab>Modify panel
	**Trim/Extend Multiple Elements**	• **Ribbon:** *Modify* tab>Modify panel
	**Trim/Extend Single Element**	• **Ribbon:** *Modify* tab>Modify panel
	**Trim/Extend to Corner**	• **Ribbon:** *Modify* tab>Modify panel • **Shortcut:** TR
	**Unpin**	• **Ribbon:** *Modify* tab>Modify panel • **Shortcut:** UP
Select Tools		
	**Drag elements on selection**	• **Ribbon:** All tabs>Expanded Select panel • **Status Bar**
	**Filter**	• **Ribbon:** *Modify* | *Multi-Select* tab> Filter panel • **Status Bar**
	**Select Elements By Face**	• **Ribbon:** All tabs>Expanded Select panel • **Status Bar**

	**Select Links**	• **Ribbon:** All tabs>Expanded Select panel • **Status Bar**
	**Select Pinned Elements**	• **Ribbon:** All tabs>Expanded Select panel • **Status Bar**
	**Select Underlay Elements**	• **Ribbon:** All tabs>Expanded Select panel • **Status Bar**
Additional Tools		
	**Aligned Dimension**	• **Ribbon:** *Modify* tab>Measure panel • Quick Access Toolbar
	**Detail Line**	• **Ribbon:** *Annotate* tab>Detail panel • **Shortcut:** DL
	**Model Line**	• **Ribbon:** *Architectural* tab>Model panel • **Shortcut:** LI
	**Reference Plane**	• **Ribbon:** *Architecture/Structure/ Systems* tab> Work Plane panel

Starting Architectural Projects

Starting a project in Autodesk Revit begins by using a template. You can then link in a CAD file or an existing Revit model, if these are available. From there, you can add the framework for a building including levels, which define vertical heights, as well as grids, which define the structural layout for architectural and structural columns.

Learning Objectives in this Chapter

- Link and import CAD files to be used as a basis for developing a design.
- Link existing Revit models to develop and coordinate with other disciplines.
- Add and modify levels to define floor to floor heights and other vertical references.
- Add and modify structural grids that provide locations for columns.
- Add architectural (decorative) and structural (load-bearing) columns.

3.1 Linking and Importing CAD Files

Many firms have legacy drawings from vector-based CAD programs, or could be working with consultants that use such programs. For example, you may want to link a DWG plan into your project (as shown in Figure 3–1), that you would then trace over using the Autodesk Revit tools. You can print a hybrid drawing - part Autodesk Revit project and part imported/linked drawing.

When you select an imported or linked CAD file you can see that it is called an Import Symbol.

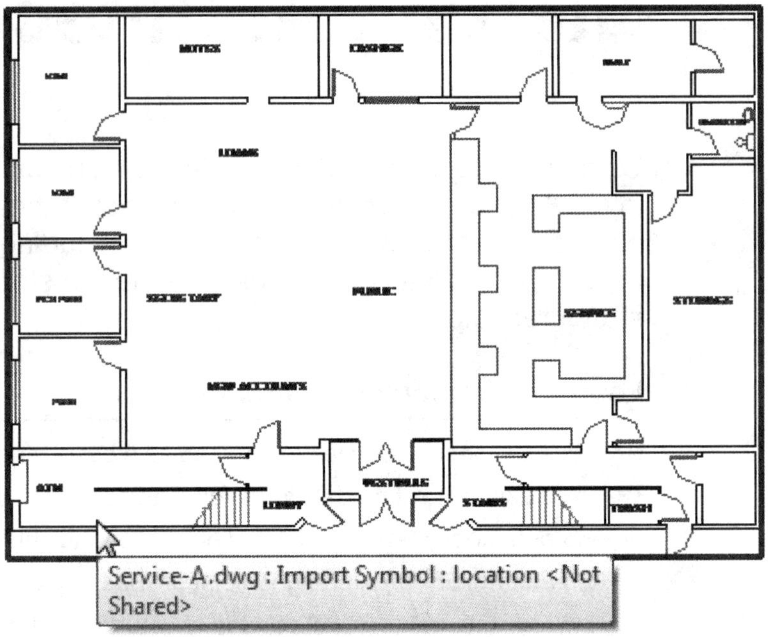

Figure 3–1

CAD file formats that can be imported or linked include: AutoCAD® (DWG and DXF), MicroStation (DGN), 3D ACIS modeling kernel (SAT), and SketchUp (SKP).

Linking vs. Importing

- **Link:** A connection is maintained with the original file and the link updates if the original file is updated.
- **Import:** No connection is maintained with the original file. It becomes a separate element in the Autodesk Revit model.

The dialog boxes for Link CAD Formats and Import CAD Formats are the same.

How To: Link or Import a CAD File

1. Open the view into which you want to link or import the file.
   - For a 2D file, this should be a 2D view. For a 3D file, open a 3D view.
2. In the *Insert* tab>Link panel, click  (Link CAD), or in the *Insert* tab>Import panel, click  (Import CAD).
3. In the Link CAD Formats or Import CAD Formats dialog box (shown in Figure 3–2), select the file that you want to import.
   - Select a file format in the Files of Type drop-down list to limit the files that are displayed.

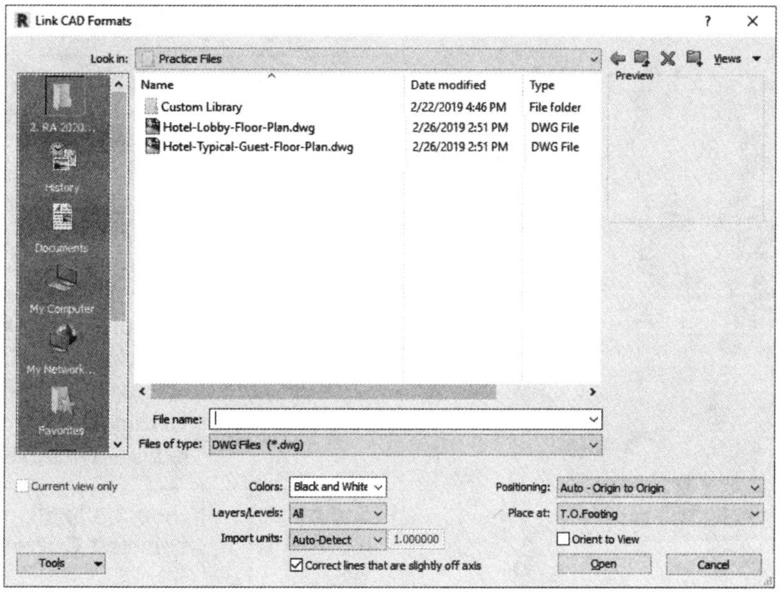

Figure 3–2

4. Set the other options, as shown in Figure 3–3.

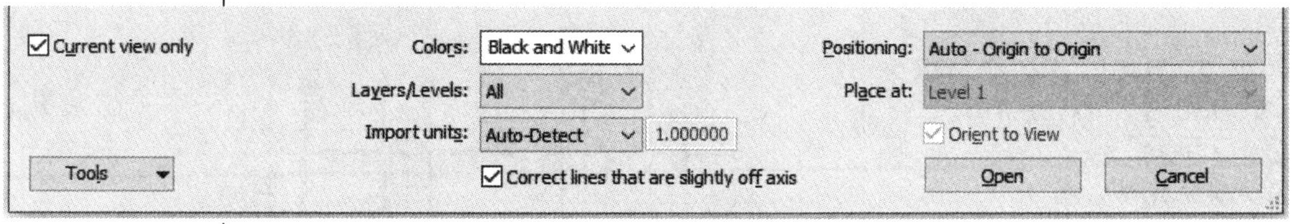

Figure 3–3

5. Click **Open**.

> **Hint: Importing PDFs**
>
> You can import a PDF into Autodesk Revit as a raster image. If the PDF contains vector data, you can snap to the elements in the PDF. In the *Insert* tab> Import panel, click  (PDF).

Link and Import Options

Current view only	Determine whether the CAD file is placed in every view, or only in the current view. This is especially useful if you are working with a 2D floor plan that you only need to have in one view.
Colors	Specify the color settings. Typical Autodesk Revit projects are mainly black and white. However, other software frequently uses color. You can **Invert** the original colors, **Preserve** them, or change everything to **Black and White**.
Layers/Levels	Indicates which CAD layers are going to be brought into the model. Select how you want layers to be imported: **All**, **Visible**, or **Specify...**.
Import units	Select the units of the original file, as required. **Auto-Detect** works in most cases.
Correct Lines...	If lines in a CAD file are off axis by less than 0.1 degree selecting this option straightens them. It is selected by default.
Positioning	Specify how you want the imported file to be positioned in the current project: **Auto-Center to Center**, **Auto-Origin to Origin**, **Manual-Origin**, **Manual-Base Point**, or **Manual-Center**. The default position is **Auto-Origin to Origin.** If linking the file, **Auto-By Shared Coordinates** is also available.
Place at	Select a level in which to place the imported file. If you selected **Current view only**, this option is grayed out.

- When a file is positioned **Auto-Origin to Origin**, it is pinned in place and cannot be moved. To move the file, click on the pin to unpin it, as shown in Figure 3–4.

For more information on importing and linking CAD files, see the Autodesk Revit Collaboration Tools guide.

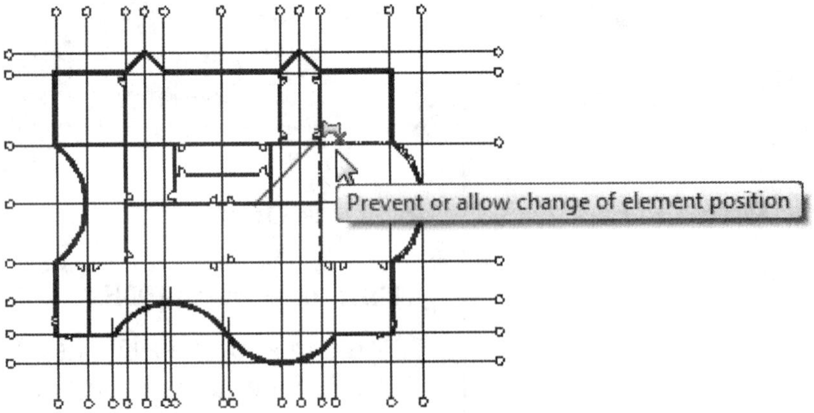

Figure 3–4

Setting an Imported or Linked File to Halftone

To see the difference between new elements and the linked or imported file, you can set the file to Halftone, as shown in Figure 3–5.

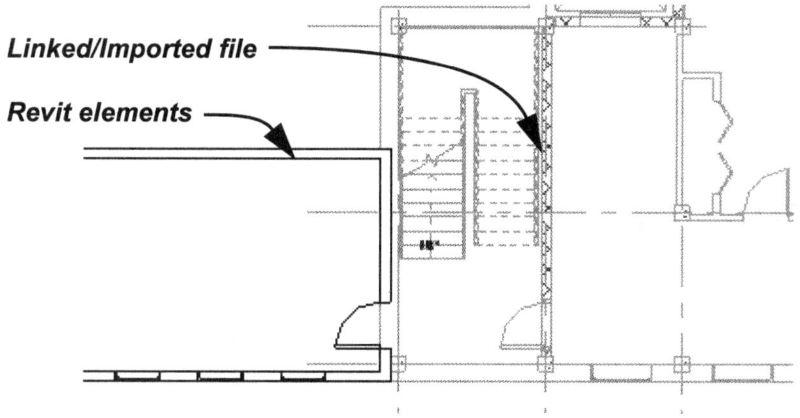

Figure 3–5

How To: Set an Element Halftone

1. Select the imported file.
2. Right-click and select **Override Graphics in View>By Element....**
3. In the View Specific Element Graphics dialog box, select **Halftone**, as shown in Figure 3–6.

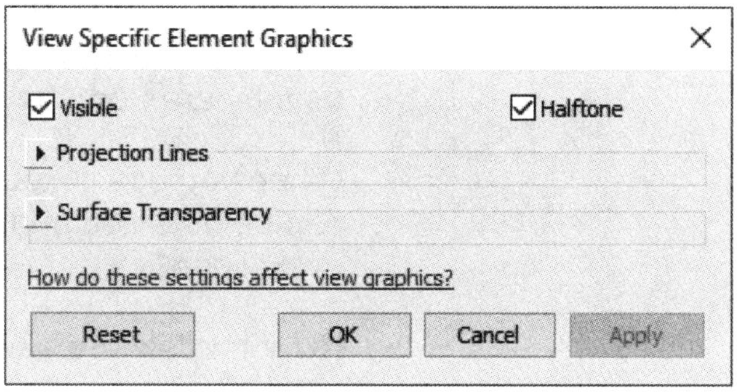

Figure 3–6

4. Click **OK**.

- You can use this method to set any element or category to halftone.

Hint: Draw Layer

Linked CAD files are typically in the background of a view. To change this, select the CAD file and in the Options Bar or in Properties, in the *Other* area, change the *Draw Layer* to **Foreground**.

3.2 Linking in Revit Models

You can link Autodesk Revit models directly into a project.These models can be an existing building that you are creating an addition to (as shown in Figure 3–7) or engineering models that you are checking to ensure that they line up with your model. They are also used for campus-like projects where the same building is repeated multiple times.They are full 3D models.

A linked model automatically updates when the original file is changed.

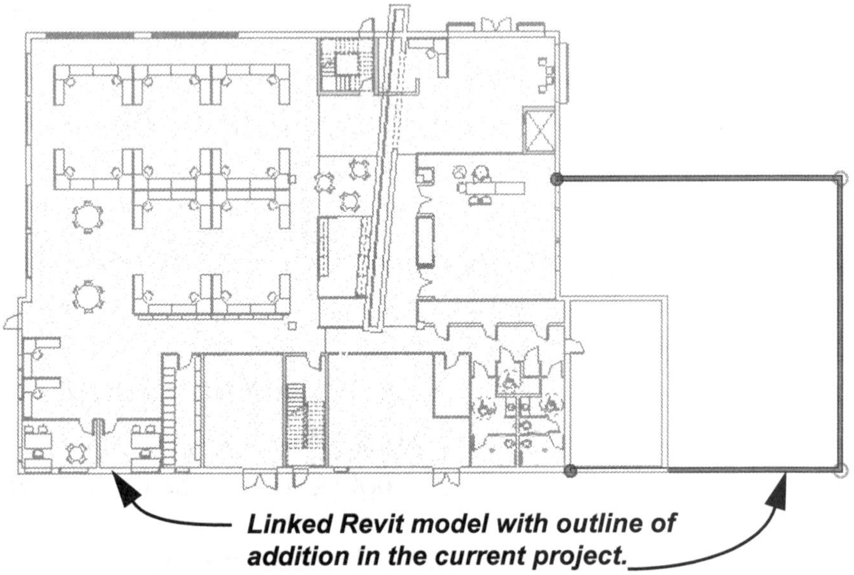

Figure 3–7

- Architectural, structural, and MEP models created in the Autodesk Revit software can be linked to each other as long as they are from the same release cycle.
- When you use linked models, clashes between disciplines can be detected and information can be passed between disciplines.
- Revit models are always linked. They cannot be imported.

How To: Add a Linked Model to a Host Project

1. In the *Insert* tab>Link panel, click (Link Revit).
2. In the Import/Link RVT dialog box, select the file that you want to link. Before opening the file, set the *Positioning*, as shown in Figure 3–8.

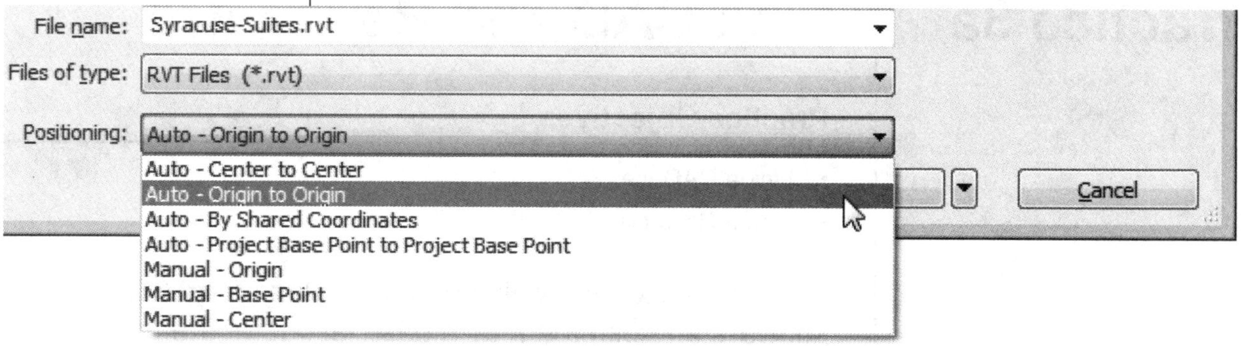

Figure 3–8

3. Click **Open**.
4. Depending on how you decide to position the file, it is automatically placed in the project or you can manually place it with the cursor.

As the links are loading, do not click on the screen or click any buttons. The more links present in a project, the longer it takes to load.

Multiple Copies of Linked Models

Copied instances of a linked model are typically used when creating a master project with the same building placed in multiple locations, such as a university campus with six identical student residence halls.

- Linked models can be moved, copied, rotated, arrayed, and mirrored. There is only one linked model, and any copies are additional instances of the link.
- Copies are numbered automatically. You can change their names in Properties when the instance is selected.
- When you have placed a link in a project, you can drag and drop additional copies of the link into the project from the Project Browser>**Revit Links** node, as shown in Figure 3–9.

Figure 3–9

- For more information on linking Revit files, see the *Autodesk Revit Collaboration Tools* guide.

Practice 3a Link CAD and Revit Files

Practice Objectives

- Link a CAD file.
- Link a Revit file.

In this practice, you will import floor plans from the AutoCAD software and use them as a base layout for the first floor lobby and for a typical guest floor. You will then link in a Revit model that includes a standard pool house and platform for the building, as shown in Figure 3–10.

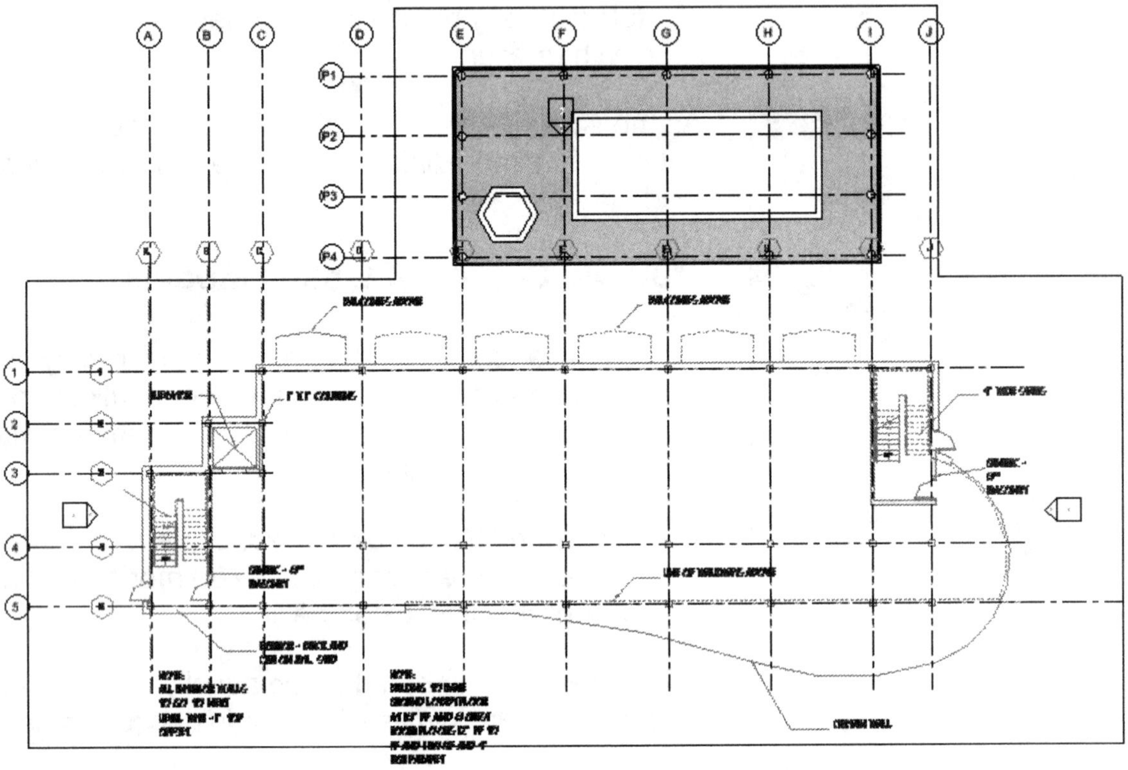

Figure 3–10

Task 1 - Link a CAD file.

1. Open the project **Modern-Hotel-Start.rvt** from the practice files folder. (There are no elements in this file.)

2. Open the **Floor Plans: Level 1** view.

3. In the *Insert* tab>Link panel, click  (Link CAD).

4. In the Link CAD Formats dialog box, select the file **Hotel-Lobby-Floor-Plan.dwg** and set the following options:
   - Select **Current view only**.
   - *Colors:* **Black and White**
   - *Layers/Levels:* **All**
   - *Import Units:* **Auto-Detect**
   - *Positioning:* **Auto-Origin to Origin**
5. Click **Open**. The linked CAD file is placed in the project on the **Floor Plans: Level 1** view.
6. Select the linked CAD file. It is all in one element and pinned in place because it was imported origin to origin.
7. In the Options Bar, change *Background* to **Foreground**.
8. With the CAD file still selected, right-click and select **Override Graphics in View>By Element....**
9. In the View-Specific Element Graphics dialog box, select **Halftone** and click **OK**.
10. Click in empty space to release the selection. The linked file displays in halftone, as shown in Figure 3–11.

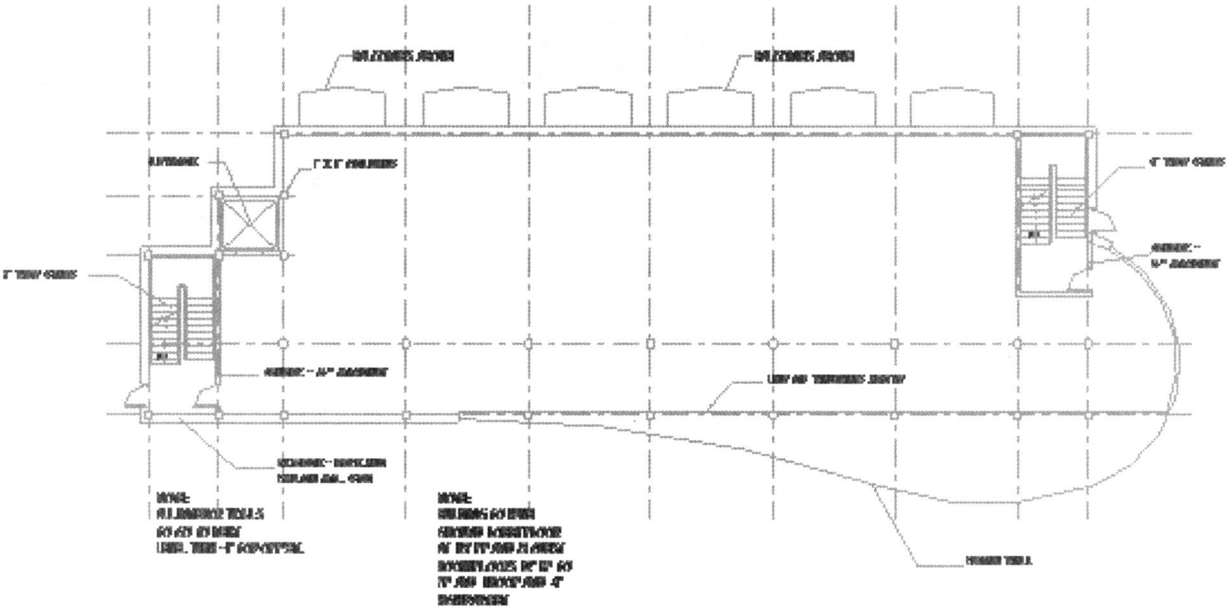

Figure 3–11

11. Open the **Floor Plans: Level 2** view. The CAD file linked to *Level 1* does not display because it was only linked in the **Level 1** view.

12. Link the CAD file **Hotel-Typical-Guest-Floor-Plan.dwg** using the options that were used for **Level 1**.

13. Override the graphics and set the linked file to **Halftone**.

14. Save the project.

Task 2 - Link in a Revit file.

1. Open the **Default 3D** view. Neither of the linked CAD files display in this view.

2. In the *Insert* tab>Link panel, click  (Link Revit).

3. Navigate to the practice files folder and select **Modern-Hotel-Pool.rvt.**

4. Verify that the *Positioning* is set to **Auto - Origin to Origin** and click **Open**.

5. Type **ZF** to fit the model to the view, as shown in Figure 3–12.

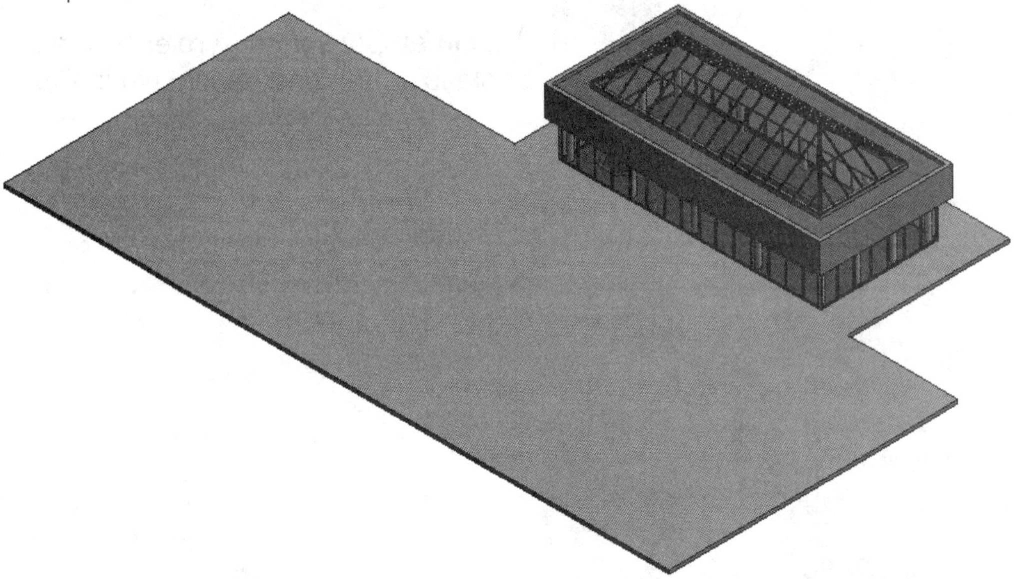

Figure 3–12

6. Select the *Level 1* tab to open this view. Both the linked CAD file and linked Revit file display in this view.

   - If you do not see the full linked CAD file, select the text that is part of the CAD file below the platform (as shown in Figure 3–13) and in Properties, in the *Other* area, change the *Draw Layer* to **Foreground**.

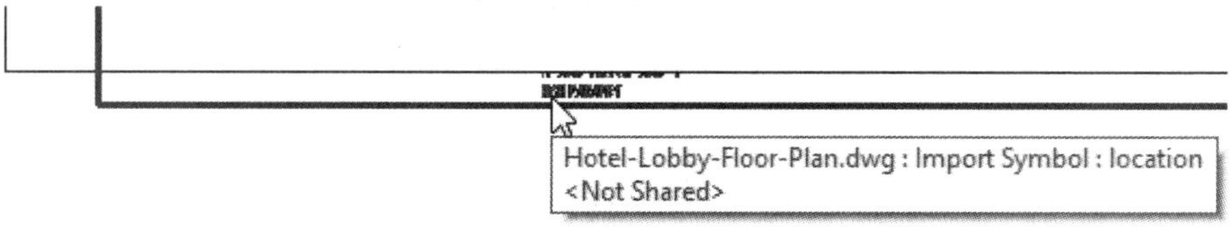

Figure 3–13

7. Save the project.

3.3 Setting Up Levels

Levels define stories and other vertical heights (such as a parapet or other reference heights), as shown in Figure 3–14. The default template includes two levels, but you can define as many levels in a project as required. They can go down (for basements) as well as up.

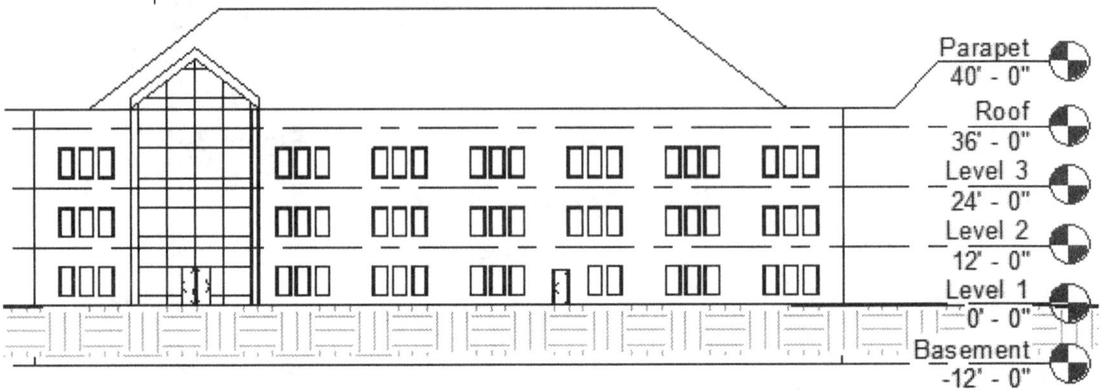

Figure 3–14

- You must be in an elevation or section view to define levels.
- Once you constrain an element to a level it moves with the level when the level is changed.

How To: Create Levels

1. Open an elevation or section view.
2. In the *Architecture* tab>Datum panel, click (Level), or type **LL**.
3. In the Type Selector, set the Level Head type if required.
4. In the Options Bar, select or clear **Make Plan View** as required. You can also click **Plan View Types...** to select the types of views to create when you place the level.
5. In the *Modify | Place Level* tab>Draw panel, click either (Pick Lines) to select an element or (Line) to sketch a level.
6. Continue adding levels as required.

- Level names are automatically incremented as you place them. This automatic numbering is most effective when you use names such as Floor 1, Floor 2, etc. (as opposed to First Floor, Second Floor, etc.). In addition, this makes it easier to find the view in the Project Browser.

- A fast way to create multiple levels is to use the (Pick Lines) option. In the Options Bar specify an *Offset,* select an existing level, and then pick above or below to place the new level, as shown in Figure 3–15.

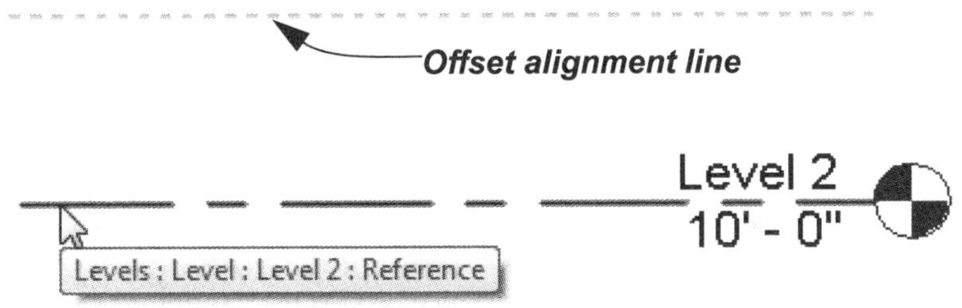

Figure 3–15

- When using the (Line) option, alignments and temporary dimensions help you place the line correctly, as shown in Figure 3–16.

You can sketch the level lines from left to right or right to left depending on where you want the bubble. However, ensure they are all sketched in the same direction.

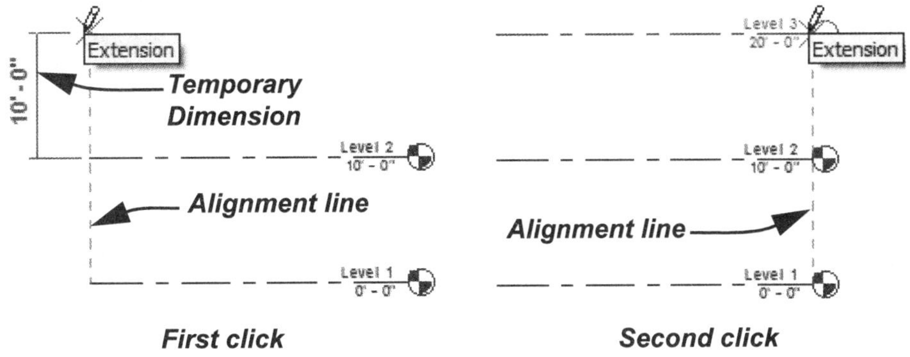

Figure 3–16

- You can also use (Copy) to duplicate level lines. The level names are incremented but a plan view is not created.

- Levels display in the default 3D view. They can be modified and copied, but cannot be created in this view.

- Levels can be hidden in any view.

Modifying Levels

You can change levels using standard controls and temporary dimensions, as shown in Figure 3–17. You can also make changes in the Properties palette.

Figure 3–17

- (Hide / Show Bubble) displays on either end of the level line and toggles the level head symbol and level information on or off.

- 2D 3D (Switch to 3d / 2d extents) controls whether any movement or adjustment to the level line is reflected in other views (3D) or only affects the current view (2D).

- (Modify the level by dragging its model end) at each end of the line enables you to drag the level head to a new location.

- (Create or remove a length or alignment constraint) controls whether the level is locked in alignment with the other levels. If it is locked and the level line is stretched, all of the other level lines stretch as well. If it is unlocked, the level line stretches independent of the other levels.

- Click (Add Elbow) to add a jog to the level line as shown in Figure 3–18. Drag the shape handles to new locations as required. This is a view-specific change.

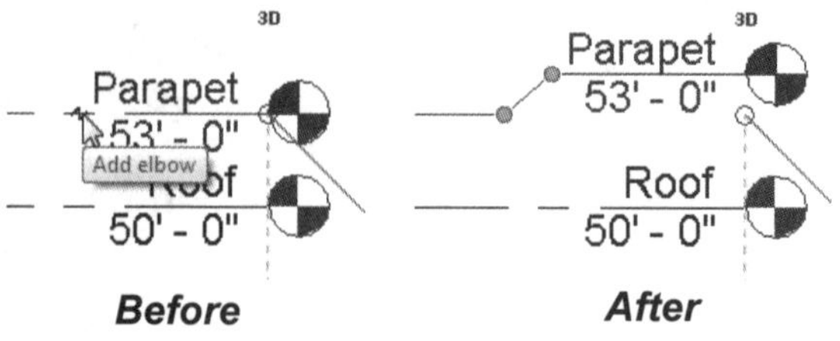

Figure 3–18

- To change the level name or elevation, double-click on the information next to the level head, or select the level and modify the *Name* or *Elevation* fields in Properties, as shown in Figure 3–19.

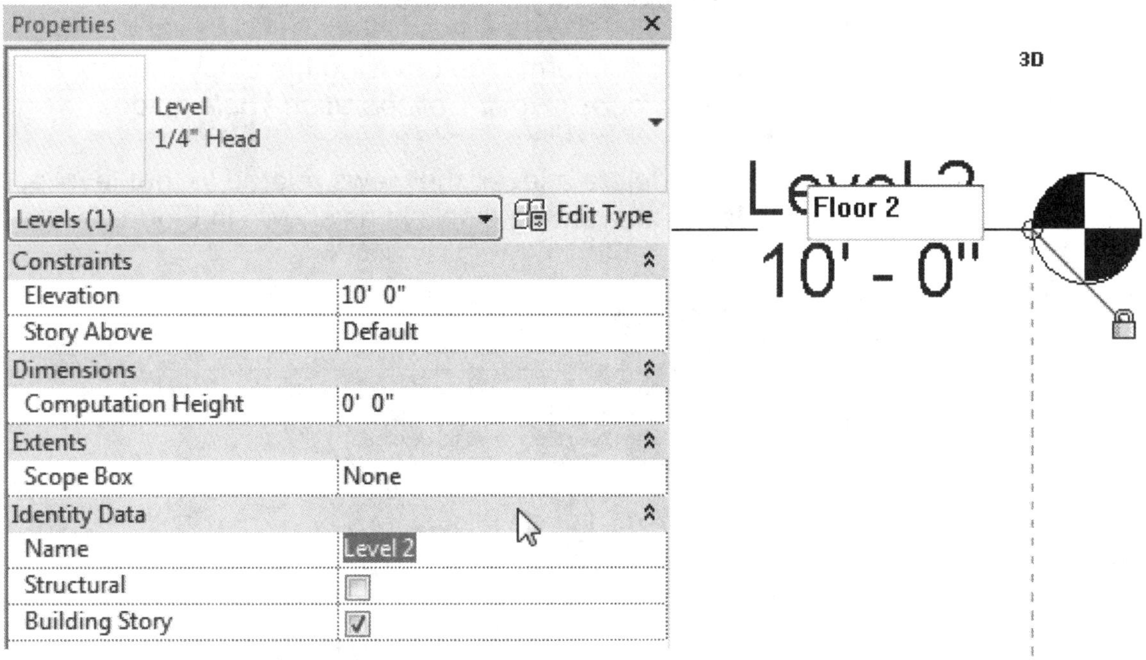

Figure 3–19

- When you rename a Level, an alert box opens, prompting you to rename the corresponding views as shown in Figure 3–20.

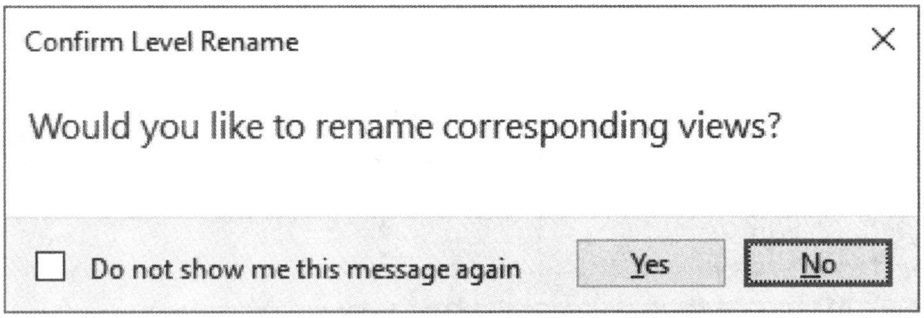

Figure 3–20

- The view is also renamed in the Project Browser.

Hint: Copying Levels and Grids from other projects

Levels and grid lines can be added by drawing over existing levels or grids in an imported or linked CAD file. It can also be copied and monitored from a linked Autodesk® Revit® file. Some projects might require both methods.

- For more information on using the Copy/Monitor tools, see the *Autodesk Revit Collaboration Tools* guide.

- If you delete a level, the views related to that level are also delete. A warning displays as shown in Figure 3–21.

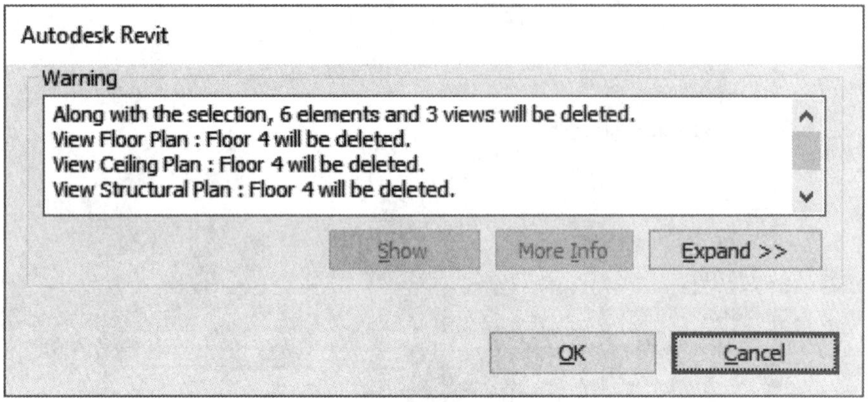

Figure 3–21

Creating Plan Views

Typically, you do not need to create plan views for levels that specify data, such as the top of a storefront window or the top of a parapet.

By default, when you place a level, plan views for that level are automatically created. If **Make Plan View** was toggled off when adding the level, or if the level was copied, you can create plan views to match the levels.

- Level heads with views are blue and level heads without views are black, as shown in Figure 3–22.

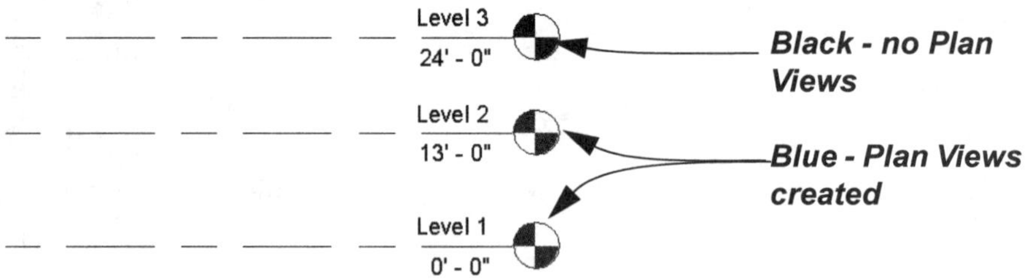

Figure 3–22

How To: Create Plan Views

1. In the *View* tab>Create panel, expand (Plan Views) and select the type of plan view you want to create, as shown on the left in Figure 3–23.
2. In the New Plan dialog box (shown on the right in Figure 3–24), select the levels for which you want to create plan views. Hold <Ctrl> to select more than one level.

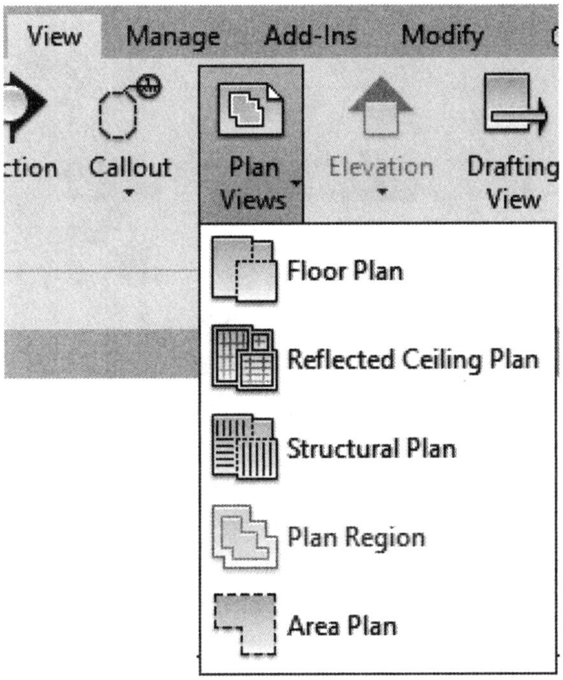

Figure 3–23

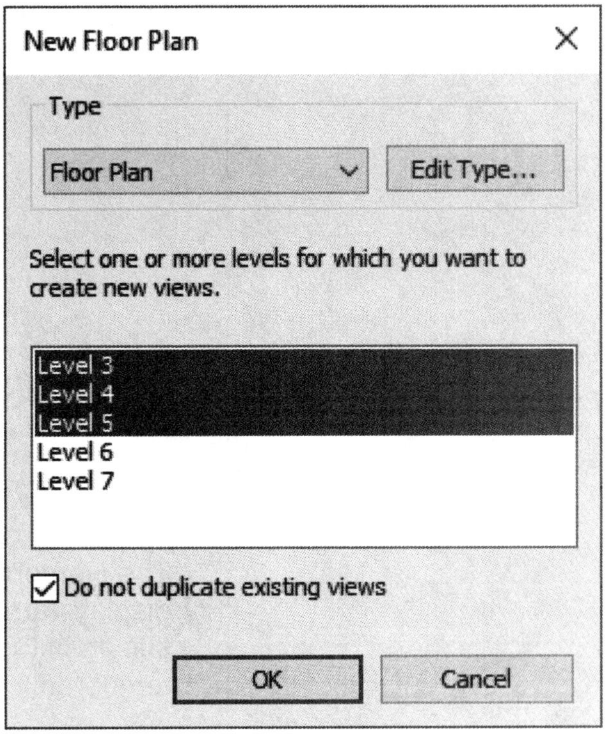

Figure 3–24

3. Click **OK**.

- Once a plan view is made from a level, you can double-click on the level head to open the related floor plan view.

Hint: Temporary Hide/Isolate

You might want to temporarily remove elements from a view, modify the project, and then restore the elements. Instead of completely toggling the elements off, you can temporarily hide them.

Select the elements you want to hide (make invisible) or isolate (keep displayed while all other elements are hidden) and click  (Temporary Hide/Isolate). Select the method you want to use, as shown in Figure 3–25.

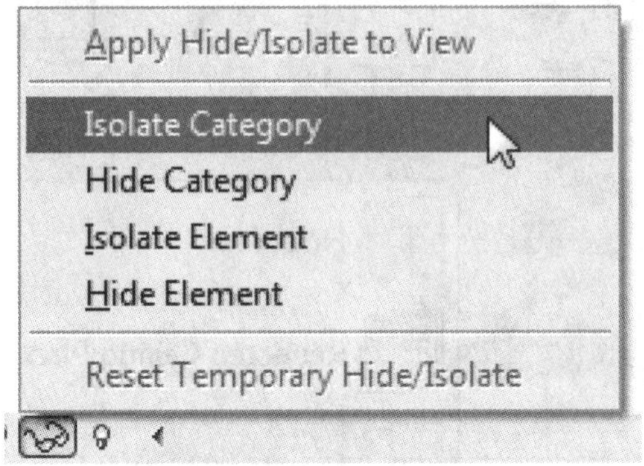

Figure 3–25

The elements or category are hidden or isolated. A cyan border displays around the view with a note in the upper left corner, as shown in Figure 3–26. It indicates that the view contains temporarily hidden or isolated elements.

Figure 3–26

- Click  (Temporary Hide/Isolate) again and select **Reset Temporary Hide/Isolate** to restore the elements to the view.
- If you want to permanently hide the elements in the view, select **Apply Hide/Isolate to View**.
- Elements that are temporarily hidden in a view are not hidden when the view is printed.

Practice 3b Set Up Levels

Practice Objective

- Add and modify levels.

In this practice, you will set up the levels required in the Modern Hotel project, including the floors, the top of the footing, and the parapet, as shown in Figure 3–27.

Figure 3–27

- The linked Revit file is hidden in this view.

Task 1 - Add and Modify Levels.

1. Open the project **Modern-Hotel-Levels.rvt** from the practice files folder.
2. Open the **Elevations (Building Elevation): North** view.

3. The project has two existing levels named **Level 1** and **Level 2**. These were defined in the template. You will also see the **Floor 1** and **Floor 2** levels that are part of the linked Revit file.

4. Select the linked Revit file.

5. In the View Control Bar, expand  (Temporary Hide/ Isolate) and select **Hide Element**. This toggles off the entire linked Revit file.

6. Zoom in on the level names.

7. Double-click on the name *Level 1* and rename it to **Floor 1**, as shown in Figure 3–28. Press <Enter>.

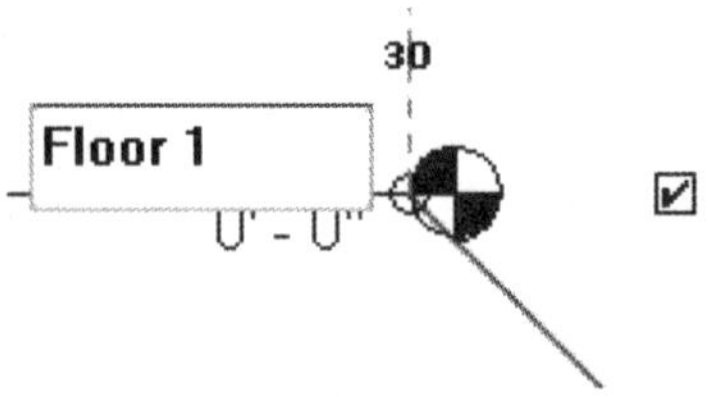

Figure 3–28

8. Click **Yes** (press <Enter> or type **Y**) when prompted to rename the corresponding views.

9. Repeat the process and rename *Level 2* as **Floor 2**. Double-click on the height of Floor 2 (10'-0") and change it to **18'- 0"**.

10. In the *Architecture* tab>Datum panel, click  (Level).

11. In the Options Bar, verify that **Make Plan View** is select. Click **Plan View Types...** and select only *Ceiling Plan* and *Floor Plan*, as shown in Figure 3–29. Click **OK**.

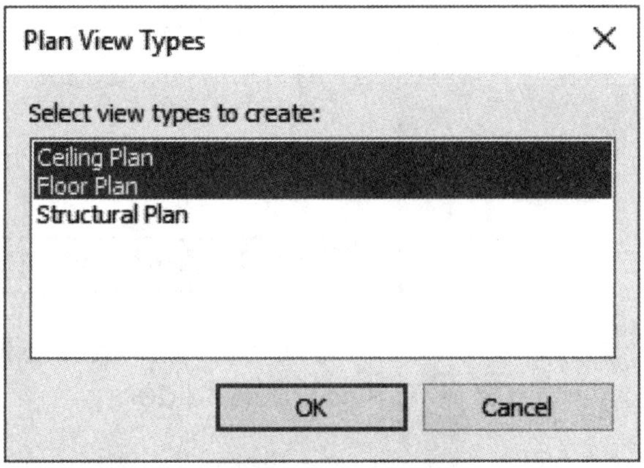

Figure 3–29

12. In the *Modify | Place Level* tab>Draw panel, click  (Pick Lines). In the Options Bar, set the *Offset* to **12' - 0"**.
13. Hover the cursor over the level line of **Floor 2** and move the cursor slightly upward so that the offset level line is displayed above the **Floor 2** level. Click to create the new level **Floor 3**.
14. Create additional levels until there are a total of eight levels above Floor 1 (up to Floor 9).
15. Click **Modify** and select the **Floor 9** level.
16. Rename *Floor 9* as **Roof**. (Rename the corresponding views.)
17. Start the **Level** command again.
18. In the Options Bar, clear the **Make Plan View** option and set the *Offset* to **5' 0"**. Create one additional level above the highest level, **Roof**. This level does not need a plan view.
19. Rename the top level as **Parapet**, as shown in Figure 3–30.

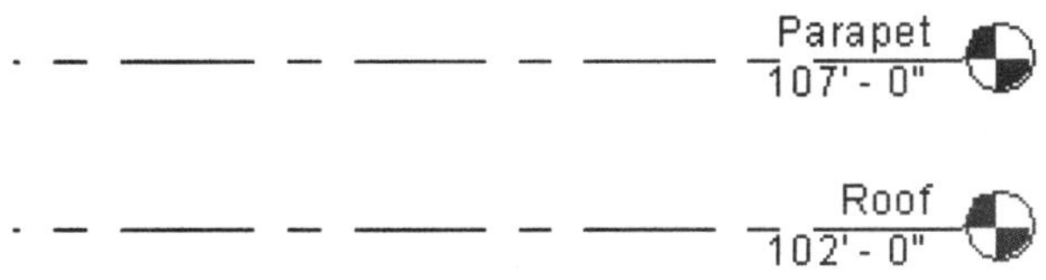

Figure 3–30

20. Add two levels below **Floor 1**. Name them **Basement** and **T.O. Footing** and set the heights as shown in Figure 3–31. You can modify the levels for clarity using controls such as **Add Elbow**.

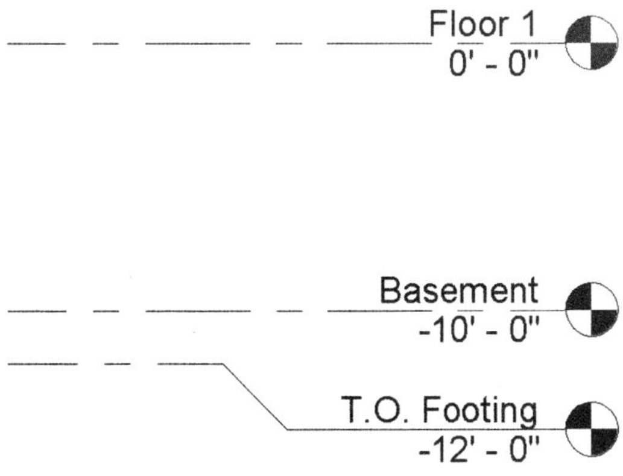

Figure 3–31

21. Zoom out to display the entire project.

22. In the View Control Bar, expand (Temporary Hide/Isolate) and select **Reset Temporary Hide/Isolate**. The pool displays again.

23. Open the Default 3D view. You can see the levels display in this view as well.

24. Save the project.

3.4 Creating Structural Grids

The structural grid indicates how to space the bays of a building and where to place columns, as shown in Figure 3–32. Any changes to the grid influences the elements that are referenced to them.

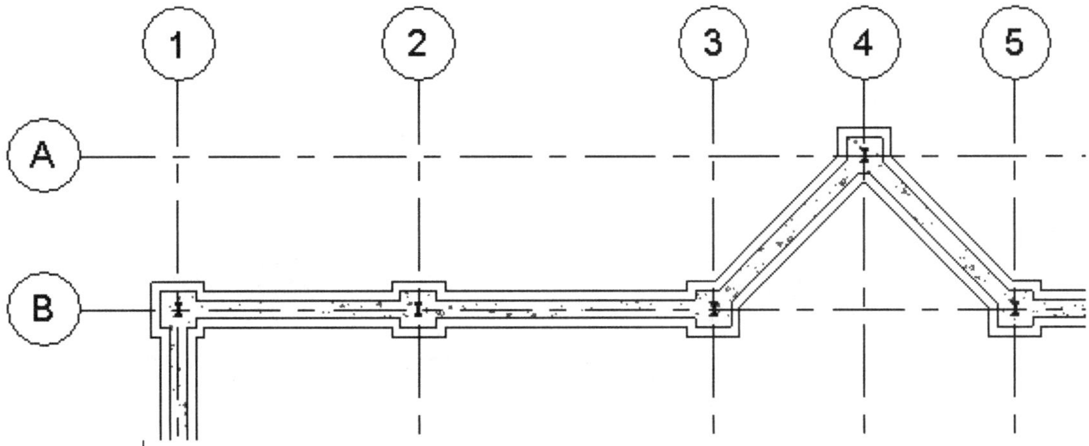

Figure 3–32

Each line or arc in a grid is a separate entity and can be placed, moved, and modified individually.

How To: Create a Structural Grid

1. In the *Architecture* tab>Datum panel, click  (Grid) or type **GR**.
2. In the Type Selector, select the Grid type which controls the size of the bubble and the linestyle.
3. In the *Modify | Place Grid* tab>Draw panel (shown in Figure 3–33) select the method you want to use.

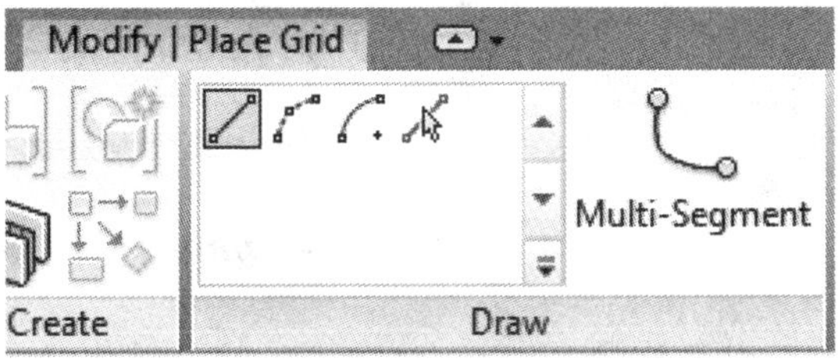

Figure 3–33

4. In the Options Bar, set the *Offset* if required.
5. Continue adding grid lines as required.

- Grids can be sketched at any angle, but you should ensure that all parallel grids are sketched in the same direction (i.e., from left to right, or from bottom to top).
- When using the Multi-Segment tool (shown in Figure 3–34), sketch the line and click (Finish Edit Mode) to complete the command.

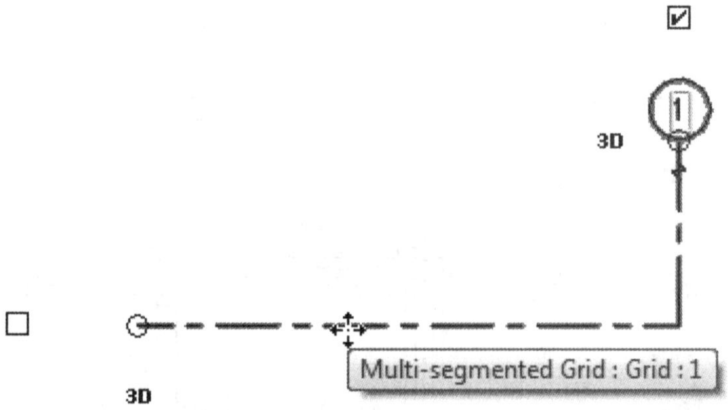

Figure 3–34

Modifying Grid Lines

Grid lines are very similar to Level lines. You can modify grid lines using controls, alignments, and temporary dimensions (as shown in Figure 3–35), as well as in the Properties palette and Type Selector.

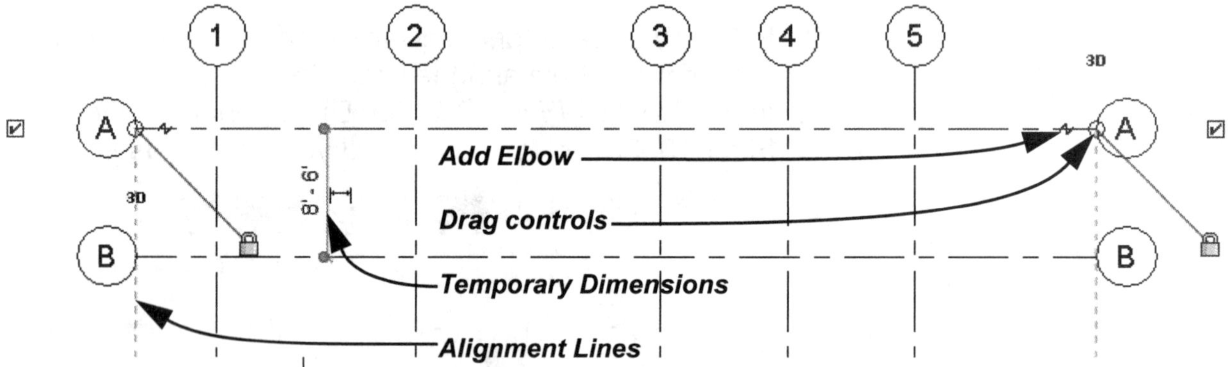

Figure 3–35

- To modify a grid number, double-click on the number in the bubble and type the new number. Grid numbers can be numbers, letters, or a combination of the two.
- Grid numbers increment automatically.

3.5 Adding Columns

The Autodesk Revit software includes two types of columns: architectural and structural, as shown in Figure 3–36. Architectural columns are placeholders or decorative elements, while structural columns include more precise information relative to strength and load-bearing parameters.

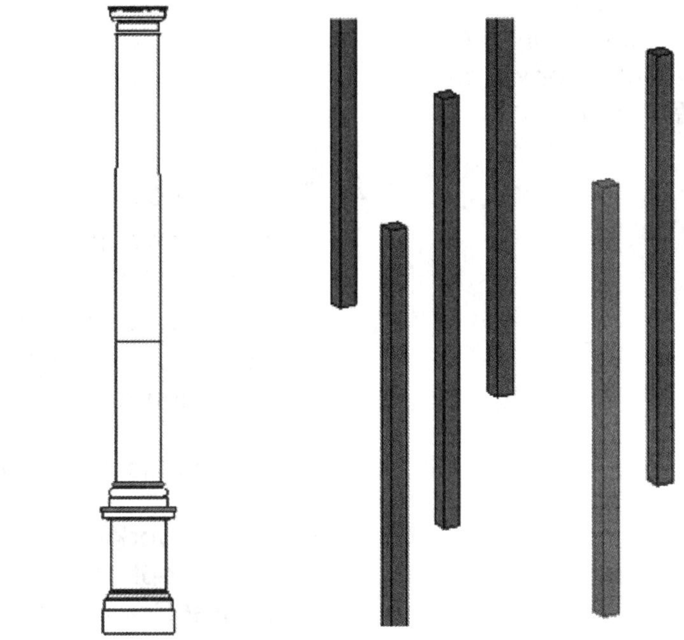

Architectural Column ***Structural Columns***

Figure 3–36

How To: Add Columns

Structural Column is the default.

1. In the *Architecture* tab>Build panel, expand (Column) and click either (Column: Architectural) or (Structural Column).
2. In the Type Selector, select the column you want to use, as shown in Figure 3–37.

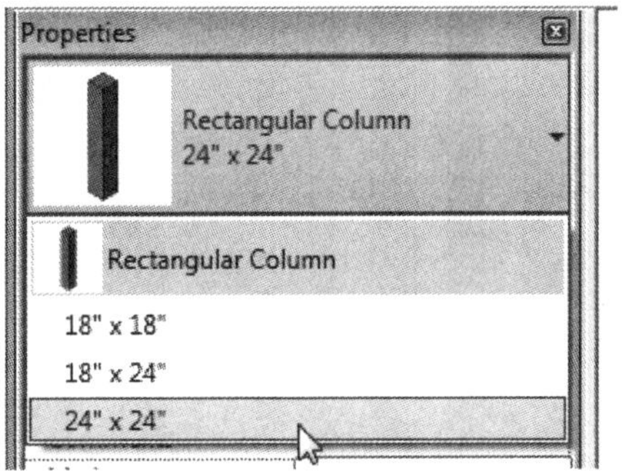

Figure 3–37

3. In the Options Bar, set the *Height* (or *Depth*) for the column. You can select a level (as shown in Figure 3–38), or select **Unconnected** to specify a height.

Architectural columns are typically placed from the level that you are on up to a specific height. Structural columns are typically placed from the level you are on down to a specific depth.

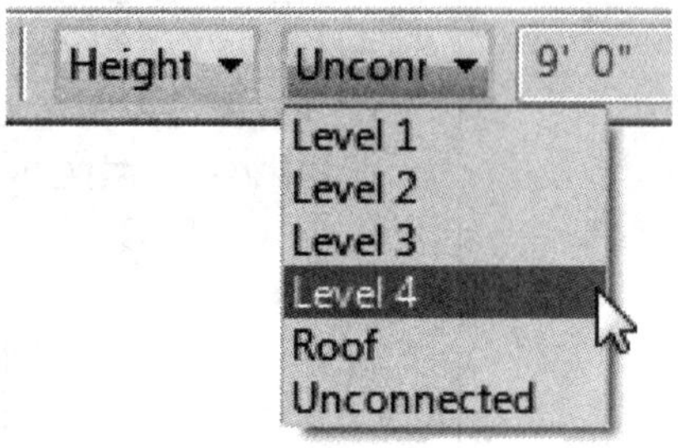

Figure 3–38

4. Place the column as required. It snaps to grid lines and walls.
   - Columns can be placed as a free instance unconnected to any grid lines.
   - If you select **Rotate after placement**, you are prompted for a rotation angle after you select the insertion point for the column.

5. Continue placing columns as required.

- If you are working with structural columns, you have two additional options for placing columns in the *Modify | Place Structural Column* tab>Multiple panel:
  - To place columns at the intersection of grid lines, click (At Grids) and select the grid lines. Columns will only be placed at the intersections of the selected grid lines.
  - To place structural columns wherever you have an architectural column, click (At Columns) and select the architectural columns. The structural columns are placed at the center of the architectural columns, as shown in Figure 3–39.

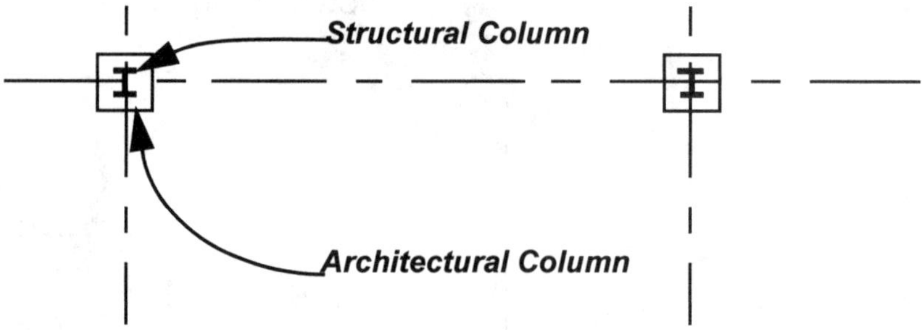

Figure 3–39

- An architectural column placed in a wall is automatically cleaned up if the material of the column and wall match. Structural columns remain separate even if they are the same material as the surrounding walls, as shown in Figure 3–40.

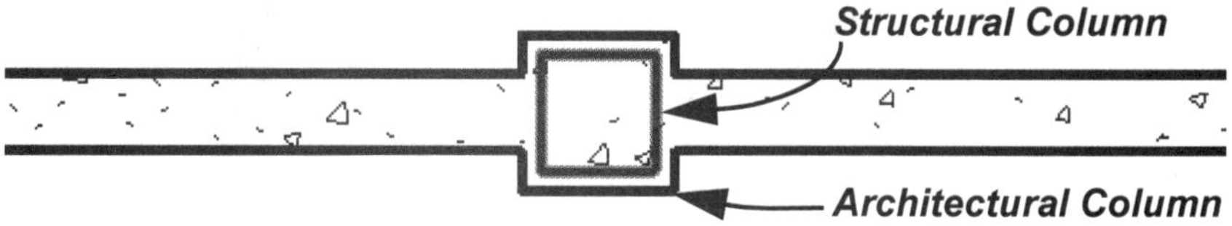

Figure 3–40

Loading Columns

Select additional column types from the Autodesk Revit Library.

In the *Modify* | *Place Column* tab>Mode panel, click (Load Family). In the Load Family dialog box, navigate to the *Columns* folder (as shown in Figure 3–41) for architectural columns, or to the *Structural Columns* folder and sub-folders for *Concrete*, *Light Gauge Steel, Precast Concrete*, *Steel*, and *Wood*.

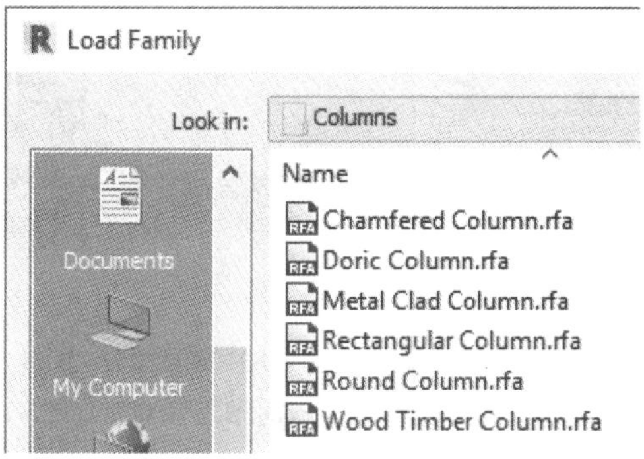

Figure 3–41

- When you open a structural column family, you are prompted to choose from a list of types, as shown in Figure 3–42. Hold <Ctrl> or <Shift> to select more than one.

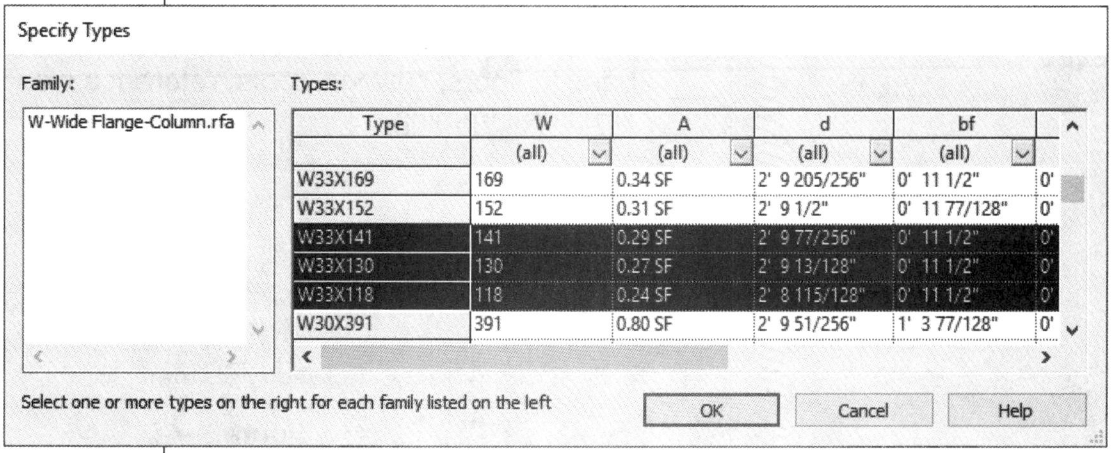

Figure 3–42

Modifying Columns

Structural columns have additional parameters.

- In Properties, you can change the *Base Level* and *Top Level*, as well as the offsets from these levels and several other options, as shown in Figure 3–43.

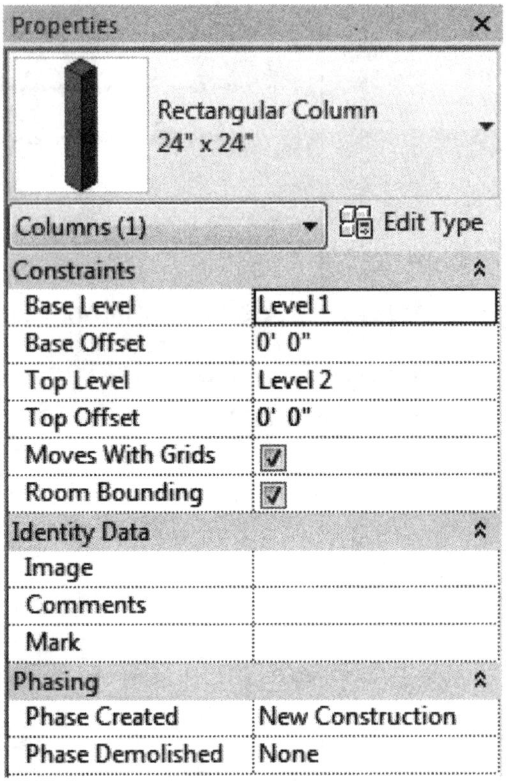

Figure 3–43

- Deleting a grid line or wall does not delete the columns placed on them.
- By default, columns move with nearby grids although you can still move them independently. Select the column(s) and, in the Options Bar or Properties, select or clear **Move With Grids** to change the method.
- In the *Modify | Column* tab>Modify Column panel (shown in Figure 3–44), you can attach or detach a column's top and base to floors, ceilings, roofs, reference planes, and structural framing.

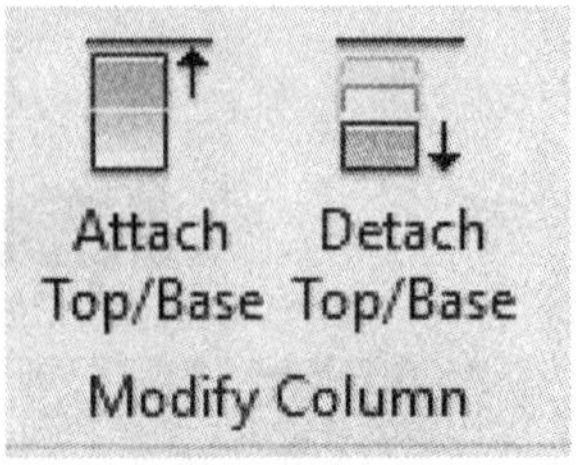

Figure 3–44

Practice 3c Add Structural Grids and Columns

Practice Objectives

- Add and modify structural grid lines.
- Add structural columns.

In this practice, you will add grid lines using information in the imported file.You will then add structural columns to the grids and modify the height of the columns, as shown in Figure 3–45.

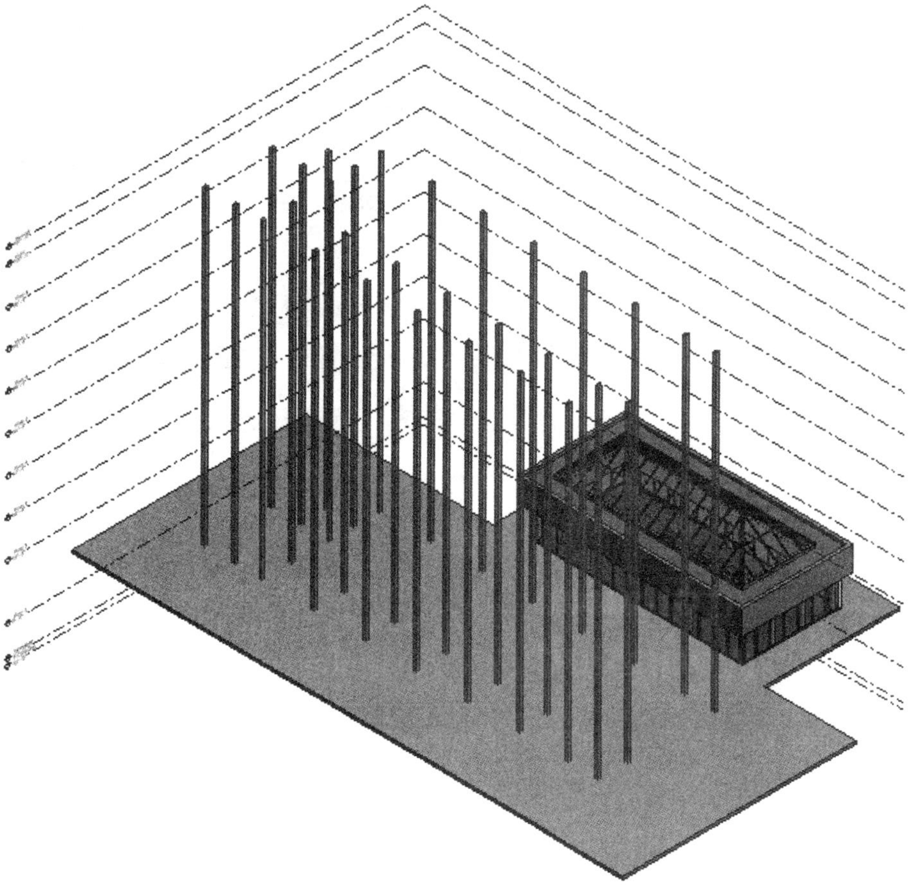

Figure 3–45

Task 1 - Create structural grids.

1. Open the project **Modern-Hotel-Grids.rvt** from the practice files folder.
2. Open the **Floor Plans: Floor 1** view.

3. Select the linked Revit file with the pool. In the View Control Bar, expand (Temporary Hide/Isolate) and select **Hide Element**.
4. In the *Architecture* tab>Datum panel, click (Grid).
5. In the *Modify | Place Grid* tab>Draw panel, click (Pick Lines).
6. Select the first vertical grid line on the left of the linked file. Click inside the bubble, type **A**, and press <Enter>.
7. Continue selecting the vertical grid lines displayed in the imported file. The letters automatically increment.
8. Click the first horizontal grid line and change the letter in the bubble to **1**.
9. Continue selecting the horizontal grid lines. The numbers automatically increment.
10. Click (Modify).
11. Select the CAD file. In the View Control Bar, expand (Temporary Hide/Isolate) and select **Hide Element**.
12. Only the grids should now display, as shown in Figure 3–46. Check the lengths of all grid lines. Modify the length by dragging the ends if required.

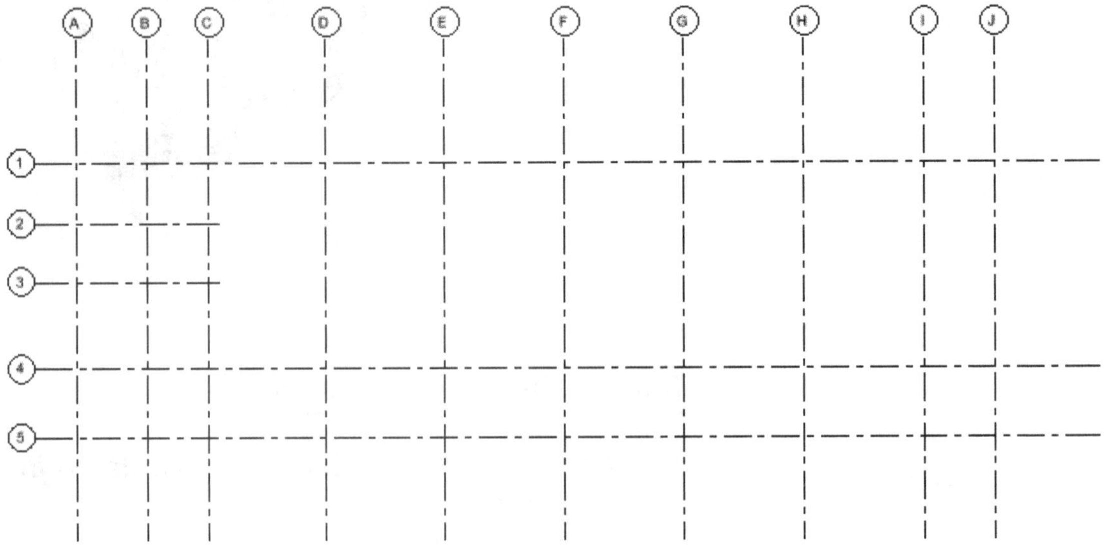

Figure 3–46

13. Save the project.

Task 2 - Add columns.

1. In the *Architecture* tab>Build panel, click (Structural Column).
2. In the Type Selector, select **Precast-Square Column: 12" x 12"**.
3. In the Options Bar, change *Depth* to **Height**, then set the *Height* to **Floor 2**.

Verify that Height (not Depth) is selected in the Options Bar.

4. In the *Modify | Place Structural Column* tab>Multiple panel, click (At Grids).
5. Select all of the horizontal and vertical grid lines in the project.

You can use a crossing window from right to left to select the grids. All other elements are automatically filtered out.

6. In the *Modify | Place Structural Column>At Grid Intersection* tab>Multiple panel, click (Finish).
7. Return to the **Modify** command.
8. Delete the columns at locations **A1**, **A2**, **A4**, **B1**, and **B4**. The project displays as shown in Figure 3–47.

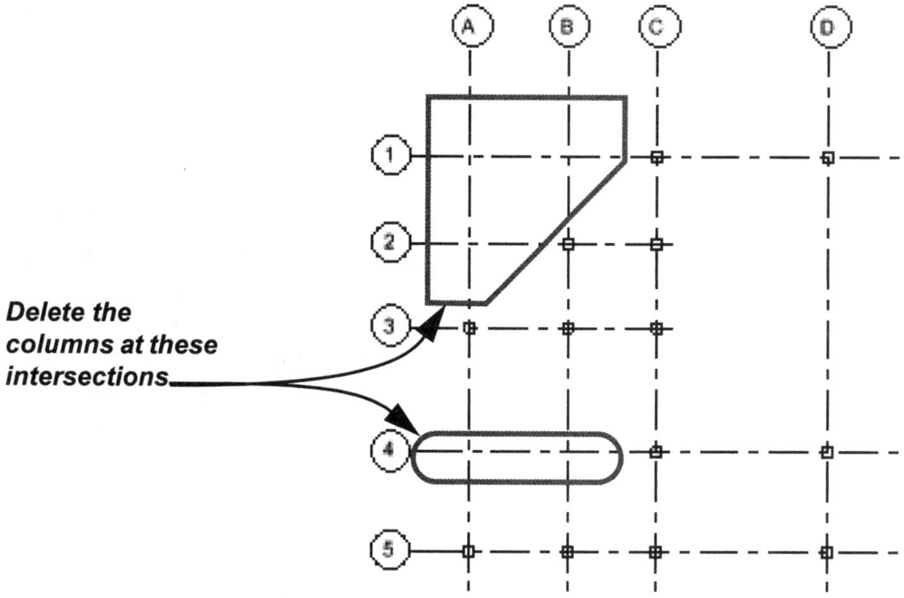

Figure 3–47

9. In the View Control Bar, expand (Temporary Hide/ Isolate) and select **Reset Temporary Hide/Isolate**.
10. Save the project.

Task 3 - Modify the Columns.

1. In the Quick Access Toolbar, click  (Default 3D View). The columns are only set to the height of the 2nd floor (Floor 2), as shown in Figure 3–48.

The linked file does not display in the 3D view because it was only linked to the plan view.

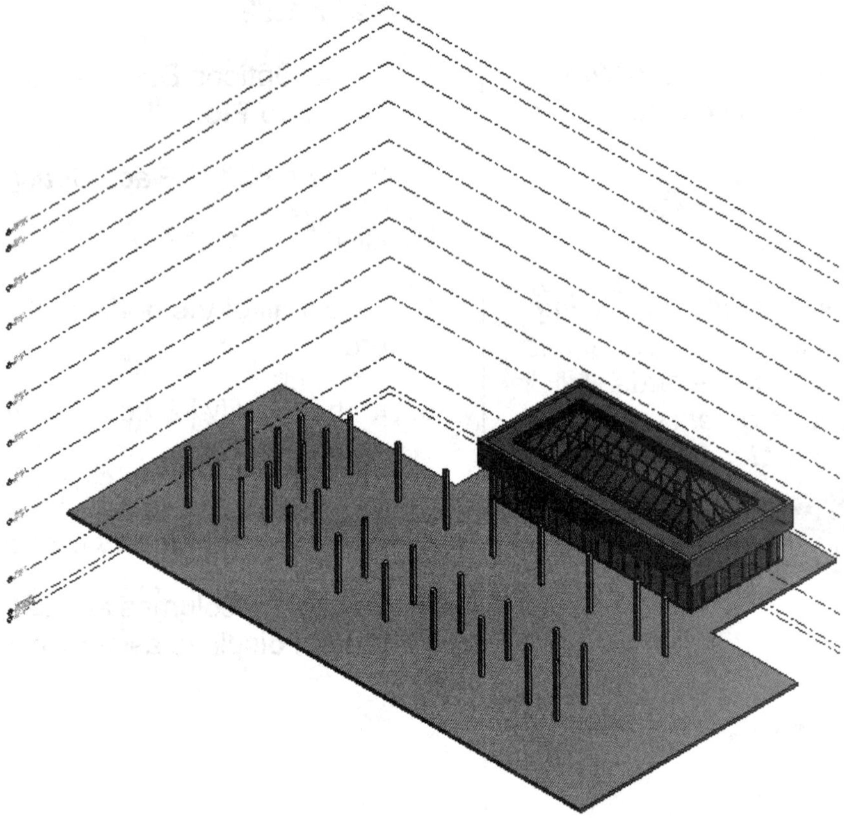

Figure 3–48

2. Select all of the columns. You can select one column, then right-click and select **Select All Instances>Visible in View**.
3. In Properties, in the *Constraints* area, change the *Base Level* to **T.O. Footing** and the *Top Level* to **Roof**. Click **Apply** or move the cursor into the view window. The columns now extend from the top of the footing to the roof.
4. Click in space to release the selection.

*Type **ZA** to zoom out in the view if required.*

5. View several different floor plan views to verify the grids and columns display.
6. Return to the **3D** view.
7. Save the project.

Chapter Review Questions

1. What type of view do you need to be in to add a level to your project?

   a. Any non-plan view.

   b. As this is done using a dialog box, the view does not matter.

   c. Any view except for 3D.

   d. Any section or elevation view.

2. How do you line up grid lines that might be different lengths, as shown in Figure 3–49?

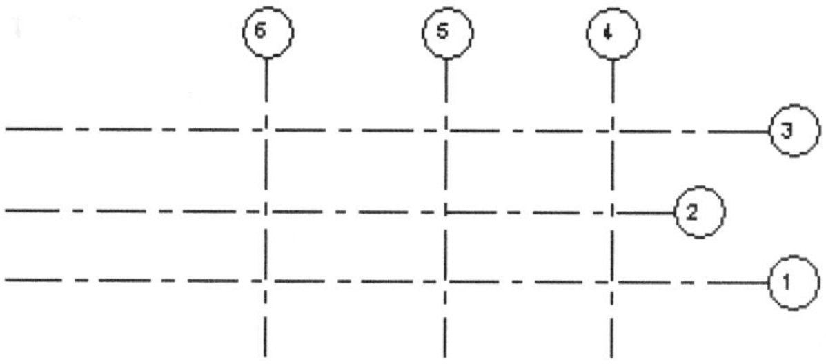

Figure 3–49

   a. Use  (Trim/Extend Multiple Elements) to line them up with a common reference line.

   b. Select the grid line and use the drag control to line up with the other grid lines.

   c. Select the grid line, right-click and select **Auto-Align**.

   d. In Properties, change the *Length* and then use  (Move) to get them into position.

3. Where can columns (whose command access is shown in Figure 3–50) be placed?

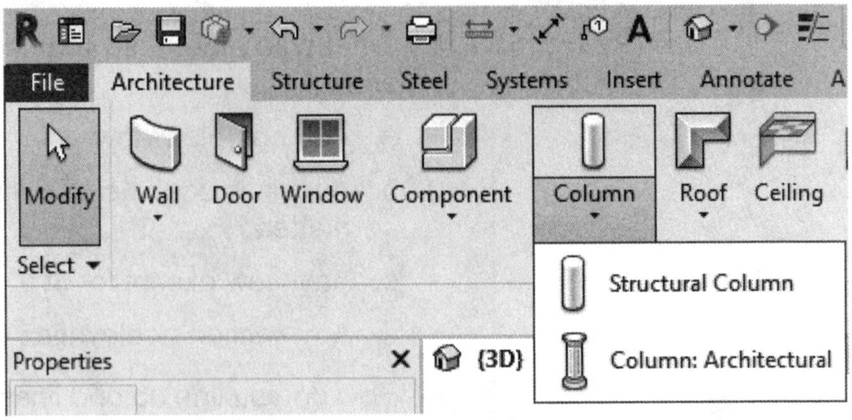

Figure 3–50

a. Columns can only be placed on grids.

b. Architectural columns can be placed anywhere, but structural columns can only be placed on grids.

c. Both types of columns can be placed wherever you want.

d. Grid-based column types must be placed on the grid, but free-standing column types can be placed anywhere.

4. Which of the following types of CAD formats can you import into the Autodesk Revit software? (Select all that apply.)

a. .DWG

b. .XLS

c. .SAT

d. .DGN

Command Summary

Button	Command	Location
	**At Columns**	• **Ribbon:** *Modify | Place Structural Column* tab>Multiple panel
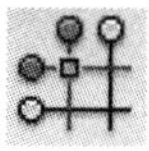	**At Grids**	• **Ribbon:** *Modify | Place Structural Column* tab>Multiple panel
	**Column**	• **Ribbon:** *Architecture* tab>Build panel
	**Column> Column: Architectural**	• **Ribbon:** *Architecture* tab>Build panel>expand Column
	**Column> Structural Column**	• **Ribbon:** *Architecture* tab>Build panel>expand Column
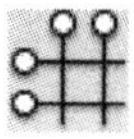	**Grid**	• **Ribbon:** *Architecture* tab>Datum panel • **Shortcut:** GR
	**Import CAD**	• **Ribbon:** *Insert* tab>Import panel
	**Level**	• **Ribbon:** *Architecture* tab>Datum panel • **Shortcut:** LL
	**Link CAD**	• **Ribbon:** *Insert* tab>Link panel
	**Link Revit**	• **Ribbon:** *Insert* tab>Link panel
	**Multi-Segment (Grid)**	• **Ribbon:** *Modify | Place Grid* tab>Draw panel
	**PDF**	• **Ribbon:** *Insert* tab>Import panel
	**Propagate Extents**	• **Ribbon:** *Modify | Grids* or *Modify | Levels*> Datum panel
	**Temporary Hide/Isolate**	• **View Control Bar**

Design Development Phase

The second section of this guide focuses on teaching you how to use the tools available in the Autodesk® Revit® software to create the building model. It also describes the viewing tools required to produce the model.

This section includes the following chapters:

- Chapter 4: Modeling Walls
- Chapter 5: Working with Doors and Windows
- Chapter 6: Working with Curtain Walls
- Chapter 7: Working with Views
- Chapter 8: Adding Components
- Chapter 9: Modeling Floors
- Chapter 10: Modeling Ceilings
- Chapter 11: Modeling Roofs
- Chapter 12: Modeling Stairs, Railings, and Ramps

Chapter 4

Modeling Walls

Walls are the primary elements that define rooms in buildings. The Autodesk® Revit® software contains a variety of wall types that are available in different widths and materials. You can change the height, length, and type as required. After you have added walls, you can add room elements to areas defined by the walls.

Learning Objectives in this Chapter

- Model walls using specific wall types.
- Modify walls by changing the wall type, height, and length.
- Define how walls join at intersections.
- Add wall openings that are not cased or filled with a door or window.
- Add room elements and tags that display the room name and room number.

4.1 Modeling Walls

Walls in the Autodesk® Revit® software are more than just two lines on a plan. They are full 3D elements that store detailed information, including height, thickness, and materials. This means they are useful in 2D and 3D views, and also impact material takeoff schedules, as shown in Figure 4–1.

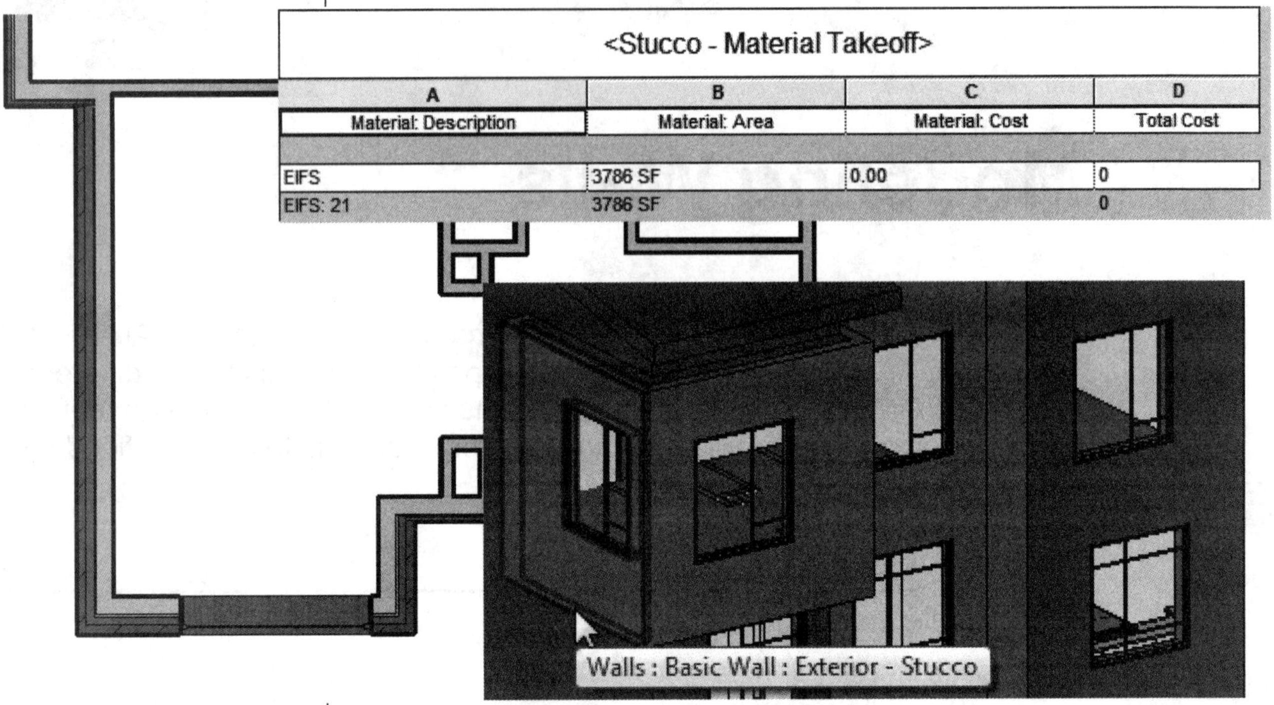

<Stucco - Material Takeoff>			
A	B	C	D
Material: Description	Material: Area	Material: Cost	Total Cost
EIFS	3786 SF	0.00	0
EIFS: 21	3786 SF		0

Figure 4–1

There are three broad categories of walls:

- *Basic walls:* Compound walls that contain on or more layers (e.g., blocks, air space, bricks, etc.).
- *Curtain Walls:* Non-bearing walls made of glass with mullions.
- *Stacked walls:* Includes one wall type above another wall type, such as a brick wall over a concrete wall.

- To display the hatching in the walls in plan views, in the View Control Bar, set the *Detail Level* to **Medium** or **Fine**, as shown in Figure 4–2.

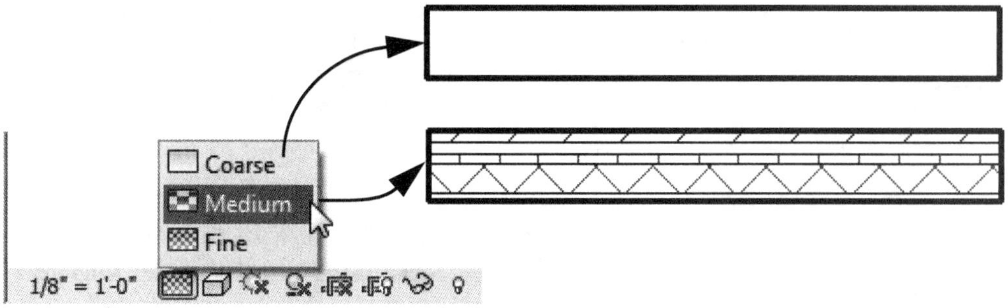

Figure 4–2

How To: Model a Wall

1. In the *Architecture* tab>Build panel, click (Wall) or type the shortcut **WA**.
2. In the Type Selector, select a wall type as shown in Figure 4–3.

You can use the Search box to quickly find specific types of walls.

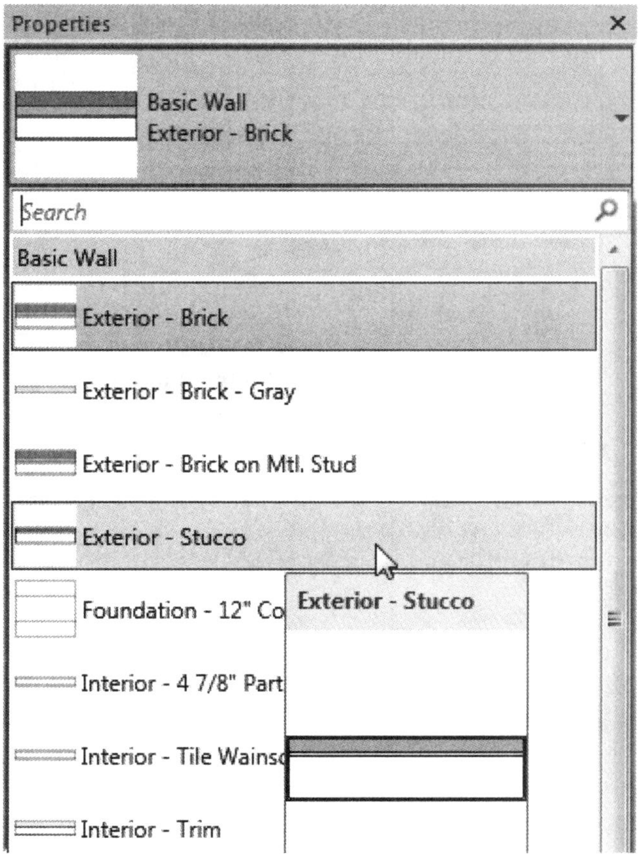

Figure 4–3

3. In the Options Bar (shown in Figure 4–4), specify the following information about the wall before you start modeling:

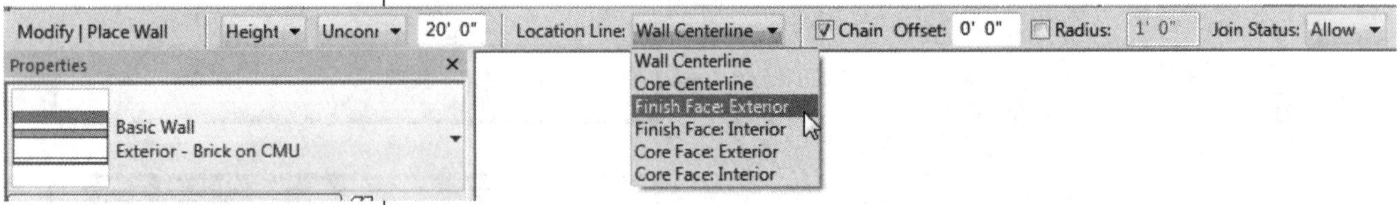

Figure 4–4

- *Height:* Set the height of a wall to either **Unconnected** (with a specified height) or to a level.
- *Location Line:* Set the justification of the wall using the options shown in Figure 4–4, above.
- *Chain:* Enables you to model multiple connected walls.
- *Offset:* Enables you to enter the distance at which a new wall is created from an existing element.
- *Radius:* Adds a curve of a specified radius to connected walls as you model.
- *Join Status:* Allow or Disallow automatic wall joins.

4. In the *Modify | Place Wall* tab>Draw panel (shown in Figure 4–5), select one of the options to create the wall.

Figure 4–5

- Use alignment lines, temporary dimensions, and snaps to place the walls.
- As you are sketching you can press <Spacebar> to flip the orientation of compound walls.
- When using the *Chain* option, press <Esc> to finish the string of walls and remain in the Wall command.

4.2 Modifying Walls

There are several methods of modifying walls. You can change the type of wall using the Type Selector, modify the Properties, use controls and shape handles to modify the length and wall orientation, and use temporary and permanent dimensions to change the location or length of a wall in 2D and 3D, as shown in Figure 4–6. Additional tools enable you to modify wall joins, edit the profile of a wall, and add wall openings.

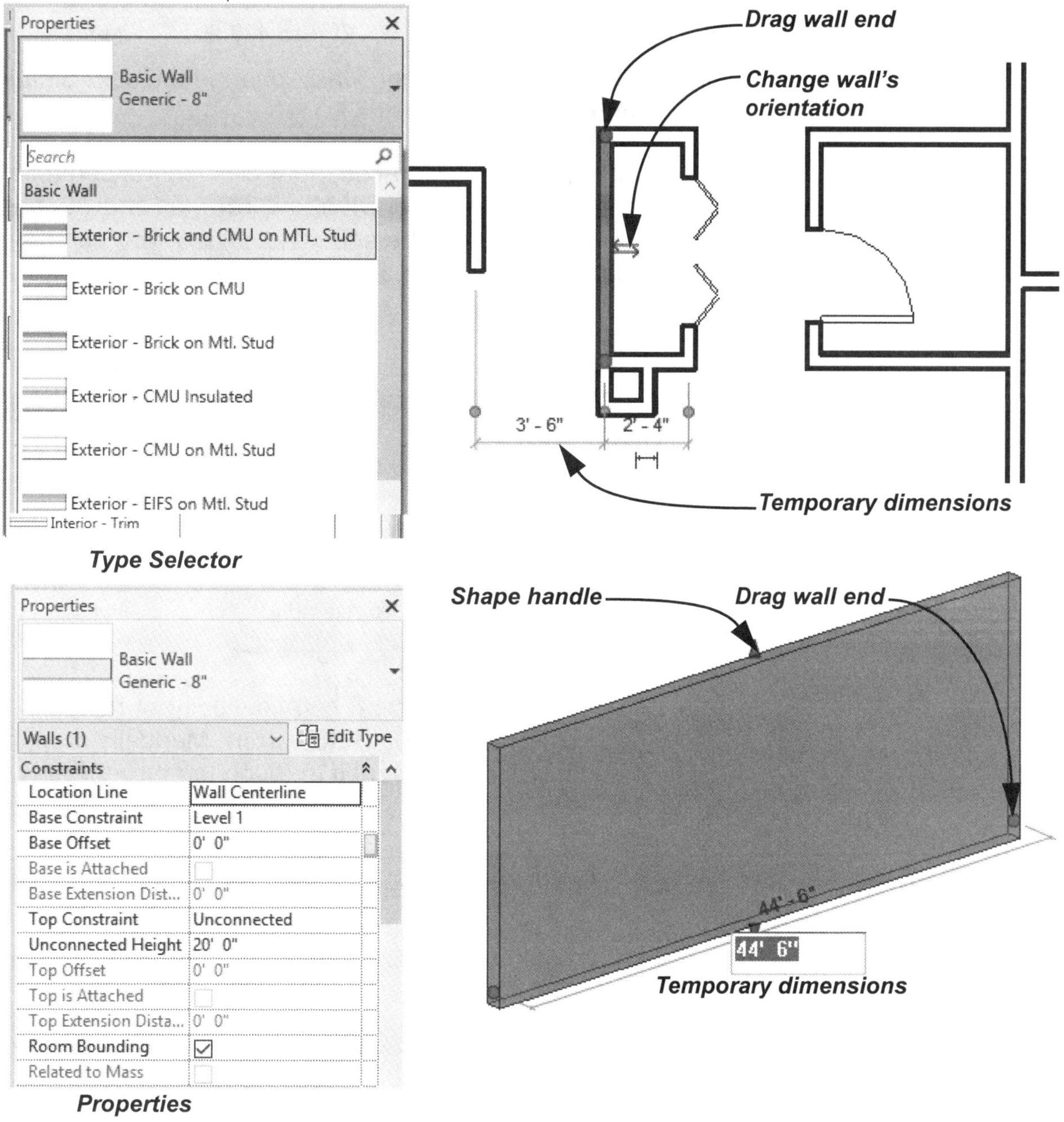

Figure 4–6

Wall Joins

The software automatically joins walls with common materials when they come together at an intersection, as shown on the left in Figure 4–7. However, there are times when you do not want the walls to clean up, such as when one fire-rated wall butts into another, or when a wall touches a column surround, as shown on the right in Figure 4–7.

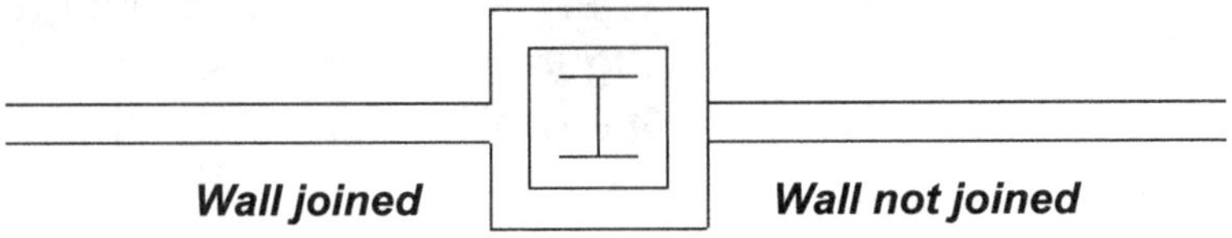

Figure 4–7

- While you are creating walls, change the *Join Status* to **Disallow** in the Options Bar.
- If a wall is already placed, right-click on the control at the end of the wall and select **Disallow Join**, as shown on the left in Figure 4–8. Once the end is not joined, you can drag it to the appropriate location, as shown on the right in Figure 4–8.

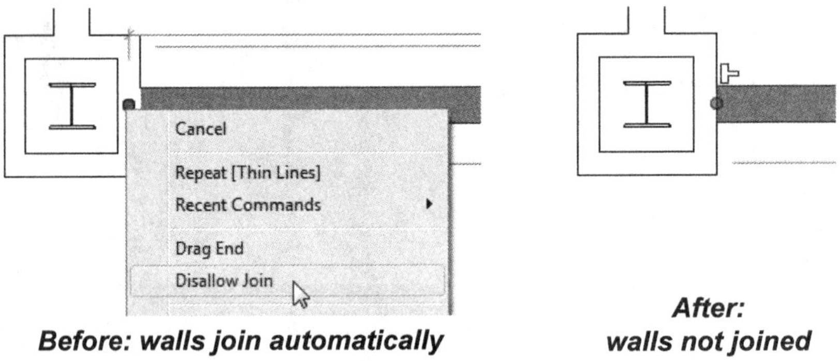

Figure 4–8

- To rejoin the walls, click (Allow Join) or right-click on the end control and select **Allow Join**. Manually drag the wall back to where you want it to touch the target wall

Hint: Using Thin Lines

The software automatically applies line weights to views, as shown for a section on the left in Figure 4–9. If a line weight seems heavy or obscures your work on the elements, toggle off the line weights. In the Quick Access Toolbar or in the *View* tab>Graphics panel, click  (Thin Lines) or type **TL**. The lines display with the same weight, as shown on the right in Figure 4–9.

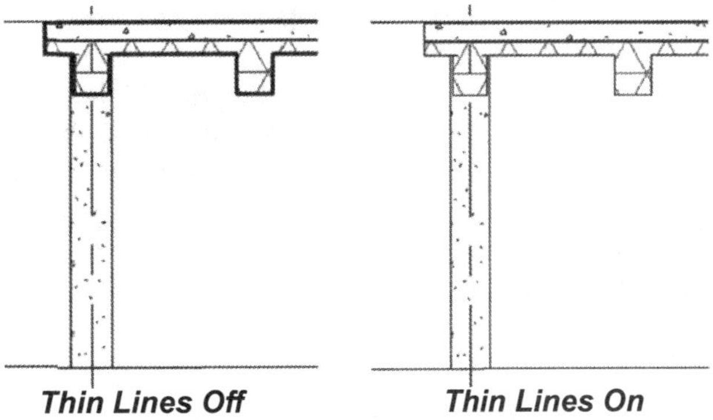

Figure 4–9

- The **Thin Line** setting is remembered until you change it, even if you shut down and restart the software.

Editing Wall Profiles

Walls often follow the contours of a site or an angle, such as following a line of stairs, as shown in Figure 4–10. If required, you can edit the profile of a wall.

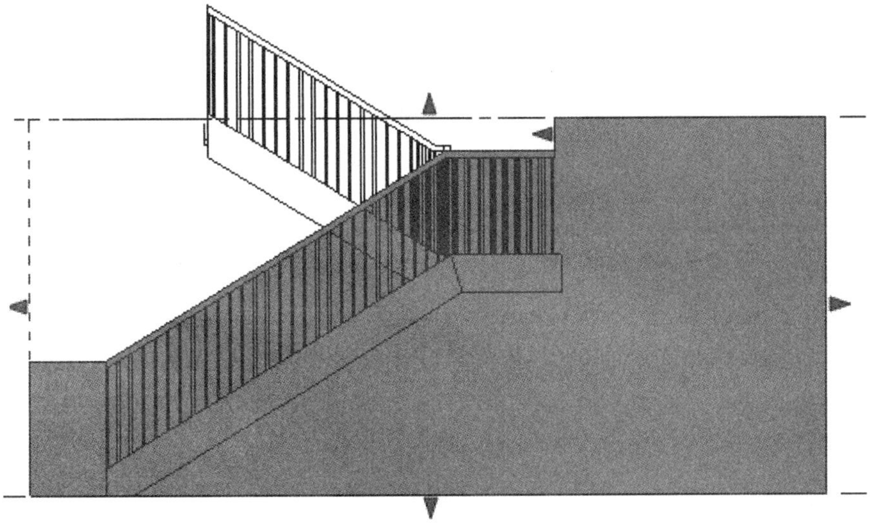

Figure 4–10

How To: Edit the Profile of a Wall

You can also double-click on a wall to edit the profile.

1. Open an elevation or section view in which you can see the face of the wall that you want to edit.
2. Select the wall (by highlighting the wall boundary).
3. In the *Modify | Walls* tab>Mode panel, click (Edit Profile). The wall is outlined in magenta indicating the profile of the wall.
4. In the *Modify | Walls>Edit Profile* tab>Draw panel, use the tools to modify the profile sketch of the wall, as shown on the top in Figure 4–11.
5. Once the profile is complete, click (Finish Edit Mode). The wall now follows the new profile, as shown on the bottom in Figure 4–11.

The sketch must form a continuous loop. Verify that the lines are clean without any gaps or overlaps. Use any of the tools in the Modify panel to clean up the sketch.

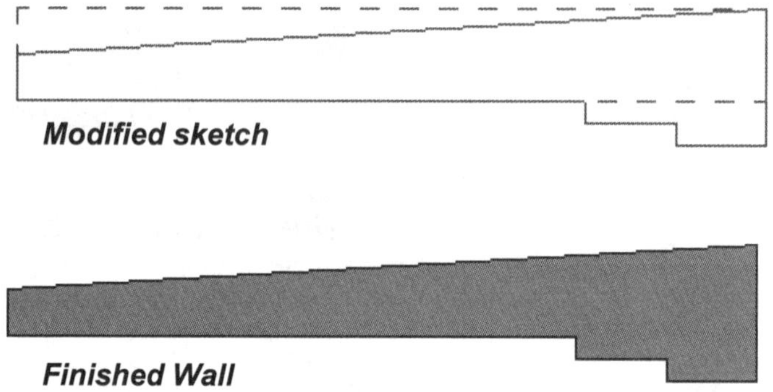

Figure 4–11

- For more information about editing walls and wall joins see *Appendix B.2 Editing Wall Joins* and *B.3 Wall Sweeps and Reveals.*

Wall Openings

You can add openings in walls that are not windows or doors by using the **Wall Opening** tool. This creates rectangular openings for both straight and curved walls, as shown in Figure 4–12.

Figure 4–12

How To: Add Wall Openings

1. Open an elevation, section, or 3D view.
2. In the *Architecture* tab>Openings panel, click (Wall Opening).
3. Select the wall.
4. Pick two points on the diagonal to determine the opening size.

- You can use temporary dimensions to size the opening while in the command and both temporary dimensions and shape handles to modify the opening when it is selected, as shown in Figure 4–13.

Figure 4–13

Hint: Matching Properties

You can select an existing wall and use it to assign the wall type and instance properties to other walls by using the **Match Type** command. This command also works with all elements that have types.

1. In the *Modify* tab>Clipboard panel, click (Match Type) or type **MA**. The cursor changes to an arrow with a clean paintbrush.
2. Select the source element that you want all of the others to match. The paintbrush changes to look as if it has been dipped in black paint as shown in Figure 4–14.

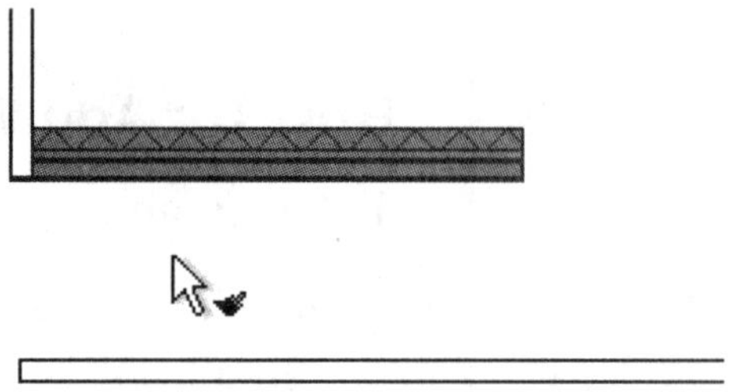

Figure 4–14

3. To select more than one element, in the *Modify | Match Type* tab>Multiple panel, click (Select Multiple). You can then use windows, crossings, <Ctrl>, and <Shift> to create a selection set of elements to change.
4. Select the elements that you want to change. For multiple selections, click (Finish) to apply the type to the selection.

- Click in an empty space in the project to empty the brush so that you can repeat the command with a different element.
- Elements to be matched must be of the same type (e.g., all walls, all doors, etc.).

Practice 4a

Model the Exterior Shell

Practice Objectives

- Add walls by tracing over lines in an imported DWG file.
- Add curtain walls.

In this practice, you will add exterior walls, including a curtain wall, to create the exterior shell of the project. You will use an imported file to help establish the location of the walls. The completed model is shown in Figure 4–15.

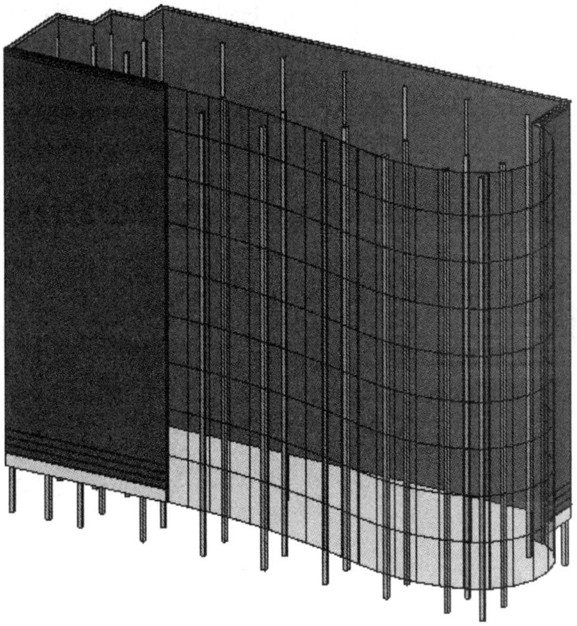

Figure 4–15

Task 1 - Add walls by picking lines.

1. Open the project **Modern-Hotel-Walls.rvt** from the practice files folder.
2. Verify that you are in the **Floor Plans: Floor 1** view.
3. In the View Control Bar, set the *Detail Level* to (Medium). Doing so enables the multiple layers of the wall that is going to be added to be displayed.
4. In the *Architecture* tab>Build panel, click (Wall).
5. In the Type Selector, select **Basic Wall: Exterior - Brick and CMU on MTL. Stud**.

6. In the Options Bar or Properties, set or verify the following options:

   - *Height:* **Parapet**
   - *Location Line:* **Finish Face: Exterior**
   - Select **Chain**.
   - *Join Status:* **Allow**
   - *Base Offset:* **0' 0"**
   - *Top Offset:* **0' 0"**

7. In the Draw panel, click (Pick Lines).

8. Select one of the exterior walls in the imported file, as shown in Figure 4–16. Ensure the dashed line displays inside the wall. This wall is a compound wall and you want the brick to display on the outside.

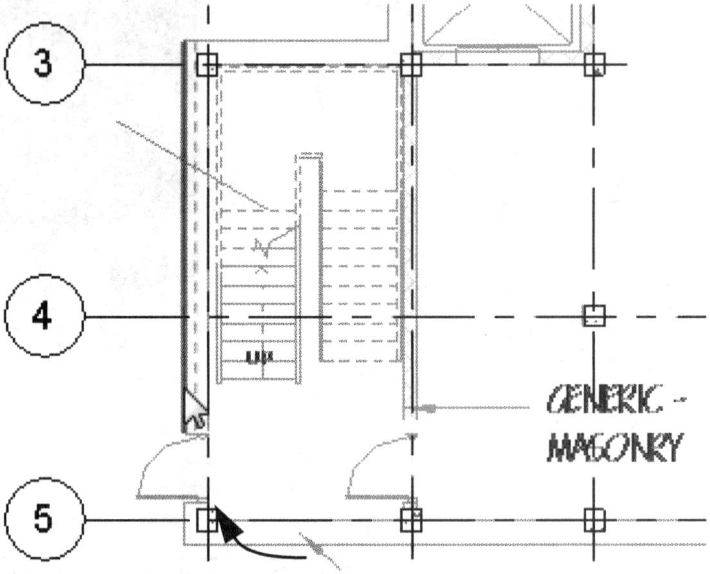

Do not place a wall

Figure 4–16

9. Continue selecting lines around the exterior of the building. Do not select the curved curtain wall lines.

   - Use (Flip) to change the wall's orientation if the brick side of the wall is not on the outside.

10. Click (Modify).

11. At the door openings on either end of the building, do not add walls on either side of the door. Instead, use the **Drag Wall End** control, as shown in Figure 4–17, to lengthen the wall across the opening. The intersections should clean up automatically.

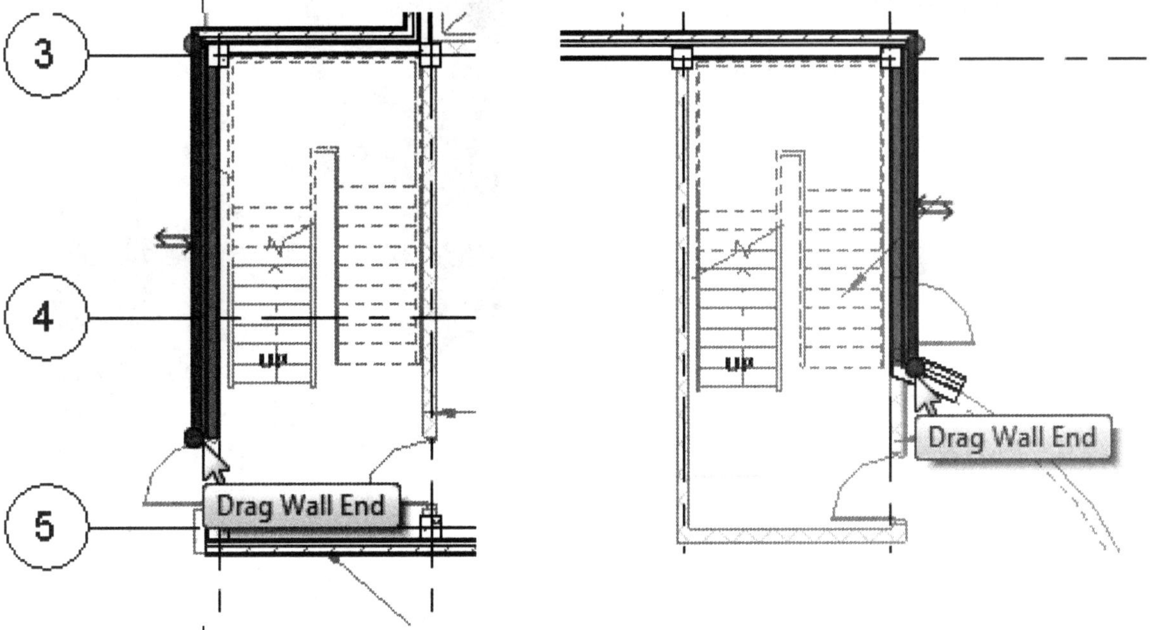

Figure 4–17

12. Save the project.

Task 2 - Add basic curtain walls.

1. Click (Wall).

2. In the Type Selector, select **Curtain Wall: Exterior Glazing** and set the following properties:
   - *Base Constraint:* **Floor 1**
   - *Base Offset:* **0**
   - *Top Constraint:* **Up to level: Parapet**
   - *Top Offset:* **0**

This places the top of the curtain wall below the roof level.

3. Use (Pick Lines) and select the three curved lines.

4. Click **Modify**.

The columns are hidden to make this graphic more readable.

5. In the Quick Access Toolbar, click (3D View).
6. In the View Control Bar, set the *Visual Style* to (Consistent Colors) to see the glass in the curtain walls, as shown in Figure 4–18.

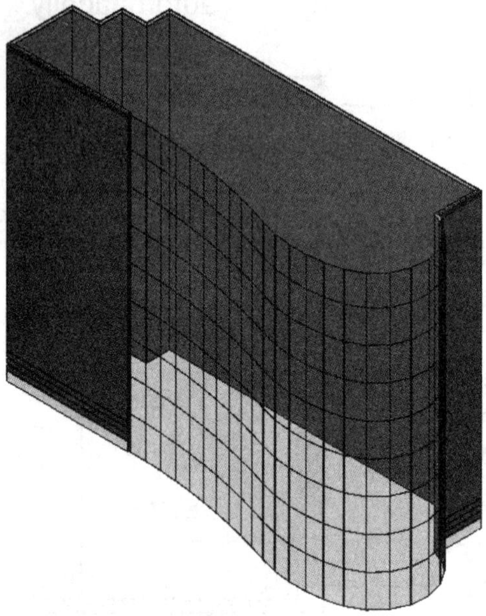

Figure 4–18

7. Save the project.

- An additional task to add a parapet to the exterior wall can be found in *Practice 4d (Optional) Model Additional Walls*

Extra credit

Practice 4b

Add Interior Walls

Practice Objectives

- Model and modify walls.
- Use modify tools including **Align**, **Offset**, **Trim/Extend**, **Copy**, and **Mirror**.

In this practice, you will add interior walls to the first floor plan, as shown in Figure 4–19, and use **Offset**, **Split Element**, **Trim**, and **Align** to help create them.

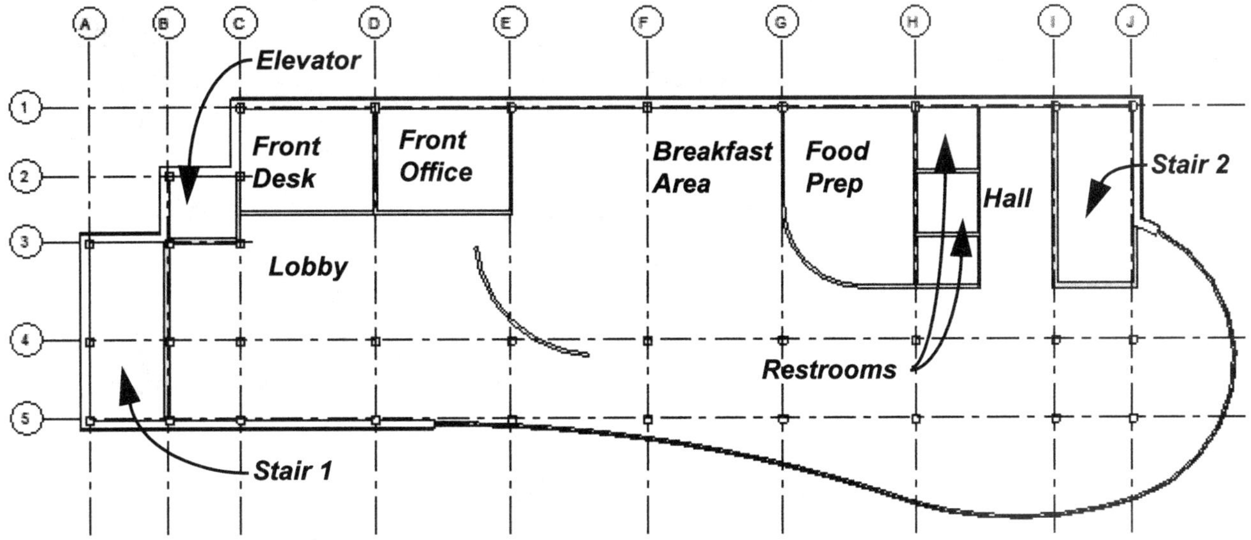

Figure 4–19

Task 1 - Add and align the stair and elevator walls.

1. Open the project **Modern-Hotel-Interior-Walls.rvt** from the practice files folder.
2. Open the **Floor Plans: Floor 1** view.
3. Zoom in on the stair and elevator area on the left side of the building.
4. Start the **Wall** command.

5. In the Options Bar and Properties, set the following options:
    - *Wall Type:* **Basic Wall: Generic 8" Masonry**
    - *Base Constraint:* **Basement**
    - *Base Offset:* **0'-0"**
    - *Top Constraint:* **Up to level: Roof**
    - *Top Offset:* **0' 0"**
    - Clear the **Chain** option.
6. Draw the stair and elevator walls, as shown in Figure 4–20. Draw each wall separately from column to column.

*If you leave the **Chain** option on, the wall will snap to other walls rather than the columns.*

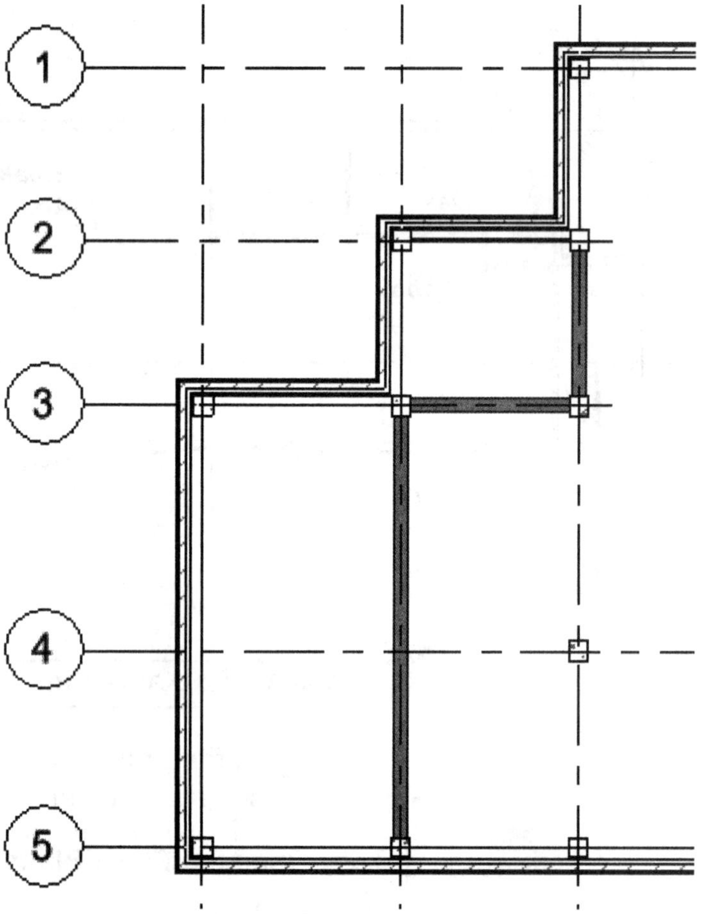

Figure 4–20

7. Click (Modify).

*If required, you can use the **Align** command to ensure that the walls are in the right place.*

8. Pan over to the other stair. Using the same wall type and other information, but with the **Chain** option toggled on, add the walls, as shown in Figure 4–21.

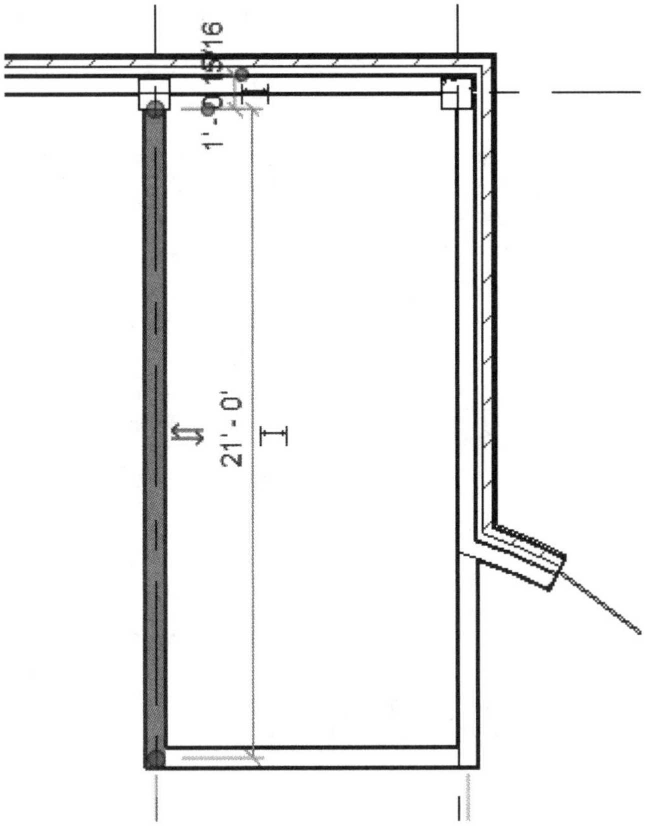

Figure 4–21

9. Zoom out to display the entire building floor plan.

10. Save the project.

Task 2 - Add the front desk and office walls.

Setting the Top Offset to a negative number leaves room for the floor above.

1. Start the **Wall** command and set the following properties:
    - *Wall type:* **Basic Wall: Interior - 4 7/8" Partition (1-hr)**
    - *Height:* **Floor 2**
    - *Location Line:* **Wall Centerline**
    - *Top Offset:* (negative) **-1' 0"**

2. Draw the walls shown in Figure 4–22.

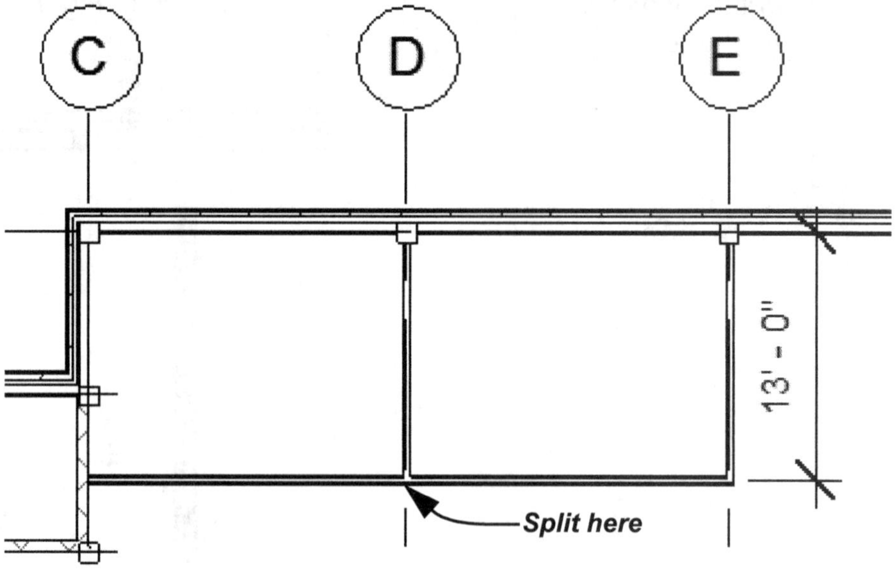

Figure 4–22

3. In the *Modify | Place Wall* tab>Modify panel, click (Split Element).

4. Click the horizontal wall at the point shown in Figure 4–22.

5. Click (Modify) and select the wall on the left. Change the *Top Constraint* to **Unconnected** and the *Unconnected Height* to **4'-0"**. This becomes the base for the Front Desk shelf.

6. Modify the lower wall to butt up against the taller walls, as shown in Figure 4–23.

In the Quick Access Toolbar, click (Thin Lines) to make the close-up easier to see.

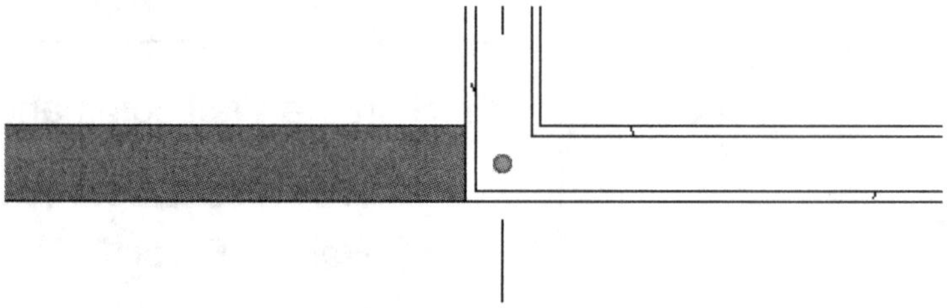

Figure 4–23

Using the Offset command would create a replica of the outside wall.

Task 3 - Add the support room walls.

1. Pan over to the other stairwell and add the walls shown in Figure 4–24. Use the same wall type and properties as the other main interior walls.

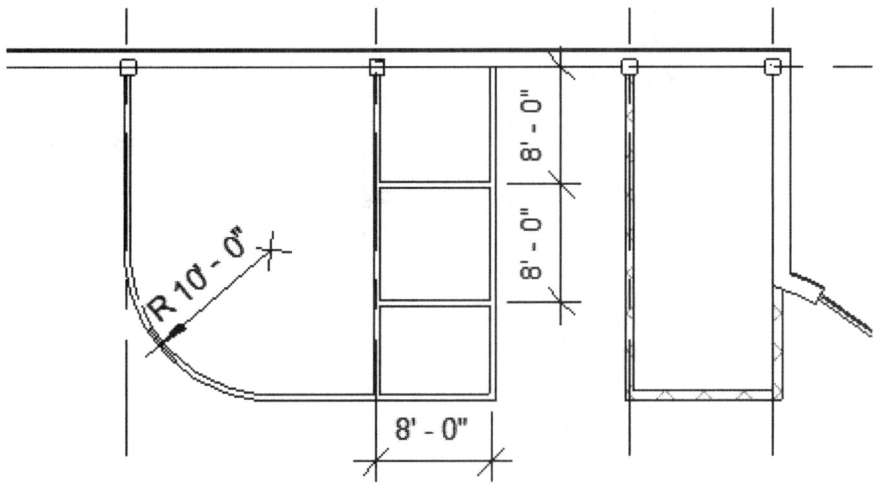

Figure 4–24

- When adding the restroom walls, use the **Wall** command and set the *Offset* to (negative) **-8'-0"**. Then, sketch the new walls relative to the outside walls.
- Use (Align) to match up the front face of the lower wall with the front face of the stairwell wall.
- To create the arc wall, add two straight walls first. Click (Fillet Arc), set the *Fillet radius* to **10' 0"**, and select the two walls to create the arc at the corner.
- Use (Trim/Extend to Corner), (Trim/Extend Single), and (Trim/Extend Multiple) as required to get the walls in place.

The exact size and location does not matter, but ensure there is enough room for people to get by on both sides.

2. Zoom out and add a **8'-0"** high curved wall using the same interior wall type to separate the Lobby from the Breakfast area, as shown in Figure 4–25.

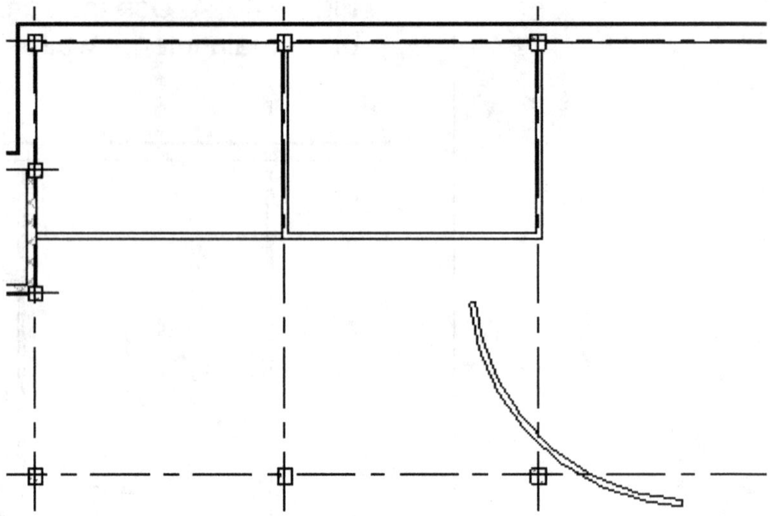

Figure 4–25

3. Zoom out and save the project.

- Additional wall practices are found in *Practice 4d (Optional) Model Additional Walls*

4.3 Adding Room Elements

Room elements are important for room names and numbers, as well as adding room information to schedules. You can place a room element in any space bounded by walls (as shown in Figure 4–26) or by room separation lines. Room separation lines enable you to divide an open space into more rooms.

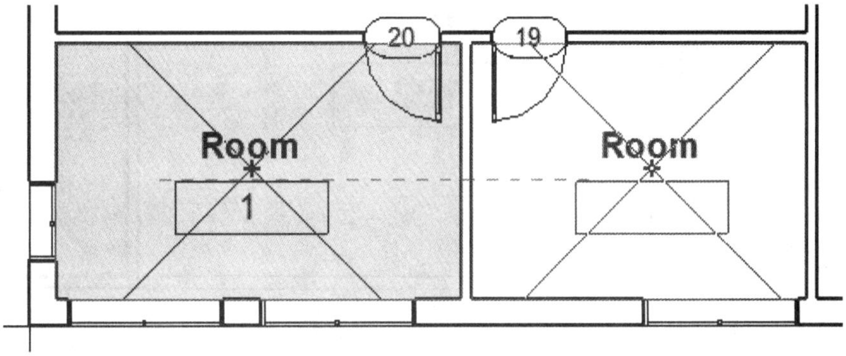

Figure 4–26

How To: Add Rooms

1. In the *Architecture* tab>Room & Area panel, click (Room) or type **RM**.
2. Move the cursor inside a boundary and click to place a room element. If you have **Tag on Placement** active, it also places the tag at the point you selected.
3. Continue clicking inside boundaries to add other rooms.

- To add multiple rooms at once, in the *Modify | Place Room* tab>Room panel, click (Place Rooms Automatically). Rooms are added in every bounded area that does not already have a room.
- Rooms are inserted with the default name of *Room*. Numbers increment automatically as you place rooms. Select the first room on a floor, change the number as required, and then add the rest of the room locations.

- To select rooms, hover the cursor near the room tag to highlight the room element, as shown in Figure 4–27.

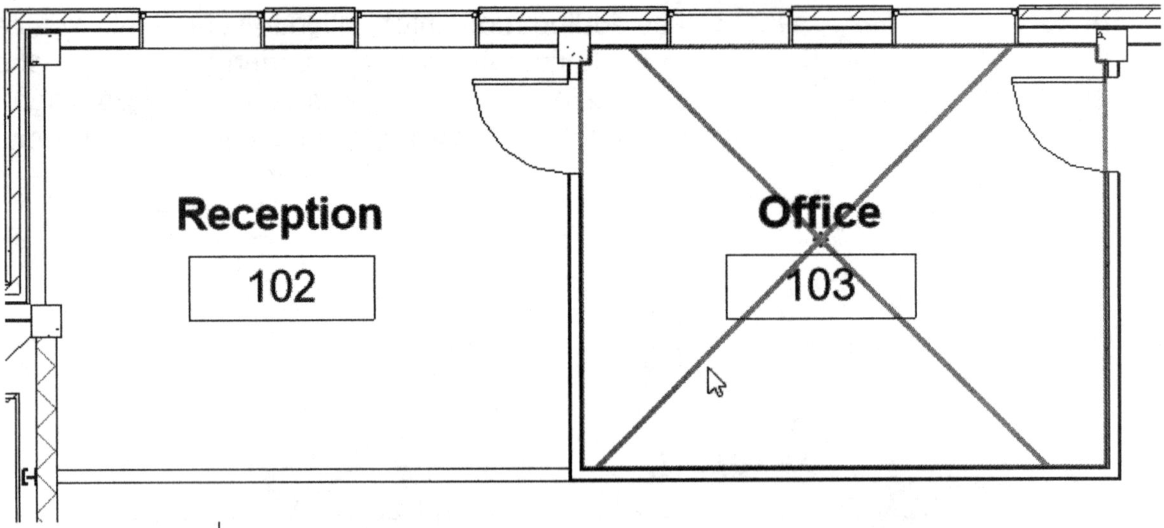

Figure 4–27

- To change the names of several rooms to the same name, select the room elements and in Properties, change the *Name* parameter, as shown in Figure 4–28.

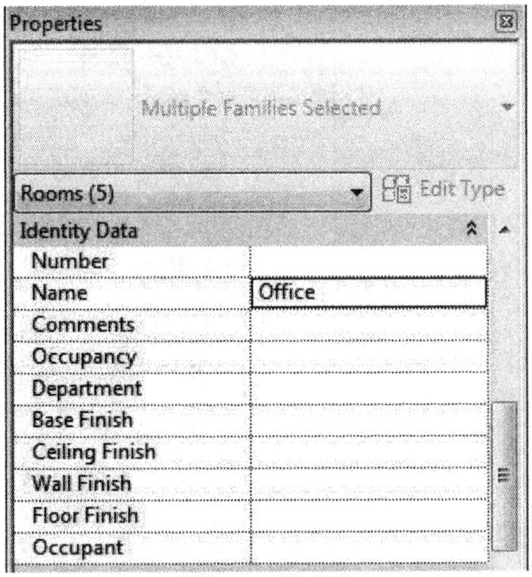

Figure 4–28

- Other information, such as finishes, can also be added in the room properties. This information is made available to schedules.

Hint: Making Rooms Visible

If rooms are not visible in a view, in the Visibility/Graphic Overrides dialog box, expand **Rooms** and select **Interior Fill** and/or **Reference**, as shown in Figure 4–29.

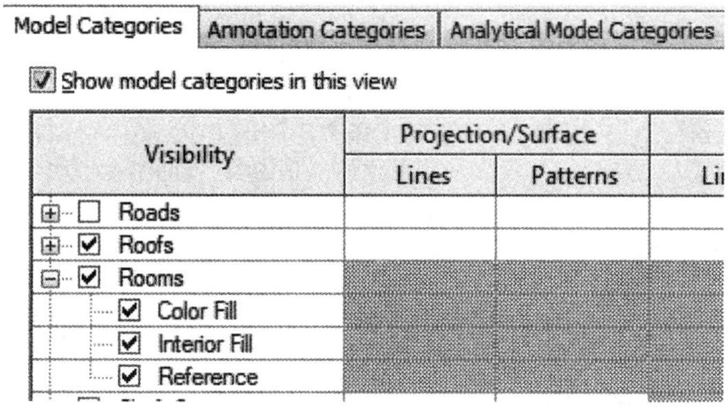

Figure 4–29

- Color Fill is used when a color scheme is applied to a view.

Add Room Separation Lines

1. In the *Architecture* tab>Room & Area panel, click  (Room Separator).
2. Use the Draw tools to place lines that divide the spaces.
3. After creating the room separation lines, use the **Room** command to add the rooms, as shown in Figure 4–30.

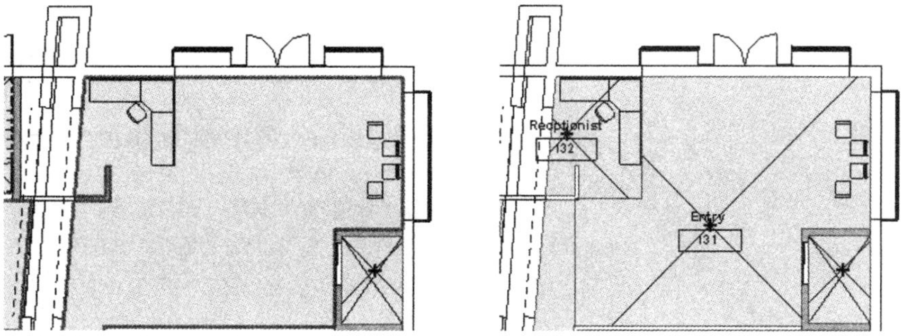

Before Room Separation Lines ***With Room Separation Lines***

Figure 4–30

Practice 4c

Extra credit

Add Room Elements

Practice Objectives

- Set up a view that displays rooms.
- Add rooms and room separation lines.

In this practice, you will add rooms to the model. You will change the names and numbers of rooms using tags and Properties. You will add room separation lines to break up the larger open areas, as shown in Figure 4–31.

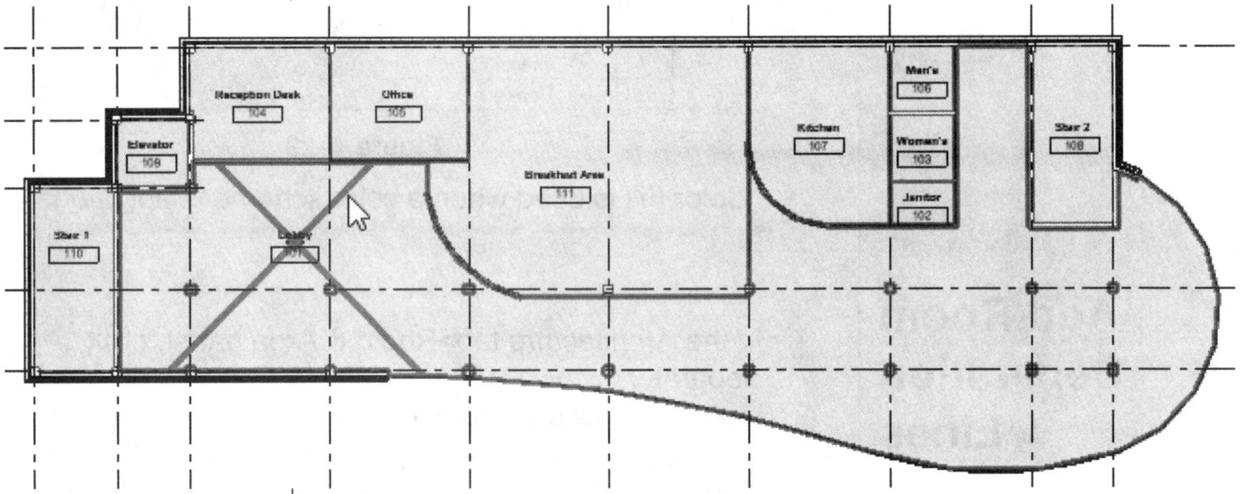

Figure 4–31

Task 1 - Add rooms and room tags.

1. Open the project **Modern-Hotel-Rooms.rvt**.
2. Open the **Floor Plans: Floor 1 - Rooms** view. The room elements have been turned on in this view so you can see them as you create them.
3. In the *Architecture* tab>Room & Area panel, click (Room).
4. In the *Modify* | *Place Room* tab>Tag panel, verify that (Tag on Placement) is selected.
5. Place a room element inside the lobby area.
6. Zoom in on the room tag.

Changing this first room number ensures that the rest of the numbers increment correctly.

7. Click **Modify**. Click on the tag and change the room name to **Lobby** and number to **101**, as shown in Figure 4–32. Click in empty space to finish the command.

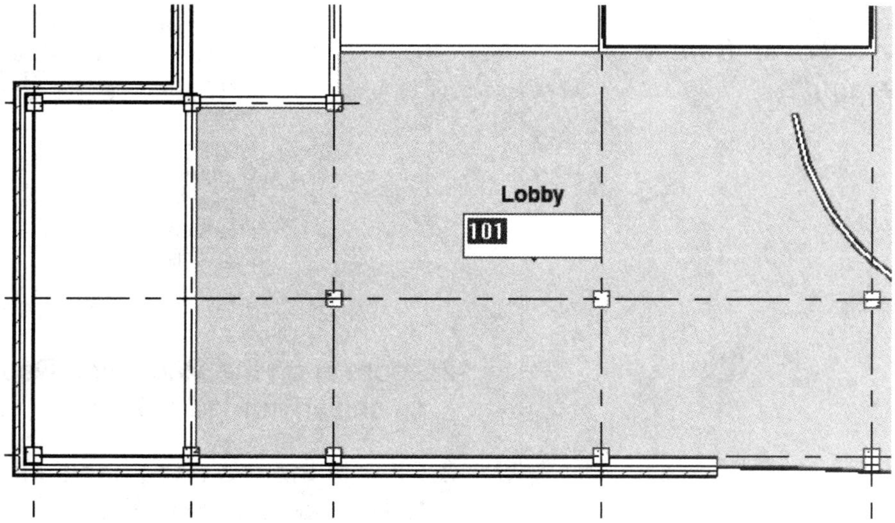

Figure 4–32

8. Zoom out and start the **Room** command again

9. In the *Modify* | *Place Room* tab>Room panel, click (Place Rooms Automatically). The rest of the rooms are added to the model, as shown in Figure 4–33. Click **Close** in the dialog box.

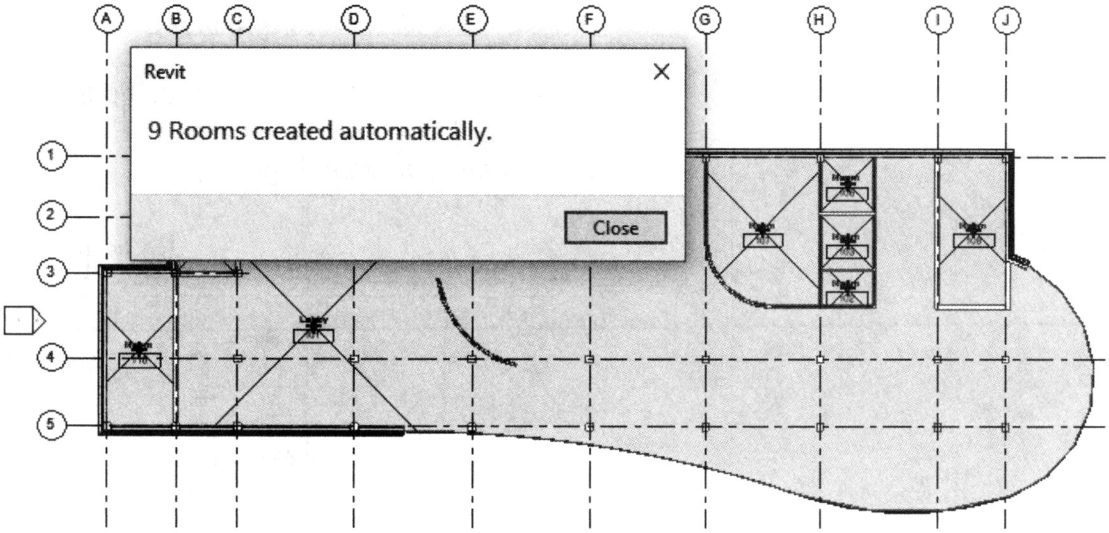

Figure 4–33

10. Select the room (not the tag) directly behind the hotel entrance.

11. In Properties, in the *Identity Data* area, note that the *Number* is automatically incremented. Set the *Name* to **Reception Desk** (as shown in Figure 4–34) and click **Apply**.

Your room number might differ from this example.

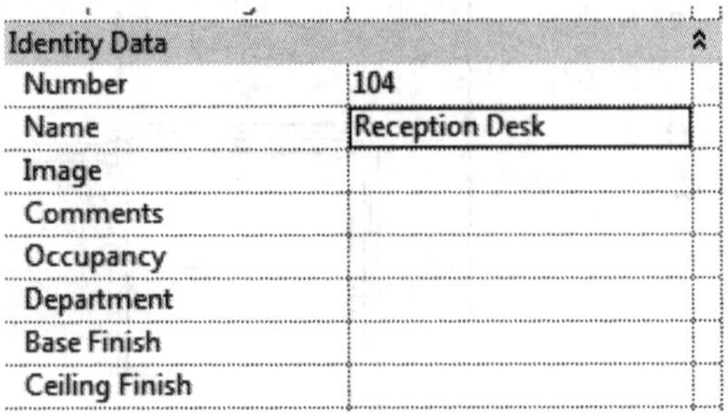

Figure 4–34

12. Zoom in on the Reception Desk area to see the updated tag, as shown in Figure 4–35.

13. Click in the room tag beside it and change the name to **Office**, as shown in Figure 4–35.

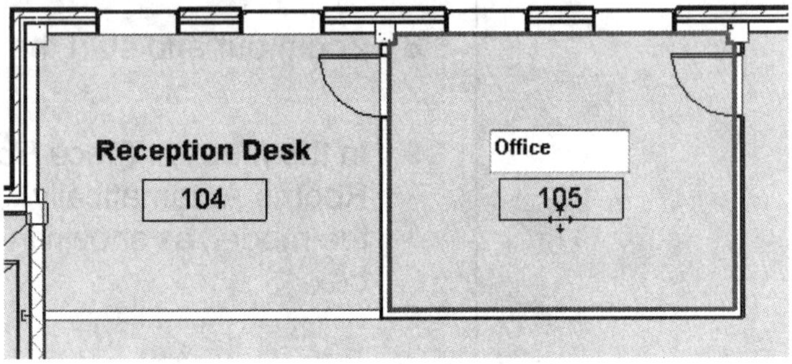

Figure 4–35

14. Rename the rest of the rooms by using the tag or by selecting the room and changing the name in Properties. Several examples are shown in Figure 4–36.

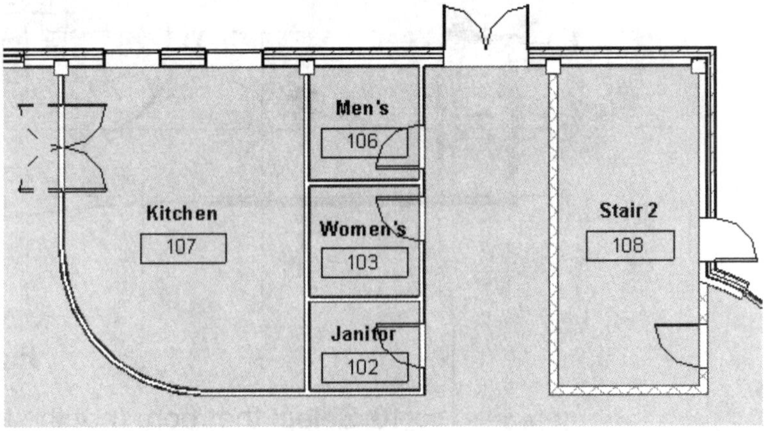

Figure 4–36

15. Save the project.

Task 2 - Add Room Separation Lines and additional rooms.

1. In the *Architecture* tab>Room & Area panel, click (Room Separator).
2. Draw room separation lines to separate the breakfast area from the main lobby, as shown in Figure 4–37.

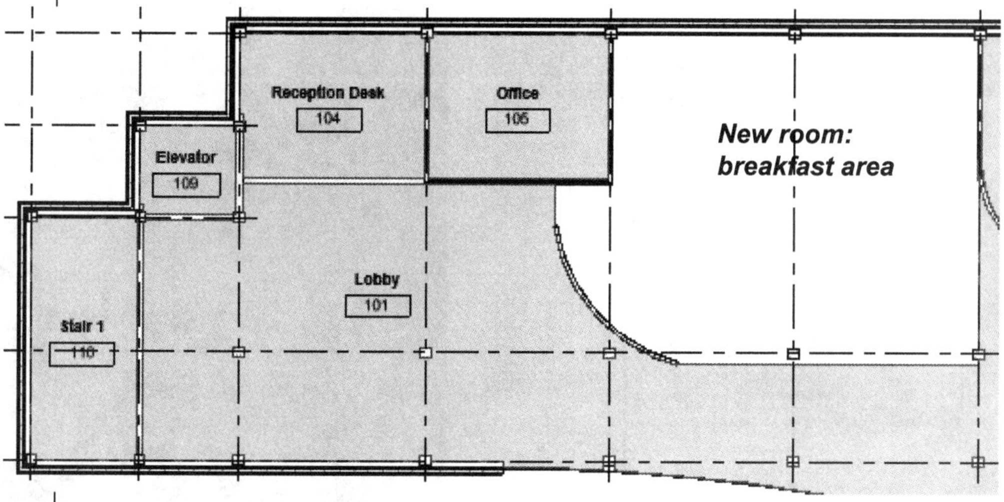

Figure 4–37

3. Start the **Room** command and verify that **Tag on Placement** is toggled on. In Properties, in the *Name* field, type **Breakfast Area**, and then place the room in the location shown in Figure 4–37.
4. Move tags around, if required.
   - Toggle on **Leader** if you want to move a tag outside of its room, otherwise the tag is orphaned from the room.
5. Save the project.

Practice 4d

(Optional) Model Additional Walls

If time permits, you can add a parapet above the curtain walls (as shown in Figure 4–38), as well as walls to the second floor, basement, and footings.

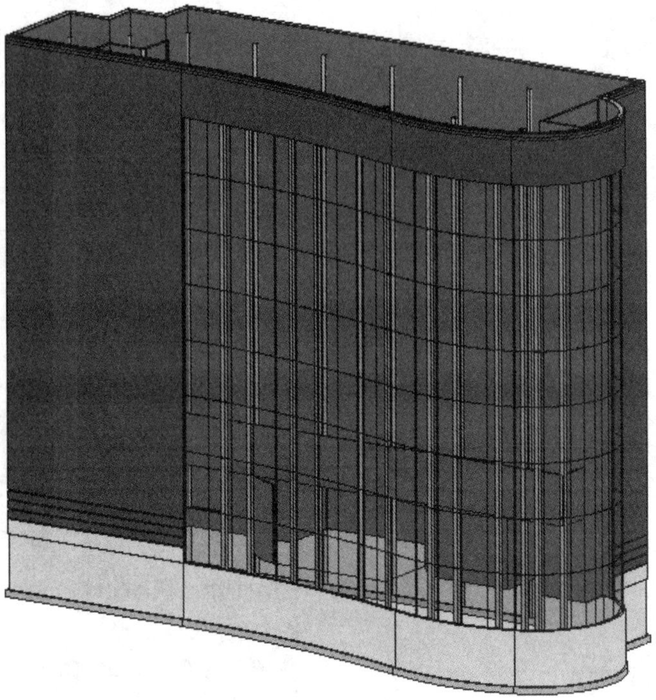

Figure 4–38

Task 1 - Add a parapet.

1. Open **Modern-Hotel-Additional-Walls.rvt**
2. Open the **Floor Plans: Roof** view.
3. Select the three curtain walls.
4. In Properties, set the *Top Constraint* to **Up to Level: Roof** and the *Top Offset* to (negative) **-6'-0"**.
5. In the View Control Bar, set the *Detail Level* to (Medium) to display the layers of the walls.

6. Select the small curved piece of wall at the northeast corner of the building on Column Line J. Right-click on the right end point grip and select **Disallow Join,** as shown in Figure 4–39.

Some walls, when they try to automatically clean up, cause problems. Disallowing a join can resolve the issue.

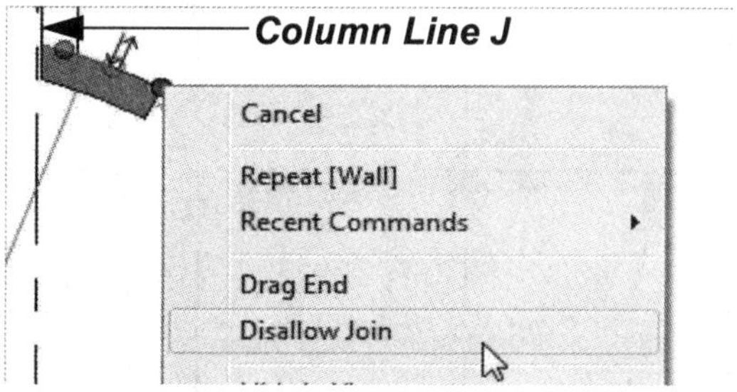

Figure 4–39

7. Repeat the process again on the other wall that connects to the curtain wall near the intersection of Grid D5.

8. Start the **Wall** command.

9. In the Type Selector, select **Basic Wall: Exterior - Brick on MTL. Stud - parapet**.and set the following properties:
   - *Base Constraint:* **Roof**
   - *Base Offset:* (negative) **-6' 0"**
   - *Top Constraint:* **Up to level: Parapet**
   - *Top Offset:* **0' 0"**

10. In the Draw panel, click (Pick Lines). Move the cursor over the middle curved curtain wall and press <Tab> until the curtain wall reference displays as shown in Figure 4–40 and then click to place the wall.

Ensure that you are selecting the main line of the curtain wall or a grid line and not one of the curtain wall panels.

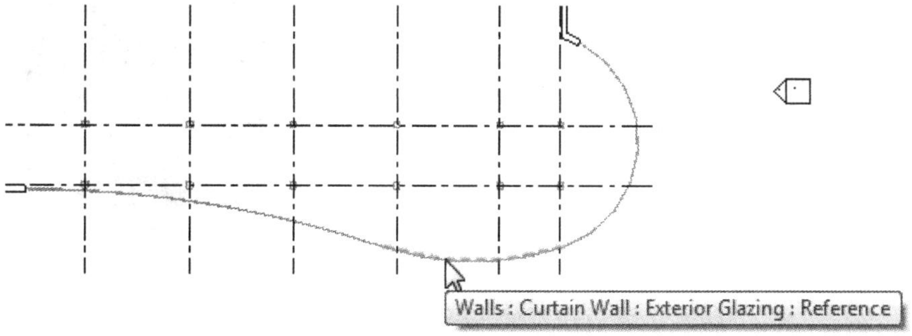

Figure 4–40

11. In the *Modify | Place Wall* tab>Draw panel, click (Start-End-Radius Arc).

12. Select the points in the order shown in Figure 4–41. Ensure that you select the endpoints before selecting the tangent point on the arc.

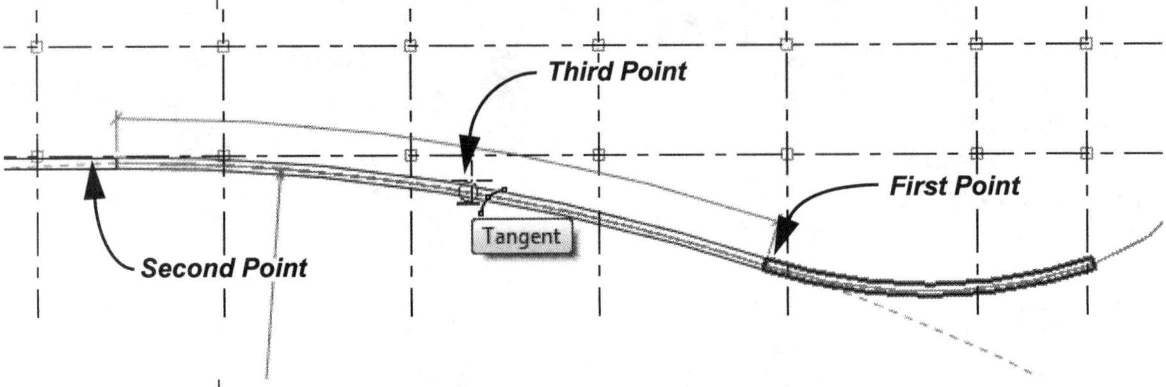

Figure 4–41

- Creating the wall this way solves some issues because the center line of the curtain wall is at a slight offset from the main wall.
- If a warning displays about a wall sweep you can ignore it.

13. Repeat the process in a similar manner for the other part of the arc, starting with the endpoint of the small wall, and then the endpoint of the curved wall, and finally the tangent point.

14. Click (Modify).

15. Type **ZA** to display the full floor plan.

16. Return to the 3D view. The new parapet wall over the curtain wall displays, as shown in Figure 4–42.

The columns are hidden to clarify the image.

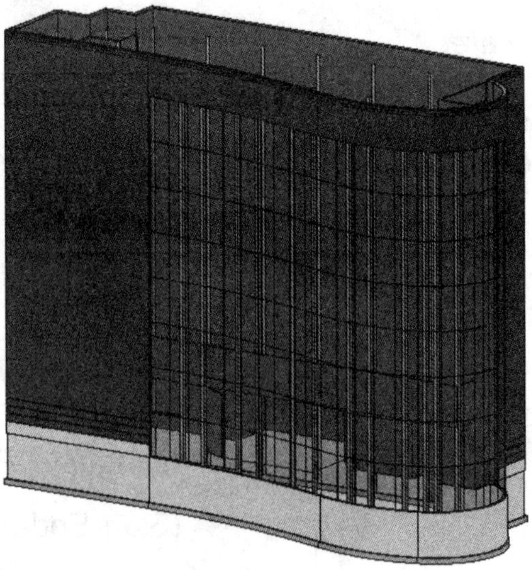

Figure 4–42

commercial doors use 36"

17. Save the project.

Revitcity.com

Task 2 - Add typical guest floor walls.

1. Open the **Floor Plans: Floor 2** view. The view displays the walls created in the project and the linked drawing of the second floor.

2. Add walls for the guest rooms, as shown in Figure 4–43, using the following options:
   - *Wall type:* **Interior - 4 7/8" Partition (1-hr)**
   - *Height:* **Floor 3**
   - *Top Offset:* (negative) **-1' 0"**.
   - Align the center of the vertical walls to the grids.
   - Ignore all of the door openings.
   - You can use  (Copy) and  (Mirror) to duplicate the walls once you have modeled one guest room layout.

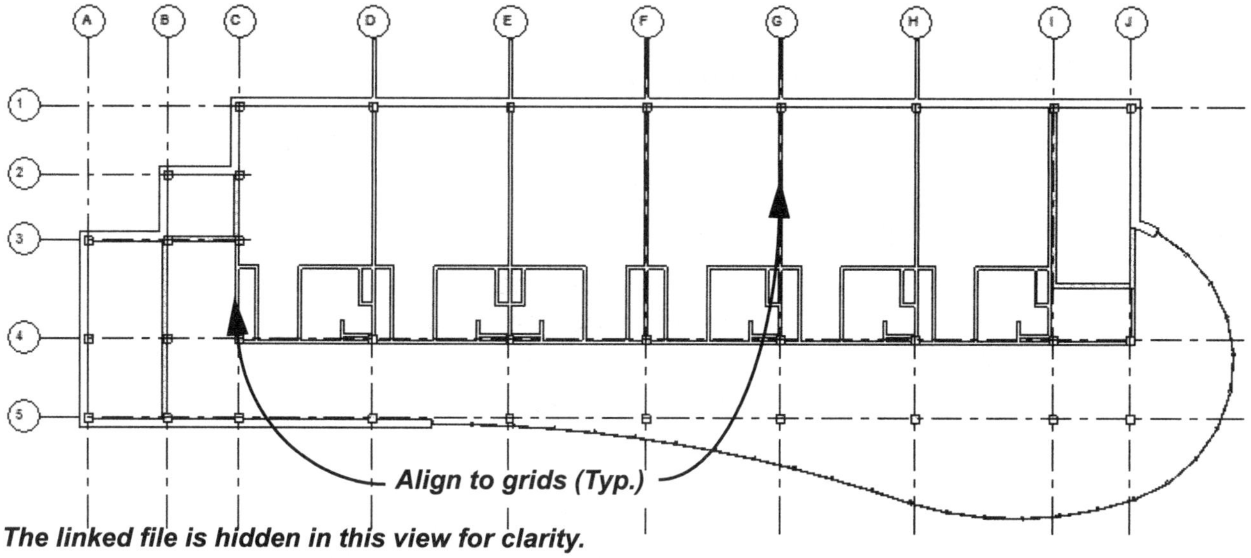

Figure 4–43

3. Return to **Floor Plans: Floor 1** view.

Task 3 - Add basement walls.

1. Open the **Floor Plans: T.O. Footing** view. In this view, the column grids have been toggled off and an underlay of Floor 1 displays so you can see where the walls must be placed.

2. In the *Architecture* tab>Build panel, click  (Wall).

3. In Properties, set the following options: (Reset the constraints if required.)
   - *Wall type:* **Basic Wall: Generic - 12" Masonry**
   - *Location Line:* **Core Centerline**
   - *Base Constraint:* **T.O. Footing**
   - *Base Offset:* **0' 0"**
   - *Top Constraint:* **Up to Level: Floor 1**
   - *Top Offset:* **0' 0"**
4. Create the walls as shown in Figure 4–44.

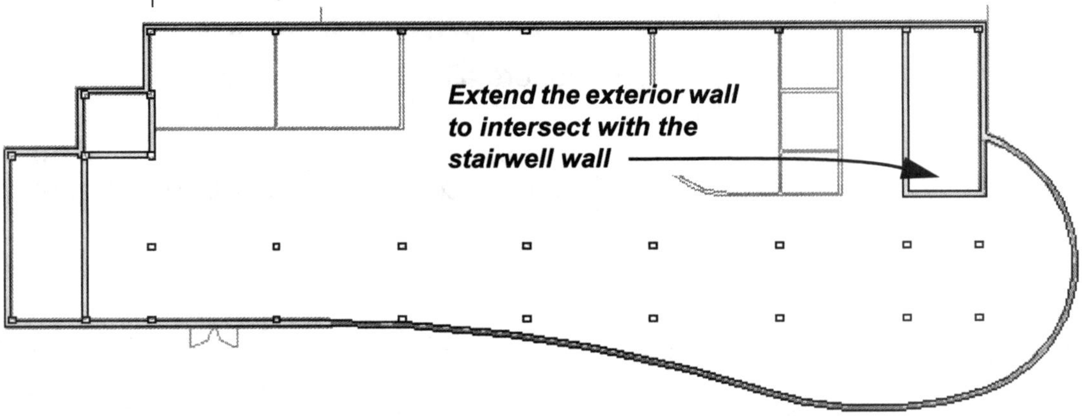

Figure 4–44

Hover the cursor over a wall and then press <Tab> until the center line displays.

   - Use (Pick Lines) and select the core center line of the exterior walls and curtain walls.
   - Zoom into the stairwells to add the interior walls, using **Align** and other modify tools to get them in place.
5. Click (Modify).
6. Save the project.

Task 4 - Add footings to the walls.

1. Click (Wall).
2. In Properties or the Options Bar, set the following options:
   - *Wall type:* **Basic Wall: Generic - 24" Concrete**
   - *Location Line:* **Core Centerline**
   - *Base Constraint:* **T.O. Footing**
   - *Base Offset:* (negative) **-1' 6"**
   - *Top Constraint:* **Up to Level:T.O.Footing**
   - *Top Offset:* **0' 0"**

You might need to zoom in to highlight the core center line.

3. Click (Pick Line) and select the core center line of all the foundation walls. The wall footings display, as shown in Figure 4–45. You add column footings later.

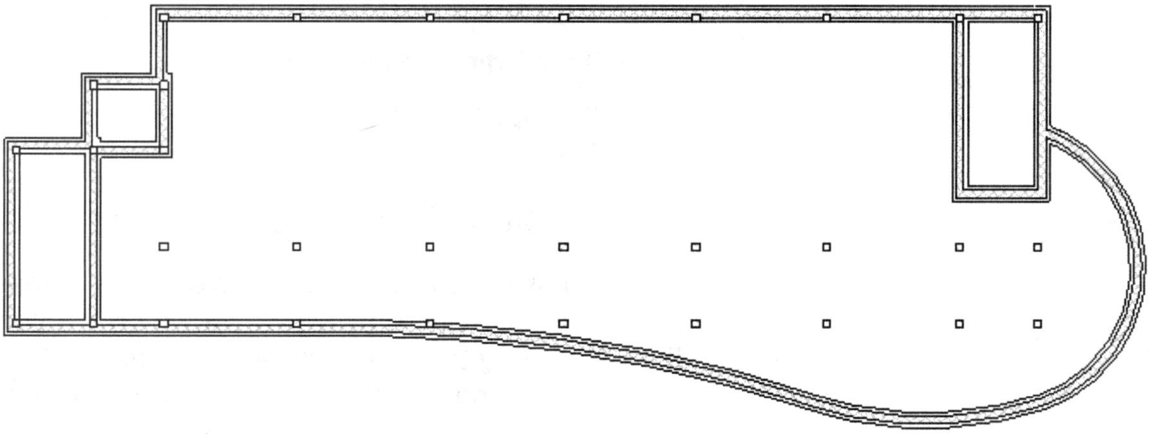

Figure 4–45

4. Save the project.

Chapter Review Questions

1. Where do you specify the height of a wall before you start modeling it?
   a. In the *Modify | Place Wall* tab.
   b. In the Options Bar.
   c. In the Status Bar.
   d. In the Quick Access Toolbar.

2. Some walls are made from multiple layers of materials, such as brick, block, and drywall, as shown on the bottom in Figure 4–46. If the hatching for these materials is not displayed (as shown at the top in Figure 4–46), how do you change this?

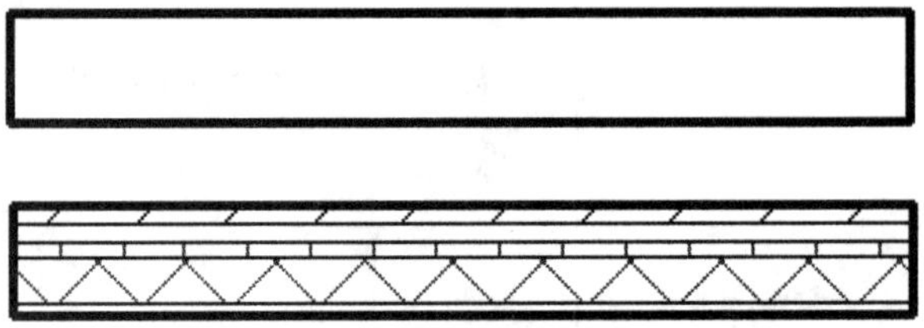

Figure 4–46

   a. Set the *Visual Style* to **Realistic**.
   b. Set the *Detail Level* to **Medium**.
   c. Set the *View Scale* to be higher.
   d. Set the *Phase* to **New**.

3. Which of the following tools enables you to change a wall from one made out of studs and brick, to one made out of concrete?
   a. Properties
   b. Change Wall
   c. Type Selector
   d. Edit Wall

4. Match the names for the following controls with the numbers shown in Figure 4–47.

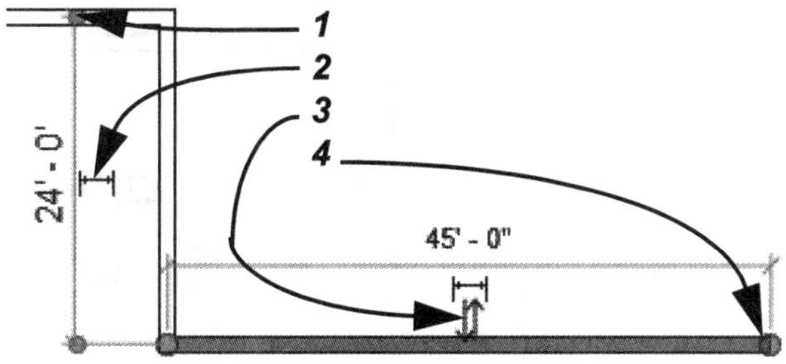

Figure 4–47

Control	Number
Drag wall end	
Flip	
Move witness line	
Make this temporary dimension permanent	

5. Which of the following are potential differences between the column surround wall and the associated walls, as shown in Figure 4–48? (Select all that apply.)

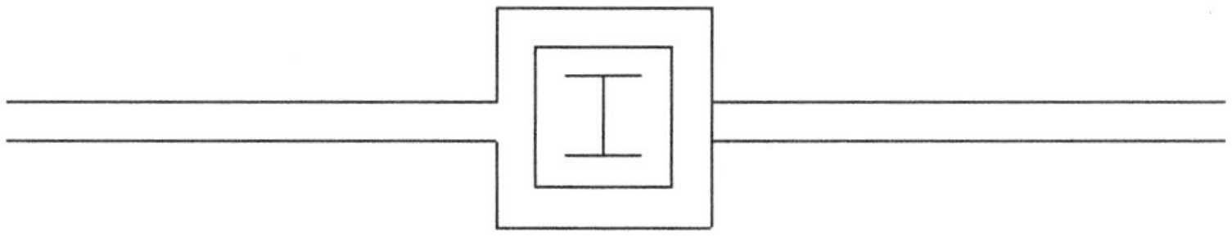

Figure 4–48

   a. The column surround and wall on the left are made with the same wall type, while the wall type on the right is different.
   b. The wall on the left has been joined together with the column surround, while the wall on the right was set to **Disallow Join**.
   c. The wall on the left was trimmed against the column surround.
   d. The wall on the right was extended to the column surround.

6. Which of the following would be true if you changed the top constraint of a wall from an unconnected height to a level?
   a. All walls of that type would also change height.
   b. Only that wall would change height.

7. When you want to add rooms with the same name (as shown in Figure 4–49), you need to modify each one separately.

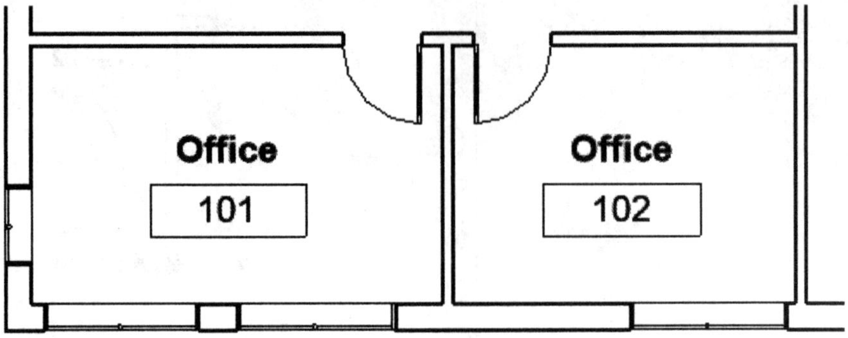

Figure 4–49

a. True

b. False

Command Summary

Button	Command	Location
	**Detail Level: Coarse**	• **View Control Bar**
	**Detail Level: Fine**	• **View Control Bar**
	**Detail Level: Medium**	• **View Control Bar**
	**Edit Profile**	• **Ribbon:** (when a wall is selected) *Modify* | *Walls* tab>Mode panel
	**Match Type**	• **Ribbon:** *Modify* tab>Clipboard panel • **Shortcut:** MA
	**Properties**	• **Ribbon:** *Modify* tab>Properties panel • **Shortcut:** PP
N/A	**Type Selector**	• **Properties palette** • **Ribbon:** *Modify* tab (*Optional*) • **Quick Access Toolbar** (*Optional*)
	**Wall**	• **Ribbon:** *Architecture* tab>Build panel
	**Wall Opening**	• **Ribbon:** *Architecture* tab>Opening panel
	**Room**	• **Ribbon:** *Architecture* tab>Room & Area panel • **Shortcut:** RM
	**Room Separator**	• **Ribbon:** *Architecture* tab>Room & Area panel

Working with Doors and Windows

Doors and windows are host elements that are placed in walls. There are many different types of doors and windows available in the Autodesk® Revit® libraries, and you can easily create additional sizes of the types that come with the software to meet your design requirements.

Learning Objectives in this Chapter

- Insert doors and windows in walls.
- Modify door and window locations and properties that can be referenced in schedules.
- Load additional door and window types from the library.
- Create additional door and window sizes of a selected type.

5.1 Inserting Doors and Windows

Doors and windows in the Autodesk Revit software are designed to be hosted by walls. You can use temporary dimensions (as shown in Figure 5–1) as well as alignment lines and snaps to help place the openings exactly where you need them in the walls.

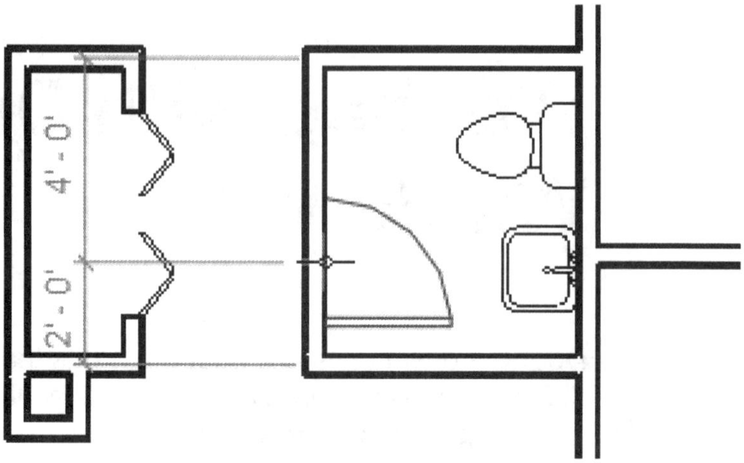

Figure 5–1

How To: Add a Door or Window

1. In the *Architecture* tab>Build panel, click (Door) or (Window). The keyboard shortcuts are **DR** for doors and **WN** for windows.
2. To insert a tag with each door or window, verify that (Tag on Placement) is toggled on. You can specify the tag options using the Options Bar, as shown in Figure 5–2.

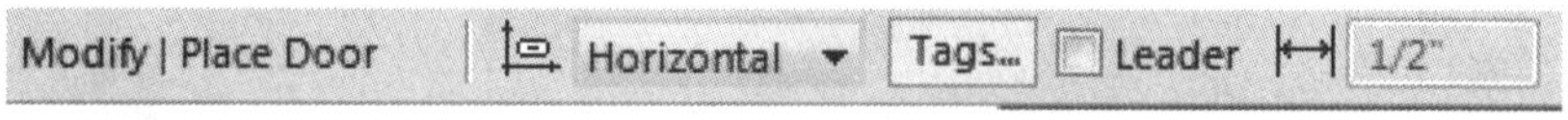

Figure 5–2

3. In the Type Selector, select the type of door or window required.
4. Select the wall to place the door or window.
   - Press <Spacebar> to change the swing of the door before placing it.
5. Continue adding other doors or windows as required.

- While placing or modifying doors or windows, you can adjust the element using temporary dimensions and the **Flip the instance facing** and **Flip the instance hand** controls to change the swing and hinge locations, as shown in Figure 5–3. With windows, you can flip the interior and exterior using the same technique.

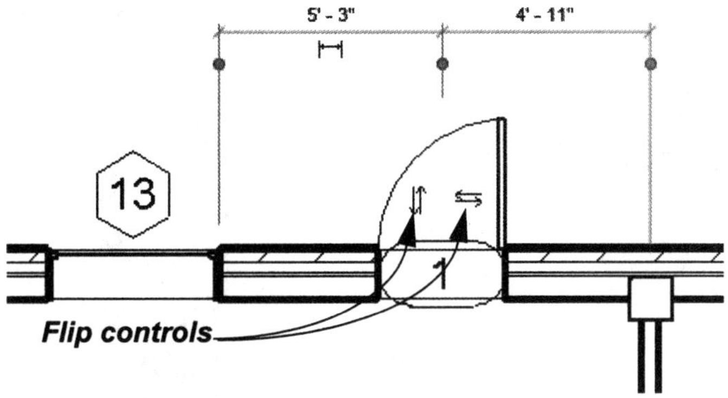

Figure 5–3

- If you are including window tags, select a point close to the outside of the wall when inserting the window so that the tag is placed on the outside.

- To move a door or window tag, select the tag. A control displays, as shown in Figure 5–4, which enables you to drag the tag to a new location.

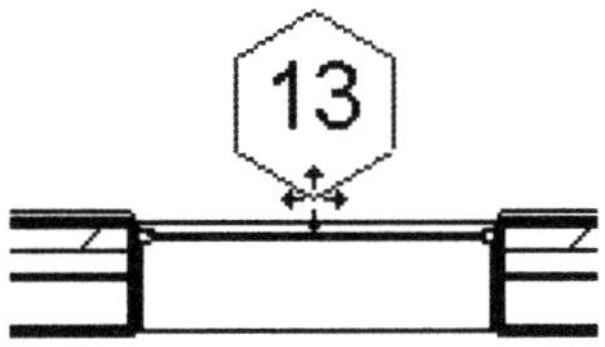

Figure 5–4

Modifying Door and Window Properties

The door or window types control most of their properties. To change the property information, you change the type in the Type Selector. You can also change Instance Parameters (as shown in Figure 5–5) that impact the specific door or window in the associated schedule. Instance Parameters include things such as the *Swing Angle, Masonry* or *Drywall Frame*, etc.

The exact properties vary according to the door or window selected.

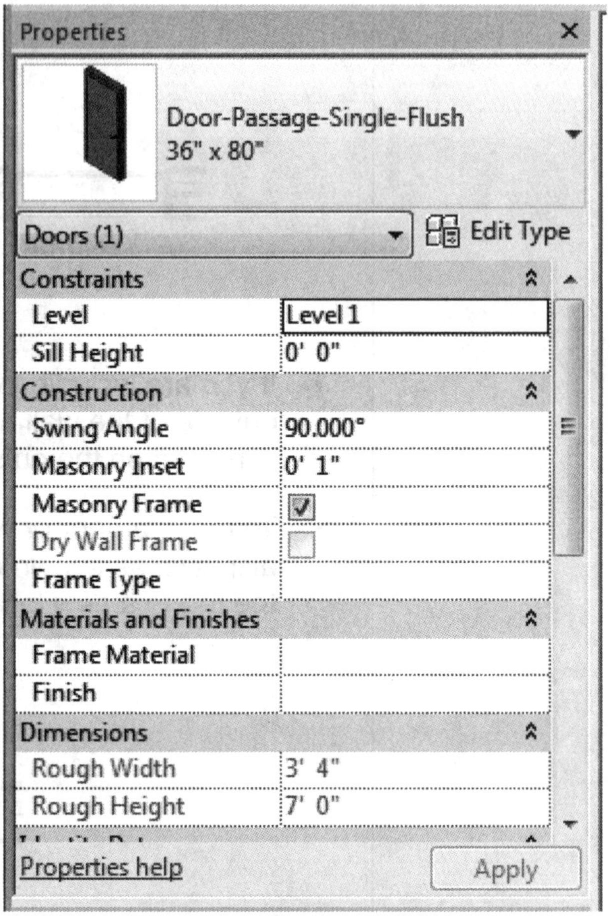

Figure 5–5

Hint: Copying Elements to Levels

The standard Windows commands (Cut or <Ctrl>+<X>), (Copy To Clipboard or <Ctrl>+<C>), and (Paste From Clipboard or <Ctrl>+<V>) work in the Autodesk Revit software just as they do in other Windows-compatible software. They are available in the *Modify* tab>Clipboard panel, but not in the shortcut menu.

In the software, you can also paste elements aligned to various views or levels, as shown in Figure 5–6.

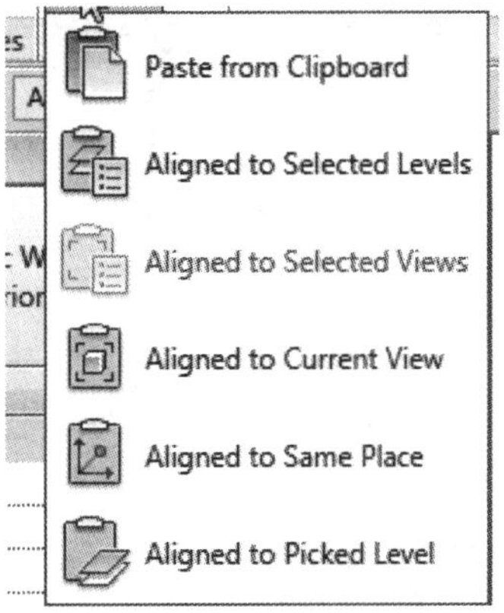

Figure 5–6

- **Aligned to Selected Levels:** Opens a dialog box where you can select the level to which you want to copy. This enables you to copy items on one level and paste them to the same location on another level (e.g., windows in a high-rise building).
- **Aligned to Selected Views:** Copies view-specific elements (such as text or dimensions) into a view that you select in a dialog box. Only the Floor Plan or Reflected Ceiling Plan views are available.
- **Aligned to Current View:** Pastes elements copied in one view to the same location in another view.
- **Aligned to Same Place:** Pastes elements to the same location in the same view.
- **Aligned to Picked Level:** Pastes elements to the level you select in an elevation or section view.

Practice 5a Insert Doors and Windows

Practice Objectives

- Add doors and windows.
- Copy elements to multiple levels.

In this practice, you will add doors and windows to a model, as shown for Floor 1 in Figure 5–7. You will use controls and temporary dimensions to help you place the doors and windows. You will also copy windows to multiple levels.

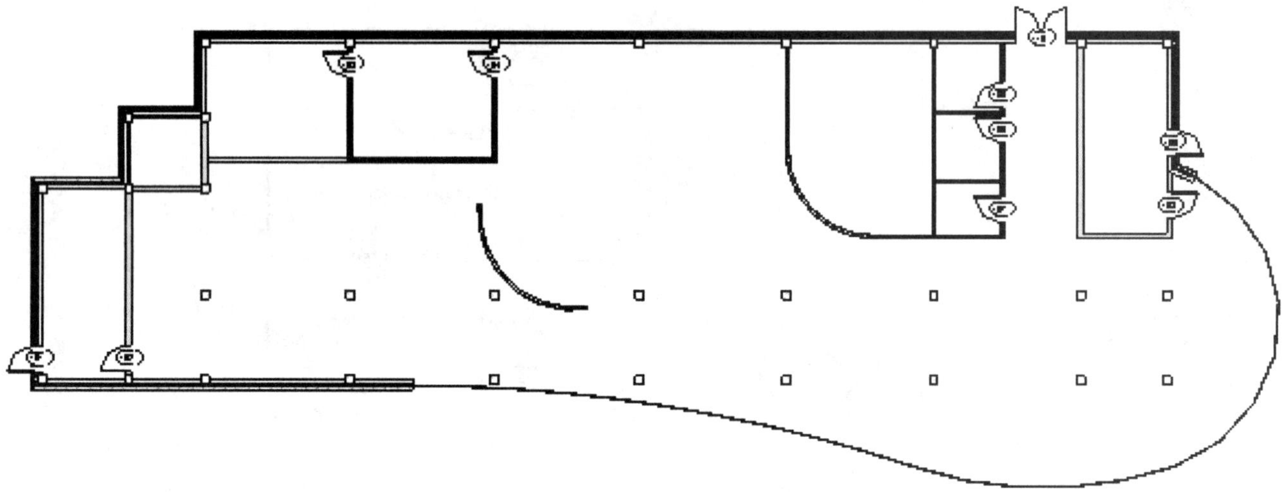

Figure 5–7

Task 1 - Add doors.

1. Open the project **Modern-Hotel-Doors.rvt** from your practice files folder.
2. Open the **Floor Plans: Floor 1** view.
3. In the *Architecture* tab>Build panel, click (Door).
4. In the Type Selector, select **Single-Flush: 36" x 80"**.
5. In the *Modify* | *Place Door* tab>Tag panel, verify that (Tag on Placement) is on.

6. Place the door near the lower left corner of the building, as shown in Figure 5–8. Use the flip arrows to make it swing in the right direction and use temporary dimensions to place it to the correct location on the wall. Click on the tag and change the number to **101**.

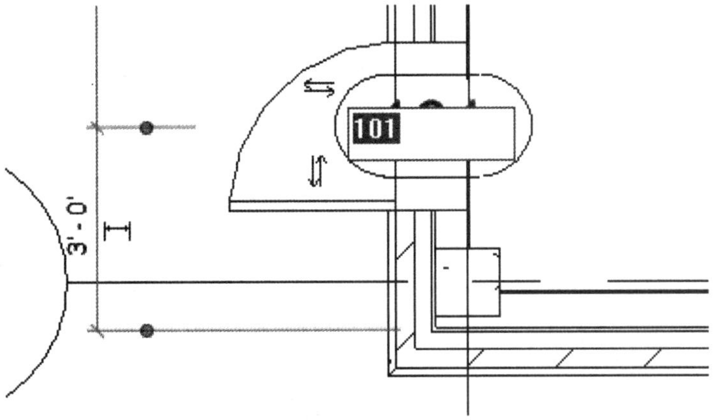

Figure 5–8

7. Continue adding single flush doors in the project, similar to the locations shown in Figure 5–9. Use the same door type. The tag number automatically increments.

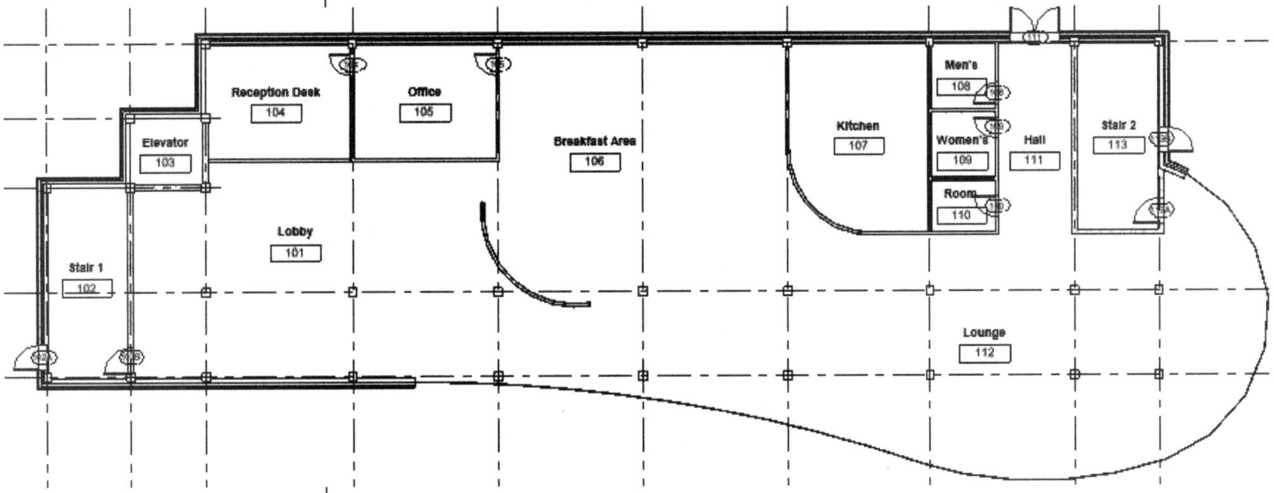

Figure 5–9

8. Click (Modify) and select the two sets of stairwell doors (two doors on the left side and two doors on the right side of the building).

   - If you select multiple categories, use (Filter) to help select only the doors.

9. In the Type Selector, select **Single-Flush Vision: 36" x 84"**.

10. Zoom in on the upper right corner of the building, in the area of the Stair 2 and Hall.

11. Click (Door) and in the Type Selector, select **Double-Glass 1: 72" x 84"**.

12. Place the door at the end of the hall, pointing to the exterior, as shown in Figure 5–10.

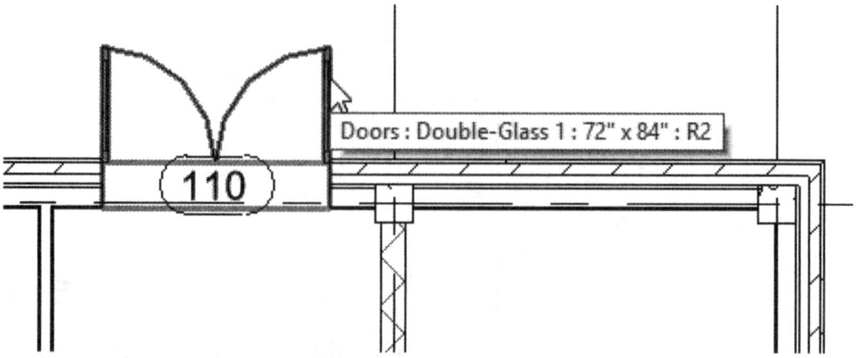

Figure 5–10

13. Zoom out to see the full floor plan.

14. Optionally, you can modify the door numbers to match the room numbers similar to the pattern shown in Figure 5–11, or using your office standard if you have one.

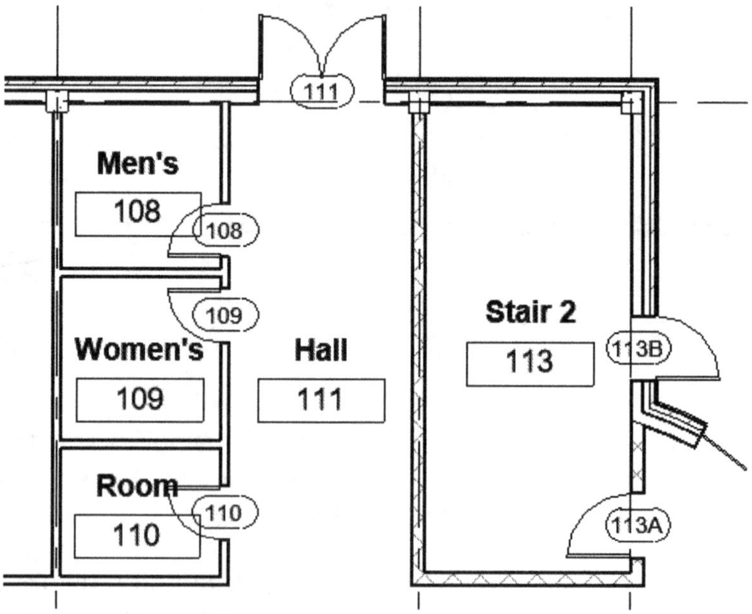

Figure 5–11

15. Save the project.

Task 2 - Add windows and space them equally apart.

1. Open the **Floor Plans: Floor 2** view.
2. The linked CAD file is still displayed in this view. Select it and in the Status Bar, click (Temporary Hide/Isolate)>**Hide Elements**.
3. In the *Architecture* tab>Build panel, click (Window).
4. In the *Modify* | *Place Window* tab>Tag panel, verify that (Tag on Placement) is toggled on.
5. In the Type Selector, select **Casement 3x3 with Trim: 48" x 48"**.
6. Add the window close to Stair 1, as shown in Figure 5–12. Use temporary dimensions to move it so it is 5'-0" from the grid line, as shown in Figure 5–12. You might need to move the witness line so that it references the grid, rather than a wall.

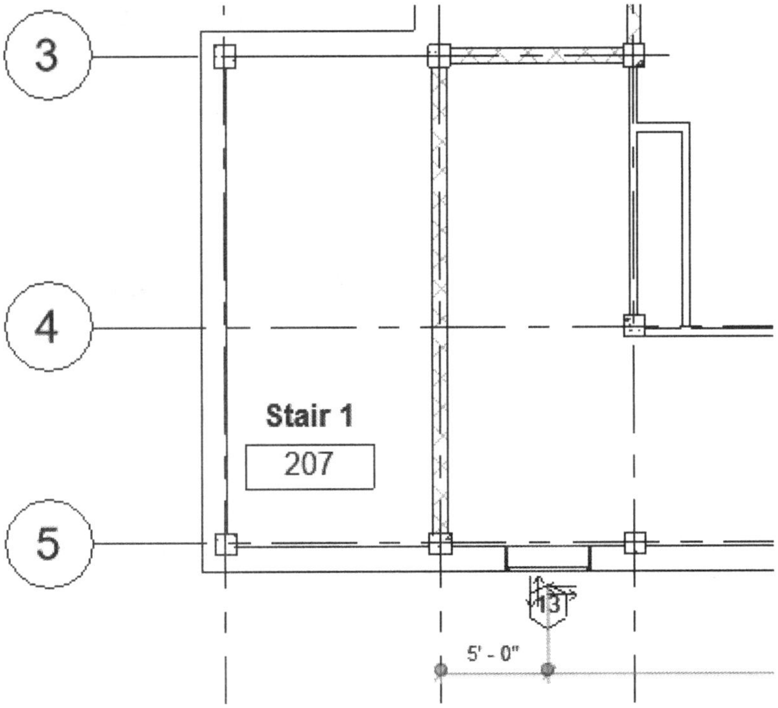

Figure 5–12

7. Click **Modify** and select the window and the window tag.

8. In the *Modify | Windows* tab>Modify panel, click (Copy).

9. In the Options Bar, select **Multiple**.

10. Select a point on the window as the move start point.

Autodesk Revit interprets 8 as 8'-0".

11. Move the cursor to the right and type **8** for the distance. Move the cursor over past the new window and type **8** again. Move the cursor over one last time and type **8**, as shown in Figure 5–13. Four evenly spaced windows are created.

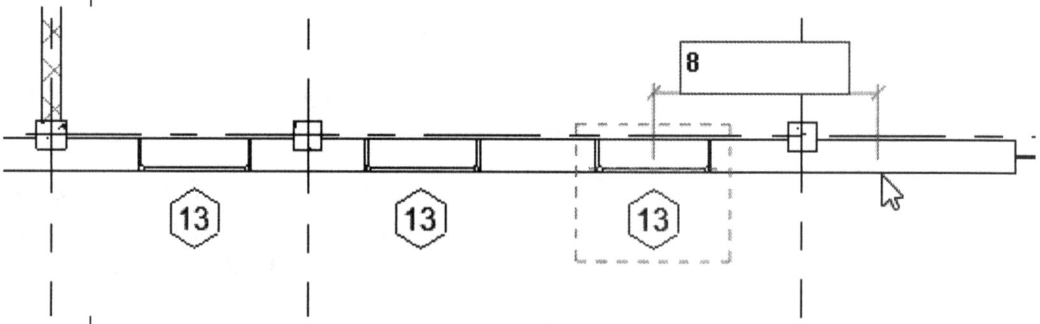

Figure 5–13

12. Save the project.

Task 3 - Copy windows to multiple levels.

1. Open the 3D view and verify that the front of the building where the windows are located is displayed.

2. Select all four windows by holding <Ctrl> and selecting each one.

3. In the *Modify | Windows* tab>Clipboard panel, click (Copy to Clipboard).

4. In the Clipboard panel, expand (Paste) and click (Aligned to Selected Levels).

5. In the Select Levels dialog box, select the floors between and including **Floor 3** and **Floor 8**, as shown in Figure 5–14.

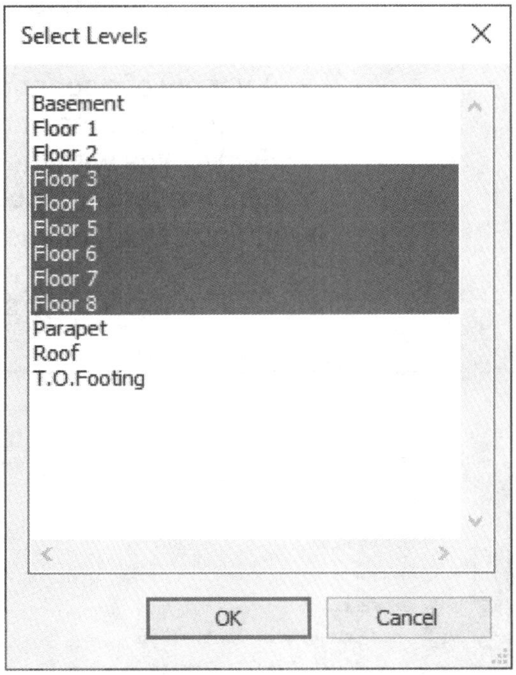

Figure 5–14

6. Click **OK**. The windows are copied up the side of the building, as shown in Figure 5–15.

Additional doors and windows will be placed using storefront curtain walls.

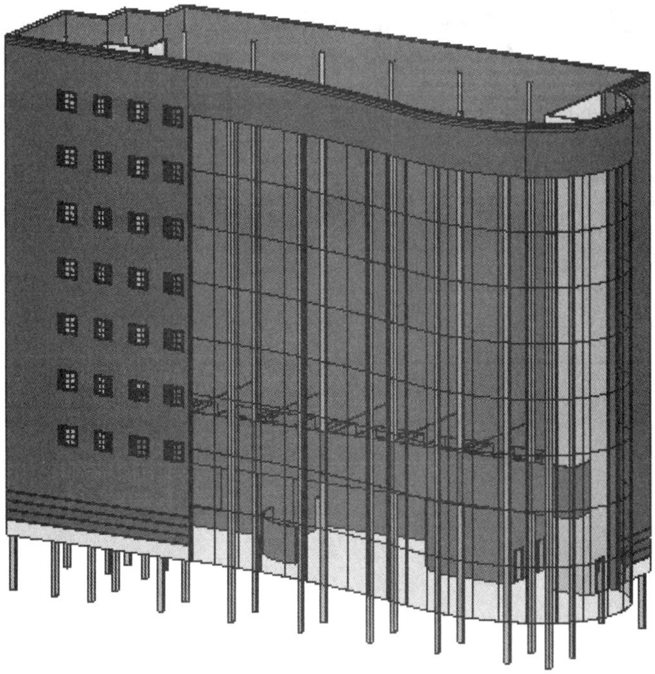

Figure 5–15

7. Save the project.

5.2 Loading Door and Window Types from the Library

A variety of door and window styles are available in the Autodesk Revit Library, as shown in Figure 5–16. They are grouped in *Family* files with the extension .RFA. For example, when you load the family **Door-Double-Glass.rfa** you can then select various sizes of this door you want to use in the project.

- The process is similar for loading all types of families.

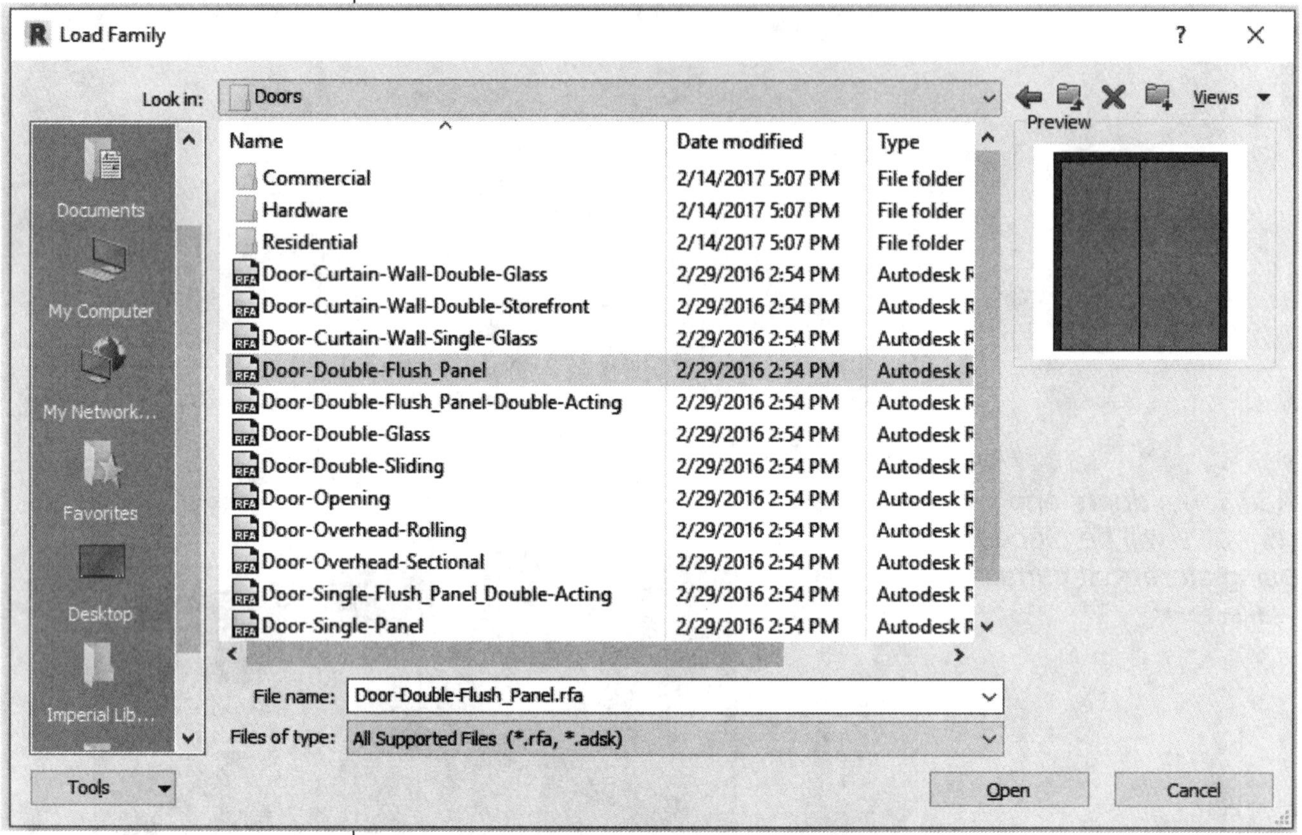

Figure 5–16

How To: Load a Family

1. In the *Insert* tab>Load from Library panel, click (Load Family). Alternatively, start a family-based command such as **Door** or **Window** and in the *Modify | contextual* tab>Mode panel, click (Load Family).
2. In the Load Family dialog box, navigate to the folder that contains the family you want to load and select the family.
3. Click **Open**.
4. For some families the Specify Types dialog box displays, as shown for a door in Figure 5–17. Select the types you want to include in your project and click **OK**.

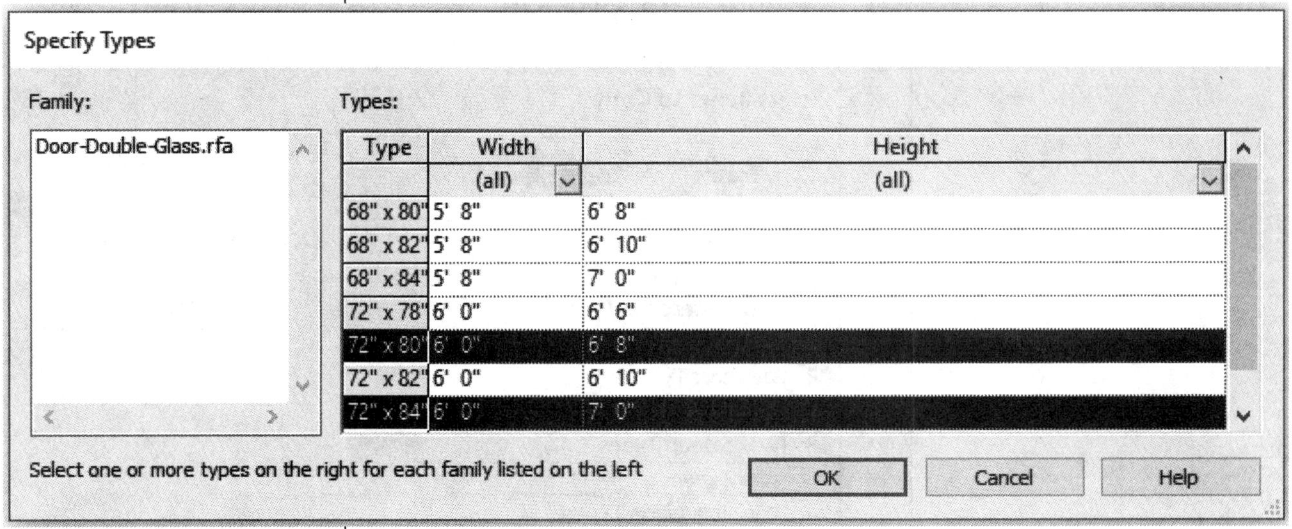

Figure 5–17

- To select more than one type, hold <Ctrl> as you select.
- You can use the drop-down lists under the columns to filter the sizes.

5. Once the family is loaded, in the Type Selector, select the type you want to use.

- When you are working with a command such as **Door** or **Window**, you can only load families that are from that category of elements. For example, you cannot load window families while working in the **Door** command.

- There are several families used for openings. In the *Doors* folder: **Door-Opening.rfa** and in the *Windows* folder: **Window-Round Opening.rfa** and **Window-Square Opening.rfa**.

Hint: Transferring Project Standards

Some elements (such as wall types) are not accessible from a specific library. However, you can copy them from other projects.

1. Open the project from which you want to copy information.
2. Open the project to which you want to copy the information.
3. In the *Manage* tab>Settings panel, click (Transfer Project Standards).
4. In the Select Items To Copy dialog box, select an option in the Copy from drop-down list and then select the settings you want to copy into the current file, as shown in Figure 5–18. Click **OK**.

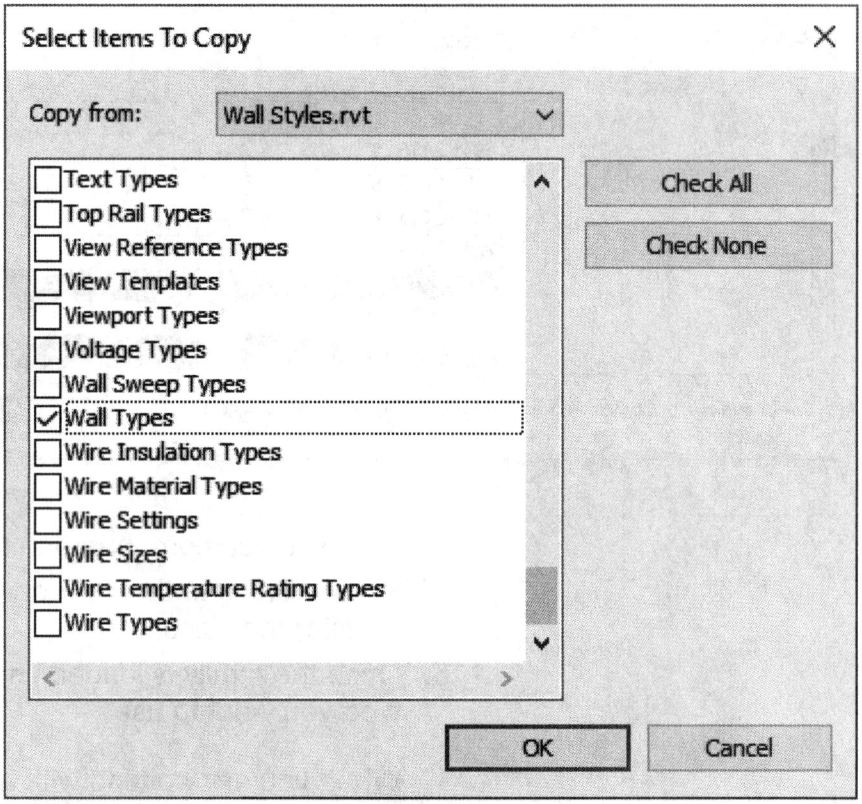

Figure 5–18

5. In the Duplicate Types dialog box, click either **Overwrite** or **New Only** to apply the settings to the current project.

5.3 Creating Additional Door and Window Sizes

You can specify materials for door and window sub-elements in the Type Properties.

The parameters might be different depending on the door or window you selected.

You can easily add additional sizes to existing families of doors or windows that have been loaded into a project. To do this, you create a new type of the required size based on an existing type, as shown in Figure 5–19.

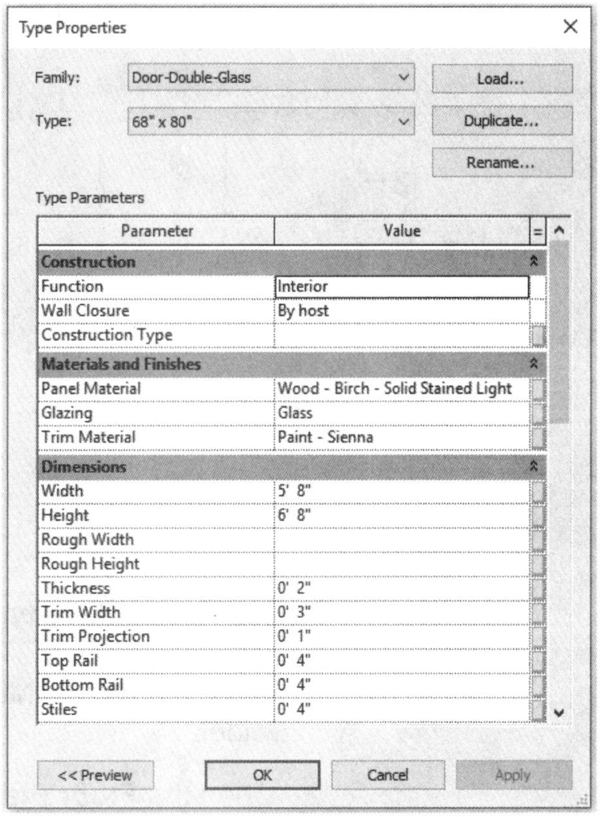

Figure 5–19

How To: Create Additional Door and Window Sizes

1. Start the **Door** or **Window** command.
2. In the Type Selector, select the type you want to modify. In Properties, click (Edit Type) or in the *Modify* tab> Properties panel, click (Type Properties).
3. In the Type Properties dialog box, click **Duplicate**.
4. Type a new name for the element and click **OK**.
5. In the Type Properties dialog box, change the *Height* and *Width* parameters to match the size.
6. Click **OK** to close the dialog box. The new window or door type is now available for use.

Practice 5b Load and Create Door Types

Practice Objectives

- Load door types.
- Duplicate and modify a door type.

In this practice, you will load specialty door types used in the guest rooms, create a new door size, and add doors to the second floor, as shown in Figure 5–20.

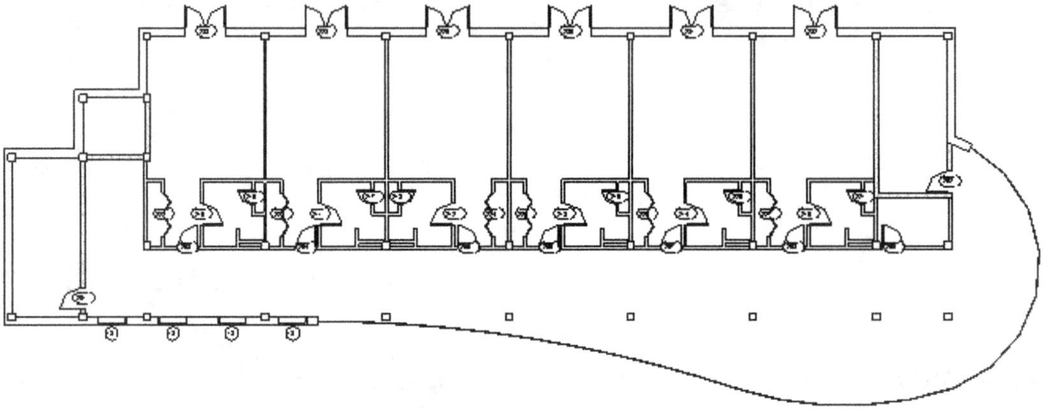

Figure 5–20

Task 1 - Load door types.

1. Open the project **Modern-Hotel-Load.rvt** from the class folder.
2. Open the **Floor Plans: Floor 1** view and zoom in on the kitchen area.
3. In the *Architecture* tab>Build panel, click  (Door).
4. In the *Modify | Place Door* tab>Mode panel, click  (Load Family).
5. In the Load Family dialog box, navigate to the *Doors* folder and select **Door-Double-Flush_Panel-Double-Acting.rfa**. Click **Open.**

6. In the Specify Types dialog box, select the *Type* **72"x 80"**, as shown in Figure 5–21 and click **OK**.

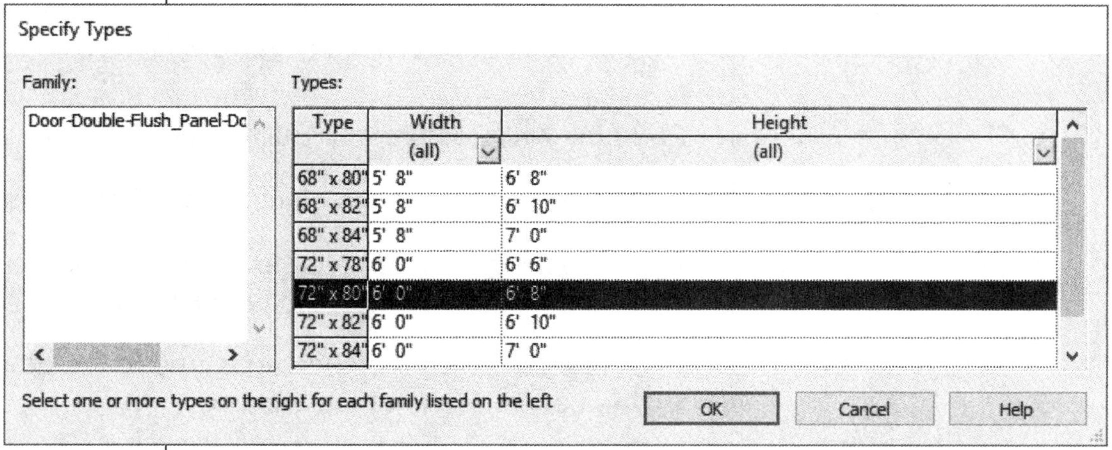

Figure 5–21

7. Start the Load Family command again. (Hint: Press <Enter> to repeat the last command.)

8. In the Load Family dialog box, navigate to the *Doors> Residential* folder and select **Door-Interior-Single-6 _Panel-Wood.rfa.** Click **Open**.

9. In the Specify Types dialog box, scroll down the *Type* list, select **36" x 80"**, and click **OK**.

10. In the Type Selector, select **Door-Double-Flush_Panel-Double-Acting: 72" x 80"**, and place an instance of it in the wall between the kitchen and dining area, as shown in Figure 5–22.

Renumber the door to match the Kitchen room number, if required.

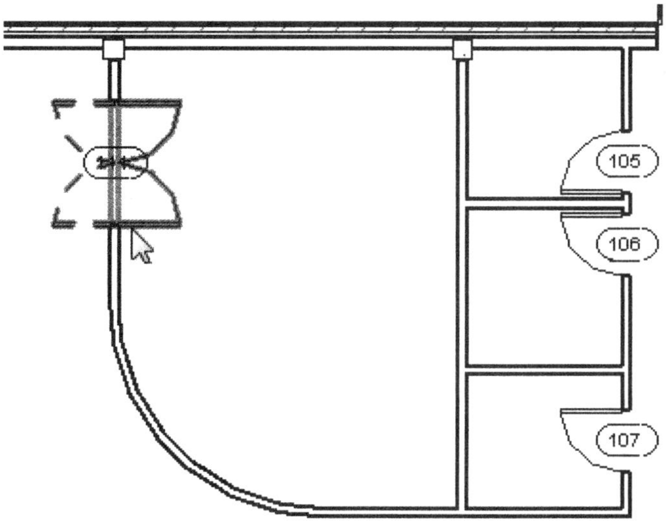

Figure 5–22

11. Zoom to the extents of the view and save the project.

Task 2 - Add doors to Floor 2.

1. Open the **Floor Plans: Floor 2** view. The linked CAD file is displayed to help you place the doors.
2. In the *Architecture* tab>Build panel, click (Door).
3. In the Type Selector, select **Single-Flush-Vision: 36" x 80".**
4. Place the first door in the lower left stairwell as shown in the linked file and change the tag number to 210
5. Add another door of the same type to the other stairwell at the opposite end of the building.
6. Change the door type to **Door-Interior-Single-6_Panel-Wood: 36" x 80"** and place a door at the entrance of Guest Room 201. Change the door number to **201**.
7. Continue placing doors at the entrance of each guest room allowing the number to increment.
8. Use the same type to add doors to the bathrooms. (Disregard the door numbers at this time. They can be changed later when the rest of the doors are all placed, if required.)

The door to the small closet in the guest bathroom is smaller than the existing door sizes. Therefore, you need to find out what size it is and create a new size.

9. Change the door type to **Single Flush: 30" x 80"**.
10. In Properties, click (Edit Type) or in the *Modify | Place Door* tab>Properties panel, click (Type Properties).
11. In the Type Properties dialog box, click **Duplicate**.
12. Enter **24" x 80"** for the name and click **OK**.
13. In the Type Properties dialog box, change the *Width* property to **2'-0"**. You can type either **2** or **24"** but you must add the **"** symbol to the value if you are using inches.
14. Click **OK** to close the dialog box. The new door type is available for use. Add it to the small closets.

15. Continue adding other doors using different door styles (i.e., **Bifold 72" x 80"** for the closets and **Double-Glass 72" x 84"** for the balconies). The rooms should look similar to the layout shown in Figure 5–23, though the numbering might be different.

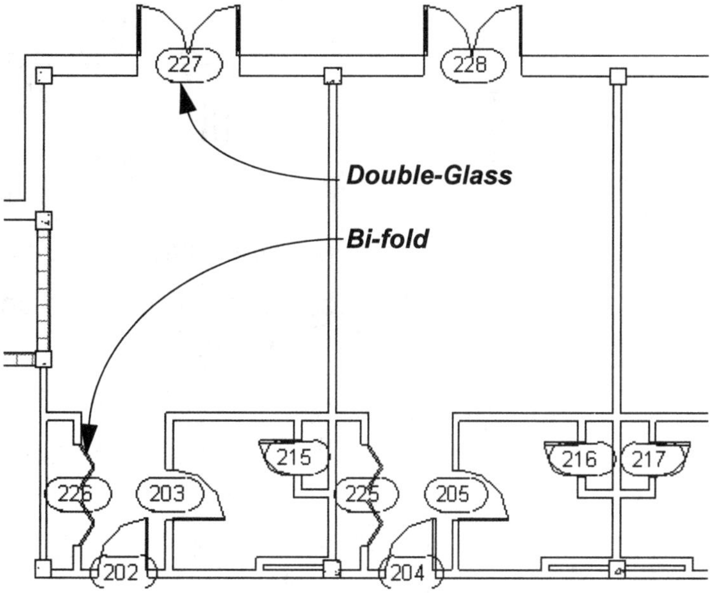

Figure 5–23

16. Renumber the doors in the guest rooms based on the room number if you have time.

17. Save the project.

Chapter Review Questions

1. How do you change the swing direction of a door, as shown in Figure 5–24? (Select all that apply.)

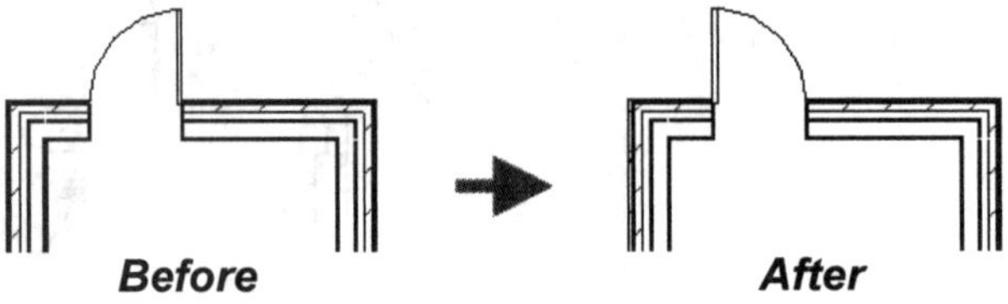

Figure 5–24

   a. When placing the door, press <Spacebar>.

   b. When placing the door, right-click and select **Change Swing**.

   c. Select an existing door and select the flip arrows.

   d. Select an existing door, right-click and select **Change Swing**.

2. How do you add additional window or door families to a project?

   a. Find the window or door family using Windows Explorer, right-click and select **Import into Revit Project**.

   b. Import them from the Window or Door Catalog.

   c. Load them from the Library.

   d. Use the Window/Door tool to create new families.

3. How do you include a tag with a door or window, as shown in Figure 5–25?

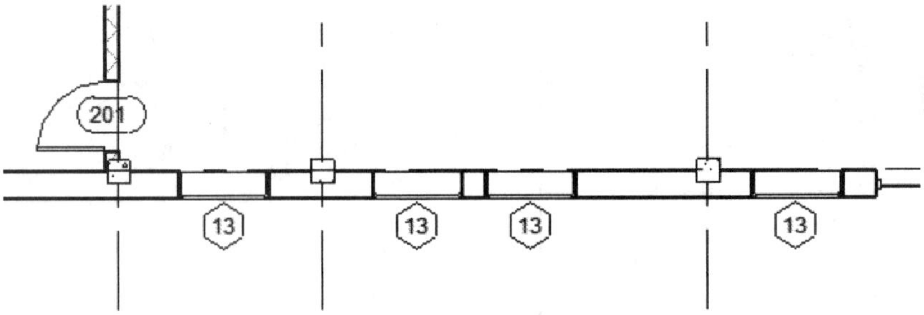

Figure 5–25

   a. Select a door or window family that includes a tag.

   b. Select the Tag box in the Options Bar before placing the door or window.

   c. Tags can only be used after placing the door or window.

   d. Select **Tag on Placement** in the contextual tab.

4. Where are the door and window sizes stored?
   a. In Properties.
   b. In Type Properties.
   c. In Door/ Window Settings.
   d. In the template file.
5. How do you create additional door or window sizes, as shown in Figure 5–26?

Figure 5–26

   a. Select the required door or window and use the Size tool to specify a new size.
   b. Select the required door or window and in Type Properties, duplicate an existing door and modify it.
   c. Find the existing door or window family in the Project Browser, right-click and select **New Size**.
   d. Select the door or window in the view, and edit it using size controls to the required size.

Command Summary

Button	Command	Location
Clipboard		
	**Copy to Clipboard**	• **Ribbon:** *Modify* tab>Clipboard panel • **Shortcut:** <Ctrl>+<C>
	**Cut to the Clipboard**	• **Ribbon:** *Modify* tab>Clipboard panel • **Shortcut:** <Ctrl>+<X>
	**Paste - Aligned to Current View**	• **Ribbon:** *Modify* tab>Clipboard panel> expand Paste
	**Paste - Aligned to Same Place**	• **Ribbon:** *Modify* tab>Clipboard panel> expand Paste
	**Paste - Aligned to Selected Levels**	• **Ribbon:** *Modify* tab>Clipboard panel> expand Paste
	**Paste - Aligned to Selected Views**	• **Ribbon:** *Modify* tab>Clipboard panel> expand Paste
	**Paste - Aligned to Picked Level**	• **Ribbon:** *Modify* tab>Clipboard panel> expand Paste
	**Paste from Clipboard**	• **Ribbon:** *Modify* tab>Clipboard panel • **Shortcut:** <Ctrl>+<V>
Doors and Windows		
	**Door**	• **Ribbon:** *Architecture* tab>Build panel • **Shortcut:** DR
	**Edit Type/ Type Properties**	• **Properties palette:** Edit Type • **Ribbon:** *Modify* tab>Properties panel
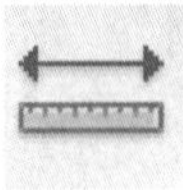	**Measure**	• **Quick Access Toolbar** • **Ribbon:** *Modify* tab>Measure panel
	**Window**	• **Ribbon:** *Architecture* tab>Build panel • **Shortcut:** WN

Working with Curtain Walls

Curtain walls are the "skin" of a building, and are often used to create complex windows and storefronts. Curtain walls are created based on a curtain wall type to which additional grids and mullions can be added and individual panels swapped out to create the required pattern.

Learning Objectives in this Chapter

- Create basic curtain walls and storefronts using curtain wall types.
- Modify the curtain grid pattern.
- Switch out curtain wall panels with other types, doors, or windows.
- Add mullions to curtain wall grids.

6.1 Creating Curtain Walls

Curtain walls are non-bearing walls consisting of panels laid out in a grid pattern. They can encase an entire building like a membrane or, as shown in Figure 6–1, fill a cutout in a standard wall, often called a storefront.

Figure 6–1

How To: Create a Curtain Wall.

Panels can be a specific material (such as glass or stone) or can incorporate doors, windows, or other wall types.

1. In a plan view, model a wall using a curtain wall type.
2. In an elevation or 3D view, add grids to the curtain wall.
3. Modify the panels of the curtain wall.
4. Add mullions to separate the panels.

The components of a curtain wall are shown in Figure 6–2.

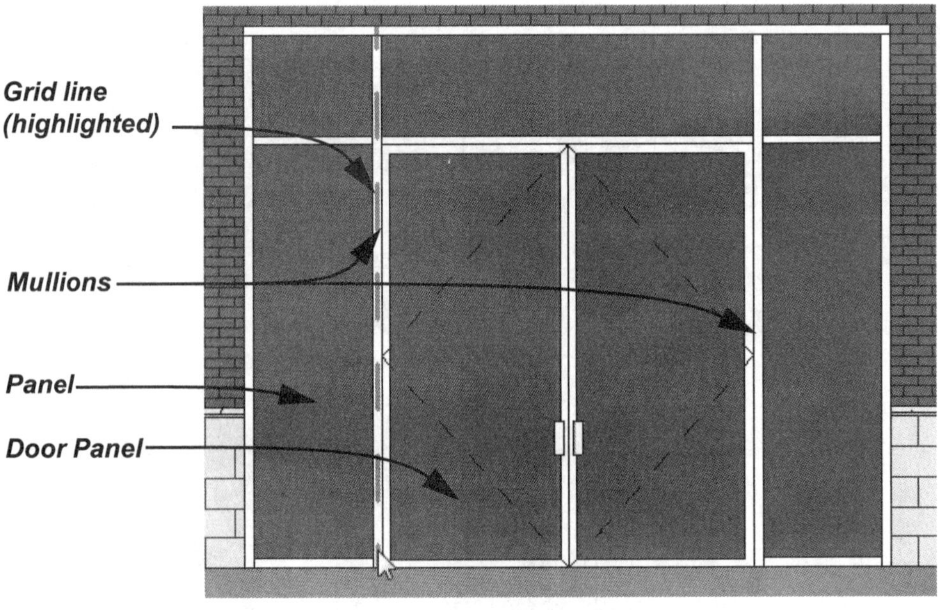

Figure 6–2

- The simplest way to create a curtain wall is to use a curtain wall type with a preset uniform grid already applied to it, such as the three types that come with the software, as shown in Figure 6–3.

Curtain Wall 1 ***Exterior Glazing*** ***Storefront***

Figure 6–3

- Many curtain walls do not have a uniform pattern of exact distances between grids, as shown in Figure 6–4. Therefore, you need to create these designs directly on the curtain wall. You can start with a curtain wall type that has a basic uniform grid, if applicable.

Figure 6–4

- For more information on creating curtain wall Types, see *Appendix B.4 Creating Curtain Wall Types with Automatic Grids*.

Creating Storefronts

Some curtain walls are embedded into other walls, as shown in Figure 6–5. They can also be used to create what looks like a complex set of windows. The **Storefront** curtain wall type is designed to be embedded in another wall.

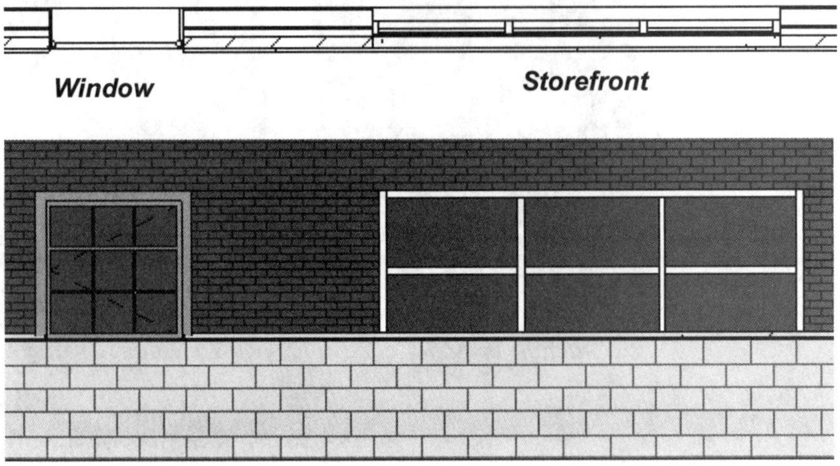

Figure 6–5

How To: Add a Storefront Wall in an Existing Wall

1. In the *Architecture* tab>Build panel, click (Wall).
2. In the Type Selector, select the curtain wall type you want to use. In Properties, set the *Base Constraint, Top Constraint*, and *Offsets* as required.The height can be less than the height of the wall in which you are embedding.
3. Select a point on the existing wall, as shown in Figure 6–6.

Figure 6–6

4. Select the second point along the wall. (Hint: Press <Tab> to cycle from the default Horizontal and Nearest snap to the dynamic dimension and then type the distance for the embedded curtain wall.) The wall displays, as shown in Figure 6–7.

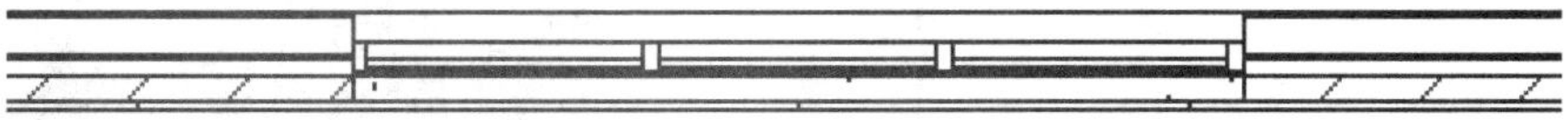

Figure 6–7

5. Open the appropriate elevation view. Select the outside edge of the curtain wall and use the shape handles and dynamic dimensions, as shown in Figure 6–8, to place the storefront in the wall as required.

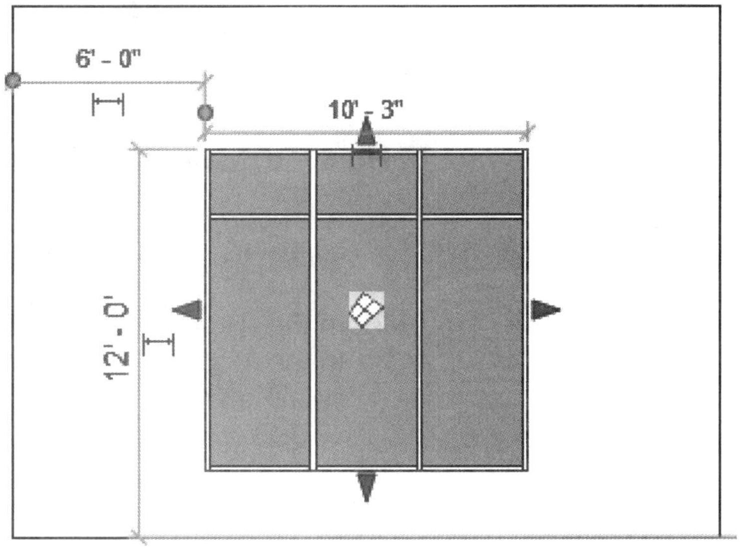

Figure 6–8

6.2 Adding Curtain Grids

Once you have a curtain wall in place with at least one panel, you need to separate it into multiple panels for the design. Each grid line divides a panel into two or more smaller panels, as shown in Figure 6–9.

Figure 6–9

How To: Create a Curtain Grid

1. After you have modeled the base curtain wall in a plan view, switch to an elevation or 3D view.
2. In the *Architecture* tab>Build panel, click (Curtain Grid).
3. In the *Modify | Place Curtain Grid* tab>Placement panel, select an insertion method, as described below.

(All Segments)	Creates a grid line through the entire curtain wall height or width.
(One Segment)	Creates a grid line between only the selection point and the next line. The entire grid line is established, but only one segment displays. You can add other segments later.
(All Except Picked)	Creates a grid line through the entire grid and permits you to go back and remove segments of the grid line. The removed segment displays as a dashed line until you add another grid line or start another command.

4. Move the cursor over an edge of the curtain wall or an existing curtain grid line. Dynamic dimensions are displayed, as shown in Figure 6–10. The new grid line is perpendicular to the edge at the point you select. Click at the required location.

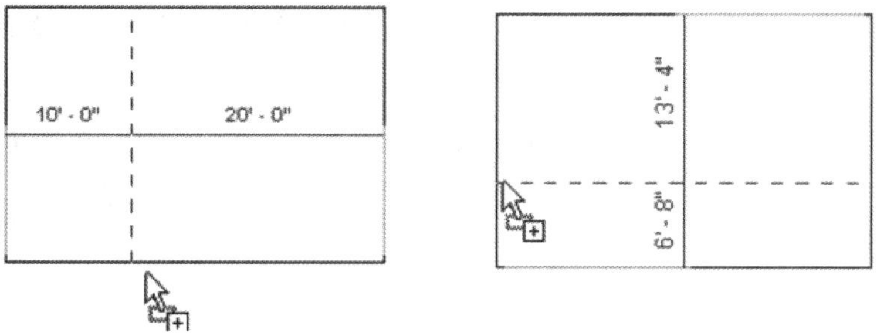

Figure 6–10

- Curtain grids automatically snap to the midpoint or 1/3 point of the panel. They also snap to levels, column grids, and reference planes.

- You can (Copy) and (Array) curtain grid lines. This method can be the fastest way of creating grids across the length of a wall.

Modifying Curtain Grids

Once you have placed the grid lines, they might not be exactly where you want them or overlap other lines where you do not want them to overlap. You can modify the location of lines in the grid and add or remove segments from the lines, as shown in Figure 6–11.

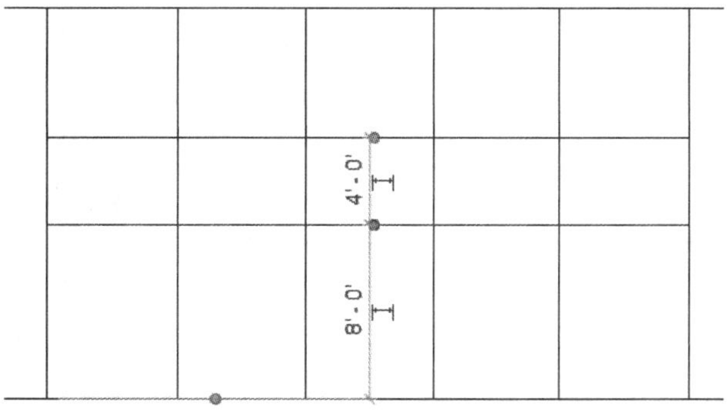

Figure 6–11

- To modify the grid, you must select a grid line, not a wall or the mullion. Press <Tab> to cycle through elements.

- To move a grid line, select it and use dynamic dimensions or (Move).

- If you select a grid line that was created using a curtain wall type, (Prevent or allow change of element position) is displayed, indicating that the element is constrained to a host element. Click the icon to enable you to move the line.

How To: Add or Remove Segments of Curtain Grids

1. Select a grid line to modify.
2. In the *Modify |Curtain Wall Grids* tab>Curtain Grid panel, click (Add/Remove Segments).
3. Click on the part of the grid that you want to add or remove. The line displays as dashed when you click to remove a segment, as shown in Figure 6–12. You must select grid lines, one at a time, with this command.

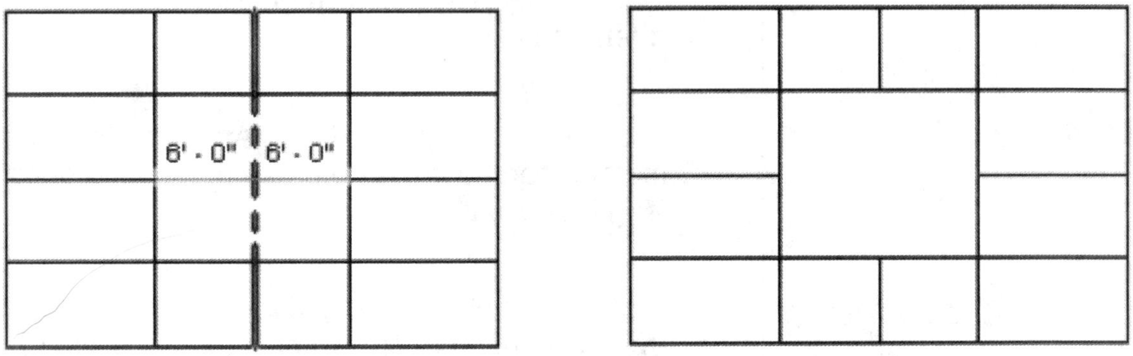

Figure 6–12

4. Click in empty space to finish the command.

- You can create non-rectangular panels by removing individual grid segments.

Hint: Aligning and Locking

When you use the **Align** command, you can also lock the lines together so if one moves, the other does as well. However, locking also causes the software to slow down. Therefore, be careful how much you use the **Lock** option and apply it only when you expect to make a lot of modifications.

Practice 6a Work with Curtain Walls

Practice Objectives

- Modify curtain wall properties.
- Add curtain wall grid lines.

In this practice, you will modify a curtain wall using Properties to ensure that the lines match up with other elements. You will also add grid lines that follow the pattern of a nearby wall. The finished elevation is shown in Figure 6–13.

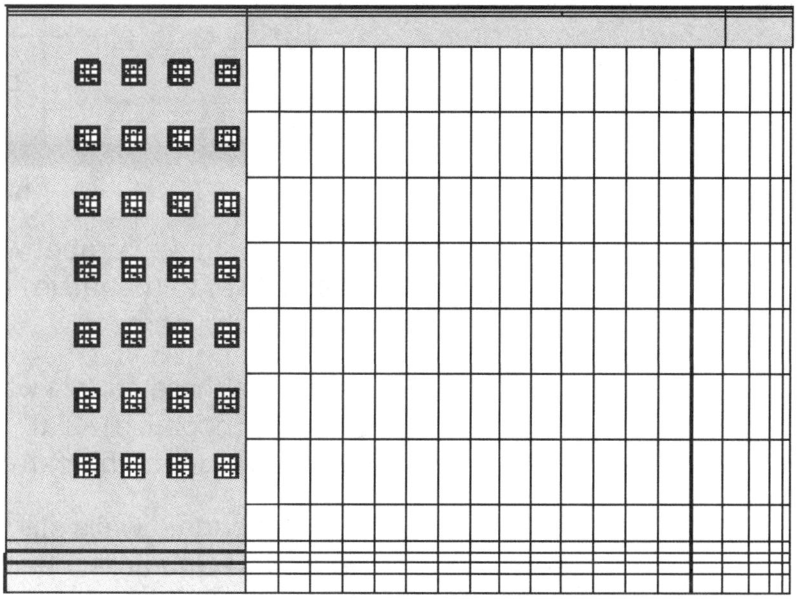

Figure 6–13

Task 1 - Modify the curtain wall.

1. Open the project **Modern-Hotel-Curtain-Walls.rvt**.
2. Open the **Elevations (Building Elevation):South** view.
3. To make the view easier to understand, select one grid line and one level line (hold <Ctrl> to select more than one element.) Then, right-click and select **Hide in View> Category**.

The curtain wall grid does not match up with any of the other features, as shown in Figure 6–14.

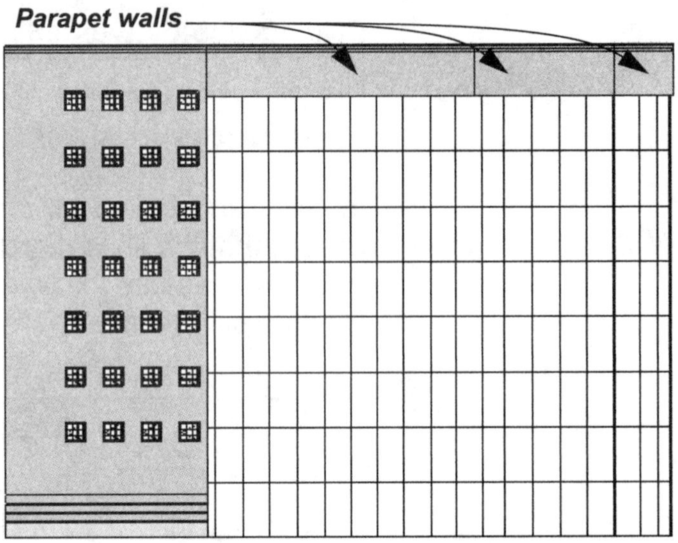

Figure 6–14

4. Select the three parapet walls. In Properties, change the *Base Offset* to (negative) **-2' 0"** and click **Apply**. This shortens the parapet.

5. Select the three curtain walls. In Properties, change the *Top Offset* to (negative) **-2' 0"** and click **Apply**. This extends the curtain wall up to the parapet.

6. With the curtain walls still selected, in Properties in the *Horizontal Grid* area, change the *Offset* to **4' 0"**, as shown in Figure 6–15. The grid now fits better, as shown in Figure 6–16.

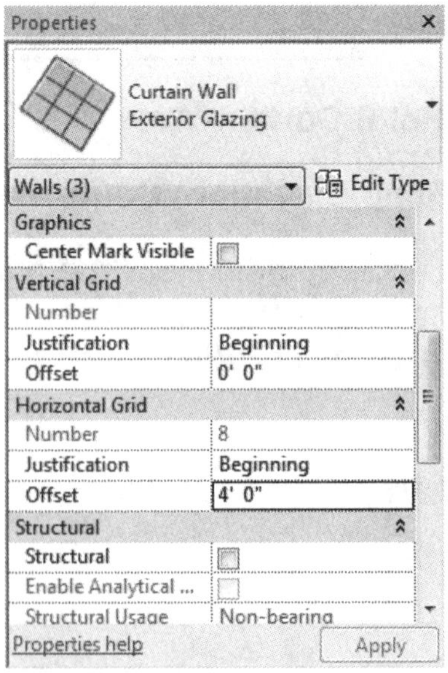

Figure 6–15

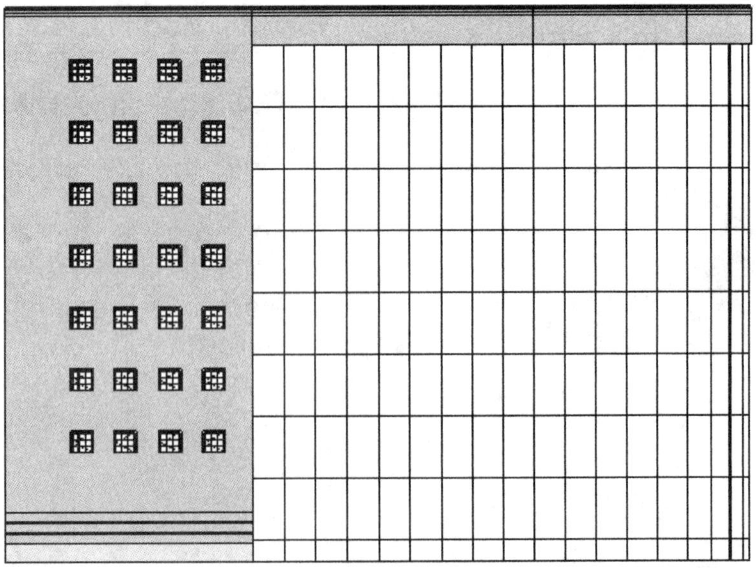

Figure 6–16

Task 2 - Add grid lines.

In this task, you will add grid lines to match up with multiple lines at the bottom of the building.

1. Zoom in to the bottom edge of the building and ensure that the brick/CMU and the curtain wall is displayed. Select the grid line and unpin it, as shown in Figure 6–17.

*If you cannot see the raised brick courses easily, in the Quick Access Toolbar, toggle off **Thin Lines**.*

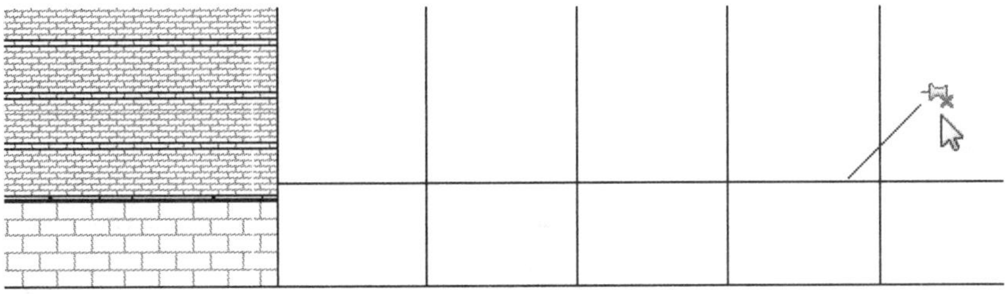

Figure 6–17

2. Use  (Align) to move the curtain grid line so it matches with the top of the CMU sill, as shown in Figure 6–18.

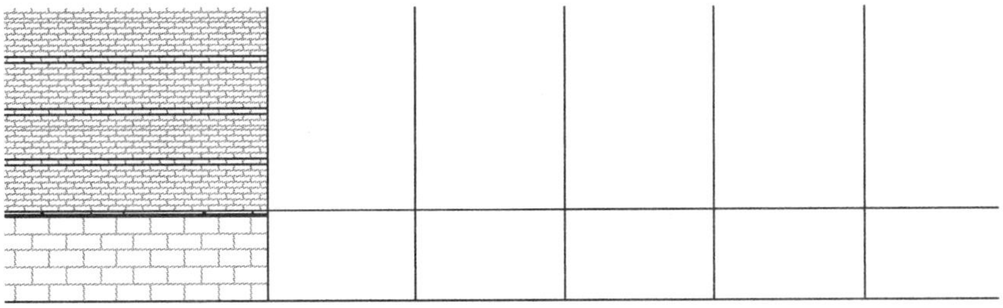

Figure 6–18

3. In the *Architecture* tab>Build panel, click  (Curtain Grid).
4. Add three grid lines and align them with the top of the reveals in the brick, as shown in Figure 6–19.

Zoom in until the heavier lines of the brick reveals are displayed.

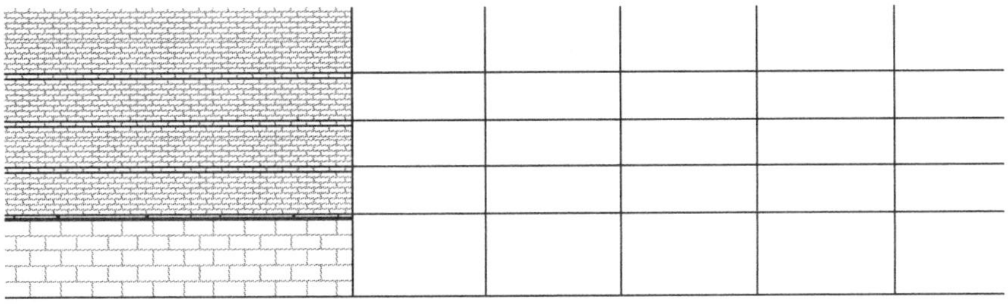

Figure 6–19

5. Select these four curtain grid lines (hold <Ctrl> and select each line individually) and move them down **1 1/4"**. Ensure you drag the cursor down before entering the move value. This places them correctly for the mullions, that are added later.

6. Pan over, add and align curtain grid lines to the other two parts of the curtain wall, as shown in Figure 6–20. Ensure you unpin the existing horizontal curtain grid lines before aligning them.

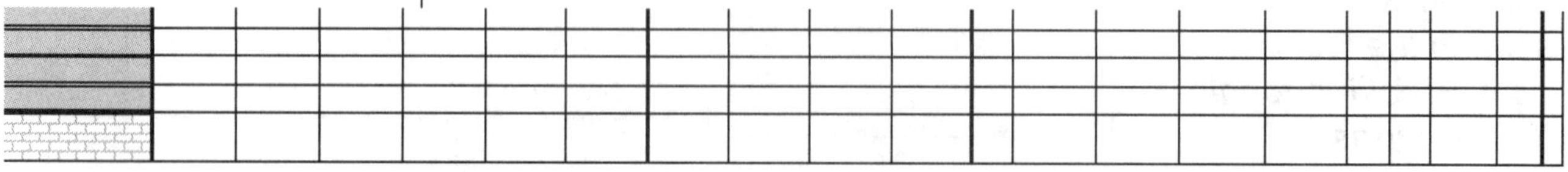

Figure 6–20

7. Zoom out until the entire front of the building is displayed.

8. Save the project.

6.3 Working with Curtain Wall Panels

The default panel for a curtain wall is typically a glazed panel. As you create the curtain grid and refine the wall design, you might want to use other materials for some of the panels, as shown in Figure 6–21. You can select the existing panels and in the Type Selector, select a panel type with the material you want to use.

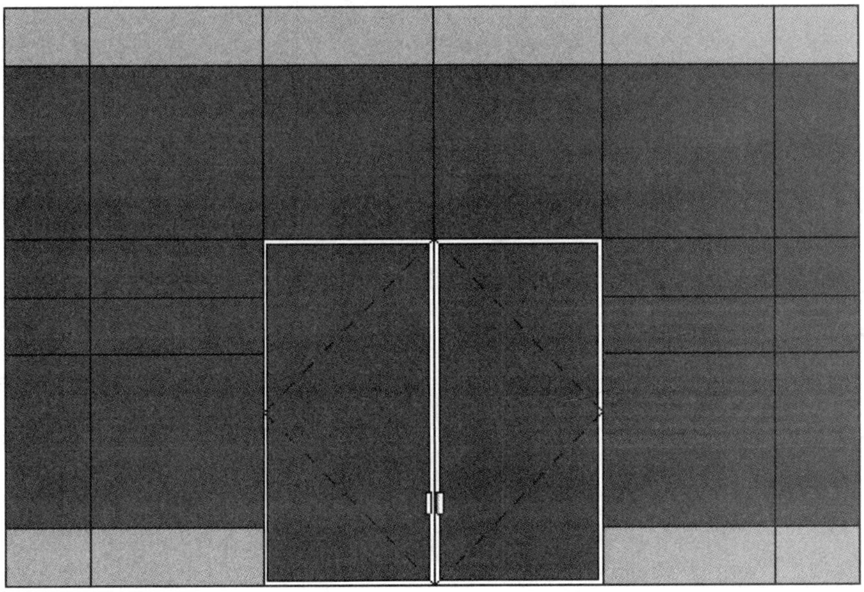

Figure 6–21

- Additionally, the panel type controls the thickness and can define a door or window for the panel.
- To select a panel, move the cursor over its edge, press <Tab> until it highlights, and then click to select it.
- To select all of the panels, select the edge of the curtain wall, right-click, and select **Select Panels on Host.**

- If  (Prevent or allow change of element position) displays (as shown in Figure 6–22), it indicates that the panel is locked and that changes to the element are not permitted. Click the icon to toggle off the lock and modify the panel.

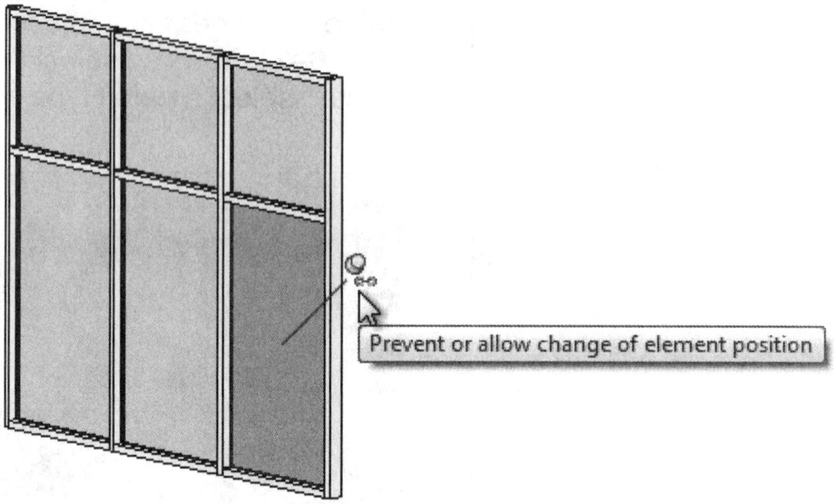

Figure 6–22

- To unpin multiple panels, select them and type **UP** (for **Unpin**).

Default Panel Types

Three panel types come with the default project template:

Empty Panel	You cannot delete a panel in a curtain wall, but you can change the panel type to an empty panel.
Glazed Panel	A typical panel type with glass as its material.
Solid Panel	A panel type using a solid material. You can create variations of this type with other materials.

- You can use any other wall type (including other curtain wall types) to fill in a panel.

- Door and window panels are available through the Library. Similar to other panel types, door and window panels fill the size of the panel to which they are applied. Adjust the curtain grid for the correct sizes, as shown in Figure 6–23.

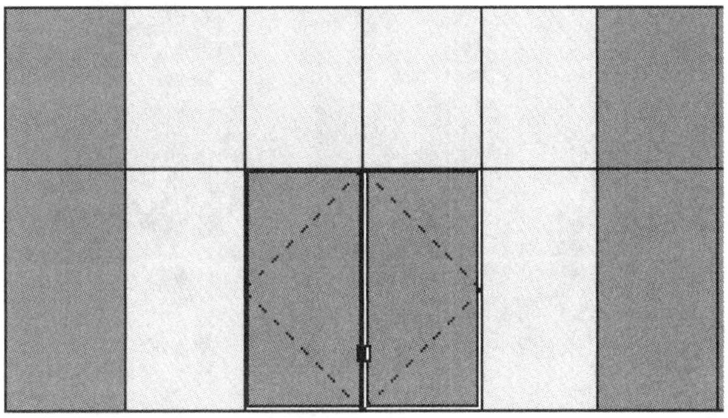

Figure 6–23

How To: Place Doors and Windows in Curtain Wall Panels

1. Load the door or window type that can be used as a curtain wall panel, such as the **Door-Curtain-Wall-Double-Glass.rfa** shown in Figure 6–24.

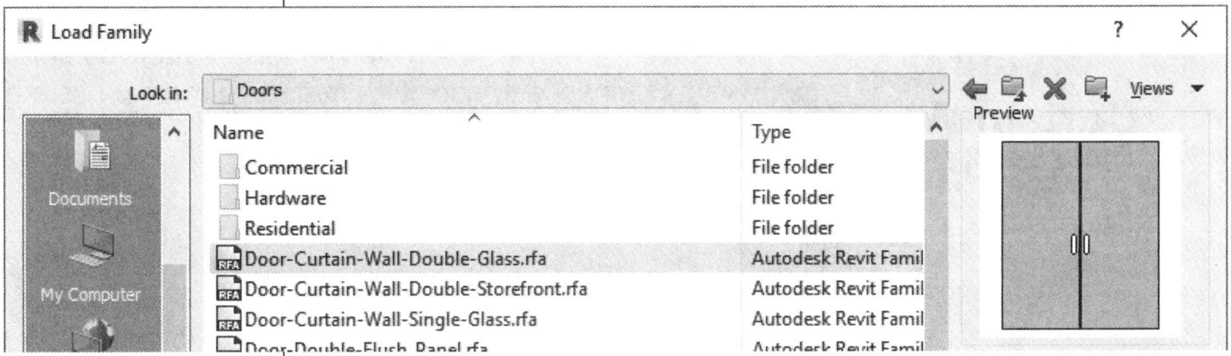

Figure 6–24

2. Modify the curtain grid layout to ensure that the size of the opening in the curtain wall matches the size of the door you want to use.
3. Select the curtain wall panel.

4. In the Type Selector, select the type that you want to use as the panel, as shown in Figure 6–25.

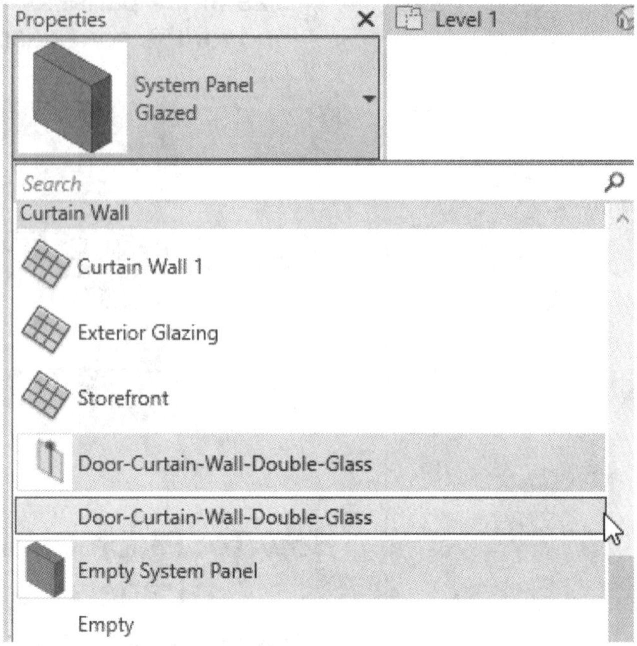

Figure 6–25

5. The door or window fills the panel area.

Creating a Curtain Wall Panel

While you can create curtain wall panels in many complex ways, a basic technique is to specify a material for a flat system panel, as shown in Figure 6–26.

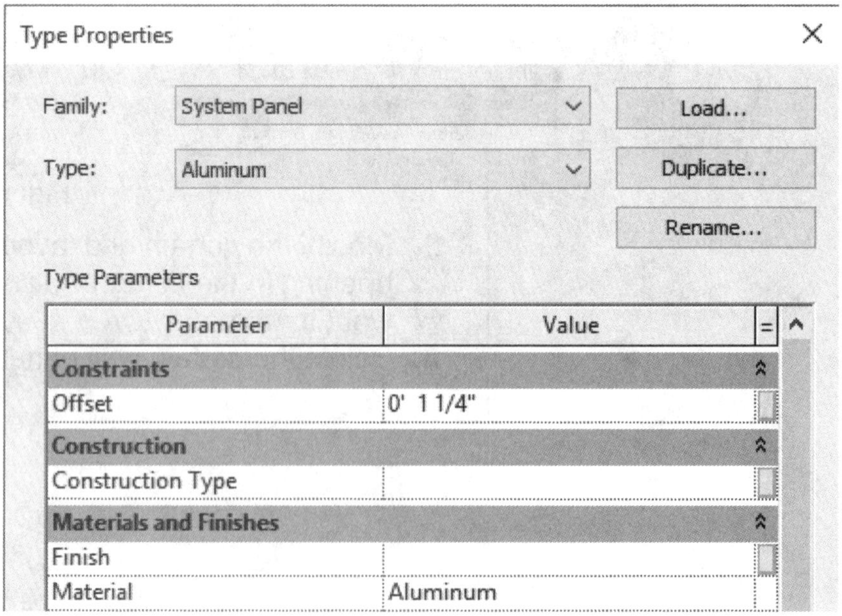

Figure 6–26

How To: Create a Curtain Wall Panel

1. Select a panel similar to the one you want to create (e.g., select a solid panel to create a new solid panel type). If it is locked, unlock it by clicking (Prevent or allow change of element position).
2. In Properties, click (Edit Type), or, in the *Modify | Curtain Panels* tab>Properties panel, click (Type Properties).
3. In the Type Properties dialog box, click **Duplicate** to create a copy of the existing family type.
4. Give the panel a new name that describes its purpose (e.g., **Brick** or **Aluminum**). The new name automatically includes the family name, such as **System Panel**.
5. Set the *Thickness*, *Offset*, and *Material* and any other parameters as required. Many materials are available in the Material Browser that opens when you click (Browse) in the Materials list.
6. Click **OK** to close the dialog box and finish the panel. It is automatically applied to the panel you selected for modification.

- The *Thickness* of the material is centered on the grid if you did not specify an *Offset*. If you want the panel to be recessed in the wall, use a negative offset. If you want the panel to stand out from the wall, use a positive offset.
- Materials with patterns, such as the glass block shown in Figure 6–27, do not display the pattern when the view is zoomed out far. Zoom in to view the material.

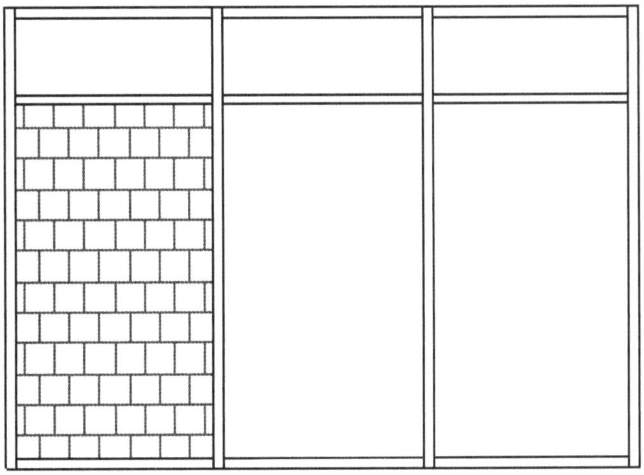

Figure 6–27

6.4 Attaching Mullions to Curtain Grids

Mullions are the frameworks for curtain wall panels, as shown in Figure 6–28. They can be many sizes, shapes, and materials. Add them as the final step in your curtain wall design after you have placed the grid lines.

Figure 6–28

How To: Add Mullions

1. In the *Architecture* tab>Build panel, click  (Mullion).
2. In the Type Selector, select the mullion style. There are no modifiable properties when you insert a mullion.
3. In the *Modify | Place Mullion* tab>Placement panel, select a *Create Mullion on* method:  (Grid Line),  (Grid Line Segment), or  (All Grid Lines), as shown in Figure 6–29.

Mullions must be placed individually; they cannot be copied or arrayed.

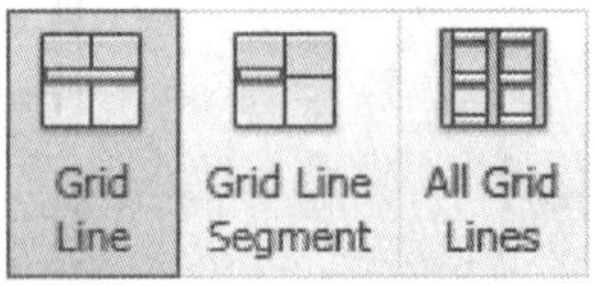

Figure 6–29

4. Select the grid line on which you want to place the mullion. If the grid line is inside a grid, the mullion is placed on the grid's center line. If it is on the edge of the wall, the mullion is placed so that its exterior is flush with the outside of the wall.

- Hold <Shift> to place a mullion only on the selected segment.
- Hold <Ctrl> to place the mullion on all empty grid segments (i.e., all without mullions).

- Corner mullion types are designed for the intersection of two curtain walls. They adjust to fit the angle of the intersection.

Modifying Mullions

To quickly select mullions, right-click on the edge of the curtain wall and select **Select Mullions**. The mullion options include **On Vertical Grid** or **On Horizontal Grid**, **Inner Mullions**, **Border Mullions**, or **Mullions on Host**, as shown in Figure 6–30.

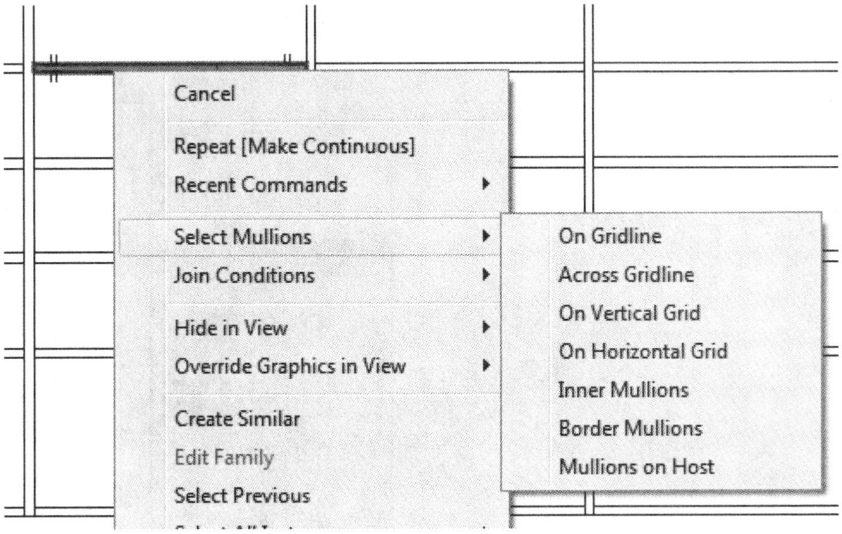

Figure 6–30

- Modify mullion styles by changing their type in the Type Selector.
- If you move a grid line, the mullion moves with it.
- If you delete a grid line, the mullion is also deleted. However, if you delete a mullion, the grid line is not deleted.
- You can change the way mullions intersect. Select the mullion and in the *Modify | Curtain Wall Mullions* tab>Mullion panel, click 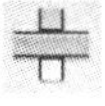 (Make Continuous) or  (Break at Join). Alternatively, select the mullion and click the **Toggle Mullion Join** control, as shown in Figure 6–31.

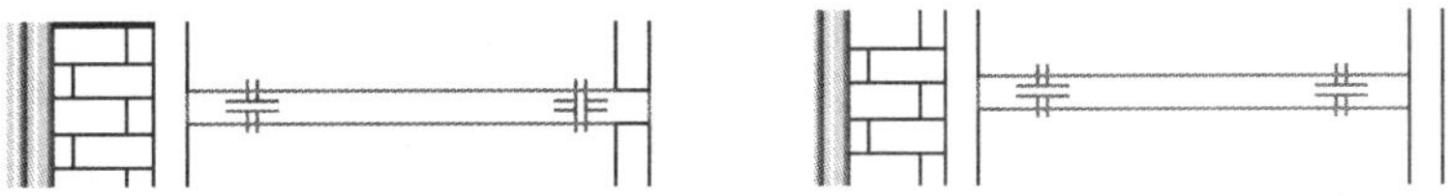

Before ***After***

Figure 6–31

Practice 6b

Add Mullions and Panels to Curtain Walls

Practice Objectives

- Add and modify mullions.
- Add a storefront entrance and door panel.

In this practice, you will add and modify mullions along the curtain walls. You will also create a storefront that includes a door panel as the front entrance of the building. The finished elevation is shown in Figure 6–32.

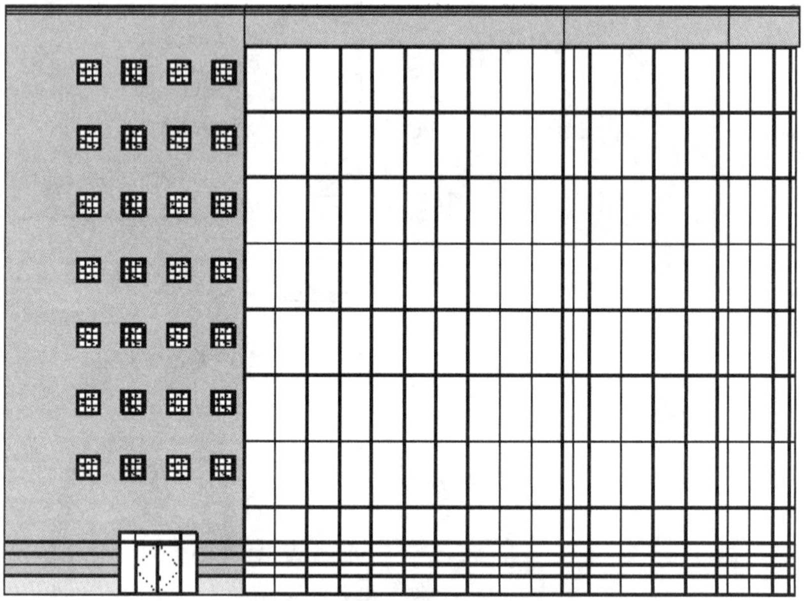

Figure 6–32

Task 1 - Add and modify mullions.

1. Open the project **Modern-Hotel-Mullions.rvt**.
2. Open the **Elevations (Building Elevations): South** view, or work in the 3D view.
3. In the *Architecture* tab>Build panel, click (Mullion).
4. In the *Modify* | *Place Mullion* tab>Placement panel, click (All Grid Lines).
5. Select each of the curtain walls. Mullions are place on all of the grid lines.

6. Click (Modify).

7. At the two lines where the curtain walls meet, extra mullions are added, as shown in Figure 6–33. These are not required and should be removed.

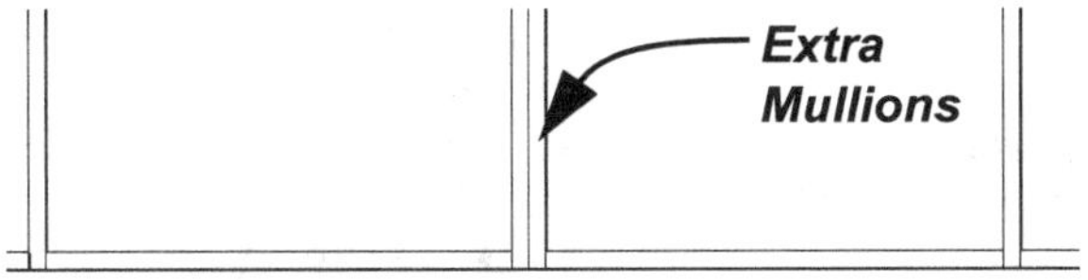

Figure 6–33

8. Select one of the mullions.

9. In the View Control Bar, click (Temporary Hide/Isolate) and select **Isolate Category**. This makes selecting the mullions you want to delete easier.

10. Select one vertical mullion where the two curtain walls meet. Right-click and select **Select Mullions>On Gridline** and then press <Delete>. Repeat for the other duplicate set of mullions.

11. Zoom out until all of the curtain walls are displayed.

12. Select the entire bottom row of mullions. You can use the Window selection box to select the entire row.

13. In the *Modify | Curtain Wall Mullions* tab>Mullion panel, click (Make Continuous). This changes the mullion direction, as shown in Figure 6–34.

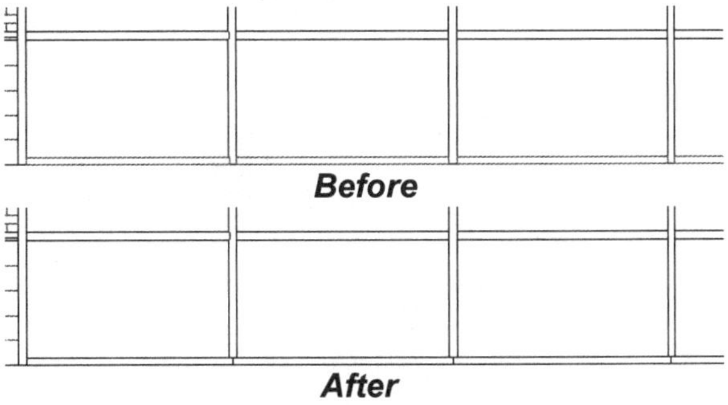

Figure 6–34

14. Repeat with the top row of mullions.

15. In the View Control Bar, click (Temporary Hide/Isolate) and select **Reset Temporary Hide/Isolate**.

16. Save the project.

Task 2 - Add the storefront entrance.

1. Open the **Floor Plans: Floor 1** view.
2. In the *Architecture* tab>Build panel, click  (Wall).
3. In the Type Selector, select **Curtain Wall:Storefront**.
4. In Properties, enter the following values:
   - *Base Constraint:* **Floor 1**
   - *Base Offset:* **0' 0"**.
   - *Top Constraint:* **Up to level: Floor 2**
   - *Top Offset:* (negative) **-6' 0"**
5. Draw the storefront, working from left to right, in the existing wall **1'-3"** off of the right gridline, as shown in Figure 6–35.

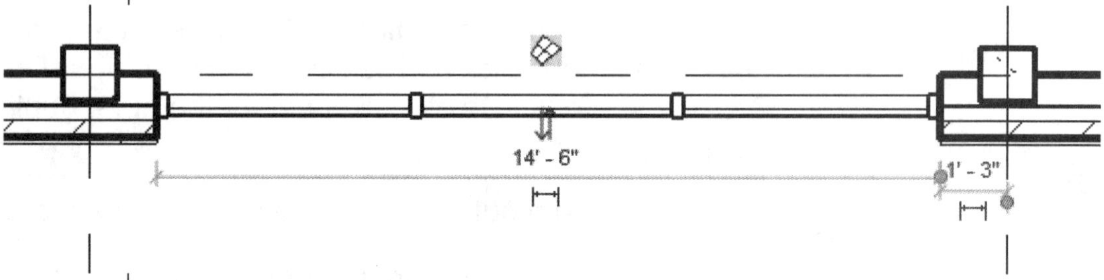

Figure 6–35

6. Open the **Elevations (Building Elevation): South** view and zoom in on the storefront.

*Type **UP** to unpin the elements, as shown in Figure 6–37.*

7. Window around to select the storefront. Because it was created with a preset type, all of the grids and panels are pinned, as shown on the left in Figure 6–36.

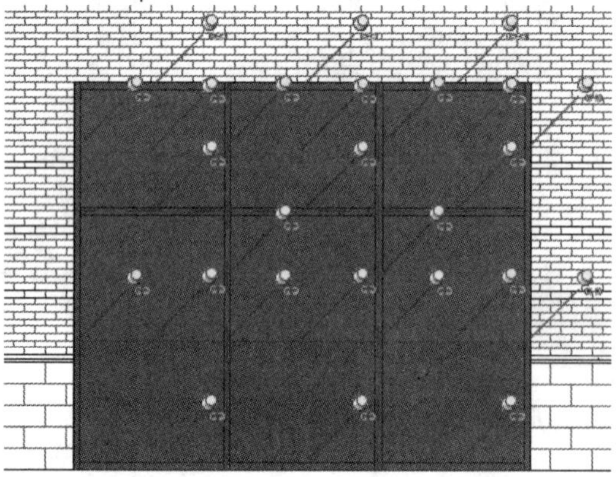

Figure 6–36

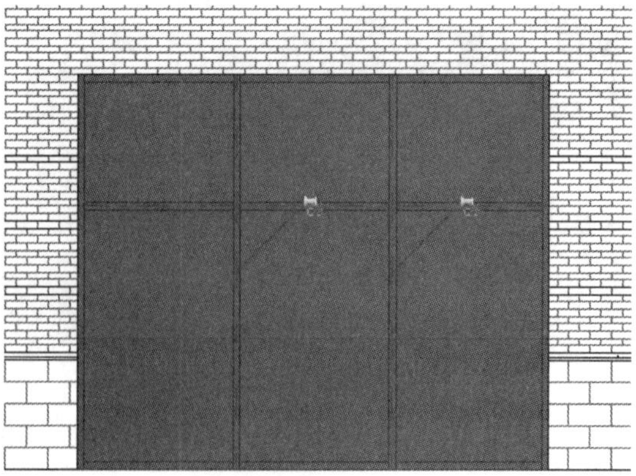

Figure 6–37

8. Modify the storefront, as shown in Figure 6–38. Align the horizontal line with the curtain grid line in the main curtain wall and use temporary dimensions to locate the vertical grid lines.

Ensure you are selecting curtain grid lines as you work and not the mullions. Use <Tab> to cycle through the elements.

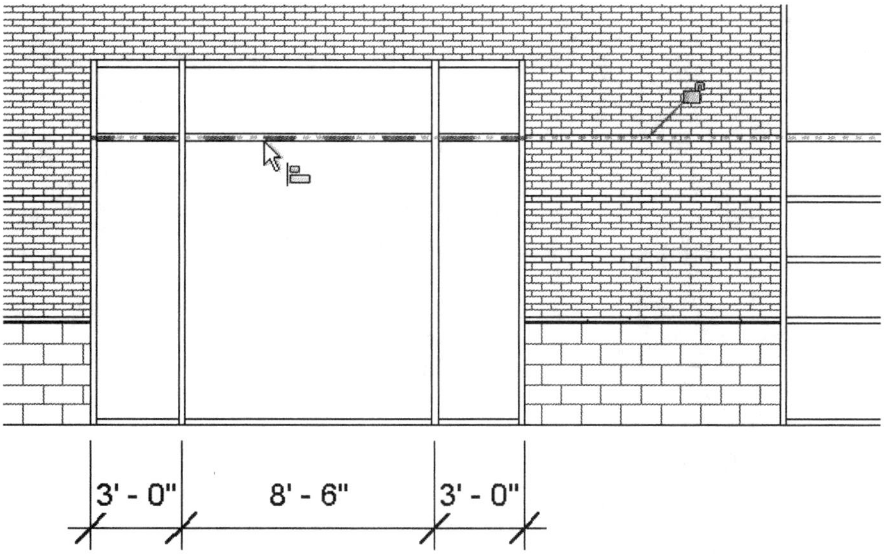

Figure 6–38

9. Select the mullions at the top of the storefront and toggle the mullion joins to the top bar so that it is straight across, as shown in Figure 6–39.

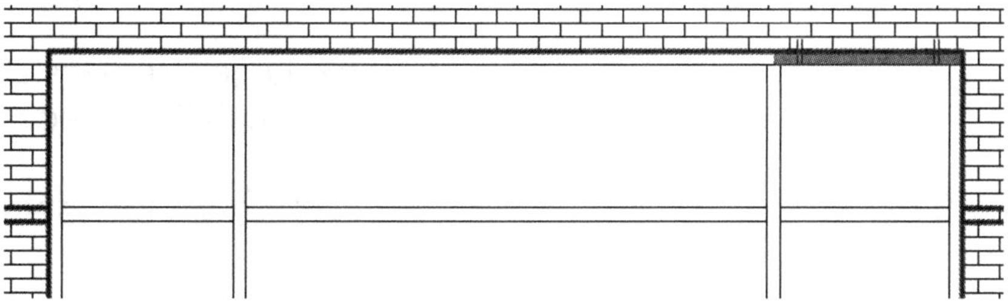

Figure 6–39

10. Save the project.

Task 3 - Add a door in the storefront.

1. In the *Insert* tab>Load from Library panel, click (Load Family). Use this more generic method of loading the curtain wall door family because you cannot use the **Door** command to place doors in curtain walls.

2. In the Load Family dialog box, in the *Doors* folder, select the door **Door-Curtain-Wall-Double-Storefront.rfa**, as shown in Figure 6–40. Click **Open**.

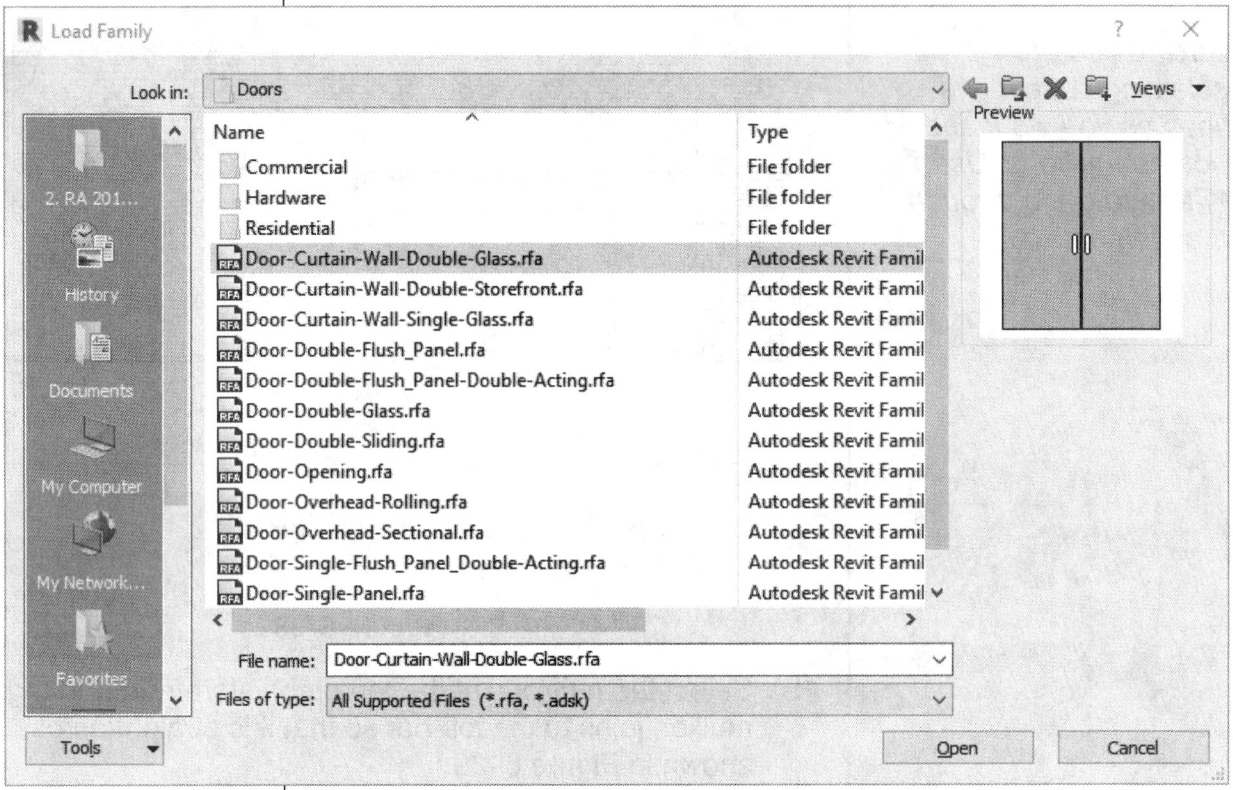

Figure 6–40

3. Select the large panel, as shown in Figure 6–41. Use <Tab> to cycle through the selections and then click to select it.

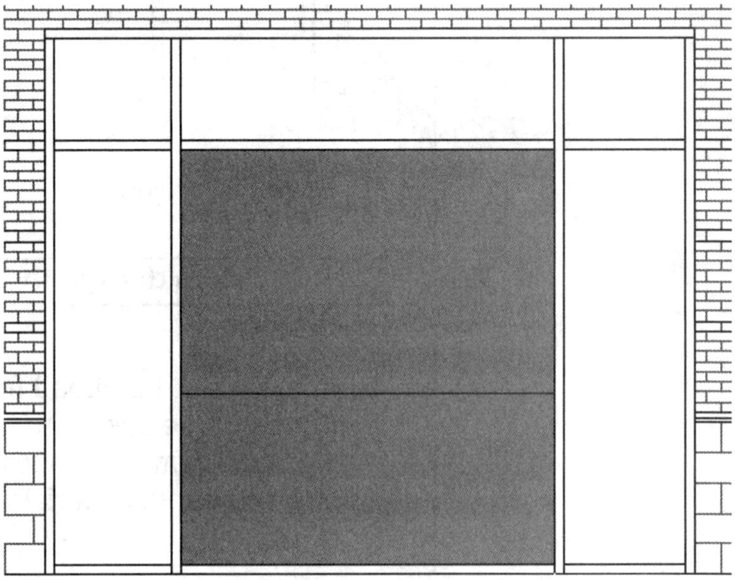

Figure 6–41

4. In the Type Selector, select **Door-Curtain-Wall-Double-Storefront.** The panel changes to the door. Delete the mullion at the bottom of the door, as shown in Figure 6–42.

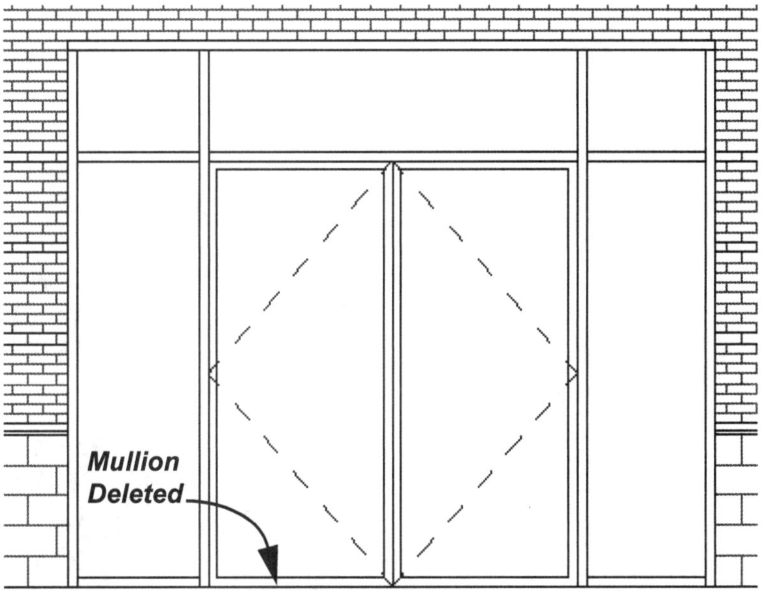

Figure 6–42

5. Zoom out until the entire front elevation is displayed.
6. View the project in 3D.
7. Save the project.

Chapter Review Questions

1. Which command do you start with to create a curtain wall?

    a.  (Wall)

    b.  (Curtain Grid)

    c.  (Curtain System)

2. You are placing a curtain grid and it keeps snapping to one dimension, such as the TWO-THIRDS OF CURTAIN PANEL shown in Figure 6–43, when you want it to be another. What should you do?

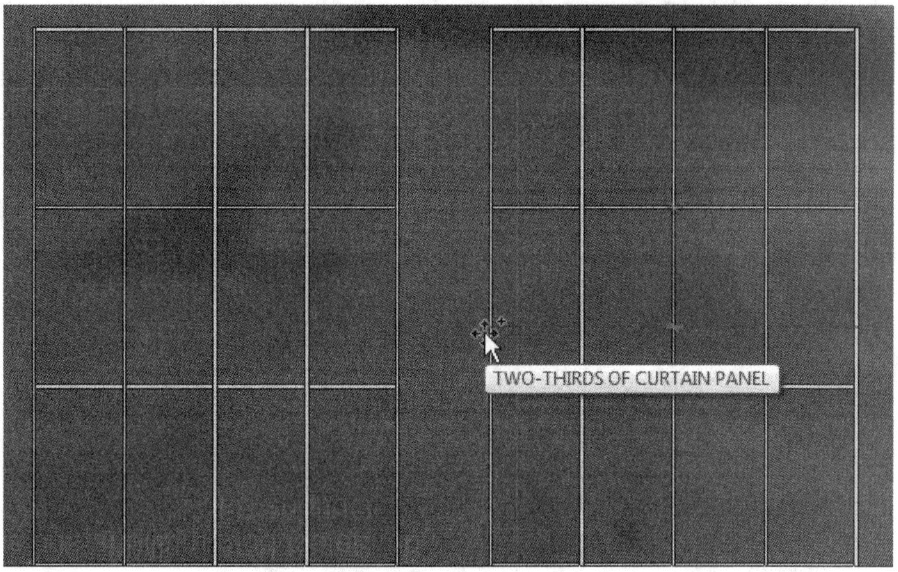

Figure 6–43

    a. Change the snap settings.

    b. Edit the Curtain Wall Type to permit manual grid placement.

    c. Use a Non-Uniform Curtain Wall Type instead of a Uniform one.

    d. Place the curtain grid anyway, select the temporary dimension, and change it to the required value.

3. How do you select one panel to modify it?
   a. Select the middle of the panel.
   b. Point to the edge of the panel and press <Tab> until it is identified.
   c. Select the curtain wall, right-click and select **Panel Select**.
   d. In the Selection Priority drop-down list, select **Curtain Panel**.
4. Once you select a panel, what can you swap it for? (Select all that apply.)
   a. Empty system panel
   b. Store Front Door
   c. Blank
   d. Wall Type
5. How do you change the way in which two mullions intersect, as shown in Figure 6–44? (Select all that apply.)

Figure 6–44

   a. Select one of the mullions and press <Tab> until the correct intersection displays.
   b. Select one of the mullions and click **Make Continuous** or **Break at Join** in the contextual tab.
   c. Select one of the mullions and click the **Toggle Mullion Join** control.
   d. Select both mullions and select the **Intersect** box in the Options Bar.

Command Summary

Button	Command	Location
	**Add/Remove Segments**	• **Ribbon:** *Modify* | *Curtain Wall Grids* tab> Curtain Grid panel
	**Curtain Grid**	• **Ribbon:** *Architecture* tab>Build panel
	**Curtain Grid: All Except Picked**	• **Ribbon:** *Modify* | *Place Curtain Grid* tab> Placement panel
	**Curtain Grid: All Segments**	• **Ribbon:** *Modify* | *Place Curtain Grid* tab> Placement panel
	**Curtain Grid: One Segment**	• **Ribbon:** *Modify* | *Place Curtain Grid* tab> Placement panel
	**Mullion**	• **Ribbon:** *Architecture* tab>Build panel
	**Mullion: All Grid Lines**	• **Ribbon:** *Modify* | *Place Mullion* tab> Placement panel
	**Mullion: Break at Join**	• **Ribbon:** *Modify* | *Curtain Wall Mullions* tab>Mullion panel • **Right-click:** (with mullion selected) Join Conditions>Break at Join
	**Mullion: Grid Line**	• **Ribbon:** *Modify* | *Place Mullion* tab> Placement panel
	**Mullion: Grid Line Segment**	• **Ribbon:** *Modify* | *Place Mullion* tab> Placement panel
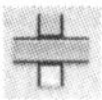	**Mullion: Make Continuous**	• **Ribbon:** *Modify* | *Curtain Wall Mullions* tab>Mullion panel • **Right-click:** (with mullion selected) Join Conditions>Make Continuous

Working with Views

Views are the cornerstone of working with Autodesk® Revit® models as they enable you to see the model in both 2D and 3D. As you are working, you can duplicate and change views to display different information based on the same view of the model. Callouts, elevations, and sections are especially important views for construction documents.

Learning Objectives in this Chapter

- Change the way elements display in different views to show required information and set views for construction documents.
- Duplicate views so that you can modify the display as you are creating the model and for construction documents.
- Create callout views of parts of plans, sections, or elevations for detailing.
- Add building and interior elevations that can be used to demonstrate how a building will be built.
- Create building and wall sections to help you create the model and to include in construction documents.
- Create 3D section views using Selection Boxes and Orient to View.

7.1 Modifying the View Display

Views are a powerful tool as they enable you to create multiple versions of a model without having to recreate building elements. For example, you can have views that are specifically used for working on the model, while other views are annotated and used for construction documents. Different disciplines can have different views that show only the features they require, as shown in Figure 7–1. Properties of a view are independent of the properties of other views.

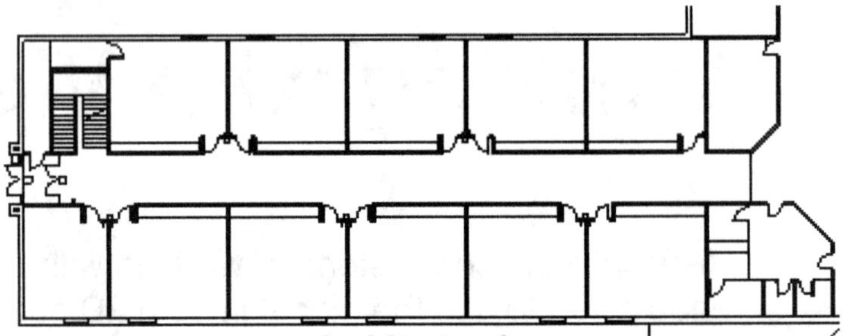

Architectural

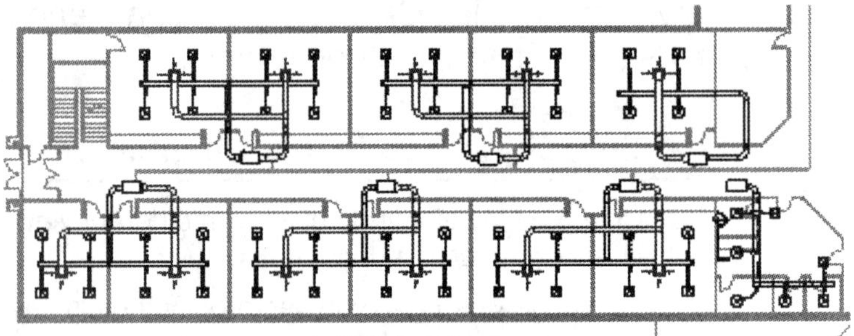

Mechanical

Figure 7–1

The view display can be modified in the following locations:

- View Control Bar
- Properties
- Shortcut menu
- Visibility/Graphic Overrides dialog box

View Properties

The most basic properties of a view are accessed using the View Control Bar, shown in Figure 7–2. These include the *Scale*, *Detail Level*, and *Visual Style* options. Additional options include temporary overrides and other advanced settings.

Figure 7–2

- The **Detail Level** controls whether you see schematic elements (Coarse or Medium Detail) or full scale elements (Fine Detail), as shown in Figure 7–3.

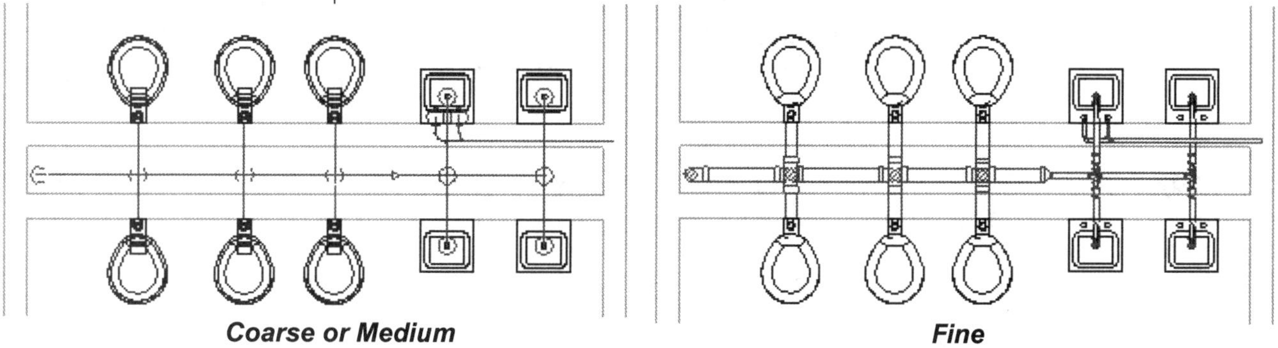

Coarse or Medium ***Fine***

Figure 7–3

Other modifications to views are available in Properties, as shown in Figure 7–4. These properties include *Underlays* and *View Range* as well as many others. The *Discipline* and *Sub-Discipline* of a view can also be set here. This is especially important for MEP projects.

The options in Properties vary according to the type of view. A plan view has different properties than a 3D view.

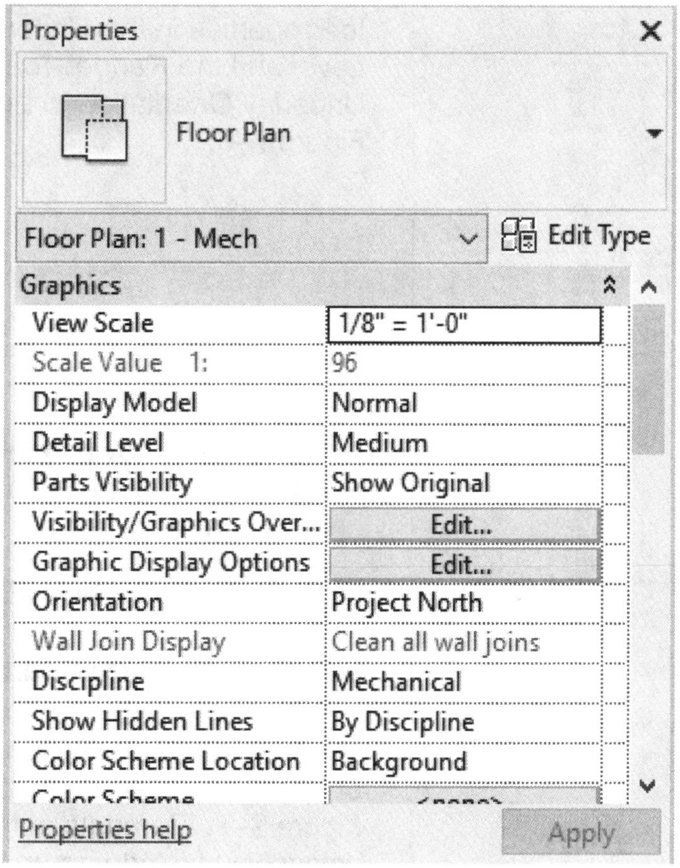

Figure 7–4

Setting an Underlay

Setting an *Underlay* is helpful if you need to display elements on a different level, such as the basement plan shown with an underlay of the first floor plan in Figure 7–5. You can then use the elements to trace over or even copy to the current level of the view.

Underlays are only available in Floor Plan and Ceiling Plan views.

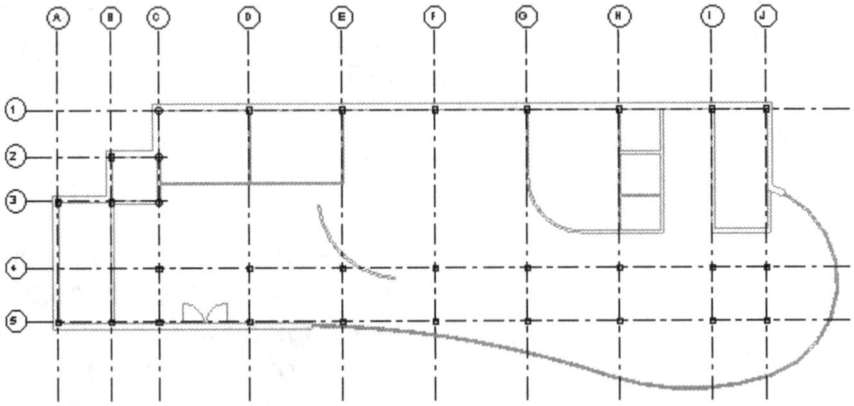

Figure 7–5

In Properties in the *Underlay* area, specify the *Range: Base Level* and the *Range: Top Level*. You can also specify the Underlay Orientation to **Look down** or **Look up**, as shown in Figure 7–6.

Underlay	
Range: Base Level	Floor 2
Range: Top Level	Floor 3
Underlay Orientation	Look down

Figure 7–6

- To prevent moving elements in the underlay by mistake, in the Select panel, expand the panel title, and clear **Select underlay elements**. You can also toggle this on/off using  (Select Underlay Elements) in the Status Bar.

Setting the View Range

The View Range controls the cut planes that control the visibility of plan views, as shown in the Sample View Range key in Figure 7–7. Elements outside the cut planes do not display unless you include an underlay.

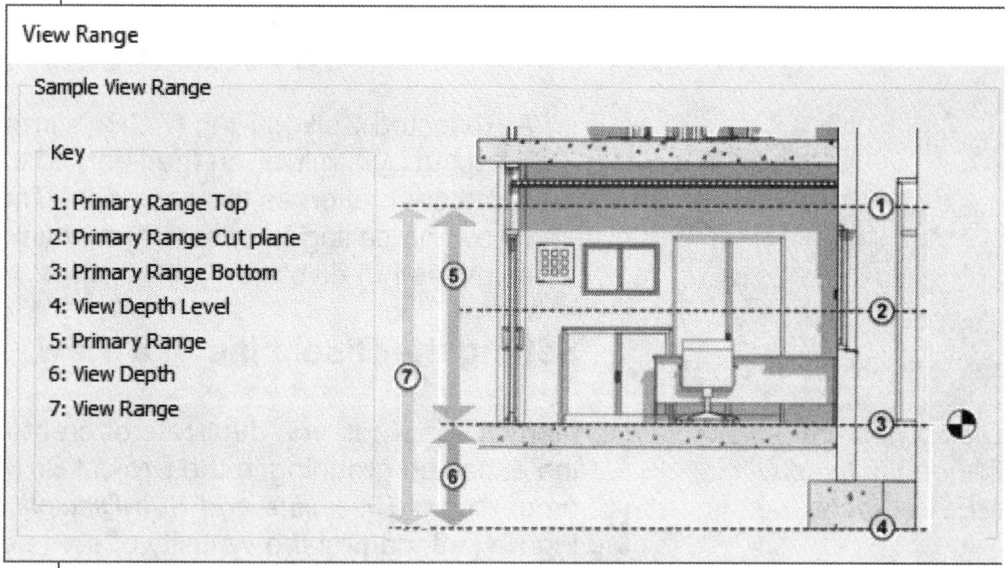

Figure 7–7

How To: Set the View Range

1. In Properties, in the *Extents* area, beside *View Range*, select **Edit…** or type **VR**.
2. In the View Range dialog box, as shown in Figure 7–8, modify the Levels and Offsets for the *Primary Range* and *View Depth.*
   - Click **<<Show** to display the Sample View Range key.
3. Click **OK**.

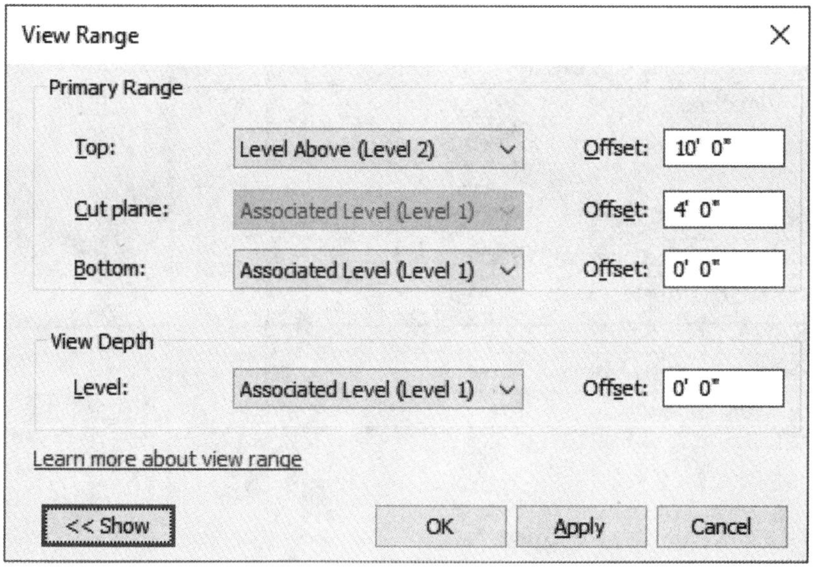

Figure 7–8

- If the settings used cannot be represented graphically, a warning displays, stating the inconsistency.
- A Reflected Ceiling Plan (RCP) is created, as if the ceiling is reflected by a mirror on the floor, so that the ceiling is the same orientation as the floor plan. The cutline is placed just below the ceiling to ensure that any windows and doors below do not display.

Setting the Discipline of a View

Disciplines are frequently used with MEP projects.

Many times when you duplicate or create a view it will not be in the expected grouping in the Project Browser. The view properties of *Discipline* and *Sub-Discipline*, as shown in Figure 7–9, control the visibility of some elements and applies grouping in the Project Browser. For example, you can separate the Plumbing Plans from the Fire Plumbing plans, as shown in Figure 7–10.

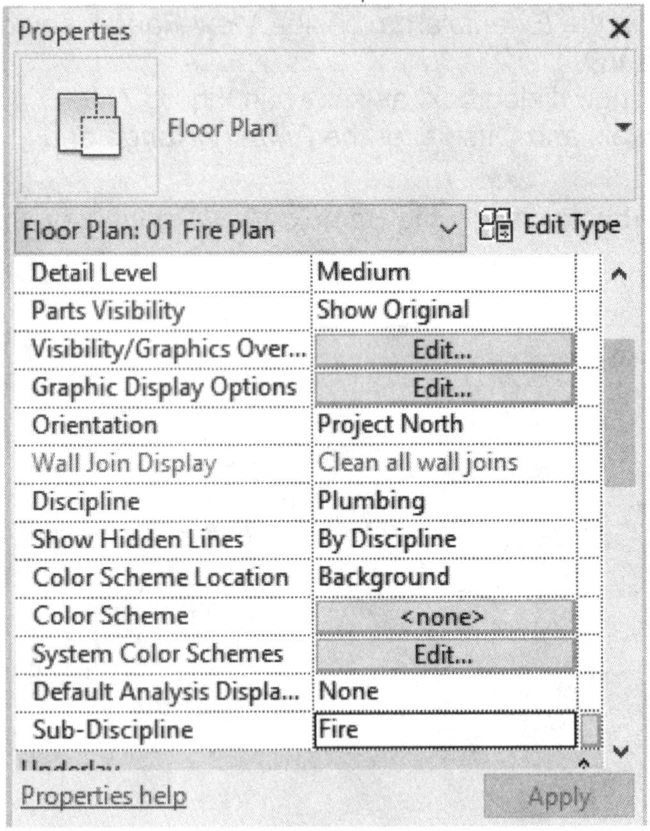

Figure 7–9

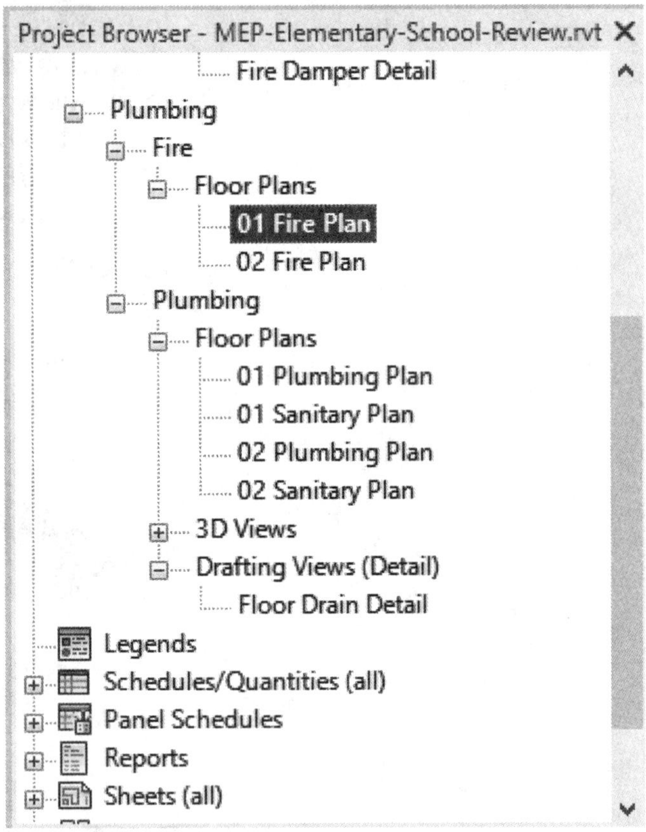

Figure 7–10

- You can add additional sub-disciplines by typing in a new name but the list of disciplines is set by the software.

Hiding and Overriding Graphics

Two common ways to customize a view are to:

- Hide individual elements or categories
- Modify how graphics display for elements or categories (e.g., altering lineweight, color, or pattern)

An element is an individual item such as one wall in a view, while a category includes all instances of a selected element, such as all walls in a view.

In the example shown in Figure 7–11, a Furniture Plan has been created by toggling off the structural grids category, and then graying out all of the walls and columns.

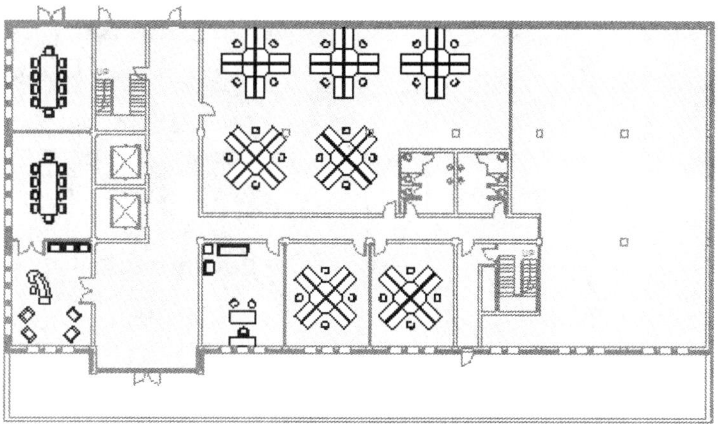

Figure 7–11

How To: Hide Elements or Categories in a view

The elements or categories are hidden in current view only.

1. Select the elements or categories you want to hide.
2. Right-click and select **Hide in View>Elements** or **Hide in View>Category**, as shown in Figure 7–12.
3. *A quick way to hide entire categories is to select an element(s) and type* ***VH****.*

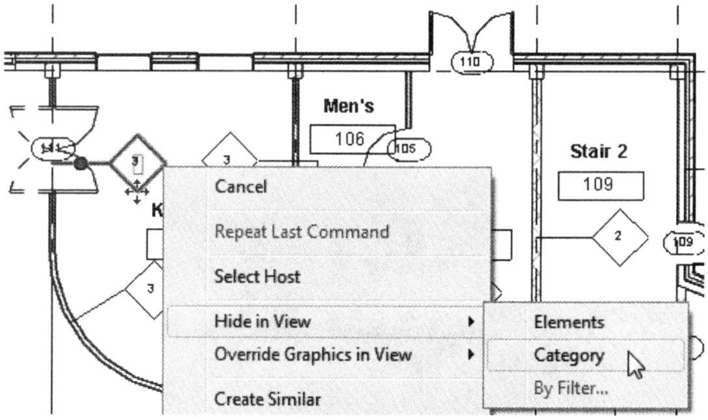

Figure 7–12

How To: Override Graphics of Elements or Categories in a View

The exact options in the dialog box vary depending on the type of elements selected.

1. Select the element(s) you want to modify.
2. Right-click and select **Override Graphics in View>By Element** or **By Category**. The View-Specific Element (or Category) Graphics dialog box opens, as shown in Figure 7–13.

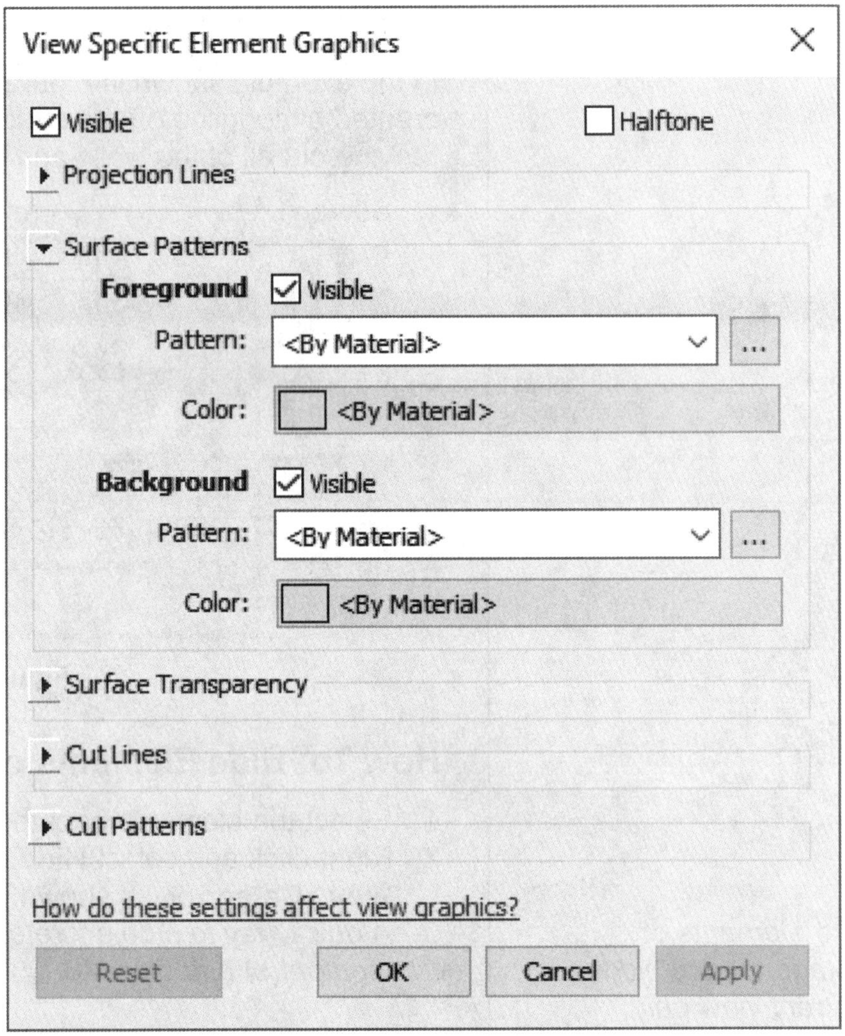

Figure 7–13

Select the changes you want to make and click **OK**.

View-Specific Options

- Clearing the **Visible** option is the same as hiding the elements or categories.
- Selecting the **Halftone** option grays out the elements or categories.
- The options for *Projection Lines* and *Cut Lines* include **Weight**, **Color**, and **Pattern**. The options for *Surface Patterns* and *Cut Patterns* include **Visibility**, **Pattern**, and **Color** for the Foreground and Background, as shown in Figure 7–13.
- **Surface Transparency** can be set by moving the slider bar, as shown in Figure 7–14.

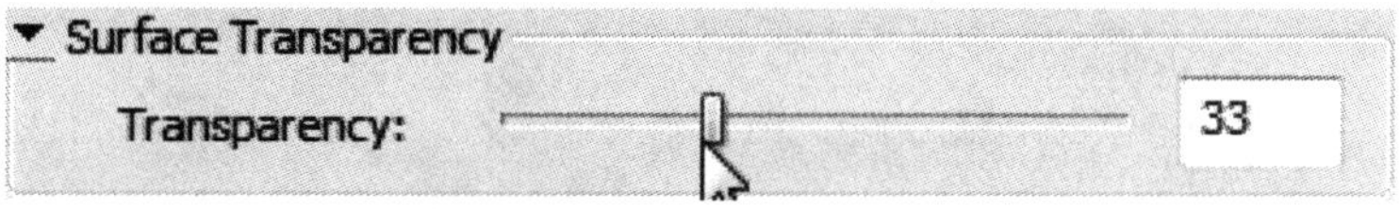

Figure 7–14

- The View-Specific Category Graphics dialog box includes **Open the Visibility Graphics dialog...**, which opens the full dialog box of options.

The Visibility/Graphic Overrides Dialog Box

The options in the Visibility/Graphic Overrides dialog box (shown in Figure 7–15) control how every category and sub-category of elements is displayed per view. You can toggle categories on and off, override the *Projection/Surface* and *Cut* information, set categories to **Halftone**, and change the *Detail Level*.

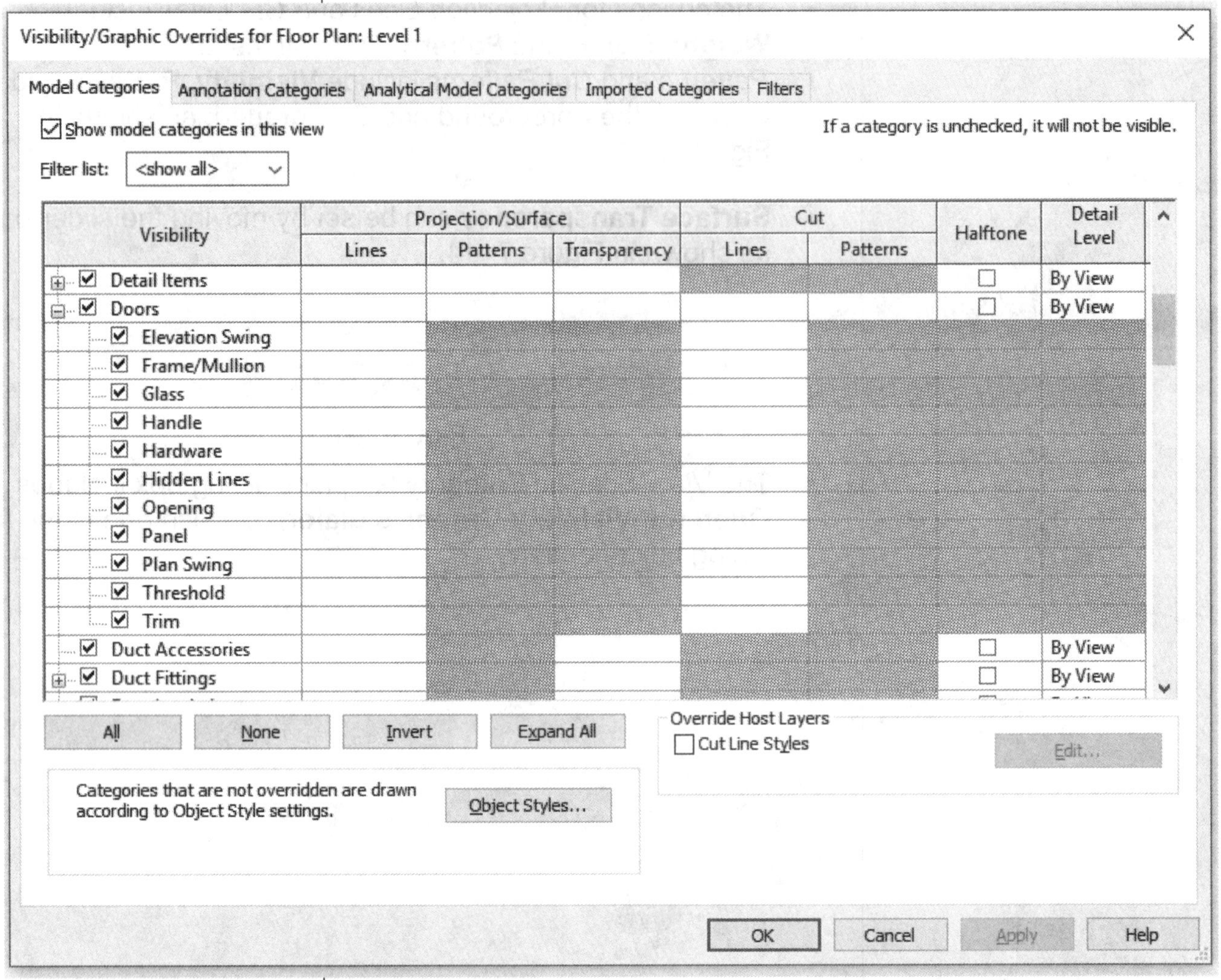

Figure 7–15

To open the Visibility/Graphic Overrides dialog box, type **VV** or **VG**. It is also available in Properties: in the *Graphics* area, beside *Visibility/Graphic Overrides*, click **Edit....**

- The Visibility/Graphic Overrides are divided into *Model*, *Annotation*, *Analytical Model*, *Imported,* and *Filters* categories.
- Other categories might be available if specific data has been included in the project, including *Design Options*, *Linked Files*, and *Worksets*.
- To limit the number of categories showing in the dialog box select a discipline from the *Filter list,* as shown in Figure 7–16

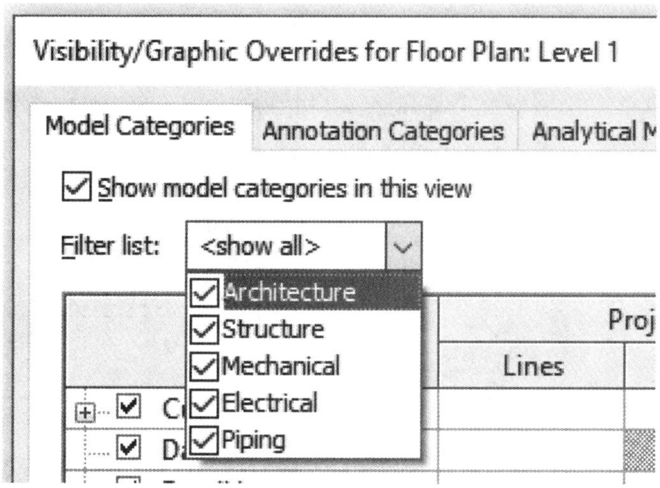

Figure 7–16

- To help you select categories, use the **All**, **None**, and **Invert** buttons. The **Expand All** button displays all of the sub-categories.

Hint: Restoring Hidden Elements or Categories

If you have hidden categories, you can display them using the Visibility/Graphic Overrides dialog box. To display hidden elements, however, you must temporarily reveal the elements first.

1. In the View Control Bar, click (Reveal Hidden Elements). The border and all hidden elements are displayed in magenta, while visible elements in the view are grayed out, as shown in Figure 7–17.

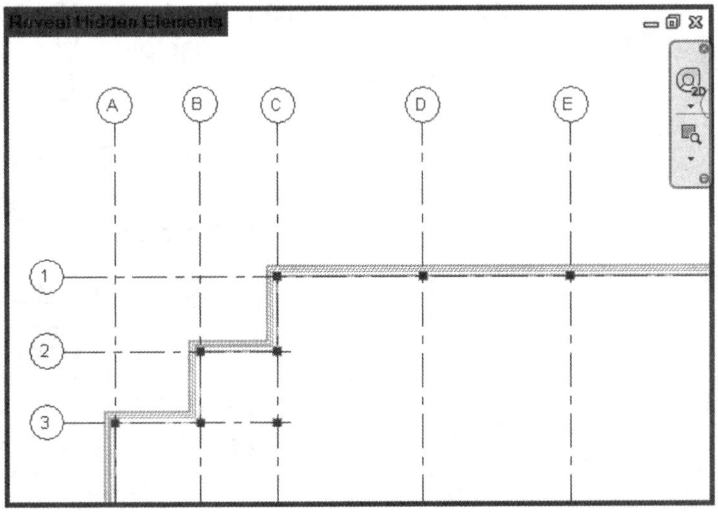

Figure 7–17

2. Select the hidden elements you want to restore, right-click, and select **Unhide in View>Elements** or **Unhide in View>Category**. Alternatively, in the *Modify* | contextual tab>Reveal Hidden Elements panel, click (Unhide Element) or (Unhide Category).
3. When you are finished, in the View Control Bar, click (Close Reveal Hidden Elements) or, in the *Modify* | contextual tab>Reveal Hidden Elements panel, click (Toggle Reveal Hidden Elements Mode).

Using View Templates

A powerful way to use views effectively is to set up a view and then save it as a View Template. You can apply view templates to views - individually or through the Properties palette. Setting the View Template using the Properties palette helps to ensure that you do not accidentally modify the view while interacting with it.

How To: Create a View Template from a View

1. Set up a view, as required.
2. In the Project Browser, right-click on the view and select **Create View Template from View**.
3. In the New View Template dialog box, type in a name and then click **OK**.
4. The new view template is listed in the View Templates dialog box. Make any required modifications.

Click **OK**.

How To: Specify a View Template for a View

1. In the Project Browser, select the view or views to which you want to apply a view template.
2. In Properties, scroll down to the *Identity Data* section and click the button beside *View Template*.
3. In the Apply View Template dialog box, select the view template from the list, as shown in Figure 7–18.

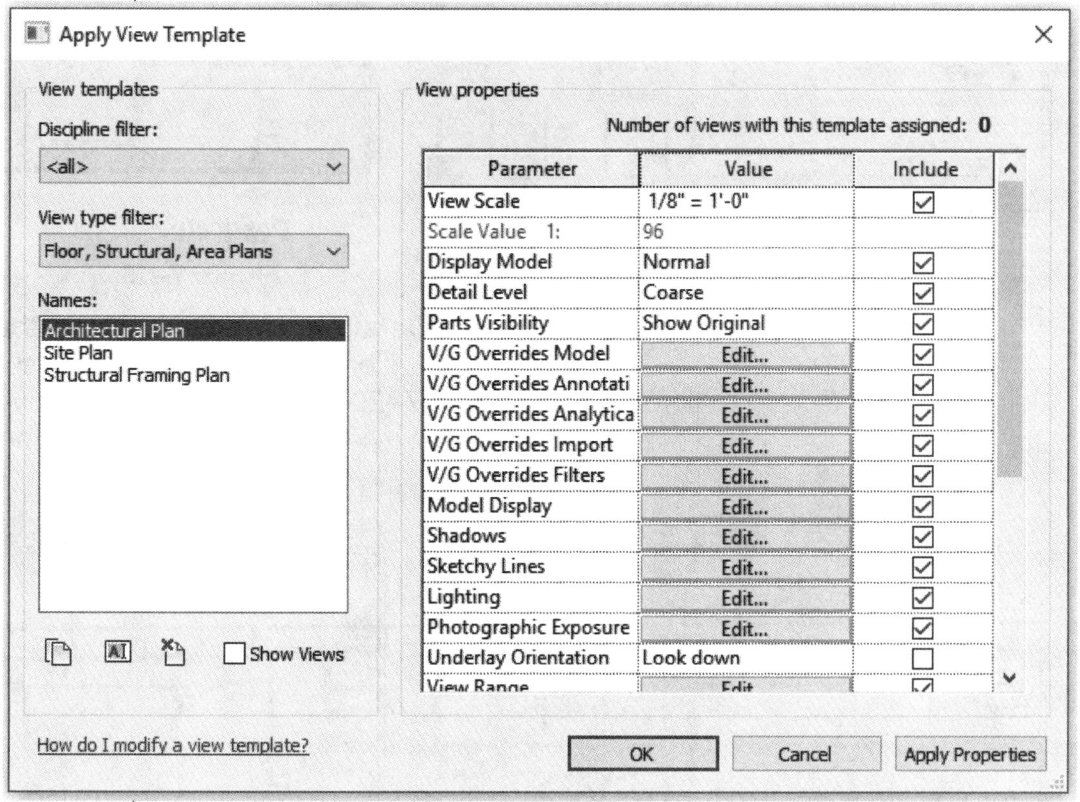

Figure 7–18

4. Click **OK**.

- In the View Control Bar, use  (Temporary View Properties) to temporarily apply a view template to a view.

7.2 Duplicating Views

Once you have created a model, you do not have to recreate the elements at different scales or copy them so that they can be used on more than one sheet. Instead, you can duplicate the required views and modify them to suit your needs.

Duplication Types

Duplicate creates a copy of the view that only includes the building elements, as shown in Figure 7–19. Annotation and detailing are not copied into the new view. Building model elements automatically change in all views, but view-specific changes made to the new view are not reflected in the original view.

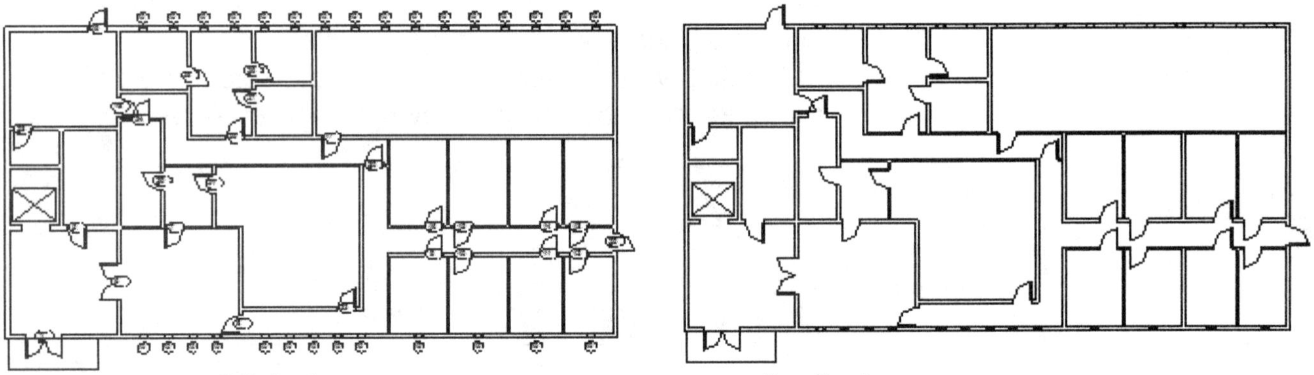

Original *Duplicate*

Figure 7–19

Duplicate with Detailing creates a copy of the view and includes all annotation and detail elements (such as tags), as shown in Figure 7–20. Any annotation or view-specific elements created in the new view are not reflected in the original view.

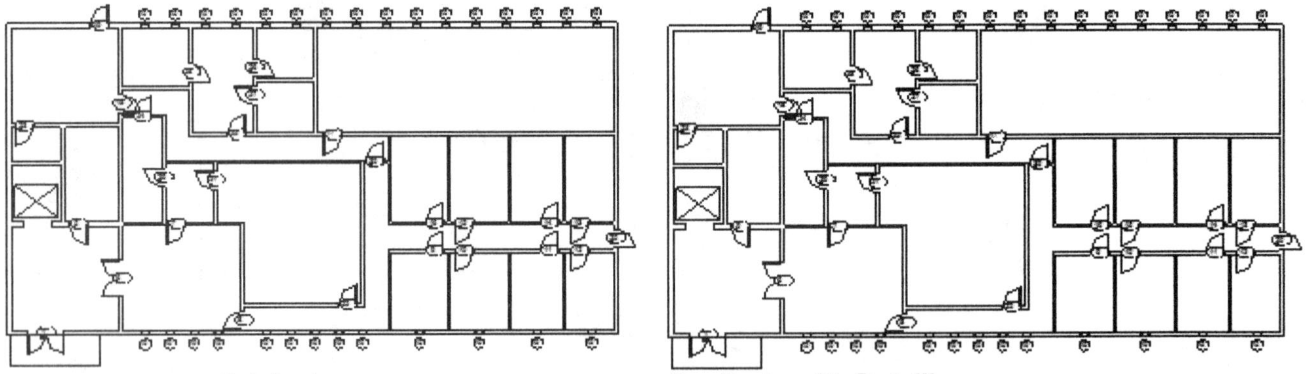

Original *Duplicate with Detailing*

Figure 7–20

Duplicate as a Dependent creates a copy of the view and links it to the original (parent) view, as shown in the Project Browser in Figure 7–21. View-specific changes made to the overall view, such as changing the *Scale*, are also reflected in the dependent (child) views and vice-versa.

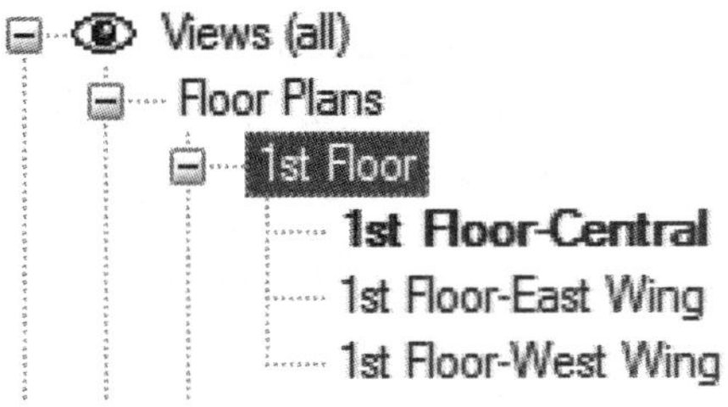

Figure 7–21

- Use dependent views when the building model is so large that you need to split the building onto separate sheets, while ensuring that the views are all same scale.
- If you want to separate a dependent view from the original view, right-click on the dependent view and select **Convert to independent view**.

How To: Create Duplicate Views

1. Open the view you want to duplicate.
2. In the *View* tab>Create panel, expand **Duplicate View** and select the type of duplicate view you want to create, as shown in Figure 7–22.

Most types of views can be duplicated.

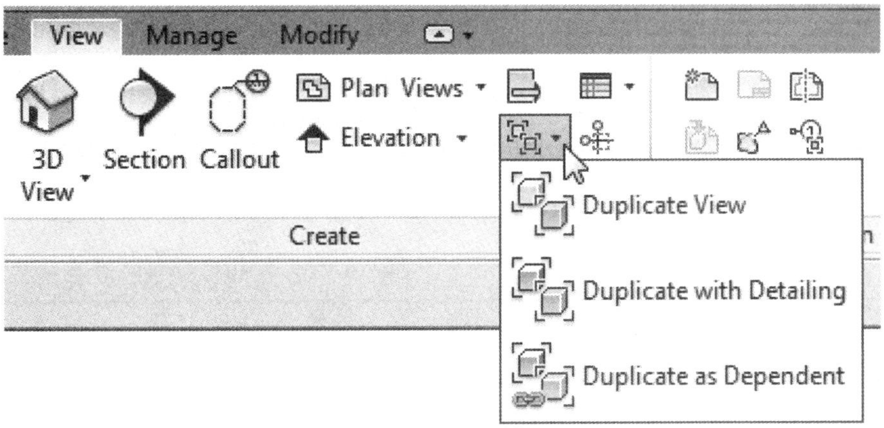

Figure 7–22

- Alternatively, you can right-click on a view in the Project Browser and select the type of duplicate that you want to use, as shown in Figure 7–23.

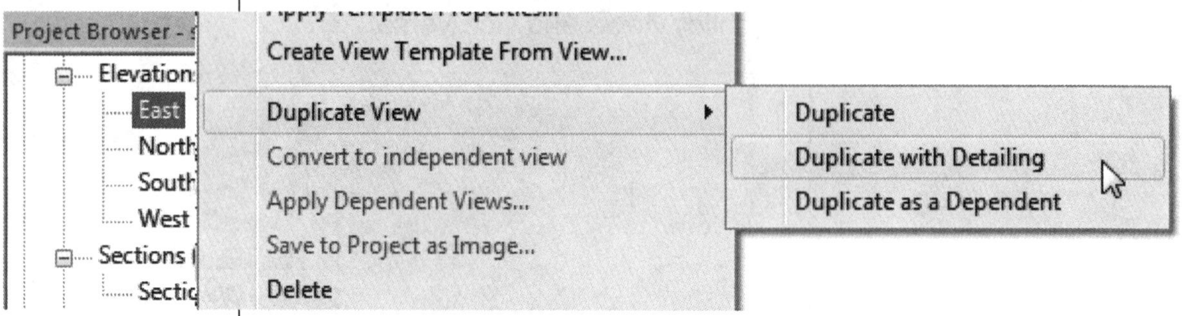

Figure 7–23

- To rename a view, double-click on the view name slowly and the text highlights, as shown in Figure 7–24. You can also right-click on a view name and select **Rename...** or press <F2>.

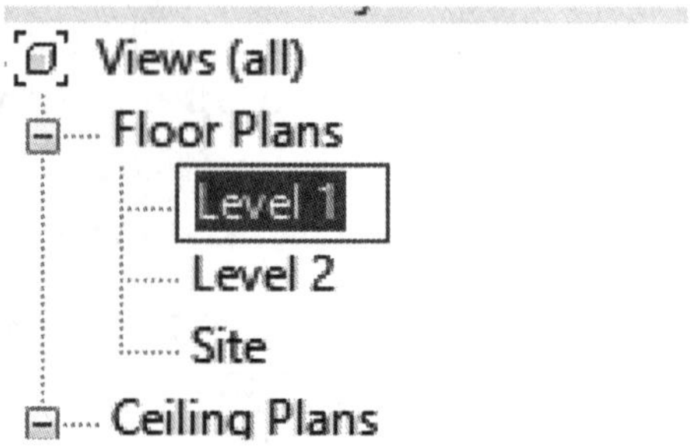

Figure 7–24

Practice 7a

Duplicate Views and Set the View Display

Practice Objectives

- Duplicate and rename views.
- Hide elements in views.
- Modify the graphic display of elements in views.

In this practice, you will duplicate views and then modify them by changing the scale, hiding some elements, and changing other elements to halftone to prepare them to be used in construction documents. The finished views of the second floor are shown in Figure 7–25.

The model used in this practice is that of the completed building.

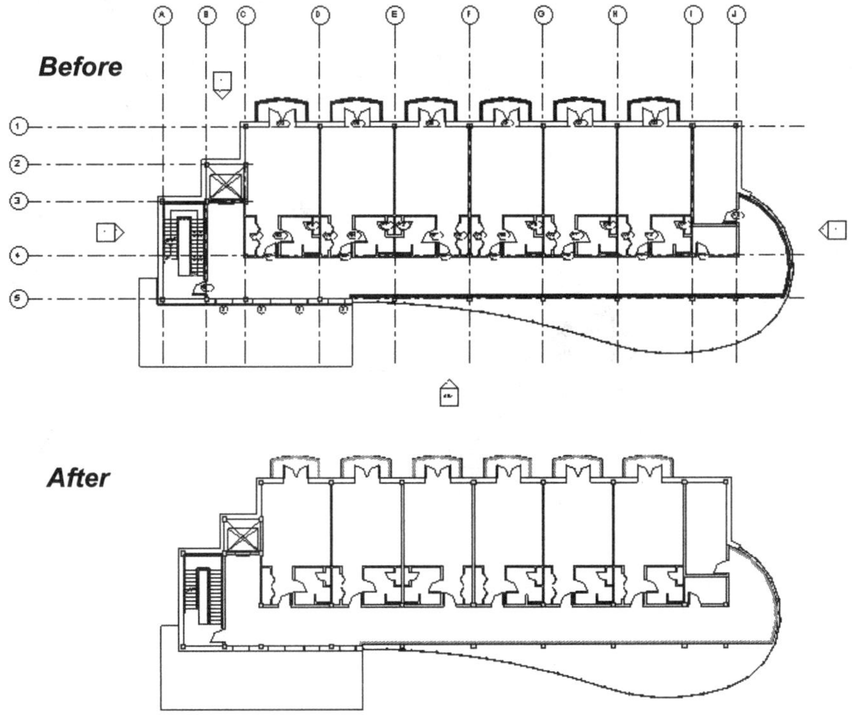

Figure 7–25

Task 1 - Duplicate and modify the first floor plan view.

1. Open the project **Modern-Hotel-Display.rvt**.
2. Close any other projects you may have open.
3. Open the **Floor Plans: Floor 1** view. This view includes a variety of tags.

4. In the Project Browser, right-click on the **Floor Plans: Floor 1** view and select **Duplicate View>Duplicate with Detailing**. This creates a view with all of the tags.

5. In the Project Browser, slowly double-click on the duplicated view name. Rename it **Floor 1 - Reference**. You will use this view later to place callouts and sections.

6. In the Project Browser, right-click on the **Floor Plans: Floor 1** view and select **Duplicate View>Duplicate**. This creates a view without all of the tags, but includes the grids and elevation markers.

7. Rename it to **Floor 1 - Overall**.

8. In the View Control Bar, change the *Scale* to **1/16"=1'-0"**. All of the annotations become larger, as they need to plot correctly at this scale.

9. Type **WT** to tile the 4 open windows and then **ZA** to zoom out to fit all the view in their new windows. Compare the various floor plans as shown in Figure 7–26.

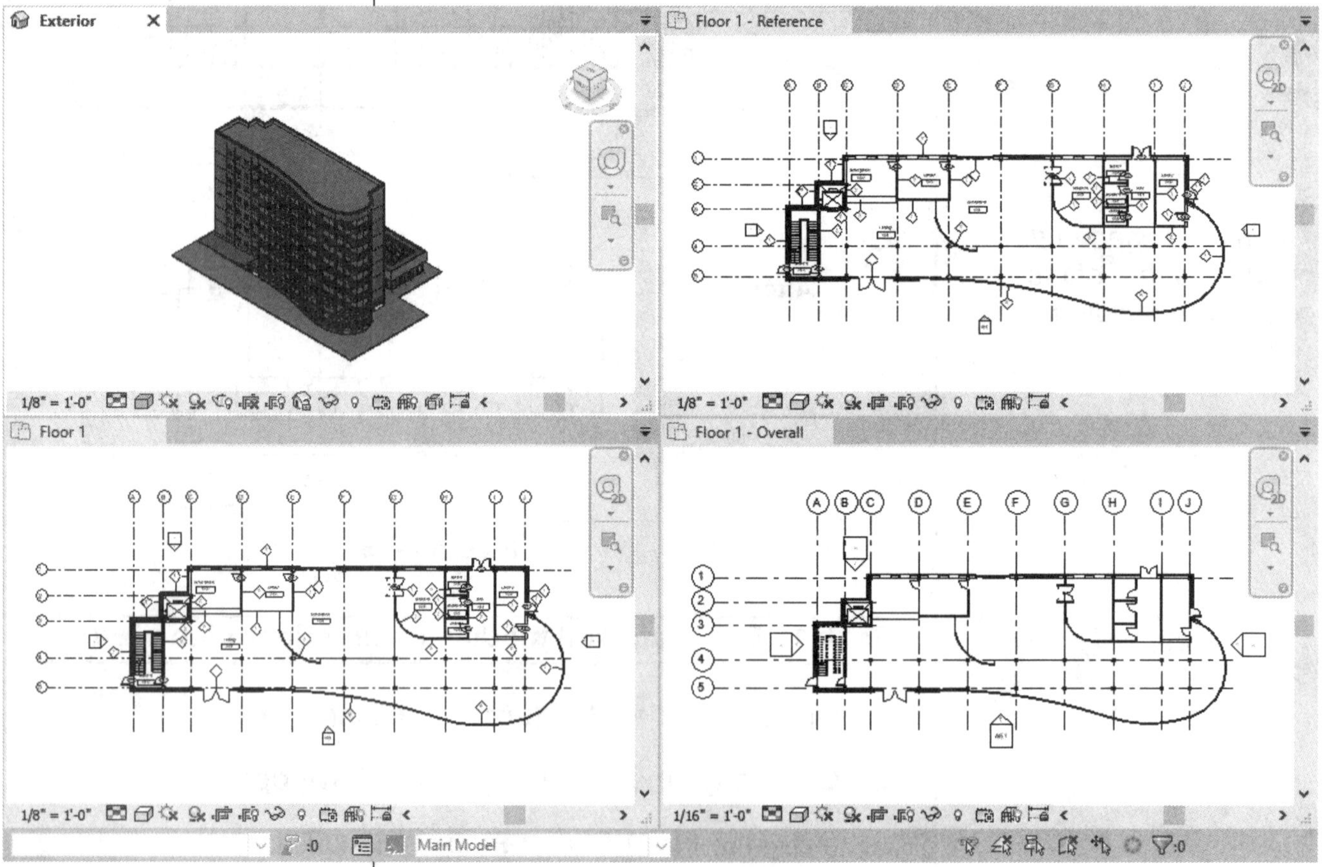

Figure 7–26

10. Save the project.

Task 2 - Duplicate and modify a second floor plan view.

1. Type **TW** to return to the tab views.
2. Click on the X, as shown in Figure 7–27, to close the **Floor 1 - Reference** and **Floor 1 - Overall** views.

Figure 7–27

3. Open the **Floor Plans: Floor 2** view.
4. In the Project Browser, right-click on the same view and select **Duplicate View>Duplicate**. This creates a new view without any annotation.
5. Rename this view to **Typical Guest Room Floor Plan**.
6. Select one of the grids and one of the elevation markers and type **VH** (Hide in View Category).
7. Select one of the railings along the balconies. Right-click and select **Select All Instances>Visible in View**. The railings are selected as shown in Figure 7–28.

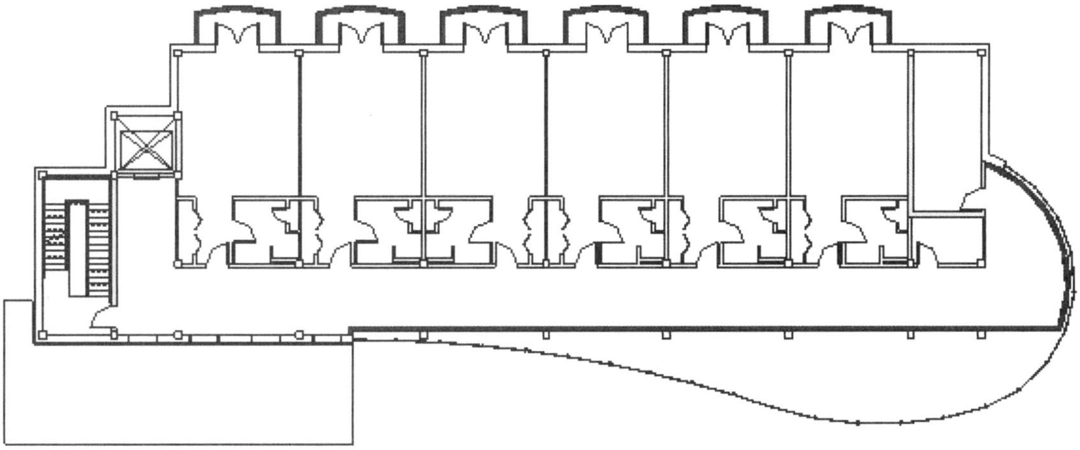

Figure 7–28

8. Right-click again and select **Override Graphics in View > By Element...**.

9. In the View Specific Element Graphics dialog box, select **Halftone** and click **OK**.
10. Click in the view to release the selection. The railings are now gray and not as prominent.
11. Type **WT** to tile the four windows and then type **ZA** so the model displays fully in the view so that you can see the differences in the views.
12. Save the project.

7.3 Adding Callout Views

Callouts are details of plan, elevation, or section views. When you place a callout in a view, as shown in Figure 7–29, it automatically creates a new view clipped to the boundary of the callout, as shown in Figure 7–30. You can create rectangular or sketched callout boundaries.

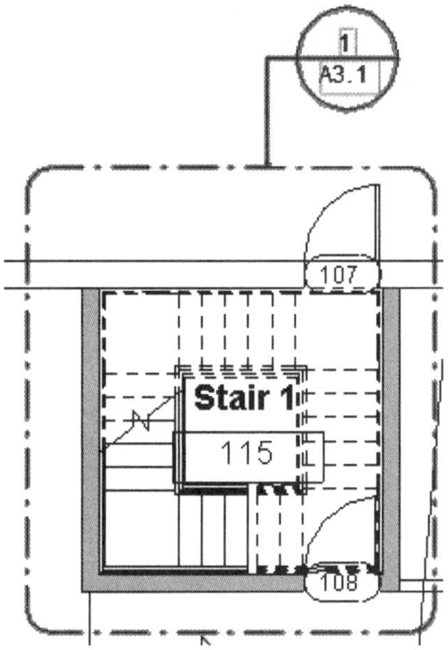

Callout in a view

Figure 7–29

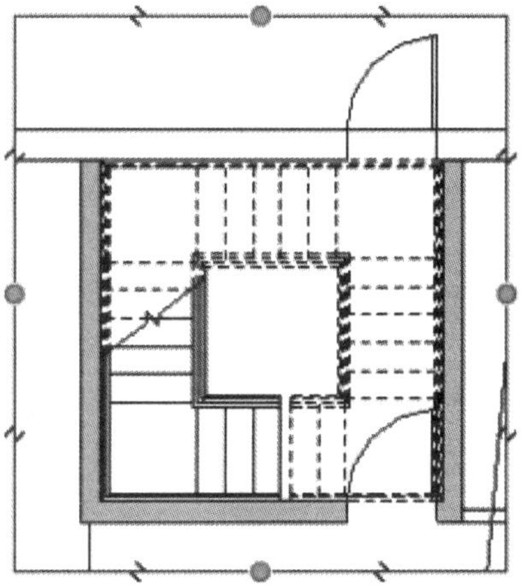

Callout view

Figure 7–30

- Callout views are saved in the same node in the Project Browser as the original view. For example, the callout of a floor plan is placed in the Floor Plans node.

- To open the callout view, double-click on its name in the Project Browser or on the callout bubble (verify that the callout itself is not selected before you double-click on it).

How To: Create a Rectangular Callout

1. In the *View tab>Create panel,* click **(Callout)**.
2. Select points for two opposite corners to define the callout box around the area you want to detail.
3. Select the callout and use the shape handles to modify the location of the bubble and any other edges that might need changing.
4. In the Project Browser, rename the callout.

How To: Create a Sketched Callout

1. In the *View tab>Create panel,* expand (Callout), and click (Sketch).
2. Sketch the shape of the callout using the tools in the *Modify | Edit Profile* tab>Draw panel, as shown in Figure 7–31.

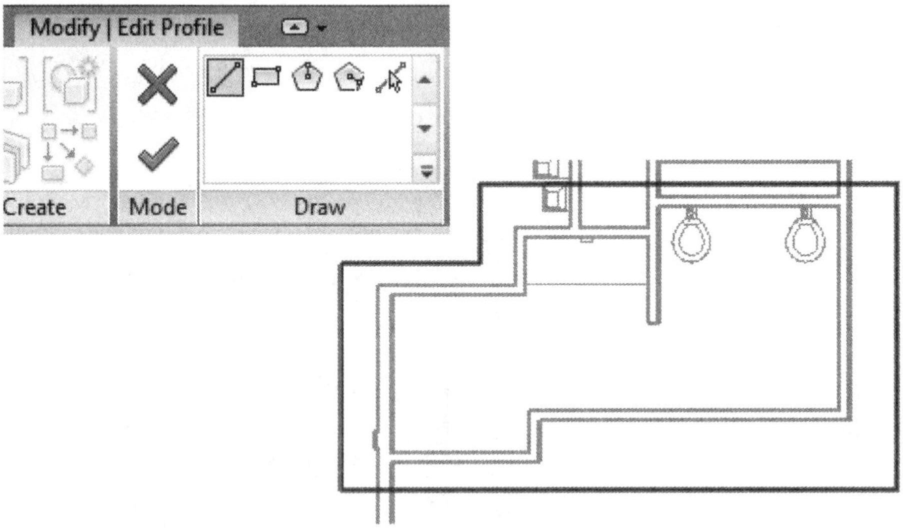

Figure 7–31

3. Click (Finish) to complete the boundary.
4. Select the callout and use the shape handles to modify the location of the bubble and any other edges that might need to be changed.
5. In the Project Browser, rename the callout.

Modifying Callouts

Callouts are cropped versions of the original view. When you modify them you are changing the Crop Region of the view.

- If you change the size of the callout box in the original view, it automatically updates the callout view and vice-versa.
- Callouts can be reshaped. Select the callout box or crop region and, in the *Modify | Floor Plan* tab>Mode panel, click (Edit Crop) and use the Draw tools to modify the sketch.
- If you want to return a sketched or modified callout or crop region to a rectangular configuration, click (Reset Crop).

Working with Crop Regions

Plans, sections, elevations, and 3D views can all be modified by changing how much of the model is displayed in a view. One way to do this is to set the Crop Region. If there are dimensions, tags, or text near the required crop region, you can also use the Annotation Crop Region to include these, as shown in Figure 7–32.

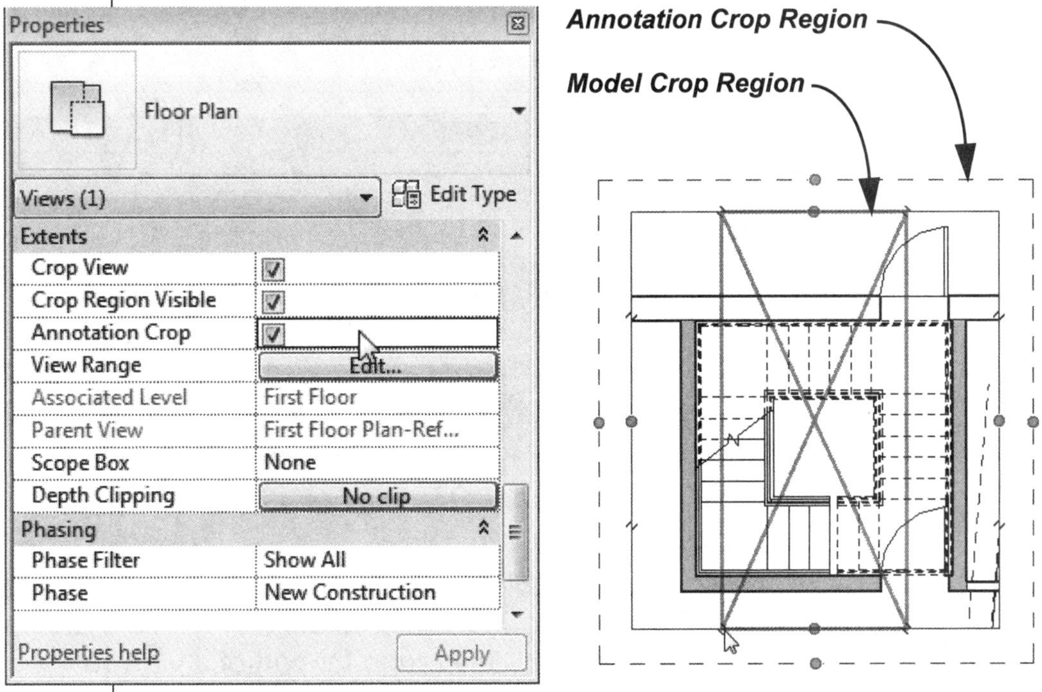

Figure 7–32

Zoom out if you do not see the crop region when you set it to be displayed.

- To display the crop region, in the View Control Bar, click (Show Crop Region). Alternatively, in Properties, in the *Extents* area, select **Crop Region Visible**. **Annotation Crop** is also available in this area.
- It is best practice to hide a crop region before placing a view on a sheet. In the View Control Bar, click (Hide Crop Region).
- Resize the crop region using the control on each side of the region.
- Click (Break Line) control to split the view into two regions, horizontally or vertically. Each part of the view can then be modified in size to display what is required and be moved independently.

Breaking the crop region is typically used with sections or details.

- You can also resize the crop region and the annotation crop region using the Crop Region Size dialog box, as shown in Figure 7–33. In the *Modify | Floor Plan* tab>Crop panel, click (Size Crop) to open the dialog box.

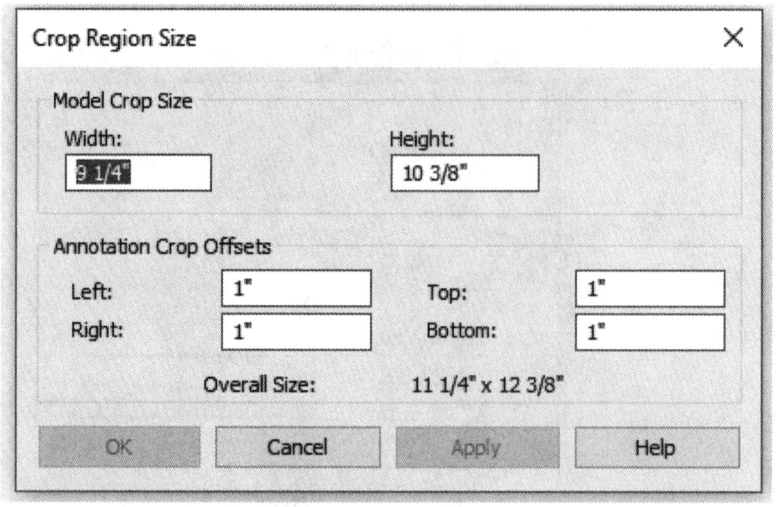

Figure 7–33

Plan Regions

When you have a plan view with multiple levels of floors or ceilings, you can create plan regions that enable you to set a different view range for part of a view (as shown in Figure 7–34) for a set of clerestory windows.

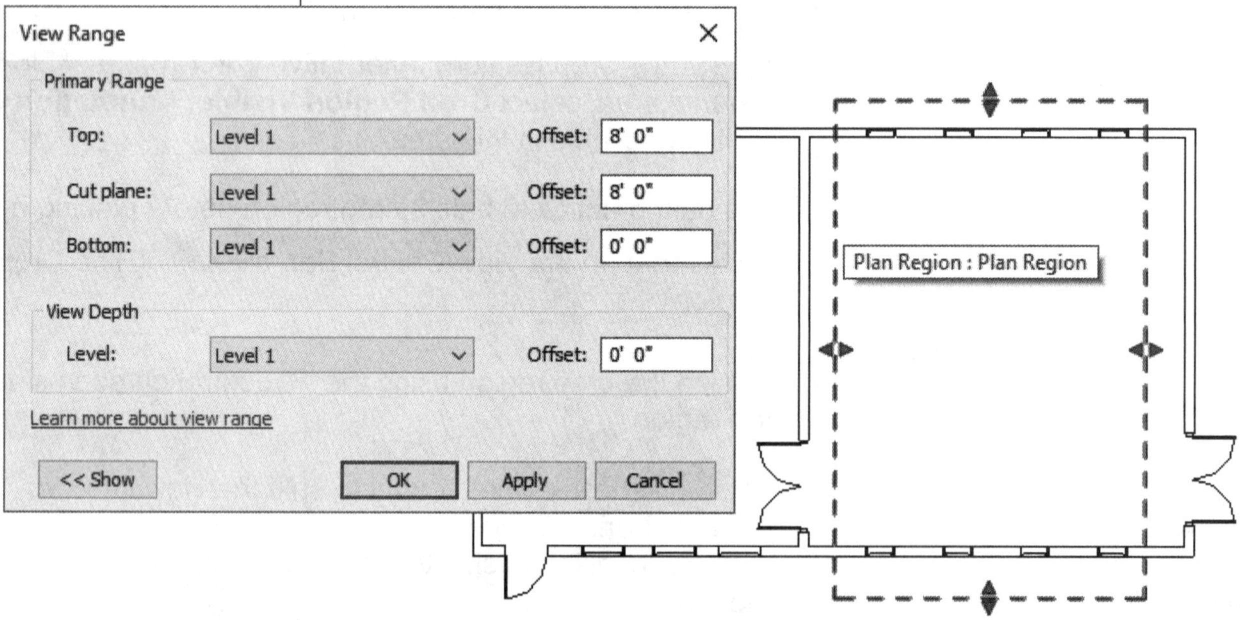

Figure 7–34

How To: Create Plan Regions

1. In a plan view, in the *View* tab>Create panel, expand (Plan Views) and select (Plan Region).
2. In the *Modify | Create Plan Region Boundary* tab>Draw panel, select a draw tool and create the boundary for the plan region.
   - The boundary must be closed and cannot overlap other plan region boundaries, but the boundaries can be side by side.
3. Click (Finish Edit Mode).
4. In the *Modify | Plan Region t*ab>Region panel, click (View Range).
5. In the View Range dialog box, specify the offsets for the plan region and click **OK**. The plan region is applied to the selected area.

- Plan regions can be copied to the clipboard and then pasted into other plan views.
- You can use shape handles to resize plan region boundaries without having to edit the boundary.
- If a plan region is above a door, the door swing displays, but the door opening does not display, as shown in Figure 7–35.

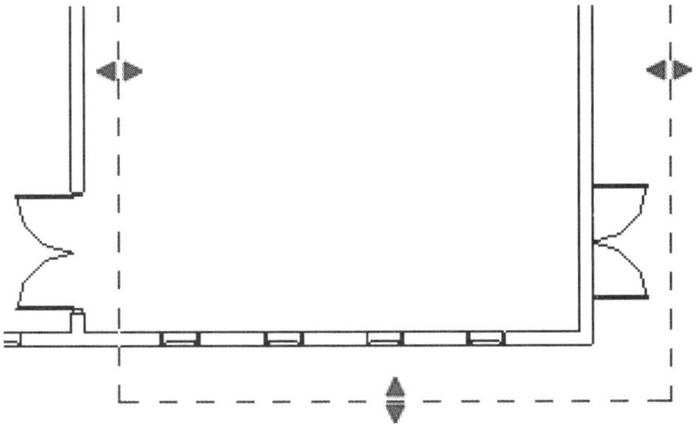

Figure 7–35

- Plan Regions can be toggled on and off in the Visibility/ Graphic Overrides dialog box on the *Annotation Categories* tab. If they are displayed, the plan regions are included when printing and exporting.

Hint: Depth Clipping and Far Clipping

Depth Clipping, shown in Figure 7–36, is a viewing option which sets how sloped walls are displayed if the *View Range* of a plan is set to a limited view.

Far Clipping (shown in Figure 7–37) is available for section and elevation views.

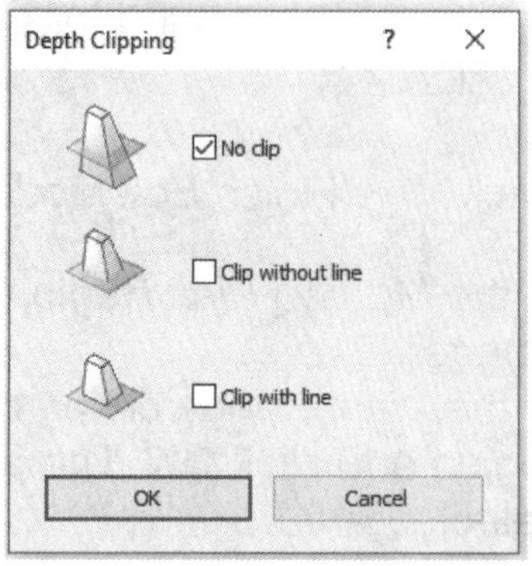

Figure 7–36

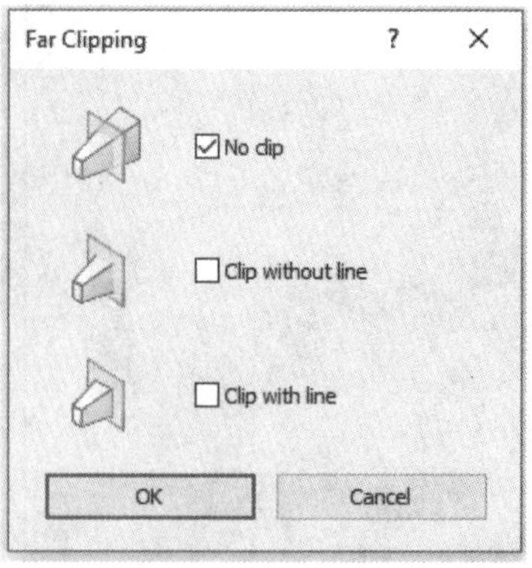

Figure 7–37

- An additional Graphic Display Option enables you to specify *Depth Cueing*, so that items that are in the distance will be made lighter.

Practice 7b Add Callout Views

Practice Objective

- Modify crop regions.
- Create callouts.
- Override visibility and graphic styles in views.

In this practice, you will create callout views of a guest room and make modifications to the visibility graphics so that one does not display the furniture and the other one does, as shown in Figure 7–38. You will also add callout views for other areas that need enlarged plans.

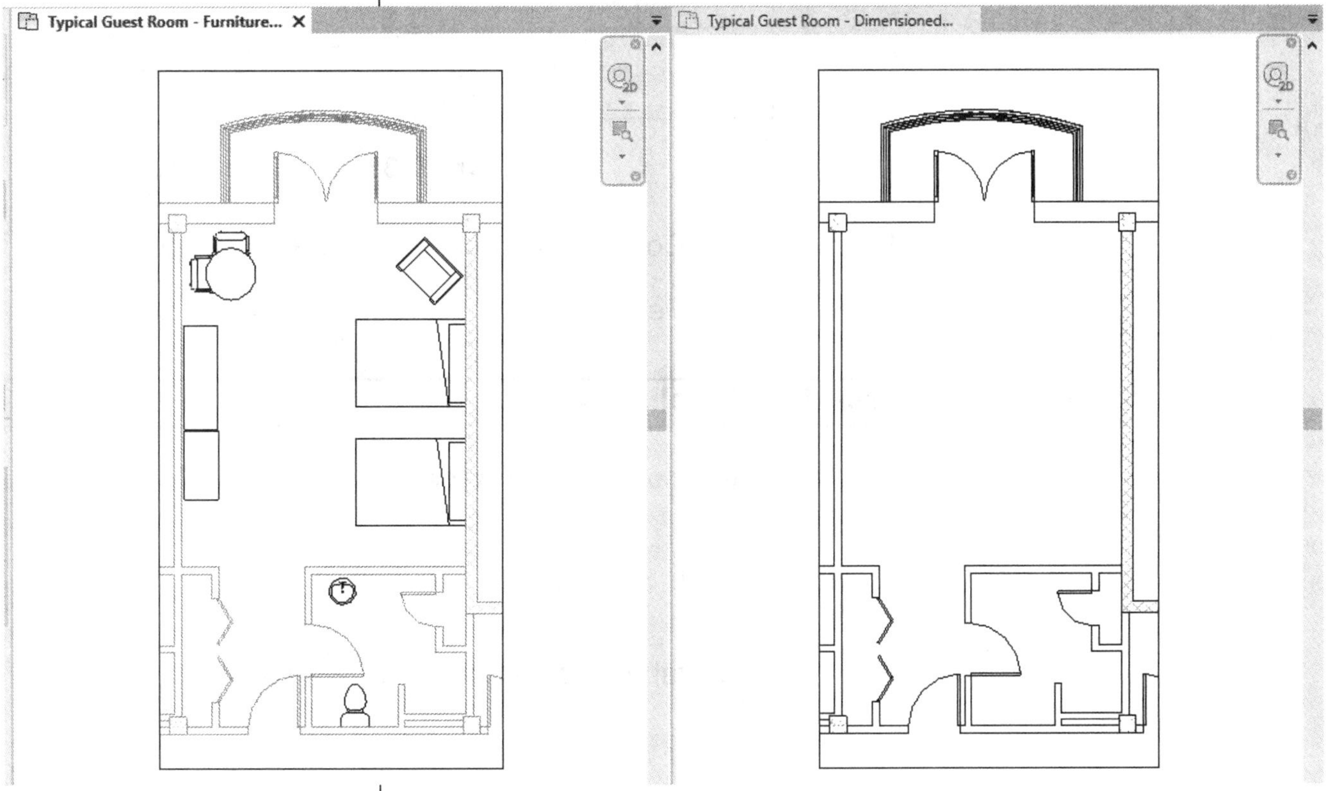

Figure 7–38

Task 1 - Modify the Crop Region of a View.

1. Open the project **Modern-Hotel-Callouts.rvt**.
1. Open the **Floor Plans: Floor 1 - Overall** view.
2. In the View Control Bar, click (Show Crop Region).
3. Select the crop region and drag the control on the top until the pool house displays, as shown in Figure 7–39.

4. Select one of the vertical grid lines and drag them so they are above the poolhouse, as shown in Figure 7–39.

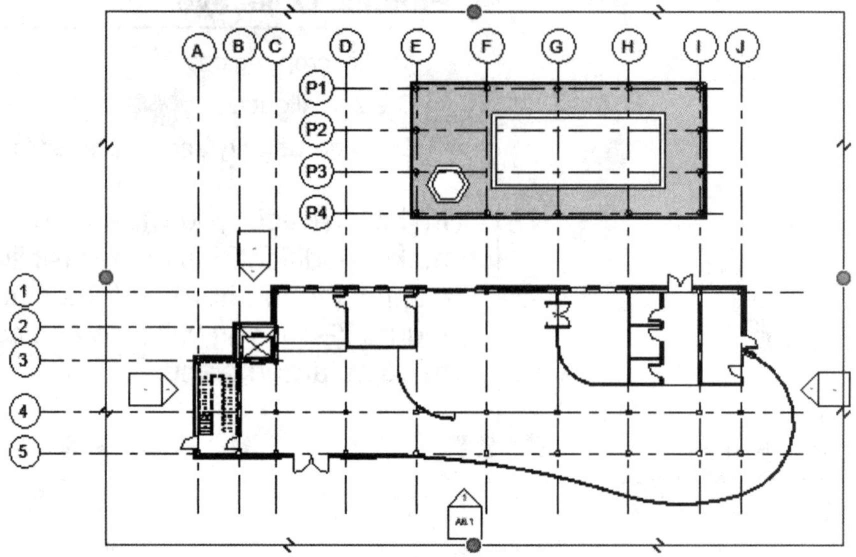

Figure 7–39

5. In the View Control Bar, click (Hide Crop Region).
6. Save the project.

Task 2 - Add callout views.

---

1. Open the **Floor Plans: Typical Guest Room Floor Plan** view.
2. Note that the *Scale* is set to **1/8" =1'-0"**.
3. In the *View* tab>Create panel, click (Callout).

4. Place a callout around the guest room with furniture, as shown in Figure 7–40. Move the bubble as required.

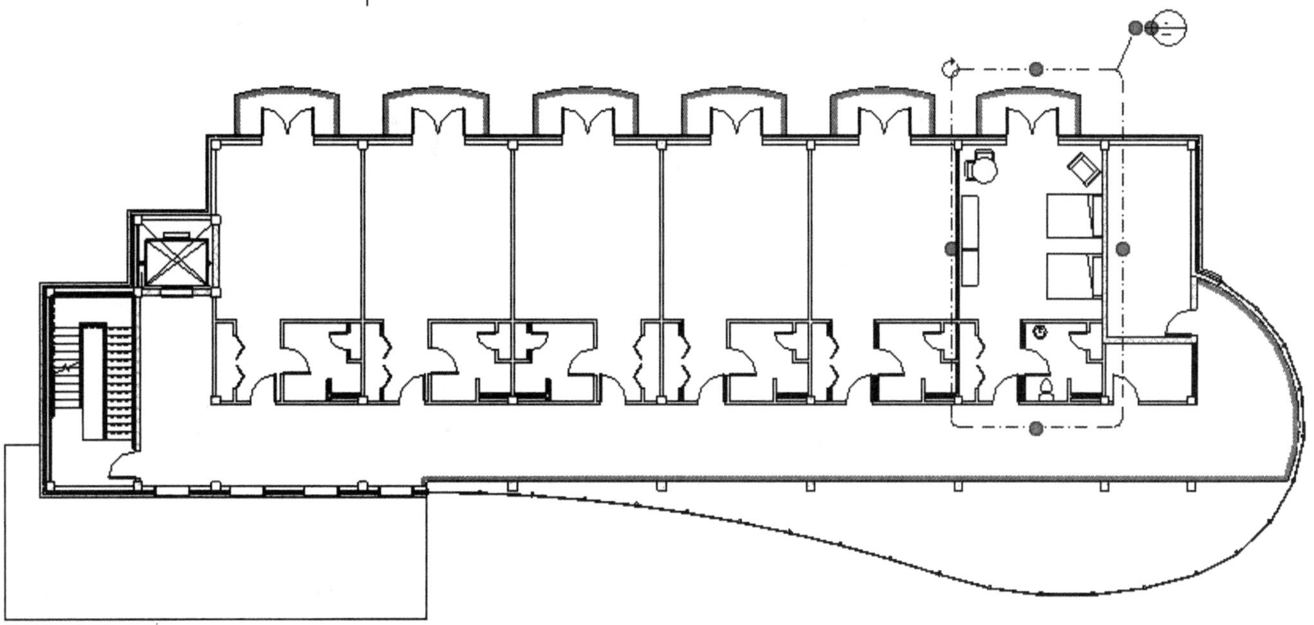

Figure 7–40

5. Click in empty space to release the selection.

6. Double-click on the callout view bubble to display the view. Note that the *Scale* is automatically set to **1/4"= 1'-0"**, as it is a partial plan view.

7. Rename the view to **Typical Guest Room - Dimension Plan**.

8. Duplicate the callout view and rename it to **Typical Guest Room - Furniture Plan**.

9. Close all other views except the Dimension and Furniture Plans.

10. Type **WT** to tile the windows and **ZA** to zoom out in both of them, as shown in Figure 7–41.

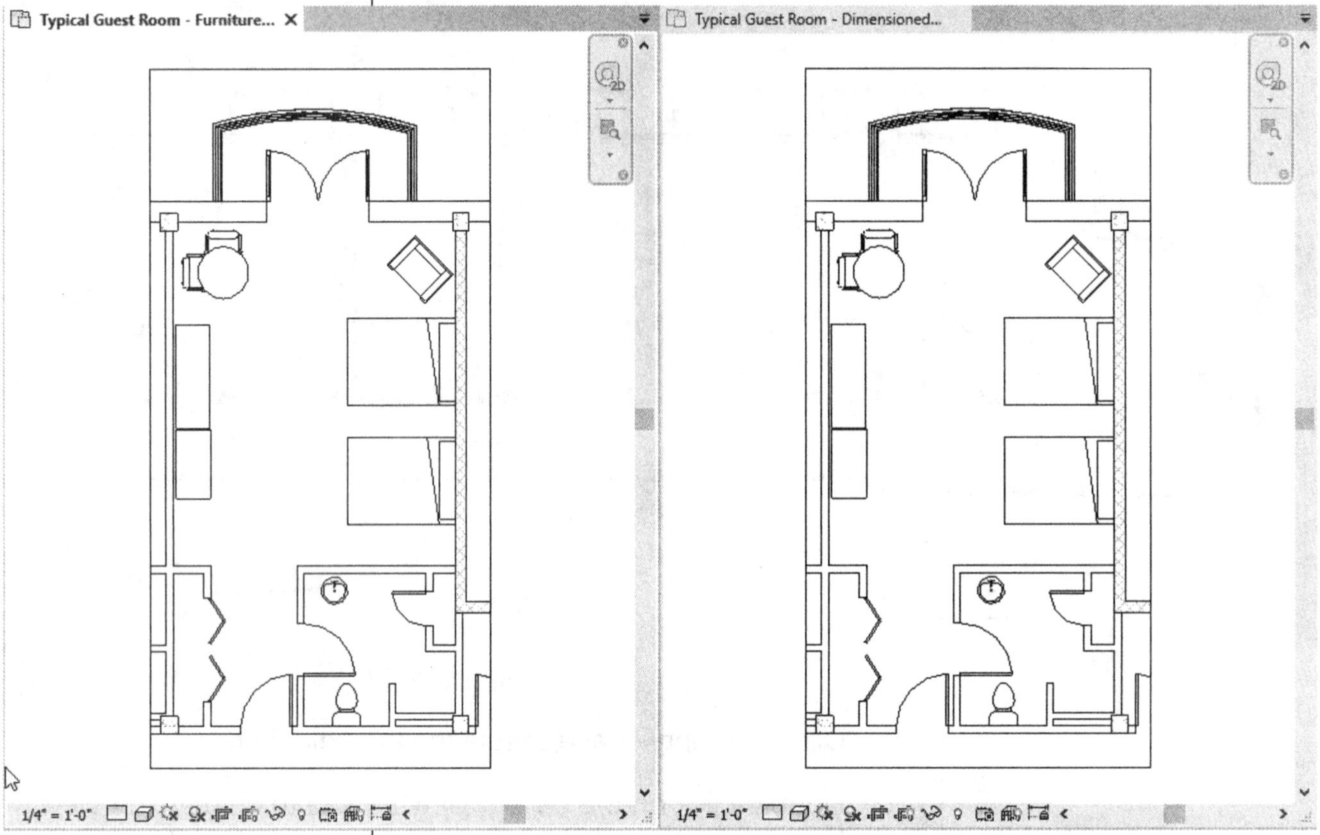

Figure 7–41

11. Save the project.

Task 3 - Override graphics in views.

1. Click in the **Floor Plans: Typical Guest Room - Dimension Plan** view.
2. Open the Visibility/Graphic Overrides dialog box by typing **VV**.

3. In the dialog box, set the *Filter list* to **Architecture** (by clearing the checkmarks for the other options). In the *Visibility* column, clear **Casework**, **Furniture**, **Furniture Systems** (as shown in Figure 7–42) and **Plumbing Fixtures** (not shown).

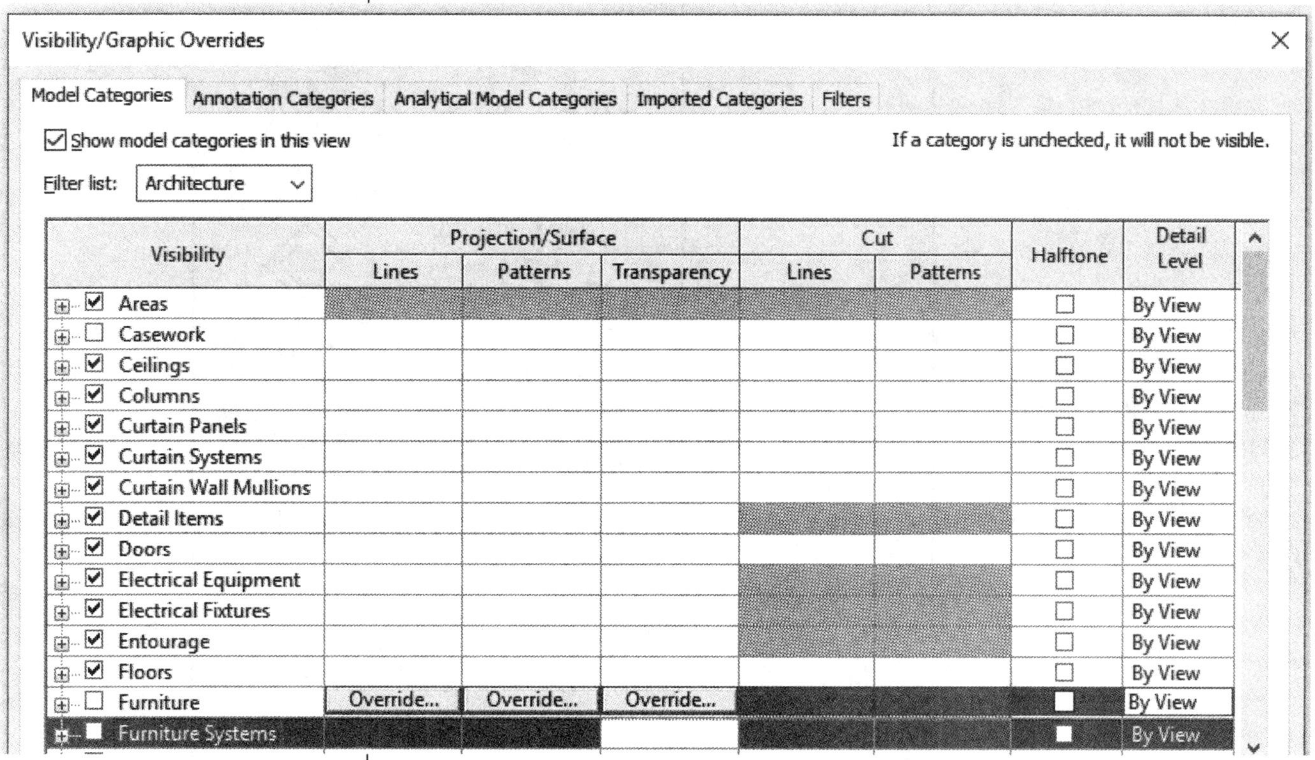

Figure 7–42

4. Click **OK**. The furniture is removed from the view.
5. Click in the **Floor Plans: Typical Guest Room - Furniture Plan** view.
6. Reopen the Visibility/Graphic Overrides dialog box. Below the table, click **All** and place a checkmark in one of the *Halftone* columns. All of the elements are set to halftone.
7. Click **None** to clear all categories.
8. In the *Halftone* column, clear the **Casework**, **Furniture**, **Furniture Systems**, and **Plumbing Fixtures** categories.
9. Click **Apply** to set the changes without exiting the dialog box.
10. In the *Annotation Categories* tab, clear **Show annotation categories in this view**. No annotations elements will display in this view even if they are added in other views of this part of the model.

11. Click **OK** to close the dialog box. The view should display with all existing elements in halftone, as shown in Figure 7–43.

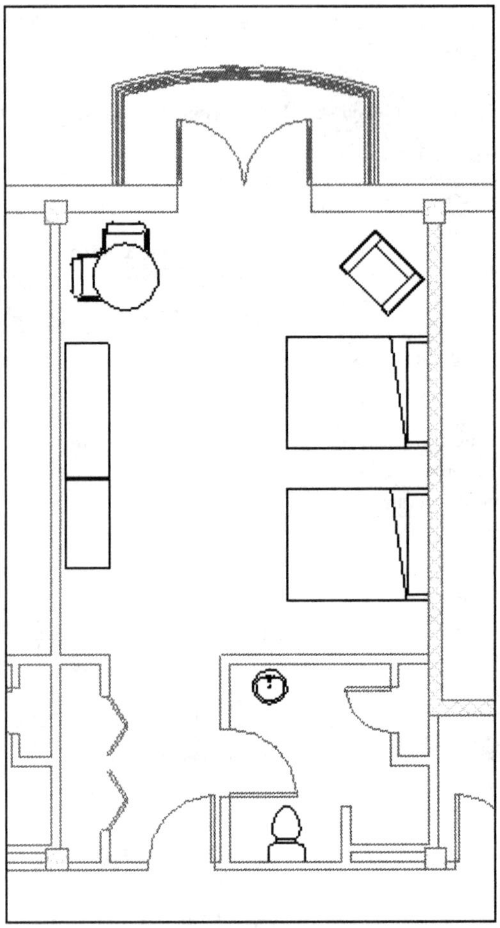

Figure 7–43

12. Save the project.

Task 4 - Additional Callouts

1. Open the **Floor Plans: Floor 1 - Reference** view.

2. In the *View* tab>Create panel, click (Callout) and add callouts to the stairs and restrooms. Name the views as shown in Figure 7–44.

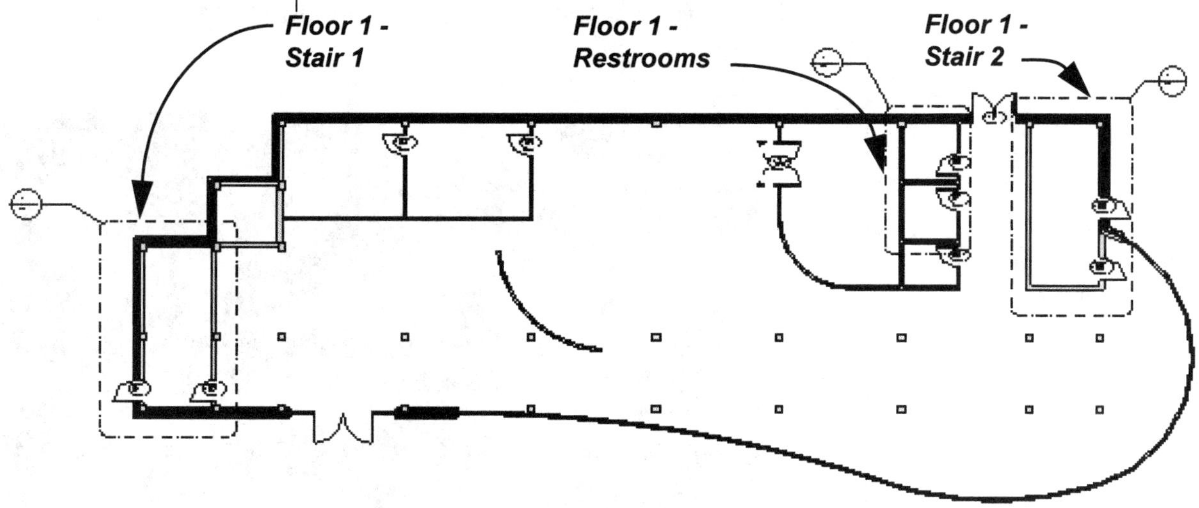

Figure 7–44

- The view has been simplified for clarity.

3. Save the project.

7.4 Creating Elevations and Sections

Elevations and sections are critical elements of construction documents and can assist you as you are working on a model. Any changes made in one of these views (such as the section in Figure 7–45), changes the entire model and any changes made to the project model are also displayed in the elevations and sections.

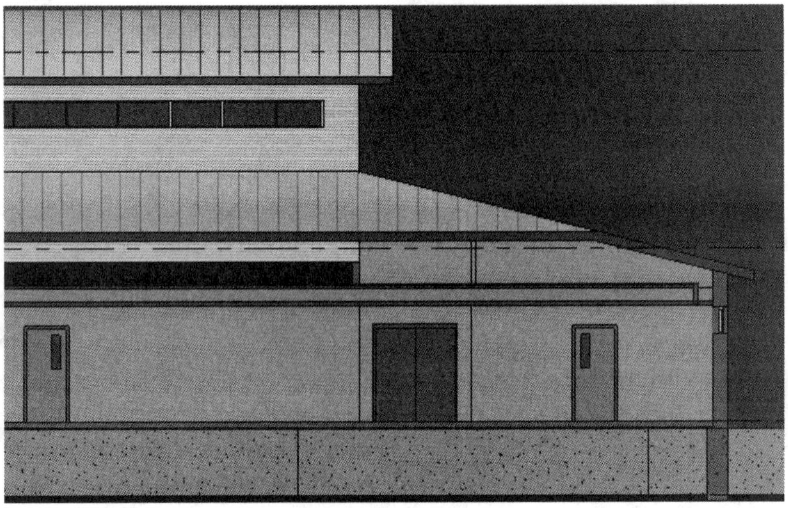

Figure 7–45

- In the Project Browser, elevations are separated by elevation type and sections are separated by section type, as shown in Figure 7–46.

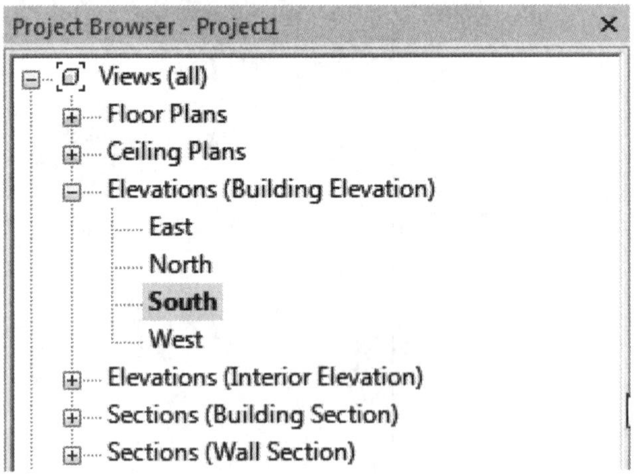

Figure 7–46

- To open an elevation or section view, double-click on the marker arrow or on its name in the Project Browser.

- To give the elevation or section a new name, in the Project Browser, slowly double-click on the name or right-click on it and select **Rename...**.

Elevations

Elevations are *face-on* views of the interiors and exteriors of a building. Four Exterior Elevation views are defined in the default template: **North**, **South**, **East**, and **West**. You can create additional building elevation views at other angles or interior elevation views, as shown in Figure 7–47.

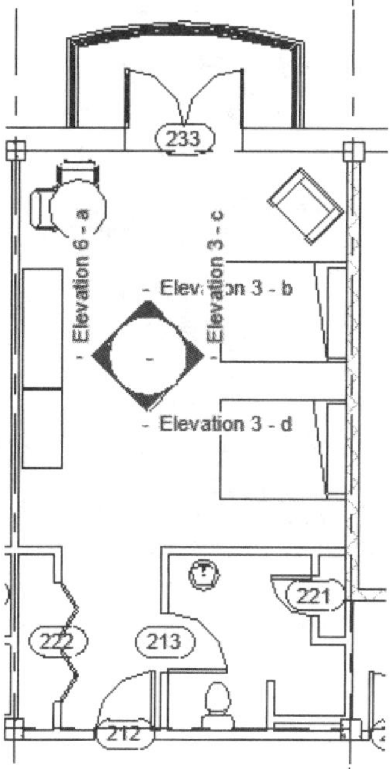

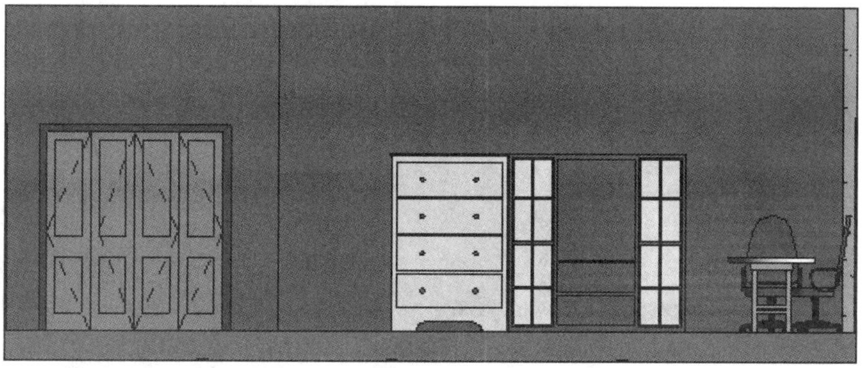

Figure 7–47

- Elevations must be created in plan views.
- When you add an elevation or section to a sheet, the detail and sheet number are automatically added to the view title.

How To: Create an Elevation

The software remembers the last elevation type used, so you can click the top button if you want to use the same elevation command.

1. In the *View* tab>Create panel, expand (Elevation) and click (Elevation).
2. In the Type Selector, select the elevation type. Two types come with the templates: **Building Elevation** and **Interior Elevation**.
3. Move the cursor near one of the walls that defines the elevation. The marker follows the angle of the wall.
4. Click to place the marker.

- The length, width, and height of an elevation are defined by the walls and ceiling/floor at which the elevation marker is pointing.
- When creating interior elevations, ensure that the floor or ceiling above is in place before creating the elevation or you will need to modify the elevation crop region so that the elevation markers do not show on all floors.

Sections

Sections are slices through a model. You can create a section through an entire building, as shown in Figure 7–48, or through one wall for a detail.Sections can be created in plan, elevation, and other section views.

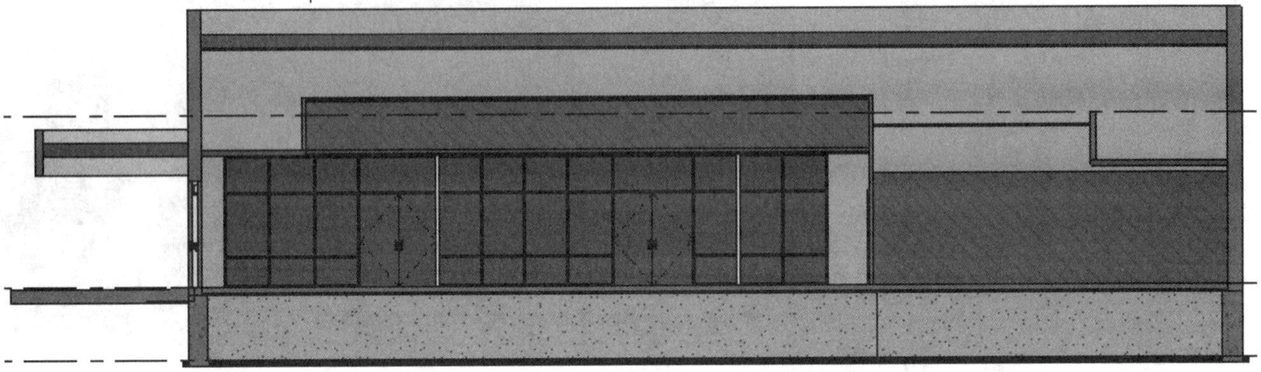

Figure 7–48

How To: Create a Section

1. In the *View* tab>Create panel or in the Quick Access Toolbar, click (Section).
2. In the Type Selector, select **Section: Building Section** or **Section: Wall Section.** If you want a section in a Drafting view select **Detail View: Detail.**
3. In the view, select a point where you want to locate the bubble and arrowhead.
4. Select the other end point that describes the section.
5. The shape controls display. You can flip the arrow and change the size of the cutting plane, as well as the location of the bubble and flag.

- When placing a section you can snap to other elements in the model as the start and end points of the section line. You can also use the Align command to reorient a section line to an element such as an angled wall.

- Section lines can also be used as an alignment object and can be snapped to when placing other geometry.

Modifying Elevations and Sections

There are two parts to modifying elevations and sections:

- To modify the markers (as shown in Figure 7–49), use the controls to change the length and depth of elevations and sections. There are other specific type options as well.
- To modify the view (as shown in Figure 7–50), use the controls to modify the size or create view breaks.

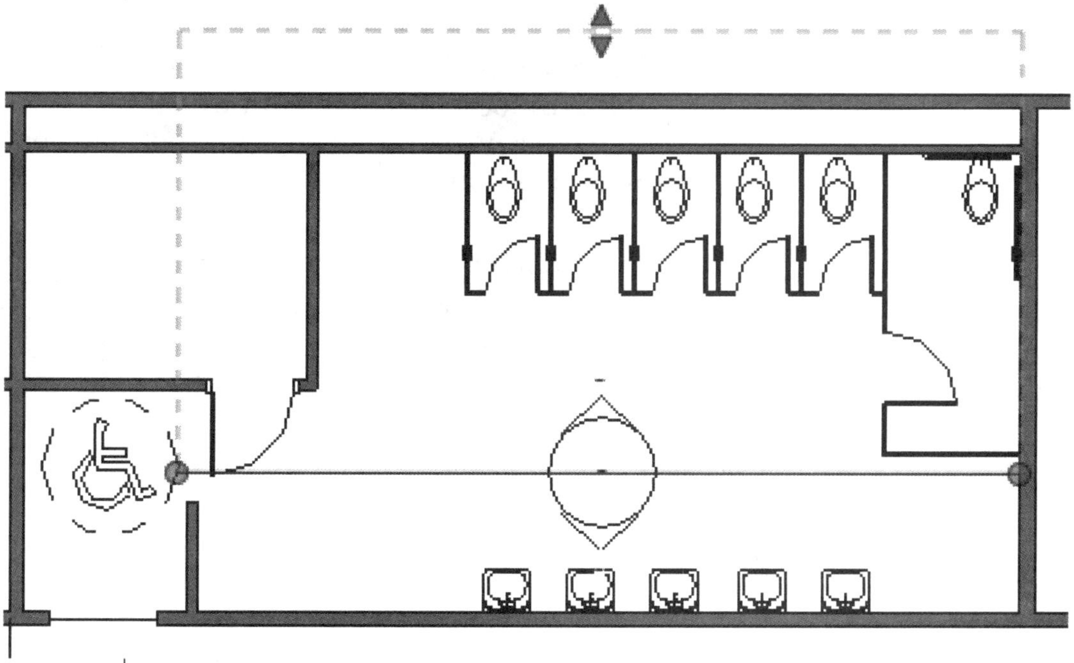

Figure 7–49

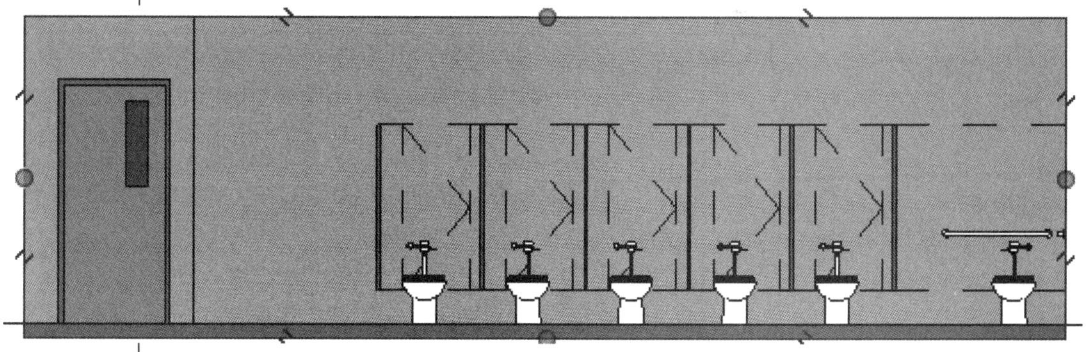

Figure 7–50

Modifying Elevation Markers

When you modify elevation markers, you can specify the length and depth of the clip plane, as shown in Figure 7–51.

- Select the arrowhead of the elevation marker (not the circle portion) to display the clip plane.
- Drag the round shape handles to lengthen or shorten the elevation.
- Adjust the (Drag) controls to modify the depth of the elevation.

To display additional interior elevations from one marker, select the circle portion (not the arrowhead) and place a checkmark in the Show Arrow box in the directions that you want to display, as shown in Figure 7–51.

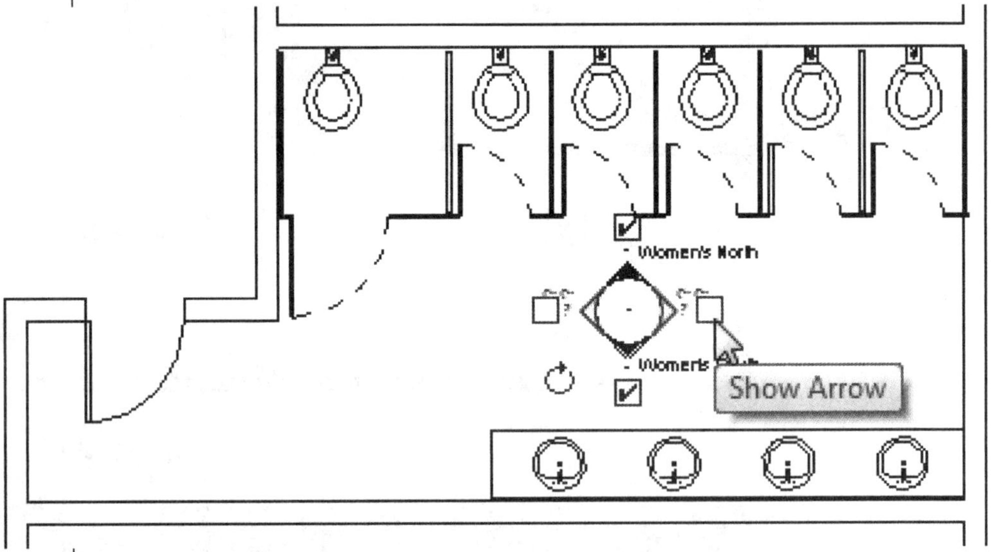

Figure 7–51

- Use the (Rotate) control to angle the marker (i.e., for a room with angled walls).

Modifying Section Markers

When you modify section markers, various shape handles and controls enable you to modify a section, as shown in Figure 7–52.

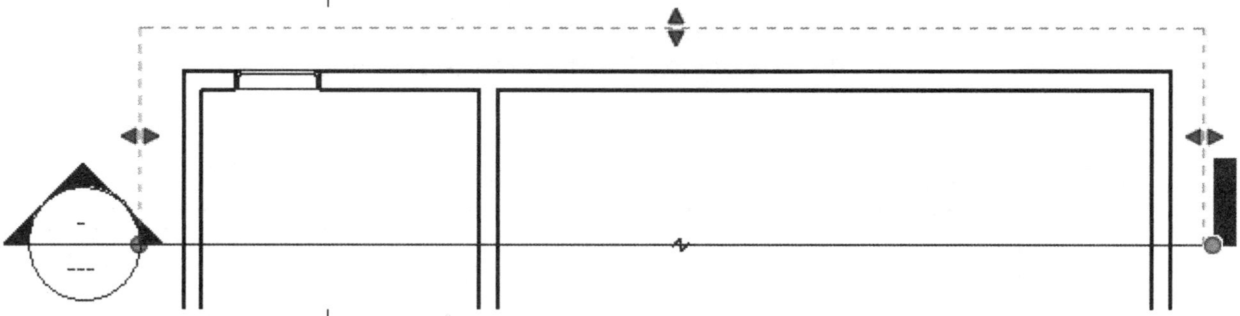

Figure 7–52

- Adjust the (Drag) controls to change the length and depth of the cut plane.
- Drag the circular controls at either end of the section line to change the location of the arrow or flag without changing the cut boundary.
- Click (Flip Section) to change the direction of the arrowhead, which also flips the entire section.
- Click (Cycle Section Head/Tail) to switch between an arrowhead, flag, or nothing on each end of the section.
- Click (Gaps in Segments) to create an opening in section lines, as shown in Figure 7–53. Select it again to restore the full section cut.

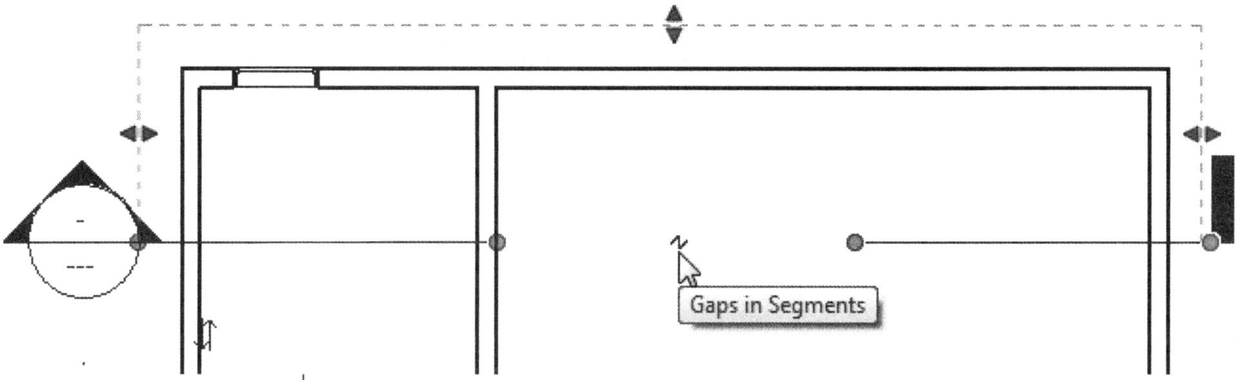

Figure 7–53

How To: Add a Jog to a Section Line

1. Select the section line you want to modify.
2. In the *Modify | Views* tab> Section panel, click (Split Segment).
3. Select the point along the line where you want to create the split, as shown in Figure 7–54.
4. Specify the location of the split line, as shown in Figure 7–55.

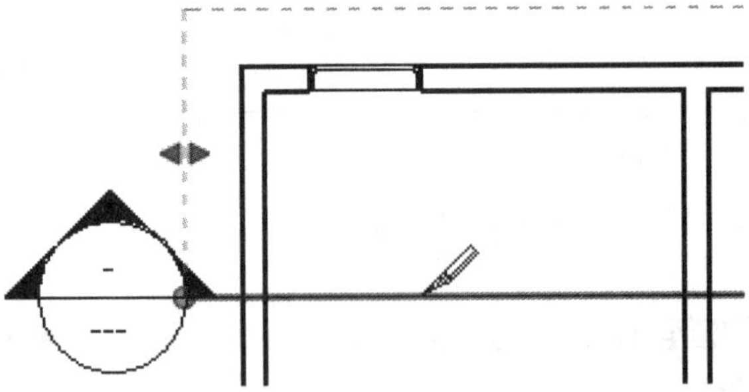

Figure 7–54

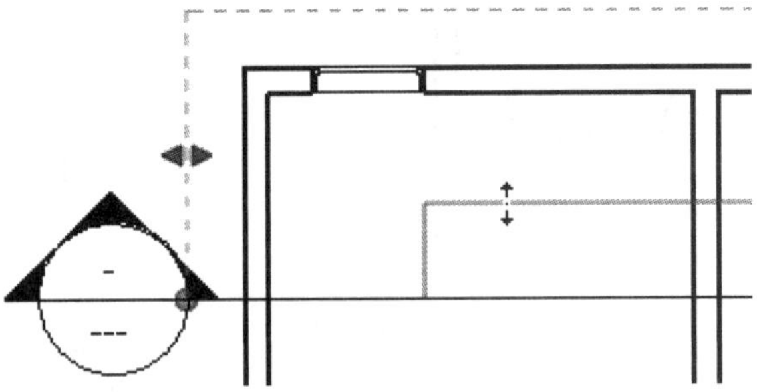

Figure 7–55

- If you need to adjust the location of any segment on the section line, modify it and drag the shape handles along each segment of the line, as shown in Figure 7–56.

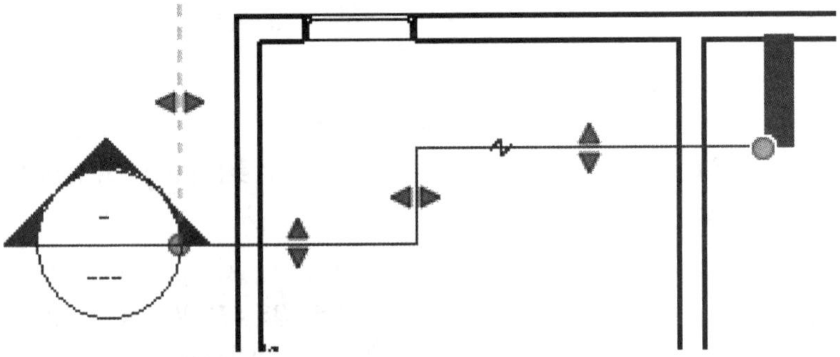

Figure 7–56

To bring a split section line back into place, use a shape handle to drag the jogged line until it is at the same level with the rest of the line.

- For more information on enhancing views such as sections and elevation, see *Appendix B.5 Enhancing Views*.

3D Section Views

There are two ways you can create section views of your 3D model: Creating a Selection Box, as shown in Figure 7–57, and Orienting to a view. Both of these are very helpful as you are working and also can be used in construction documents and presentations.

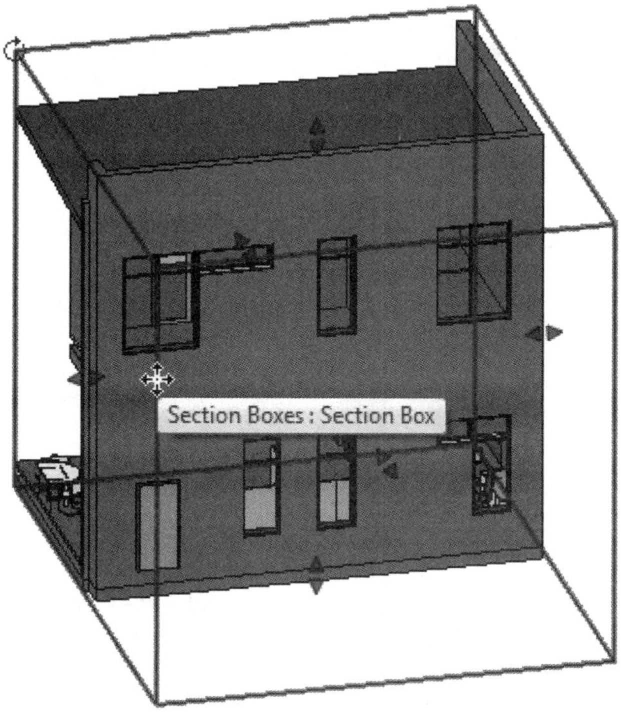

Figure 7–57

How To: Create a Selection Box

1. In a 3D view, select the elements you want to isolate. In the example shown in Figure 7–57, the front wall was selected.
2. In the *Modify* tab>View panel, click (Selection Box) or type **BX**.
3. The view is limited to a box around the selected item(s).
4. Use the controls of the Section Box to modify the size of the box to show exactly what you want.

- To toggle off a section box and restore the full model, in the view's Properties, in the *Extents* area, clear the check from **Section Box**.

How To: Orient a 3D View to a View

1. Open a 3D view.
2. Right-click on the ViewCube and select **Orient to View>Floor Plans, Elevations, Sections,** or **3D Views**, as shown in Figure 7–58, and select the view from the list.

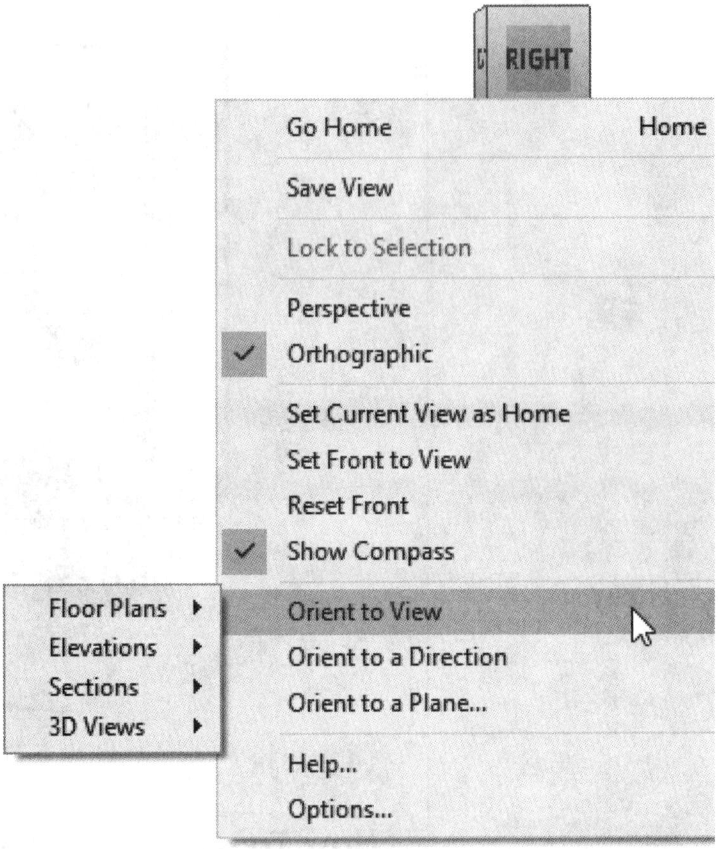

Figure 7–58

3. The view displays as shown, in the partial floor plan view of a stair, in Figure 7–59. Use the 3D view rotation tools to navigate around the 3D model, as shown in Figure 7–60.

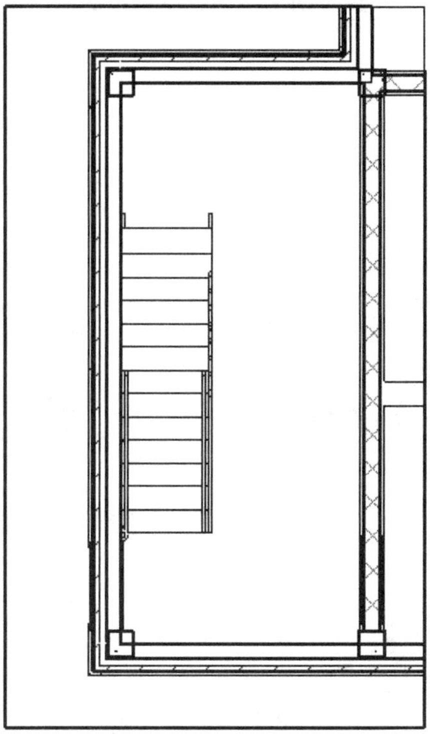

Figure 7–59

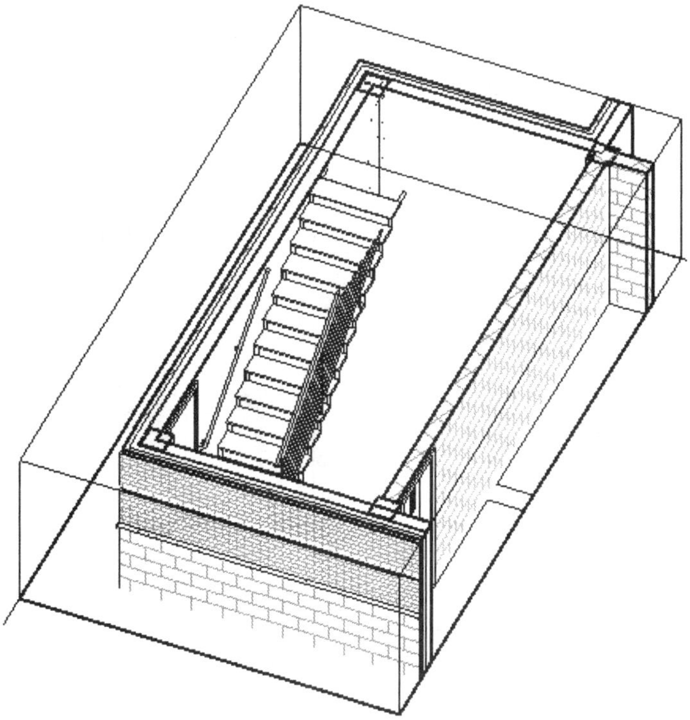

Figure 7–60

- **Orient to a Direction** allows you to rotate the view to a specific direction, as shown in Figure 7–61. This is similar to using the orientation planes of the ViewCube.

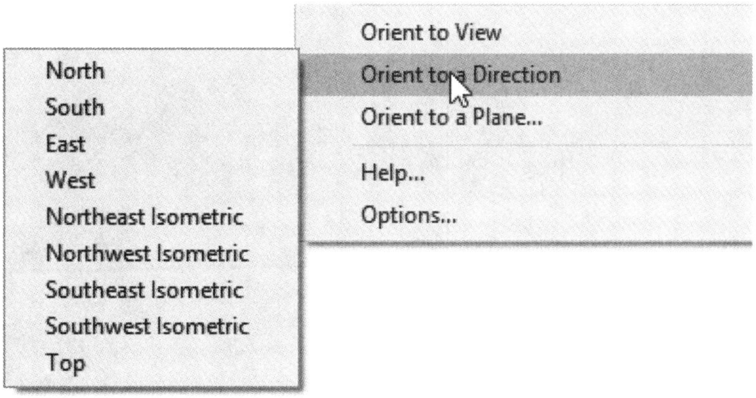

Figure 7–61

- **Orient to a Plane** opens the Select Orientation Plane dialog box and allows you to specify a Level, Grid, or named Reference Plane, or pick a plane or a line, as shown in Figure 7–62. The view is not cut at the plane but oriented in that direction.

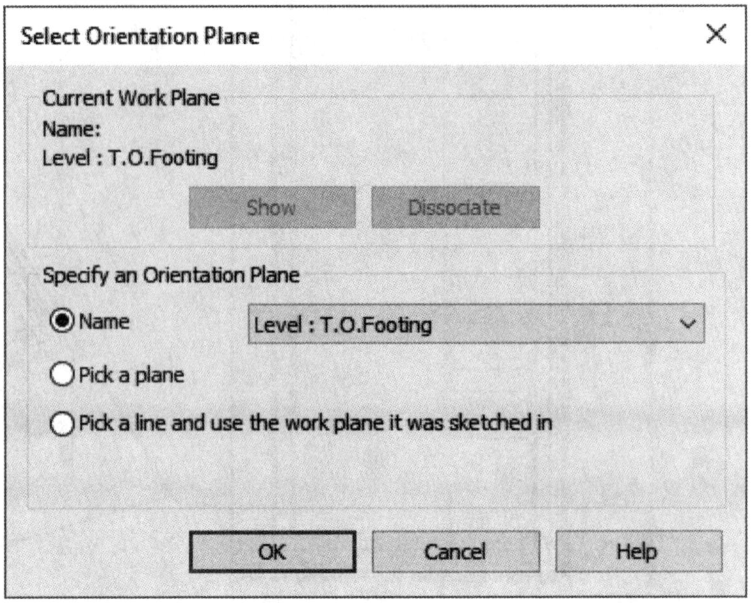

Figure 7–62

Practice 7c Create Elevations and Sections

Practice Objectives

- Create exterior and interior elevations.
- Add building sections and wall sections.

In this practice, you will create exterior elevations of the poolhouse and interior elevations of the restrooms. You will also add building sections, as shown in Figure 7–63, and several wall sections to the project.

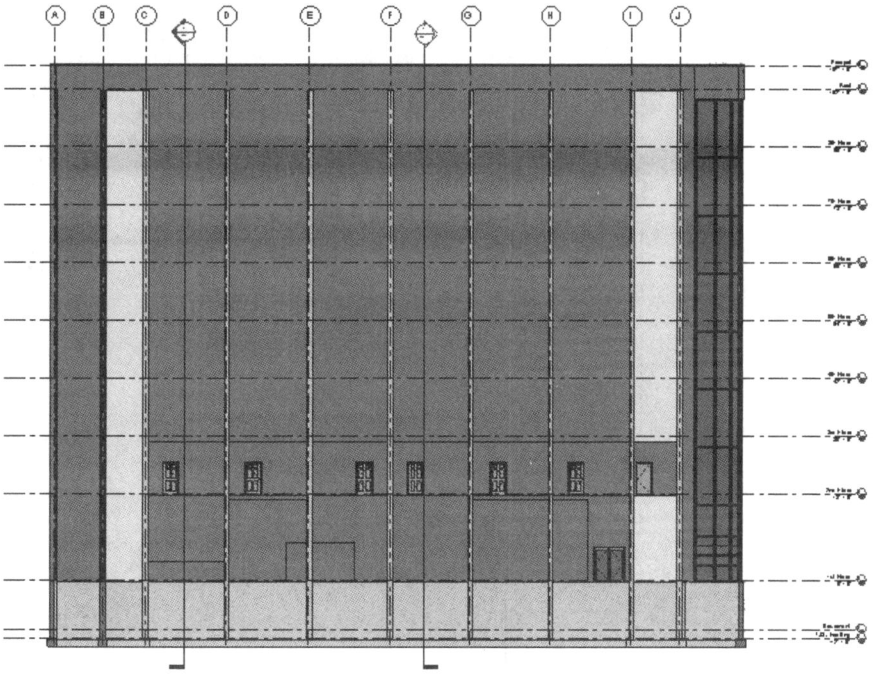

Figure 7–63

Task 1 - Add exterior elevations.

1. Open the project **Modern-Hotel-Elevations.rvt**.
2. Open the **Floor Plans: Floor 1 Overall** view.
3. In the View Control Bar, click (Show Crop Region).
4. Ensure that there is enough space above the pool house to add an elevation mark at this scale, if not, move the crop region up.

5. In the *View* tab>Create panel, expand (Elevation) and click (Elevation). In the Type Selector, select **Elevation: Building Elevation**.
6. Place an elevation marker outside of the pool building, as shown in Figure 7–64.

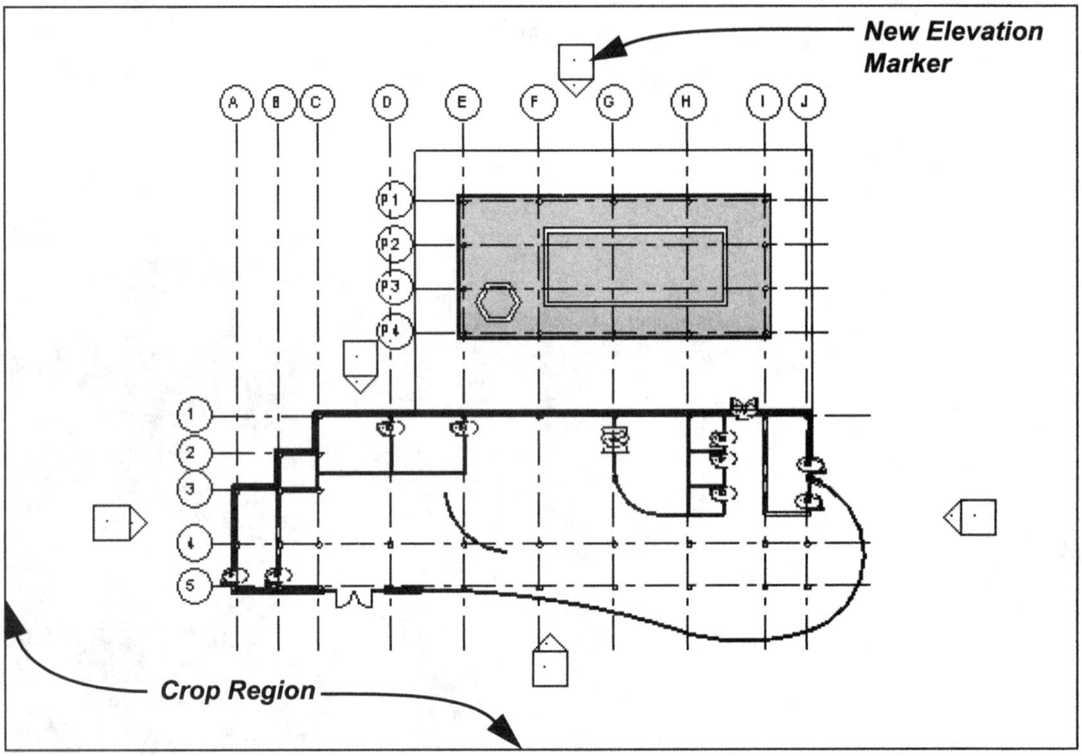

Figure 7–64

7. Click (Modify) and select the pointed side of the new elevation marker.
8. Change the length and depth of the elevation boundaries so only the poolhouse is displayed, as shown in Figure 7–65.

Grids are hidden to clarify the view.

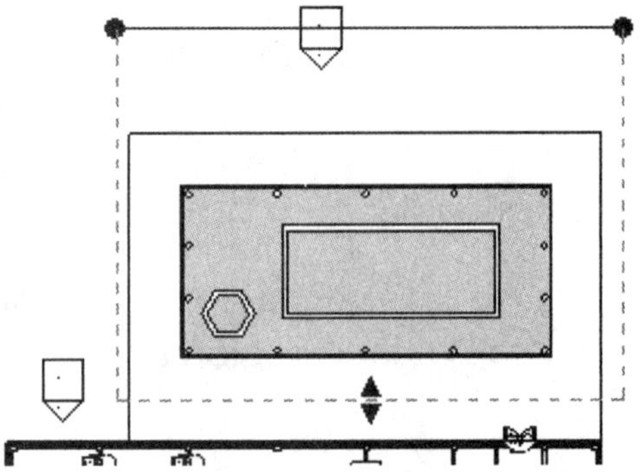

Figure 7–65

9. Double-click on the pointed side of the elevation marker to open the elevation view.

10. Change the crop region so that the height is up to **Floor 3** and the bottom is just below the floor line. Bring the sides in close to the pool building.

11. Hide the grids and levels so that the elevation is similar to that shown in Figure 7–66.

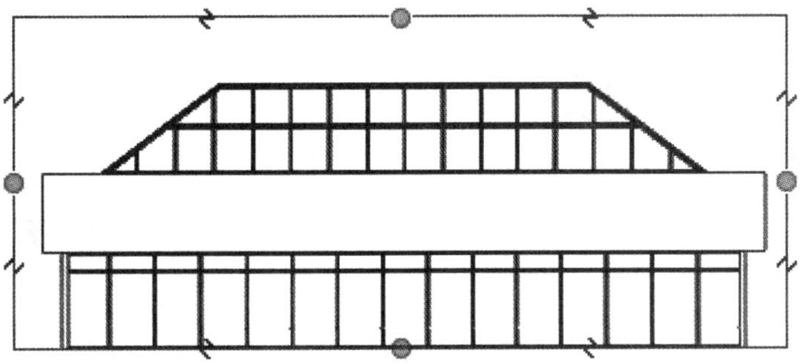

Figure 7–66

12. Hide the crop region.

In this project, North is considered the top of the project.

13. In the Project Browser, in the *Elevations (Building Elevation)* area), rename the elevation (Elevation 1 -a if you selected this direction first) as **Pool-North**.

14. Return to the **Floor Plans: Floor 1 Overall** view.

15. Add elevation markers to the other sides of the poolhouse.

16. Open the new elevations. Resize and rename them as required.

17. Save the project.

Task 2 - Add interior elevations.

1. Open the **Floor Plans: Floor 1 - Restrooms** view.
2. Select the floor that shows the floor drain slopes and hide it.
3. In the *View* tab>Create panel, click  (Elevation).
4. In the Type Selector, select **Elevation: Interior Elevation**.

5. Place an elevation in one of the restrooms and then in the other restroom.

6. Click  (Modify and select the circle part of one of the elevation markers and check each of the boxes, as shown in Figure 7–67. This places an elevation in each direction.

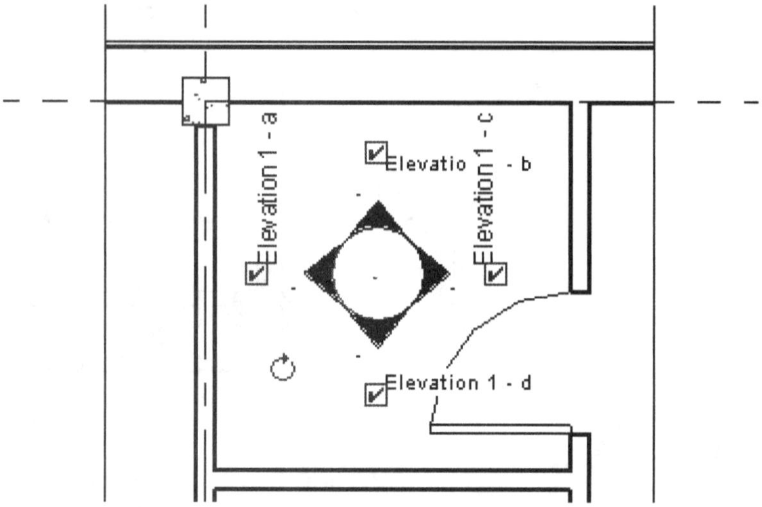

Figure 7–67

7. Repeat for the other restroom.

8. In the Project Browser, under *Elevations (Interior Elevation)*, as shown in Figure 7–68, rename the top restroom elevations as **Men's Restroom-North**, **South**, **East**, **West** and the bottom restroom elevations as **Women's Restroom-North**, **South**, **East**, **West**.

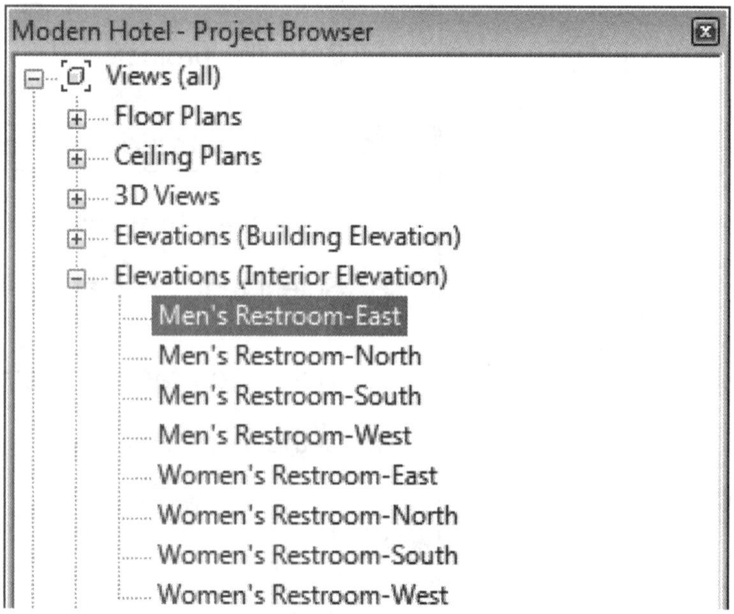

Figure 7–68

Doing this keeps these markers from showing up in other plans at larger scales.

9. Select all of the elevation marker arrows (not the circles) and, in Properties, set the *Hide at scales coarser than* to **1/4"=1'-0"**, as shown in Figure 7–69.

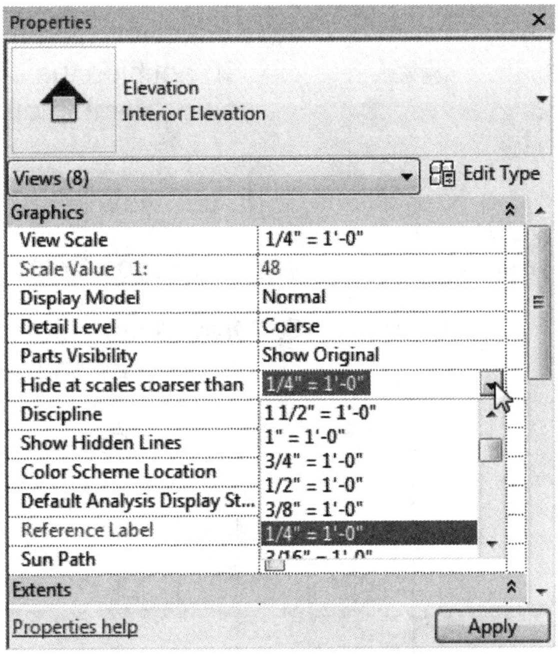

Figure 7–69

10. Open one of the elevations facing the door (**Men's Restroom-East**). The interior elevation should automatically stop at the boundaries of the walls and ceiling.

11. If the elevation is not bounded as expected, move the crop region so that it is tight against the walls, as shown in Figure 7–70.

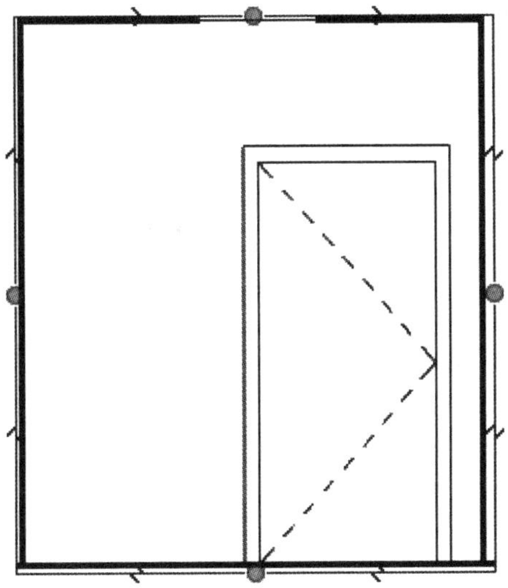

Figure 7–70

12. Save the project.

Task 3 - Clean up a view and add building sections.

1. Open the **Floor Plans: Floor 1 - Reference** view.
2. Select and hide the elevation markers facing the poolhouse. (Do not hide the category as that would also hide the markers you do want to display.)
3. In the *View* tab>Create panel, click (Section).
4. In the Type Selector, select **Section: Building Section**.
5. Draw a horizontal section and a vertical section through the building, as shown in Figure 7–71.

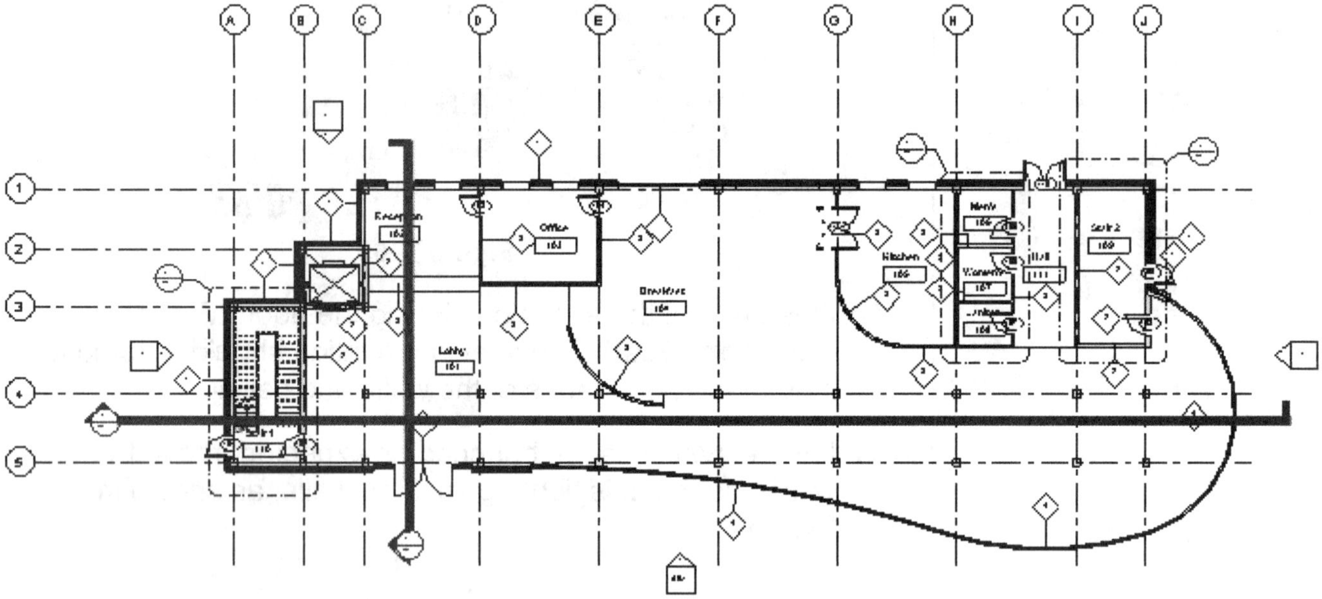

Figure 7–71

6. In the Project Browser, under *Sections*, rename them to **East-West Section** and **North-South Section**.
7. View each of the building sections.

Task 4 - Add wall sections.

*You are using the **Floor 2** view to place the wall sections, as you want to ensure they go through certain features, such as doors and windows.*

1. Open the **Floor Plans: Floor 2** view.
2. Hide by element, the elevation markers facing the poolhouse.
3. In the *View* tab>Create panel, click (Section). In the Type Selector, select **Section: Wall Section**.
4. Draw four wall sections, as shown in Figure 7–72. Ensure that the front wall section passes through a window and the back wall section passes through a door.

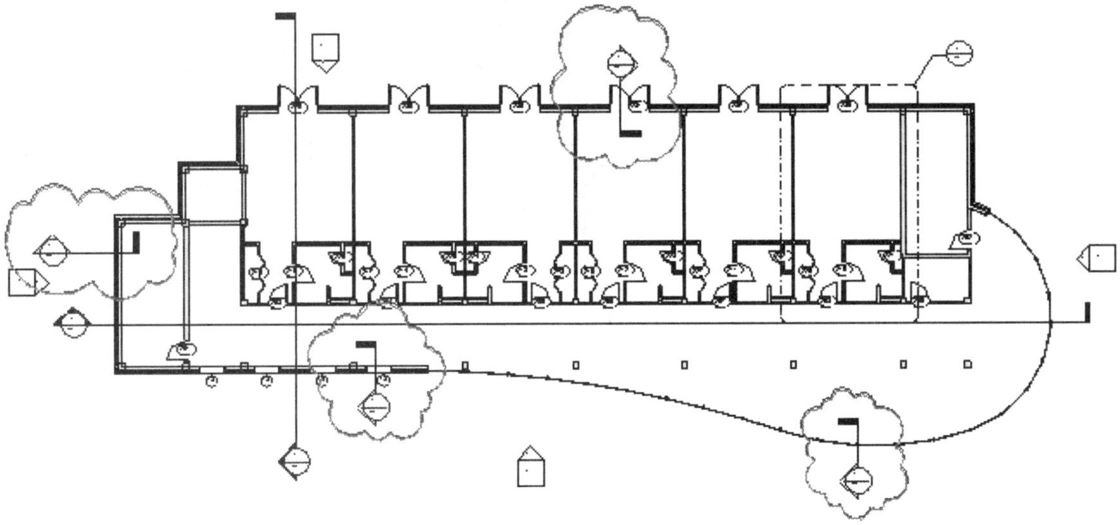

Figure 7–72

5. Move any annotation elements so they do not interfere with the section cut.
6. View each of the wall sections.
7. Save the project.

Chapter Review Questions

1. Which of the following commands shown in Figure 7–73, creates a view that results in an independent view displaying the same model geometry and containing a copy of the annotation?

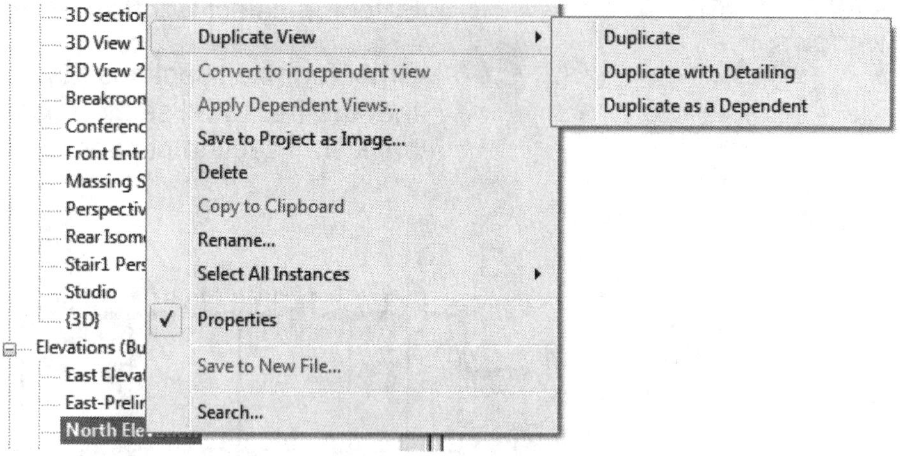

Figure 7–73

   a. Duplicate
   b. Duplicate with Detailing
   c. Duplicate as a Dependent

2. Which of the following is true about the Visibility Graphic Overrides dialog box?
   a. Changes made in the dialog box only affect the current view.
   b. It can only be used to toggle categories on and off.
   c. It can be used to toggle individual elements on and off.
   d. It can be used to change the color of individual elements.

3. If you want to see rooms in a view (as shown in Figure 7–74), but they are not displayed, what do you have to do?

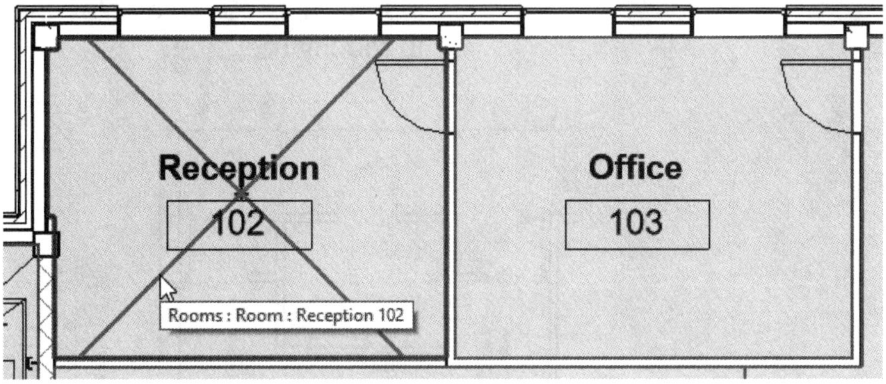

Figure 7–74

   a. Create a new Room Plan view.
   b. In the View Control Bar, toggle on **Rooms**.
   c. In the Visibility/Graphic Overrides dialog box, under Rooms toggle on **Interior Fill**.
   d. While the **Room** command is active, in the *Place Room* tab, verify that **Interior Fill** is selected.

4. The purpose of callouts is to create a...
   a. Boundary around part of the model that needs revising, similar to a revision cloud.
   b. View of part of the model for export to the AutoCAD® software for further detailing.
   c. View of part of the model that is linked to the main view from which it is taken.
   d. 2D view of part of the model.

5. You placed dimensions in a view and some of them display and others do not (as shown on the left in Figure 7–75) but you were expecting the view to display as shown on the right in Figure 7–75. To display the missing dimensions you need to modify the...

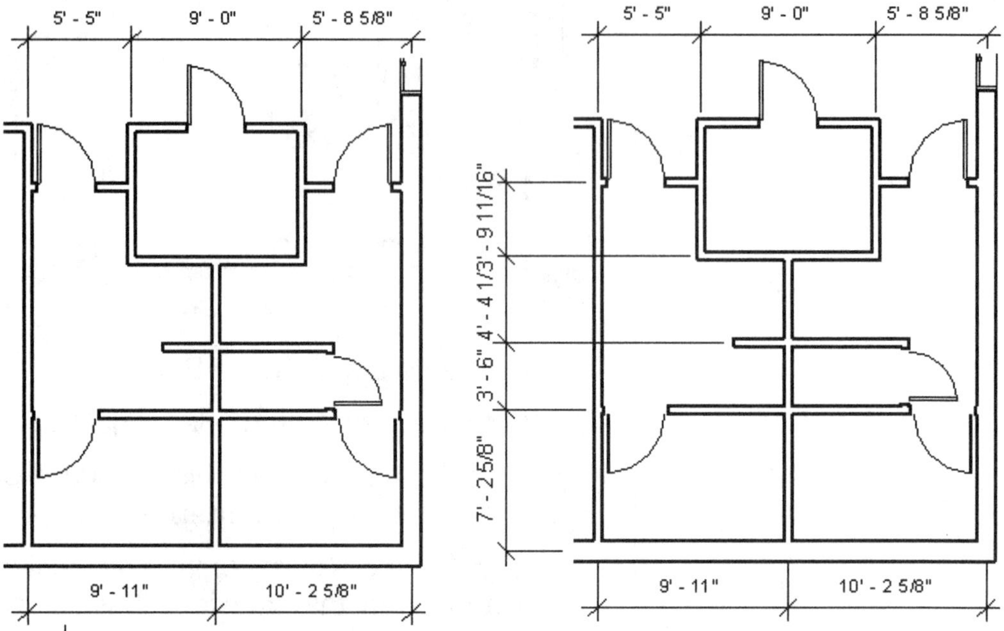

Figure 7–75

a. Dimension Settings

b. Dimension Type

c. Visibility Graphic Overrides

d. Annotation Crop Region

6. How do you create multiple interior elevations in one room?

a. Using the **Interior Elevation** command, place the elevation marker.

b. Using the **Elevation** command, place the first marker, select it and select the appropriate Show Arrow boxes.

c. Using the **Interior Elevation** command, place an elevation marker for each wall of the room you want to display.

d. Using the **Elevation** command, select a Multiple Elevation marker type, and place the elevation marker.

7. How do you create a jog in a building section, such as that shown in Figure 7–76?

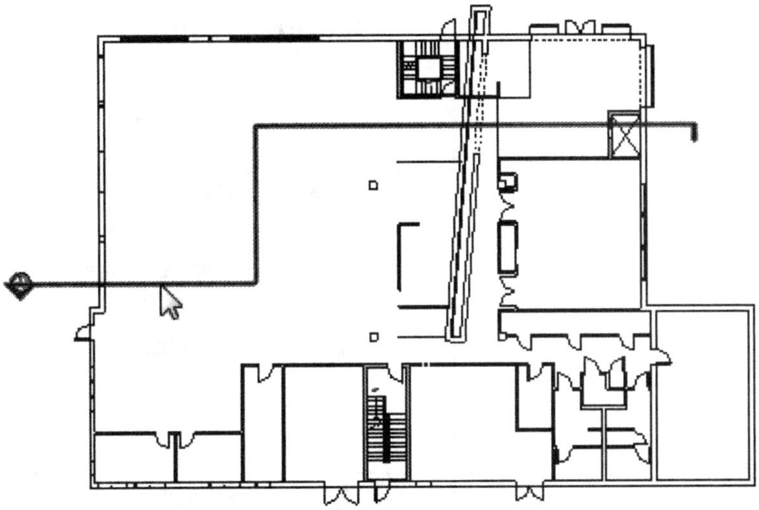

Figure 7–76

   a. Use the **Split Element** tool in the *Modify* tab>Modify panel.
   b. Select the building section and then click **Split Segment** in the contextual tab.
   c. Select the building section and click the blue control in the middle of the section line.
   d. Draw two separate sections, and use the **Section Jog** tool to combine them into a jogged section.

Command Summary

Button	Command	Location
Views		
	Elevation	• **Ribbon:** *View* tab>Create panel> expand Elevation
	Callout: Rectangle	• **Ribbon:** *View* tab>Create panel> expand Callout
	Callout: Sketch	• **Ribbon:** *View* tab>Create panel> expand Callout
	Duplicate	• **Ribbon:** *View* tab>Create panel> expand Duplicate View • **Right-click:** (*on a view in the Project Browser*) expand Duplicate View
	Duplicate as Dependent	• **Ribbon:** *View* tab>Create panel> expand Duplicate View • **Right-click:** (*on a view in the Project Browser*) expand Duplicate View
	Duplicate with Detailing	• **Ribbon:** *View* tab>Create panel> expand Duplicate View • **Right-click:** (*on a view in the Project Browser*) Duplicate View
	Plan Region	• **Ribbon:** *View* tab>Create panel> expand Plan Views
	Section	• **Ribbon:** *View* tab>Create panel • **Quick Access Toolbar**
	Split Segment	• **Ribbon:** (*when the elevation or section marker is selected*) *Modify | Views* tab> Section panel
Crop Views		
	Crop View	• **View Control Bar** • **View Properties:** Crop View (*check*)
	Do Not Crop View	• **View Control Bar** • **View Properties:** Crop View (*clear*)
	Edit Crop	• **Ribbon:** (*when the crop region of a callout, elevation, or section view is selected*) *Modify | Views* tab>Mode panel
	Hide Crop Region	• **View Control Bar** • **View Properties:** Crop Region Visible (*clear*)
	Reset Crop	• **Ribbon:** (*when the crop region of a callout, elevation or section view is selected*) *Modify | Views* tab>Mode panel

	Show Crop Region	• **View Control Bar** • **View Properties:** Crop Region Visible (*check*)
	Size Crop	• **Ribbon:** (*when the crop region of a callout, elevation or section view is selected*) *Modify | Views* tab>Mode panel
View Display		
	Hide in View	• **Ribbon:** *Modify* tab>View Graphics panel>Hide>Elements *or* By Category • **Right-click:** *(when an element is selected)* Hide in View>Elements *or* Category
	Override Graphics in View	• **Ribbon:** *Modify* tab>View Graphics panel>Hide>Elements *or* By Category • **Right-click:** *(when an element is selected)* Override Graphics in View>By Element *or* By Category • **Shortcut:** *(category only)* VV or VG
	Plan Region	• **Ribbon:** *View* tab>Create panel expand Plan Views.
	Selection Box	• **Ribbon:** *Modify* tab>View panel • **Shortcut: BX.**
	Reveal Hidden Elements	• **View Control Bar**
	Temporary Hide/Isolate	• **View Control Bar**
	Temporary View Properties	• **View Control Bar**

Chapter 8

Adding Components

As you construct a building model, you add component families such as furniture, lighting fixtures, mechanical equipment, and structural framing elements. These components can be loaded from your company's template, the Autodesk® Revit® library, or a custom library.

Learning Objectives in this Chapter

- Place components in a project to further develop the design.
- Load components from the Autodesk Revit library.
- Change component types and locations.
- Purge unused component elements to increase the processing speed of the model.

8.1 Adding Components

Many types of elements are added to a project using component families. These can include freestanding components, such as the furniture, floor lamp, and table lamp shown in Figure 8–1. They can also include wall, ceiling, floor, roof, face and line-hosted components. These hosted components must be placed on the referenced element, such as the fluorescent light fixtures in Figure 8–1.

Figure 8–1

- Several components are included in the default template, making them automatically available in new projects. You can load more components into a project or create your own as required.
- Components are located in family files with the extension RFA. For example, a component family named Desk.rfa can contain several types and sizes.

How To: Place a Component

1. In the *Architecture* tab>Build panel, click  (Place a Component), or type **CM**.
2. In the Type Selector, select the component you want to add to the project.
3. Proceed as follows, based on the type of component used:

If the component is...	Then...
Not hosted	Set the *Level* and *Offset* in Properties, as shown in Figure 8–2.
Wall hosted	Set the *Elevation* in Properties, as shown in Figure 8–3.
Face hosted	Select the appropriate method in the contextual tab> Placement panel, as shown in Figure 8–4. • Vertical Faces include walls and columns. • Faces include ceilings, beams, and roofs. • Work Planes can be set to levels, faces, and named reference planes.

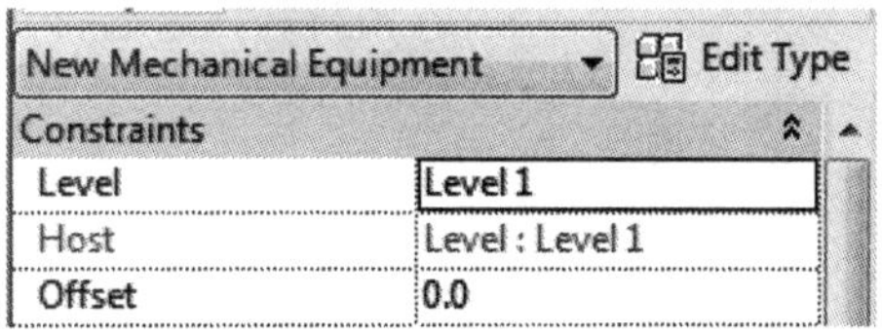

Figure 8–2

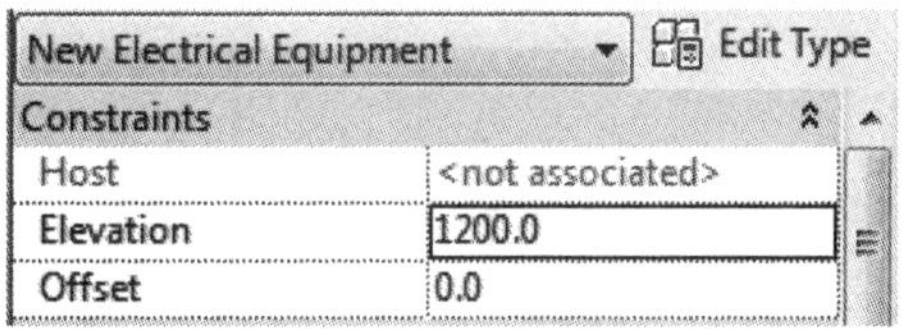

Figure 8–3

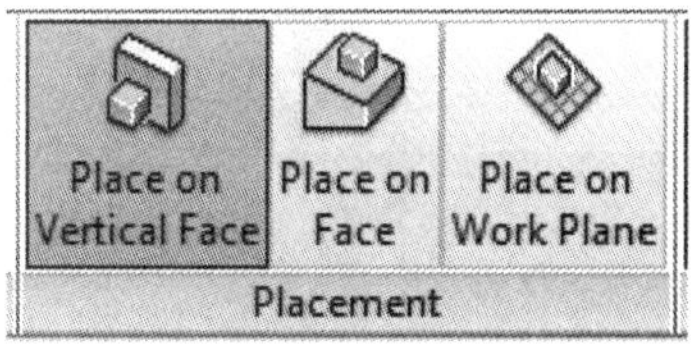

Figure 8–4

4. Place the component in the model.

Create Similar works with all elements.

- A fast way to add components that match those already in your project is to select one, right-click on it, and select **Create Similar**. This starts the **Component** command with the same type selected.

Loading Components

If the components you are looking for are not available, you can look in the Autodesk Revit Library, which contains many options. You can also check which custom components your company has and find vendor-specific components.

- You can also copy a component to the clipboard in one project and past it into a different project.

How To: Load a Family

You can also load a family from the Modify | Place Component tab> Mode panel when placing a component.

1. In the *Insert* tab>Load from Library panel, click  (Load Family).
2. In the Load Family dialog box, locate the folder that contains the family or families you want to load and select them, as shown in Figure 8–5. To load more than one family at a time, hold <Ctrl> while selecting.

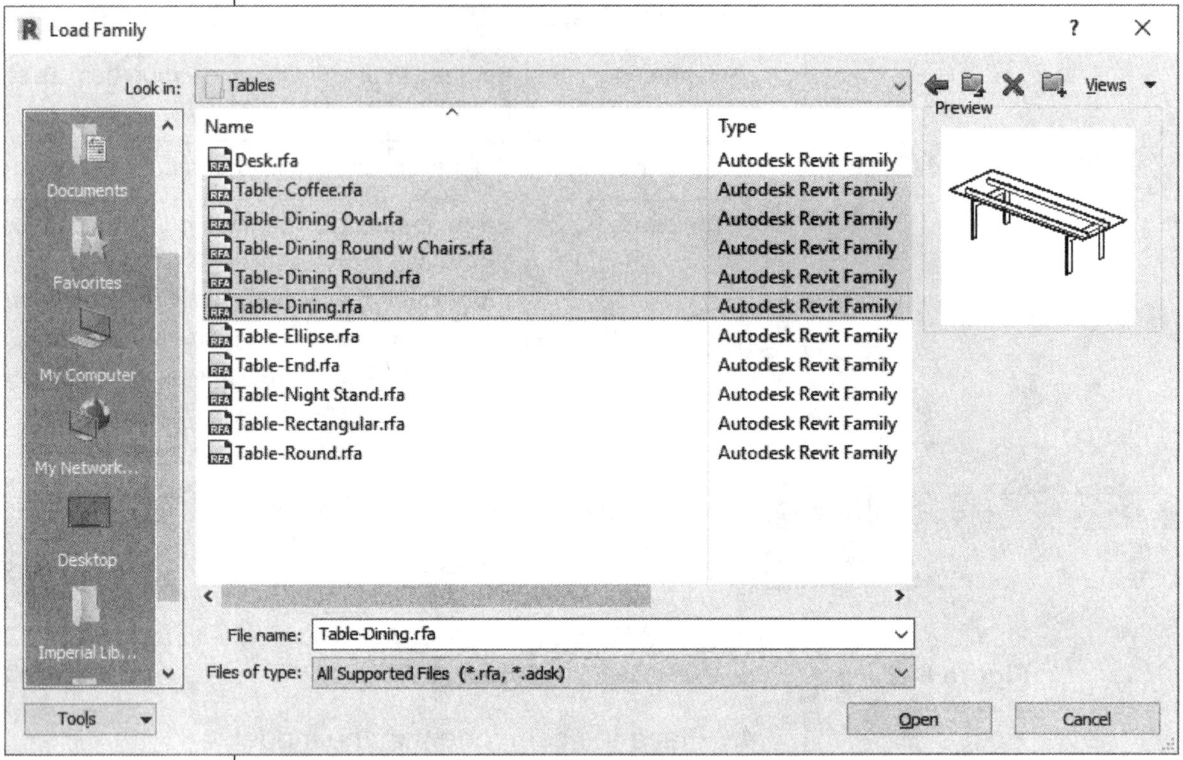

Figure 8–5

- The program remembers the last used folder.

3. Click **Open**.
4. Once the family (or families) is loaded, click  (Component) and select the type you want to use from the Type Selector, as shown in Figure 8–6.

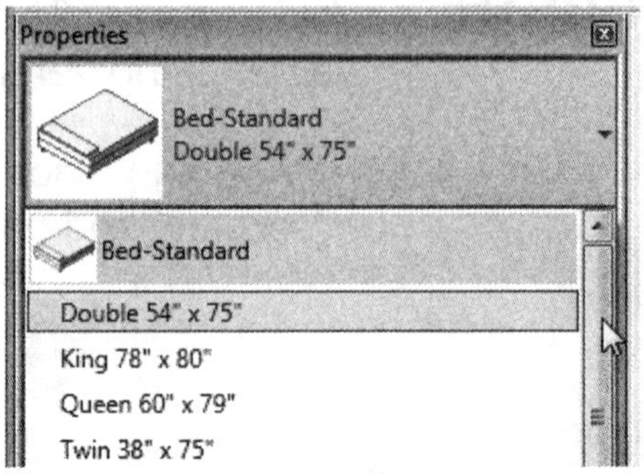

Figure 8–6

8.2 Modifying Components

Components can be modified when they are selected by changing the type in the Type Selector. For example, you might have placed a task chair in a project (as shown in Figure 8–7), but now you need to change it to an executive chair. With some types, you can use controls to modify the component. You can also select a new host for a component and move components with nearby elements.

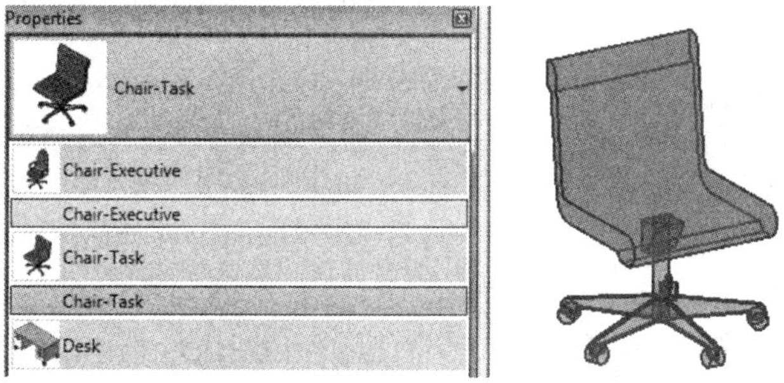

Figure 8–7

Working with Host Elements

If you need to move a component from the level on which it was inserted, you can change its host. For example, one of the desks in Figure 8–8 is floating above the floor. It was placed on Level 1 when it was inserted, but needs to be located on the floor that is below the level.

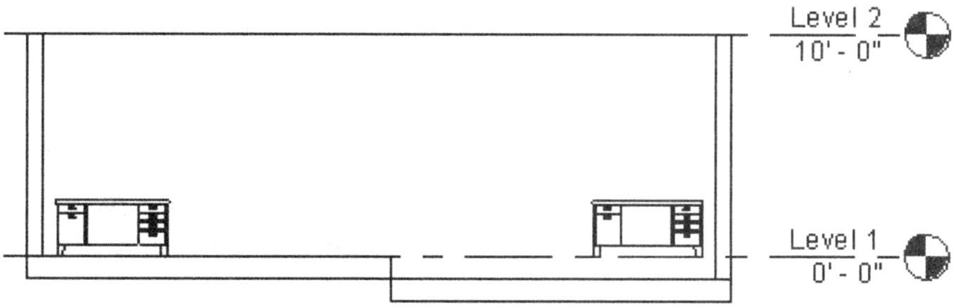

Figure 8–8

How To: Pick a New Host Element

1. Select a component.
2. In the *<component type>* contextual tab>Host panel, click (Pick New Host).
3. Select the new host (e.g., the floor).

- You can select a floor, surface, or level to be the new host for the components depending on the requirements of the component.

Moving with Nearby Host Elements

Components have the capacity to move with nearby host elements (such as walls) when they are moved. Select the component and in the Options Bar select **Moves With Nearby Elements**. The component is automatically assigned to the closest host elements.

For example, a desk near the corner of two walls is linked to those two walls. If you move either wall, the desk moves as well. However, you can still move the desk independently of the walls.

- You cannot specify which elements the component should be linked to; the software determines this automatically. This option only works with host elements (such as walls), not with other components.

Purging Unused Elements

You can remove unused elements from a project, including individual component types, as shown in Figure 8–9.

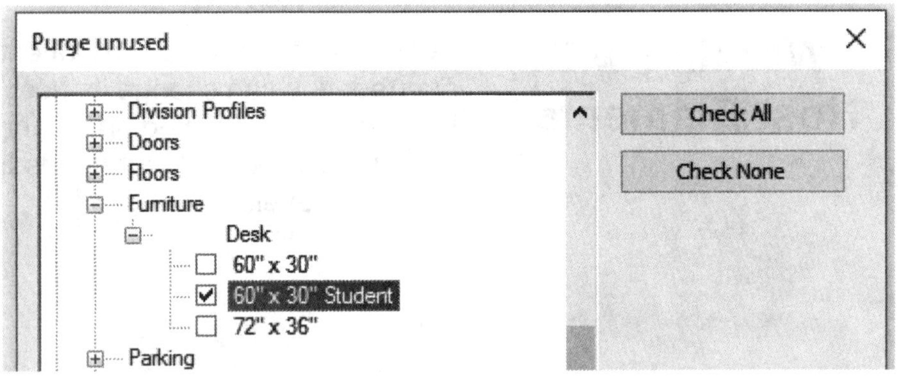

Figure 8–9

- Some elements are nested in other elements and it might require several rounds of purging the project to remove them.

How To: Purge Unused Elements

1. In the *Manage* tab>Settings panel, click  (Purge Unused).
2. In the Purge unused dialog box, click **Check None** and select the elements you want to purge.
3. Click **OK**.

- Purging unused components not only helps simplify the component list, but more importantly, reduces the project file size.

Practice 8a

Add Components

Practice Objective

- Load and add components.

In this practice, you will add furniture to the lobby of the hotel, as shown in Figure 8–10. You will load a component from a custom library and use controls to modify the placement. If you have time, add casework and equipment to the Breakfast and Preparation areas. Finally, you will add footing components to the base of the columns.

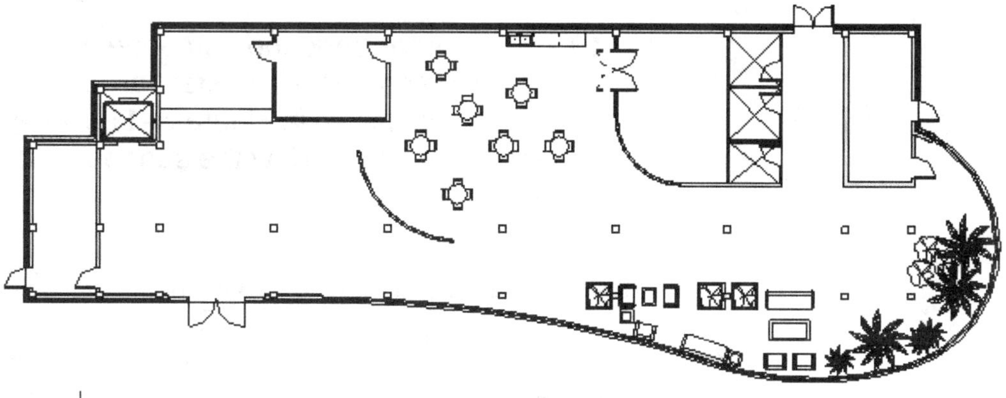

Figure 8–10

Task 1 - Add furniture to the lobby.

1. Open the project **Modern-Hotel-Components.rvt**.
2. Open the **Floor 1 - Furniture Plan** view.
3. In the *Architecture* tab>Build panel, expand (Component) and click (Place a Component).
4. In the Type Selector, review the various furniture components that are available for the project. Select **Chair-Corbu** and place it in the lobby area near the curved curtain walls.
5. Open the **Floor Plans: Floor 1** view. The chair does not display in this view because the Furniture category (and several others) has been toggled off.
6. Return to the **Floor Plans: Floor 1 Furniture Plan**.
7. Start the **Component** command.

8. In the *Modify | Place Component* tab>Mode panel, click  (Load Family).

9. In the Load Family dialog box, in the Revit Library, navigate to the folders and open the families listed below:

   - In the *Furniture>Tables* folder: **Table-Dining Round w Chairs.rfa**.
   - In the *Planting* folder: **RPC Plant-Tropical.rfa** **RPC Tree-Tropical.rfa**.
   - In the *Site>Accessories* folder: **Planter.rfa**.

10. Place and arrange the components as required, placing the dining tables in the breakfast area and other elements in the lounge, as shown in Figure 8–11. Place at least one plant in a planter.You can follow the suggested layout or create your own design.

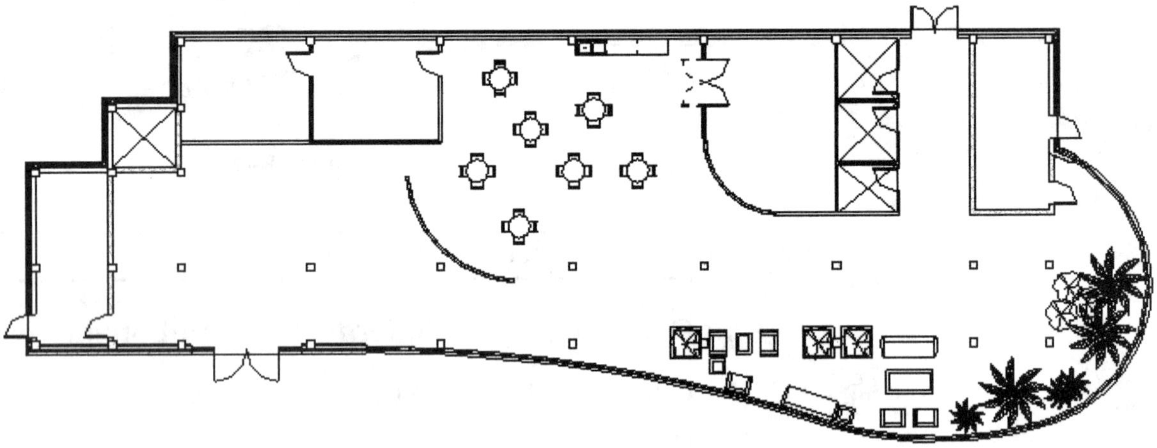

Figure 8–11

Task 2 - Load and place custom components.

1. Start the **Component** command and, in the *Modify | Place Component* tab>Mode panel, click  (Load Family).

2. In the Load Family dialog box, navigate to your practice files folder and open the *Custom Library* folder. Load the following components:

   - **Countertop-Lobby.rfa**
   - **Elevator-Door-Center.rfa**
   - **Elevator-Electric.rfa**

3. Zoom in on the office area near the elevator where there is a partial height wall.

4. In the Type Selector, select **Countertop-Lobby 24" Depth**.

5. In Properties, set the *Offset* to **1' 1 5/8"**.

6. Place the Countertop component over the partial height wall. Modify its length using the controls on each end, as shown in Figure 8–12. Extend it so that it touches the vertical walls on both ends.

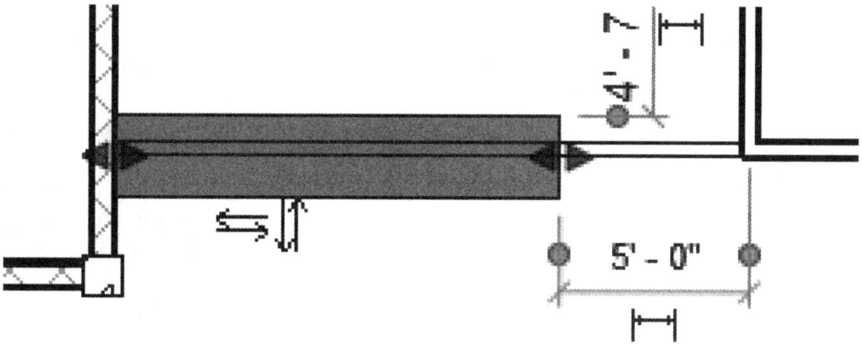

Figure 8–12

- Countertops are automatically set to 3'-0" above the level where they are placed. This wall is 4'-0" high and the countertop thickness is about 1 1/2".

7. Pan over to the elevator.

8. Place the **Elevator-Electric 2500 lbs** inside the elevator shaft and place the **Elevator Door - Center 42" x 84"** in the wall, as shown in Figure 8–13. Note that the door is also a component.

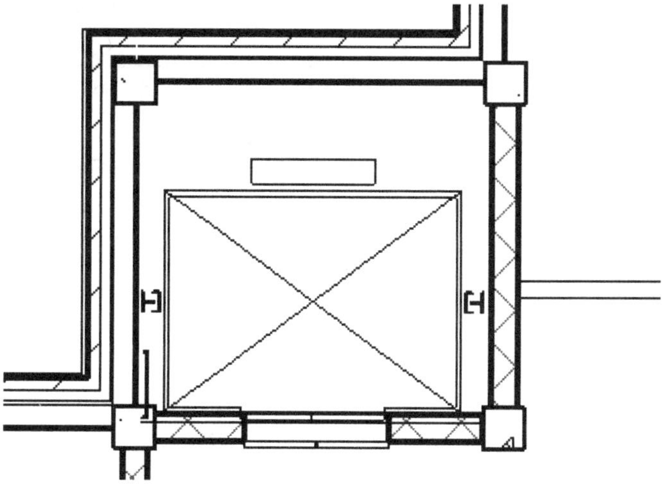

Figure 8–13

9. Select the Elevator Door component.

.rta = family
.rvt = revit file
.rte = template

10. In the *Modify* | *Specialty Equipment* tab>Clipboard panel, click (Copy to the Clipboard).

11. In the Clipboard panel, expand (Paste) and click (Aligned to Selected Levels).

12. In the Select Levels dialog box, select **Basement** and **Floor 2** through **Floor 8**, as shown in Figure 8–14. Click **OK**. This copies the door to the rest of the levels.

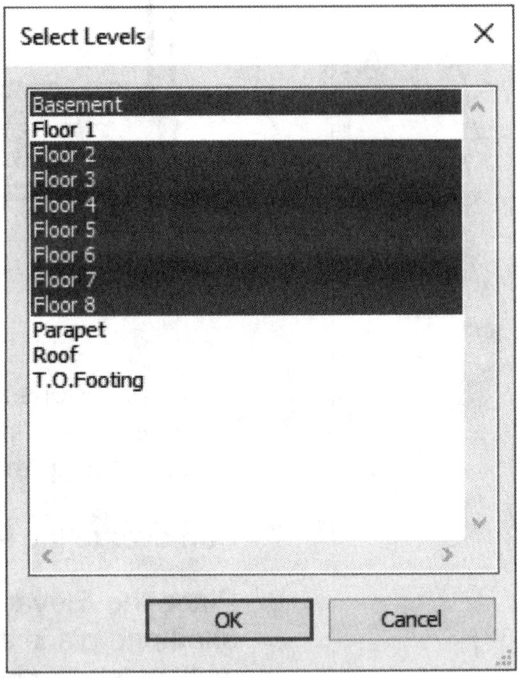

Figure 8–14

13. Save the project.

Task 3 - Add column footings.

1. Open the **Floor Plans: T.O. Footing** view and select everything in the view.
2. In the Status Bar (or in the *Modify* | *Multi-select* tab>Selection panel), click (Filter).
3. In the Filter dialog box, clear **Structural Columns** and click **OK**.

4. In the Status Bar, expand (Temporary Hide/Isolate) and select **Hide Element.** Everything except the columns should be hidden, as shown in Figure 8–15. It is now easier to identify the locations of the footings.

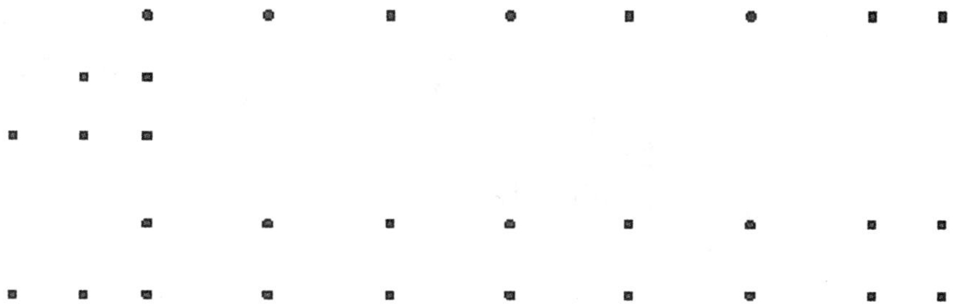

Figure 8–15

5. In the *Architecture* tab>Build panel, click (Component).

6. In the *Modify | Place Component* tab>Mode panel, click (Load Family).

7. In the Autodesk Revit Library>*Structural Foundations* folder, select **Footing-Rectangular.rfa** and click **Open**.

8. In the Type Selector, select **Footing-Rectangular:72" x 48" x 18"**. Set the *Level* to **T.O. Footing**.

9. Place a footing at each column. Once you have placed at least one footing, you can use **Copy** to add the others. Ensure that you are copying from the column midpoint, as shown in Figure 8–16.

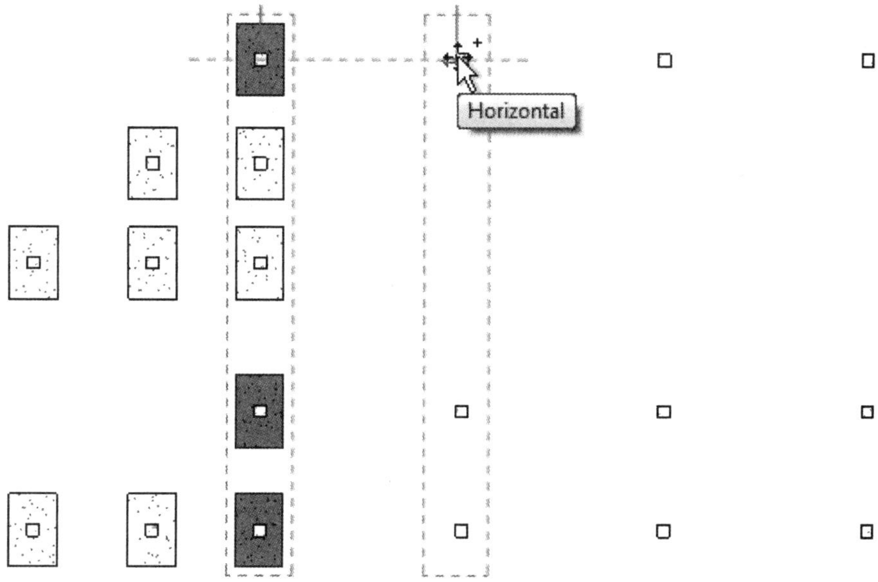

Figure 8–16

10. In the View Control Bar, click (Temporary Hide/Isolate) and select **Reset Temporary Hide/Isolate**. The entire footing system displays, as shown in Figure 8–17.

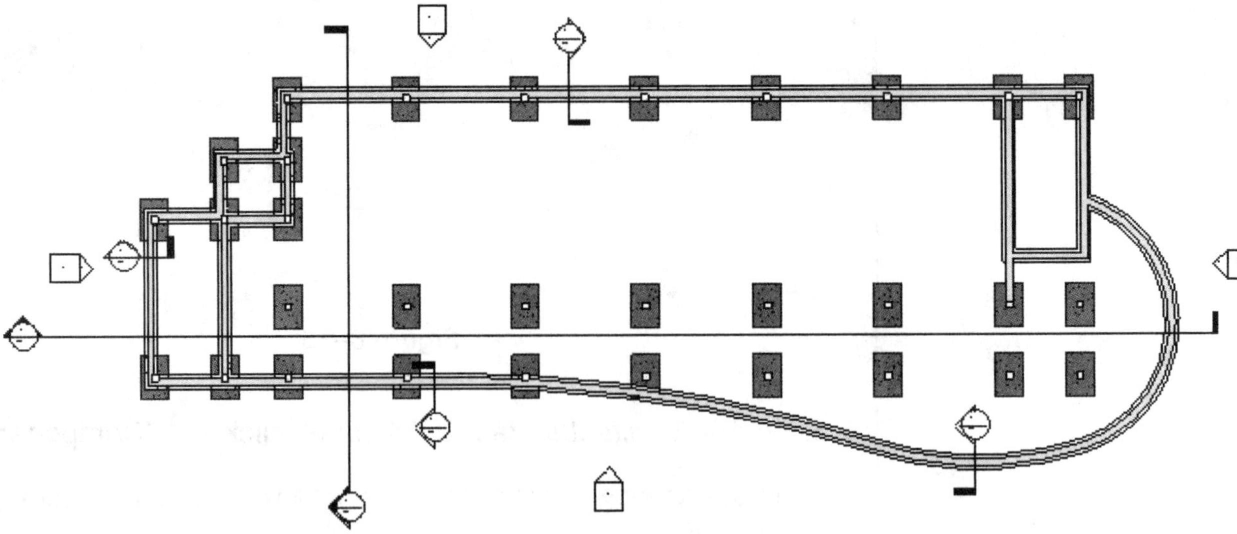

Figure 8–17

11. Save the project.

Chapter Review Questions

1. When inserting a component, you select the family that you want to use in the...
    a. Quick Access Toolbar
    b. Type Selector
    c. Options Bar
    d. Properties Palette
2. If the component you want to use is not available in the current project, where do you go to get the component? (Select all that apply.)
    a. In another project, copy the component to the clipboard and paste it into the current project.
    b. In the current project, use  (Insert from File) and select the family from the list in the dialog box.
    c. In the current project, use  (Load Family) and select the family from the list in the dialog box.
    d. Search a manufacturers site for a component and download it.
3. When you use the **Moves with Nearby Elements** option, can you control which elements a component moves with?
    a. Yes, select the element with which you want it to move.
    b. No, it moves with the closest host element.

4. Which of the following commands would you use if you want to move a furniture component to a floor that is lower than the level where it was original placed, as shown in Figure 8–18?

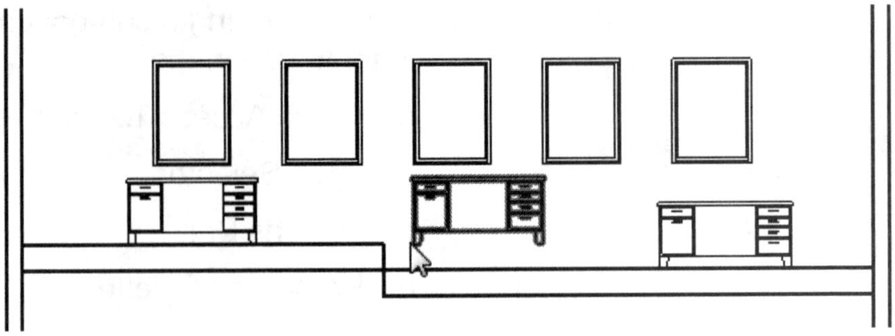

Figure 8–18

a. Use  (Level) and add a Level at the height of the lower floor.

b. Use  (Ref Plane) and draw a plane aligned with the lower floor.

c. Use  (Pick New Host) and select the lower floor.

d. Use  (Edit Family) and change the work plane in the family so that it matches the height of the lower floor.

Command Summary

Button	Command	Location
	**Load Family**	• **Ribbon:** *Modify* | *Place Component* tab>Load panel or *Insert* tab>Load from Library panel
	**Pick New Host**	• **Ribbon:** *Modify* | *Multi-Select* or *component type* contextual tab>Host panel
	**Place Component**	• **Ribbon:** *Architecture* tab>Build panel> expand Component • **Shortcut:** CM
	**Place on Face**	• **Ribbon**: *Modify* | *Place Component* tab> Placement panel
	**Place on Vertical Face**	• **Ribbon**: *Modify* | *Place Component* tab> Placement panel
	**Place on Work Plane**	• **Ribbon**: *Modify* | *Place Component* tab> Placement panel
	**Purge Unused**	• **Ribbon:** *Manage* tab>Settings panel

Modeling Floors

Floors in the Autodesk® Revit® software can be used as full depth floors, or as a thin veneer that shows floor material placed on an underlying floor. You can customize floors by creating slopes for drainage, cutting holes, or creating shafts that cut through multiple floors.

Learning Objectives in this Chapter

- Sketch and modify floor boundaries.
- Join geometry between floors and walls for a cleaner visual presentation.
- Add a shaft opening that cuts through multiple floors.
- Slope a floor in one or more directions for drainage.

9.1 Modeling Floors

The **Floor** command can generate any flat or sloped surface, such as floors, balconies, decks, and patios, as shown in Figure 9–1. Typically created in a plan view, the floor can be based either on bounding walls or on a sketched outline.

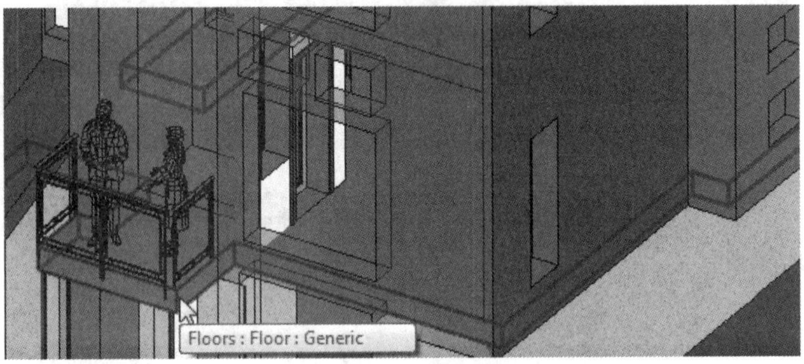

Figure 9–1

- The floor type controls the thickness of a floor.

How To: Add a Floor

1. In the *Architecture* tab>Build panel, expand (Floor) and click (Floor: Architectural) or (Floor: Structural). You are placed in sketch mode where other elements in the model are grayed out.
2. In the Type Selector, set the type of floor you want to use. In Properties, set any other options you might need.
3. In the *Modify | Create Floor Boundary* tab>Draw panel, click (Boundary Line).
   - Click (Pick Walls) and select the walls, setting either the inside or outside edge. If you have selected a wall, you can click (Flip) to switch the inside/outside status of the boundary location, as shown in Figure 9–2.
   - Click (Line) or one of the other Draw tools and sketch the boundary edges.
4. Click (Slope Arrow) to define a slope for the entire floor.

The lines in the sketch must form a closed loop. Use tools in the Modify panel to adjust intersections.

The span direction is automatically placed on the first sketch line.

5. Click (Span Direction), as shown in Figure 9–2, to modify the direction of the structural elements in the floor.

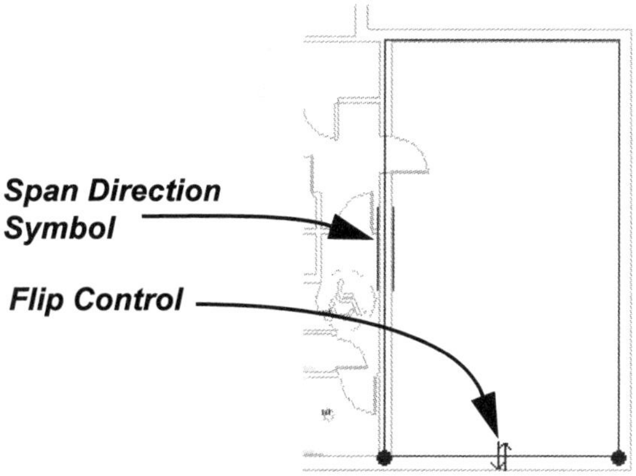

Figure 9–2

6. Click (Finish Edit Mode) to create the floor.

- If you are using (Pick Walls), select the **Extend into wall (to core)** option in the Options Bar if you want the floor to cut into the wall. For example, the floor would cut through the gypsum wall board and the air space but stop at a core layer such as CMU.
- If you select one or more of the boundary sketch lines, you can also set *Cantilevers* for *Concrete* or *Steel*, as shown in Figure 9–3.

Figure 9–3

- To create an opening inside the floor, create a separate closed loop inside the first one, as shown in Figure 9–4.

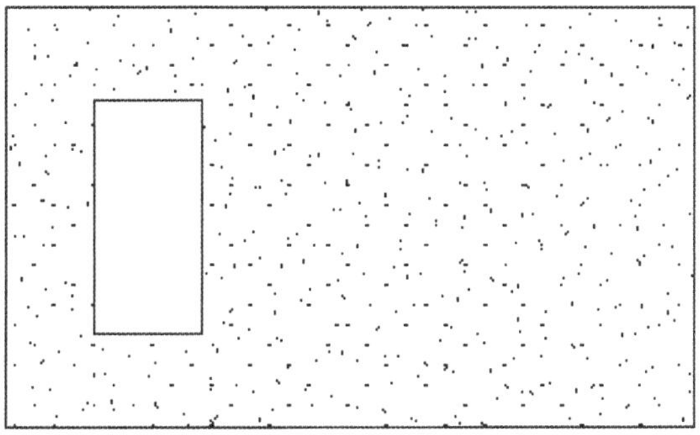

Figure 9–4

Hint: Sketched Arcs and Tangent Lock.

If you are adding arcs or ellipses to a sketch that are tangent to other lines, you can lock the geometry in place by clicking on the tangency lock (Toggle Join Tangency), as shown in Figure 9–5.

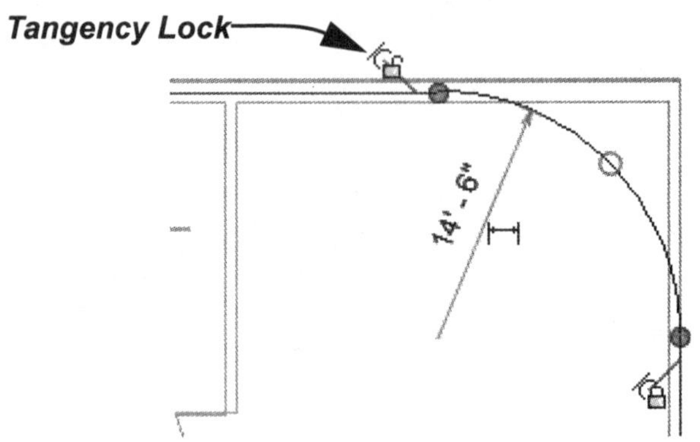

Figure 9–5

- This lock is available whenever you are in sketch mode.

- If you create a floor on an upper level, an alert box displays prompting if you want the walls below to be attached to the underside of the floor and its level. If you have a variety of wall heights, it is better to click **No** and attach the walls separately.

- Another alert box might open as shown in Figure 9–6. You can automatically join the geometry or can do so at a later time.

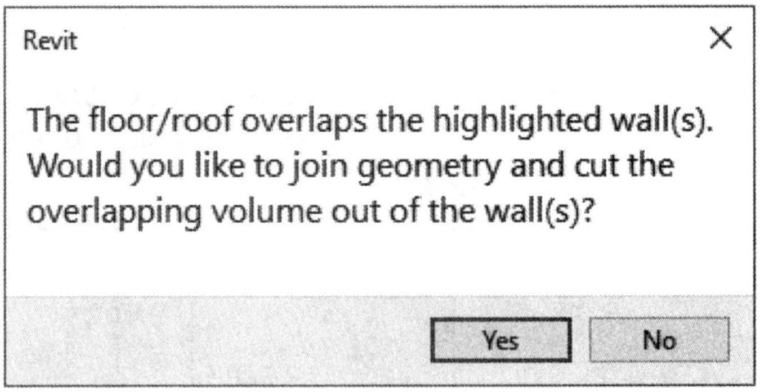

Figure 9–6

- Floors can be placed on top of floors. For example, a structural floor can have a finish floor of tile or carpet placed on top of it, as shown in Figure 9–7. These floors can then be scheduled separately.

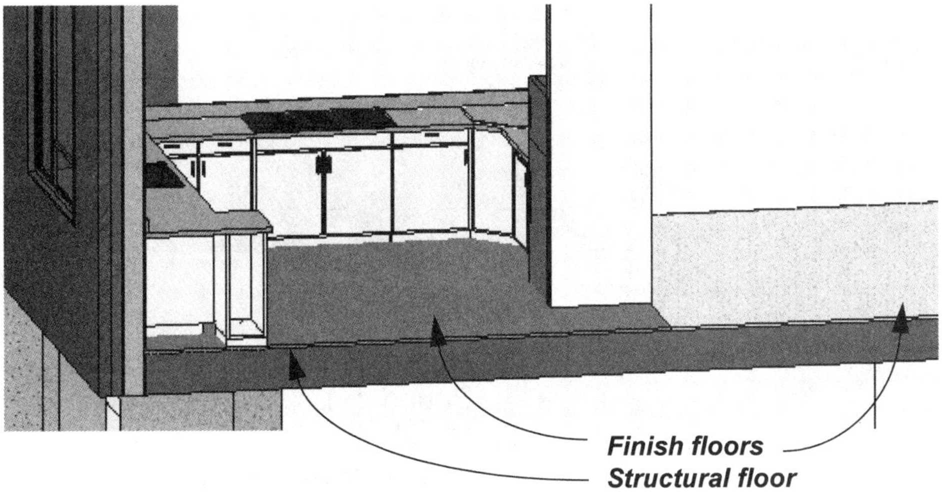

Figure 9–7

Modifying Floors

You can change a floor to a different type using the Type Selector. In Properties, you can modify parameters including the *Height Offset From Level*, as shown in Figure 9–8. When you have a floor selected, you can also edit the boundaries.

Many of the parameters in Properties are used in schedules, including Elevation at Top (Bottom) and Elevation at Top (Bottom) Core for multi-layered floors.

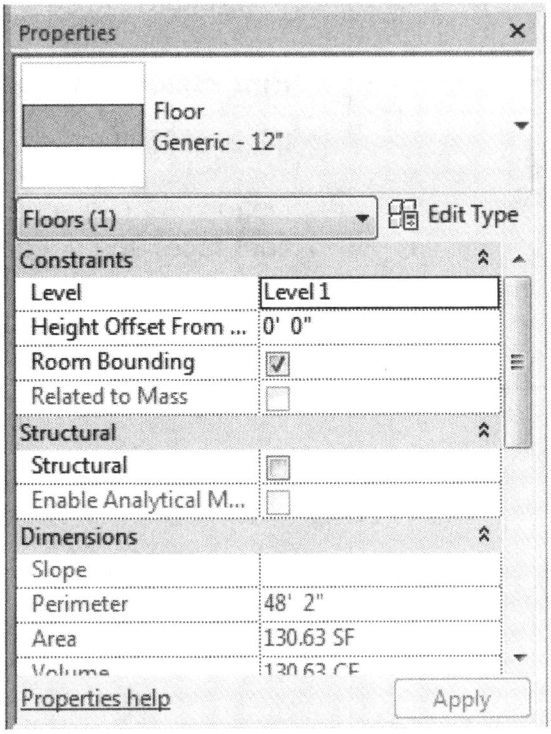

Figure 9–8

How To: Modify the Floor Sketch

1. Select a floor. You might need to highlight an element near the floor and press <Tab> until the floor type displays in the Status Bar or in a tooltip, as shown in Figure 9–9.

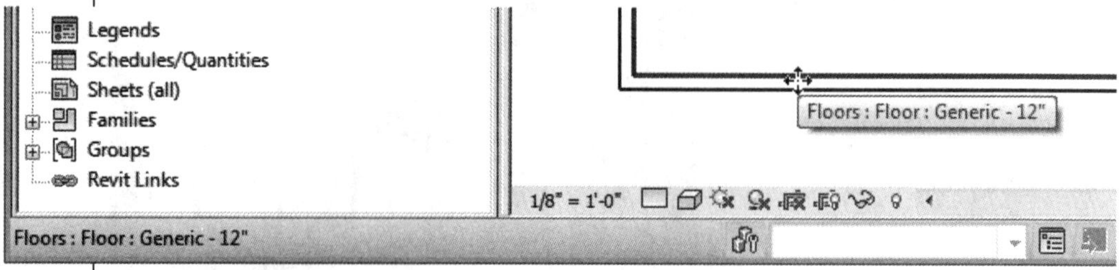

Figure 9–9

2. In the *Modify | Floors* tab>Mode panel, click (Edit Boundary). You are placed in sketch mode.
3. Modify the sketch lines using the draw tools, controls, and the various modify tools.
4. Click (Finish Edit Mode).

- Double-click on a floor to move directly to editing the boundary.
- Floor sketches can be edited in plan and 3D views, but not in elevations. If you try to edit in an elevation view, you are prompted to select another view in which to edit.

Hint: Selecting Floor Faces

If it is difficult to select the floor edges, toggle on the Selection Option (Select Elements by Face). Then can select the floor face, and not only the edges.

Joining Geometry

Cutting a section through the objects you want to join helps to display them more clearly.

Join Geometry is a versatile command used to clean up intersections. The elements remain separate, but the intersections are cleaned up. It can be used with many types of elements including floors, walls, and roofs. In Figure 9–10, the wall on the left and the floor have been joined, but the wall on the right has not been joined with the floor and therefore does not display the lines that define the intersection edges.

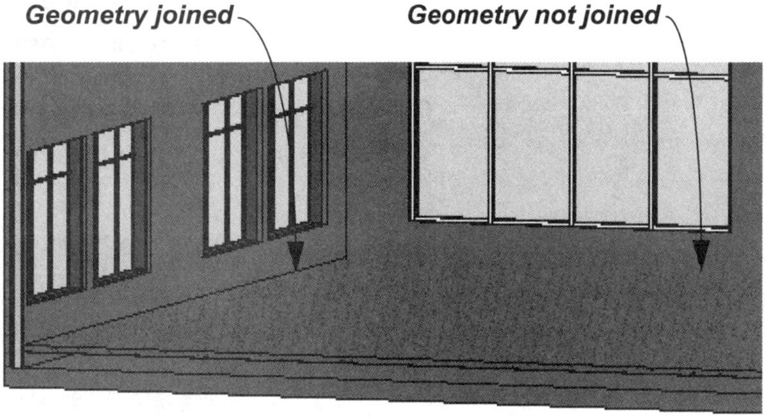

Figure 9–10

How To: Join Geometry

1. In the *Modify* tab>Geometry panel, expand  (Join) and click  (Join Geometry).
2. Select the elements to join.

- If you toggle on the **Multiple Join** option in the Options Bar, you can select several elements to join to the first selection.
- To remove the join, expand  (Join), click  (Unjoin Geometry), and select the elements to unjoin.

Practice 9a Model Floors

Practice Objectives

- Add floors.
- Copy a floor to multiple levels.

In this practice, you will create or modify floors in the Basement, first floor, and second floor of a project. You then copy the floor on the second floor to other related levels and clean up connections between the floors and wall.The second floor with balconies is shown in Figure 9–11.

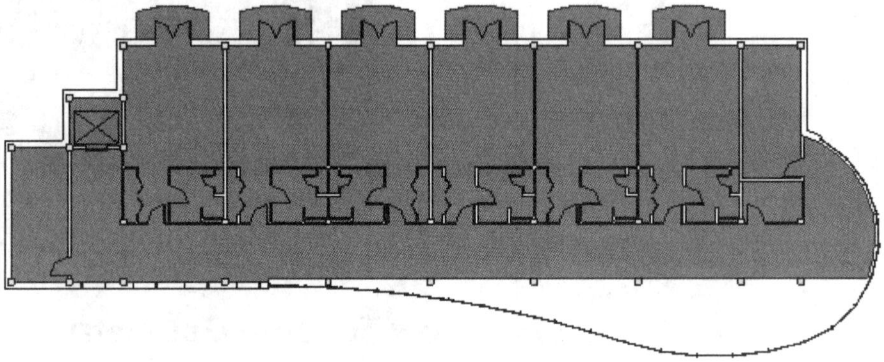

Figure 9–11

Task 1 - Add the basement floor.

1. Open the project **Modern-Hotel-Floors.rvt**.
2. Open the **Floor Plans: Basement** view.
3. In the *Architecture* tab>Build panel, click  (Floor).
4. In the Type Selector, select **Floor: Concrete-1-'0"**.
5. In the *Modify | Create Floor Boundary* tab>Draw panel, click  (Pick Walls) and select the inside face of the exterior foundation walls. Use the Modify tools to ensure that the boundary is a closed loop.
6. Click  (Finish Edit Mode).

7. When the alert box about joining geometry opens, click **Yes**. The floor pattern displays as shown in Figure 9–12.

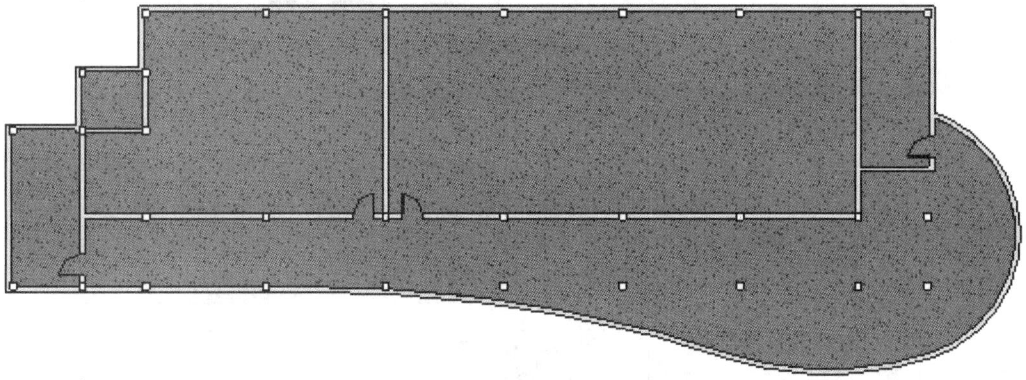

Figure 9–12

8. Click in empty space to release the floor selection.

Press <Enter> to repeat the last command.

9. Start the **Floor** command again.

10. In the Type Selector, select **Floor: Tile**. In Properties, set the *Height Offset from Level* to **1/4"** to match the thickness of the tile.

11. Draw the boundary around the stair wells and hall as shown in Figure 9–13.

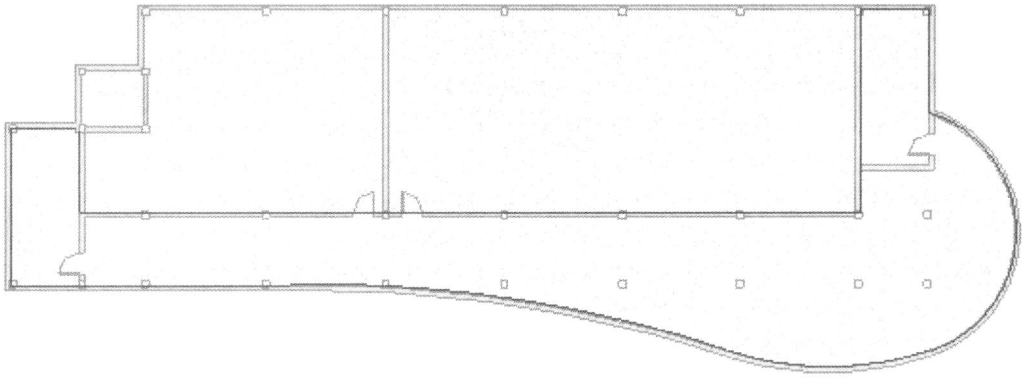

Figure 9–13

12. Click  (Finish Edit Mode).

13. When prompted to join overlapping geometry, click **Yes**.

14. Click in empty space to release the selection and zoom in to display the different floor coverings, as shown in Figure 9–14.

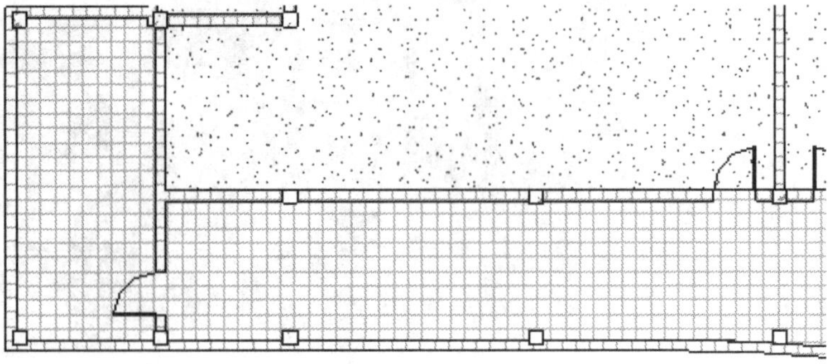

Figure 9–14

15. Save the project.

Task 2 - Modify a floor as a platform for the building.

1. Open the **Floor Plans**: **Floor 1 with Pool** view.
2. Select the existing floor outside the pool building. In the *Modify* | *Floors* tab>Mode panel, click (Edit Boundary).
3. Modify the boundary as shown in Figure 9–15.

Modifying the boundary of this floor creates a platform for the building.

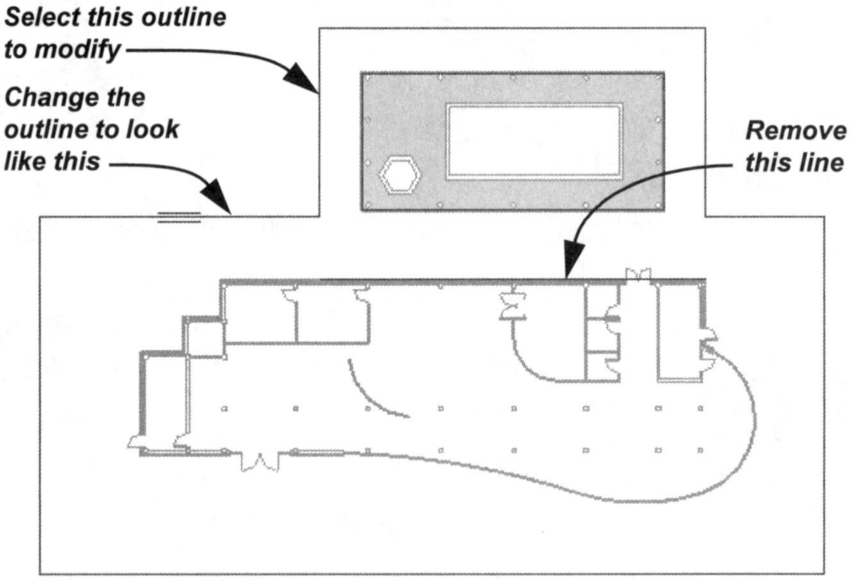

Figure 9–15

4. Click ✓ (Finish Edit Mode).
5. When prompted to attach walls to the floor, click **No**. Some of the walls need to be attached, but not all of them.
6. Click in empty space to release the selection.
7. View the building in 3D. It now has a base to rest on.
8. Save the project.

Task 3 - Add the second floor with balconies.

1. Open the **Floor Plans: Floor 2** view.
2. In the *Architecture* tab>Build panel, click (Floor) and set the following options:
   - In the Type Selector, select **Floor: Generic - 12"**.
   - In the Options Bar, set the *Offset* to **0' 0"** and select **Extend into wall (to core)**.
   - In Properties set the *Height Offset From Level* to **0'-0"**.
3. Use (Pick Walls) and select the main outside walls. Do not select the three curved walls.
4. Change to (Pick Lines) and select the lines of walkways in the linked CAD file as shown in Figure 9–16.

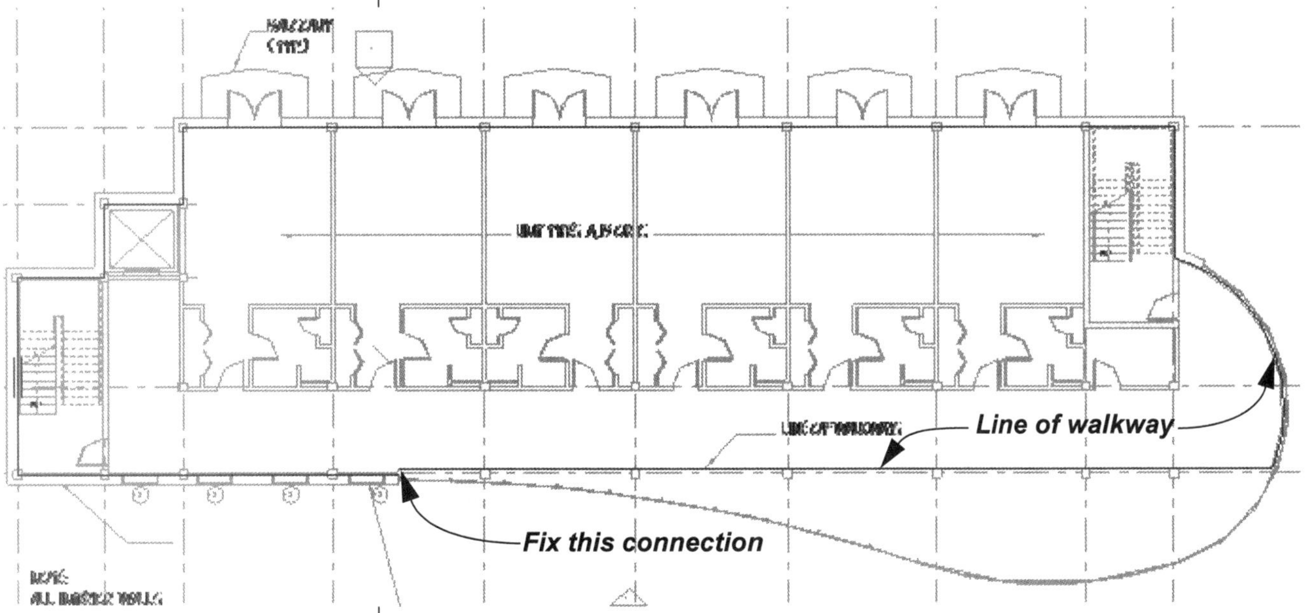

Figure 9–16

5. Zoom in and fix the connection at the front wall and walkway, as shown in Figure 9–17, and check the other connections.

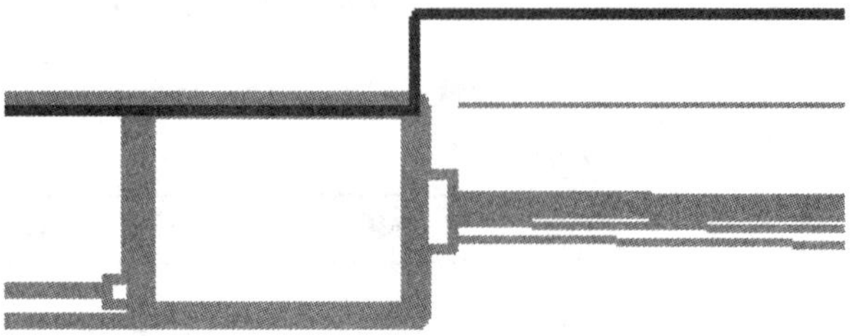

Figure 9–17

6. Pan over to one of the balconies.

7. Use  (Pick Lines) to create the outline of the balcony.

8. Use drag controls to have the balcony lines meet the floor line.

9. Use  (Split Element) with **Delete Inner Segment** selected on the Options Bar, and cut the line as shown in Figure 9–18.

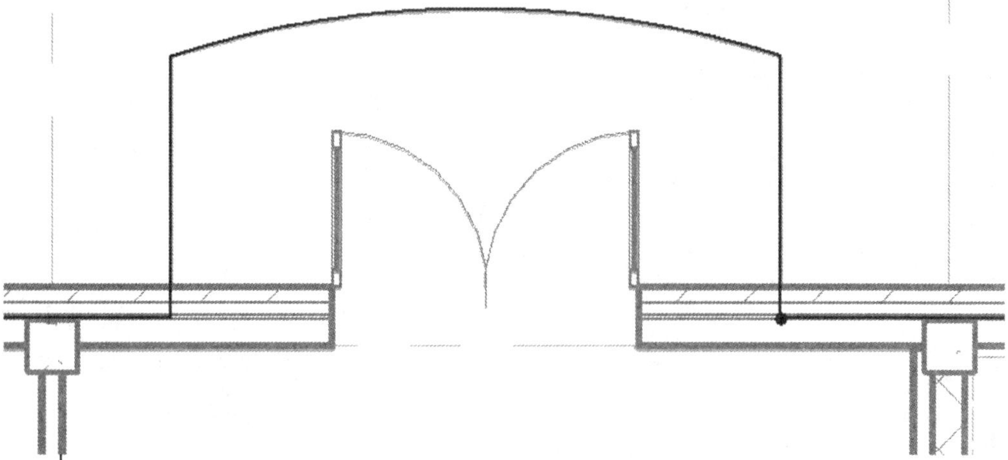

Figure 9–18

10. Click (Modify) and select the balcony elements.

11. Copy the elements to the other balconies and split the lines to create one continuous sketch.

12. Click (Finish Edit Sketch).

13. When the first alert box displays (as shown in Figure 9–19), click **No**. You do not want to attach the walls to this floor.

14. When the alert box shown in Figure 9–20 displays, click **Yes** to cut overlapping geometry out of the walls.

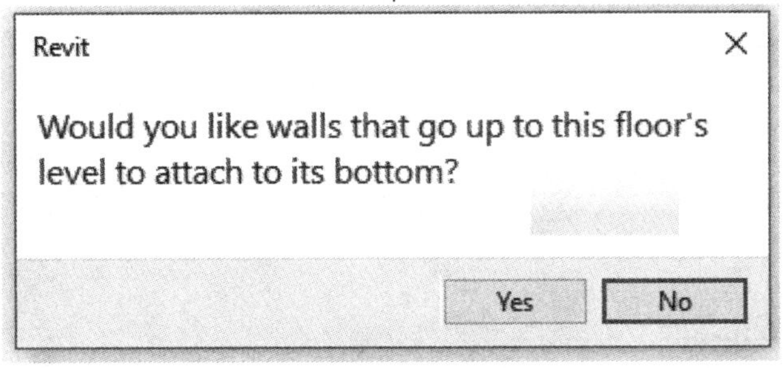

Figure 9–19

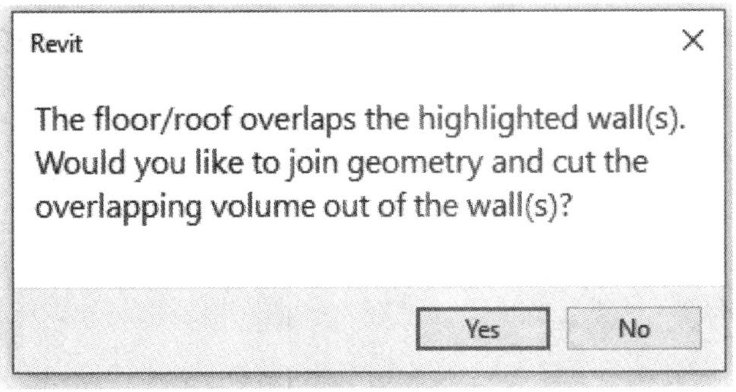

Figure 9–20

15. Click in empty space to release the floor selection.

16. Select the imported CAD file and type **VH** to hide it in the view.

17. Save the project.

Task 4 - Copy the second floor to other floors and clean up floor connections with the walls.

1. In the **Floor Plans: Floor 2** view, select the new floor. (**Hint:** the easiest way is to select one of the balconies.)

2. Hold <Ctrl> and select all of the balcony doors.

3. In the *Modify | Multi-Select* tab>Clipboard panel, click (Copy to the Clipboard).

4. In the Clipboard panel, expand (Paste) and click (Aligned to Selected Levels).

This method can also be used to copy the interior walls and doors to the other levels.

5. In the Select Levels dialog box, select **Floor 3** through **Floor 8**, as shown in Figure 9–21. Click **OK**.

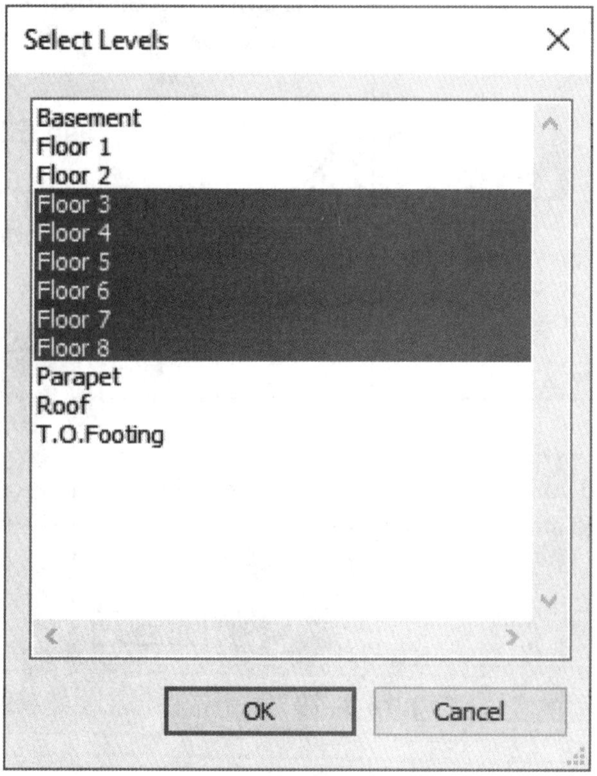

Figure 9–21

6. Open a 3D view and rotate it to display the new doors and floors placed in the building, as shown in Figure 9–22.

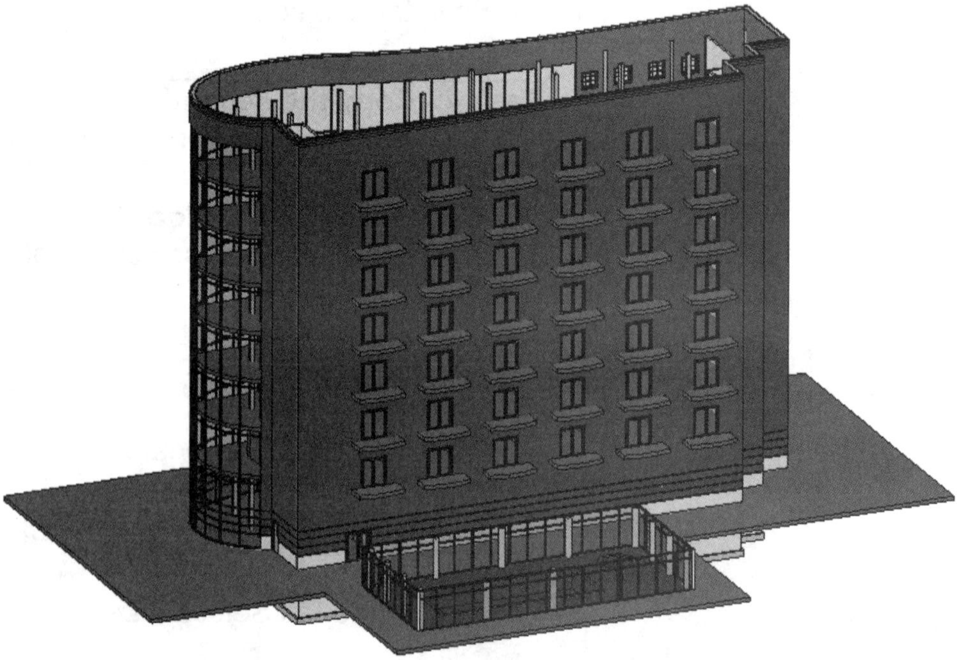

Figure 9–22

7. Zoom in on the back of the building. The floor slabs that extend to the balconies are not joined with the walls and therefore do not display a line across the connection between the wall and balcony, as shown in Figure 9–23. Zoom out to display all of the floors.

8. In the *Modify* tab>Geometry panel, expand (Join) and click (Join Geometry). In the Options Bar, select **Multiple Join**.

9. Select the back exterior wall and then select each floor with a balcony to join the wall and floors, as shown in Figure 9–24. Floor 2 is already joined and does not need to be selected.

Figure 9–23

Figure 9–24

10. Click **Modify** to end the command and then click in space to clear the selection.

11. Zoom out to see the entire building.

12. Save the project.

9.2 Creating Shaft Openings

Shaft Openings only cut floors, roofs, and ceilings. They do not cut walls, beams, or other objects.

Openings can be added to floors (as well as roofs and ceilings) by drawing a closed sketch in the existing sketch. When you have elevator shafts or other floor openings that span more than one floor, create a Shaft Opening, as shown in plan and 3D in Figure 9–25.

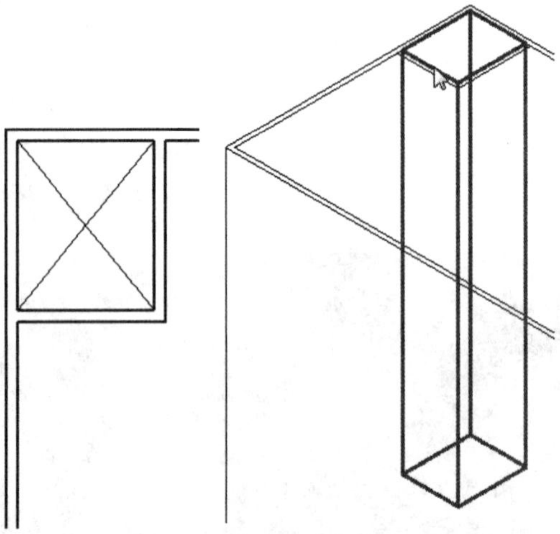

Figure 9–25

How To: Add a Shaft Opening

1. In the *Architecture* tab>Opening panel, click (Shaft).
2. In the *Modify | Create Shaft Opening Sketch* tab>Draw panel, click (Boundary Line) and sketch a line to define the opening.
3. In the Draw panel, click (Symbolic Line) and add lines that show the opening symbol in plan view.
4. In Properties, set the following:
   - *Base and Top Constraint*
   - *Base and Top Offset* or *Unconnected Height*
5. Click (Finish Edit Mode) to create the opening.

- A Shaft Opening element can include symbolic lines that repeat on each level, displaying the shaft in a plan view.
- Shafts are a separate element from the floor, roof, ceiling, or wall, and can be deleted without selecting a host element.

9.3 Creating Sloped Floors

Floors can have slopes applied to them. To make a floor slope in one direction, you place a *slope arrow* in the sketch of the floor, as shown in Figure 9–26.

The slope arrow only displays while Sketch mode is active.

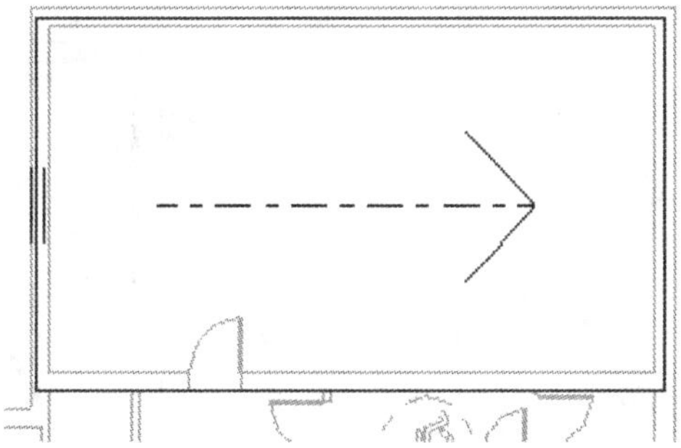

Figure 9–26

- Once the floor is created, you can add multiple drainage points and cause the floor to warp toward them.
- These tools also work with roofs and structural slabs.

How To: Slope a Floor in One Direction

1. Select the floor you want to slope. In the *Modify | Floors* tab> Mode panel, click (Edit Boundary).
2. In the *Modify | Floors>Edit Boundary* tab>Draw panel, click (Slope Arrow).
3. Select two points to define the arrow. The first point is the tail and the second is the head. The tail and head locations are points at which you can specify heights. The direction of the arrow determines the orientation of the slope.
4. In Properties, specify the *Level* and *Offset* at the *Tail* and *Head*, as shown in Figure 9–27.

Constraints	
Specify	Height at Tail
Level at Tail	Default
Height Offset at Tail	1' 0"
Level at Head	Default
Height Offset at Head	0' 0"

Figure 9–27

Creating Multiple Slopes for Drainage

Restrooms, labs, garages, and other rooms often need to have floors that slope towards drains, as shown in Figure 9–28. In addition, all flat roofs are not actually flat, but also slope towards drains. Several tools provide ways of creating points for the drain locations, as well as creating lines to define how the slope is going to drain.

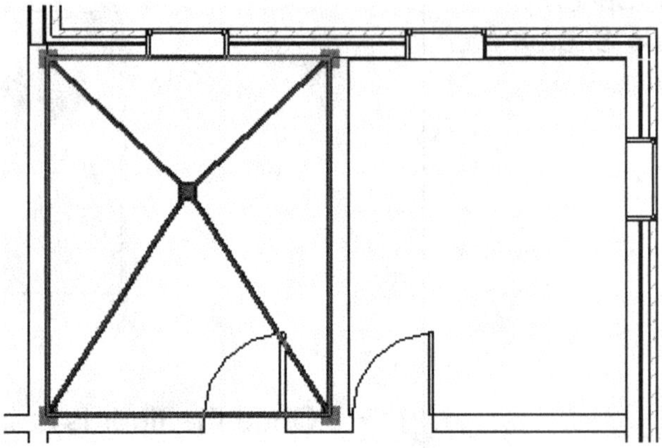

Figure 9–28

- These tools work with floors, roofs, and structural floors.

How To: Create Multiple Slopes for Drainage

1. Select the required flat floor, roof, or slab.
2. In the *Modify | Floors* tab>Shape Editing panel, as shown in Figure 9–29, select the tools that you want to use to define the slopes.

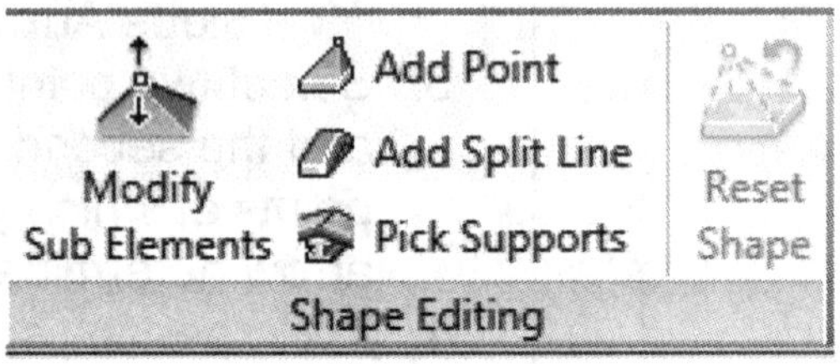

Figure 9–29

Add Point: Specify the location of the low or high points on the surface. In the Options Bar, set the *Elevation*. •By default, the elevation is relative to the top of the surface. Clear the **Relative** option if you want to use the project elevation.

-  displays when you place the point. Slope lines are automatically added from the corners of the surface to the point.

	**Add Split Line:** Define smaller areas on the surface when you place more than one drain. Depending on the size of the area you are working with, you might want to create these before you add the drains. Select the **Chain** option if you want to add more than one connected segment.
	**Pick Supports:** Select structural beams that define the split lines.
	**Modify Sub-Elements:** Change the elevation of edges and points and change the location of points. You can also move points using shape handles without clicking  (Modify Sub-Elements), as shown in the figure below. Press <Tab> to cycle through the options to reach the element you want to modify. 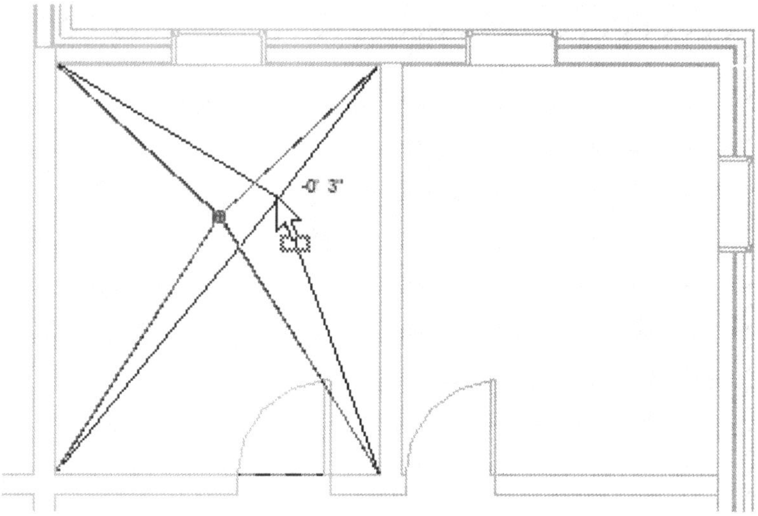

- If you want to remove the slopes from a surface, click  (Reset Shape).
- Floors, roofs, and slabs use styles set to a constant thickness (where the entire element slopes) or to a variable thickness (where only the top layer slopes), as shown in Figure 9–30.

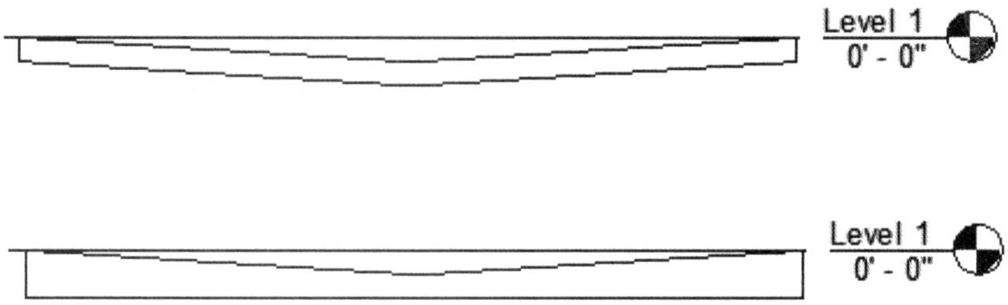

Figure 9–30

Practice 9b Create Shaft Openings and Sloped Floors

Practice Objectives

- Create a shaft opening.
- Slope floors.

In this practice, you will add a shaft opening for the elevator, as shown on the left in Figure 9–31. You will also slope floors for drainage in the restrooms and janitors closet using the Shape Editing tools, as shown on the right in Figure 9–31.

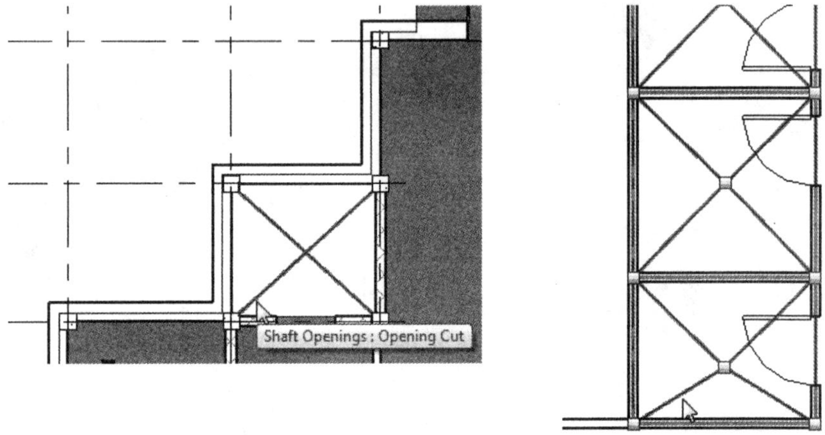

Figure 9–31

Task 1 - Create a shaft opening.

1. Open the project **Modern-Hotel-Shaft.rvt**.
2. Open the **Floor Plans: Floor 1** view and zoom in to the elevator area.
3. Temporarily hide the elevator.
4. In the *Architecture* tab>Opening panel, click (Shaft).
5. In the *Modify | Create Shaft Opening Sketch* tab>Draw panel, verify that (Boundary Line) is selected.

Shafts do not cut through structural elements.

6. Use (Pick Walls) to create the boundary. Then use (Trim/Extend to Corner) to ensure that the boundary is closed, as shown in Figure 9–32.

7. In the Draw panel, click (Symbolic Line) and add two lines crossing the opening, as shown in Figure 9–32.

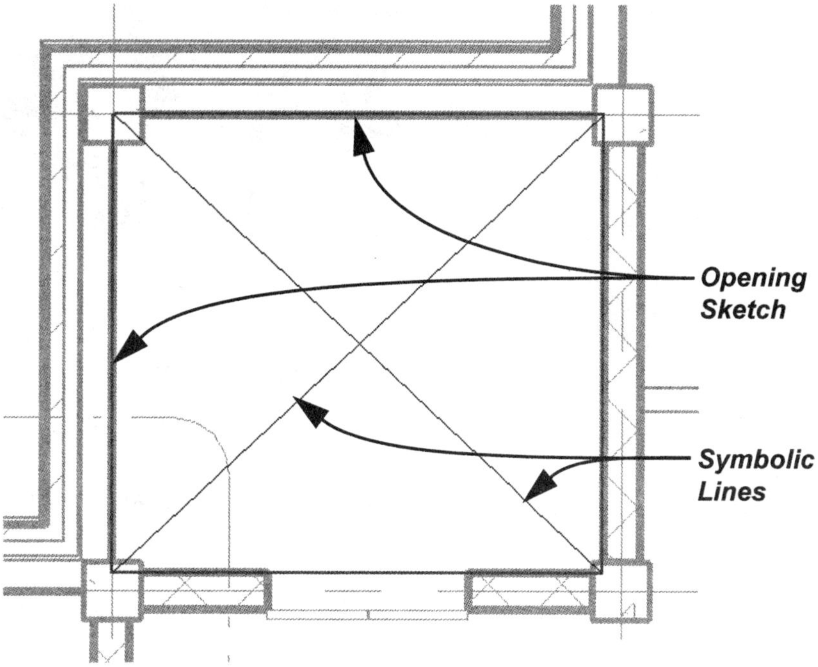

Figure 9–32

8. In Properties, verify that the *Base Constraint* is **Floor 1**. Set the *Base Offset* to (negative) **-1' 0"** and the *Top Constraint* to **Up to Level:Roof**.

9. Click (Finish Edit Mode).

10. Reset **Temporary Hide/Isolate** and zoom out to fit the view.

11. Open the **Floor Plans: Floor 2** view.

12. In the View Control Bar, change the *Visual Style* to (Consistent Colors) to display the opening.

13. Return the *Visual Style* to (Hidden Line).

14. Open the 3D view and rotate it to display the shaft as it goes through all of the floors, as shown in Figure 9–33.

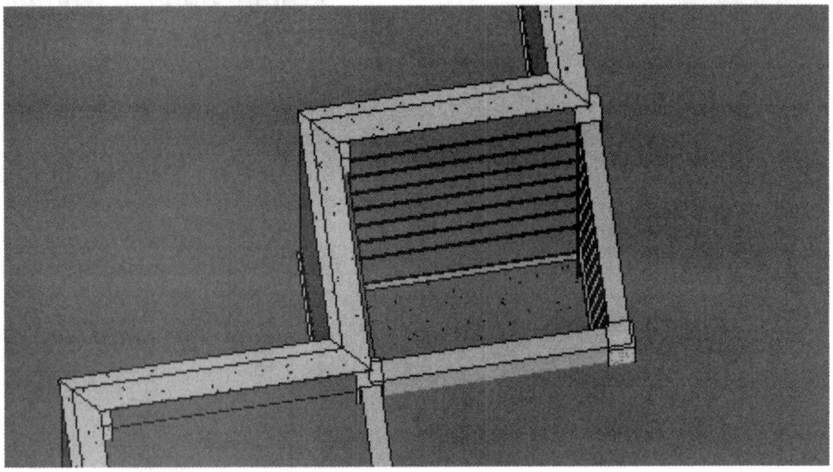

Figure 9–33

15. Open a couple other full floor plan views.The symbolic lines display in all views.

16. Return to the **Floor Plans: Floor 1** view.

17. Zoom out to display the entire view, if required.

18. In the Quick Access Toolbar, click  (Close Inactive Views).

19. Save the project.

Task 2 - Slope floors for drainage.

1. Open the **Floor Plans: Floor 1 Restrooms** view.

2. Expand the size of the crop region so the janitor's closet below is also included in the plan.

3. Select one of the elevation markers and hide the category.

4. The edge of the floor does not display in this view, so you cannot select it using the standard method. In the Status Bar, click  (Select Elements by Face), and then click on the face of the floor to select it.

5. In the *Modify | Floors* tab>Shape Editing panel, click  (Add Split Line). Draw the lines, as shown in Figure 9–34.

*Use the **Chain** option and add all of the outside edges first.*

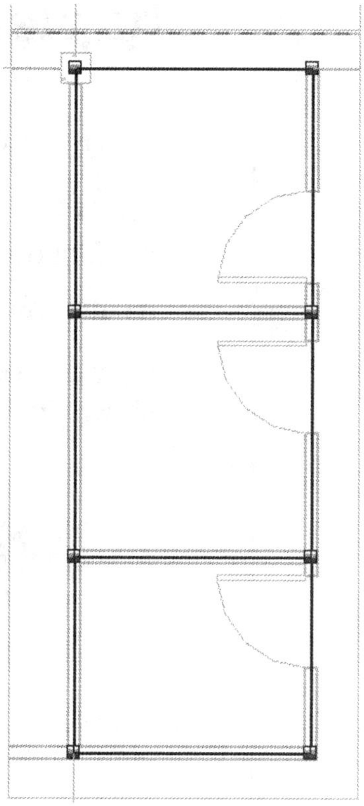

Figure 9–34

6. In the Shape Editing panel, click (Add Point). In the Options Bar, set the *Elevation* to (negative) **-1/2"**. Place a point in the center of each room, as shown for one of them in Figure 9–35.

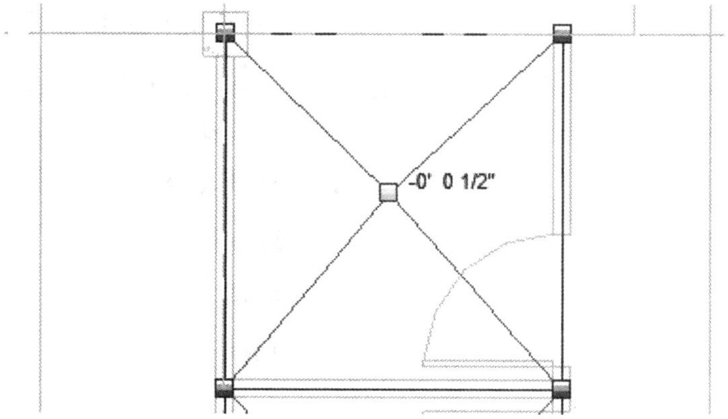

Figure 9–35

7. End the command.

8. In the Status Bar, toggle off (Select Elements by Face).

9. Open the 3D view, zoom out and save the project.

Chapter Review Questions

1. When creating a floor the boundary sketch must be...
   a. Open
   b. Closed
   c. It does not matter.
2. How do you change the thickness of a floor, such as those shown in Figure 9–36?

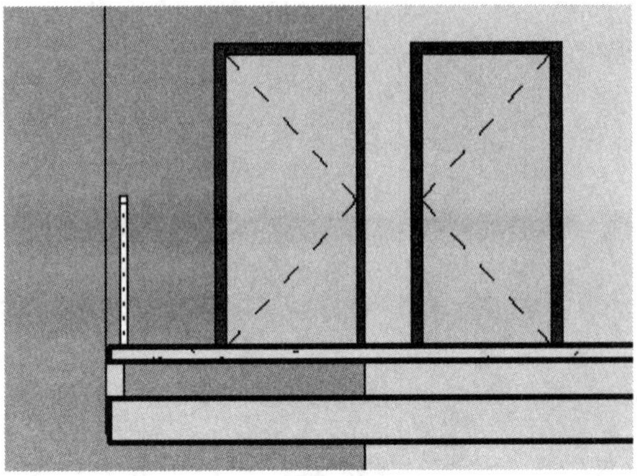

Figure 9–36

   a. In the Type Selector, change the *Floor Type*.
   b. In the Options Bar, change the *Floor Thickness*.
   c. In Properties, change the *Floor Thickness*.
   d. In the contextual ribbon, change the *Offset*.
3. Which of the following Opening commands cuts an opening in multiple floors at the same time?
   a. **By Face**
   b. **Shaft**
   c. **Wall**
   d. **Vertical**
4. When creating a sloped floor,  (Add Point) places a point at...
   a. The end of the floor where you want the slope to end.
   b. The end of the floor where you want the slope to begin.
   c. The high or low points of a floor.
   d. A point where two slopes converge.

Command Summary

Button	Command	Location
	**Floor: Architectural**	• **Ribbon:** *Architecture* tab>Build panel>expand Floor
	**Floor: Structural**	• **Ribbon:** *Architecture* tab>Build panel>expand Floor
	**Shaft**	• **Ribbon:** *Architecture* tab>Opening panel
Shape Editing Tools		
	**Add Point**	• **Ribbon:** *Modify* | *Floors* tab>Shape Editing panel
	**Add Split Line**	• **Ribbon:** *Modify* | *Floors* tab>Shape Editing panel
	**Modify Sub Elements**	• **Ribbon:** *Modify* | *Floors* tab>Shape Editing panel
	**Pick Supports**	• **Ribbon:** *Modify* | *Floors* tab>Shape Editing panel
	**Reset Shape**	• **Ribbon:** *Modify* | *Floors* tab>Shape Editing panel

Chapter 10

Modeling Ceilings

In the Autodesk® Revit® software, ceilings are modeled using reflected ceiling plans. You can add ceilings by selecting a room boundary, or by sketching ceilings that do not fill an entire room. You can create basic ceilings made of acoustical tile grids, or you can create custom ceilings of different heights with a soffit wall added between. In addition to creating a ceiling, you can also place ceiling fixtures directly onto ceiling elements.

Learning Objectives in this Chapter

- Add automatic ceilings that fill an entire room boundary and sketched ceilings that are customized to suit a design.
- Modify ceiling boundaries and the grid locations for acoustical tiles to ensure that the tiles fit the room correctly.
- Add ceiling components, including lighting and mechanical fixtures.
- Add soffit walls in the gap between ceilings of different heights.

10.1 Modeling Ceilings

Adding ceilings to Autodesk Revit models is a straightforward process. To place a ceiling, click inside areas that are bounded by walls, and the ceiling is created, as shown in the large room on the right in Figure 10–1. You can also sketch custom ceilings when required. Any fixtures you attach to a ceiling displays in reflected ceiling plans, as well as in sections and 3D views.

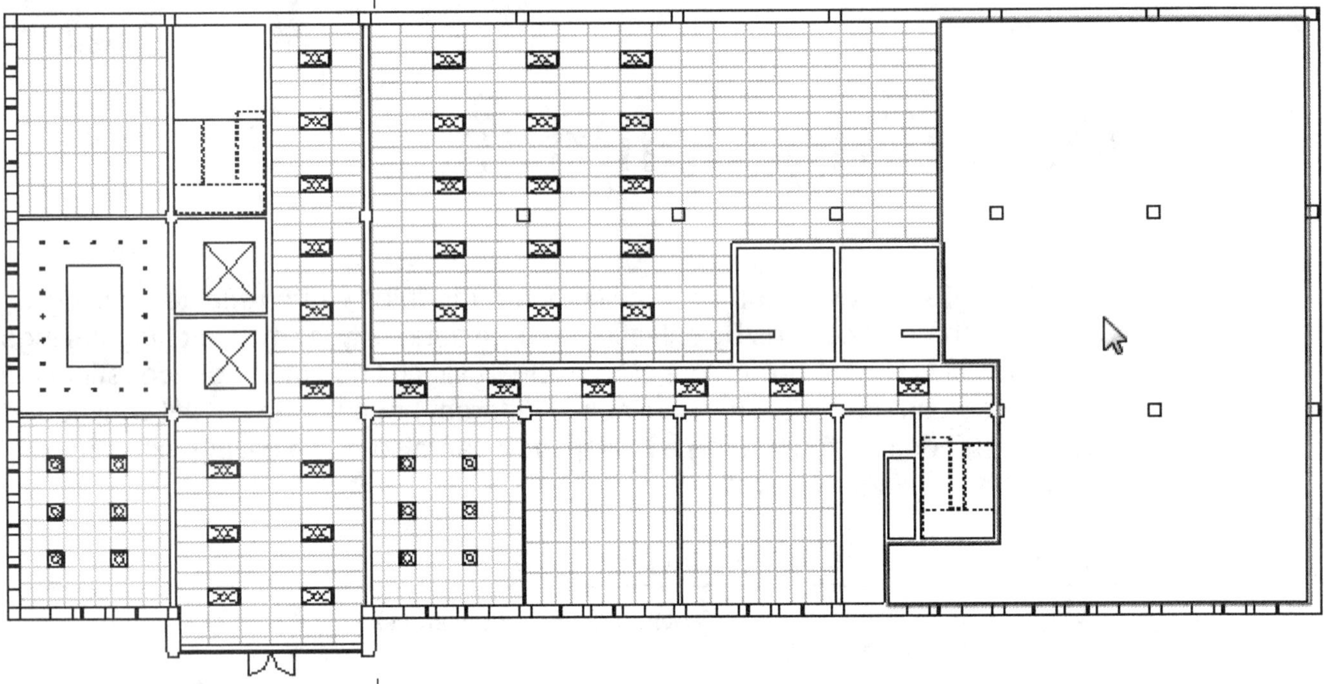

Figure 10–1

- Ceiling plans are typically created by default when you add a level with a view, as shown in Figure 10–2.

*If you do not want a level to have a ceiling plan, you can right-click on its name in the Project Browser and select **Delete**.*

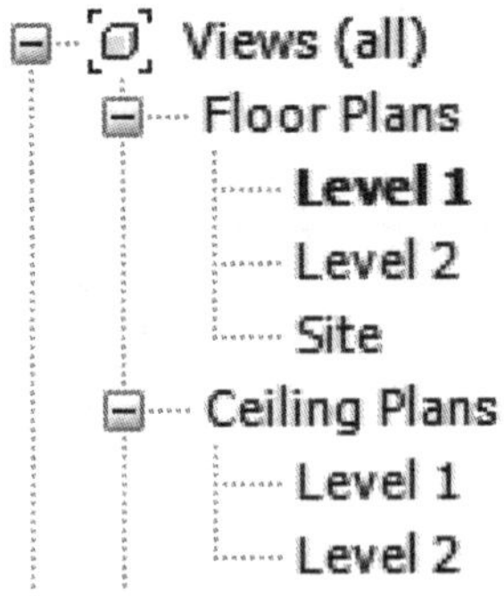

Figure 10–2

How To: Create an Automatic Boundary Ceiling

1. Switch to the appropriate Ceiling Plan view.
2. In the *Architecture* tab>Build panel, click (Ceiling).
3. In the Type Selector, select the ceiling type. In Properties, set the *Height Offset from Level*.
4. In the *Modify | Place Ceiling* tab>Ceiling panel, verify that (Automatic Ceiling) is selected. Click inside a room to create a ceiling, as shown in Figure 10–3.

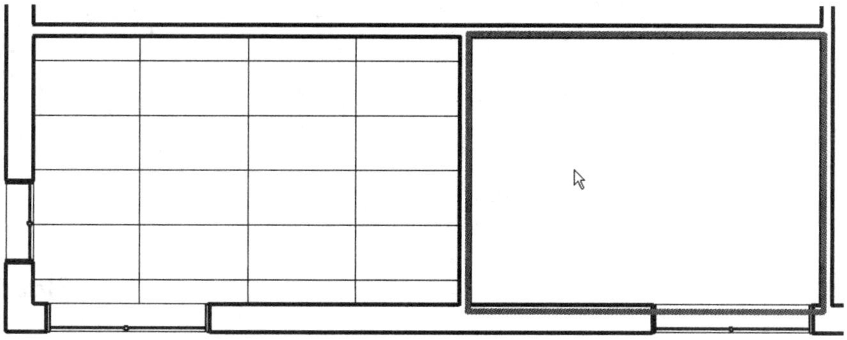

Figure 10–3

5. Continue adding ceilings to other rooms, as required.

Hint: Room Bounding Status

Elements (such as walls, floors, ceilings, and roofs) have a *Room Bounding* property set in Properties. In most cases, this is toggled on by default as these elements typically define areas and volumes.

The **Automatic Ceiling** tool uses this property to identify walls that set the outline of a ceiling. If you toggle off this property for a wall (such as a partial height wall), the **Automatic Ceiling** tool ignores the wall.

Ceilings can also be used as a Room Bounding for volume calculations.

- To modify a ceiling boundary, select a ceiling and either:
  - In the *Modify |Ceilings* tab>Mode panel, click (Edit Boundary), or
  - Double-click on the ceiling.

Sketching Ceilings

To add a ceiling to part of a room (as shown in Figure 10–4) or to have two different ceiling types at separate levels, you need to sketch a ceiling.

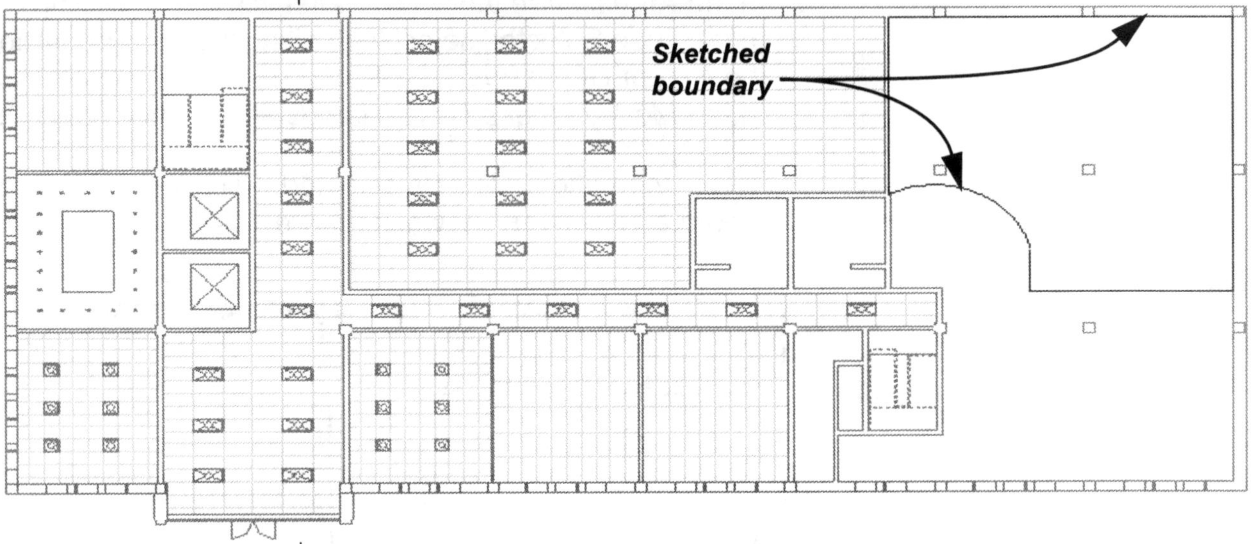

Figure 10–4

How To: Sketch a Ceiling

1. In the *Architecture* tab>Build panel, click (Ceiling).
2. In the *Modify | Place Ceiling* tab>Ceiling panel, click (Sketch Ceiling).
3. In the Draw panel, click (Line) or (Pick Walls) and define a closed loop for the ceiling boundary, similar to sketching a floor boundary.
4. Click (Finish Edit Mode) to create the ceiling.

- To include a hole in a ceiling, include the hole as part of the sketch. The hole must be a closed loop completely inside the ceiling boundary.
- In the *Architecture* tab>Opening panel, you can also use (Opening By Face), (Shaft Opening) or (Vertical Opening) to cut a hole in a ceiling that is separate from the sketch.

Modifying Ceiling Grids

To change a rectangular ceiling tile pattern from horizontal to vertical, select a grid line and rotate it 90 degrees.

When using acoustical tile ceiling types, you can reposition the grid locations by moving or rotating the grid lines, as shown in Figure 10–5.

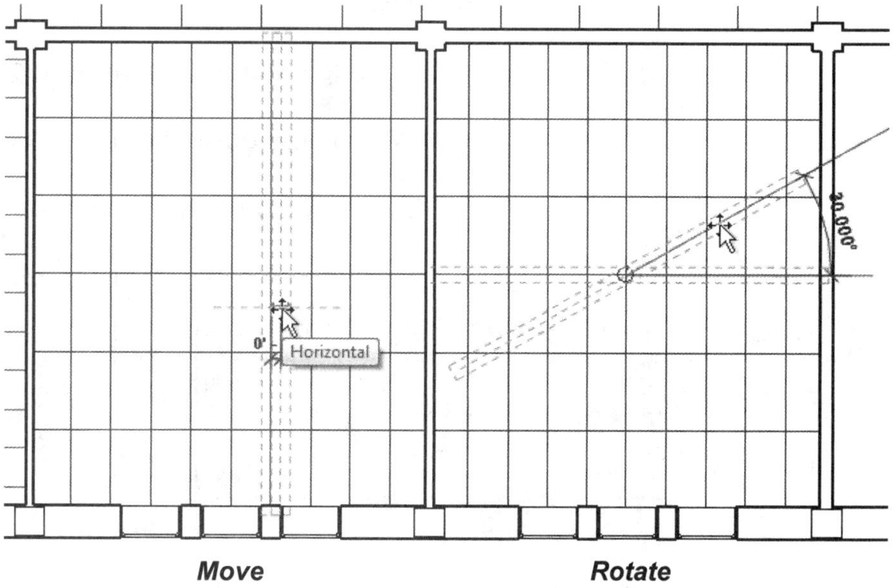

Figure 10–5

How To: Move a Ceiling Grid

1. Select a grid line in the ceiling that you want to modify.
2. In the *Modify | Ceilings* tab>Modify panel, click  (Move).
3. Move the cursor to one side and type a distance, typically an increment of the ceiling grid size.

How To: Rotate a Ceiling Grid

1. Select a grid line in the ceiling that you want to modify.
2. In the *Modify | Ceilings* tab>Modify panel, click  (Rotate).
3. In the Options Bar, type an *Angle* or use  (Rotate) to visually select the angle.

10.2 Adding Ceiling Fixtures

Several groups of components are commonly used with ceilings, such as:

- Lighting fixtures (shown in Figure 10–6)
- Mechanical equipment (for registers and diffusers)
- Specialty equipment (such as exit signs or sprinklers)

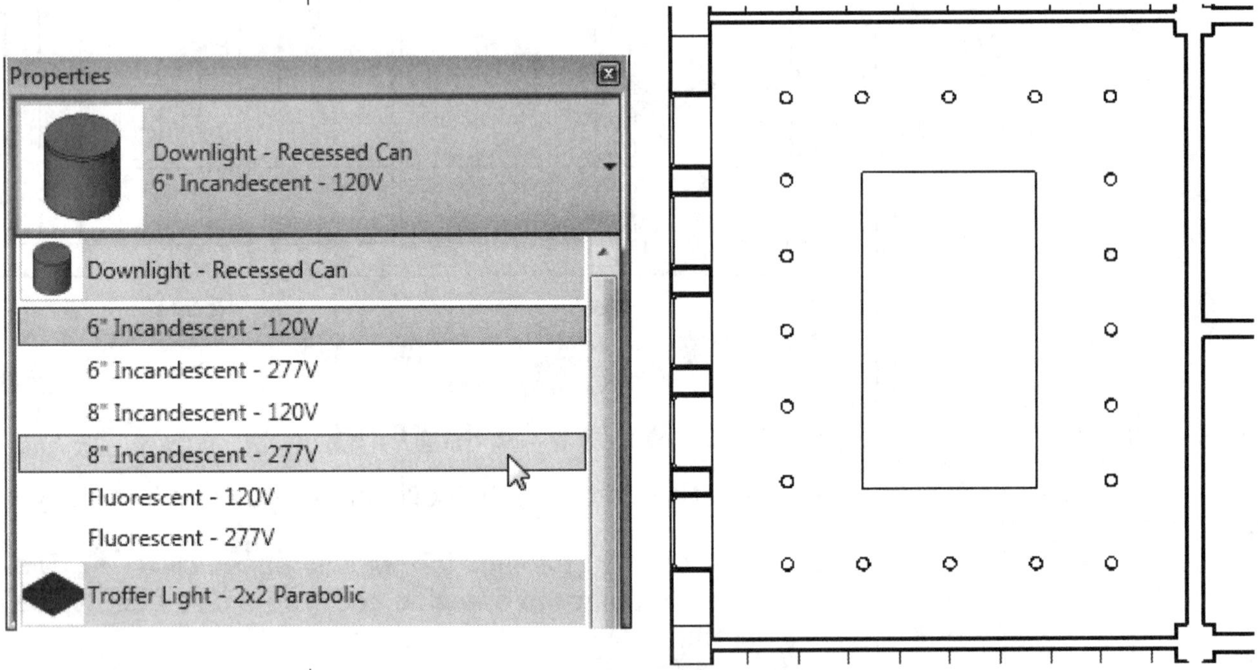

Figure 10–6

After placing a component, press <Spacebar> to rotate it in 90-degree increments.

- Use (Component) to place ceiling fixtures in the ceiling view.
- The Autodesk Revit Library contains a variety of light fixtures and mechanical ceiling fixtures.
- Many light fixtures include types that specify the voltage of the lamp, as shown in Figure 10–6.
- Some light fixtures are wall-based, instead of ceiling-based, and need to be placed on a wall in a floor plan view. These include items such as sconces.

- When you delete a ceiling, the associated components (such as light fixtures) are also deleted.
- Components come in based on their center point and respond to the nearby walls, not to the ceiling grid. Place an instance of the component and use **Move** or **Align** to get it to the correct location on the grid. Then use **Copy** to place additional instances on the grid.
- Some light fixtures can display the light source, as shown in the section in Figure 10–7. To display the light source, in the Visibility/Graphic Overrides dialog box, *in the Model Categories* tab, expand **Lighting Fixtures** and select **Light Source,** as shown on the left in Figure 10–7.

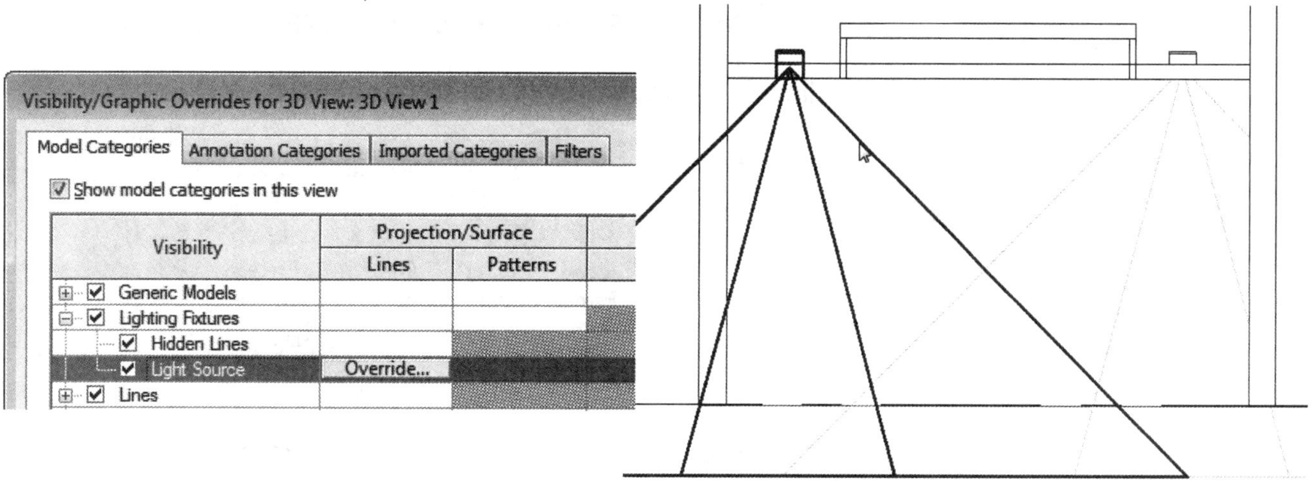

Figure 10–7

- The light sources display their true strength in renderings.

Hint: Placing Components in Rooms Without a Ceiling

If you need to place components in a room that does not have a ceiling, you can create a reference plane at the height where you want them and place workplane-based families on it. You can also place workplane-based components on the underside of a floor.

1. In a section or elevation view, sketch a reference plane at the required height.
2. Click on the <*Click to name*> field and type a name and press <Enter>.
3. Open the ceiling plan where you want to work.
4. Start the **Component** command and select a workplane-based component.
5. In the *Modify | Place Component* tab>Placement panel, click (Place on Workplane), as shown in Figure 10–8.

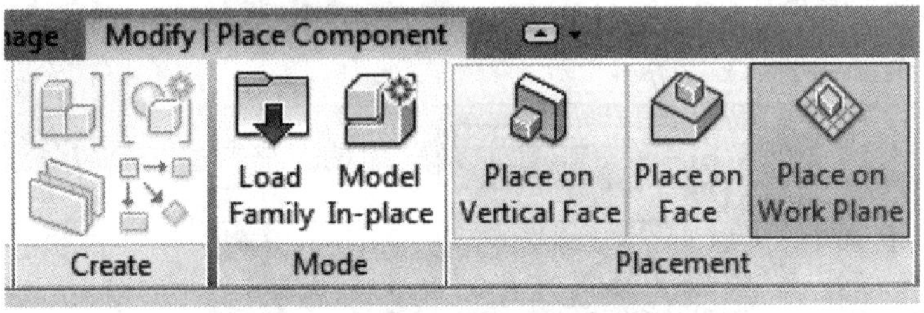

Figure 10–8

6. In the Options Bar, specify the named reference plane from the Placement Plane drop-down list, as shown in Figure 10–9.

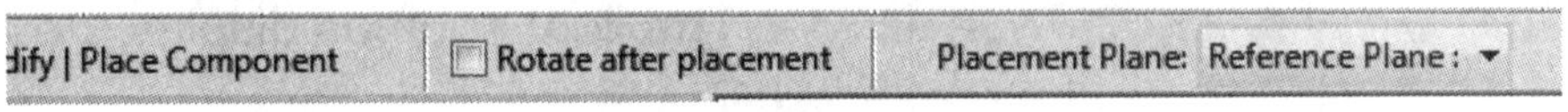

Figure 10–9

7. Place the component.

- These options are only available if you have selected a workplane-based component.

Practice 10a Model Ceilings and Add Ceiling Fixtures

Practice Objectives

- Create automatic ceilings with grids.
- Add ceiling components.

In this practice, while working in a reflected ceiling plan, you will add acoustical tile ceilings to several support spaces. You will then add light fixtures and air terminals, as shown in Figure 10–10.

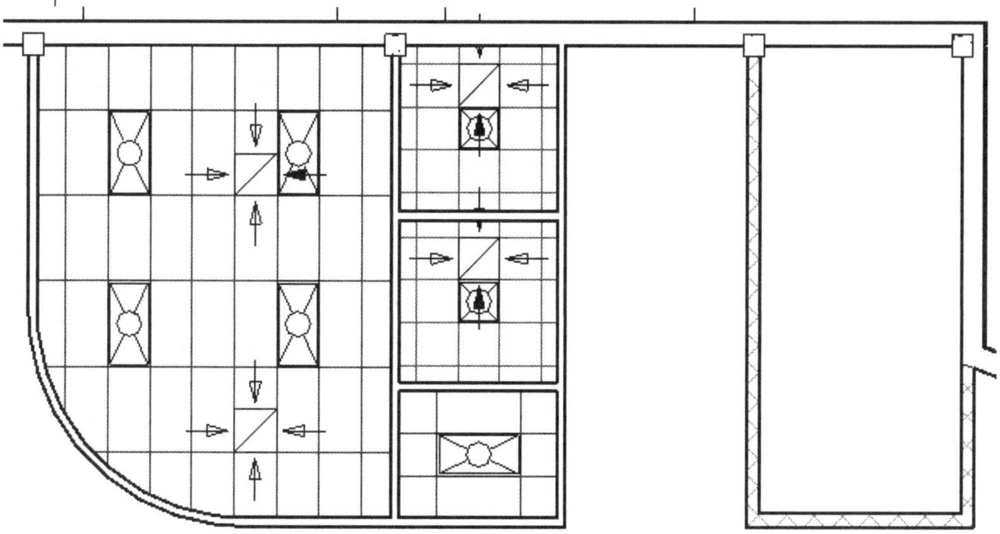

Figure 10–10

Task 1 - Create ceilings with ceiling grids.

1. Open the project **Modern-Hotel-Ceilings.rvt**.
2. Open the **Ceiling Plans: Floor 1** view.
    - To clarify the view, you might want to hide the grids, elevations, and sections categories. A quick way to do this is to select one of each element and then type **VH**.
3. In the *Architecture* tab>Build panel, click  (Ceiling).
4. In the Type Selector, verify that **Compound Ceiling: 2' x 4' ACT System** is selected.

5. Click inside the four support rooms, as shown in Figure 10–11.

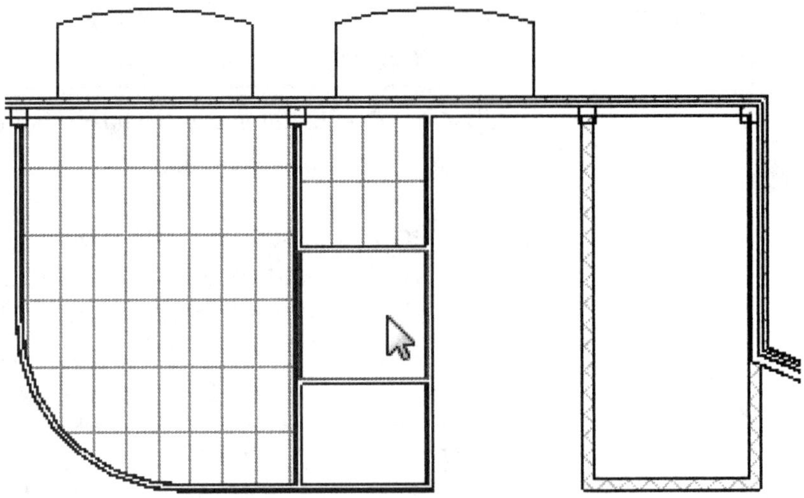

Figure 10–11

Hold <Ctrl> to select more than one element.

6. Start the **Modify** command and select one grid line in each restroom.

7. In the Type Selector, select **Compound Ceiling: 2' x 2' ACT System**. In Properties, set the *Height Offset from Level* to **9' 0"**.

8. Save the project.

Task 2 - Add ceiling components.

1. In the *Architecture* tab>Build panel, click (Component).

2. In the *Modify | Place Component*>Mode panel, click (Load Family) and load the following components from the associated folders:

   Lighting>Architectural>Internal:

   - **Downlight Recessed Can.rfa**
   - **Troffer Light 2x2 Parabolic.rfa**
   - **Troffer Light 2x4 Parabolic.rfa**

   Mechanical>MEP>Air-Side Components>Air Terminals:

   - **Return Diffuser - Hosted.rfa**
   - **Supply Diffuser - Hosted.rfa**

3. Add the ceiling fixtures, as shown in Figure 10–12.
   - Select a light fixture and place it on the grid. Press <Esc> and select the light fixture. Press <Spacebar> to rotate the light 90 degrees.
   - Use snaps or **Align** to place it exactly on the grid.
   - Copy it to the other locations.
   - Select a ceiling grid line and use **Move** to modify the grid to suit the location of the fixtures.
   - Place diffusers in each room. As you are using the hosted MEP version, in the *Modify* | *Place Component* tab> Placement panel, click (Place on Face).

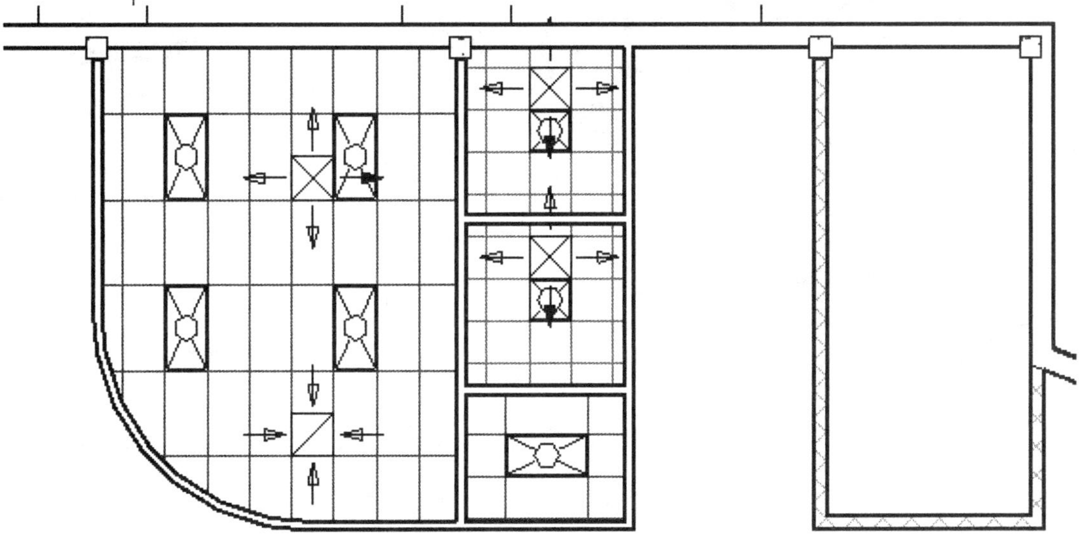

Figure 10–12

4. Save the project.

10.3 Creating Ceiling Soffits

Ceiling soffits are parts of a ceiling that have been lowered, as shown in Figure 10–13, or that connect two ceilings of different heights. Creating a ceiling soffit takes two steps. First, you create a ceiling, and then you model walls using a soffit wall type.

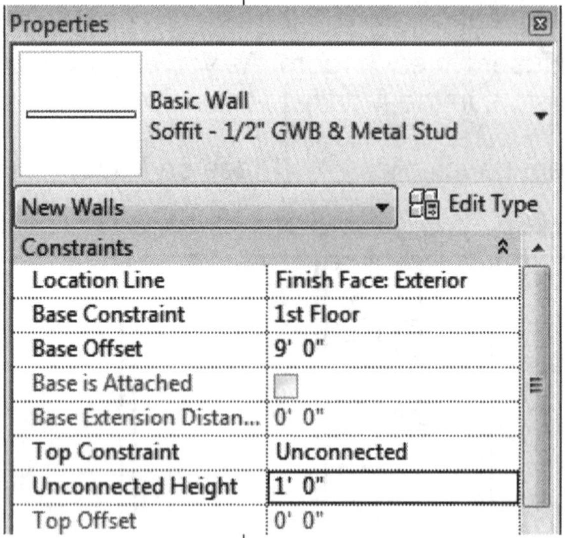

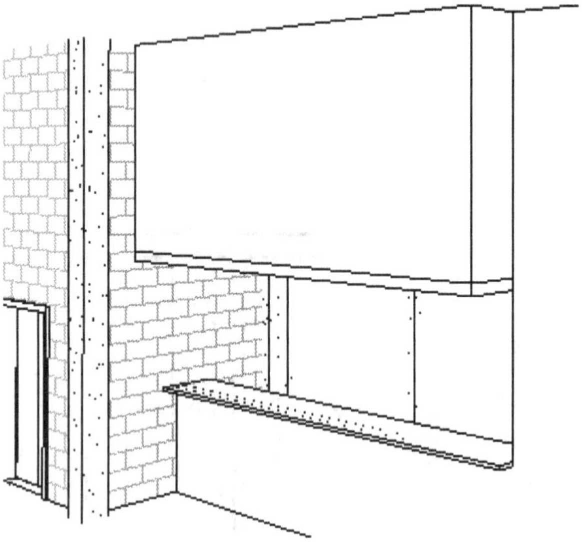

Figure 10–13

How To: Create a Ceiling with a Soffit

1. Open a ceiling plan.
2. In the *Architecture* tab>Build panel, click  (Ceiling).
3. In the Type Selector, select the ceiling type. In Properties, set the *Height Offset from Level*.
4. In the *Modify | Place Ceiling* tab>Ceiling panel, click  (Sketch Ceiling).
5. Draw the ceiling outline, such as the example shown in Figure 10–14.

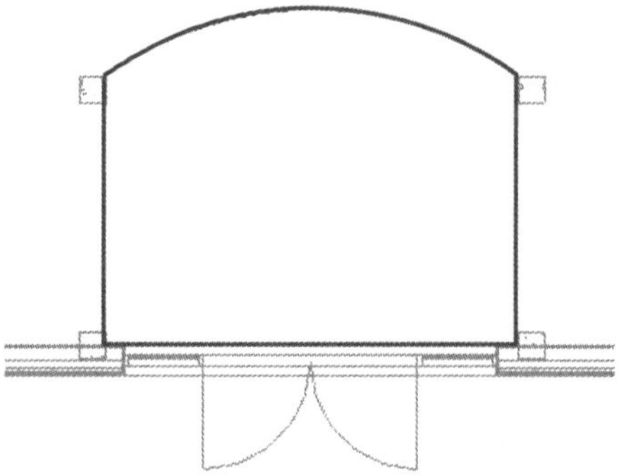

Figure 10–14

6. Click (Finish Edit Mode).
7. In *Architecture* tab>Build panel, click (Wall) to create the soffit wall.
8. In the Type Selector, select a soffit wall type. In Properties, set the *Base Offset* from the floor and set the *Top Constraint/Unconnected Height* as required to establish the height of the soffit.
   - Sometimes it is easier to set the height of the soffit walls by extending or trimming elements in a section view.
9. In the *Modify | Place Wall* tab>Draw panel, click (Pick Lines). Select the edges of the ceiling to create the walls, as shown in Figure 10–15.

If the wall is on the outside of the ceiling, flip it using the Flip control and create the rest of the walls using the opposite ***Location Line*** *option.*

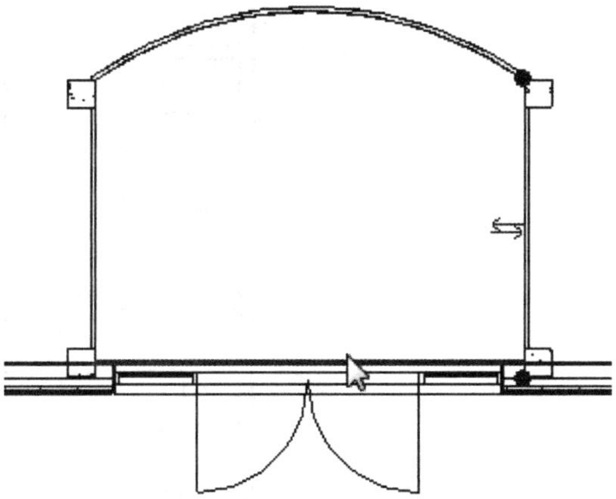

Figure 10–15

10. Display the ceiling in 3D to verify that it is displayed correctly.

Hint: Joining Geometry

When you are working with elements that are next to each other, they might need additional modification so that they display as expected. For example, one way to fix connections between walls and ceilings is to join the geometry.

In the *Modify* tab>Geometry panel, click (Join Geometry) and then select the elements to join.

Practice 10b Create Ceiling Soffits

Practice Objective

- Create ceiling soffits.

In this practice, you will sketch a ceiling, add fixtures, and create a soffit wall in the hall, as shown in Figure 10–16. Optionally, you will also add a recessed ceiling and soffit to the breakfast area.

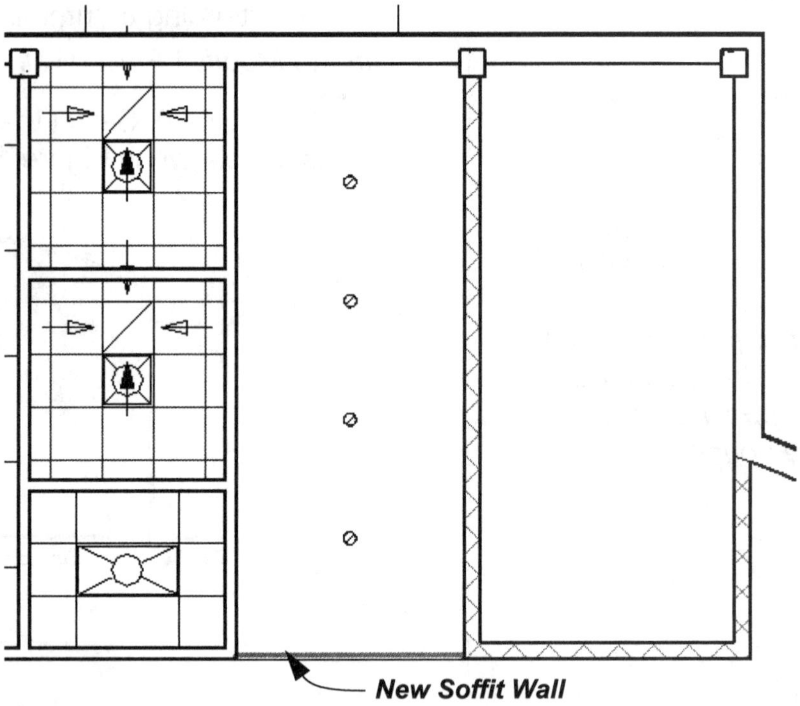

Figure 10–16

Task 1 - Sketch a ceiling.

1. Open the project **Modern-Hotel-Soffits.rvt**.
2. Open the **Ceiling Plans: Floor 1** view and zoom in on the hallway by the restrooms.
3. In the *Architecture* tab>Build panel, click  (Ceiling).
4. In the Type Selector, select **Compound Ceiling: GWB on Mtl.Stud** and in Properties, set the *Height Offset from Level* to **10' 0"**.

5. In the *Modify* | *Place Ceiling* tab>Ceiling panel, click  (Sketch Ceiling) and sketch the outline of the ceiling (as shown in Figure 10–17), in the hallway.

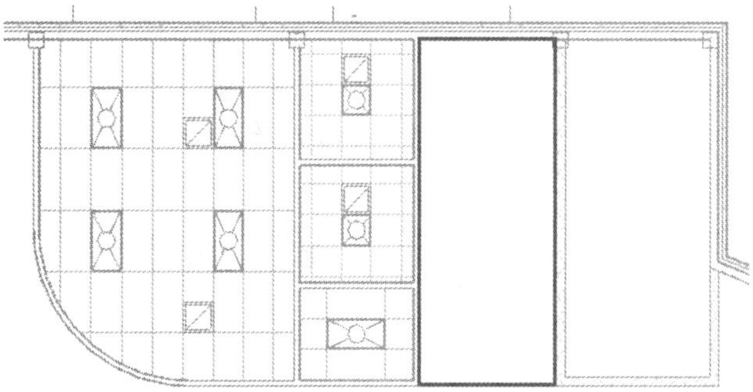

Figure 10–17

6. Click  (Finish Edit Mode).
7. Add a line of four **Downlight - Recessed Can** components down the hallway, set at an elevation of **10'-0"**.
   - Use reference planes. detail lines, dimensions set to equal, or the **Array** command to space them equally in the hallway.
8. Save the project.

Task 2 - Add a soffit.

1. Open the **Sections (Building Section): East-West Section** view and zoom in on the hallway area shown in Figure 10–18.

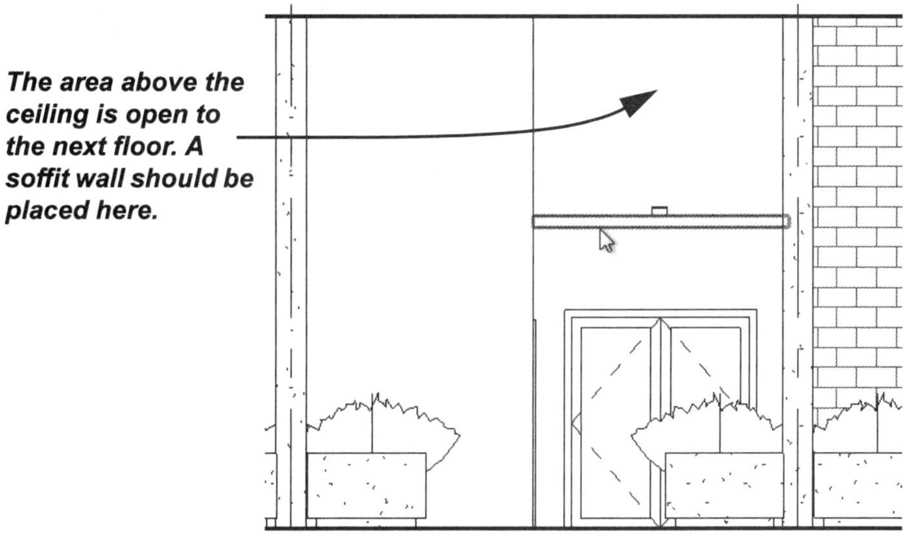

Figure 10–18

2. Return to the **Ceiling Plans: Floor 1** view.

3. Click (Wall). In the Type Selector, select **Basic Wall: Soffit 1/2" GWB & Metal Stud**.

4. In Properties, set the *Location Line* to **Finish Face: Interior**, the *Base Offset* to **10' 0"**, and the *Top Constraint* to **Up to level: Floor 2** with a *Top Offset* of (negative) **-1' 0"**.

5. Draw the wall across the face of the ceiling, as shown in Figure 10–19.

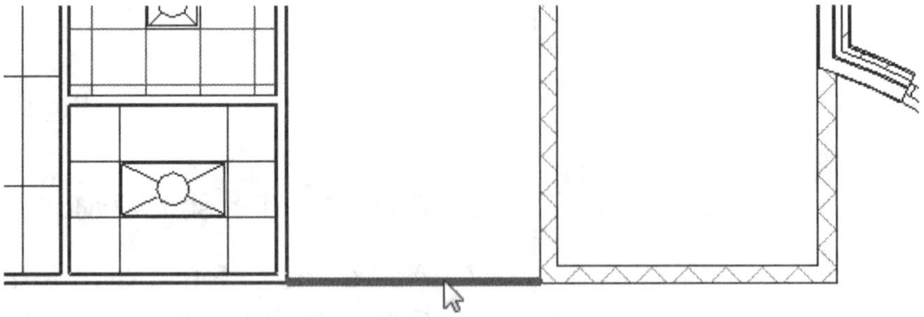

Figure 10–19

6. Open the **Sections (Building Section): East-West Section** view.

7. In the *Modify* tab>Geometry panel, click (Join).

8. Select the soffit wall above the ceiling and then select the ceiling, as shown on the left in Figure 10–20.

9. Select the ceiling again, and then the wall to the left. The elements clean up as shown on the right in Figure 10–20.

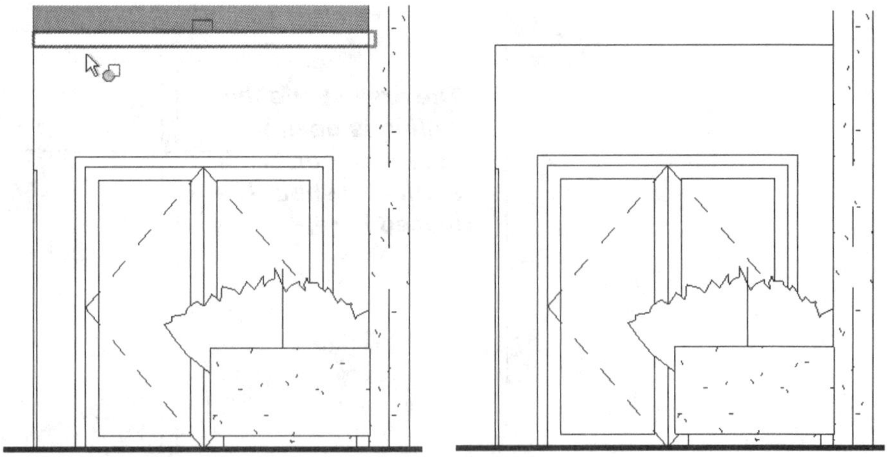

Figure 10–20

10. Save the project.

Task 3 - (Optional) Add a recessed ceiling.

1. In the **Ceiling Plans: Floor 1** view, pan over to the breakfast area near the curved wall.

2. Click (Ceiling) and click (Sketch Ceiling).

3. Create a ceiling, similar to the one shown in Figure 10–21, that has an opening in the center.

*If you have difficulty selecting the center of the curved wall, type **SC** and then select the curved wall. This snaps to the center point of the arc.*

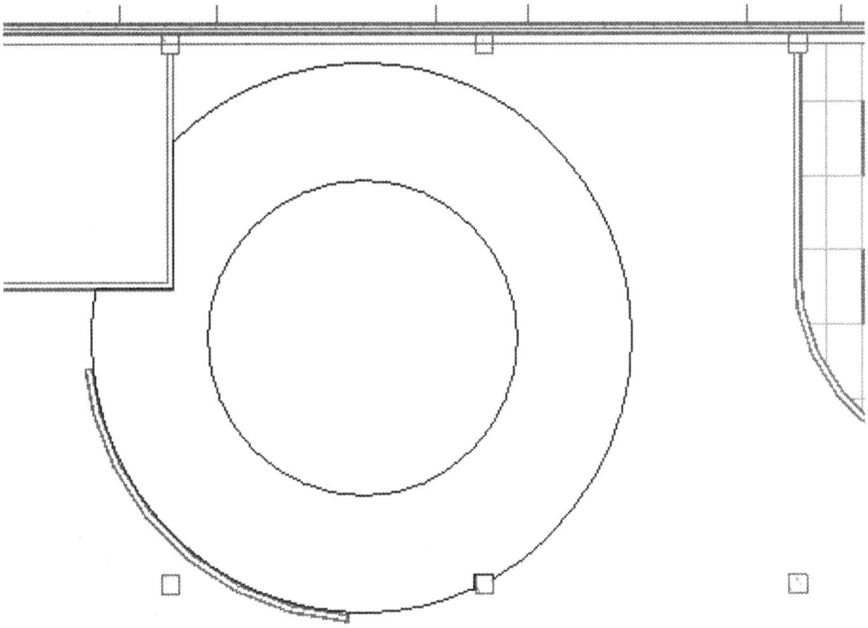

Figure 10–21

4. Click (Finish Edit Mode). The ceiling is still selected.

5. In the Type Selector, select **Compound Ceiling: GWB on Mtl. Stud** and in Properties, set the *Height Offset from Level* to **10' 0"**.

6. Click (Wall). In the type Selector, select **Basic Wall: Soffit - 1/2"GWB & Metal Stud** with the following properties:
   - *Location Line:* **Finish Face: Interior**
   - *Base Constraint:* **Floor 1**
   - *Base Offset:* **10' 0"**
   - *Top Constraint:* **Up to level: Floor 1**
   - *Top Offset:* **12' 0"**

7. In the *Modify | Place Wall* tab>Draw panel, click (Pick Lines) and select the inside hole of the ceiling, as shown in Figure 10–22.

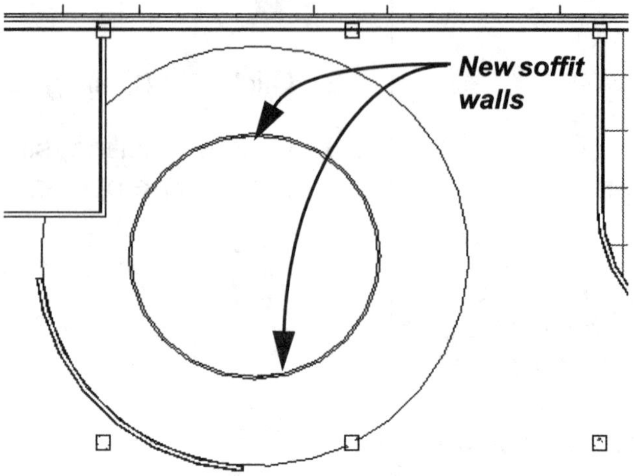

Figure 10–22

8. Click (Ceiling) again and use (Sketch Ceiling) to sketch the outline of a ceiling inside the open area. Use (Pick Walls) to select the soffit walls.

9. Click (Finish Edit Mode).

10. In the Type Selector, select **Compound Ceiling: GWB on Mtl. Stud** and in Properties, set the *Height Offset from Level* to **12' 0"**.

11. Open the **Floor Plans: Floor 1** view and create a camera view looking toward the Breakfast area, as shown in Figure 10–23.

*Use **Hide in View> Elements** to toggle off obstructing elements.*

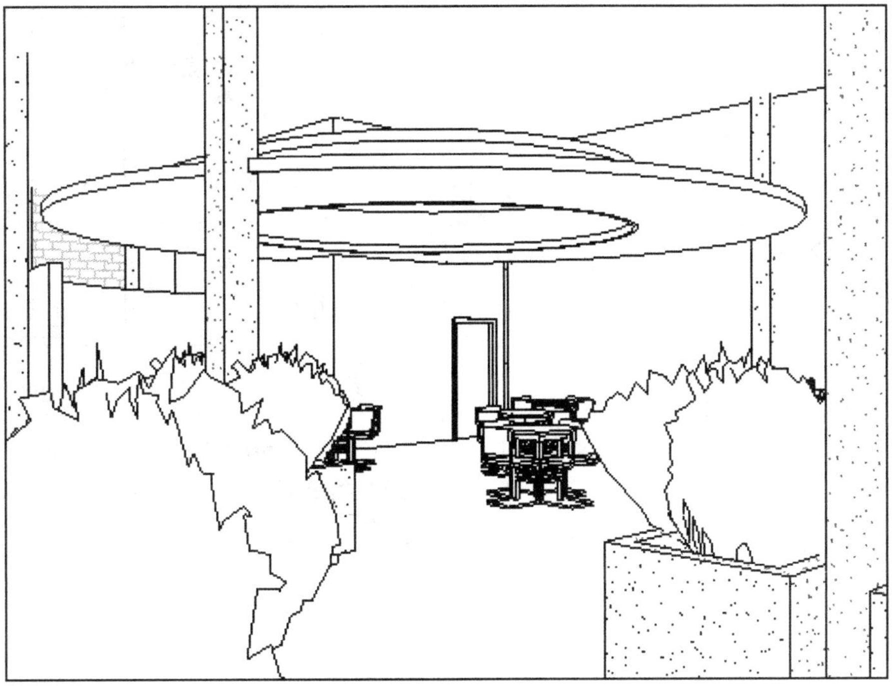

Figure 10–23

12. Save the project.

Chapter Review Questions

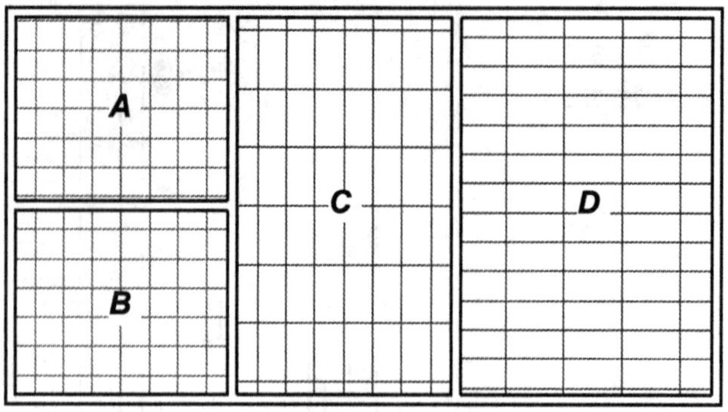

Figure 10–24

1. For the rooms labeled A and B in Figure 10–24, which command do you use to change the position of the ceiling grid?

   a. (Align)

   b. (Move)

   c. (Rotate)

   d. (Copy)

2. For the rooms labeled C and D in Figure 10–24, which command do you use to change the direction of the grids?

   a. (Align)

   b. (Move)

   c. (Rotate)

   d. (Copy)

3. Which of the following component types can be hosted by ceiling elements? (Select all that apply.)

   a. Mechanical Diffusers and Returns

   b. Lighting fixtures

   c. Curtain Grids

   d. Columns

4. Which of the following commands would you use to create a ceiling with a soffit around the edges? (Select all that apply.)

    a.  (Automatic Ceiling)

    b.  (Sketch Ceiling)

    c.  (Wall)

    d.  (Component)

5. Which of the following commands can you use to get a light fixture fitted exactly in a ceiling grid, as shown in Figure 10–25? (Select all that apply.)

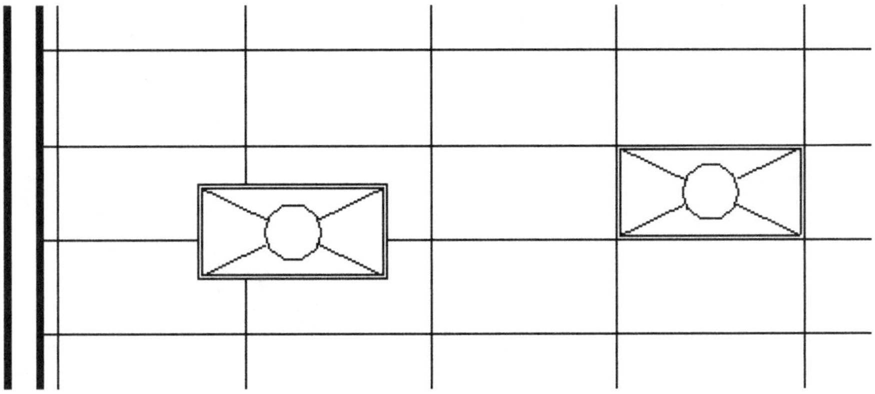

Figure 10–25

    a.  (Trim/Extend to Corner)

    b.  (Align)

    c.  (Join)

    d.  (Move)

Command Summary

Button	Command	Location
	**Ceiling**	• **Ribbon:** *Architecture* tab>Build panel
	**Place a Component**	• **Ribbon:** *Architecture* tab>Build panel

Modeling Roofs

You can create simple or very complex roofs in the Autodesk® Revit® software using two different methods. The Footprint method enables you to create roofs using a process that is similar to that for creating a floor. You can also use the Extrusion method, which is based on a profile that controls the shape of the roof.

Learning Objectives in this Chapter

- Sketch roofs using the Footprint method for flat, shed, gable, or hip roofs.
- Set Work Planes to help you create extruded roof profiles.
- Sketch a profile for the shape a roof that can then be extruded.

11.1 Modeling Roofs

The Autodesk Revit software provides two main ways of creating roofs:

- **Footprint:** Created in a floor plan view by defining the area to be covered.
- **Extrusion:** Created in an elevation or section by defining a profile sketch.

The footprint method can generate most common roof types, including flat, shed, gable, and hip roofs. The extrusion method is required for an odd-shaped roof or a roof with two slopes on the same face, as shown in Figure 11–1.

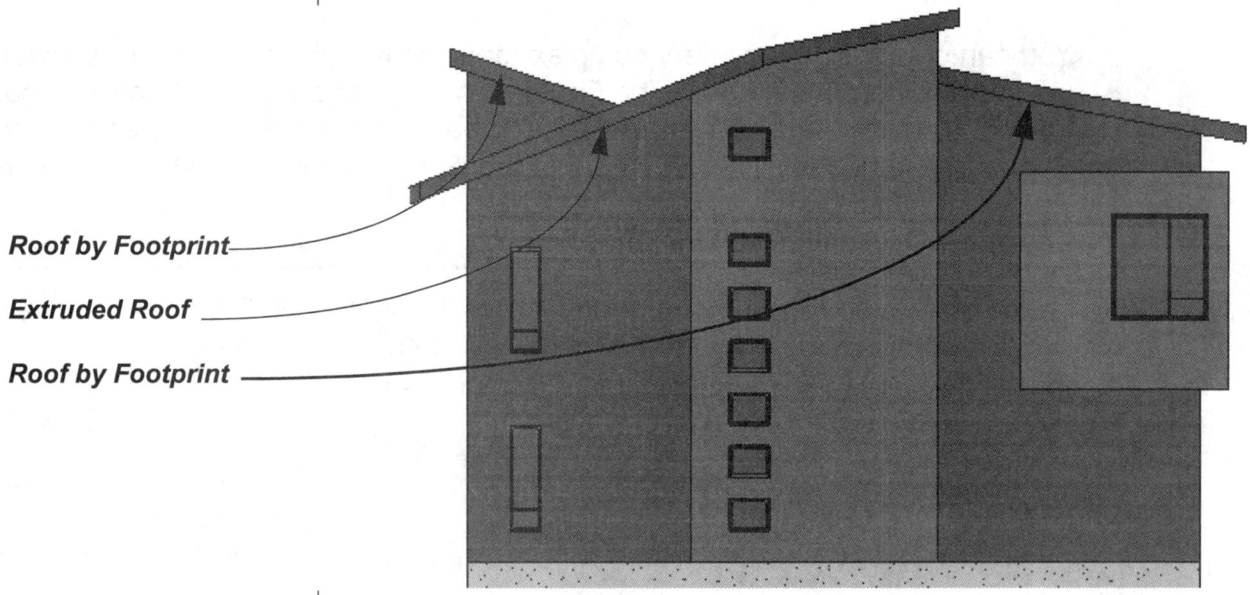

Figure 11–1

- Other roof options, found in the Roof drop-down list, include **Roof by Face**, which is used with Massing elements, **Roof Soffit**, which connects the edge of the roof to the wall, **Fascia**, which places a flat board on the outside edge of the roof and **Gutter**, which adds a gutter on the edge of the roof.

11.2 Creating Roofs by Footprint

To create a flat roof, or any basic single-sloped roofs (hip, shed, or gable), start with a plan view and define a sketch or "footprint" around the area that you want the roof to cover, as shown in Figure 11–2.

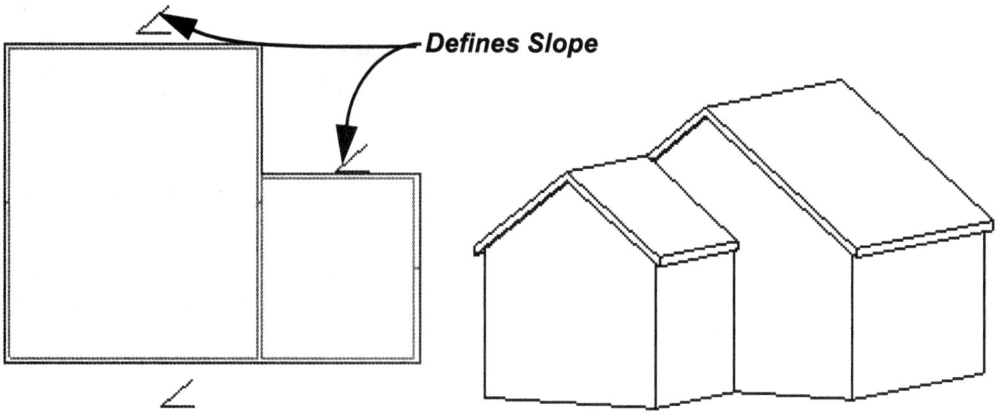

Figure 11–2

You control the type of roof by specifying which edge(s) define the slope:

- No edges sloped = flat roof
- One edge sloped = shed roof
- Two opposing edges sloped = gable roof
- All edges sloped = hip roof

How To: Add a Roof by Footprint

1. Open a plan view at the roof level of the building.
2. In the *Architecture* tab>Build panel, expand (Roof) and click (Roof by Footprint).
3. In the *Modify | Create Roof Footprint* tab>Draw panel, click (Pick Walls) or (Line) or any other Draw tool to create the roof footprint. You can include arcs in the sketch.
    - The lines must form a closed boundary with no overlapping lines.
    - Use commands such as (Trim), to modify the lines as required.

4. Select and modify each segment of the sketch as required using the Options Bar, Properties, or controls, as shown in Figure 11–3.

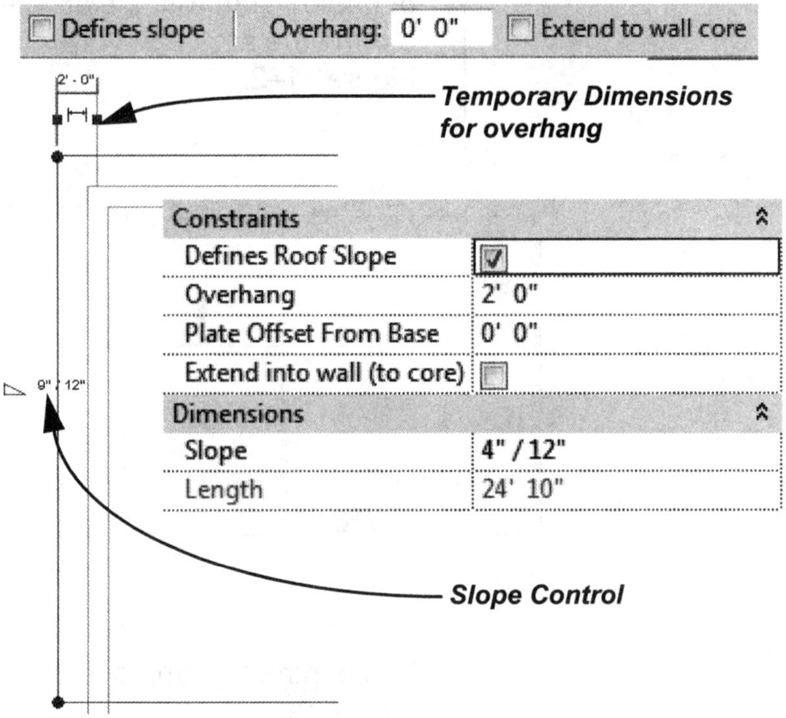

Figure 11–3

5. Click (Finish Edit Mode).
6. An alert box might open, as shown in Figure 11–4. You can attach the highlighted walls to the roof now or later.

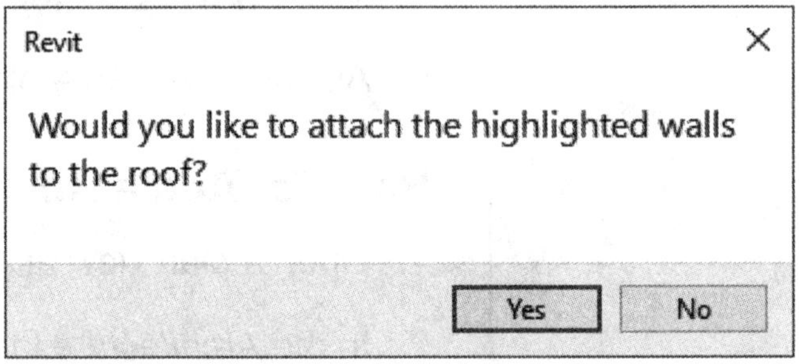

Figure 11–4

7. The roof is still selected and, in Properties, you can set the properties for the entire roof. These include roof type, *Base Offset from Level*, *Rafter Cut*, and *Cutoff Level*.

To edit a roof sketch, either:

- Double-click on the edge of the roof.

OR

- With the roof selected, click (Edit Footprint).

Attaching Walls to Roofs

Attaching walls to the roof extends the walls up to the roof, as shown in Figure 11–5. You attach walls while you are still in the roof command, or you can use the **Attach Top/Base** commands later in the design process.

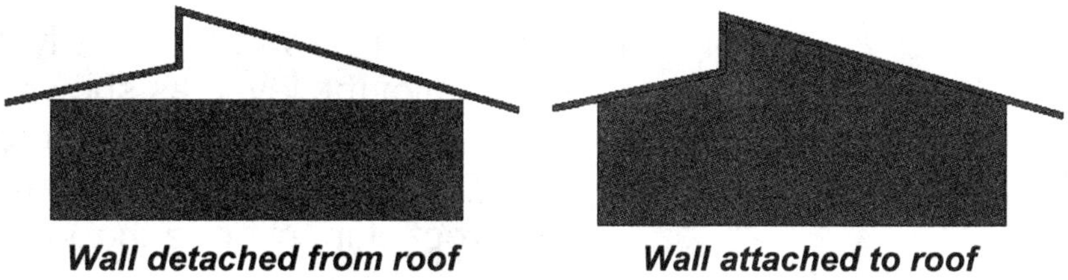

Figure 11–5

- **Attach Top/Base** can also be used with walls that are against sloping floors or topographic site features.

How To: Attach Walls to Roofs

1. Select the wall or walls that you want to attach to the roof.
2. In the *Modify* | *Walls* tab>Modify Wall panel, click (Attach Top/Base). Verify that *Attach Wall* is set to **Top**, as shown in Figure 11–6.

Figure 11–6

3. Select the roof. The walls are trimmed or extended to the roofline.

Hint: Setting Up a Roof Plan

When creating a roof, add a level with a floor plan view where the bottom of the roof should be located. If there are roofs at different heights, create a level for each location.

Most plan views are typically cut at 3'-0" to 4'-0" above the bottom of the level, as shown in Figure 11–7. However, this does not work with pitched roofs, whose structures can reach 20'-0" high or more. To change the height of the area shown in the roof plan, change the *View Range*.

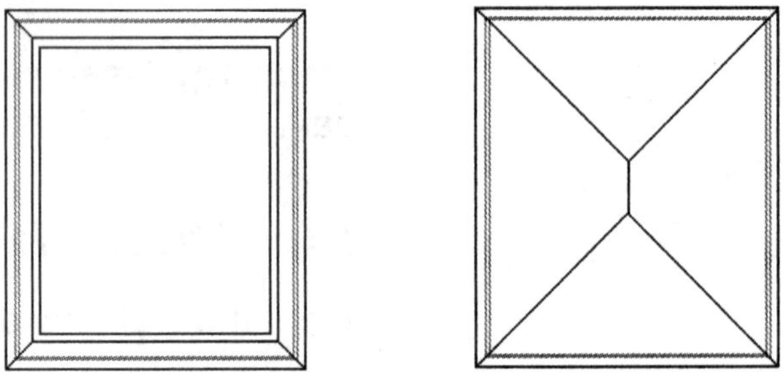

View Range Cut Plane @ 4'-0" ***View Range Cut Plane @ 30'-0"***

Figure 11–7

Practice 11a Create Roofs by Footprint

Practice Objectives

- Create flat and sloped roofs using Roof by Footprint.
- Create a roof plan view.

In this practice, you will create a flat roof on the main part of the hotel, and flat and sloped roofs over the poolhouse, as shown in Figure 11–8.

Figure 11–8

Task 1 - Create a flat roof.

1. Open **Modern-Hotel-Roof-Footprint.rvt**.
2. Open the **Floor Plans: Roof** view and set the *Underlay> Range: Base Level* to **None**.
3. Hide the grid lines and section and elevation markers.
4. In the *Architecture* tab>Build panel, expand  (Roof) and click  (Roof by Footprint).

5. In the Options Bar, clear the **Defines slope** option.
6. In the *Modify | Create Roof Footprint* tab>Draw panel, click  (Pick Walls) and select the inside of the walls around the building, as shown in Figure 11–9.

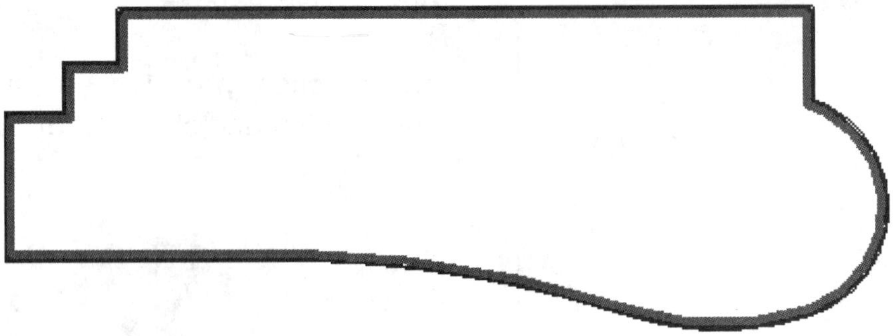

Figure 11–9

7. Click  (Finish Edit Mode).
8. In the Type Selector, select **Basic Roof: Steel Truss - Insulation on Metal Deck - EPDM**.
9. View the building in 3D to display the roof applied below the parapet wall, as shown in Figure 11–10.

Figure 11–10

10. Save the project.

Hold <Shift> and the mouse wheel to rotate in 3D view.

Task 2 - Create a roof plan.

1. Rotate the 3D view until the poolhouse at the back of the building displays. Several features are in place, including the parapet walls and roof soffit, as shown in Figure 11–11.

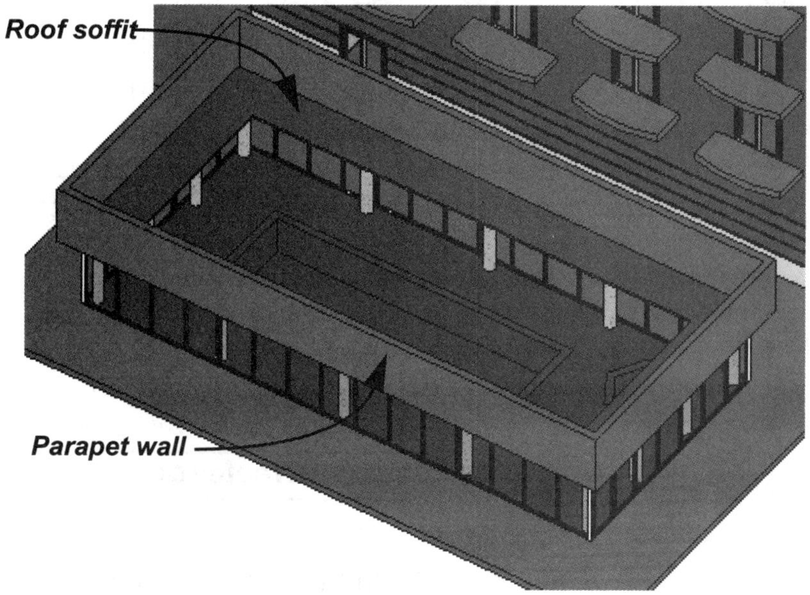

Figure 11–11

2. Duplicate a copy of the **Floor Plans: Floor 1 with Pool** view and rename it as **Roof - Poolhouse** and verify that it is open.

3. Change the *Scale* to **1/4" = 1'-0"**.

4. Open the View Range dialog box, (type **VR**), and set it up as shown in Figure 11–12. Click OK.

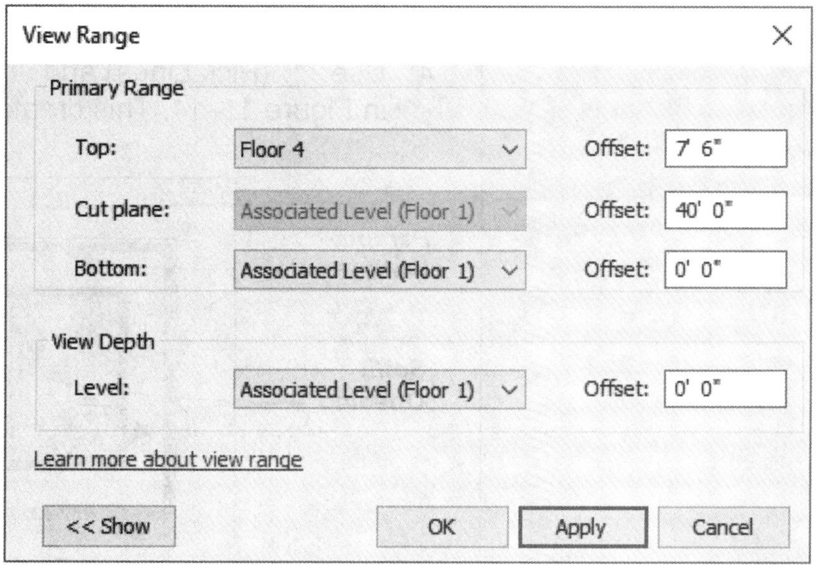

Figure 11–12

5. Modify the crop region to display only the pool area, as shown in Figure 11–13. Hide any other elements as required.

Figure 11–13

6. Hide the crop region.

Task 3 - Create roofs on the poolhouse.

1. In the *Architecture* tab>Build panel, click (Roof). The software remembers the most recently used command of **Roof by Footprint**.
2. In the Options Bar, verify that the **Defines slope** option is cleared and there is no overhang.
3. In the *Modify | Create Roof Footprint* tab>Draw panel, click (Pick Walls) and select the inside of the parapet walls, as shown in Figure 11–14.
4. Use (Pick Lines) and select the soffit opening, as shown in Figure 11–14. This creates a flat roof with an opening in it.

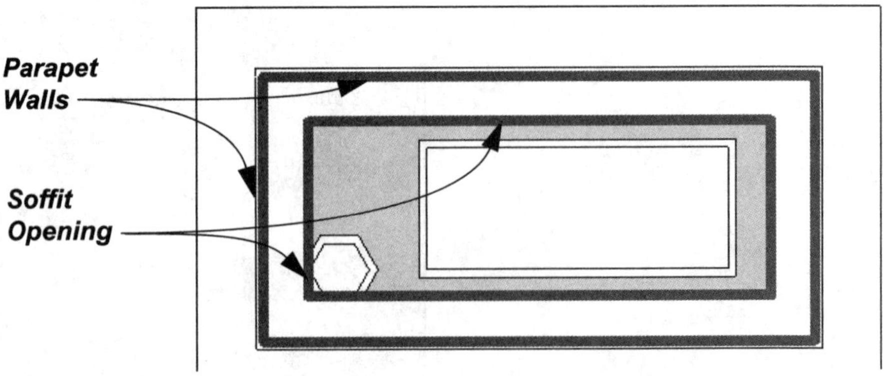

Figure 11–14

5. Click ✔ (Finish Edit Mode.) Do not attach walls to the roof.
6. With the roof still selected, set the following:
   - *Type:* **Basic Roof: Generic - 12"**
   - *Base Level:* **Floor 2**
   - *Base Offset from Level:* (negative) **-2' 0"**
7. Click in the view to release the roof.
8. Click (Wall).
9. In Properties, set the following properties:
   - *Wall Type:* **Basic Wall: Exterior - EIFS on Mtl.Stud**
   - *Location Line:* **Finish Face: Interior**
   - *Base Constraint:* **Floor 2**
   - *Base Offset:* (negative) **-1' 0"**
   - *Top Constraint:* **Unconnected**
   - *Unconnected Height:* **1' 0"**
10. Draw this short wall around the opening, as shown in Figure 11–15.

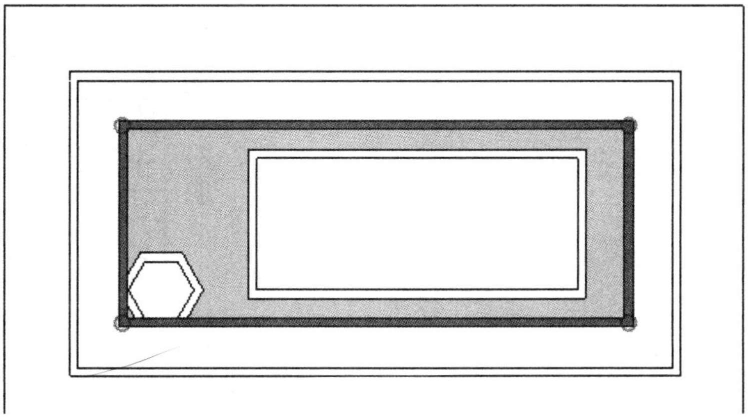

Figure 11–15

11. Start the (Roof by Footprint) command.
12. In the Options Bar, select **Defines slope**.

13. Use (Pick Walls) and select the outside of the new walls you just created, as shown in Figure 11–16.

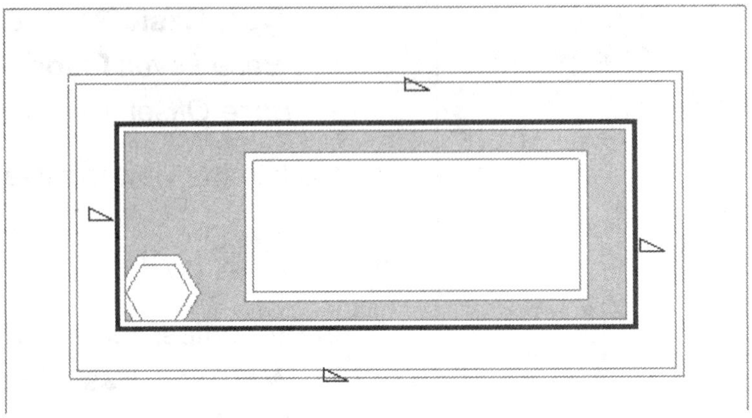

Figure 11–16

14. Click (Finish Edit Mode). In the Message dialog box, click **No** to not attach any walls to the roof.

15. In the Type Selector, select **Sloped Glazing: Sloped Glazing Pool Roof** and verify that the *Base Level* is **Floor 2**. In the *Grid 1* area, set the *Justification* to **Center**. The new roof displays, as shown in Figure 11–17.

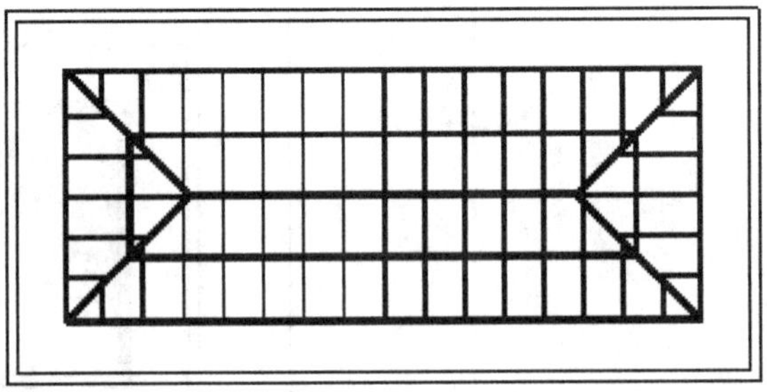

Figure 11–17

16. View the entire model in 3D.

17. Save the project.

Task 4 - (Optional) Apply slopes to the main flat roof.

If time permits, select the flat roof on the main hotel and use the Shape Editing tools on the *Modify* | *Roofs* tab to add appropriate drainage slopes.

11.3 Establishing Work Planes

In some processes, such as creating a Roof by Extrusion, you are prompted to specify a Work Plane. A Work Plane is the surface you sketch on or extrude from.

- In a plan view, the Work Plane is automatically parallel to the level.
- In an elevation or 3D view, you need to specify the Work Plane before you start sketching.

To see the current Work Plane, in the *Architecture* tab>Work Plane panel, click (Viewer). This opens the Workplane Viewer, a separate window showing the current work plane, as shown in Figure 11–18.

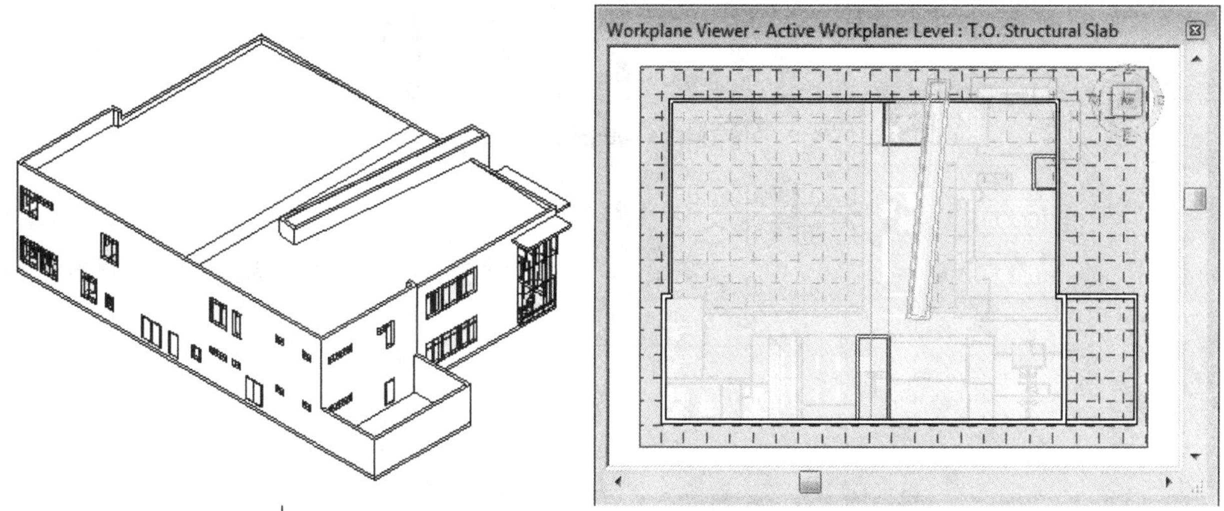

Figure 11–18

- Named reference planes can be used to specify a work plane that would otherwise not be displayed in a view. This is especially helpful when creating extruded roofs.

How To: Select a Work Plane

1. Start a command that requires a work plane or, in the *Architecture* tab>Work Plane panel, click (Set).
2. In the Work Plane dialog box, select one of the options.
   - **Name:** Select an existing level, grid, or named reference plane, as shown in Figure 11–19 and click **OK**.

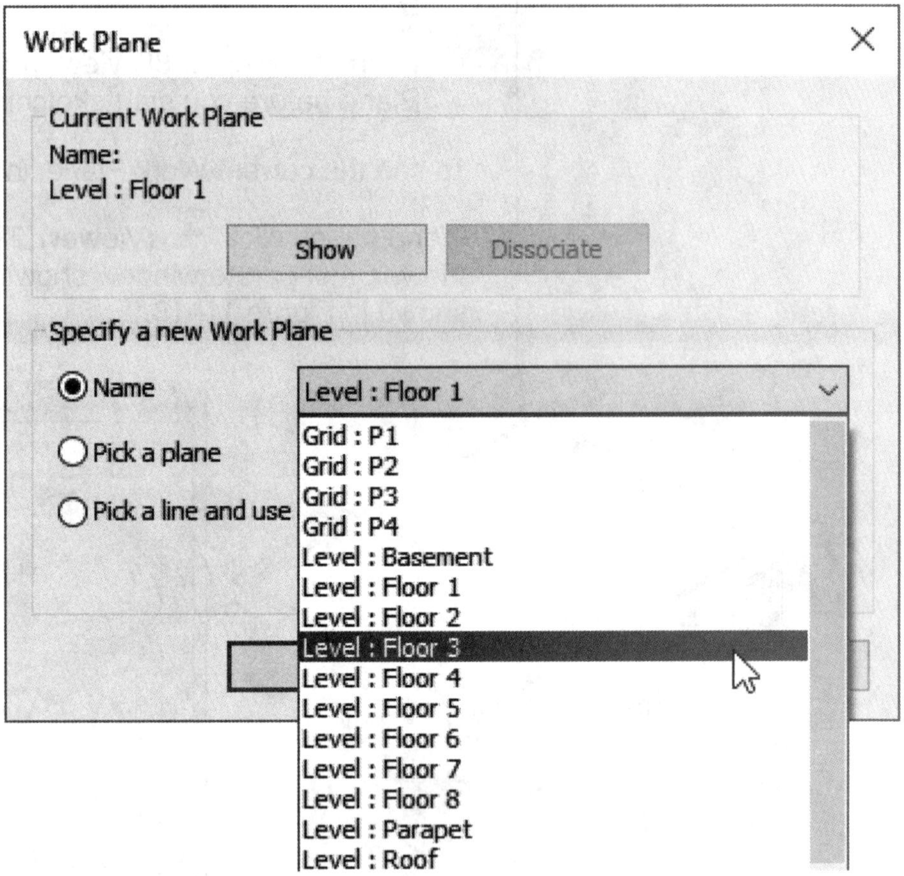

Figure 11–19

   - **Pick a plane:** Click **OK** and select a plane in the view, such as a wall face. Ensure the entire plane is highlighted before you select it.
   - **Pick a line and use the work plane it was sketched in:** Click **OK** and select a model line such as a room separation line.

- If you are in a view in which the sketch cannot be created, the Go To View dialog box opens, as shown in Figure 11–20. Select one of the views and click **Open View**.

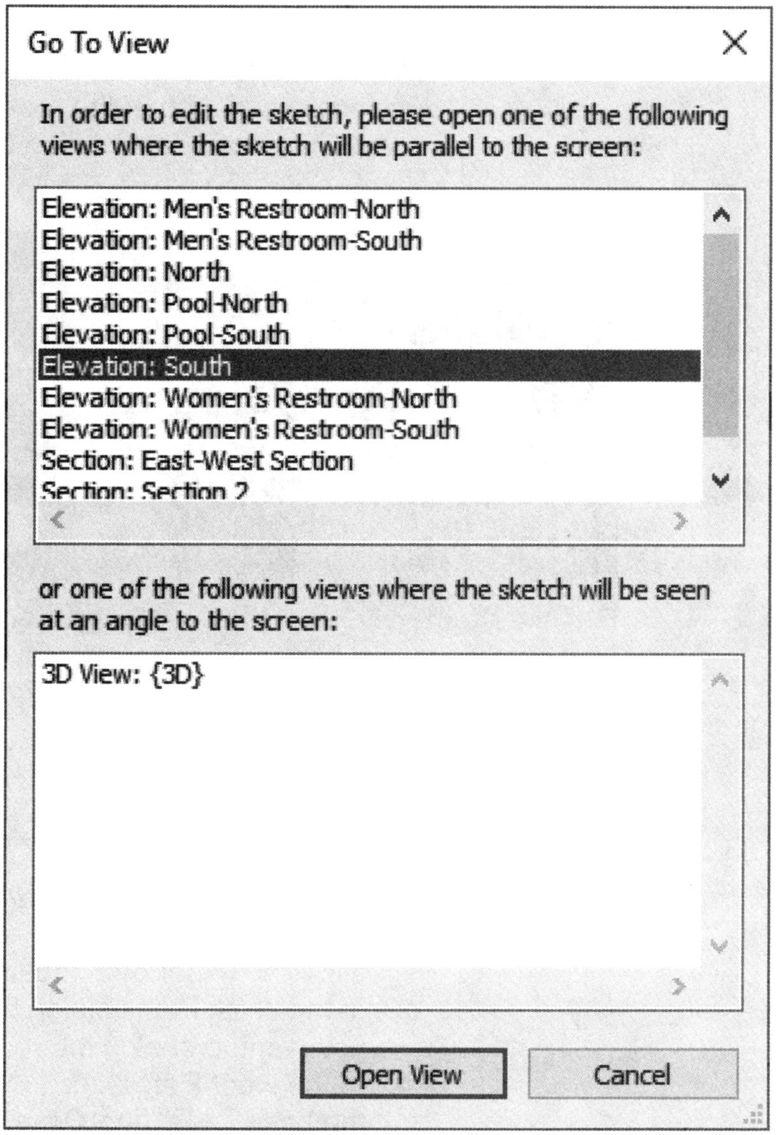

Figure 11–20

11.4 Creating Roofs by Extrusion

Extruded roofs enable you to create complex roof forms, such as the curved roof shown in Figure 11–21. Extruded roofs are based on a sketch of the roof profile in an elevation or section view. The profile is extruded between a start and end point.

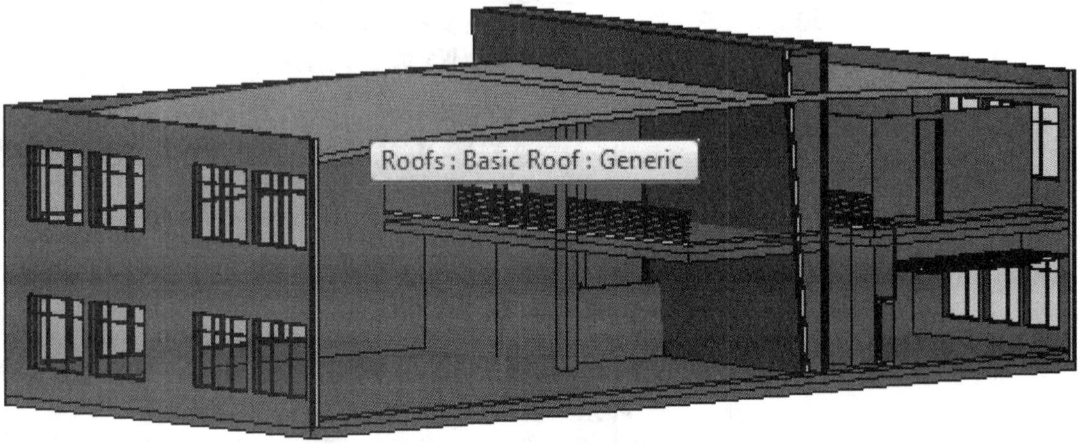

Figure 11–21

How To: Create an Extruded Roof

1. Open an elevation or a section view.
2. In the *Architecture* tab>Build panel, expand (Roof) and click (Roof by Extrusion).
3. In the Work Plane dialog box, select the Work Plane on which you want to sketch the roof profile, and click **OK.**
4. In the Roof Reference Level and Offset dialog box, specify the base *Level* and *Offset* (if any), as shown in Figure 11–22.

By default, this level is set to the highest one in the project. The offset creates a reference plane at that distance.

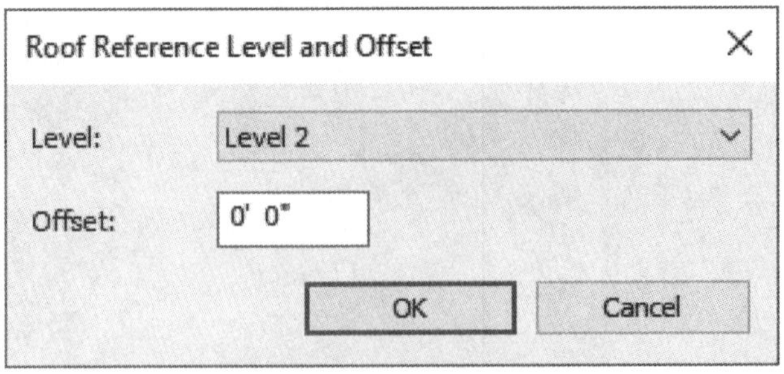

Figure 11–22

5. Draw reference planes to help you create the roof profile. Reference planes created in sketch mode do not display once the roof is finished.

6. Use the Draw tools to create the profile, as shown in Figure 11–23.

Sketch only the shape of the roof in profile, not the thickness.

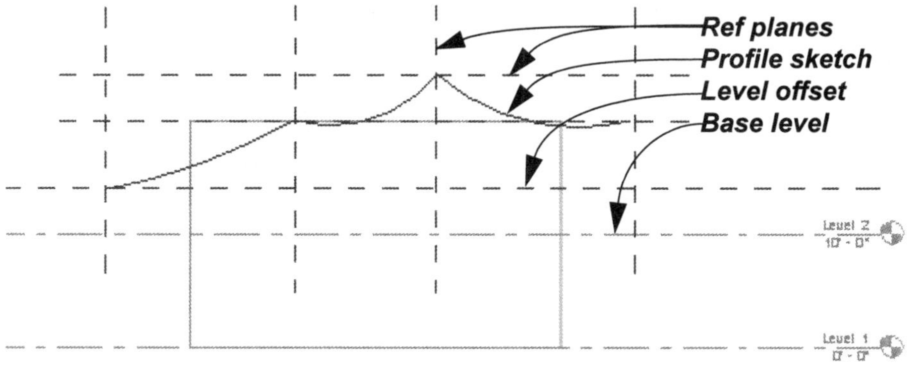

Figure 11–23

7. In Properties, set the *Extrusion Start* and *End*.
8. Click (Finish Edit Mode).
9. In the Type Selector, select the roof type.
   - The thickness, which is determined by the roof type, is added below the profile sketch line.
10. View the roof in 3D and make any other required modifications. For example, you can use the controls on the ends of the roof to extend the overhang (as shown in Figure 11–24), as well as modify the roof using temporary dimensions and Properties**.**

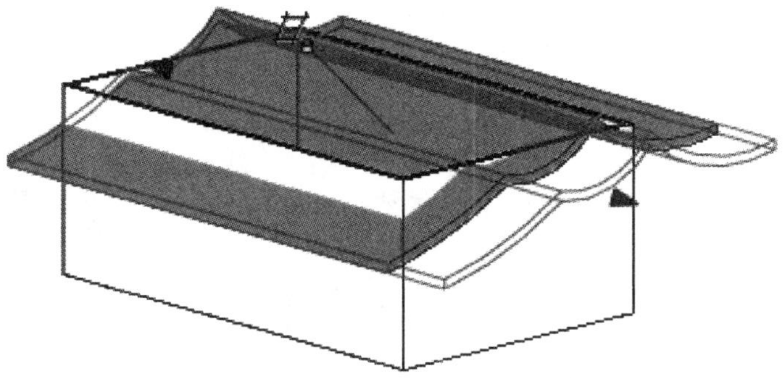

Figure 11–24

11. Attach the walls to the roof.

- You can make changes to the roof's profile in one of the following ways:
  - Double-click on the edge of the roof.
  - Select the roof. In the *Modify* | *Roofs* tab>Mode panel, click (Edit Profile).

How To: Modify the Plan View of an Extruded Roof

1. Open a plan view where the entire roof displays.
2. Select the roof.
3. In the *Modify | Roofs* tab>Opening panel, click 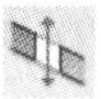 (Vertical).
4. In the *Modify | Create Extrusion Roof Profile* tab>Draw panel, use the tools to create a closed boundary.The boundary can be entirely inside the roof or touching the roof boundaries.
5. Click  (Finish Edit Mode). The extruded view now has a cutout, as shown in Figure 11–25.

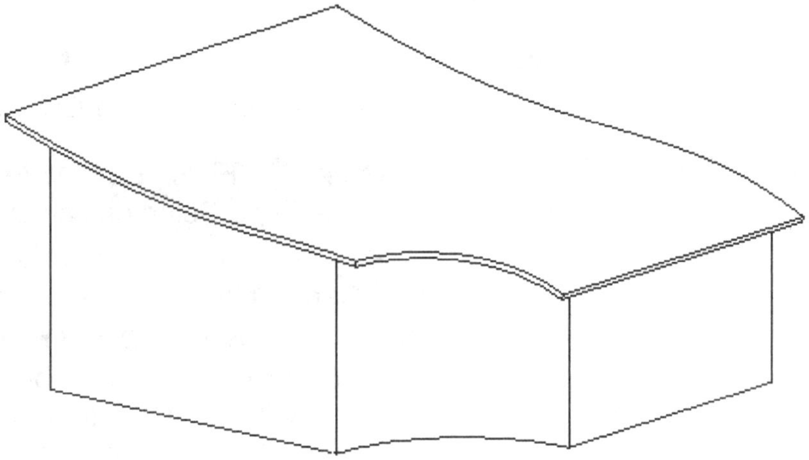

Figure 11–25

Joining Roofs

When you want to join an extruded roof to another roof, or a wall face that is taller than the roof, you can use the **Join/Unjoin Roof** command, as shown in Figure 11–26.

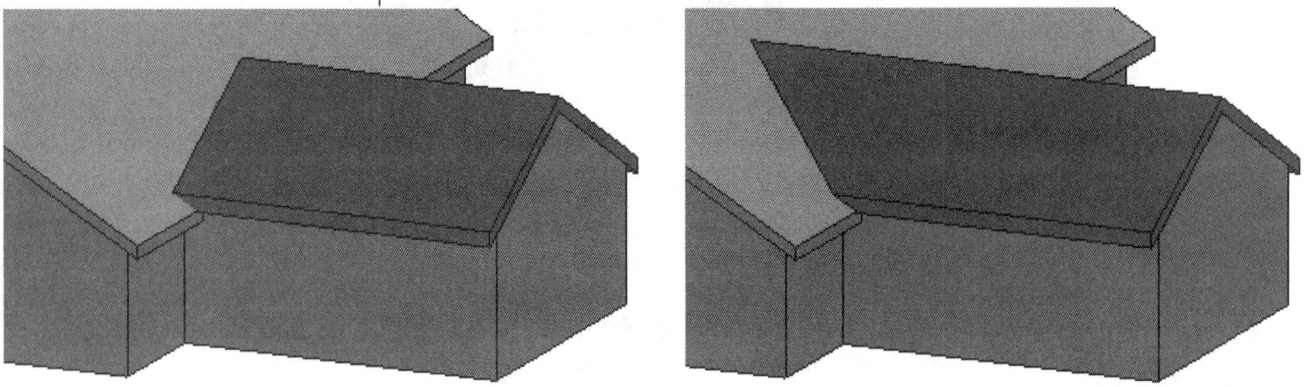

Before joining

After joining roofs

Figure 11–26

How To: Use Join/Unjoin Roof

1. In the *Modify* tab>Geometry panel, click (Join/Unjoin Roof).
2. Select one of the roof edges.
3. Select the other roof or the wall.

Hint: Join Geometry

Where roofs overlap walls or other roofs, use **Join Geometry** to clean up the intersections. The elements remain separate, but the intersections are cleaned up, as shown in Figure 11–27.

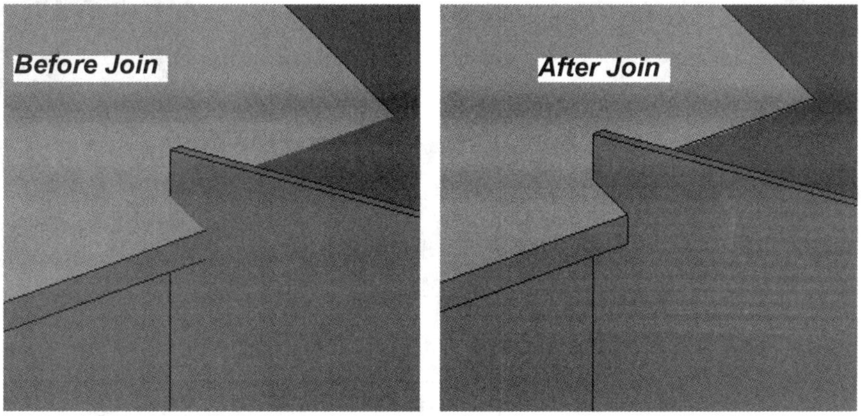

Figure 11–27

Practice 11b Create Roofs by Extrusion

Practice Objectives

- Create an extruded roof.
- Modify the plan profile of a roof.

In this practice, you will create a curved extruded roof to cover the main entrance of the building and modify its plan profile to cover the side entrance, as shown in Figure 11–28.

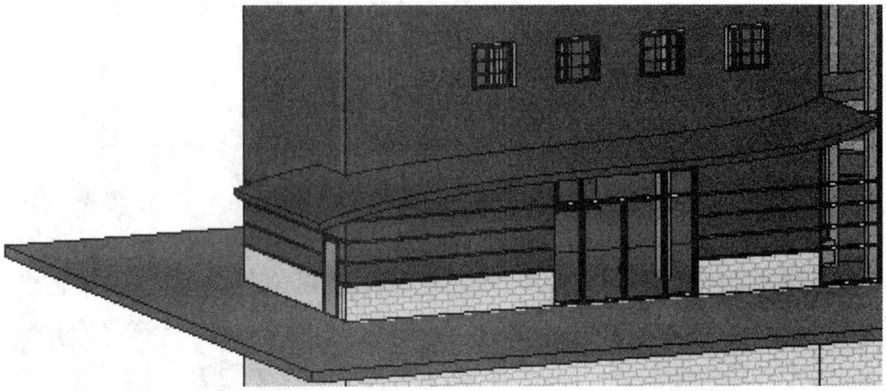

Figure 11–28

Task 1 - Create a roof by extrusion.

1. Open **Modern-Hotel-Roof-Extruded.rvt**.
2. Open the **Elevations (Building Elevation): South** view.
3. Zoom in on the area around the front entrance.
4. In the *Architecture* tab>Build panel, expand (Roof) and click (Roof by Extrusion).
5. In the Work Plane dialog box, verify that **Pick a plane** is selected, and click **OK**.
6. Select the front face of the wall.
7. In the Roof Reference Level and Offset dialog box, set the *Level* to **Floor 2** and click **OK**. A reference plane is set at this level and the model is grayed out.

The example was created using (Spline).

8. Sketch the profile of a roof similar to the one shown in Figure 11–29. It should extend beyond the building to the left but finish at the end of the brick wall on the right.

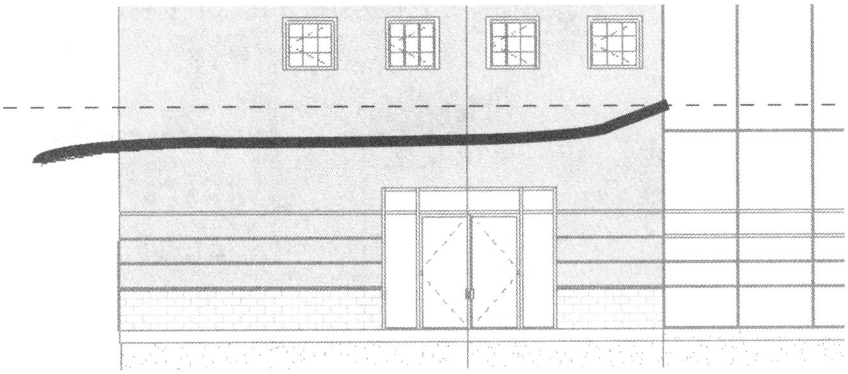

Figure 11–29

9. In Properties, set the *Extrusion End* to (negative) **-6' 0"**.

10. Click (Finish Edit Mode).

11. In the Type Selector, select **Basic Roof: Generic - 9"**.

12. View the new roof in 3D. It is mostly inside the building at this point.

Task 2 - Modify the extruded roof.

1. Open the **Floor Plans: Site** view. This view displays the entire building in plan including all of the roofs.

2. Hide the grid lines and elevation markers by category.

3. Select the Entrance roof and using controls, move the roof outward so that the length is **20' 0",** as shown in Figure 11–30.

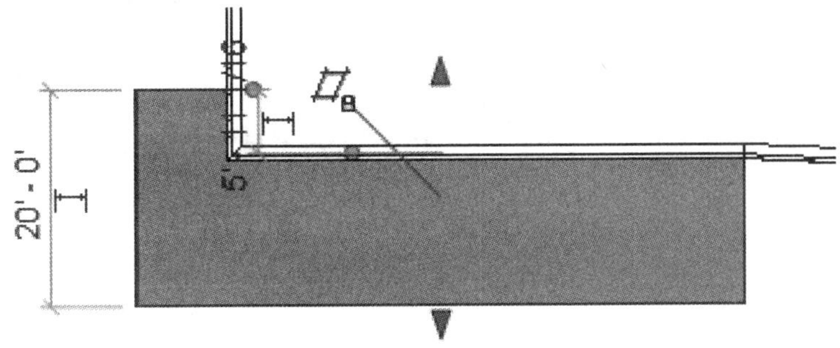

Figure 11–30

4. In the *Modify* | *Roofs* tab>Opening panel, click (Vertical).
5. Create a rectangular cutout of the roof for the portion that passes through the building, as shown in Figure 11–31.

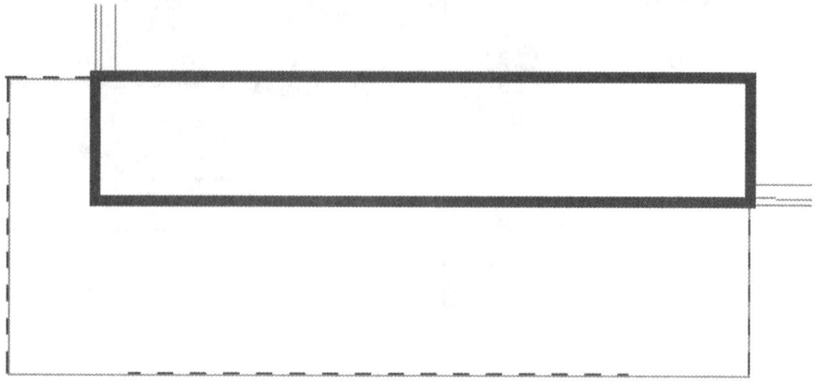

Figure 11–31

6. Click (Finish Edit Mode).
7. View the modified roof in 3D. It now wraps around the side of the building to cover the side entrance, as shown in Figure 11–32.

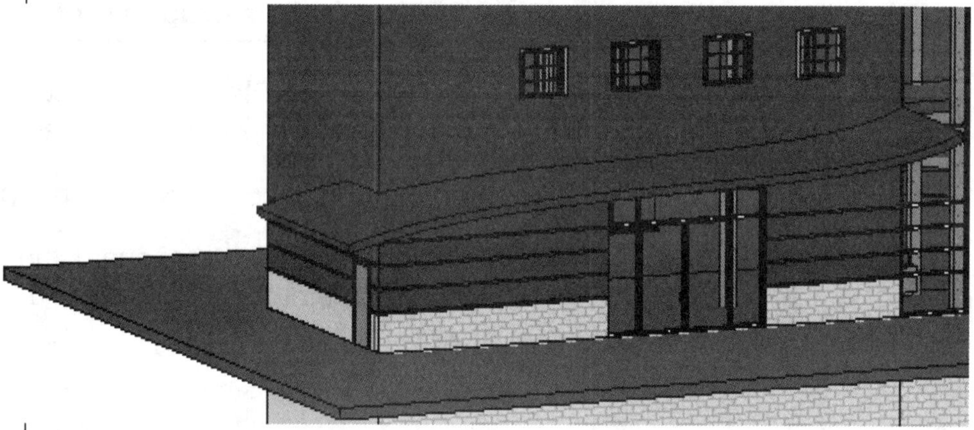

Figure 11–32

8. Save the project.

Chapter Review Questions

1. To create a roof sloping in one direction only (as shown on the front of the building in Figure 11–33), you would create a roof...

Figure 11–33

   a. By extrusion and rotate the roof to the correct angle.

   b. By footprint and specify the slope along one side.

   c. By extrusion and use the Slope Arrow to define the overall slope of the roof.

   d. By footprint and use the **Shape Editing** tools to create the slope.

2. To create a flat roof, which of the following commands would you use to sketch the boundary of the roof and to set its thickness?

   a. **Roof by Footprint** with the thickness set by the roof type.

   b. **Roof by Extrusion** with the thickness extruded from the sketch.

3. Which of the following methods makes a wall touch the underside of a roof?

   a. Select the wall and use  (Attach Top/Base).

   b. Select the roof and use  (Attach Top/Base).

   c. Select the wall and edit the profile.

   d. Select the roof and use **By Face**.

4. Which roof type and view should you use to create a curved roof as shown in Figure 11–34?

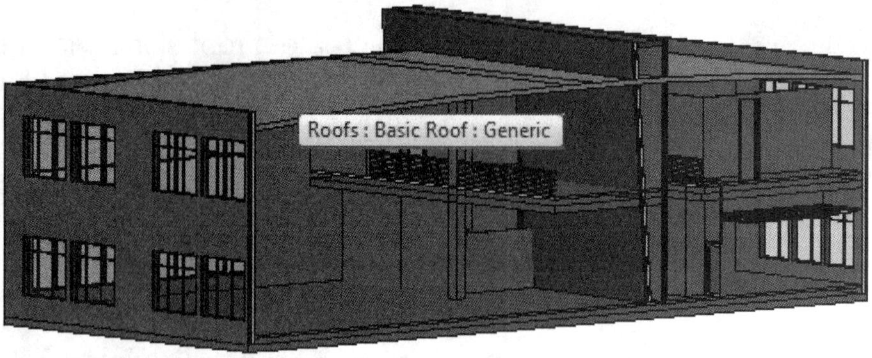

Figure 11–34

   a. Roof by Footprint, Plan View
   b. Roof by Footprint, Elevation or Section view
   c. Roof by Extrusion, Plan View
   d. Roof by Extrusion, Elevation or Section view

5. A workplane can be assigned using a named Reference Plane.
   a. True
   b. False

Command Summary

Button	Command	Location
	**Attach Top/Base**	• **Ribbon:** *Modify* | *Walls* tab>Modify Wall panel
	**Join Geometry**	• **Ribbon:** *Modify* tab>Geometry panel expand Join
	**Join/Unjoin Roof**	• **Ribbon:** *Modify* tab>Geometry panel
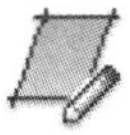	**Ref Plane**	• **Ribbon:** *Architecture* tab>Work Plane panel
	**Roof by Extrusion**	• **Ribbon:** *Architecture* tab>Build panel expand Roof
	**Roof by Footprint**	• **Ribbon:** *Architecture* tab>Build panel expand Roof
	**Set Work Plane**	• **Ribbon:** *Architecture* tab>Work Plane panel
	**Unjoin Geometry**	• **Ribbon:** *Modify* tab>Geometry panel expand Join
	**Vertical (Opening)**	• **Ribbon:** *Modify* | *Roofs*> Opening tab

Modeling Stairs, Railings, and Ramps

When modeling in the Autodesk® Revit® software you can easily create basic stairs in straight, u-shaped, and multi-landing configurations. To create more complex shapes, you can convert runs and landings to sketches. Ramps can also be created by specifying runs and landings. Railings can be added automatically with the Stair and Ramp commands, or you can sketch railings on stairs and add them to balconies and decks.

Learning Objectives in this Chapter

- Create and modify component-based stairs made of runs, landings, supports, and railings.
- Convert runs and landings to sketches.
- Add and modify railings that are connected to stairs, as well as free standing railings for balconies.
- Create ramps to make your design accessible.

12.1 Creating Component Stairs

As with other Autodesk Revit elements, stairs are *smart* parametric elements. With just a few clicks, you can create stairs of varying heights and designs, complete with railings. Stairs can be created by assembling stair components (as shown in Figure 12–1), or by sketching a custom layout.

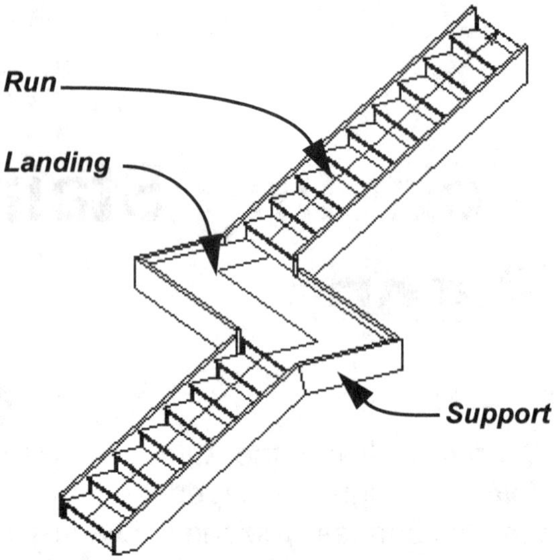

Figure 12–1

When creating component-based stairs, there are three parts of a stair that can be assembled, as shown in Figure 12–1:

- **Runs:** The actual stair tread and riser elements. These include straight runs which can be combined for multi-landing stairs, spiral stairs and L-shaped and U-shaped Winders.
- **Landings:** The platform between runs. These are typically created automatically and then modified if required.
- **Supports:** The stringer or carriage that structurally holds the stair elements. These can be created automatically or you can pick the edges where you want the different types to go. These can be placed on either side of the stairs or in the center of the stairs.
- Railings are typically added in the **Stair** command. They display after you complete the stair.
- You can select and edit each of the components while you are in stair edit mode, or after the stair has been created.

- Each component of the stair is independent but also has a relationship to the other components. For example, if steps are removed from one run they are added to connected runs to maintain the overall height, as shown in Figure 12–2.

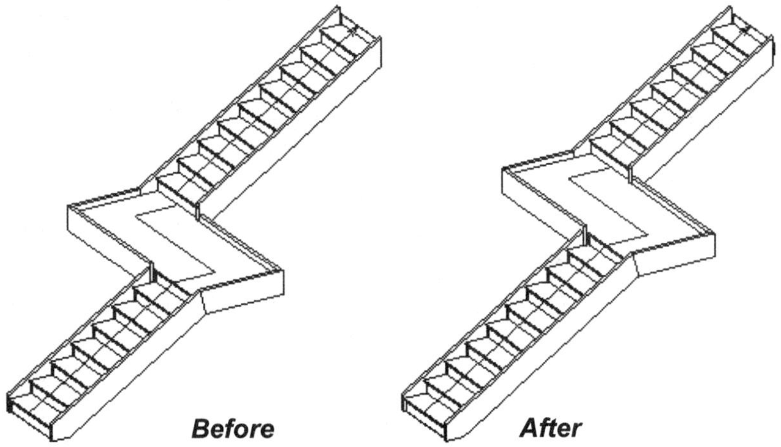

Figure 12–2

Creating Runs

To create a component stair, you must first place the run elements. There are six different options available in the Components panel, as shown in Figure 12–3, and described as follows:

Component stairs can include a mix of the different types of runs.

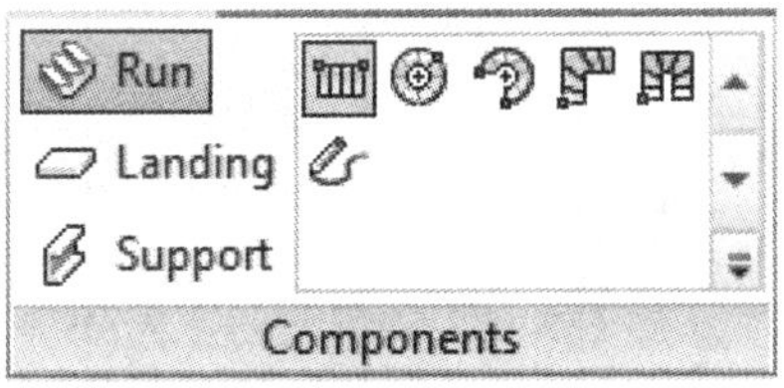

Figure 12–3

	Straight	Draws a straight run by selecting the start and end points of the run.
	Full-Step Spiral	Draws a spiral run based on a start point and radius.
	Center-Ends Spiral	Draws a spiral run based on a center point, start point, and end point.
	L-Shape Winder	Draws an L-shaped winder based on the lower end.
	U-Shape Winder	Draws a U-shaped winder based on the lower end.
	Create Sketch	Opens additional tools where you can sketch stair boundary and risers individually.

Hint: Stairs and Views

When creating stairs you can work in either plan or 3D views. It can help to have the plan view and a 3D view open and tiled side by side. Only open the views in which you want to work and type **WT** to tile the views.

How To: Create a Component-based Stair

The stair type can impact all of the other settings. Therefore, it is important to select it first.

1. In the *Architecture* tab>Circulation panel, click (Stair).
2. In the Type Selector, select the stair type, as shown in Figure 12–4.
3. In Properties (shown in Figure 12–5), set the *Base Level* and *Top Level*, and any other information that is required.

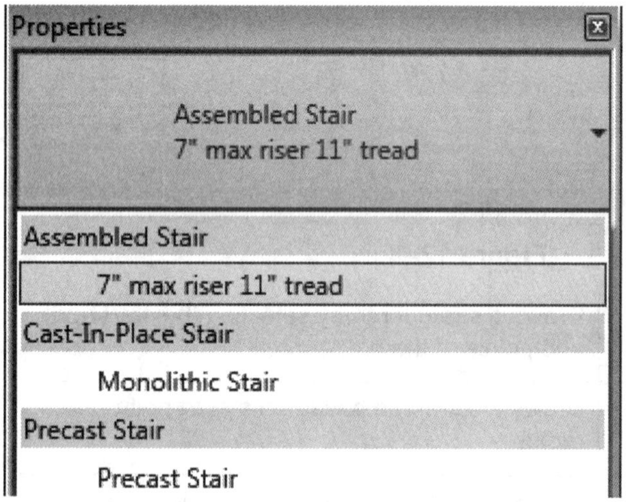

Figure 12–4

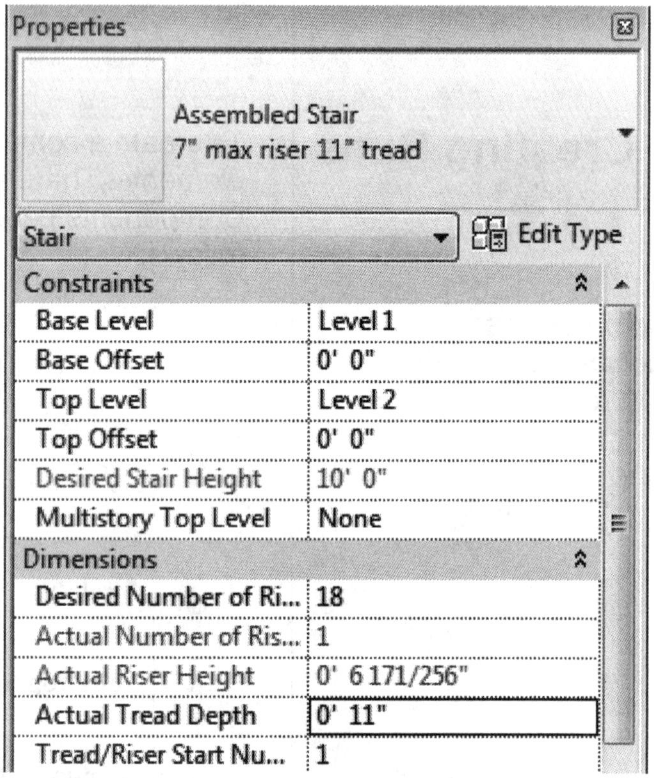

Figure 12–5

4. In the *Modify | Create Stairs* tab>Tools panel, click (Railing), select a railing type in the Railings dialog box, as shown in Figure 12–6, and specify whether the *Position* is on the **Treads** or **Stringer**. Click **OK**.

Railings can also be added and modified after the stair has been placed.

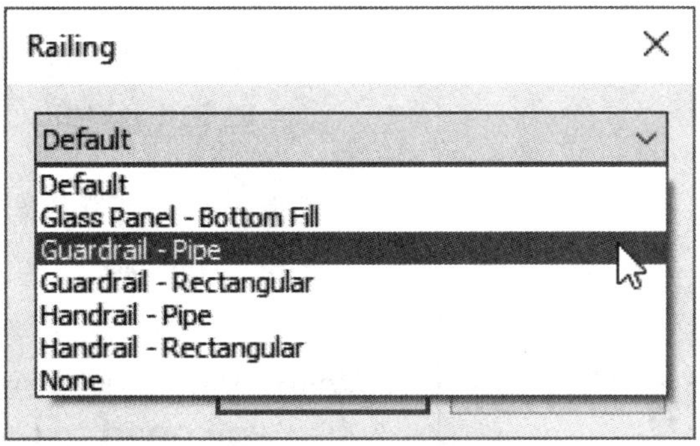

Figure 12–6

5. In the *Modify | Create Stair* tab>Components panel, click (Run) and then click (Straight).
6. In the Options Bar (shown in Figure 12–7), specify the following options:
   - **Location Line:** Select **Exterior Support: Left**, **Run: Left**, **Run: Center**, **Run: Right**, or **Exterior Support: Right**.
   - **Offset:** Specify a distance from the Location Line. This is typically used if you are following an existing wall but do not need to have the stairs directly against them.
   - **Actual Run Width:** Specify the width of the stair run (not including the supports).
   - **Automatic Landing:** Creates landings between stair runs (recommended).

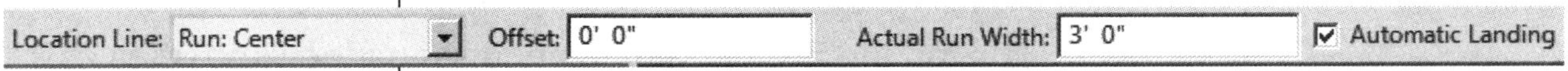

Figure 12–7

7. Click on the screen to select a start point for the run. A box displays, indicating the stair orientation and the number of risers created and remaining, as shown in Figure 12–8.

*If you are creating a complex stair pattern, sketch reference planes in the **Stairs** command, to help you select the start and end points of each run.*

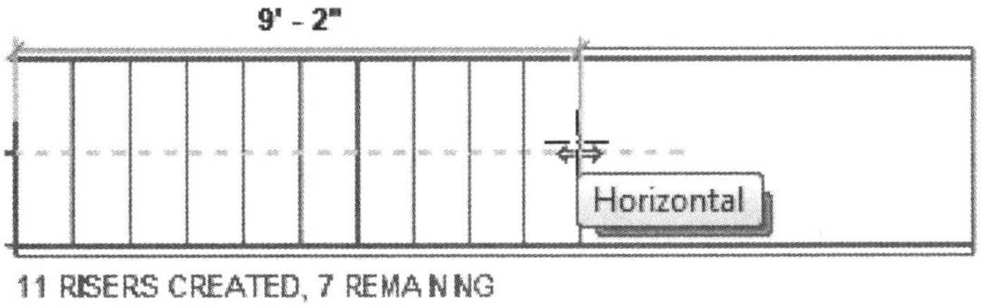

Figure 12–8

- For straight stairs of a single run, select a second point anywhere outside the box to create the run.
- For multi-landing or u-shaped stairs, select a second point inside the box for the length of the first run. Then select a start point and an end point for the next run.

- If the stair is going in the wrong direction, click (Flip) in the *Modify | Create Stair* tab>Tools panel.

8. Click (Finish Edit Mode) to create the stairs, complete with railings.

Creating Other Types of Runs

While most stairs are created using straight runs, there are times when you need to create specialty runs, such as spirals and winders or when you need to sketch a stair such as that shown in Figure 12–9.

Figure 12–9

How To: Create a Full-Step Spiral Run

1. Start the **Stair** command and set up the Properties as required.
2. In the Components panel, click (Full-Step Spiral).
3. Select the center point of the spiral.
4. Select (or type) the radius of the spiral. The run is created, as shown in Figure 12–10.

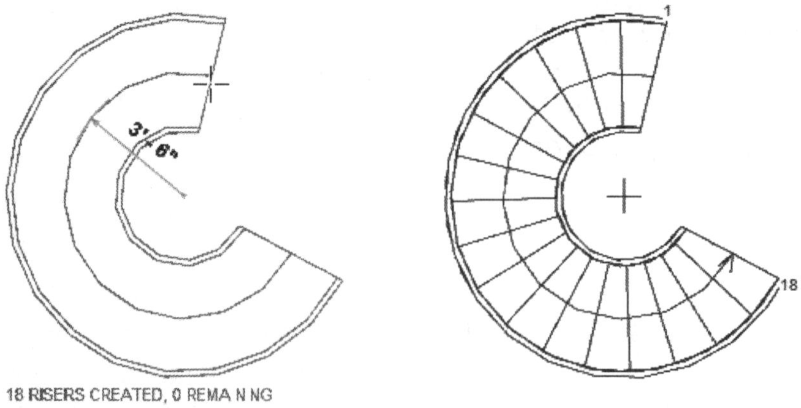

In process ***Completed***

Figure 12–10

How To: Create a Center-Ends Spiral Run

1. Start the **Stair** command and set up the Properties as required.
2. In the Components panel, click (Center-Ends Spiral).
3. Select the center of the spiral.
4. Select (or type) the radius of the spiral, as shown on the left in Figure 12–11.
5. Drag the cursor to display the number of risers, as shown on the right in Figure 12–11.

You can create spiral stairs with landings with this option.

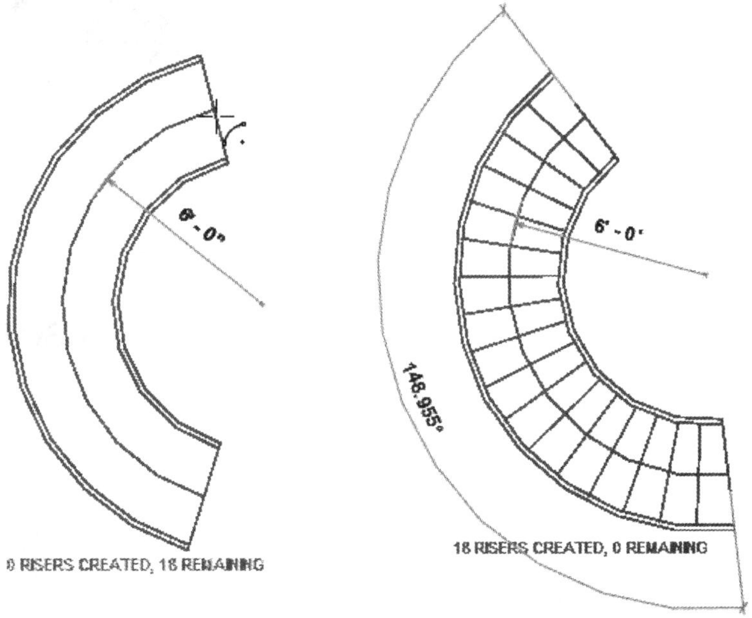

Select the radius ***Select the end of the run***

Figure 12–11

How To: Create Winder-based stairs.

1. Start the **Stair** command and set up the Properties as required.
2. In the Components panel, click (L-Shape Winder) or (U-Shape Winder).
3. Click a start point to place the overall stair.

4. Select the stair and use the arrow controls to modify the length, as shown in Figure 12–12.

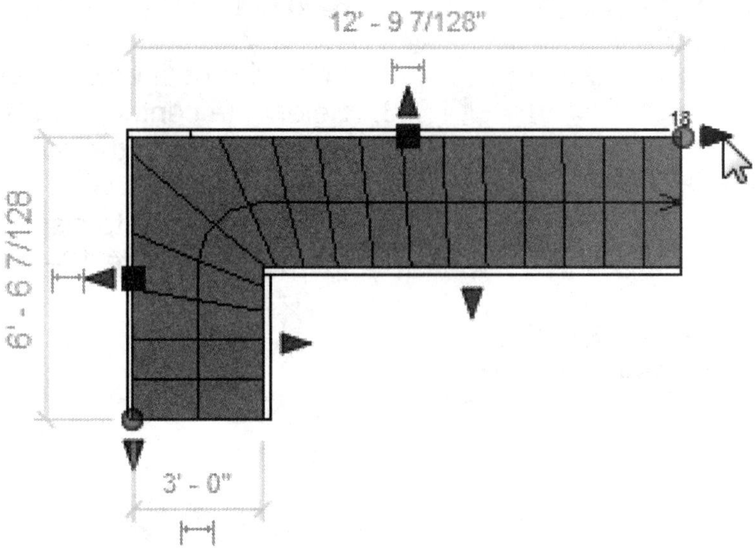

Figure 12–12

How To: Sketch a Stair

1. Start the **Stair** command and setup the Properties as required.
   - In many cases, a custom stair is shorter and should be set using a base and top offset from the same level, as shown in Figure 12–13. By default, a stair height is from level to level.

Change the level offsets before starting to sketch the stair.

Constraints	
Base Level	Level 1
Base Offset	0' 0"
Top Level	Level 1
Top Offset	2' 0"
Multistory Top Level	None

Figure 12–13

2. In the *Modify | Create Stair* tab>Components panel, click (Run) and then click (Sketch).

3. In the *Modify | Create Stair>Sketch Run* tab, use (Boundary), (Riser), and (Stair Path) to draw the parts of the stair, as shown in Figure 12–14.

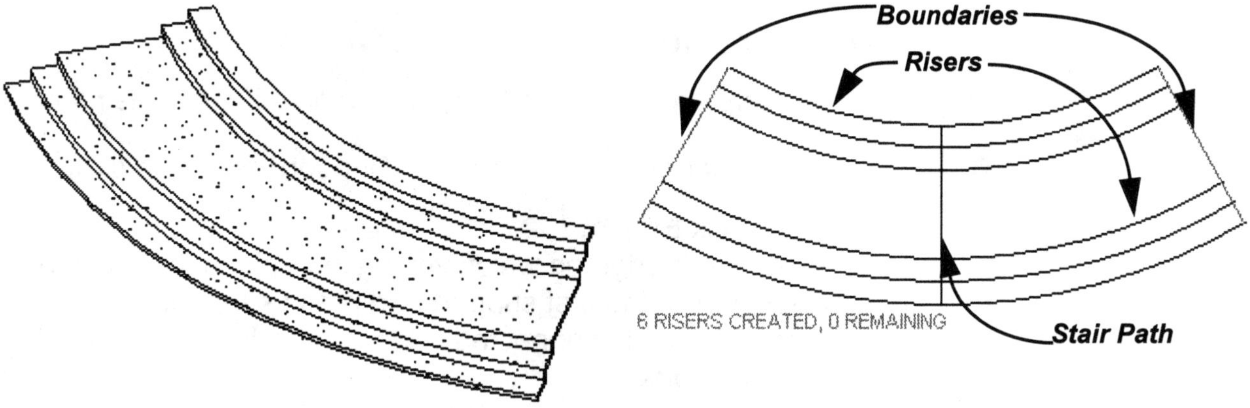

Figure 12–14

4. Click (Finish Edit Mode).
5. If you want to add a landing, you can sketch one.
6. Click (Finish Edit Mode) to complete the final assembly.

Creating Landings

Landings are typically created automatically between any breaks in runs. Once finishing the stair, you can easily modify the landings to create custom designs. There are two additional options to create landings, as shown in Figure 12–15:

- **Pick Two Runs:** Places the landing at the correct height between the runs.
- **Create Sketch:** Enables you to sketch the shape of the landing, but you must place it at the correct height.

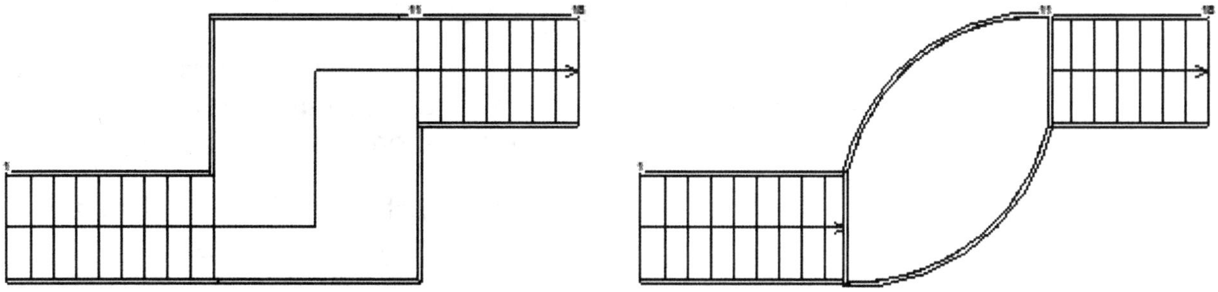

Pick Two Runs ***Create Sketch***

Figure 12–15

- You can connect runs with a landing as long as the start level and end level of the runs are at the same height.

Adding Supports

Stair supports are included in the stair type if required. However, you might want to delete them and add them later. Note that this only works if the stair type has supports that are specified in the Type properties.

How To: Add Stair Support Components

1. If there are no supports, in the *Modify* | *Create Stair* tab> Components panel, click (Support) and then click (Pick Edges).
2. Select the edge on which you want to place the support. Hover over the first support and press <Tab> if you have more than one connected edge on which you want to place the supports.
3. Finish the stair as required.

Hint: Trouble Shooting

When working with stairs and other elements, Warnings (such as the one shown in Figure 12–16), display when something is wrong, but you can keep on working. In many cases, you can close the dialog box and fix the issue or wait and do it later.

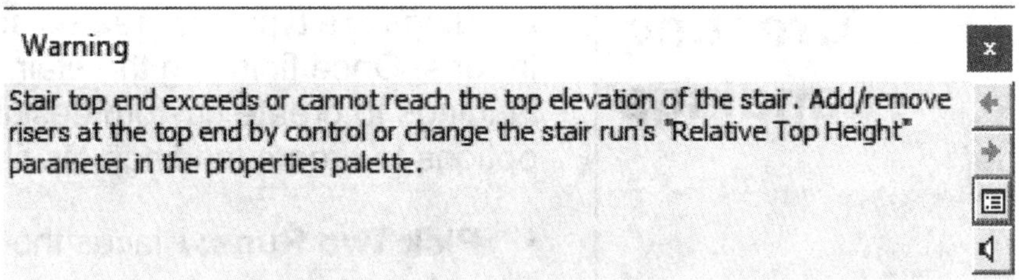

Figure 12–16

Sometimes Errors display where you must take action. These force you to stop and fix the situation.

When you select an element for which there has been a warning (Show Related Warnings) displays in the ribbon. It opens a dialog box in which you can review the warning(s) related to the selected element. You can also display a list of all of the warnings in the project by clicking (Review Warnings) in the *Manage* tab>Inquiry panel.

Practice 12a Create Component Stairs

Practice Objectives

- Create a component stairs.
- Model a custom sketch stair.

*15*In this practice, you will create u-shaped stairs in each of the stairwells, as shown in Figure 12–17. You will also create a sketched stair at the entrance to the building.

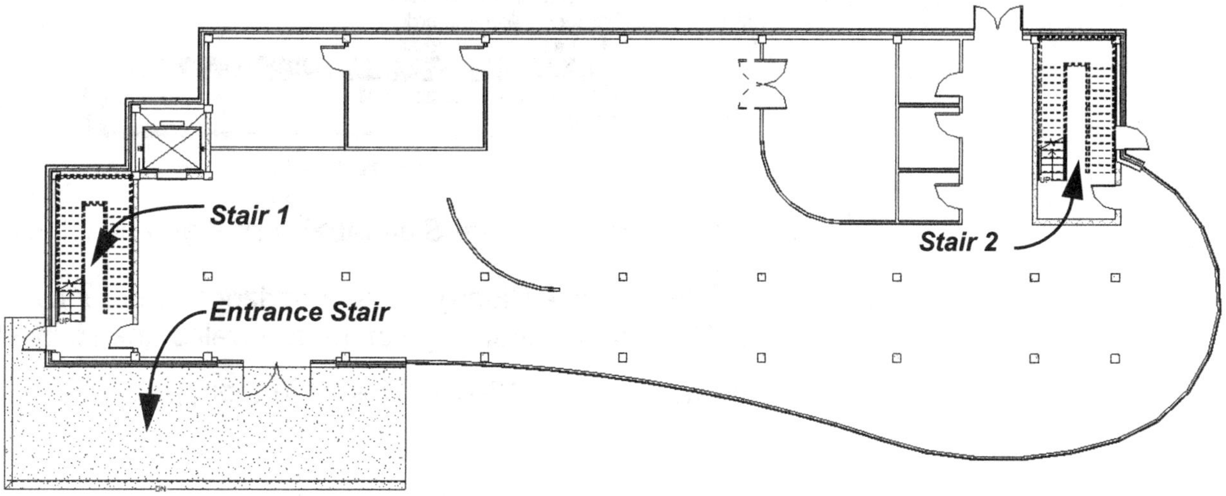

Figure 12–17

Task 1 - Create Stair 1 on the first floor.

1. Open the project **Modern-Hotel-Stairs.rvt**.
2. Open the **Floor Plans**: **Floor 1 - Stair 1** view. This is a callout from the main floor plan.
3. Hide the grid lines, sections, and crop region.
4. In the *Architecture* tab>Circulation panel, click (Stair).
5. In Properties, set or verify the following properties:
   - *Stair Type:* **Assembled Stair: Hotel Stairs**
   - *Base Level:* **Floor 1**
   - *Top Level:* **Floor 2**
   - *Base Offset:* **0' 0"**
   - *Top Offset:* **0' 0"**

6. In the *Modify | Create Stair* tab>Tools panel, click (Railing). In the Railings dialog box, select **Hotel Stair Guardrail**, as shown in Figure 12–18. Verify that the *Position* is set to **Treads** and click **OK**.

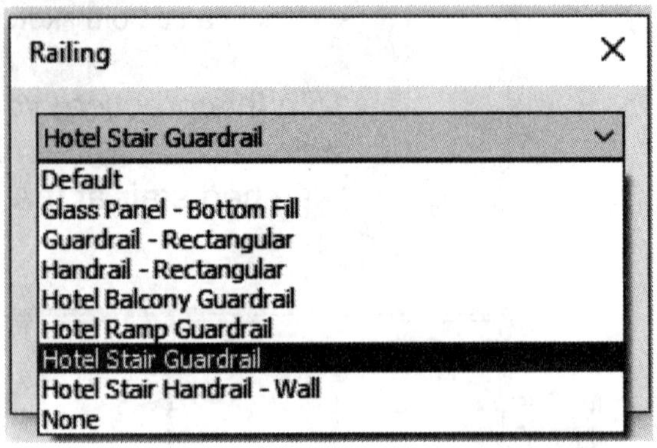

Figure 12–18

7. In the *Modify | Create Stair* tab>Work Plane panel, click (Reference Plane). Draw a horizontal reference plane **4'-0"** from the inner edge of the top wall of the stairwell, as shown in Figure 12–19. Click (Modify).

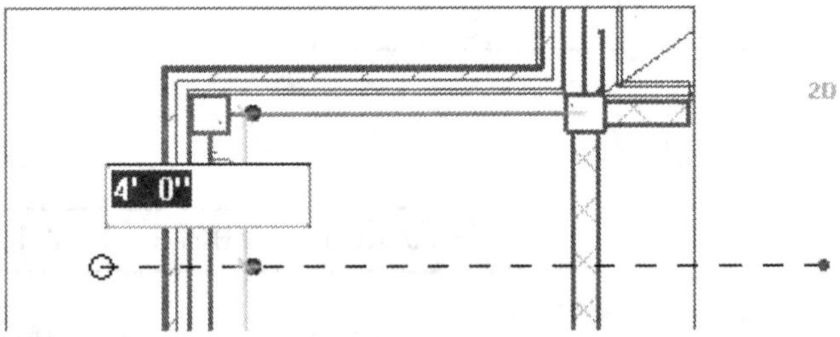

Figure 12–19

8. In the *Modify | Create Stair* tab>Components panel, click (Run).

9. In the Options Bar, set the *Location Line* to **Run: Left**, the *Offset* to **0' 0"**, the *Actual Run Width* to **3' 8"**, and select **Automatic Landing**.

10. Pick the start point of the first run on the wall close to the door, as shown in Figure 12–19. The exact location is not important at this point. Pick a second point near the reference plane.

11. Pick the start point for the second run at the intersection of the wall and reference plane, as shown in Figure 12–20. Pick the second point past the ghost image of the completed number of stairs.

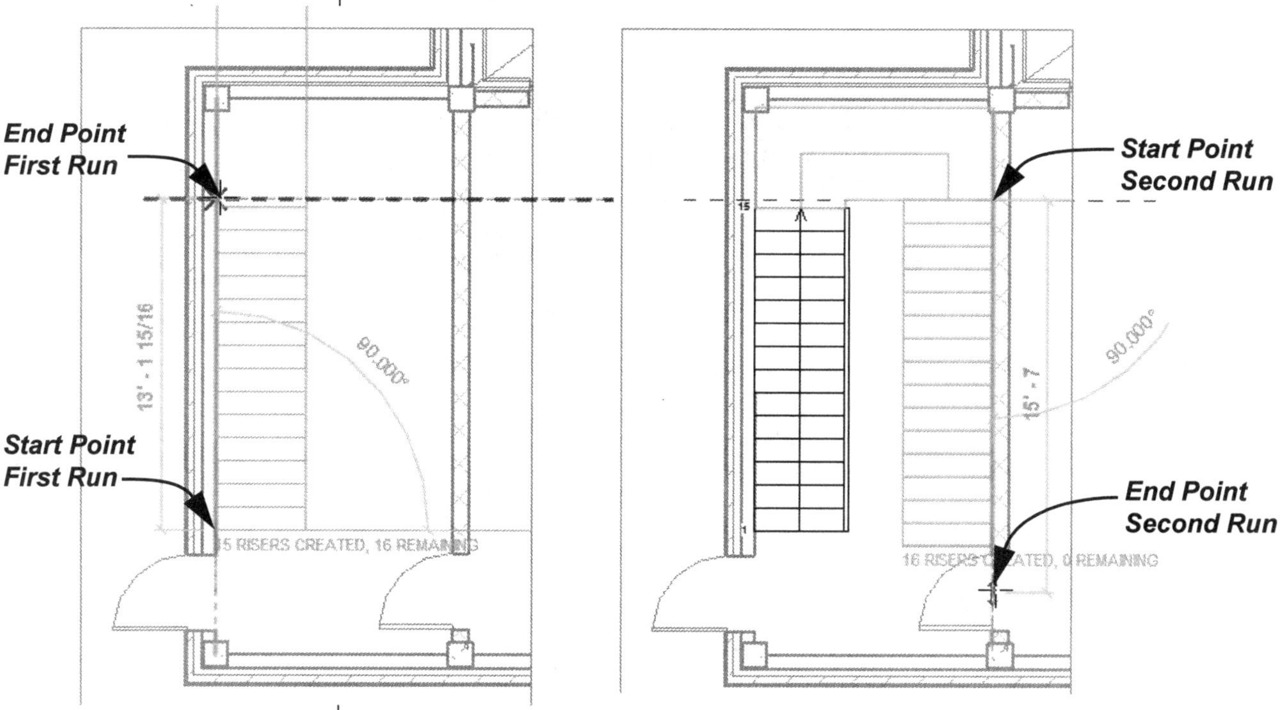

Figure 12–20

12. The run on the left wall might not be in the right place. Select the run and click (Move). Select a point on the top riser and then on the reference plane, as shown in Figure 12–21.

Make sure you select the run and not the landing.

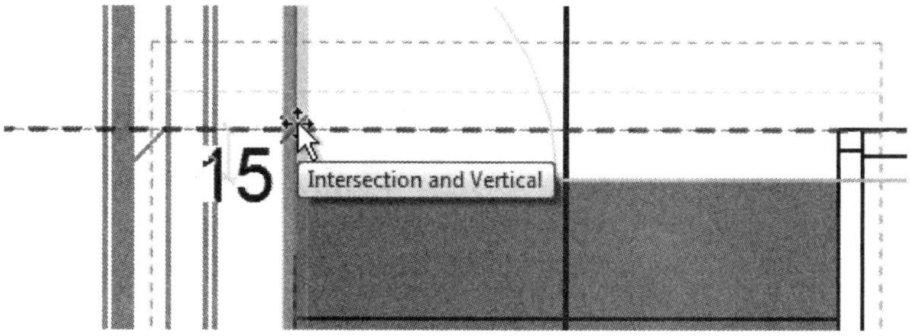

Figure 12–21

13. Depending on how you drew the runs you might also need to modify the run lengths. The left should have 1 to 16 steps and the right should have steps 17 to 31, as shown in Figure 12–22. Select the stairs on the left and use the arrow shape handle at the base of the stairs, to change the number of stairs as required.

14. Click  (Finish Edit Mode). The stairs display, as shown in Figure 12–23.

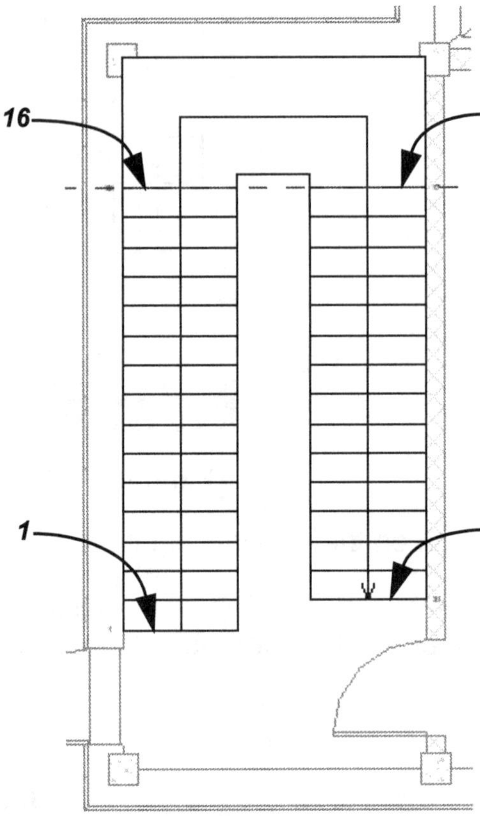

Figure 12–22

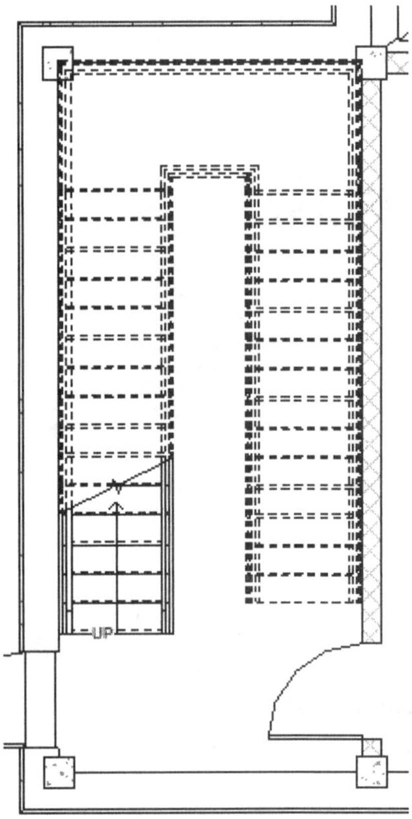

Figure 12–23

15. Save the project.

Task 2 - Create Stair 2 on the first floor.

1. Open the **Floor Plans**: **Floor 1 - Stair 2** view.

2. Repeat the process outlined above to create a stair in this stairwell, as shown in Figure 12–24.

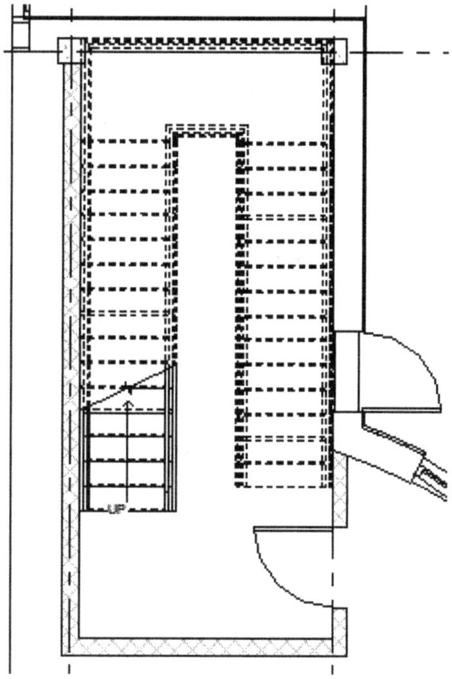

Figure 12–24

3. Save the project.

Task 3 - Create a sketched entrance stair.

1. Open the **Floor Plans: Floor 1** view.
2. Hide the gridlines and annotations by selecting one of each and typing **VH**.
3. Set the *Underlay>Range: Base Level* to **Floor 2**. This displays the outline of the entrance roof that you will use to create custom stairs.
4. In the *Architecture* tab>Circulation panel, click (Stair).
5. In the Type Selector, select **Stair: Monolithic Stair - Hotel**.
6. In Properties, set the following:
   - *Base Level:* **Floor 1**
   - *Base Offset*: (negative) **-1'-0"**
   - *Top Level*: **Floor 1**
   - *Top Offset:* **0'-0"**

7. In the *Modify | Create Stairs Sketch* tab>Tools panel, click (Railing). In the Railing dialog box, select **None** and click **OK**.

8. In the Draw panel, click (Run), (Create Sketch) then (Boundary), and (Pick Lines). Select the ends of the roof outline, as shown in Figure 12–25.

9. Click (Riser). Use the **Pick Lines** tool to select the other sides of the roof outline, as shown in Figure 12–25.

10. With (Riser) still selected, use the **Pick Lines** tool and set the offset to **1'-0"**. Offset another set of risers outside the outline, as shown in Figure 12–25.

11. Use (Trim/Extend to Corner) to clean up the intersections of the boundary lines and outside risers.

The sketch lines have been widened for emphasis.

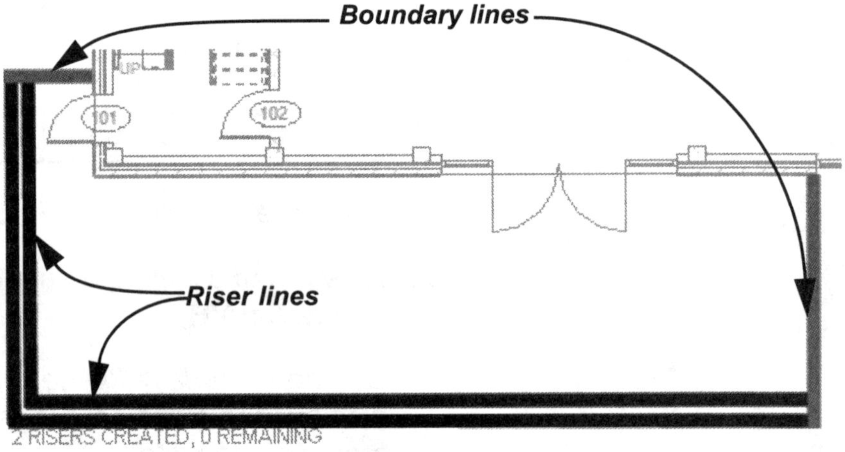

Figure 12–25

12. Click (Finish Edit Mode) to complete the stair portion of the assembly.

13. In the *Modify | Create Stair* tab>Components Panel, click (Landing) and then (Create Sketch).

14. Use **Pick Lines** to create the boundary for the landing, as shown in Figure 12–26.

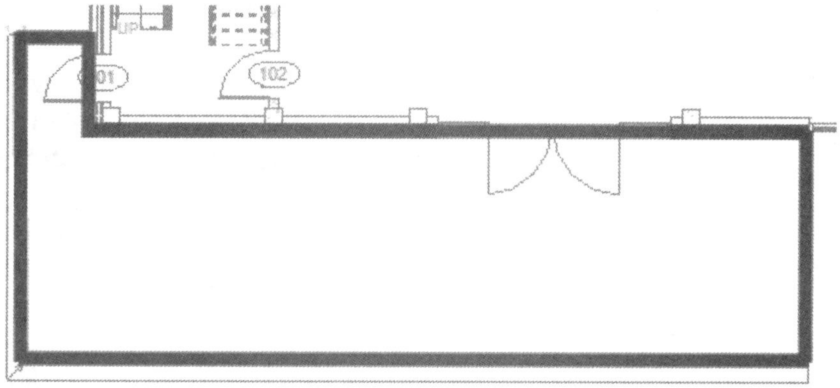

Figure 12–26

15. Click (Finish Edit Mode) twice to create the full stair assembly.

16. In Properties, set the *Underlay>Range: Base Level* to **None**.

17. View the new stairs in 3D, as shown in Figure 12–27.

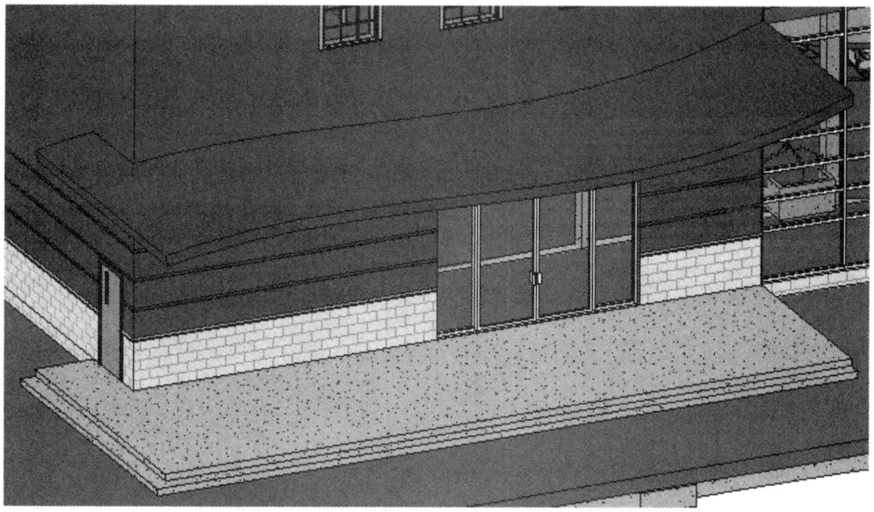

Figure 12–27

18. Save the project.

12.2 Modifying Component Stairs

Stairs can be modified in a variety of ways. For example, in Figure 12–28, a straight stair with a landing has been modified to make one run wider than the other and the landing wider than both runs, creating a balcony. The landing has been further customized by sketching a curved feature.

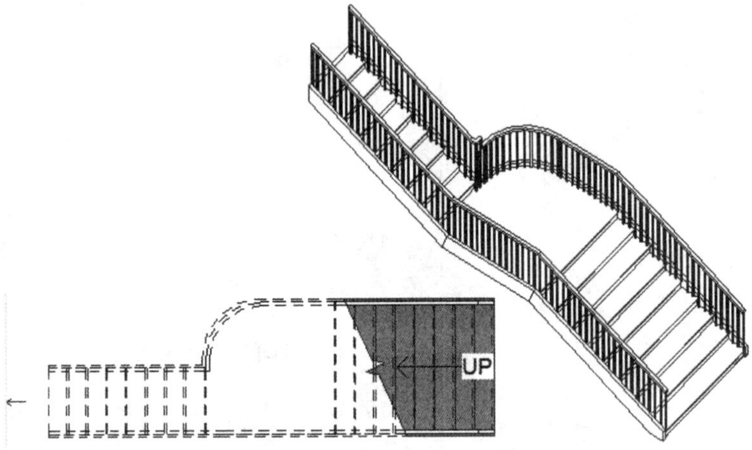

Figure 12–28

- Modifying stair components can be done when you first create the stair or later when you edit a stair.
- When working with a finished stair, you can change the type and properties, as well as flip the stair direction, as shown in Figure 12–29. You can select a stair run and use temporary dimensions to modify the length and width, as shown in Figure 12–30.

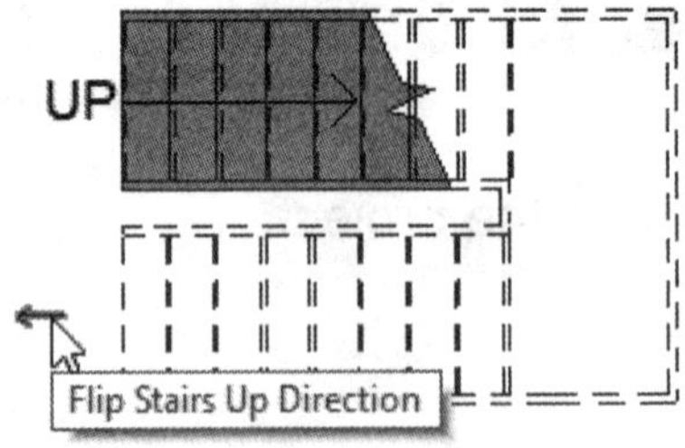

Full Stair Selected

Figure 12–29

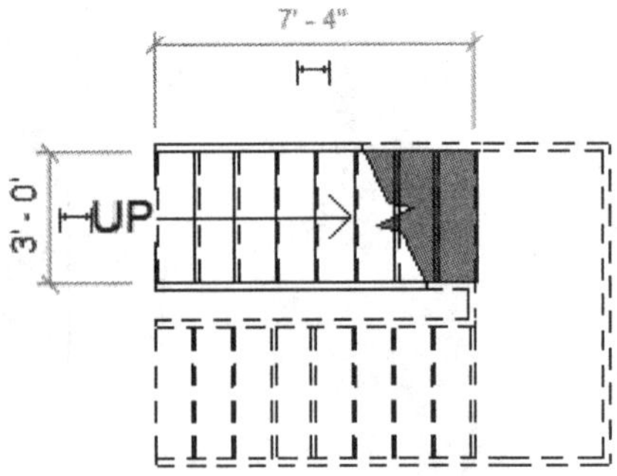

One Run Selected

Figure 12–30

- To select a stair run, hover over the stair and press <Tab> to cycle through until the one you want highlights.

Editing Individual Stair Components

Within stair edit mode, you can make more significant modifications to individual components using temporary dimensions and shape handles, as shown in Figure 12–31. Numerous snaps and alignment lines are also available as you modify the components.

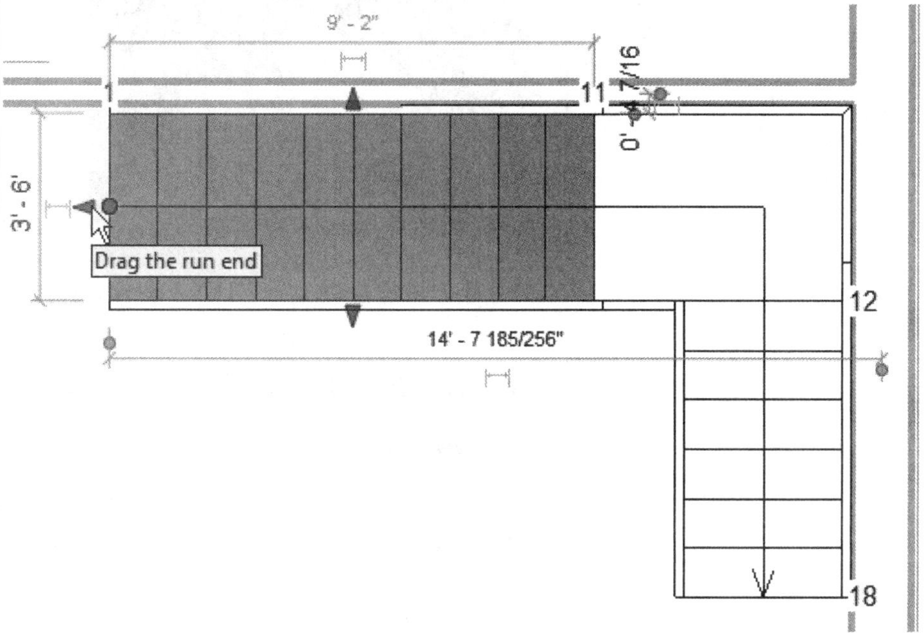

Figure 12–31

- To edit stairs, double-click on the stairs or, in the *Modify | Stairs* tab>Edit panel, click (Edit Stairs).
  - The arrow shape handle at the end of a run lengthens or shortens the run and modifies the other run so that the overall number of steps stays consistent and retains the start and end level.
  - The circle shape handle at the end of a run lengthens or shortens the run, does not modify any other runs, but changes the start and end level.
  - The arrow shape handle on the sides of the runs or landings can be used to modify the width.
  - You can use temporary dimensions for the run width and connections to other elements, but not for run lengths. Use the shape handles instead.
  - When you have finished modifying the stair, click (Finish Edit Mode).

Converting Components to Sketches

To customize a run or landing with more options, convert it into a sketch and modify the outline of the sketch as shown for a curved landing in Figure 12–32.

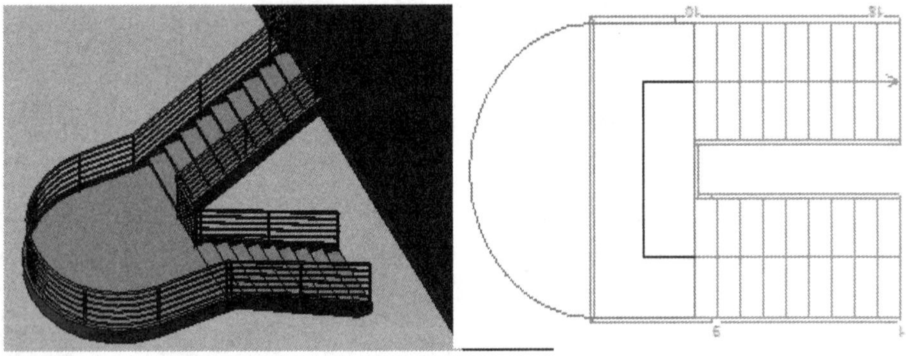

Figure 12–32

How To: Turn Stair Component into a Sketch

1. Select a stair.
2. In the *Modify | Stairs* tab>Edit panel, click (Edit Stairs).
3. Select the run or landing that you want to customize.
4. In the Tools panel, click (Convert to sketch-based). Doing so turns the component into a custom sketched element.
5. In the Tools panel, click (Edit Sketch).
6. Use the options in the *Modify | Create Stair>Sketch Landing (or Run)* tab>Draw panel, to modify the boundary, riser, or stair path, as required. The boundary of a landing is shown in Figure 12–33.

Editing an existing landing is easiest way to create a custom landing.

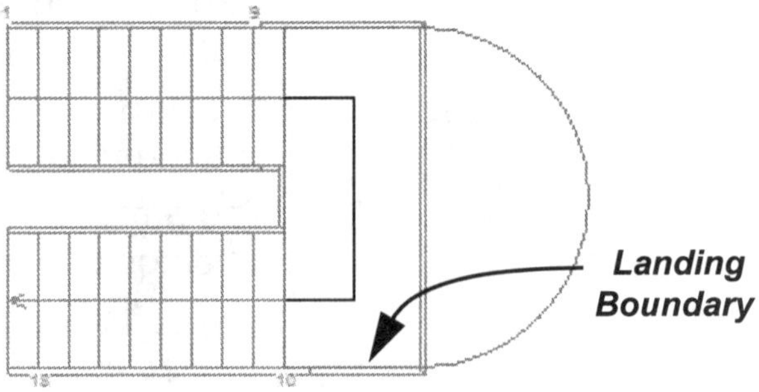

Figure 12–33

7. Click (Finish Edit Mode) to complete the sketch. Click again to return to the stair.

Multistory Stairs

Once you have created a component stair that runs from one level to another, you can expand that stair to extend to multiple building stories. You can select which levels the multistory stairs extend to, and skip levels as required, as shown in Figure 12–34.

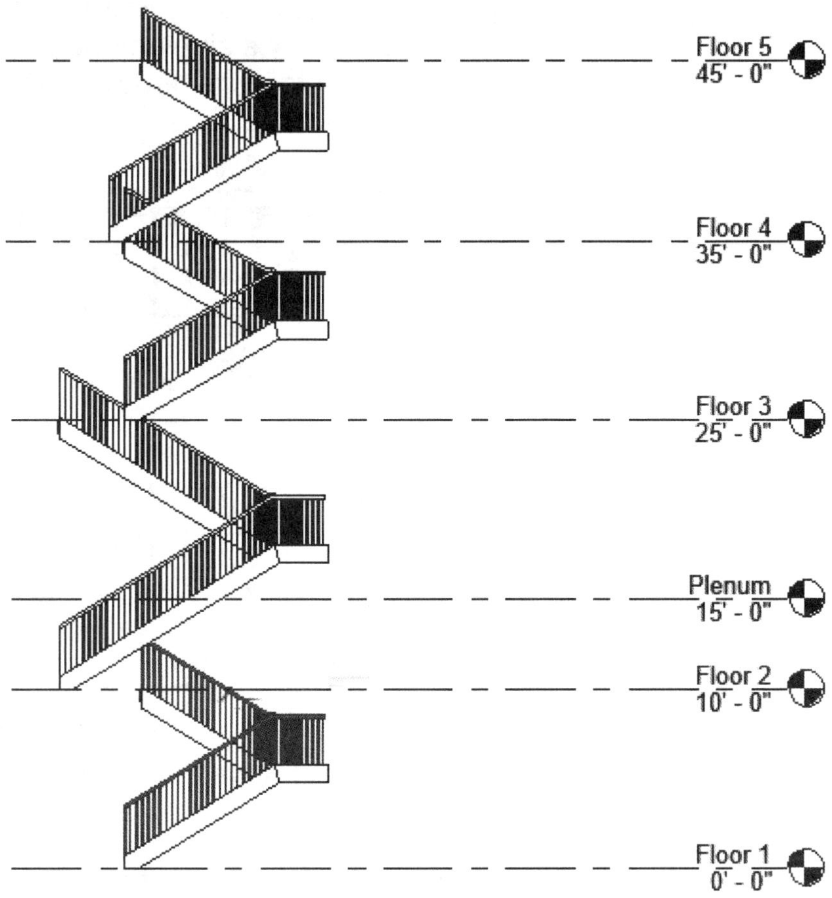

Figure 12–34

How To: Create Multistory Stairs

*You can also create multistory stairs while you are in the **Create Stair** command.*

1. Open an elevation or section view where the base stairs and levels are displayed.
2. Select the stair that you want to turn into a multistory stair.
3. In the *Modify | Stairs* tab>Multistory Stairs panel, click (Select *Levels).*
4. *In the Modify | Multistory Stairs* tab>Multistory Stairs panel, click (Connect Levels).
5. Select the levels you want to connect. Hold <Ctrl> to select multiple levels.
   - If you need to remove any levels, click (Disconnect Levels) and select the levels you want to remove.
6. Click (Finish Edit Mode).

- If you are not in an elevation or section view when you start the **Multistory Stair** command, the Go To View dialog box displays, enabling you to select and open a view by clicking **Open View**.

- To edit Multistory Stairs, ensure that you are selecting the full multistory stair element, as shown in Figure 12–35. Press <Tab> to cycle through the various components of the stairs as required.

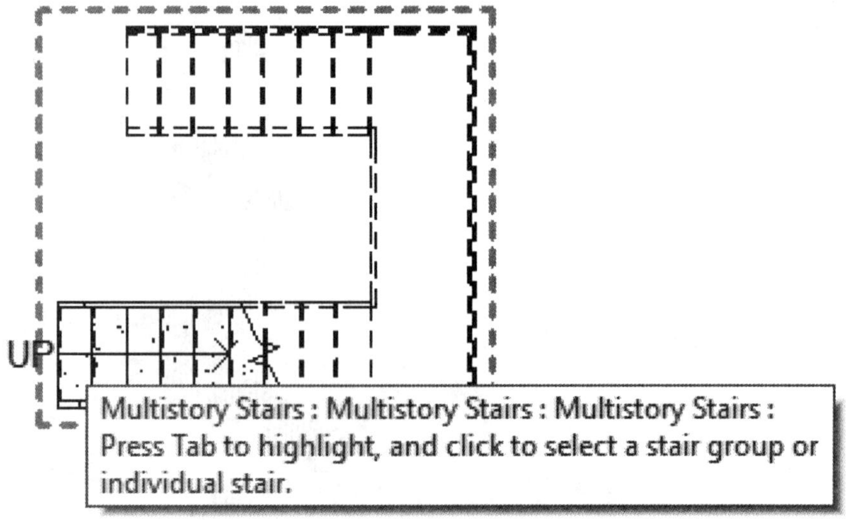

Figure 12–35

- If you change the height of a level, the stair components in the multistory stair are updated to match the new distance.

- If you change the type of a railing after a multistory stair has been placed, any runs of the same height (i.e., grouped together) are also updated. Runs of different heights would need to be modified separately.

Practice 12b Modify Component Stairs

Practice Objectives

- Expand a set of stairs to multistory stairs.
- Cut out floors where stairs penetrate them.
- Create shafts.

*10*In this practice, you will modify stairs and turn them into multistory stairs, as shown in Figure 12–36. You will also modify the floors for stair openings and add shafts to create openings for the upper floors.

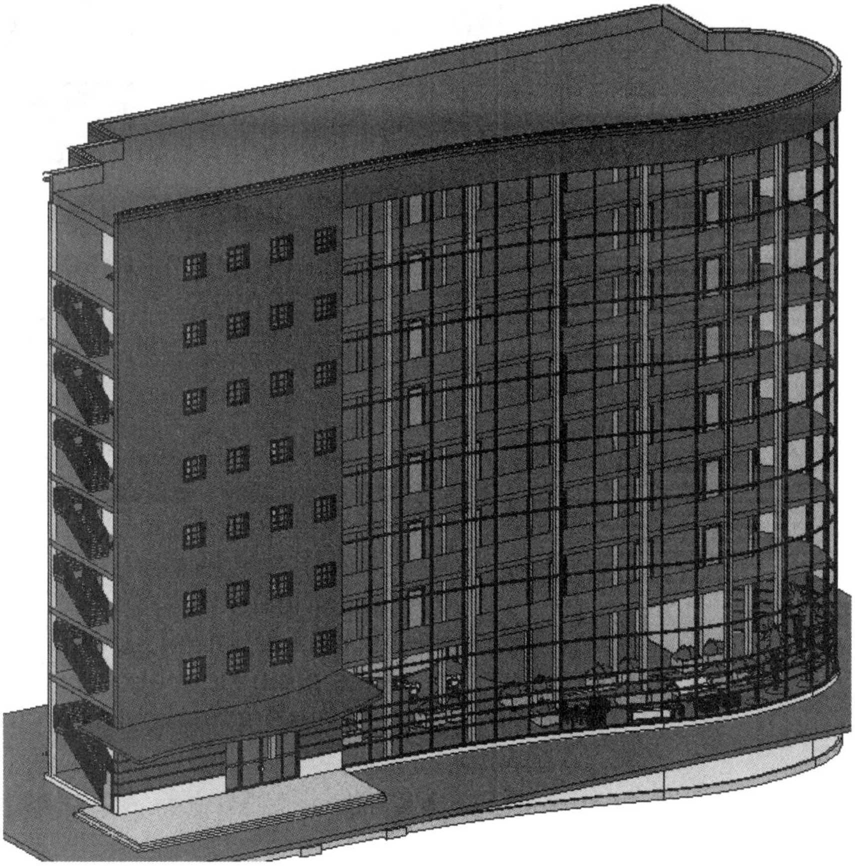

Figure 12–36

Task 1 - Create Multistory Stairs.

1. Open the project **Modern-Hotel-Stairs-Modify.rvt**.
2. Open the **Sections (Building Section): East-West Section** view.
3. Select the assembled stair shown in Figure 12–37.

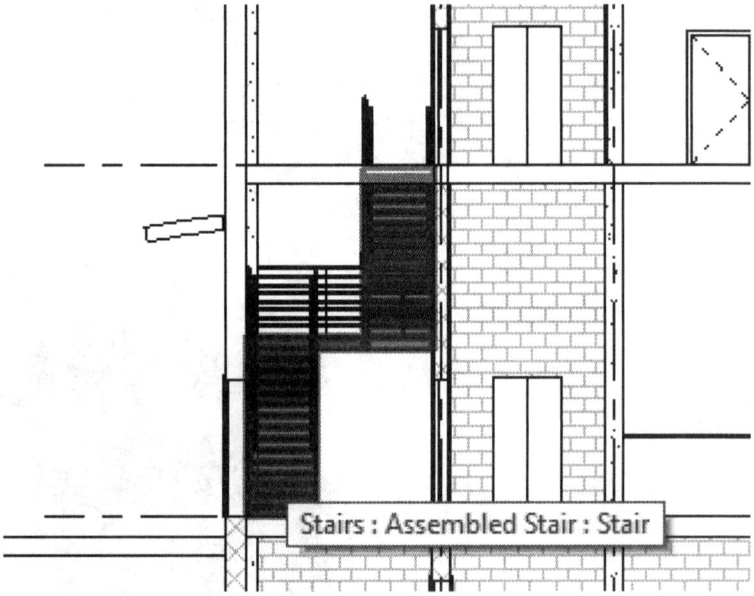

Figure 12–37

4. In the *Modify* | *Stairs* tab>Multistory Stairs panel, click  (Select Levels).
5. Hold <Ctrl> and select the level lines for **Floor 3** to **Floor 8**. (Do not select the **Roof** or **Parapet** levels.)

6. Click (Finish Edit Mode). The stairs are added between the rest of the floors as shown in Figure 12–38.

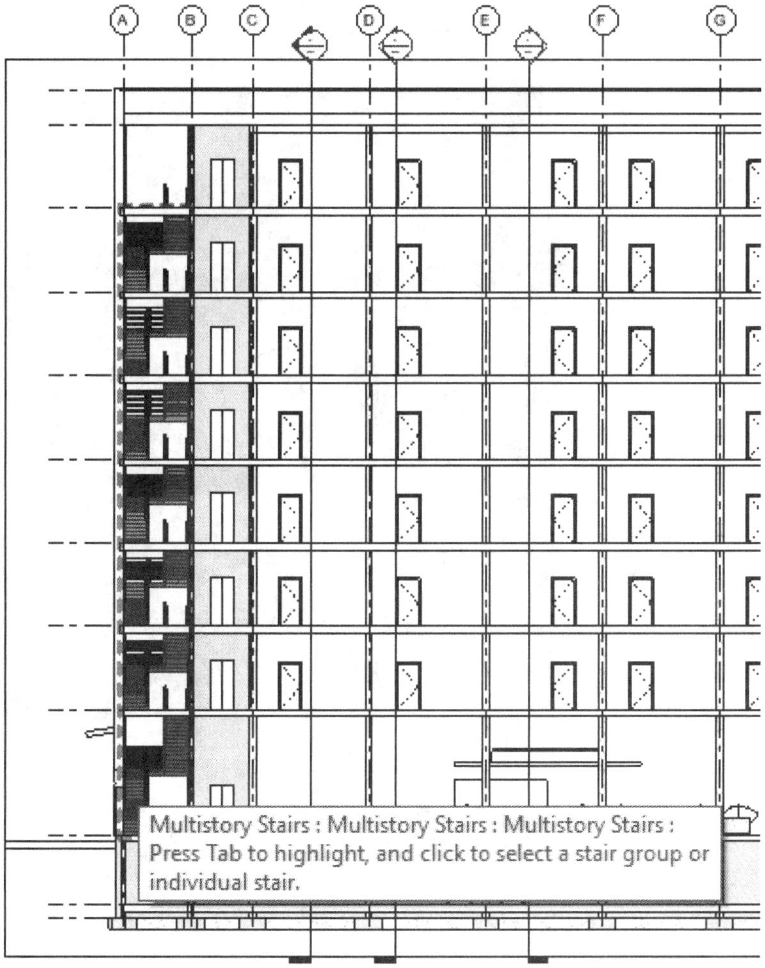

Figure 12–38

7. With the new multistory stairs still selected, in the *Modify | Multistory Stairs* tab>Multistory Stairs panel, click (Connect/Disconnect Levels).

8. Click (Connect Levels), and then select the **Basement** level line and click (Finish Edit Mode). The stairs to the basement are added.

9. Save the project.

10. To see the stairs on all of the floors, set the Visual Style to (Consistent Colors), as shown in Figure 12–39.

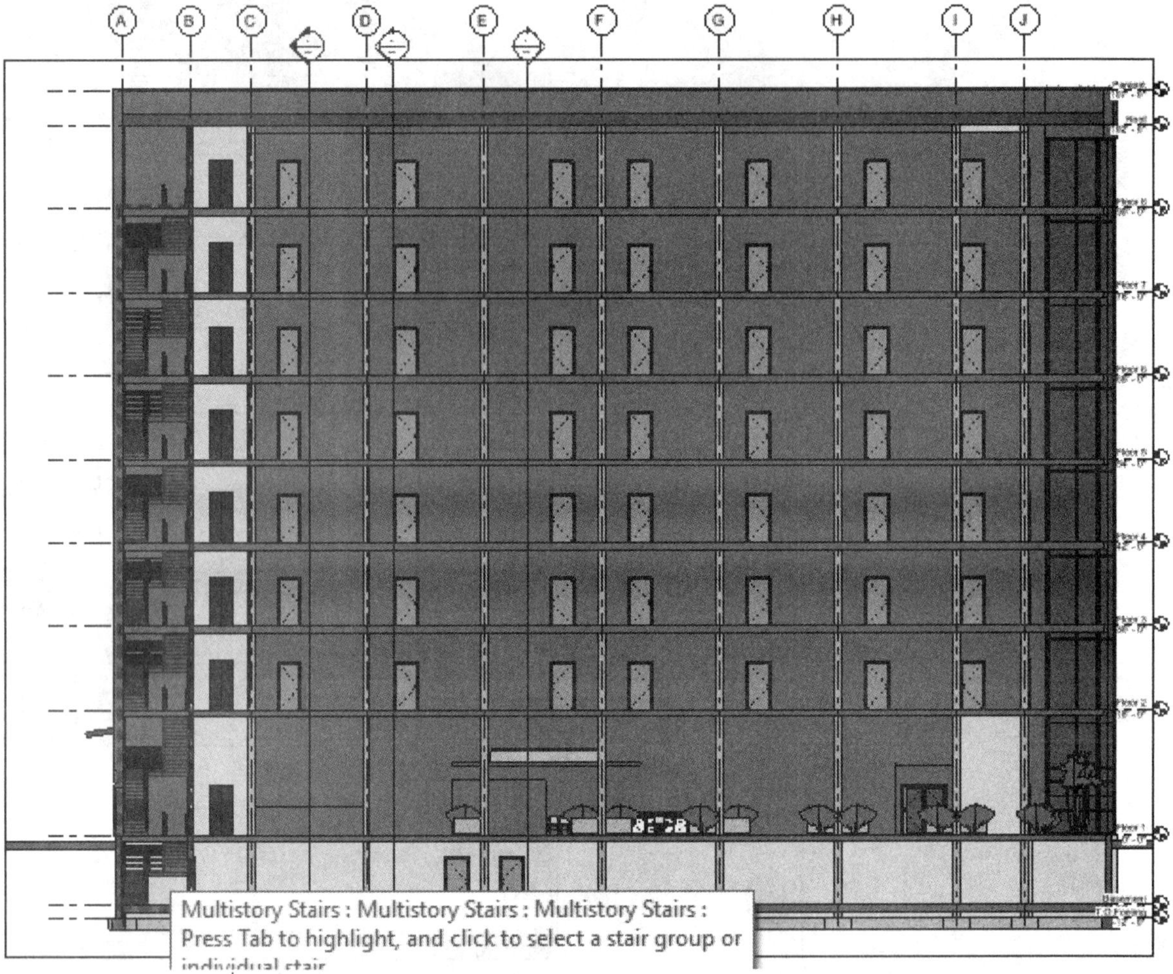

Figure 12–39

11. Save the project.
12. Return to the Floor 1 view.
13. Create another section so you can see Stair 2.
14. Repeat the process of turning this stair into a multistory stair.
15. Save the project.

Task 2 - Modify the second floor stair openings.

1. Open the **Floor Plans: Floor 2** view.
2. Select the floor. (It is easiest to select one of the balconies.)
3. In the *Modify | Floors* tab>Mode panel, click  (Edit Boundary).
4. Modify the boundary line so that it creates an opening for the stairs, as shown in Figure 12–40.

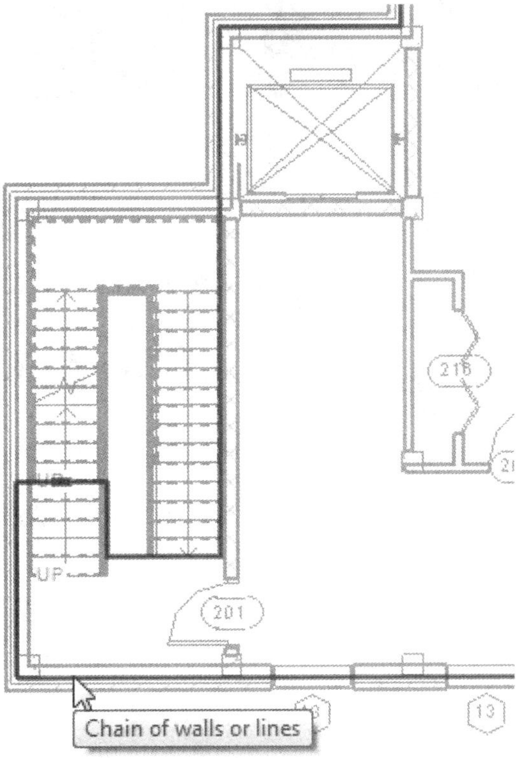

Figure 12–40

5. Pan over to the other stairwell and modify the floor boundary there as well.
6. Click  (Finish Edit Mode). Do not attach the walls to the floor.

7. Zoom out to display the entire second floor, as shown in Figure 12–41.

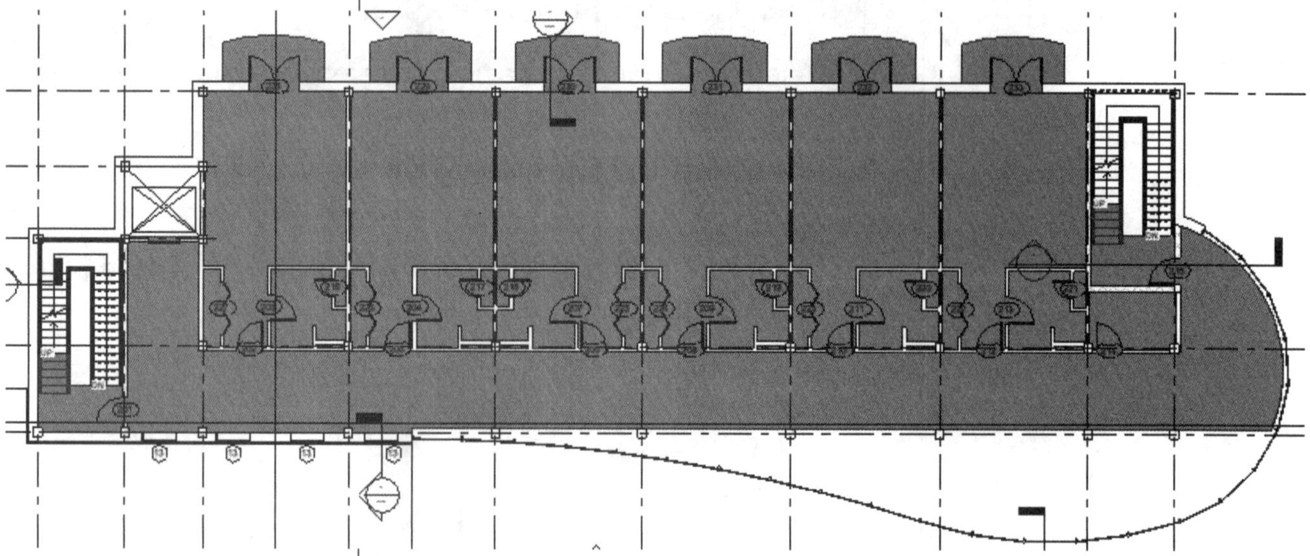

Figure 12–41

8. Save the project.

Task 3 - Add Shafts in the stairwells

1. Open the **Floor Plans: Floor 3** view.
2. Change the *Underlay* to **None** if needed.
3. In the *Architecture* tab> Opening panel click (Shaft).

You can use a shaft here because the openings are the same on all of the floors.

4. Draw the sketch of the shaft similar to that shown in Figure 12–42.

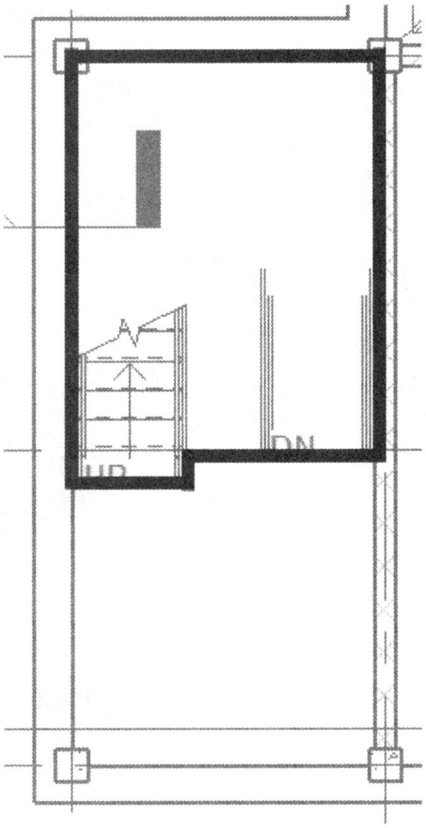

Figure 12–42

5. In Properties, set the *Base Constraint* to **Floor 3** with a *Base Offset* of (negative) **-1'-0"** and the *Top Constraint* to **Up to level: Floor 8**.
6. Repeat the process on the other stairwell.
7. Save the project.

12.3 Working with Railings

Hosts for sketched railings include floors, slabs, slab edges, the top of walls and roofs. You can also add railings to topographic surfaces.

Railings are automatically created with stairs, but you can modify or delete them independently of the stair element. You can also add railings separate from the stairs for other locations, as shown in Figure 12–43.

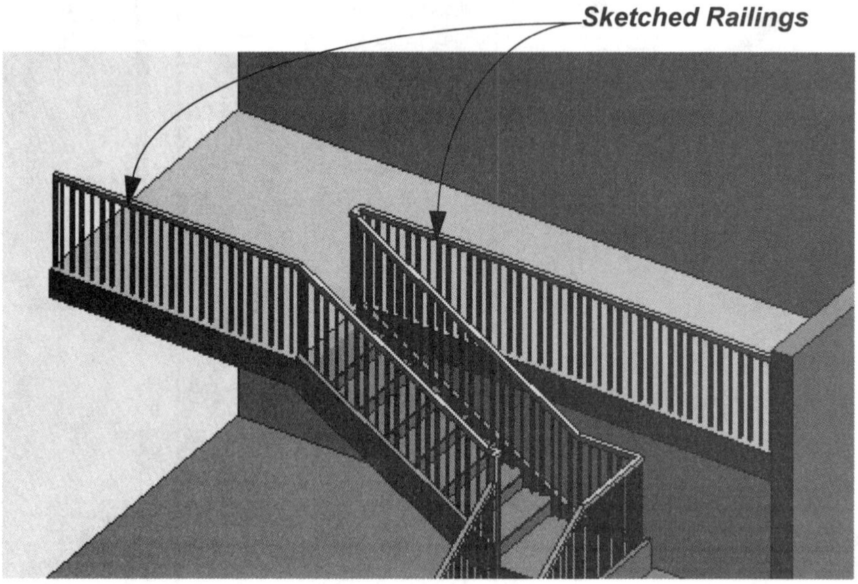

Figure 12–43

- You can add railings to existing stairs and ramps if they were not included when they were created.

How To: Add Railings by Sketching

1. Open a plan or 3D view.
2. In the *Architecture* tab>Circulation panel, expand (Railing) and click (Sketch Path).
3. In the Type Selector, specify the railing type.
4. In the *Modify | Create Railing Path* tab>Tools panel, click (Pick New Host) and select the element with which the railing is associated, such as a stair or floor or top of a wall.
   - If you are working in a 3D or section view, you can select **Preview** in the *Modify | Create Railing Path* tab>Options panel and the railing displays while you are still in edit mode. This only works if you have selected a host.

- If the host is sloped, the railing will follow the slope, as shown in Figure 12–44. The sketch displays at the hosts level.

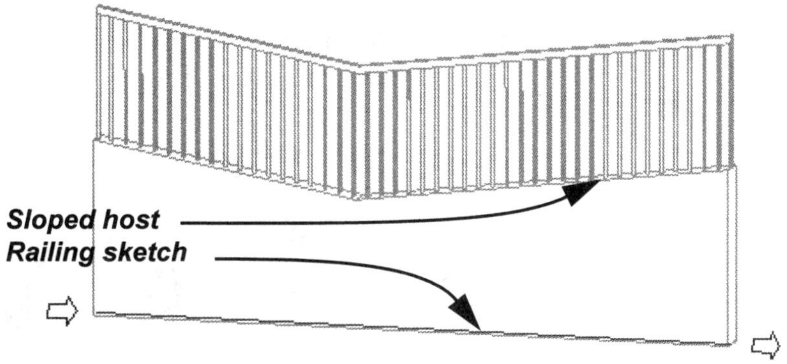

Figure 12–44

5. Use the Draw tools to sketch the lines that define the railings.
6. Click (Finish Edit Mode) to create the railing.

- The railing must be a single connected sketch. If it is not, you are prompted with a warning, such as that shown in Figure 12–45.

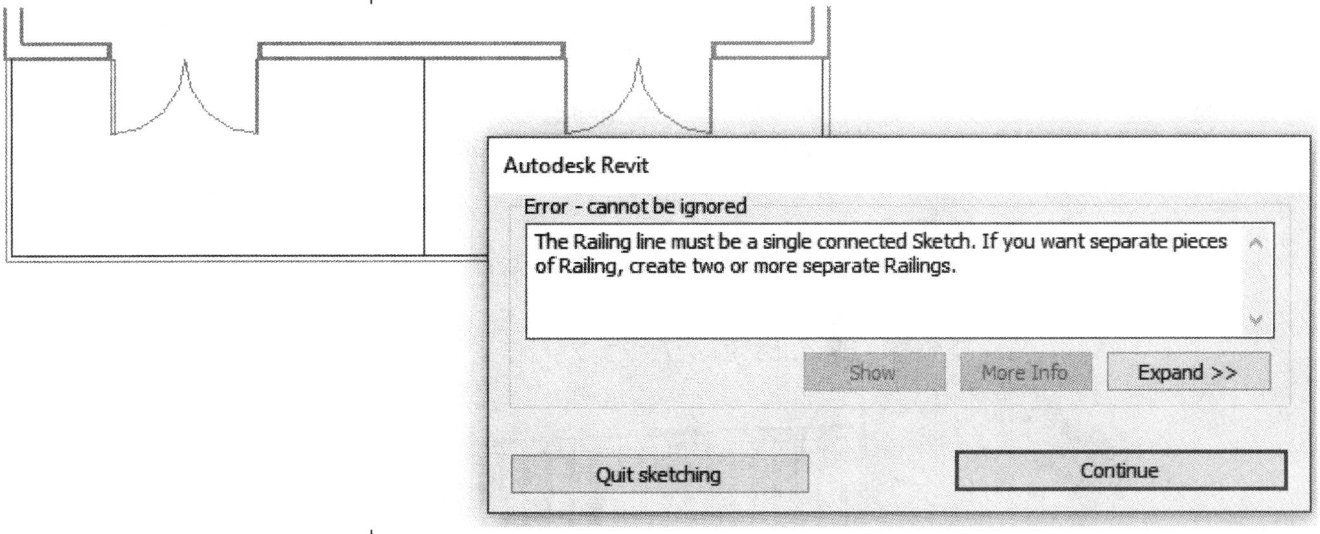

Figure 12–45

How To: Add Railings by Selecting a Host

1. In the *Architecture* tab>Circulation panel, expand (Railing) and click (Place on Host).
2. In the *Modify | Create Railing Place on Host* tab>Position panel, click (Treads) or (Stringer).
3. Select the stair or ramp where you want to add the railings.

- **Place on Host** only works if there are no railings on the stair. If you want to add an additional railing (e.g., down the middle of a wide stair) you need to sketch the railing.

Modifying Railings

Modifying railings can be as simple as changing their type, as shown in Figure 12–46. You can also edit the path of a railing.

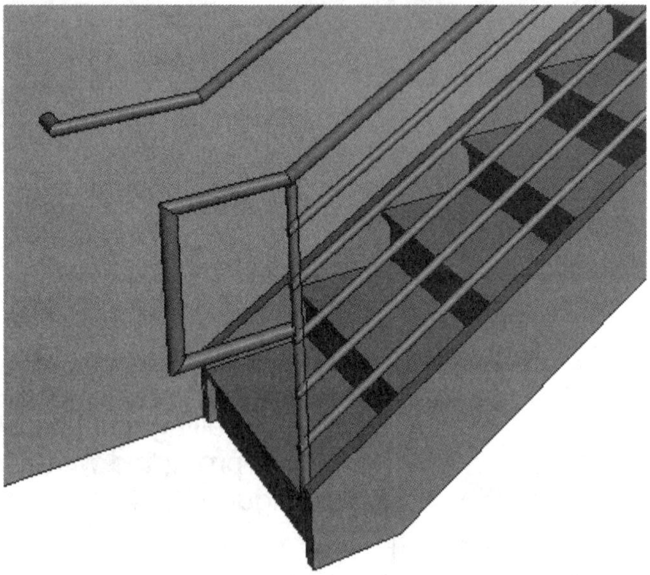

Figure 12–46

- You can delete railings separately from stairs or ramps. However, deleting a stair or ramp automatically deletes related railings.

- You can use the (Split Element) command on railings. Doing so results in separate railings, as shown in Figure 12–47.

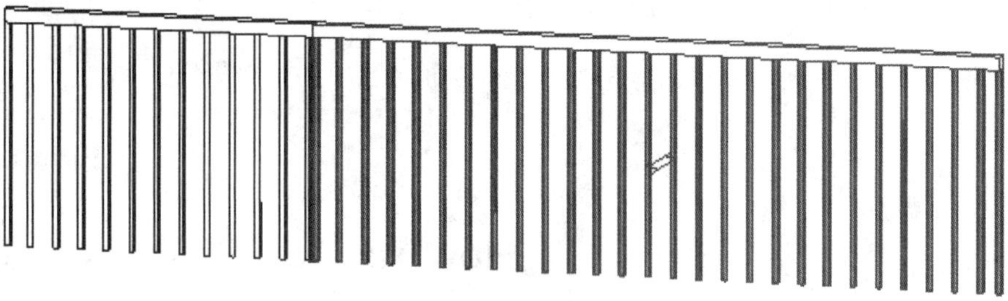

Figure 12–47

Editing the Path of a Railing

To edit the path of a railing, double-click on the railing or select the railing and in the *Modify | Railings* tab>Mode panel, click

 (Edit Path). This places you in edit mode, in which you can modify the individual lines that define the railing, as shown in Figure 12–48. You can create additional lines, but they must be connected to the existing lines.

Unlike many other elements in edit mode, railings do not have to be in a closed loop.

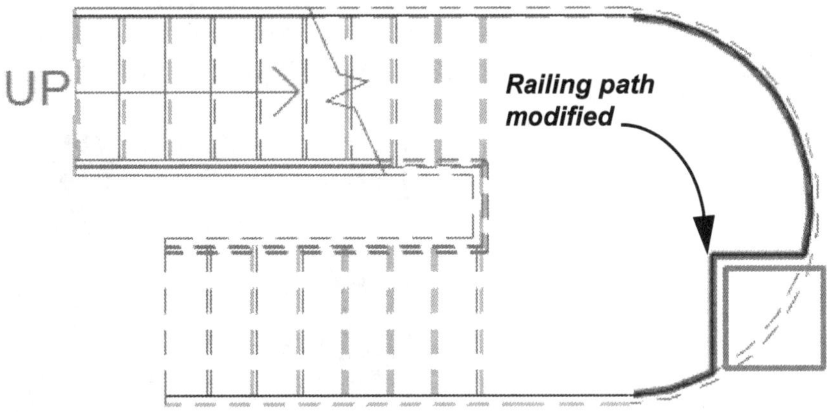

Figure 12–48

Practice 12c Work with Railings

Practice Objectives

- Modify railings and handrails.
- Add stand-alone railings.

In this practice, you will modify the railings in the stairwells by changing the railings against the wall to a new type. You will also add stand-alone railings to connect the runs of the stairs in the stairwells. You will then add railings to the interior balconies (as shown in Figure 12–49), and to the exterior balconies.

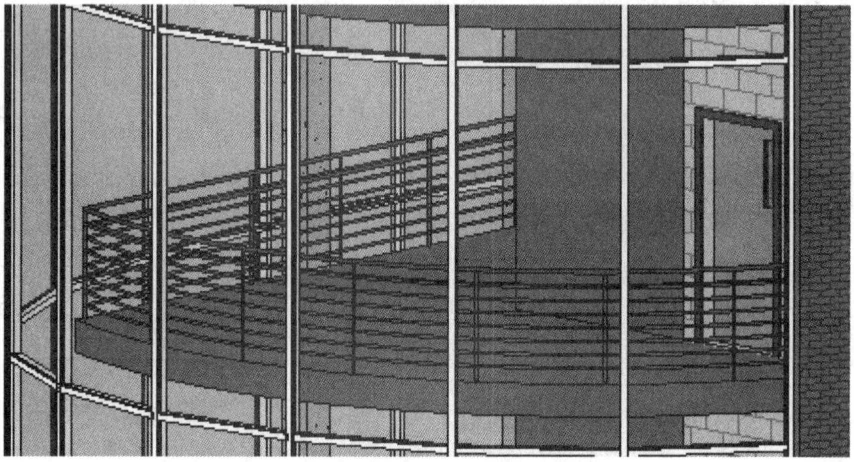

Figure 12–49

Task 1 - Modify the stairwell railings.

*Press <Ctrl>+<Tab> to move between the **3D Camera** view and the **Floor Plan** view or use the view tabs at the top of the window.*

1. Open the project **Modern-Hotel-Railings.rvt**.
2. Open the **Floor Plans: Floor 1 - Stair 1** view.
3. Create a camera view looking from the door into the stairwell to display the new stairs and railings.
4. In the Project Browser, in *3D Views*, right-click on the new 3D view and rename it as **Stair 1 - Floor 1 3D**.
5. Modify the controls as required to show the first run of the stair. and set the *Visual Style* to (Shaded).

6. Select the railing that is against the wall and in the Type Selector, select **Railing: Hotel Stair Handrail-Wall**. The railing type changes, as shown in Figure 12–50.

Figure 12–50

7. With the handrail still selected, in Properties set the *Offset from Path* to **0**. This prevents the handrail from sitting too far off the wall.

8. Open the **Floor Plans: Floor 2** view.

9. Zoom in on the stairwell and select the outside railing. In the Type Selector, change the type to **Railing: Hotel Stair Handrail-Wall** and the *Offset from Path* to **0**.

10. Select the inside railing. In the *Modify | Railing* tab>Mode panel, click (Edit Path) or double-click on the railing.

11. Select the vertical path and use the Drag Line End control to lengthen it to **10'-1"**, as shown in Figure 12–51.

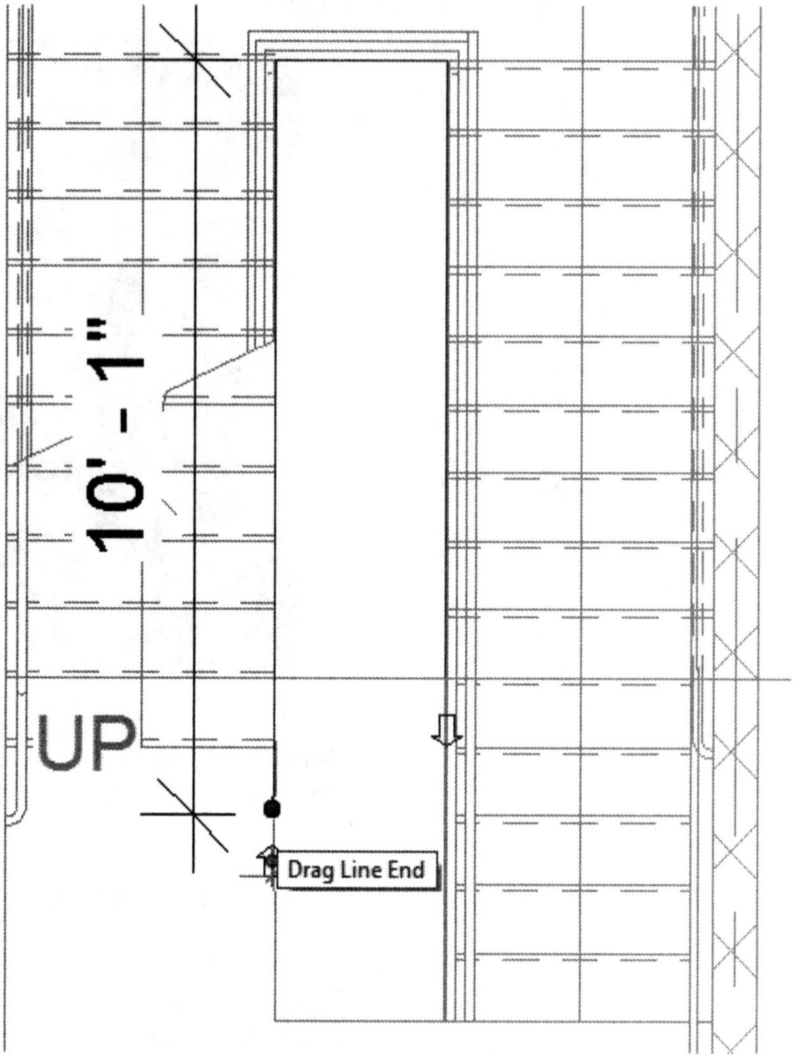

Figure 12–51

12. Click  (Finish Edit Mode).

13. In the *Architecture* tab>Circulation panel, click (Railing) and select (Sketch Path). Sketch the path from the midpoint of the guardrail on each side, as shown in Figure 12–52. Hint: Type **SM** to force a snap to the midpoint of the end of the railing.

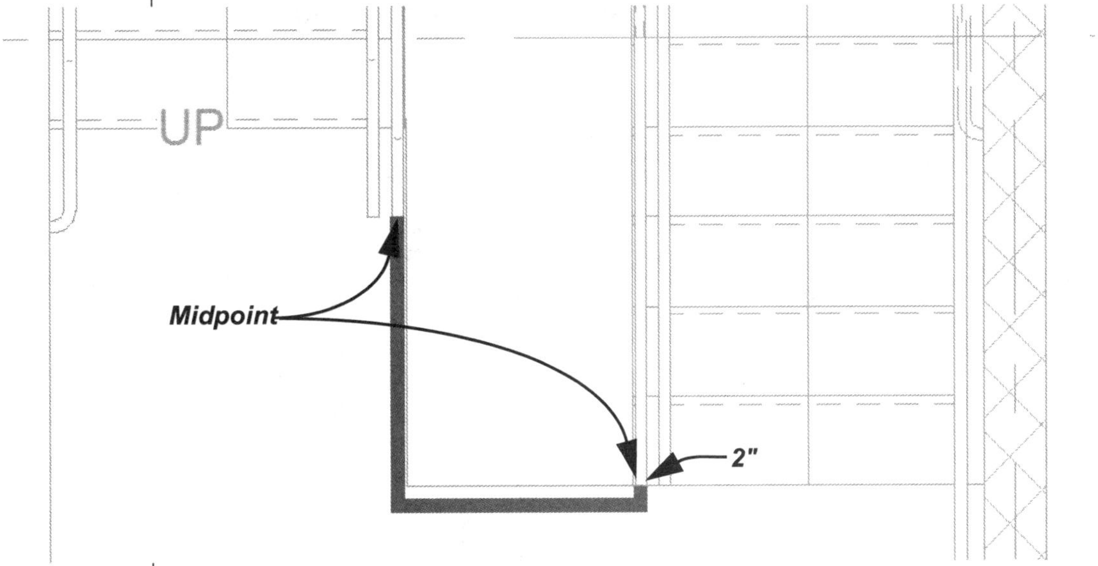

Figure 12–52

14. Click (Finish Edit Mode).

15. Select the **Flip railing direction** control if required so the guardrail and handrails match.

16. Create a camera view to display the stairs and railings, as shown in Figure 12–53.

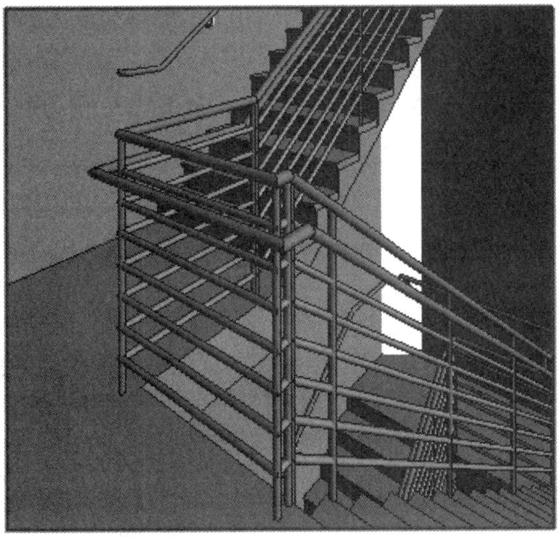

Figure 12–53

17. Rename this view as **Stair 1 - Floor 2 3D**.

18. Copy the new railing in the clipboard and use the **Paste Aligned to Selected Levels** command to copy it to Floor 3.

19. Open the **Floor Plans: Floor 3** view.

20. Modify the new railing to fit the different configuration of the stairs, as shown in Figure 12–54.

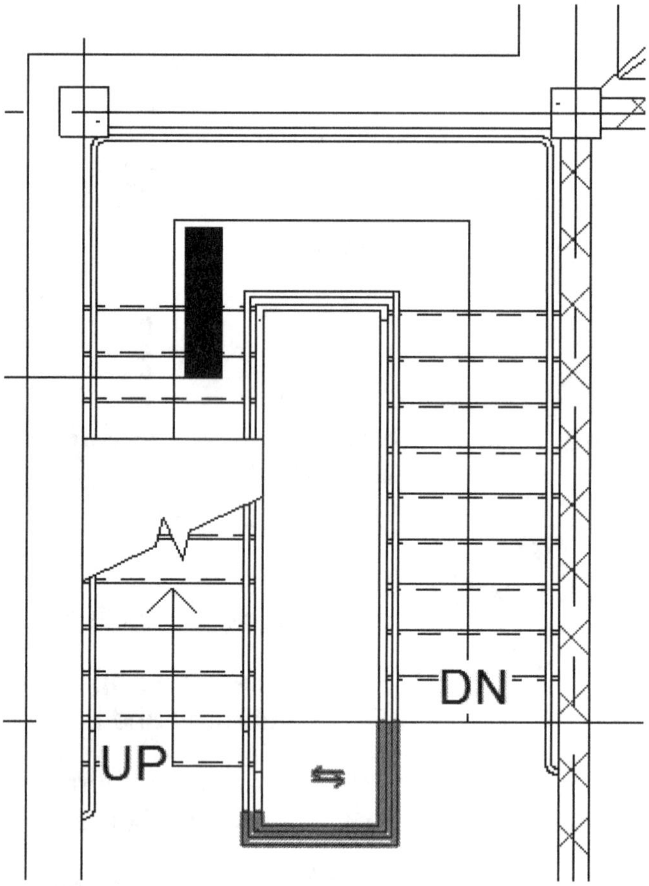

Figure 12–54

21. Copy the new railings to floors 4 through 8. If you have time, you can modify the railing on Floor 8 to fit the opening.

22. Save the project.

Task 2 - Add stand-alone railings.

1. Open the **Floor Plans: Floor 2** view and pan and zoom over to the interior balcony (walkway line) as required.

2. In the *Architecture* tab>Circulation panel, expand  (Railing) and click  (Sketch Path).

3. In the Type Selector, select **Railing: Hotel Balcony Guardrail**.

4. Draw a sketch line that is **3"** from the edge of the balcony floor over the lobby of the hotel, as shown in Figure 12–55. Ensure that you include the curved portion at the far end.

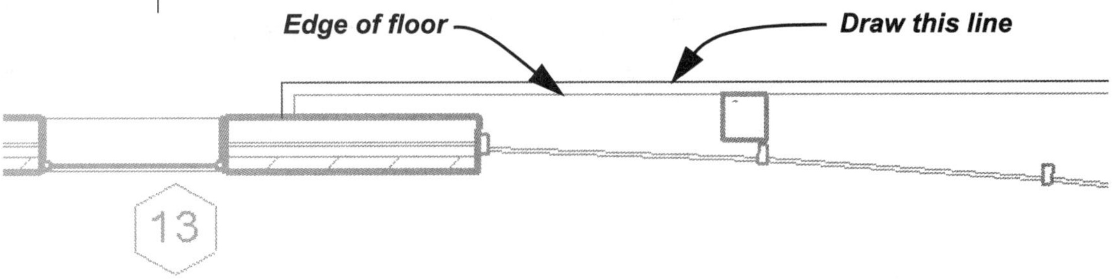

Figure 12–55

5. Click (Finish Edit Mode).

6. Zoom in on one of the outdoor balconies on the back of the building.

7. Add balcony railings, as shown in the sketch in Figure 12–56, using the same properties as the inside balcony railing.

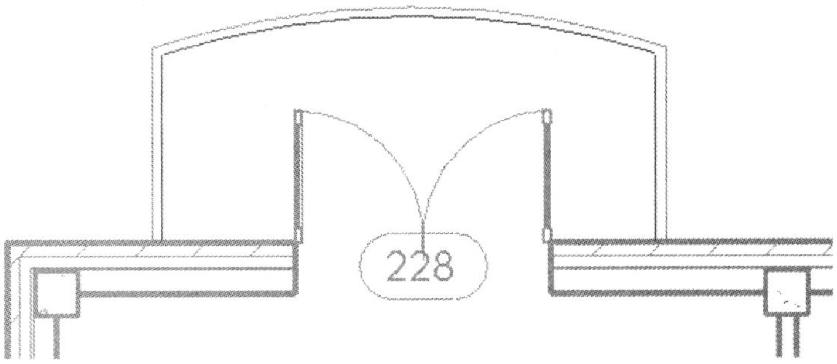

Figure 12–56

8. Click (Finish Edit Mode).

9. Copy the completed railing to the other balconies.

10. Copy all of the balcony railings, inside and out, to the other floors.

11. Open an exterior 3D view and verify the placement of all of the railings.

12. Save the project.

12.4 Creating Ramps

The process of creating ramps is similar to that of creating stairs with runs and automatic landings. You can also sketch a boundary with risers at the start and end of each slope. Ramps are most often used for short vertical distances (as shown in Figure 12–57), as they require a lot of space for their runs. Check the local building codes to determine how long a run can be before a landing is required.

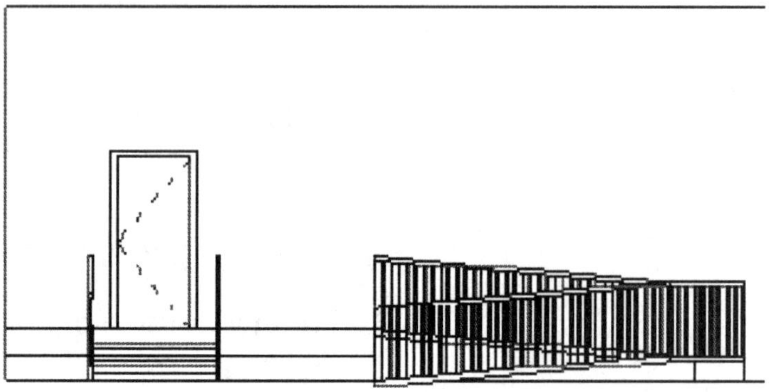

Figure 12–57

How To: Create a Ramp using Runs

1. In the *Architecture* tab>Circulation panel, click (Ramp).
2. In the Type Selector, select the ramp type.
3. In the *Modify | Create Ramp Sketch* tab>Tools panel, click (Railing) and select a railing type in the Railing Types dialog box. Click **OK**.
4. In Properties, specify the *Constraints,* especially **Base Level** and **Top Level** and their offsets as shown in Figure 12–58, and other properties. The **Width** of the ramp is set in the *Dimensions* area.

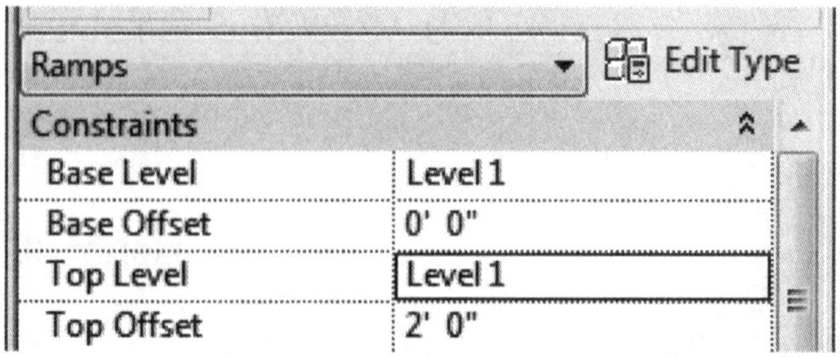

Figure 12–58

5. Draw reference planes to specify the locations of the run start and end points before creating the ramp. The run is based on the centerline of the ramp.

6. In the Draw panel, click (Run) and select a start point for the run. A preview box displays the ramp's orientation and length. Click (Line) or (Center-ends Arc) to switch between linear and curved runs.
   - Landings are automatically created between runs, as shown in Figure 12–59.

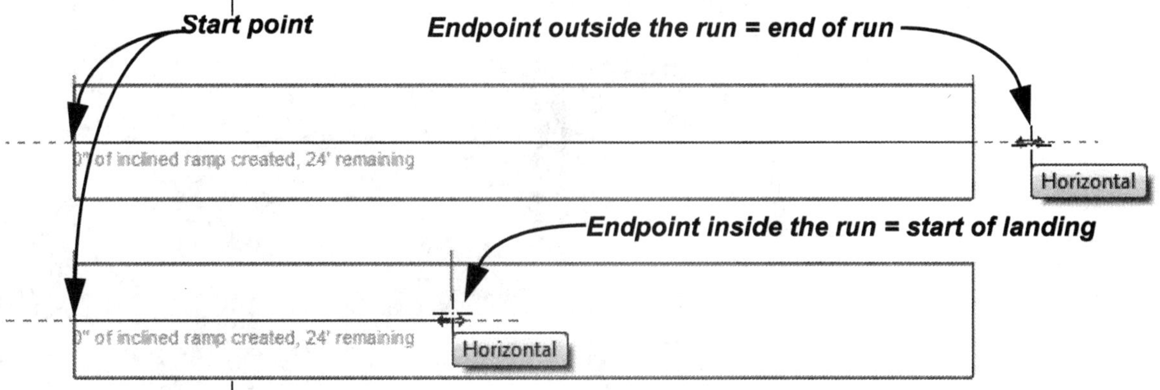

Figure 12–59

7. Click (Finish Edit Mode). The ramp (including railings) is created.

How To: Sketch a Ramp using Boundary and Riser

1. Click (Ramp) and set up the ramp type and Properties.
2. In the *Modify | Create Ramp Sketch* tab>Draw panel, click (Boundary).
3. Use the Draw tools to outline the sides (not the ends) of the ramp, as shown by the green lines in Figure 12–60.
4. In the *Modify | Create Ramp Sketch* tab>Draw panel, click (Riser).
5. Use the Draw tools to specify the ends of the slope of each ramp, as shown by the black lines in Figure 12–60.

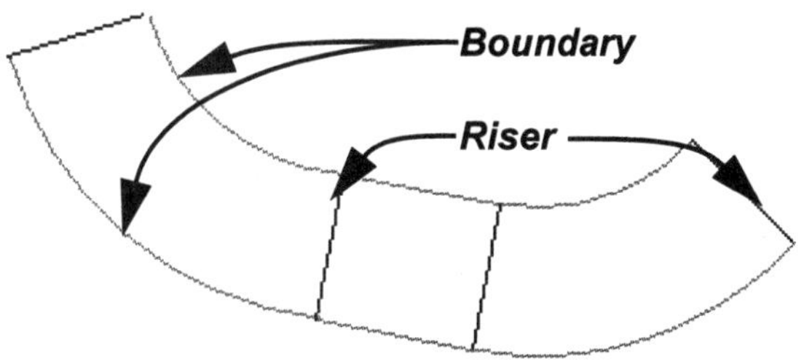

Figure 12–60

6. Click (Finish Edit Mode).

Practice 12d Create Ramps

Practice Objective

- Add a ramp.

In this practice, you will create a ramp with railings, as shown in Figure 12–61.

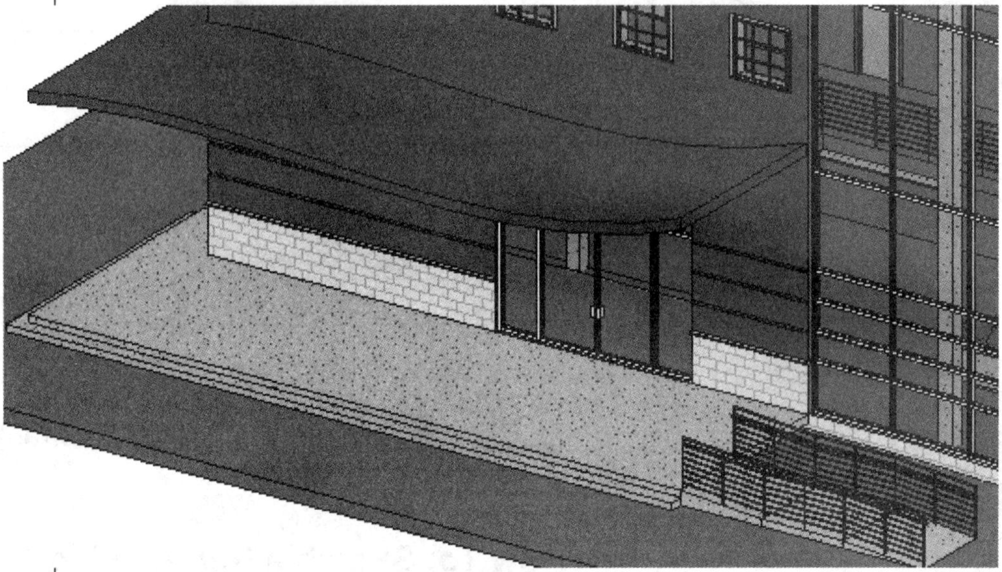

Figure 12–61

Task 1 - Adding a Ramp

1. Open the project **Modern-Hotel-Ramp.rvt**.
2. Open the **Floor Plans: Floor 1** view.
3. In the *Architecture* tab>Circulation panel, click (Ramp).
4. In the Type Selector, select **Ramp: Hotel Ramp**.
5. In Properties, set the *Base Level* to **Floor 1**, with a *Base Offset* of (negative) **-1'-0"**. Set the *Top Level* to **Floor 1**, with a *Top Offset* of **0'-0"**. Set the *Width* to **6'-0"**.
6. In the *Modify | Create Ramp Sketch* tab>Tools panel, click (Railing), select the Railing type **Hotel Ramp Guardrail**, and click **OK**.

7. In the Work Plane panel, click (Ref Plane).

8. Draw the reference planes shown in Figure 12–62.

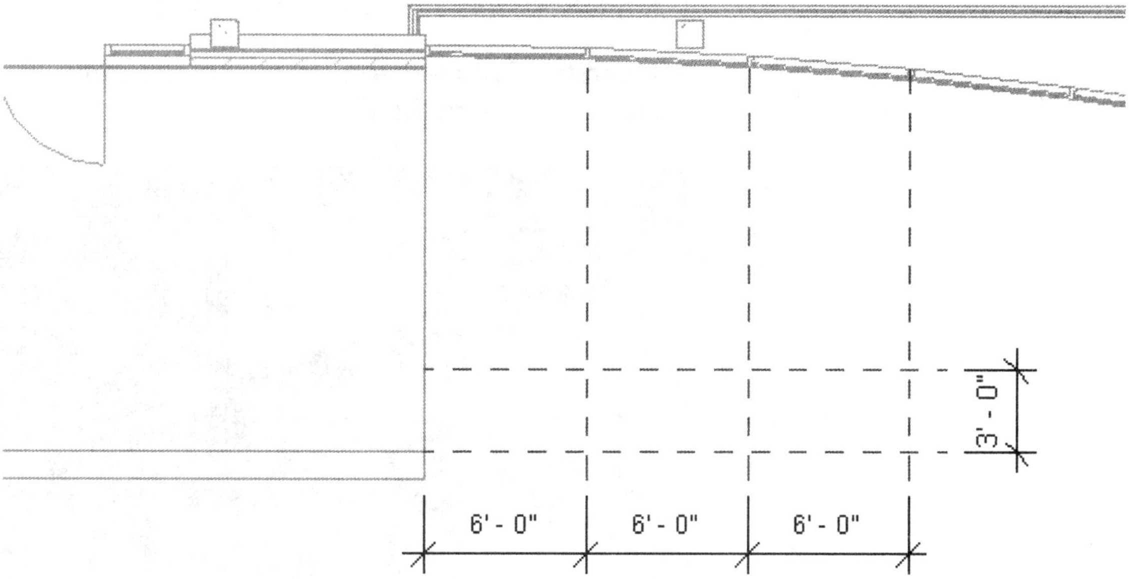

Figure 12–62

9. Click (Modify) to return to the *Modify | Create Ramp Sketch* tab in the ribbon.

10. In the Draw panel, click (Run). Start the run, as shown in Figure 12–63. Use the reference plane intersections to end the first run, and then sketch the second run.

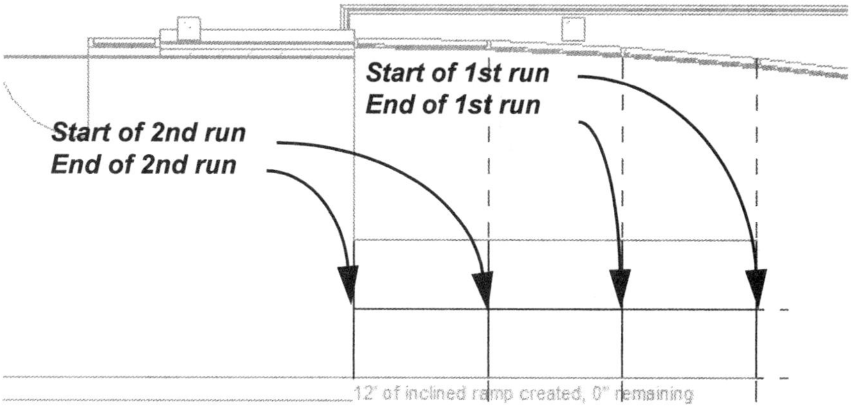

Figure 12–63

11. Click (Finish Edit Mode).

12. The Railings need to be moved so that they are fixed on the ramp. Select both of the railings and in Properties, change the *Offset* from Path to (negative) **-2"**.

13. Open the 3D View and check that the ramp displays, as shown in Figure 12–64.

Figure 12–64

14. Zoom out and save the project.

Chapter Review Questions

1. Which of the following is NOT a stair component?
   a. Runs
   b. Landings
   c. Treads
   d. Supports
2. How do you modify a stair so that it is wider at the bottom than at the top as shown in Figure 12–65?

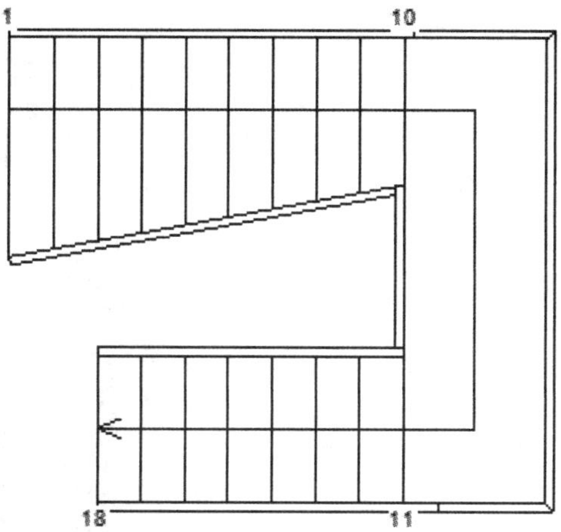

Figure 12–65

   a. Use the grips located at each corner of the stair and drag them to a new location.
   b. Convert the run to a sketch and modify the boundary and riser lines.
   c. Use <Tab> to cycle through components so that you only select the tread that you want to modify.
   d. Explode the stair into components, and then use grips to modify the stair width.

3. When do you need to use the  (Railing) command? (Select all that apply.)
   a. When you want an extra railing in the middle of very wide stairs.
   b. When you create a stair or ramp.
   c. When you create railings that are not attached to stairs or ramps.
   d. When you use the **Stair by Sketch** command.

4. To create a stair that covers multiple floors (as shown in Figure 12–66), you need to create a stair and...

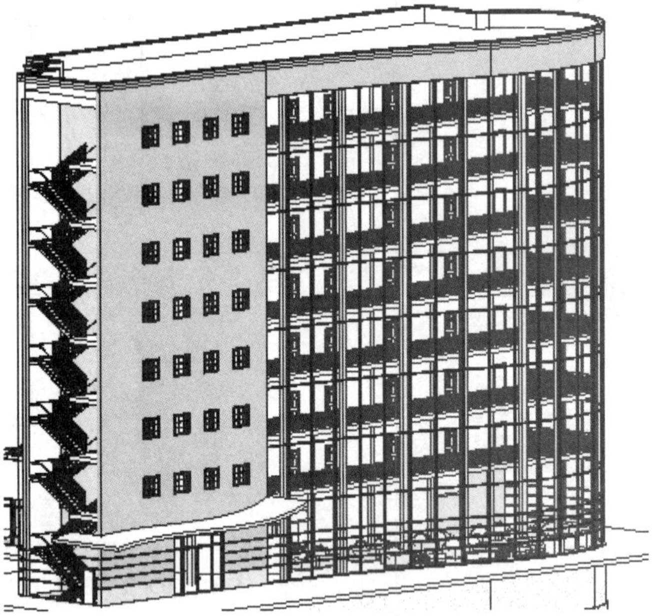

Figure 12–66

   a. In Properties, select the **Multistory Top Level** from the drop-down list of levels.
   b. Also select a stair created at the top level of the floors, right-click and select **Multistory Stair**.
   c. Copy it to the clipboard. Then use **Paste Aligned to Selected Levels** and specify the levels where you want the stairs.
   d. Select the stairs. In the ribbon, select **Connect Levels**, and then select the levels where you want.stairs.

5. Which of the following elements is most helpful in specifying the start and end runs of ramps?
   a. Walls
   b. Stairs
   c. Sketch Lines
   d. Reference Planes

Command Summary

Button	Command	Location
Stairs and Ramps		
	**Convert to sketch-based**	• **Ribbon:** *Modify* | *Create Stair* tab>Tools panel
	**Connect Levels**	• **Ribbon:** *Modify* | *Stairs* tab>Multistory Stairs panel
	**Edit Sketch**	• **Ribbon:** *Modify* | *Create Stair* tab>Tools panel
	**Edit Stairs**	• **Ribbon:** *Modify* | *Stairs* tab>Edit panel
	**Flip**	• **Ribbon:** *Modify* | *Create Stair* tab>Tools panel
	**Landing (Stair)**	• **Ribbon:** *Modify* | *Create Stair* tab>Components panel
	**Run (Stair)**	• **Ribbon:** *Modify* | *Create Stair* tab>Components panel
	**Stair**	• **Ribbon:** *Architecture* tab>Circulation panel
	**Support (Stair)**	• **Ribbon:** *Modify* | *Create Stair* tab>Components panel
	**Ramp**	• **Ribbon:** *Architecture* tab>Circulation panel
Railings		
	**Edit Path (Railings)**	• **Ribbon:** *Modify* | *Railings* tab>Mode panel
	**Railing**	• **Ribbon:** *Modify* | *Create Stair (Create Stairs Sketch) (Create Ramp)* tab>Tools panel
	**Railing>Place on Host**	• **Ribbon:** *Architecture* tab>Circulation panel>expand Railing
	**Railing>Sketch Path**	• **Ribbon:** *Architecture* tab>Circulation panel>expand Railing
	**Pick New Host**	• **Ribbon:** *Modify* | *Create Railing Path (Railings)* tab>Tools Panel

Construction Documents Phase

The third section of this guide continues to teach the Autodesk® Revit® tools, focusing on tools that help you to create accurate construction documents for a design.

This section includes the following chapters:

- Chapter 13: Creating Construction Documents
- Chapter 14: Annotating Construction Documents
- Chapter 15: Adding Tags and Schedules
- Chapter 16: Creating Details

Creating Construction Documents

The accurate creation of construction documents in the Autodesk® Revit® software ensures that the design is correctly communicated to downstream users. Construction documents are created primarily in special views call sheets. Knowing how to select titleblocks, assign titleblock information, place views, and print the sheets are essential steps in the construction documentation process.

Learning Objectives in this Chapter

- Add Sheets with titleblocks and views of a project.
- Enter the titleblock information for individual sheets and for an entire project.
- Place and organize views on sheets.
- Print sheets using the default Print dialog box.

13.1 Setting Up Sheets

While you are modeling a project, the foundations of the working drawings are already in progress. Any view (such as a floor plan, section, callout, or schedule) can be placed on a sheet, as shown in Figure 13–1.

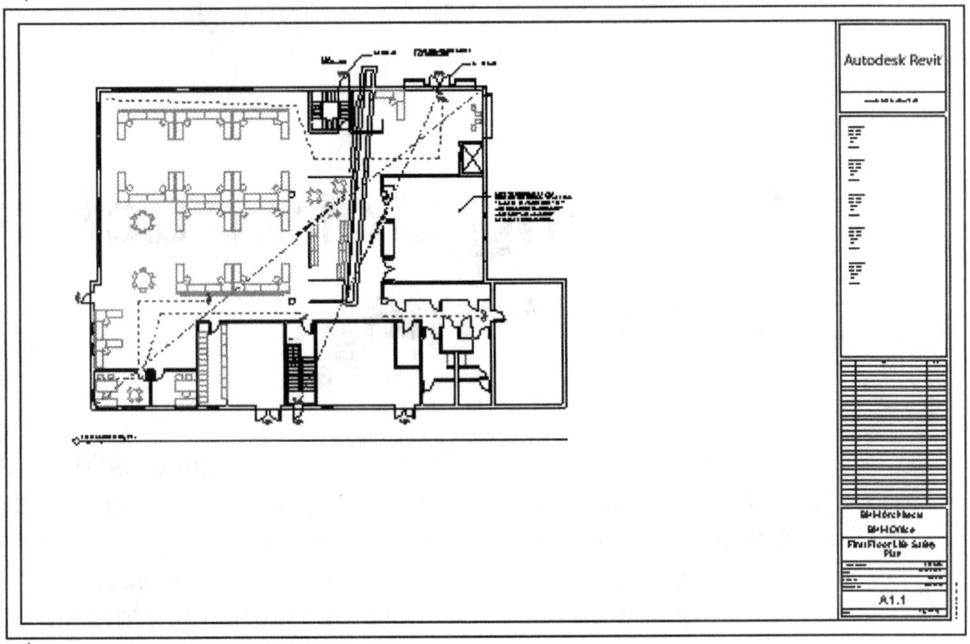

Figure 13–1

- Company templates can be created with standard sheets using the company (or project) titleblock and related views already placed on the sheet.
- The sheet size is based on the selected title block family.
- Sheets are listed in the *Sheets* area in the Project Browser.
- Most information on sheets is included in the views. You can add general notes and other non-model elements directly to the sheet, though it is better to add them using drafting views or legends, as these can be placed on multiple sheets.

How To: Set Up Sheets

1. In the Project Browser, right-click on the *Sheets* area header and select **New Sheet...** or in the *View* tab>Sheet Composition panel, click (Sheet).

2. In the New Sheet dialog box, select a titleblock from the list as shown in Figure 13–2. Alternatively, if there is a list of placeholder sheets, select one or more from the list.

*Click **Load...** to load a sheet from the Library.*

Hold <Ctrl> to select multiple placeholder sheets.

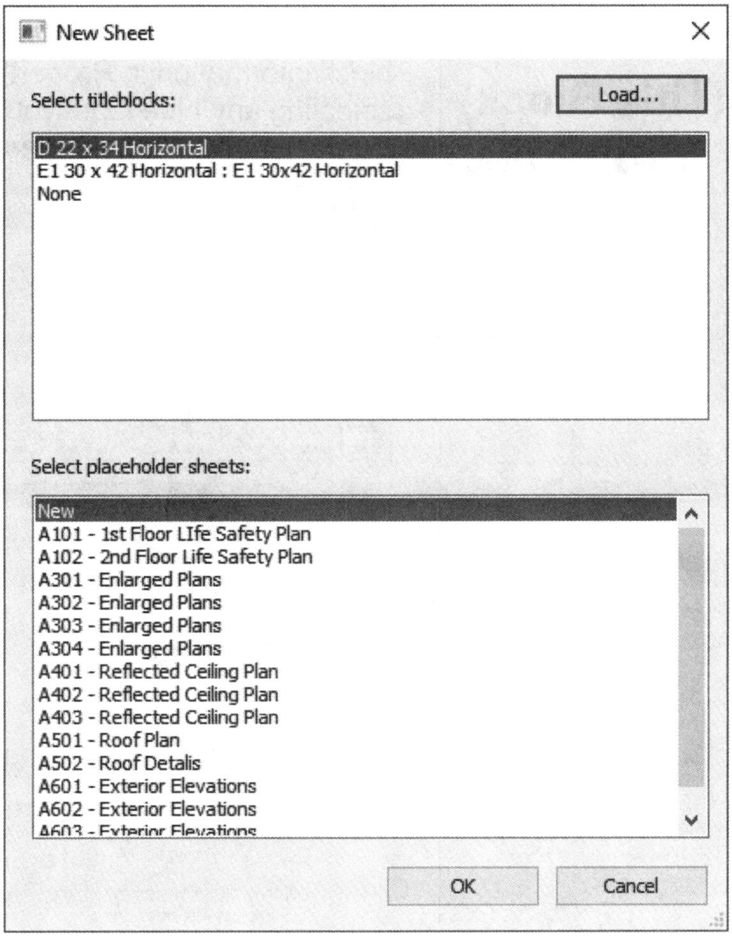

Figure 13–2

3. Click **OK**. A new sheet is created using the preferred title block.
4. Fill out the information in the title block as required.
5. Add views to the sheet.

- When you create sheets, the next sheet is incremented numerically.
- Double-click on the sheet name to change the name and number in the Sheet Title dialog box.
- When you change the *Sheet Name* and/or *Number* in the title block, it automatically changes the name and number of the sheet in the Project Browser.
- The plot stamp on the side of the sheet automatically updates according to the current date and time. The format of the display uses the regional settings of your computer.

- The Scale is automatically entered when a view is inserted onto a sheet. If a sheet has multiple views with different scales, the scale displays **As Indicated.**

Sheet (Title Block) Properties

Each new sheet includes a title block. You can change the title block information in Properties, as shown in Figure 13–3 or by selecting any blue label you want to edit (Sheet Name, Sheet Number, Drawn by, etc.), as shown in Figure 13–4.

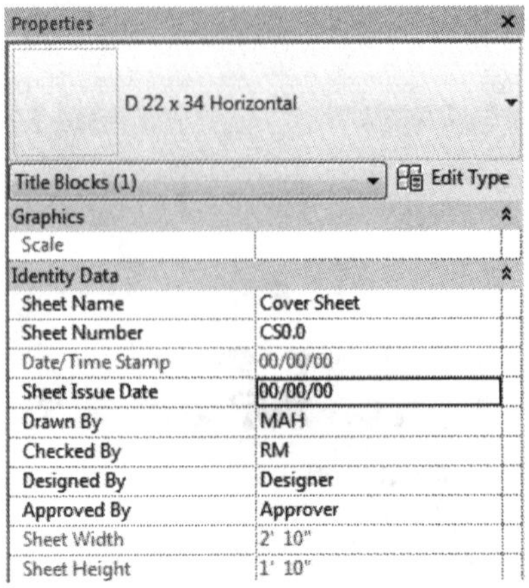

Figure 13–3

Figure 13–4

Properties that apply to all sheets can be entered in the Project Information dialog box (as shown in Figure 13–5). In the *Manage* tab>Settings panel, click (Project Information).

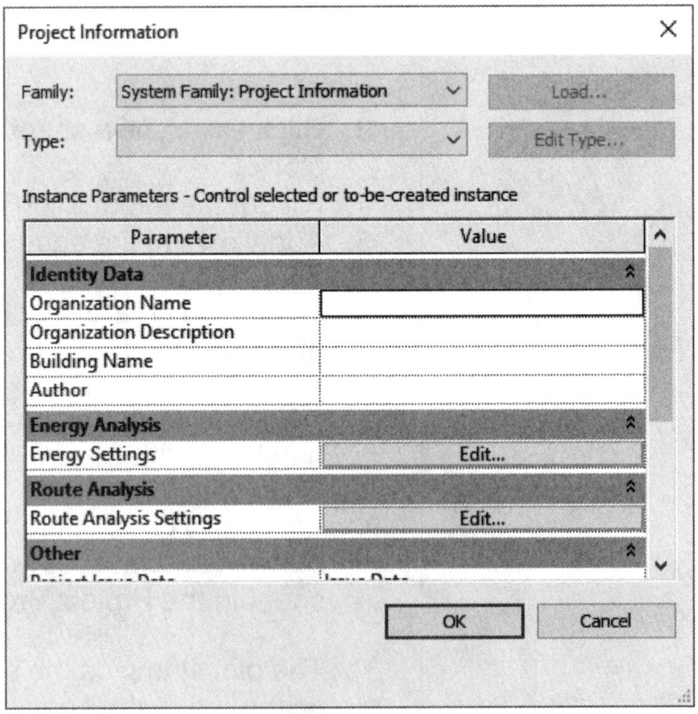

Figure 13–5

13.2 Placing and Modifying Views on Sheets

The process of adding views to a sheet is simple. Drag and drop a view from the Project Browser onto the sheet. The new view on the sheet is displayed at the scale specified in the original view. The view title displays the name, number, and scale of the view, as shown in Figure 13–6.

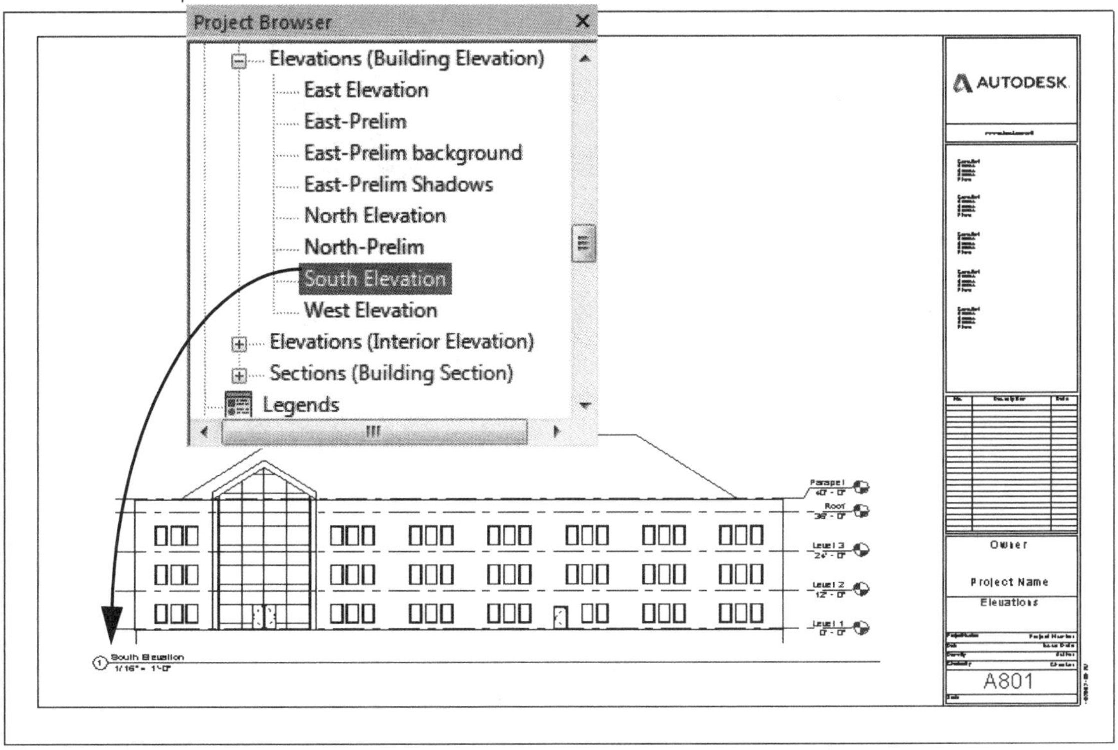

Figure 13–6

How To: Place Views on Sheets

Alignment lines from existing views display to help you place additional views.

1. Set up the view as you want it to display on the sheet, including the scale and visibility of elements.
2. Create or open the sheet where you want to place the view.
3. Select the view in the Project Browser, and drag and drop it onto the sheet.
4. The center of the view is attached to the cursor. Click to place it on the sheet.

Placing Views on Sheets

- Views can only be placed on a sheet once. However, you can duplicate the view and place that copy on a sheet.
- Views on a sheet are associative. They automatically update to reflect changes to the project.
- Each view on a sheet is listed under the sheet name in the Project Browser, as shown in Figure 13–7.

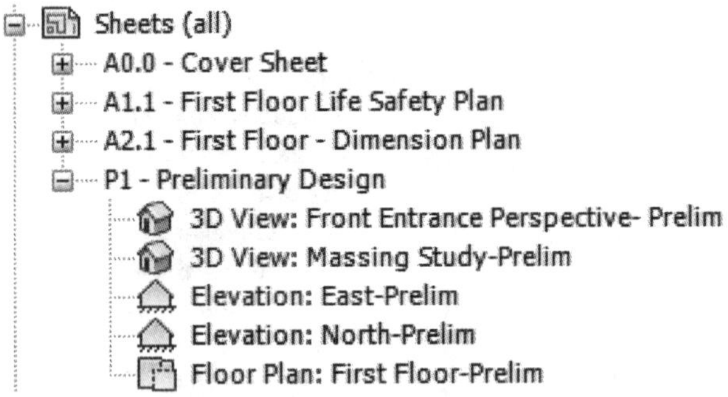

Figure 13–7

- You can also use two other methods to place views on sheets:
  - In the Project Browser, right-click on the sheet name and select **Add View...**
  - In the *View* tab>Sheet Composition panel, click (Place View).

Then, in the Views dialog box (shown in Figure 13–8), select the view you want to use and click **Add View to Sheet.**

This method lists only those views which have not yet been placed on a sheet.

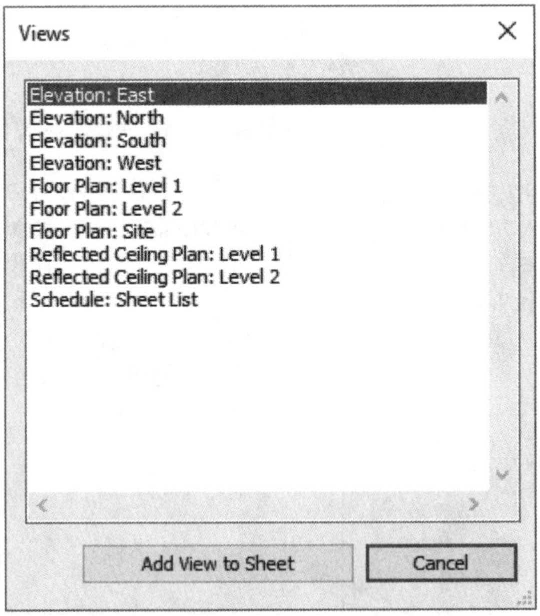

Figure 13–8

- To remove a view from a sheet, select it and press <Delete>. Alternatively, in the Project Browser, expand the individual sheet information to show the views, right-click on the view name and select **Remove From Sheet**.

Hint: Setting up the Project Browser

To view and change the Project Browser's types, select the top level node of the Project Browser (which is set to *Views (all)* by default) and select the type you want to use from the Type Selector. For example, you can set the Browser to only display views that are not on sheets, as shown in Figure 13–9.

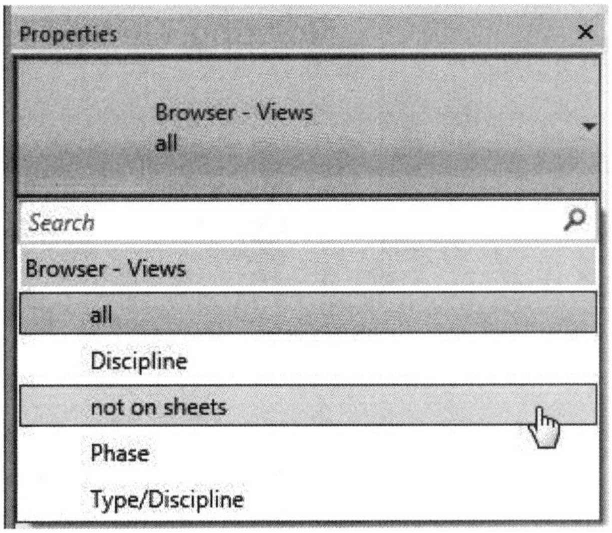

Figure 13–9

Moving Views and View Titles

*You can also use the **Move** command or the arrow keys to move a view.*

- To move a view on a sheet, select the edge of the view and drag it to a new location. The view title moves with the view.
- To move only the view title, select the title and drag it to the new location.
- To modify the length of the line under the title name, select the edge of the view and drag the controls, as shown in Figure 13–10.

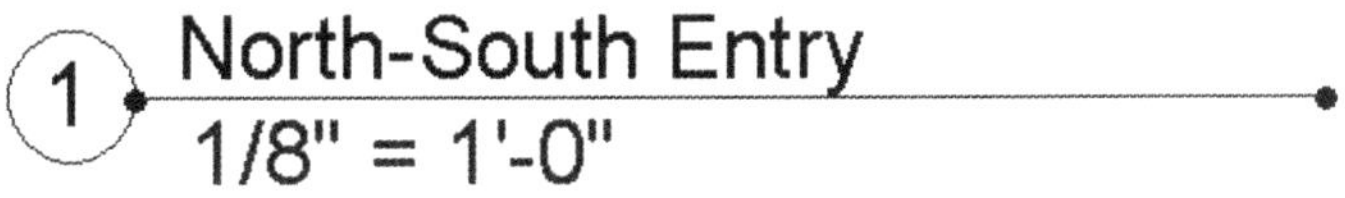

Figure 13–10

- To change the title of a view on a sheet without changing its name in the Project Browser, in Properties, in the *Identity Data* area, type a new title for the *Title on Sheet* parameter, as shown in Figure 13–11.

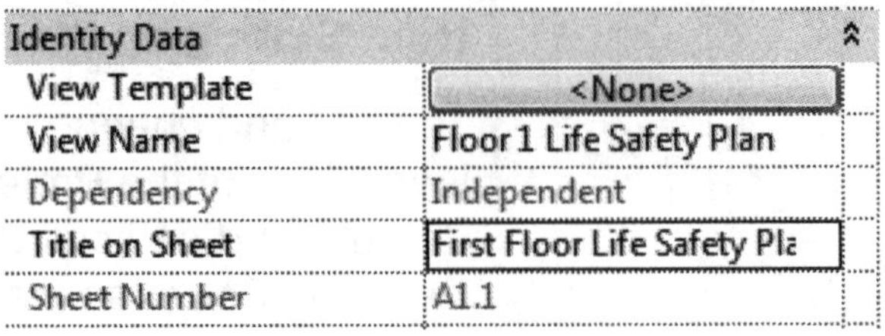

Figure 13–11

Rotating Views

- When creating a vertical sheet, you can rotate the view on the sheet by 90 degrees. Select the view and set the direction of rotation in the Rotation on Sheet drop-down list in the Options Bar, as shown in Figure 13–12.

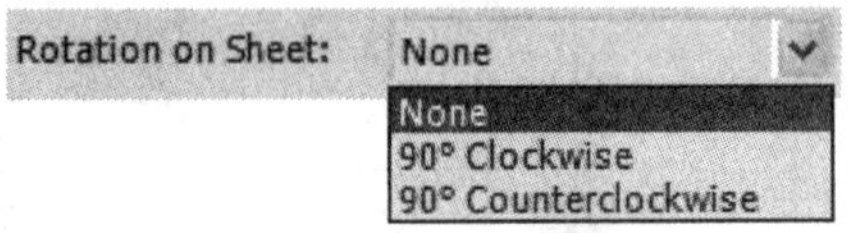

Figure 13–12

- To rotate a view to an angle other than 90 degrees, open the view, toggle on and select the crop region and use the **Rotate** command to change the angle.

Working Inside Views

To make small changes to a view while working on a sheet:

- Double-click *inside* the view to activate it.
- Double-click *outside* the view to deactivate it.

Only elements in the viewport are available for modification. The rest of the sheet is grayed out, as shown in Figure 13–13.

Only use this method for small changes. Significant changes should be made directly in the view.

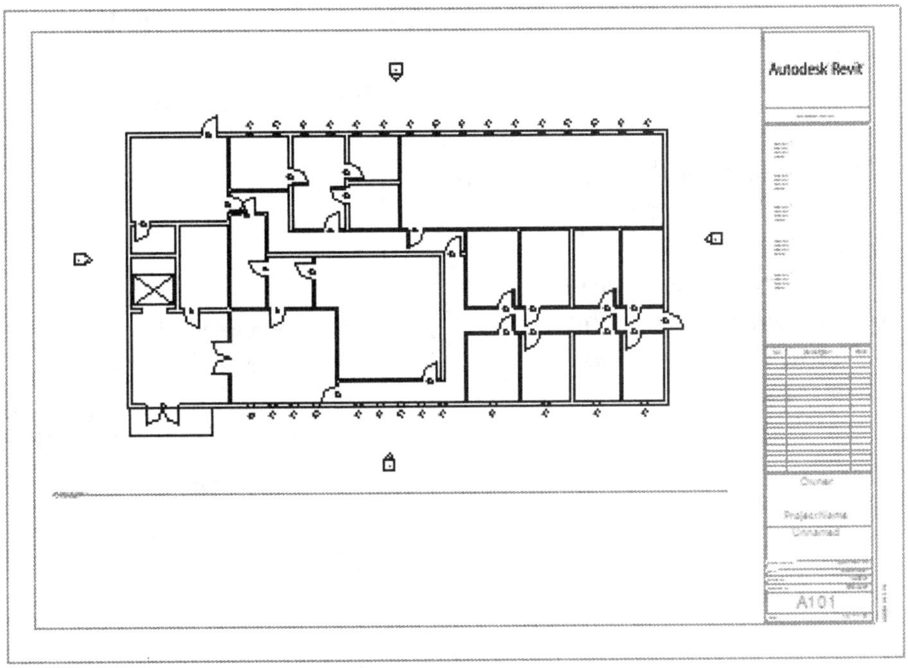

Figure 13–13

- You can activate and deactivate views by right-clicking on the edge of the view or by using the tools found on the *Modify | Viewports* and *Views* tab>Sheet Composition panel.
- Changes you make to elements when a view is activated also display in the original view.
- If you are unsure which sheet a view is on, right-click on the view in the Project Browser and select **Open Sheet**. This item is grayed out if the view has not been placed on a sheet and is not available for schedules and legends which can be placed on more than one sheet.

Resizing Views on Sheets

If the extents of the view change dramatically based on a scale change or a crop region, it is easier to delete the view on the sheet and drag it over again.

Each view displays the extents of the model or the elements contained in the crop region. If the view does not fit on a sheet (as shown in Figure 13–14), you might need to crop the view or move the elevation markers closer to the building.

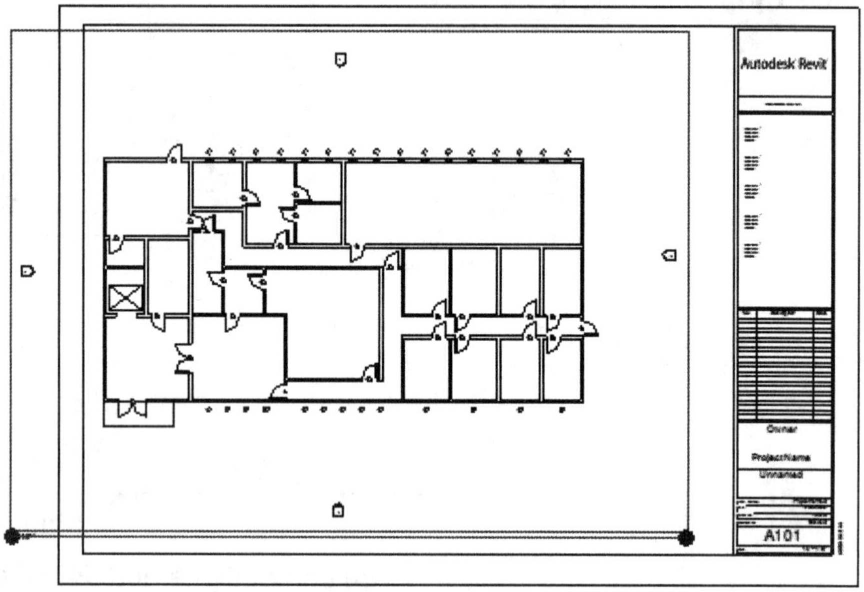

Figure 13–14

- For information about laying out views on sheets using guide grids, see *Appendix B.7 Working with Guide Grids on Sheets.*
- For information about working with revisions in views and on sheets, see *Appendix B.8 Revision Tracking*.

Hint: Add an Image to a Sheet

Company logos and renderings saved to image files (such as .JPG and .PNG) can be added directly on a sheet or in a view.

1. In the *Insert* tab>Import panel, click (Image).
2. In the Import Image dialog box, select and open the image file. The extents of the image display, as shown in Figure 13–15.

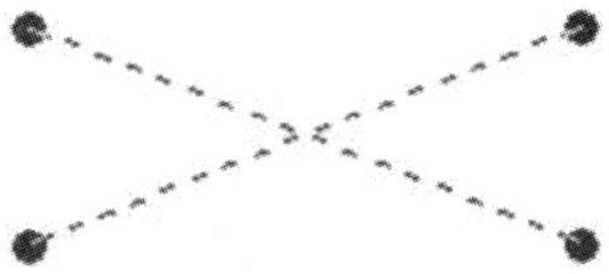

Figure 13–15

3. Place the image where you want it.
4. The image is displayed. Pick one of the grips and extend it to modify the size of the image.

- In Properties, you can adjust the height and width and also set the *Draw Layer* to either **Background** or **Foreground**, as shown in Figure 13–16.

Dimensions	
Width	1' 5 185/256"
Height	1' 1 41/64"
Horizontal Scale	1.000000
Vertical Scale	1.000000
Lock Proportions	☑
Other	
Draw Layer	Background

Figure 13–16

- You can select more than one image at a time and move them as a group to the background or foreground.

- In the *Modify | Raster Images* tab (as shown in Figure 13–17), you can access the Arrange options and Manage Images.

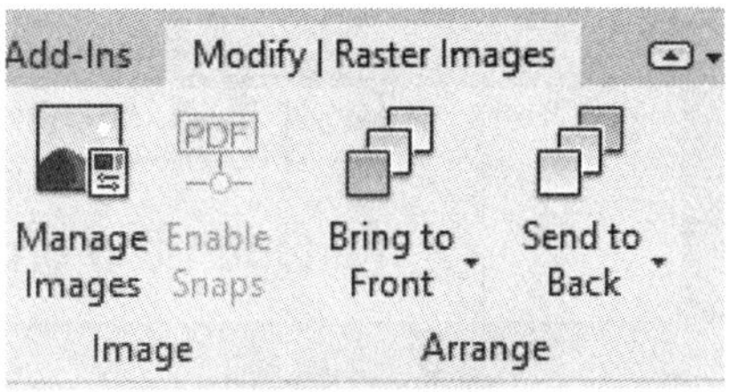

Figure 13–17

Practice 13a Create Construction Documents

Practice Objectives

- Set up project properties.
- Create sheets individually.
- Modify views to prepare them to be placed on sheets.
- Place views on sheets.

In this practice, you will complete the project information, add new sheets and use existing sheets. You will fill in title block information and then add views to sheets, such as the Wall Sections sheet shown in Figure 13–18. Complete as many sheets as you have time for.

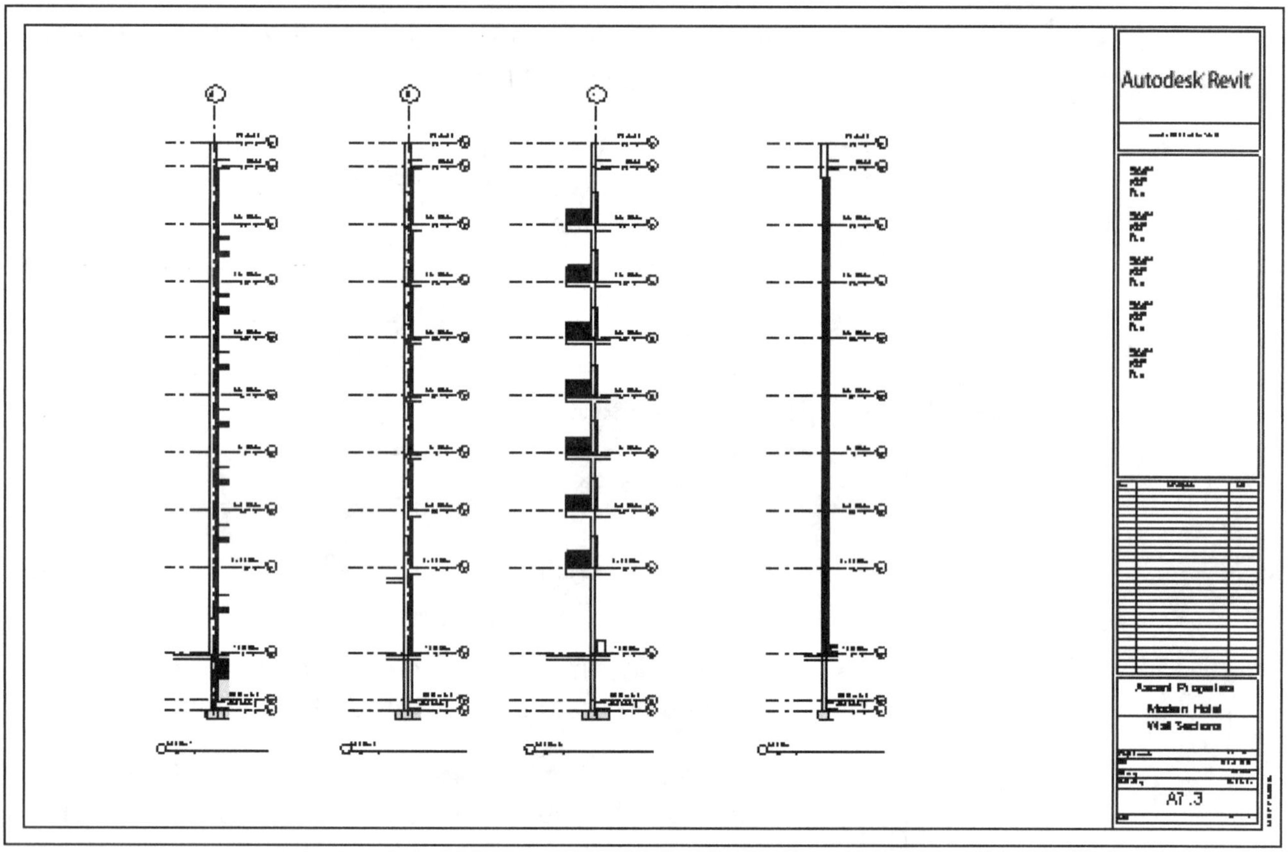

Figure 13–18

Task 1 - Complete the project information.

1. Open the project **Modern-Hotel-Sheets.rvt**.

2. In the *Manage* tab>Settings panel, click (Project Information).

These properties are used across the entire sheet set and do not need to be entered on each sheet.

3. In the Project Information dialog box, in the *Other* area, set the following parameters:
   - *Project Issue Date:* **Issue Date**
   - *Project Status:* **Design Development**
   - *Client Name:* **Ascent Properties**
   - *Project Address:* Click **Edit...** and enter your address
   - *Project Name:* **Modern Hotel**
   - *Project Number:* **1234-567**
4. Click **OK**.
5. Save the project.

Task 2 - Create a Cover Sheet and Floor Plan Sheets.

1. In the *View* tab>Sheet Composition panel, click (Sheet).
2. In the New Sheet dialog box, select the **D 22 x 34 Horizontal** titleblock.
3. Click **OK**.
4. Zoom in on the lower right corner of the title block. The Project Properties filled out earlier are automatically added to the sheet.
5. Continue filling out the title block, as shown in Figure 13–19.

Figure 13–19

6. Zoom back out to display the whole sheet.

7. In the Project Browser, expand the **3D Views** node. Drag and drop the **Exterior Front Perspective** view on to the sheet, as shown in Figure 13–20. There are two items that are not required on the cover sheet, the viewport title and crop region.

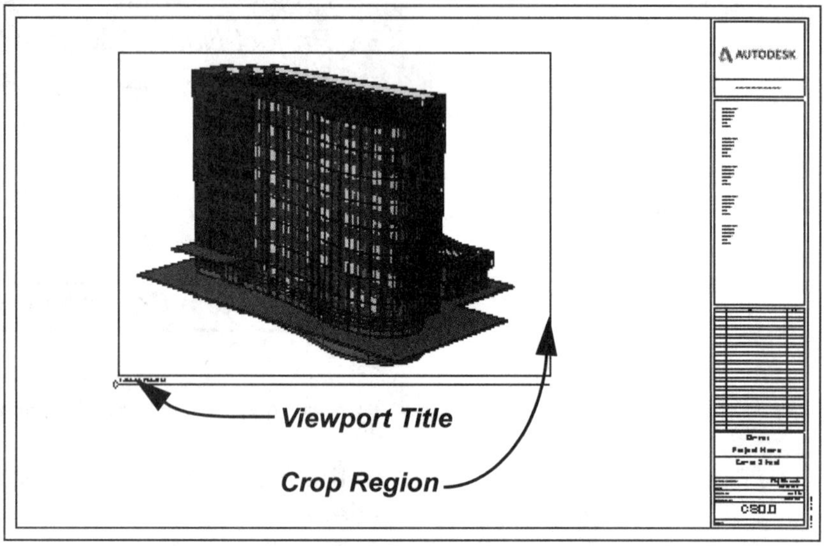

Figure 13–20

Properties box —

8. Select the edge of the viewport. In the Type Selector, select **Viewport: No Title**.

9. Double-click inside the viewport, the title block grays out and you can modify the actual view.

10. In Properties, in the *Extents* area, clear the check from **Crop Region Visible**. (This could also be done in the View Control Bar.)

11. Double-click outside the viewport to return to the sheet.

12. In the Project Browser, right-click on the **Sheets (all)** node and select **New Sheet**.

13. Using the D-sized title block, create the following new sheets:

Sheet Number and Name	View
A2.1: Ground Floor Plan	Floor 1
A2.2: Upper Floor Plan (Typical)	Typical Guest Room Floor Plan
A2.3: Roof Plan	Roof

14. Save the project.

The crop region defines the extent of the view on the sheet.

Task 3 - Set up and add views to sheets.

1. Duplicate (no detailing) the **Floor Plans: Floor 1** and **Floor 2** views and name them **Floor 1 - Life Safety Plan** and **Floor 2-8 - Life Safety Plan**.

2. Open the new views and do the following:
   - Hide all elements except the actual building elements.
   - Toggle on the crop region and ensure it is tight up against the building.
   - Toggle the crop region off.
   - In the Floor 2-8 plan, turn off the roof on the front of the building.

3. Open the sheet **A1.1 - Floor 1 - Life Safety Plan**.

4. In the Project Browser, right-click on that sheet and select **Add View...**.

5. In the Views dialog box scroll down and select **Floor Plan: Floor 1 - Life Safety Plan**, as shown in Figure 13–21. Click **Add View to Sheet** and place the view on the sheet.

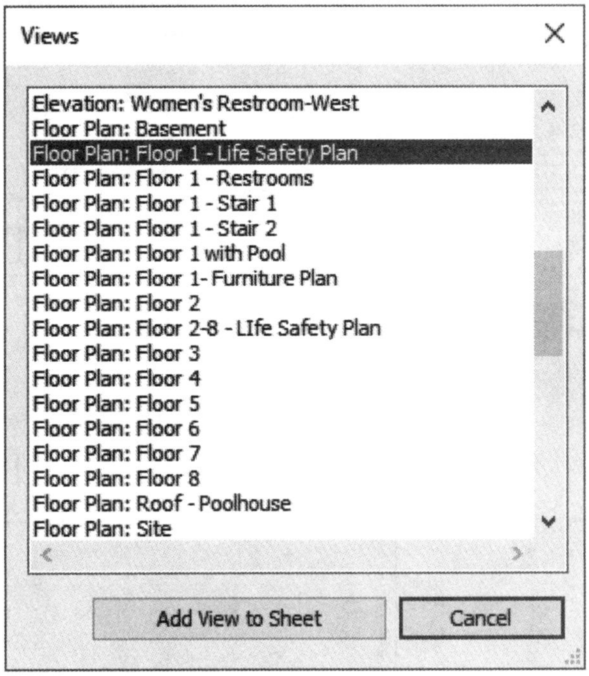

Figure 13–21

6. Repeat the process for the other floor and rename sheet **Floor 2 - Life Safety Plan** as **Floor 2-8 - Life Safety Plan**.
   - The **Floor 1 - Life Safety Plan** is no longer available because it has already been added to a sheet.

7. Repeat the process of adding views to sheets using the views you have available.
   - Modify crop regions and hide unnecessary elements in the views, as shown in Figure 13–22. Toggle off crop regions after you have modified them.

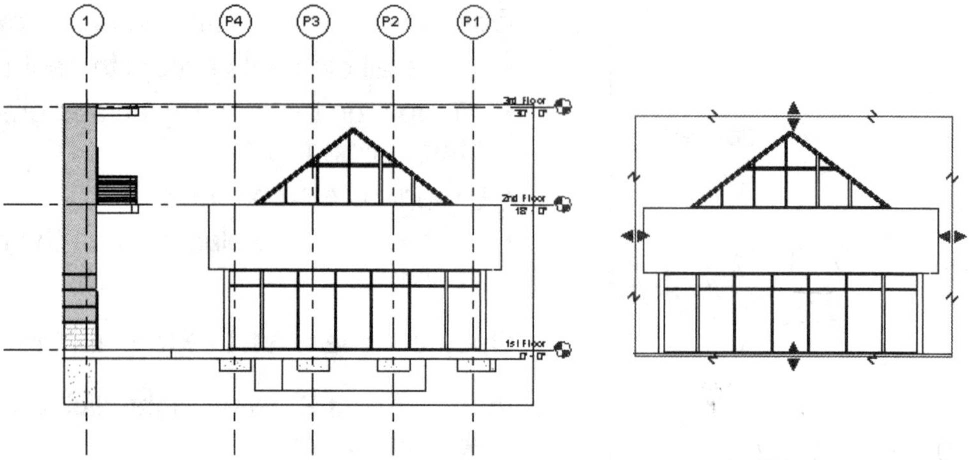

Figure 13–22

   - Verify the scale of a view in Properties before placing it on a sheet.
   - Use alignment lines to help place multiple views on one sheet, as shown in Figure 13–23.

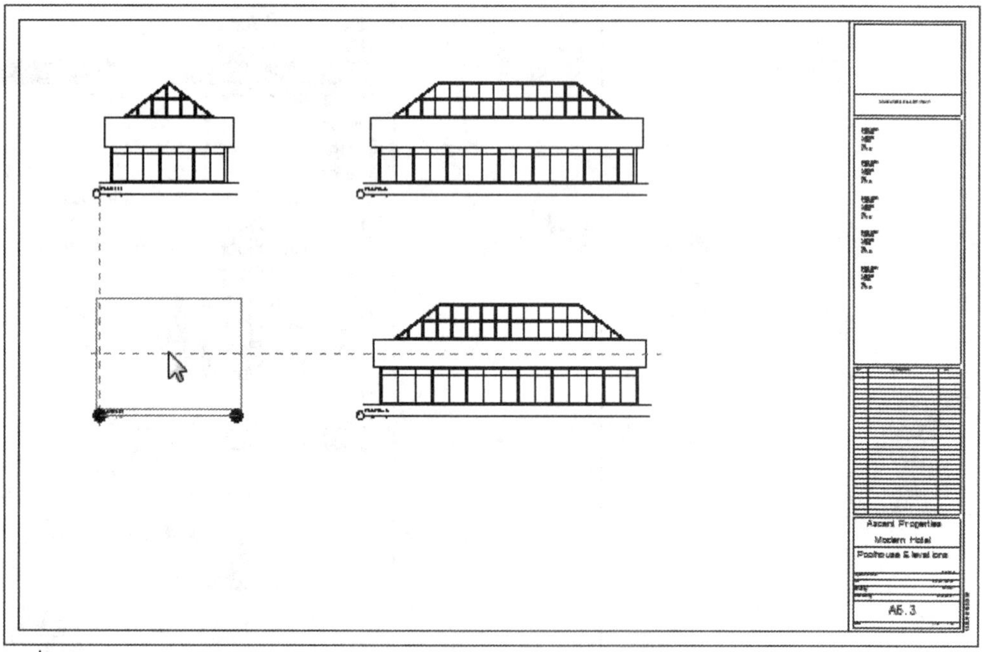

Figure 13–23

- Change the view title, if required, to more accurately describe what is on the sheet.
- To make minor changes to a view once it is on a sheet, double-click inside the viewport to activate the view. To return to the sheet, double-click outside the viewport to deactivate the view.

8. Once you have added callout, section, or elevation views to sheets, switch back to the **Floor Plans: Floor 1** view. Zoom in on one of the markers. Note that it has now been automatically assigned a detail and sheet number, as shown in Figure 13–24.

Your numbers might not exactly match the numbers in the example.

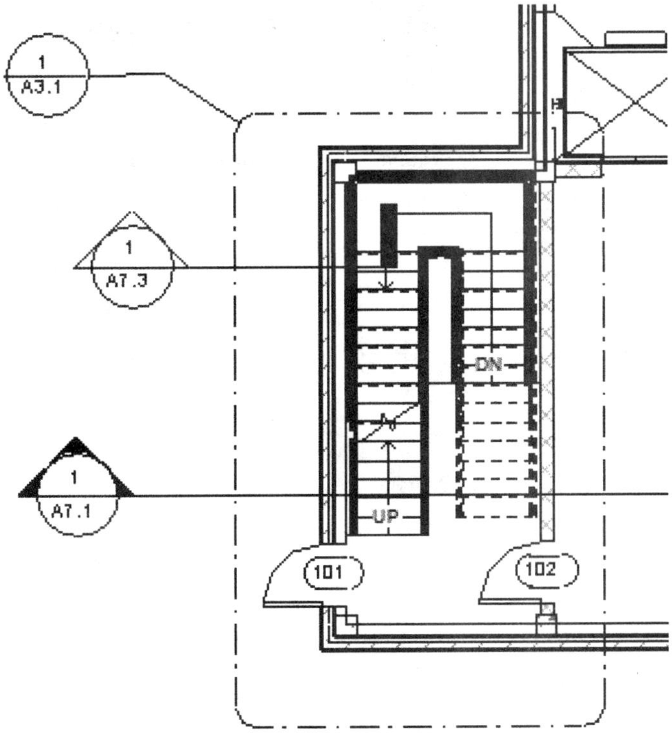

Figure 13–24

9. Save the project.

13.3 Printing Sheets

With the **Print** command, you can print individual sheets or a list of selected sheets. You can also print an individual view or a portion of a view for check prints or presentations. To open the Print dialog box (shown in Figure 13–25), in the *File* tab, click (Print).

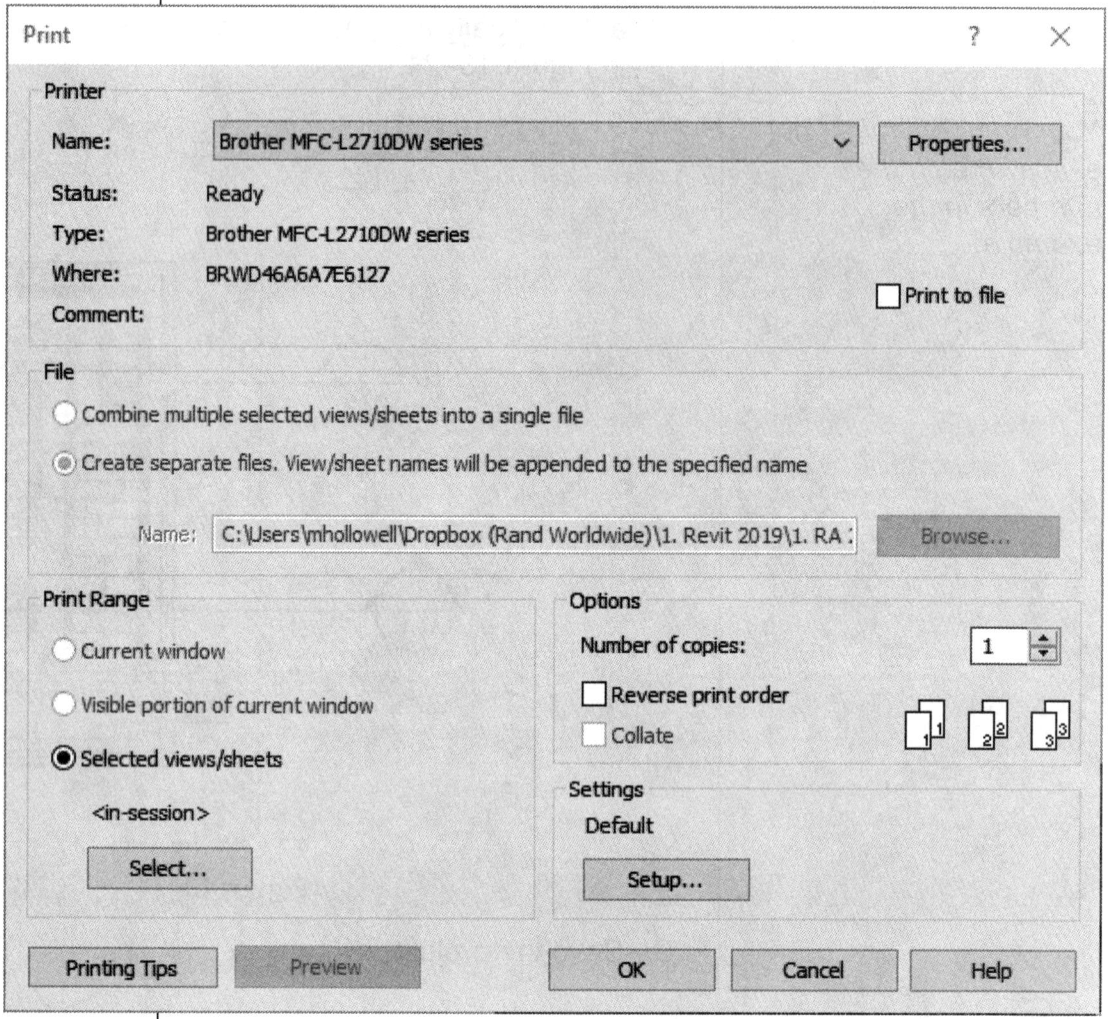

Figure 13–25

Printing Options

The Print dialog box is divided into the following areas: *Printer*, *File*, *Print Range*, *Options*, and *Settings*. Modify them as required to produce the plot you want.

- **Printing Tips**: Opens Autodesk WikiHelp online, in which you can find help with troubleshooting printing issues.
- **Preview**: Opens a preview of the print output so that you can see what is going to be printed.

Printer

Select from the list of available printers, as shown in Figure 13–26. Click **Properties...** to adjust the properties of the selected printer. The options vary according to the printer. Select the **Print to file** option to print to a file rather than directly to a printer. You can create .PLT or .PRN files.

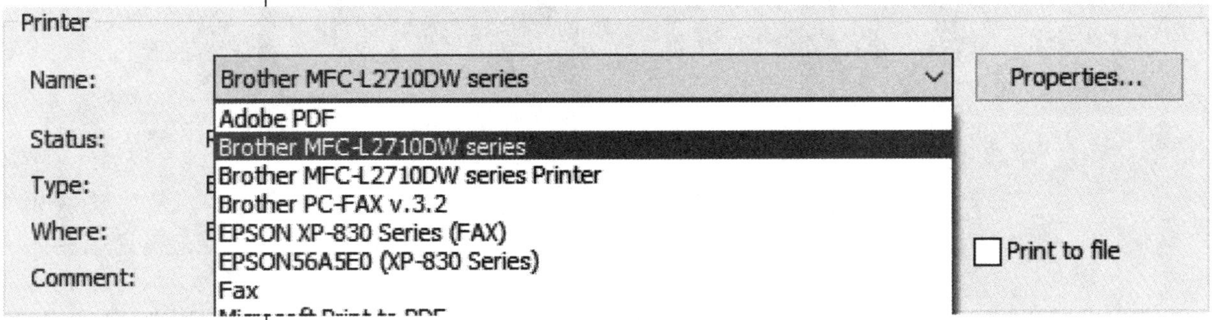

Figure 13–26

- You must have a .PDF print driver installed on your system to print to PDF.

File

The *File* area is only available if the **Print to file** option has been selected in the *Printer* area or if you are printing to an electronic-only type of printer. You can create one file or multiple files depending on the type of printer you are using, as shown in Figure 13–27. Click **Browse...** to select the file location and name.

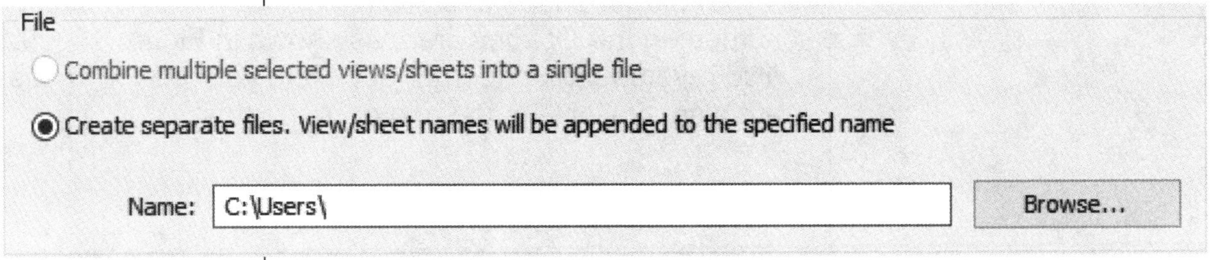

Figure 13–27

Print Range

The *Print Range* area enables you to print individual views/sheets or sets of views/sheets, as shown in Figure 13–28.

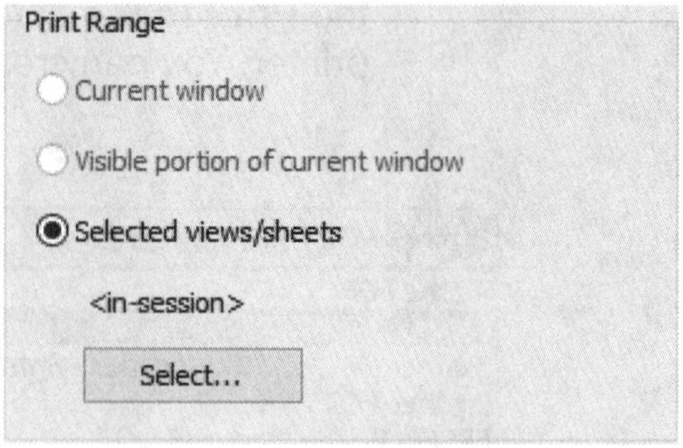

Figure 13–28

- **Current window**: Prints the entire current sheet or view you have open.
- **Visible portion of current window**: Prints only what is displayed in the current sheet or view.
- **Selected views/sheets**: Prints multiple views or sheets. Click **Select...** to open the View/Sheet Set dialog box to choose what to include in the print set. You can save these sets by name so that you can more easily print the same group again.

Options

If your printer supports multiple copies, you can specify the number in the *Options* area, as shown in Figure 13–29. You can also reverse the print order or collate your prints. These options are also available in the printer properties.

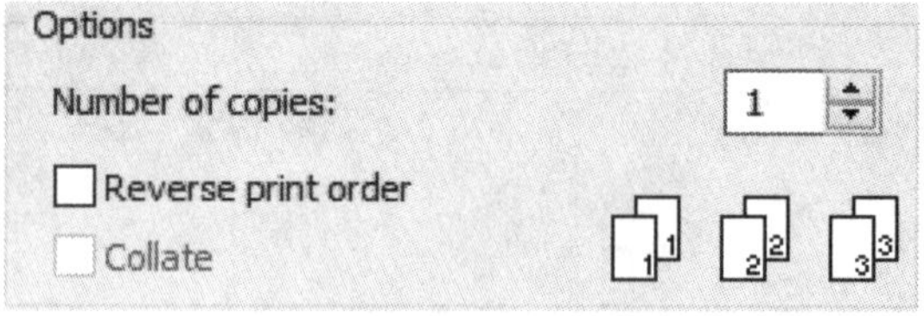

Figure 13–29

Settings

Click **Setup**... to open the Print Setup dialog box, as shown in Figure 13–30. Here, you can specify the *Orientation* and *Zoom* settings, among others. You can also save these settings by name.

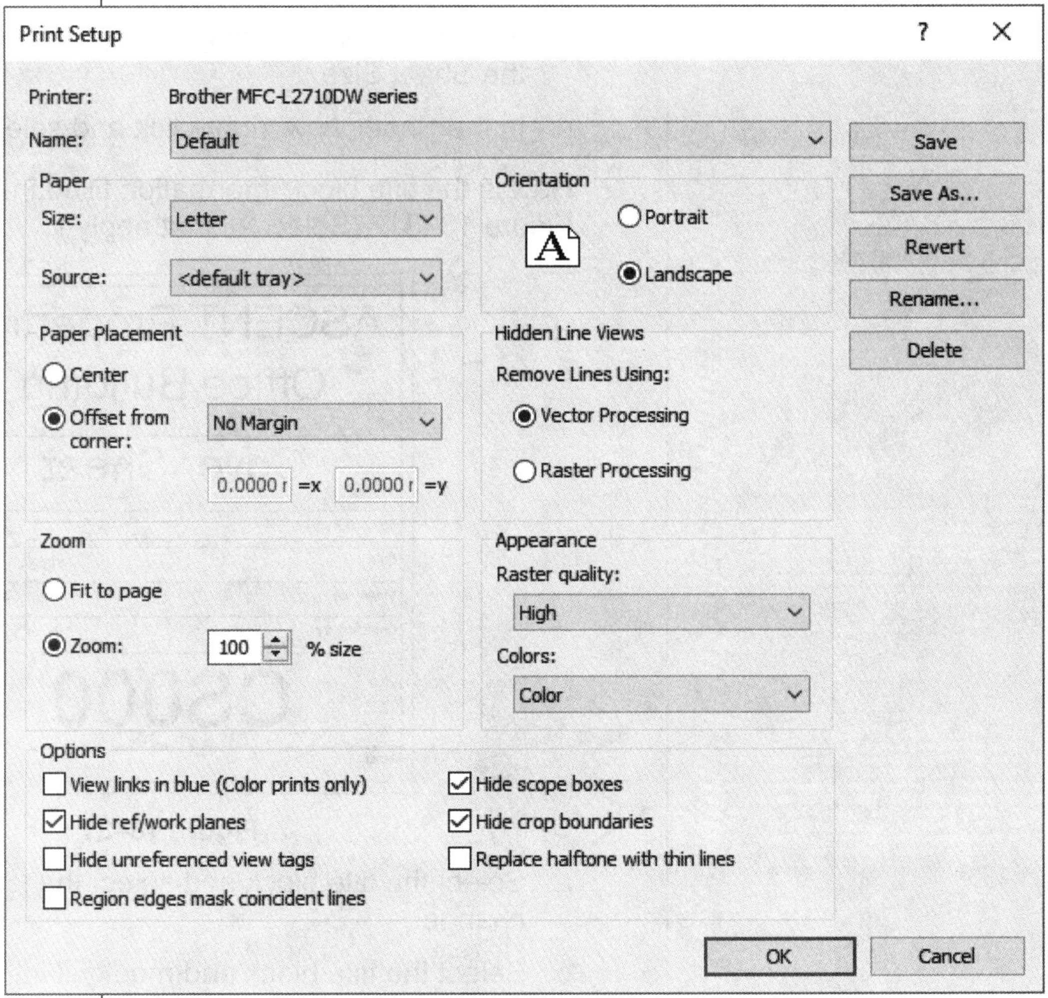

Figure 13–30

- In the *Options* area, specify the types of elements you want to print or not print. Unless specified, all of the elements in a view or sheet print.
- Sheets should always be printed at **Zoom** set to **100%** size unless you are creating a quick markup set that does not need to be exact.

Chapter Review Questions

1. How do you specify the size of a sheet?
   a. In the Sheet Properties, specify the **Sheet Size**.
   b. In the Options Bar, specify the **Sheet Size**.
   c. In the New Sheet dialog box, select a title block to control the Sheet Size.
   d. In the Sheet view, right-click and select **Sheet Size**.
2. How is the title block information filled in as shown in Figure 13–31? (Select all that apply.)

Figure 13–31

   a. Select the title block and select the label that you want to change.
   b. Select the title block and modify it in Properties.
   c. Right-click on the Sheet in the Project Browser and select **Information**.
   d. Some of the information is filled in automatically.
3. On how many sheets can a floor plan view be placed?
   a. 1
   b. 2-5
   c. 6+
   d. As many as you want.

4. Which of the following is the best method to use if the size of a view is too large for a sheet, as shown in Figure 13–32?

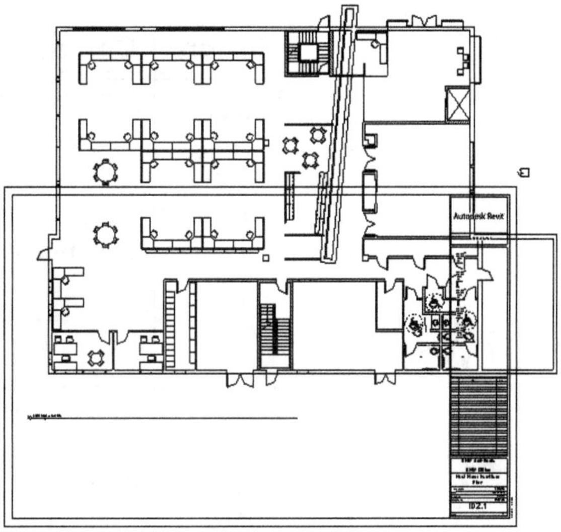

Figure 13–32

   a. Delete the view, change the scale and place the view back on the sheet.
   b. Activate the view and change the View Scale.

5. How do you set up a view on a sheet that only displays part of a floor plan, as shown in Figure 13–33?

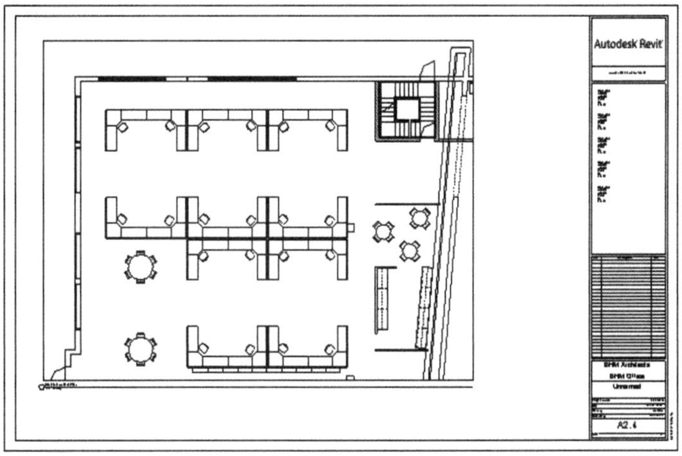

Figure 13–33

   a. Drag and drop the view to the sheet and use the crop region to modify it.
   b. Activate the view and rescale it.
   c. Create a callout view displaying the part that you want to use and place the callout view on the sheet.
   d. Open the view in the Project Browser and change the View Scale.

Command Summary

Button	Command	Location
	Activate View	• **Ribbon:** (*select the view*) *Modify | Viewports* tab>Viewport panel • **Double-click:** *(in viewport)* • **Right-click:** (*on view*) Activate View
	Deactivate View	• **Ribbon:** *View* tab>Sheet Composition panel>expand Viewports • **Double-click:** *(on sheet)* • **Right-click:** (*on view*) Deactivate View
	Place View	• **Ribbon:** *View* tab>Sheet Composition panel
	Print	• **File tab**
	Sheet	• **Ribbon:** *View* tab>Sheet Composition panel

Annotating Construction Documents

When you create construction documents, annotations are required to show the design intent. Annotations such as dimensions and text can be added to views at any time during the creation of a project. Detail lines and symbols can also be added to views as you create the working drawing sheets, while Legends can be created to provide a place to document any symbols that are used in a project.

Learning Objectives in this Chapter

- Add dimensions to the model as a part of the working drawings.
- Add text to a view and use leaders to create notes pointing to a specific part of the model.
- Create Text Types using different fonts and sizes to suit your company standards.
- Draw detail lines to further enhance the documentation view.
- Add view-specific annotation symbols for added clarity.
- Create legend views and populate them with symbols of elements in the project.

14.1 Working with Dimensions

You can create permanent dimensions using aligned, linear, angular, radial, diameter, and arc length dimensions. These can be individual or a string of dimensions, as shown in Figure 14–1. With aligned dimensions, you can also dimension entire walls with openings, grid lines, and/or intersecting walls.

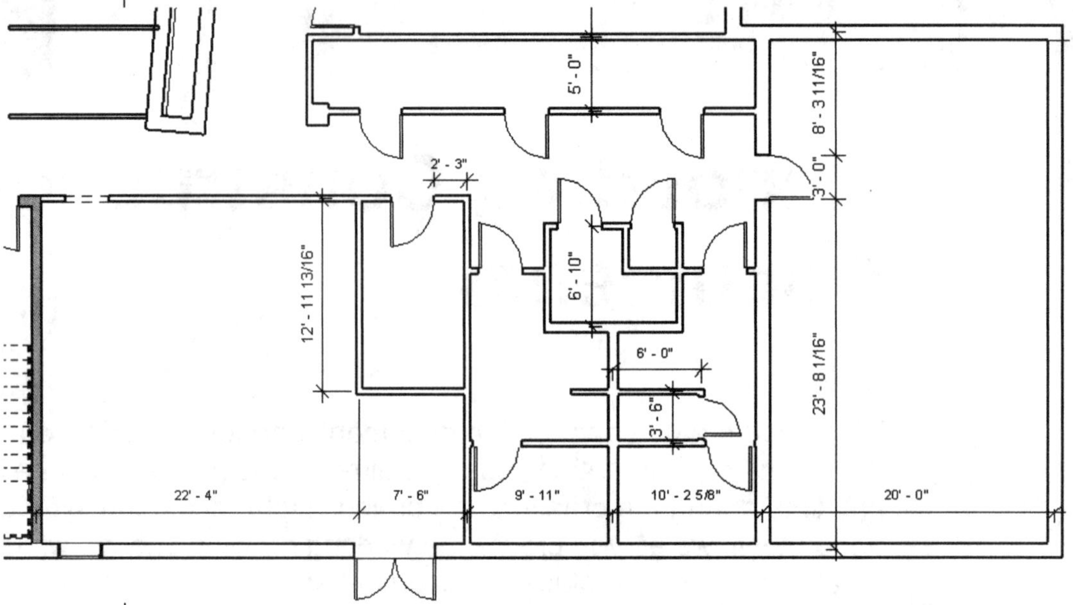

Figure 14–1

- Dimensions referencing model elements must be added to the model in a view. You can dimension on sheets, but only to items added directly on the sheets.

- Dimensions are available in the *Annotate* tab>Dimension panel and the *Modify* tab>Measure panel, as shown in Figure 14–2.

 *(Aligned) is also located in the Quick Access Toolbar.*

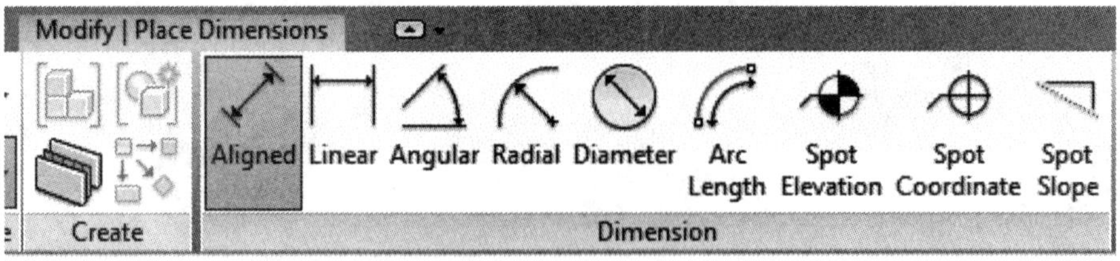

Figure 14–2

How To: Add Aligned Dimensions with Options

1. Start the  (Aligned) command or type **DI**.
2. In the Type Selector, select a dimension style.

3. In the Options Bar, select the location line of the wall to dimension from, as shown in Figure 14–3.
   - This option can be changed as you add dimensions.

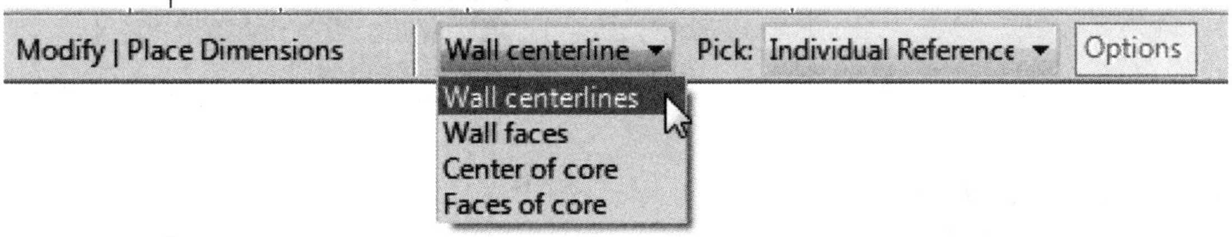

Figure 14–3

4. In the Options Bar, select your preference from the Pick drop-down list:
   - **Individual References**: Select the elements in order (as shown in Figure 14–4) and then click in empty space to position the dimension string.

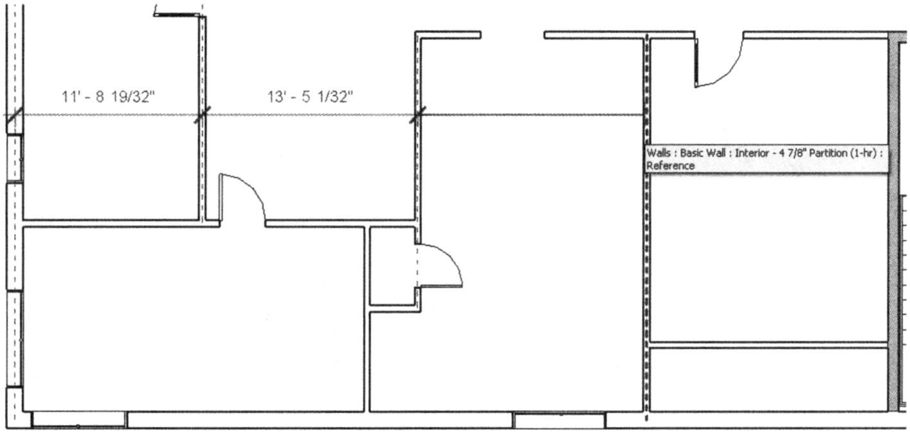

Figure 14–4

   - **Entire Walls**: Select the wall you want to dimension and then click the cursor to position the dimension string, as shown in Figure 14–5.

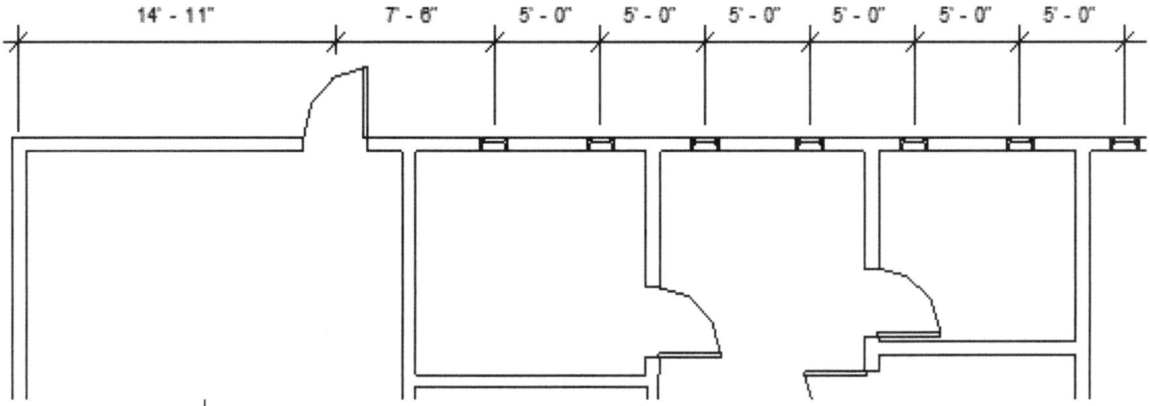

Figure 14–5

- When dimensioning entire walls you can specify how you want *Openings*, *Intersecting Walls*, and *Intersecting Grids* to be treated by the dimension string. In the Options Bar, click **Options**. In the Auto Dimension Options dialog box (shown in Figure 14–6), select the references you want to have automatically dimensioned.

*If the **Entire Wall** option is selected without additional options, it places an overall wall dimension.*

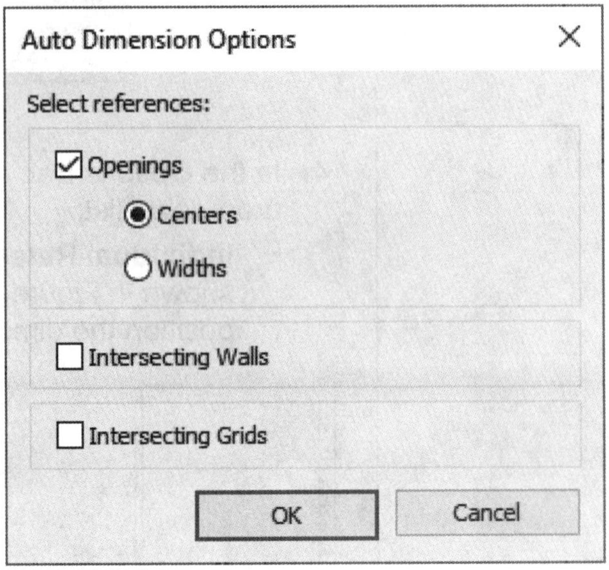

Figure 14–6

How To: Add Other Types of Dimensions

*When the **Dimension** command is active, the dimension methods are also accessible in the Modify | Place Dimensions*

1. In the *Annotate* tab>Dimension panel, select a dimension method.

	**Aligned**	Most commonly used dimension type. Select individual elements or entire walls to dimension.
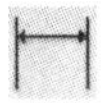	**Linear**	Used when you need to specify certain points on elements.
	**Angular**	Used to dimension the angle between two elements.
	**Radial**	Used to dimension the radius of circular elements.
	**Diameter**	Used to dimension the diameter of circular elements.
	**Arc Length**	Used to dimension the length of the arc of circular elements.

2. In the Type Selector, select the dimension type.
3. Follow the prompts for the selected method.

Modifying Dimensions

When you move elements that are dimensioned, the dimensions automatically update. You can also modify dimensions by selecting a dimension or dimension string and making changes, as shown in Figure 14–7.

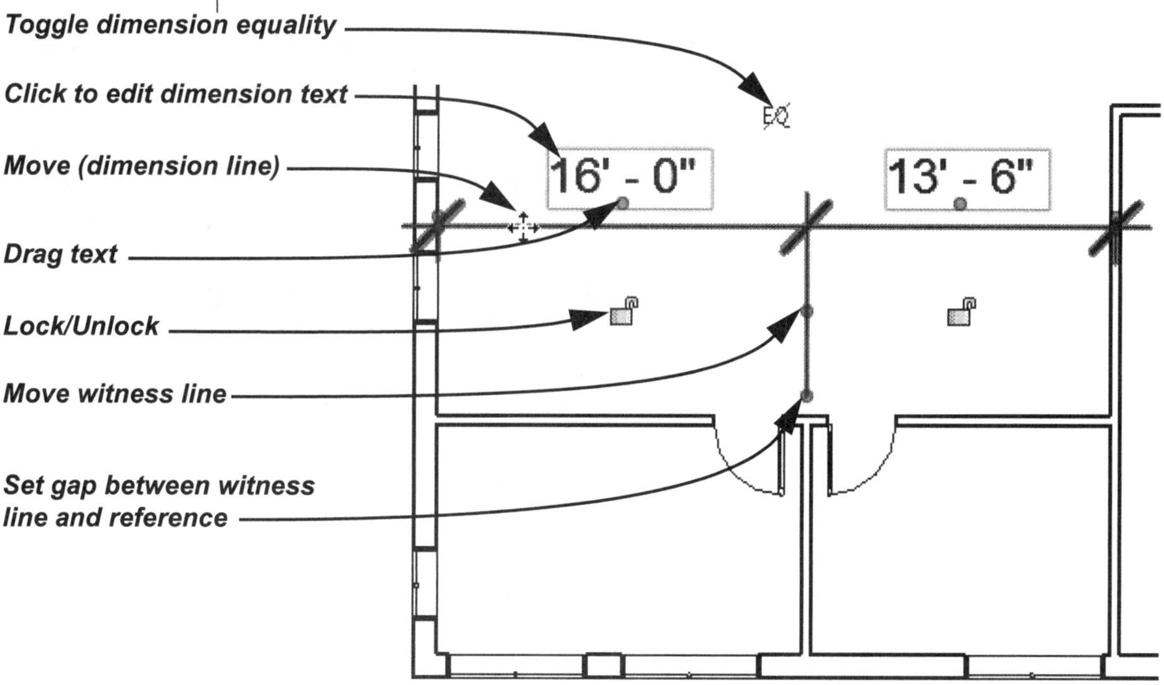

Figure 14–7

- To move the dimension text, select the **Drag text** control under the text and drag it to a new location. It automatically creates a leader from the dimension line if you drag it away. The style of the leader (arc or line) depends on the dimension style.
- To move the dimension line (the line parallel to the element being dimensioned) simply drag the line to a new location or select the dimension and drag the ✥ (Move) control.
- To change the gap between the witness line and the element being dimensioned, drag the control at the end of the witness line.
- To move the witness line (the line perpendicular to the element being dimensioned) to a different element or face of a wall, use the **Move Witness Line** control in the middle of the witness line. Click repeatedly to cycle through the various options. You can also drag this control to move the witness line to a different element, or right-click on the control and select **Move Witness Line**.

Adding and Deleting Dimensions in a String

- To add a witness line to a string of dimensions, select the dimension and, in the *Modify | Dimensions* tab>Witness Lines panel, click  (Edit Witness Lines). Select the element(s) you want to add to the dimension. Click in space to finish.
- To delete a witness line, drag the **Move Witness Line** control to a nearby element. Alternatively, you can hover the cursor over the control, right-click, and select **Delete Witness Line**.
- To delete one dimension in a string and break the string into two separate dimensions, select the string, hover over the dimension that you want to delete, and press <Tab>. When it highlights (as shown on top in Figure 14–8), pick it and press <Delete>. The selected dimension is deleted and the dimension string is separated into two elements as shown on the bottom in Figure 14–8.

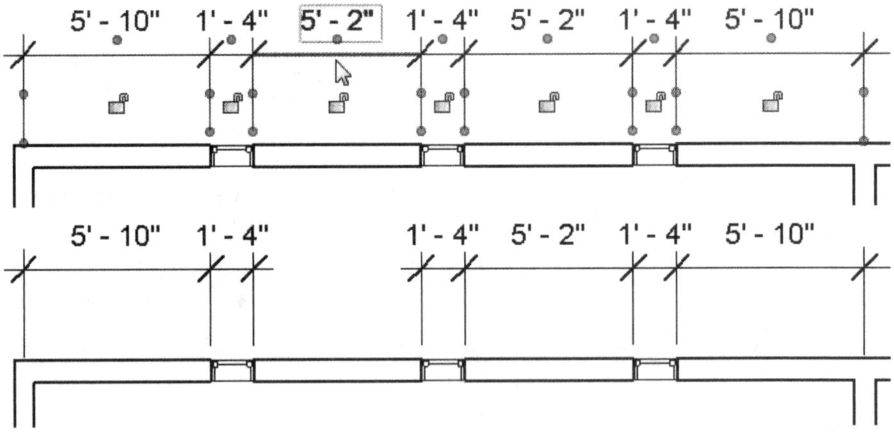

Figure 14–8

Modifying the Dimension Text

Because the Autodesk® Revit® software is parametric, changing the dimension text without changing the elements dimensioned would cause problems throughout the project. These issues could cause problems beyond the model if you use the project model to estimate materials or work with other disciplines.

You can append the text with prefixes and suffixes (as shown in Figure 14–9), which can help you in renovation projects.

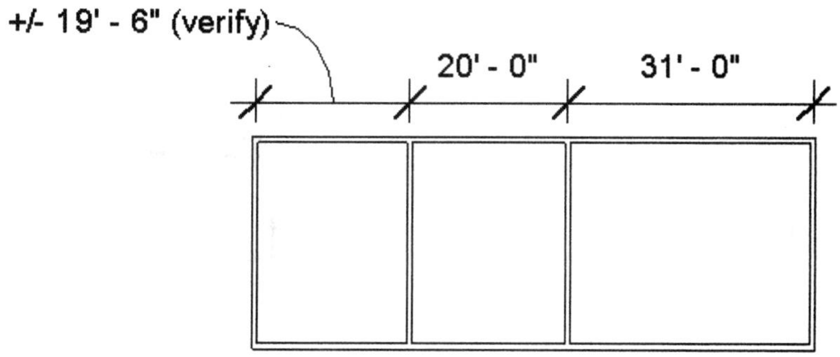

Figure 14–9

Double-click on the dimension text to open the Dimension Text dialog box, as shown in Figure 14–10, and make modifications as required.

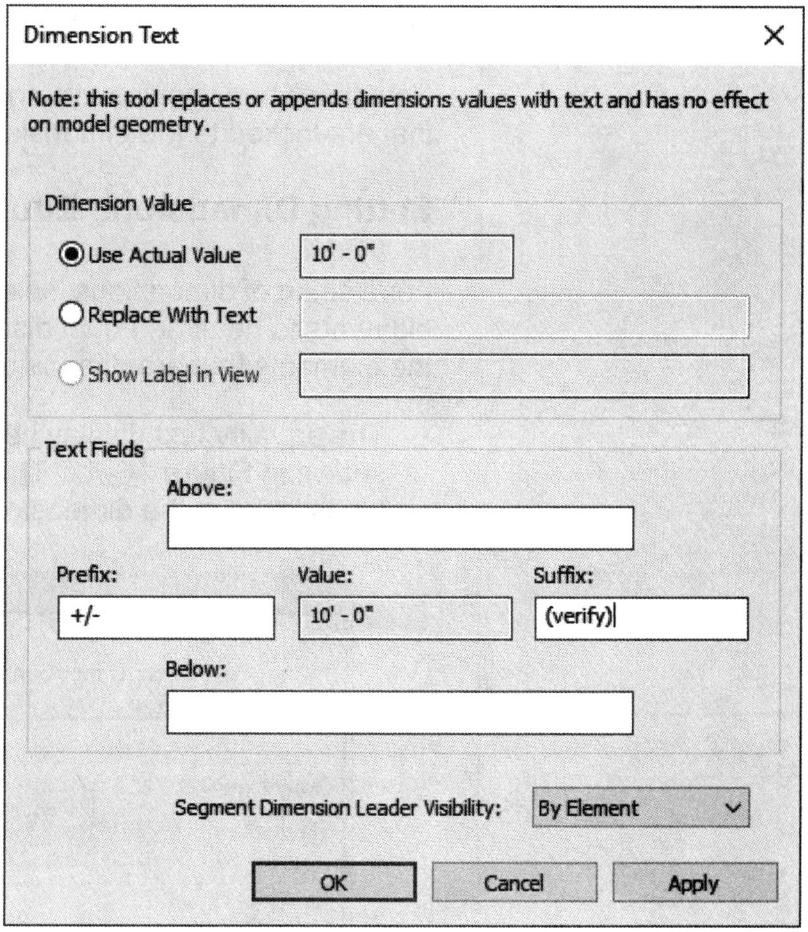

Figure 14–10

Setting Constraints

The three types of constraints that work with dimensions are locks and equal settings, as shown in Figure 14–11, as well as labels.

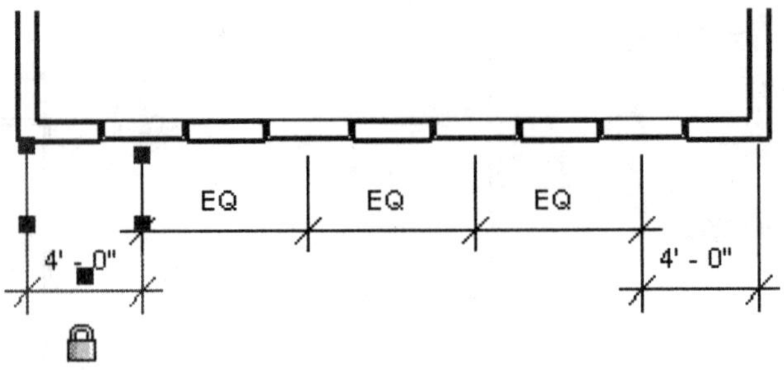

Figure 14–11

Locking Dimensions

When you lock a dimension, the value is set and you cannot make a change between it and the referenced elements. If it is unlocked, you can move it and change its value.

Note that when you use this and move an element, any elements that are locked to the dimension also move.

Setting Dimensions Equal

For a string of dimensions, select the **EQ** symbol to constrain the elements to be at an equal distance apart. This actually moves the elements that are dimensioned.

- The equality text display can be changed in Properties, as shown in Figure 14–12. The style for each of the display types is set in the dimension type.

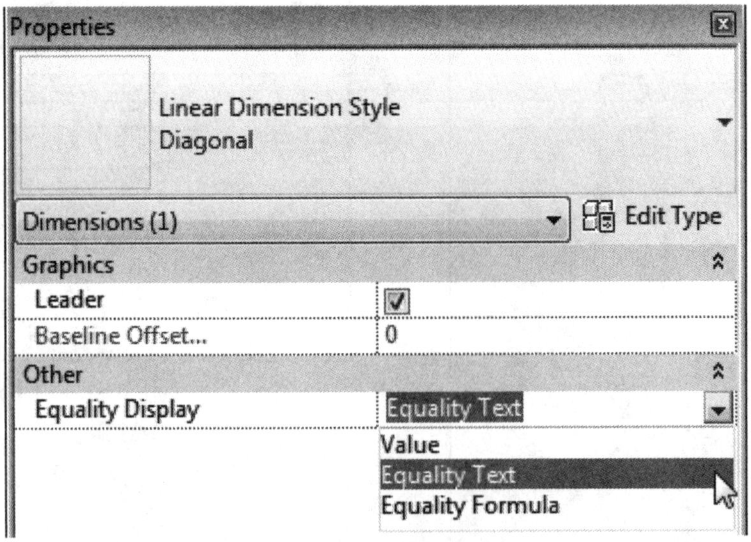

Figure 14–12

Labeling Dimensions

If you have a distance that needs to be repeated multiple times, such as the *Wall to Window* label shown in Figure 14–13, or one where you want to use a formula based on another dimension, you can create and apply a global parameter, also called a label, to the dimension.

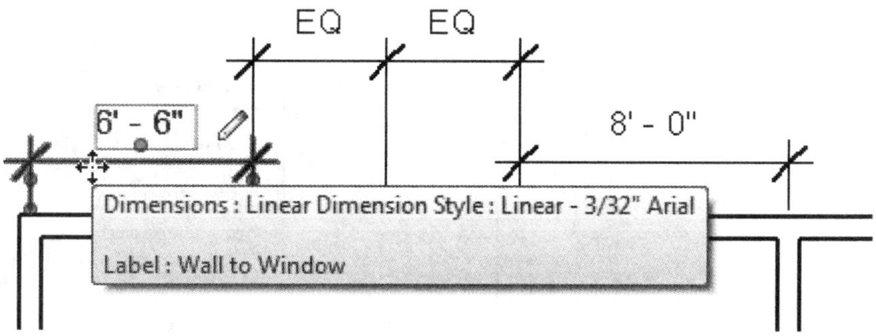

Figure 14–13

- To apply an existing label to a dimension, select the dimension and in the *Modify | Dimension* tab>Label Dimension panel, select the label in the drop-down list, as shown in Figure 14–14.

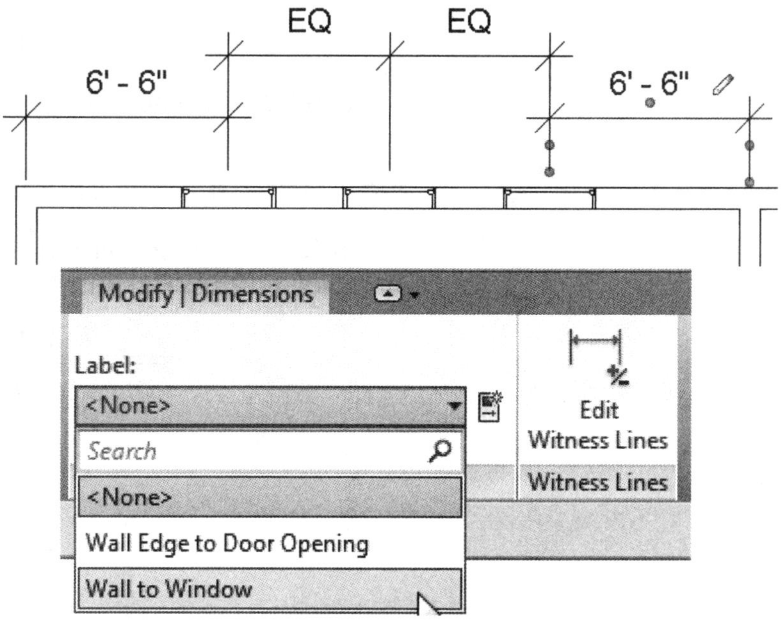

Figure 14–14

How To: Create a Label

1. Select a dimension.
2. In the *Modify | Dimension* tab>Label Dimension panel, click  (Create Parameter)
3. In the Global Parameter Properties dialog box type in a *Name* as shown in Figure 14–15 and click **OK**.

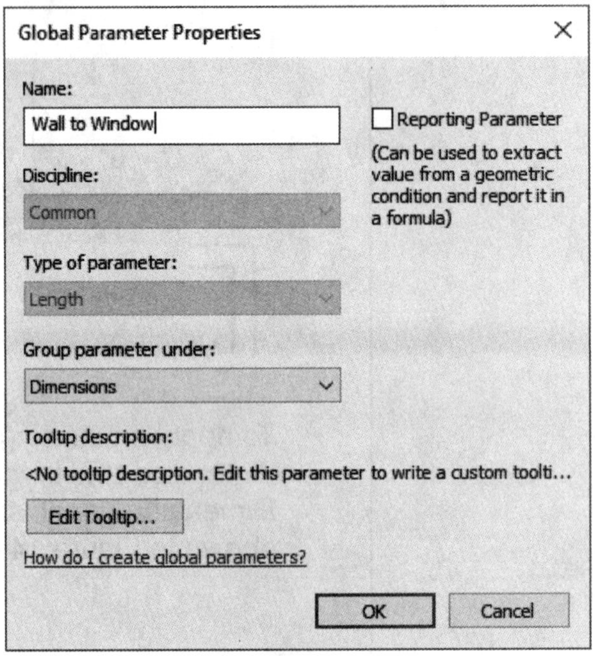

Figure 14–15

4. The label is applied to the dimension.

How To: Edit the Label Information

1. Select a labeled dimension.
2. Click **Global Parameters**, as shown in Figure 14–16.

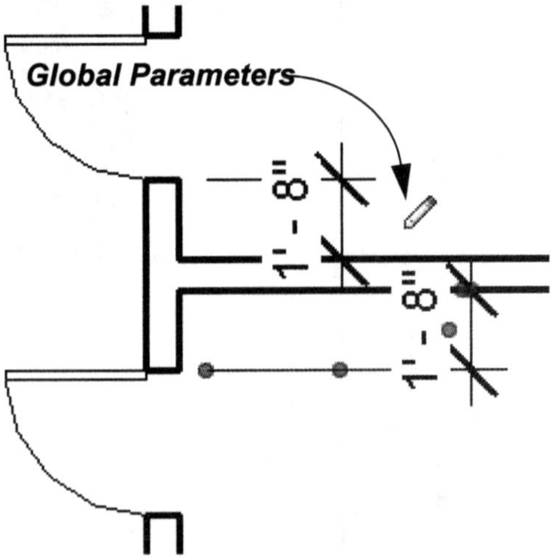

Figure 14–16

3. In the Global Parameters dialog box, in the *Value* column, type the new distance, as shown in Figure 14–17.

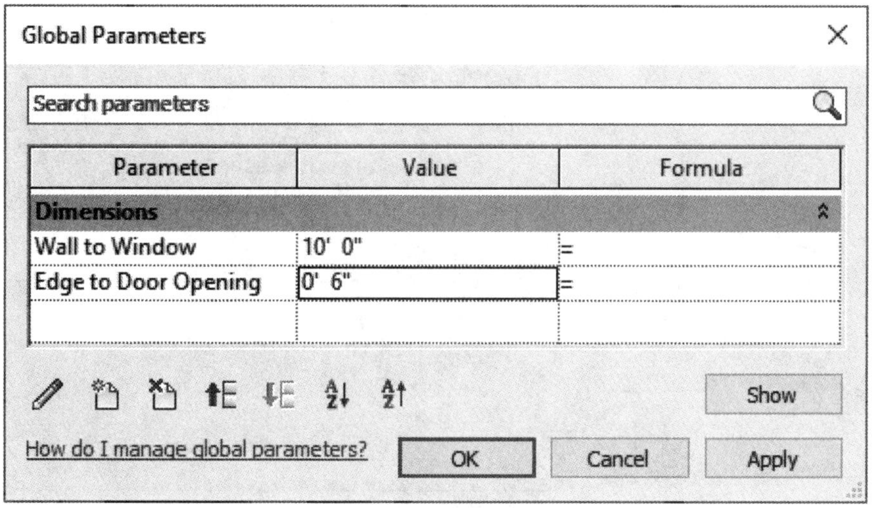

Figure 14–17

4. Click **OK**. The selected dimension and any other dimensions using the same label are updated.

- You can also edit, create, and delete Global Parameters in this dialog box.

Working with Constraints

To find out which elements have constraints applied to them, in the View Control Bar, click (Reveal Constraints). Constraints display as shown in Figure 14–18.

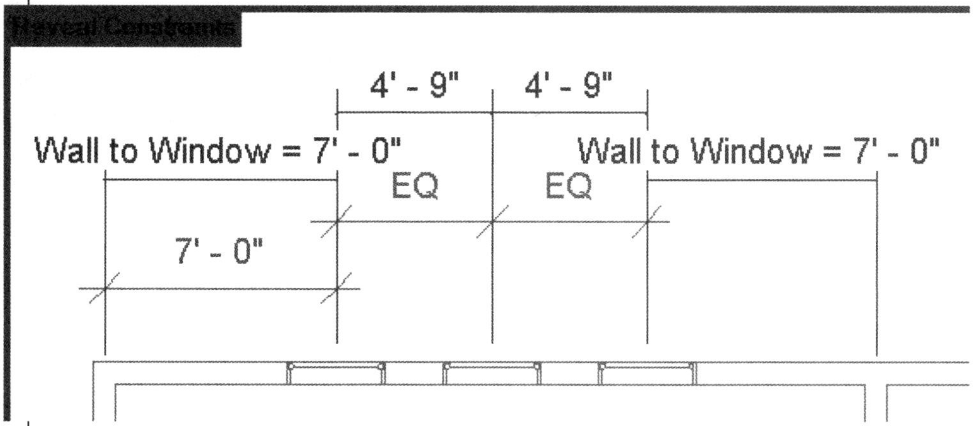

Figure 14–18

- If you try to move the element beyond the appropriate constrains, a warning dialog box displays, as shown in Figure 14–19.

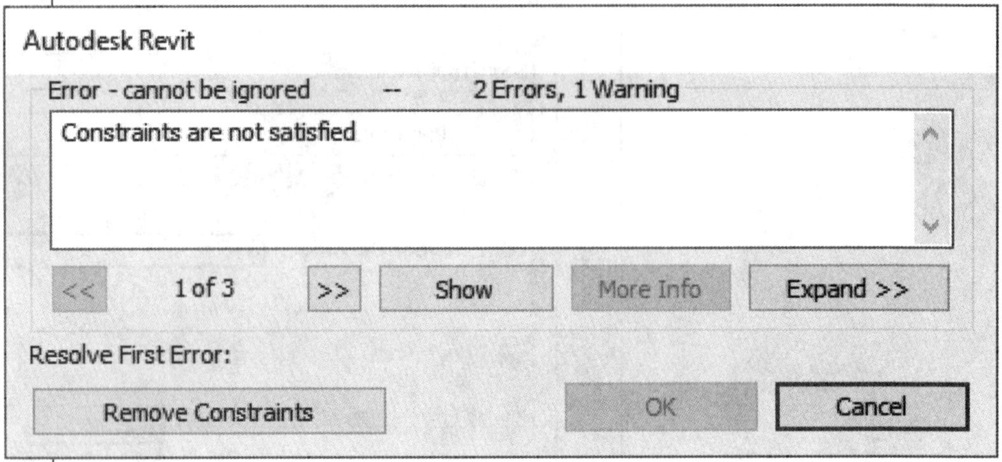

Figure 14–19

- If you delete dimensions that are constrained, a warning dialog box displays, as shown in Figure 14–20. Click **OK** to retain the constraint or **Unconstrain** to remove the constraint.

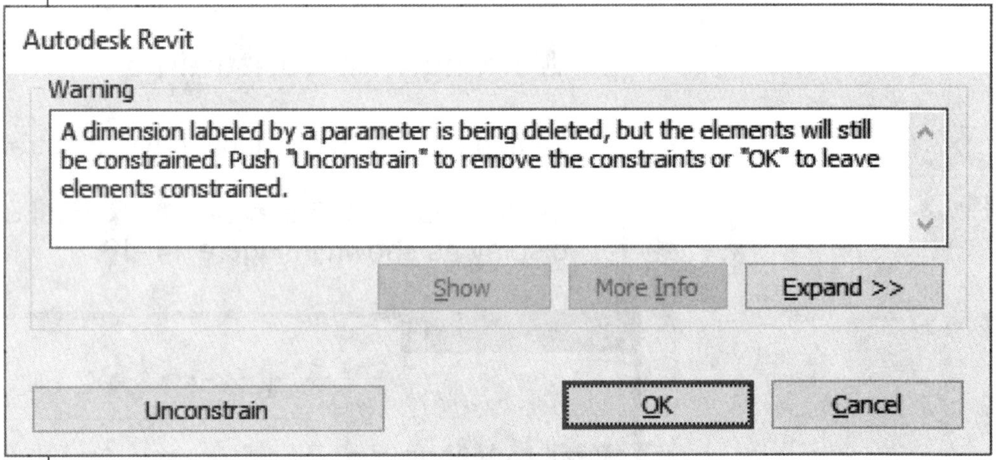

Figure 14–20

Practice 14a Work with Dimensions

Practice Objectives

- Add a string of dimensions.
- Dimension using the **Entire Walls** option.
- Edit the witness lines of dimensions.

In this practice, you will add dimensions using several different methods to a floor plan view, as shown on the sheet in Figure 14–21. You will also modify the dimensions so that they show what you are expecting. Note that some additional elements including storefront curtain walls and windows have been added at the back of the building.

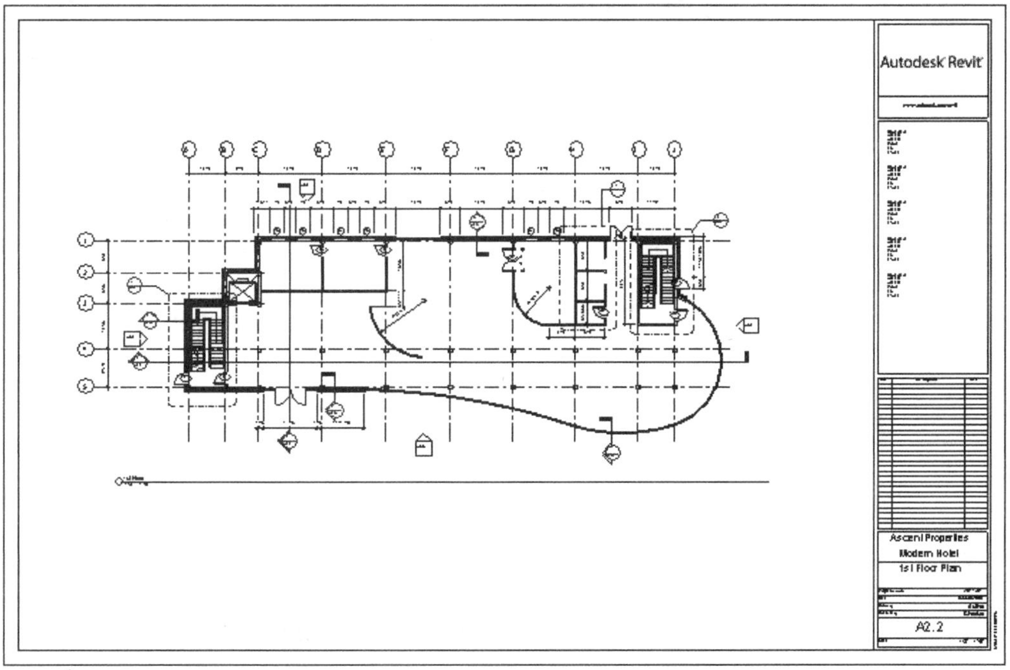

Figure 14–21

Task 1 - Add dimensions to the column grid.

1. Open the project **Modern-Hotel-Dimensions.rvt**.
2. In the Project Browser, duplicate the **Floor Plans: Floor 1** view (without detailing so that the door and window tags do not display),
3. Rename the new view to **Floor 1-Dimensioned Plan**.
4. Move the location of the grid bubbles so that there is enough room for dimensioning.

5. In the Quick Access Toolbar, click  (Aligned).

6. Dimension the column grid lines in each direction, as shown in Figure 14–22.

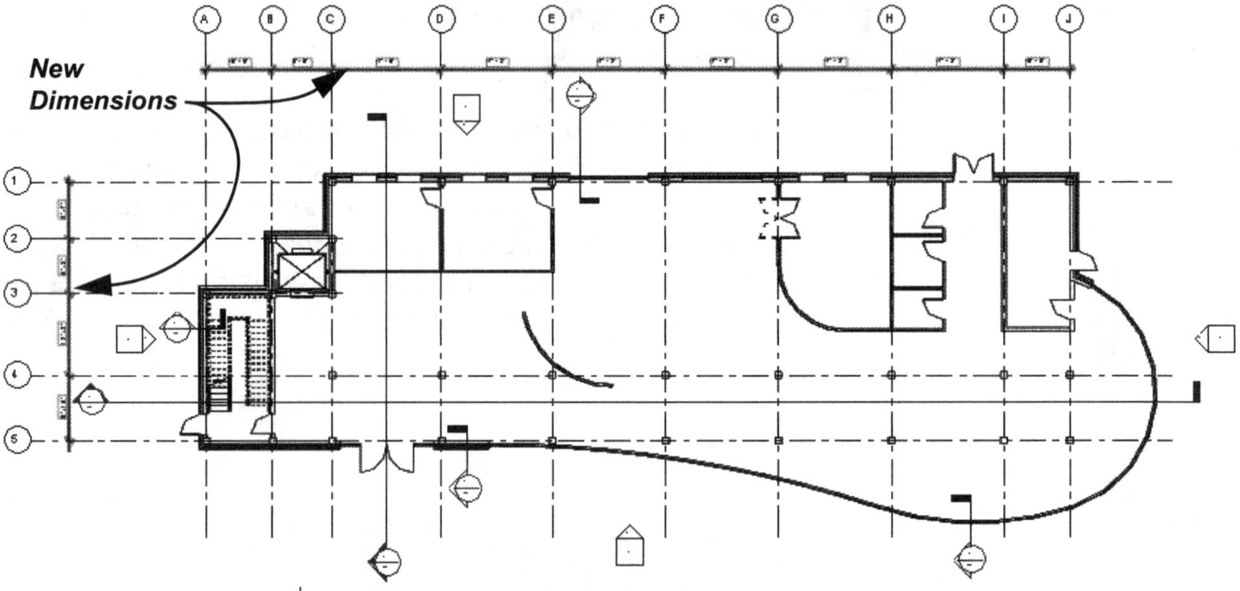

Figure 14–22

Task 2 - Dimension the exterior and interior walls.

1. Click  (Aligned).

2. In the Options Bar, select **Wall faces** and set *Pick* to **Entire Walls**.

3. Click **Options** and set the *Openings* to **Widths**, as shown in Figure 14–23. Click **OK**.

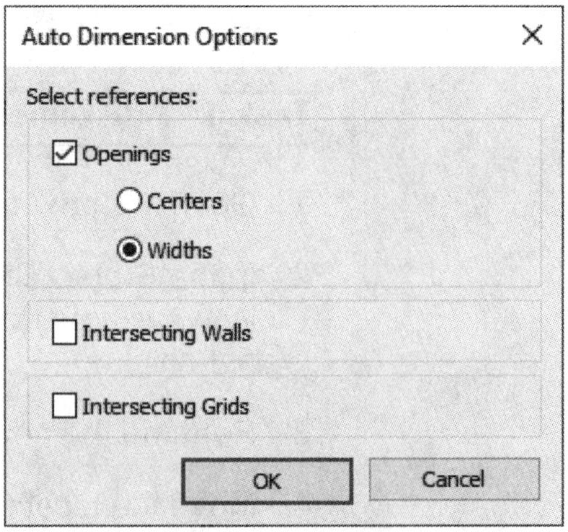

Figure 14–23

4. Select the back wall and place the dimension above it.

5. Zoom in on the upper left corner of the building. Use the **Move Witness Line** control to relocate the line from the end of the wall (as shown in Figure 14–24), to Grid Line C, the closest grid line on the right that passes through the corner column.

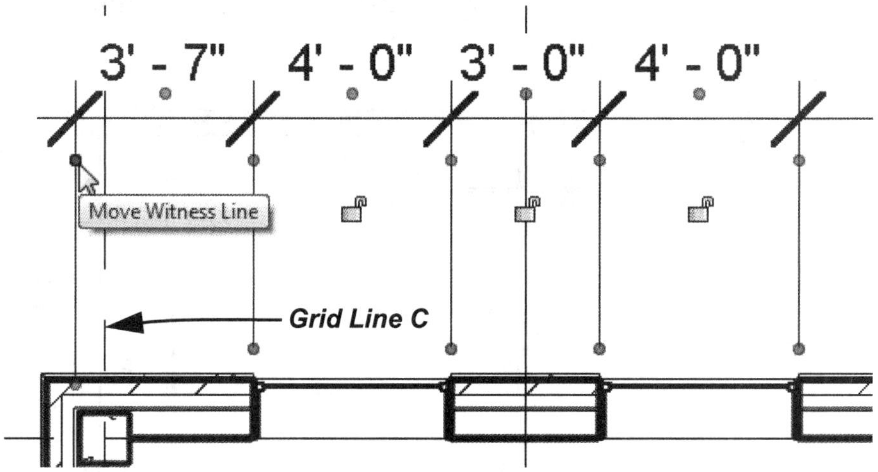

Figure 14–24

6. Click (Modify)

7. In the same wall, pan over to the right between Grid Lines E, F, and G where the storefront openings are displayed. These were not dimensioned automatically.

8. Select the wall dimension line. In the *Modify | Dimensions* tab>Witness Lines panel, click (Edit Witness Lines).

9. Select the outside edges of each side of the storefront openings to add the witness lines and then click in empty space to apply the changes. The modified dimension string displays, as shown in Figure 14–25.

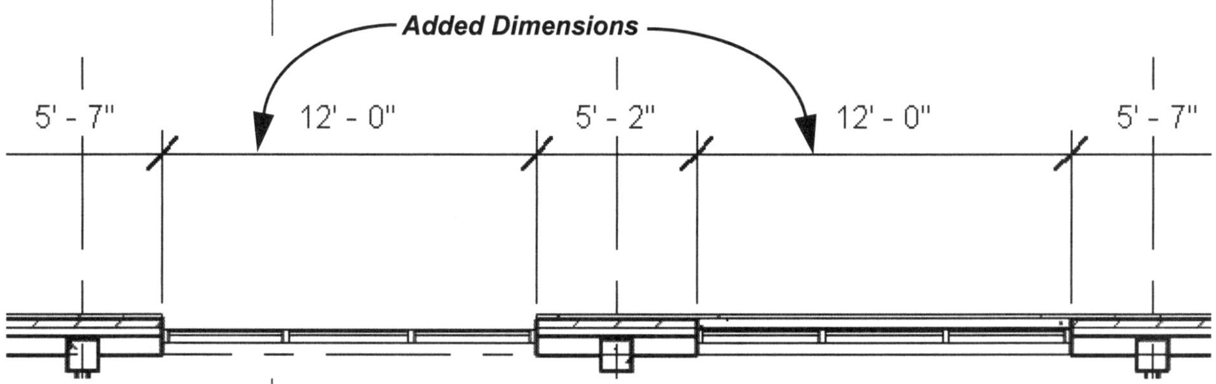

Figure 14–25

10. Move the elevation and section markers as well as the dimension line to keep the dimensions clear. You might also want to move the dimension text away from the grid lines.

11. Use the various dimensioning commands and methods to dimension the interior spaces, as shown in Figure 14–26 (Hint: don't forget to change from **Pick: Entire Walls** to **Pick: Individual References**.). The dimensions might not be exactly as shown.

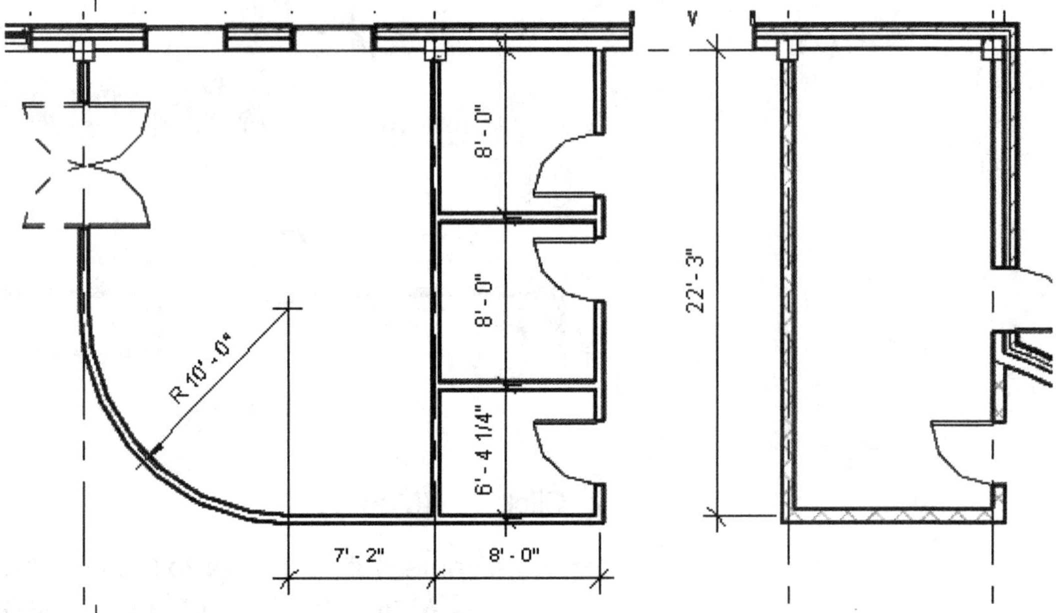

Figure 14–26

12. Save the project.

13. If time permits, dimension the **Floor Plans: Typical Guest Room - Dimension Plan** view. Make adjustments as required to the locations of the walls and doors.

14.2 Working With Text

The **Text** command enables you to add notes to views or sheets, such as the detail shown in Figure 14–27. The same command is used to create text with or without leaders.

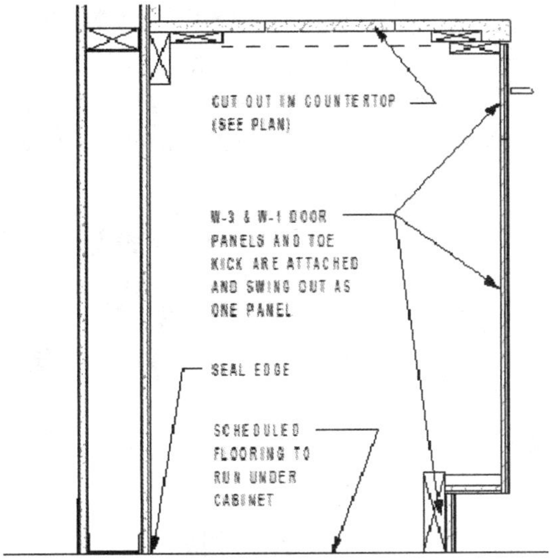

Figure 14–27

The text height is automatically set by the text type in conjunction with the scale of the view (as shown in Figure 14–28, using the same size text type at two different scales). Text types display at the specified height, both in the views and on the sheet.

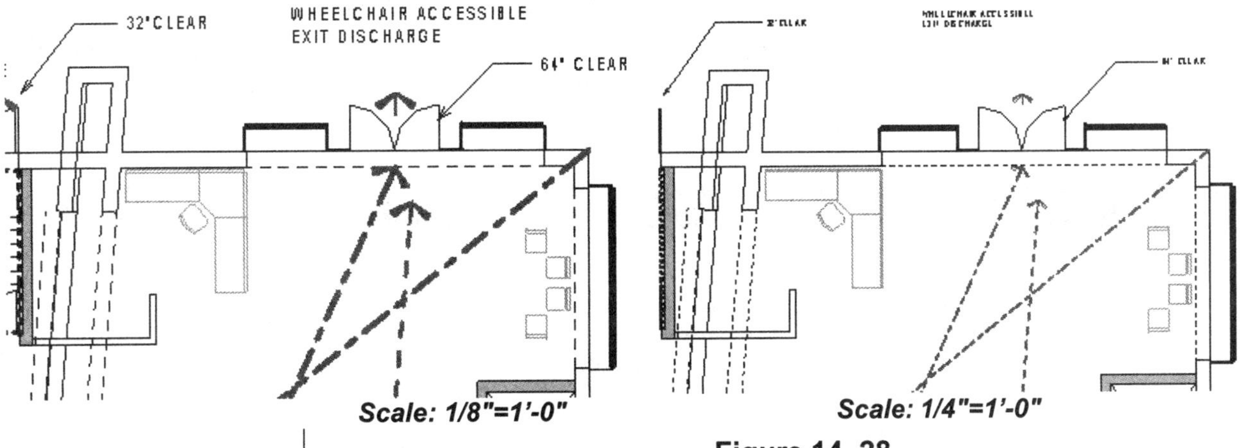

Figure 14–28

How To: Add Text

1. In the Quick Access Toolbar or *Annotate* tab>Text panel, click A (Text).

The text type sets the font and height of the text.

2. In the Type Selector, set the text type.
3. In the *Modify | Place Text* tab>Leader panel, select the method you want to use: A (No Leader), ←A (One Segment), ↙A (Two Segments), or ↙A (Curved).
4. In the Paragraph panel, set the overall justification for the text and leader, as shown in Figure 14–29.

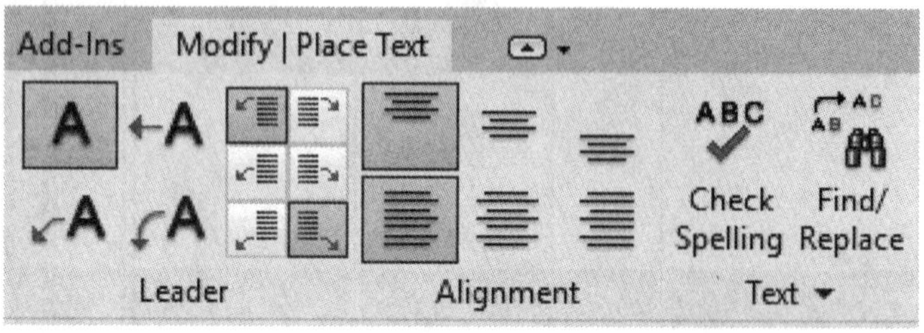

Figure 14–29

Use alignment lines to help you align the text with other text elements.

5. Select the location for the leader and text.
   - If **No leader** is selected, select the start point for the text and begin typing.
   - If using a leader, the first point places the arrow and you then select points for the leader. The text starts at the last leader point.
   - To set a word wrapping distance, click and drag to set the start and end points of the text.
6. Type the required text. In the *Edit Text* tab, specify additional options for the font and paragraph, as shown in Figure 14–30.

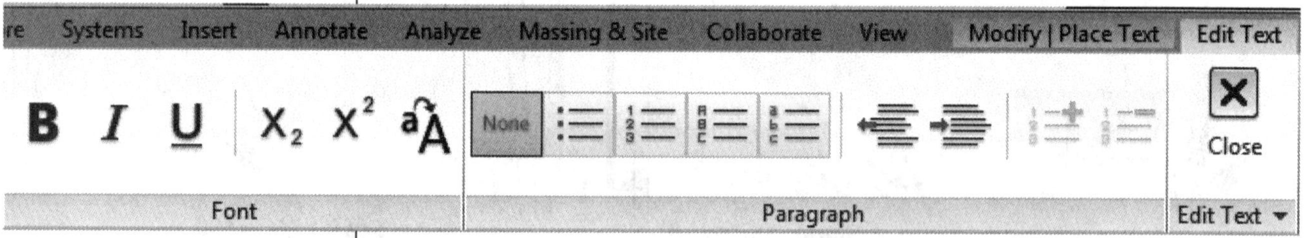

Figure 14–30

7. In the Edit Text tab>Edit Text panel, click (Close) or click outside the text box to complete the text element.
   - Pressing <Enter> after a line of text starts a new line of text in the same text window.

How To: Add Text Symbols

1. Start the **Text** command and click to place the text.
2. As you are typing text and need to insert a symbol, right-click and select **Symbols** from the shortcut menu. Select from the list of commonly used symbols, as shown in Figure 14–31.

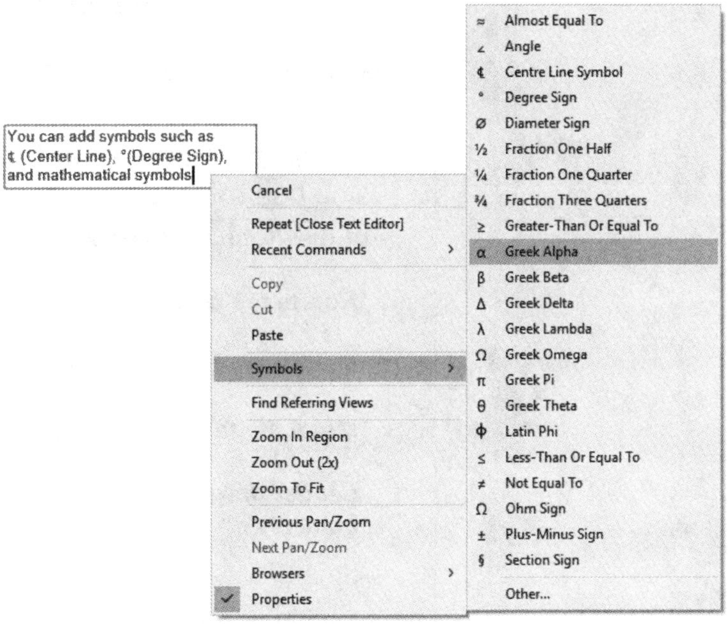

Figure 14–31

3. If the symbol you need is not listed, click **Other**.
4. In the Character Map dialog box, click on a symbol and click **Select**, as shown in Figure 14–32.

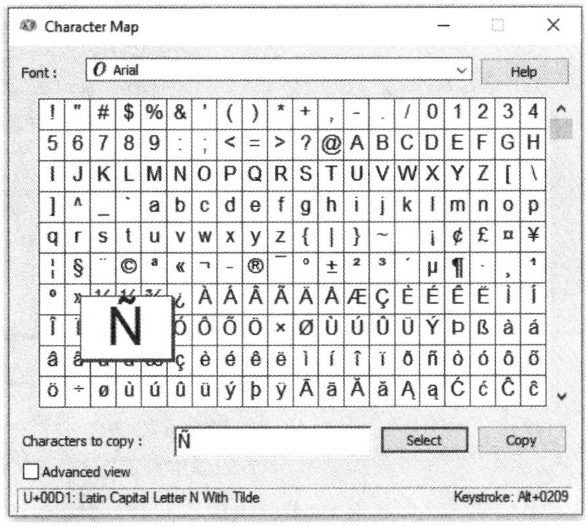

Figure 14–32

5. Click **Copy** to copy the character to the clipboard and paste it into the text box.

- The Font in the Character Map must match the font used by the text type. You cannot use a different font for symbols.

Editing Text

Editing text notes takes place at two levels:

- Modifying the text note, which includes the **Leader** and **Paragraph** styles.
- Editing the text, which includes changes to individual letters, word, and paragraphs in the text note.

Modifying the Text Note

Click once on the text note to modify the text box and leaders using controls, as shown in Figure 14–33, or using the tools in the *Modify | Text Notes* tab.

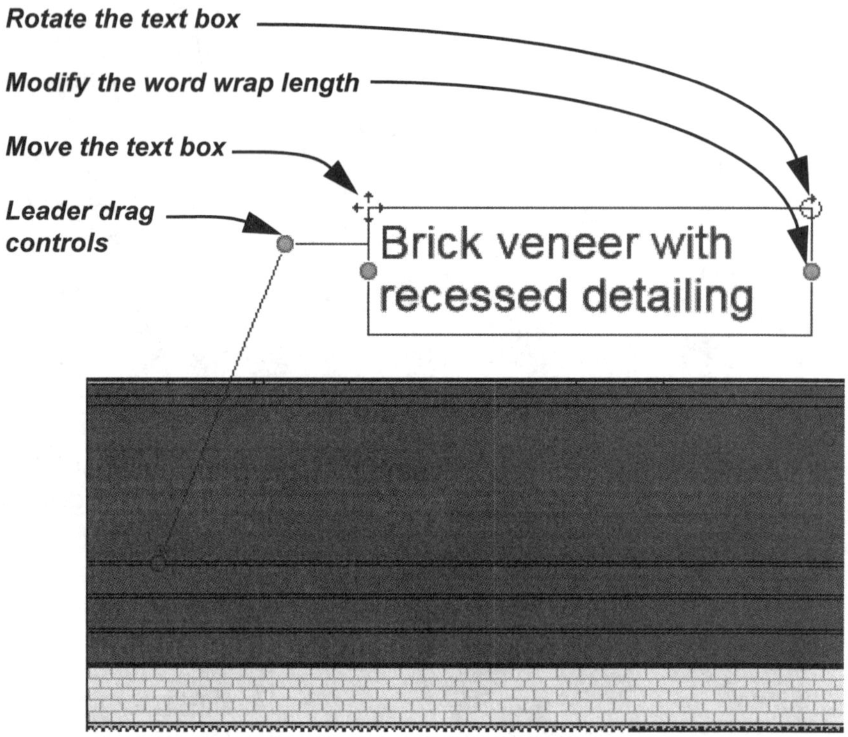

Figure 14–33

How To: Add a Leader to Text Notes

1. Select the text note.
2. In the *Modify | Text Notes* tab>Leader panel, select the direction and justification for the new leader, as shown in Figure 14–34.
3. The leader is applied, as shown in Figure 14–35. Use the drag controls to place the arrow as required.

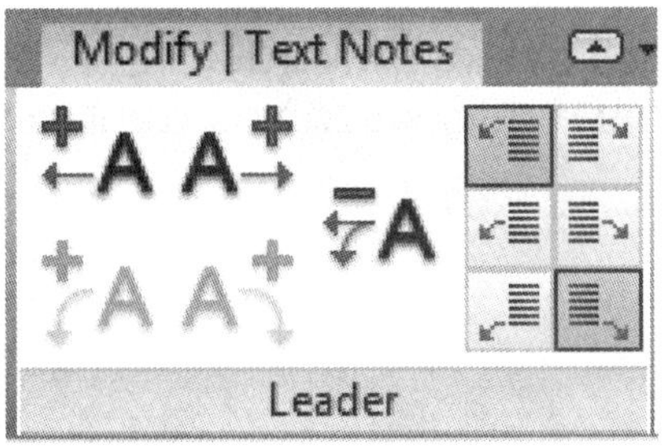

Figure 14–34

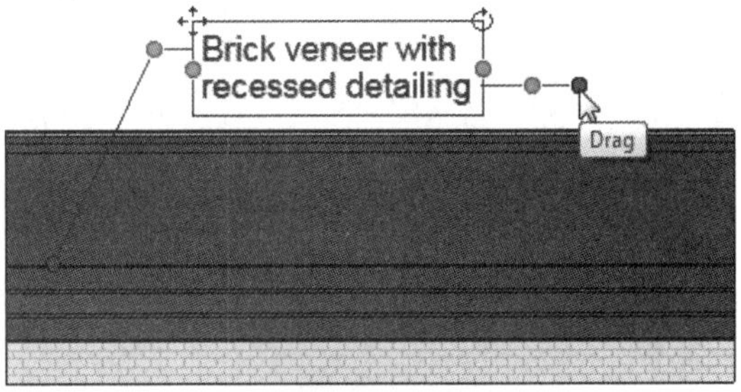

Figure 14–35

- You can remove leaders by clicking (Remove Last Leader).

Editing the Text

The *Edit Text* tab enables you to make various customizations. These include modifying the font of selected words as well as creating bulleted and numbered lists, as shown in Figure 14–36.

General Notes

1. Notify designer of intention to start construction at least 10 days prior to start of site work.
2. Installer shall provide the following:
   - 24-hour notice of start of construction
   - Inspection of bottom of bed or covering required by state inspector
   - All environmental management inspection sheets must be emailed to designer's office within 24 hours of inspection.

Figure 14–36

- You can **Cut**, **Copy**, and **Paste** text using the clipboard. For example, you can copy text from a document and then paste it into the text editor in Revit.

- To help you see the text better as you are modifying it, in the *Edit Text* tab, expand the Edit Text panel, and select one or both of the options, as shown in Figure 14–37.

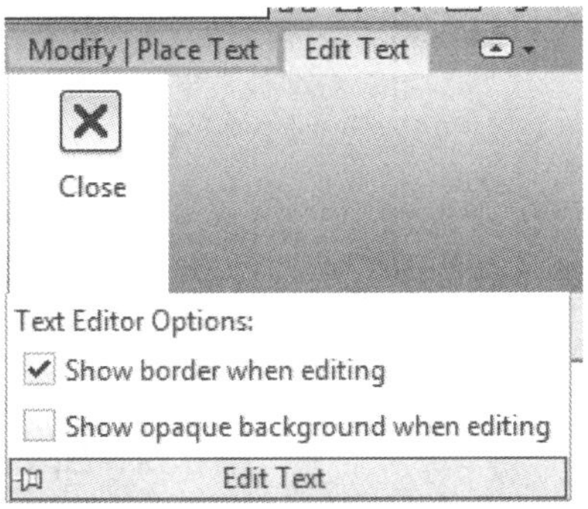

Figure 14–37

How To: Modify the Font

1. Select Individual letters or words.
2. Click on the font modification you want to include:

B (Bold)	X_2 (Subscript)
I (Italic)	X^2 (Superscript)
U (Underline)	aA (All Caps)

- When pasting text from a document outside of Autodesk Revit, font modifications (e.g, Bold, Italic, etc.) are retained.

How To: Create Lists

1. In Edit Text mode, place the cursor in the line where you want to add to a list.
2. In the *Edit Text* tab>Paragraph panel, click the type of list you want to create:

(Bullets)	(Uppercase Letters)
(Numbers)	(Lowercase Letters)

3. As you type, press <Enter> and the next line in the list is incremented.

The indent distance is setup by the Text Type Tab Size.

4. To include sub-lists, at the beginning of the next line, click (Increase Indent). This indents the line and applies the next level of lists, as shown in Figure 14–38.

4. The applicant shall be responsible:
    A. First Indent
        a. Second Indent
            • Third Indent

Figure 14–38

- You can change the type of list after you have applied the first increment. For example, you might want to use a list of bullets instead of letters, as shown in Figure 14–39.

5. Click (Decrease Indent) to return to the previous list style.

- Press <Shift>+<Enter> to create a blank line in a numbered list.

- To create columns or other separate text boxes that build on a numbering system (as shown in Figure 14–39), create the second text box and list. Then, place the cursor on one of the lines and in the Paragraph panel, click (Increment List Value) until the list matches the next number in the sequence.

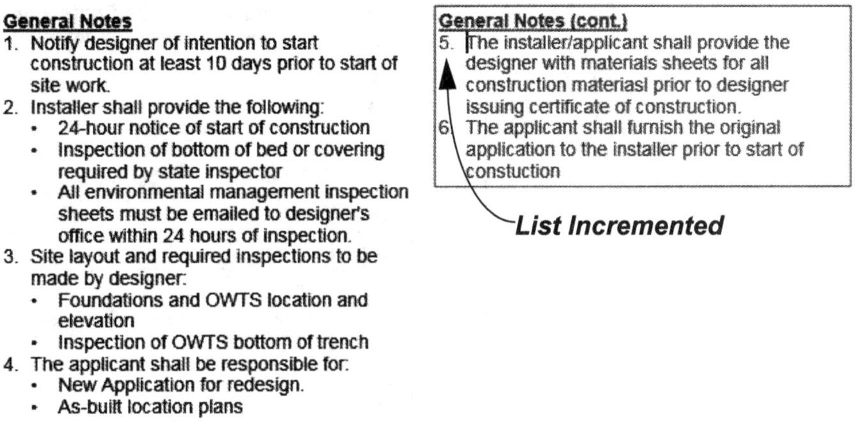

Figure 14–39

6. Click (Decrement List Value) to move back a number.

Hint: Model Text

Model text is different from annotation text. It is designed to create full-size text on the model itself. For example, you would use model text to create a sign on a door, as shown in Figure 14–40. One model text type is included with the default template. You can create other types as required.

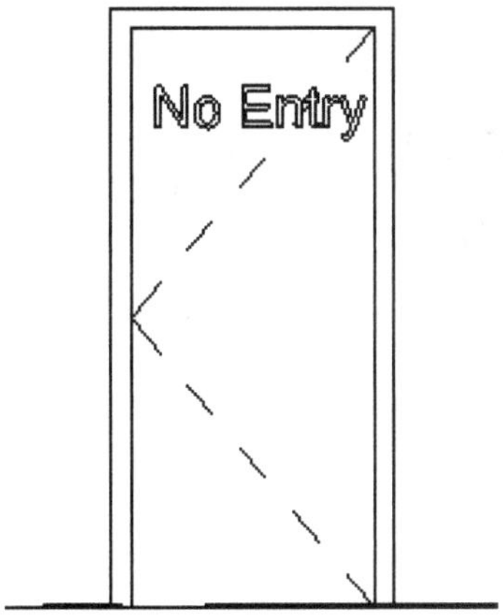

Figure 14–40

- Model text is added from the *Architecture* tab>Model panel, by clicking (Model Text).

Spell Checking

The Spelling dialog box displays any misspelled words in context and provides several options for changing them, as shown in Figure 14–41.

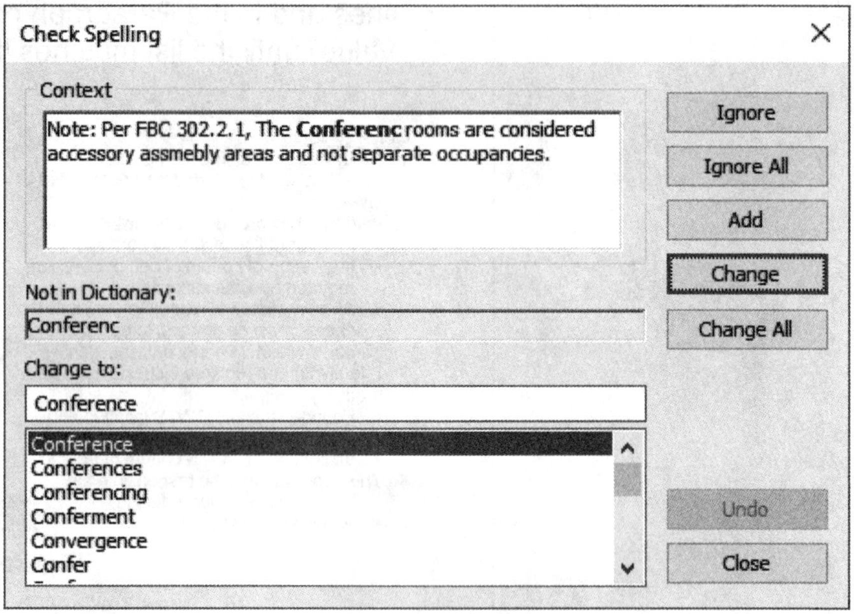

Figure 14–41

- To spell check all text in a view, in the *Annotate* tab>Text panel, click  (Spelling) or press <F7>. As with other spell checkers, you can **Ignore**, **Add**, or **Change** the word.
- You can also check the spelling in selected text. With text selected, in the *Modify | Text Notes* tab>Tools panel, click  (Check Spelling).

Creating Text Types

If you need new text types with a different text size or font (such as for a title or hand-lettering), you can create new ones, as shown in Figure 14–42. It is recommended that you create these in a project template so they are available in future projects.

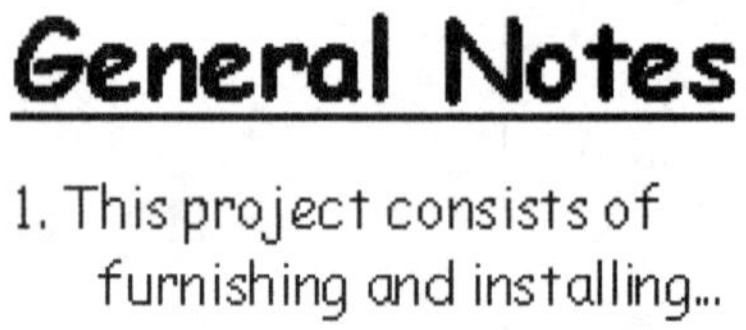

Figure 14–42

- You can copy and paste text types from one project to another or use **Transfer Project Standards**.

How To: Create Text Types

1. In the *Annotate* tab>Text panel, click (Text Types).
2. In the Type Properties dialog box, click **Duplicate**.
3. In the Name dialog box, type a new name and click **OK**.
4. Modify the text parameters, as required. The parameters are shown in Figure 14–43.

Parameter	Value
Graphics	
Color	Black
Line Weight	1
Background	Opaque
Show Border	☐
Leader/Border Offset	5/64"
Leader Arrowhead	Arrow 30 Degree
Text	
Text Font	Arial
Text Size	1/4"
Tab Size	1/2"
Bold	☐
Italic	☐
Underline	☐
Width Factor	1.000000

Figure 14–43

- The **Background** parameter can be set to **Opaque** or **Transparent**. An opaque background includes a masking region that hides lines or elements beneath the text.
- In the *Text* area, the **Width Factor** parameter controls the width of the lettering, but does not affect the height. A width factor greater than **1** spreads the text out and a width factor less than **1** compresses it.
- The **Show Border** parameter, when selected, includes a rectangle around the text.

5. Click **OK** to close the Type Properties dialog box.

Practice 14b Work with Text

Practice Objectives

- Create Text Types.
- Add text with and without leaders to a view.
- Add a numbered and bulleted list to a sheet.

*15*In this practice, you will add text with and without leaders to a view. You will also add a text note with numbered and bulleted list on a site plan sheet, as shown in Figure 14–44.

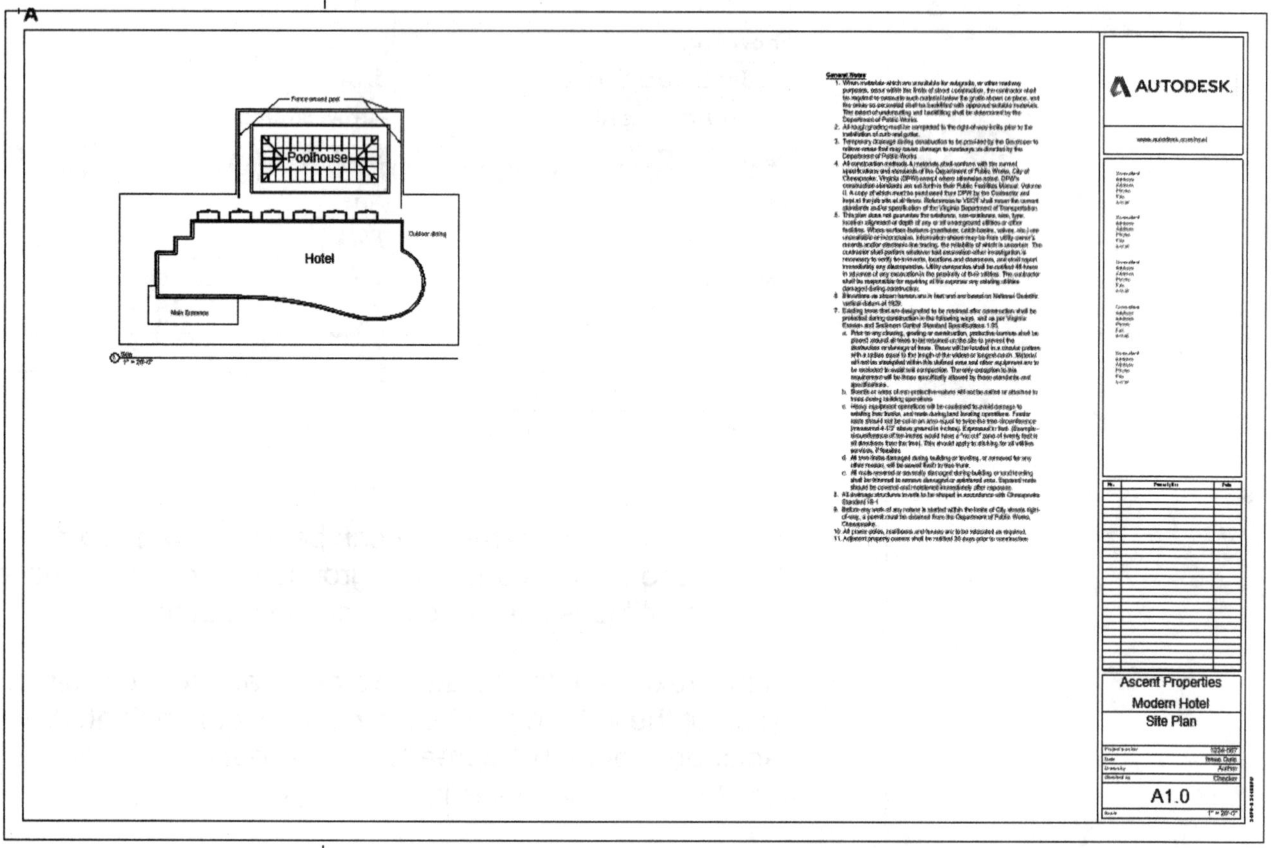

Figure 14–44

Task 1 - Create Text Types

1. Open the project **Modern-Hotel-Text.rvt**.

2. In the *Annotate* tab>Text panel, click  (Text).

3. In Properties, click  (Edit Type).

4. In the Type Properties dialog box, duplicate an existing text type and create a text type named **1/8" Arial** using the properties as outlined below.

5. Click **OK** to save the settings and close the dialog box.

6. Repeat the process to create the other two text types.

	1/8" Arial	**1/8" Arial Narrow**	**1/8" Arial Narrow Italic**
Text Font	Arial	Arial	Arial
Text Size	1/8"	1/8"	1/8"
Tab Size	1/4"	1/4"	1/4"
Width Factor	1.0	0.9	.09
Italic	No	No	Yes

7. Click **OK**.

Task 2 - Add Text to a View

1. Open the **Floor Plans: Site** view.
2. In the *Annotate* tab>Text panel, click A (Text).
3. In the Type Selector, select **Text: 1/4" Arial**.
4. Add titles for the Hotel and Poolhouse, as shown in Figure 14–45.
5. Change to **1/8" Arial Narrow** and add text for the other notes shown in Figure 14–45.

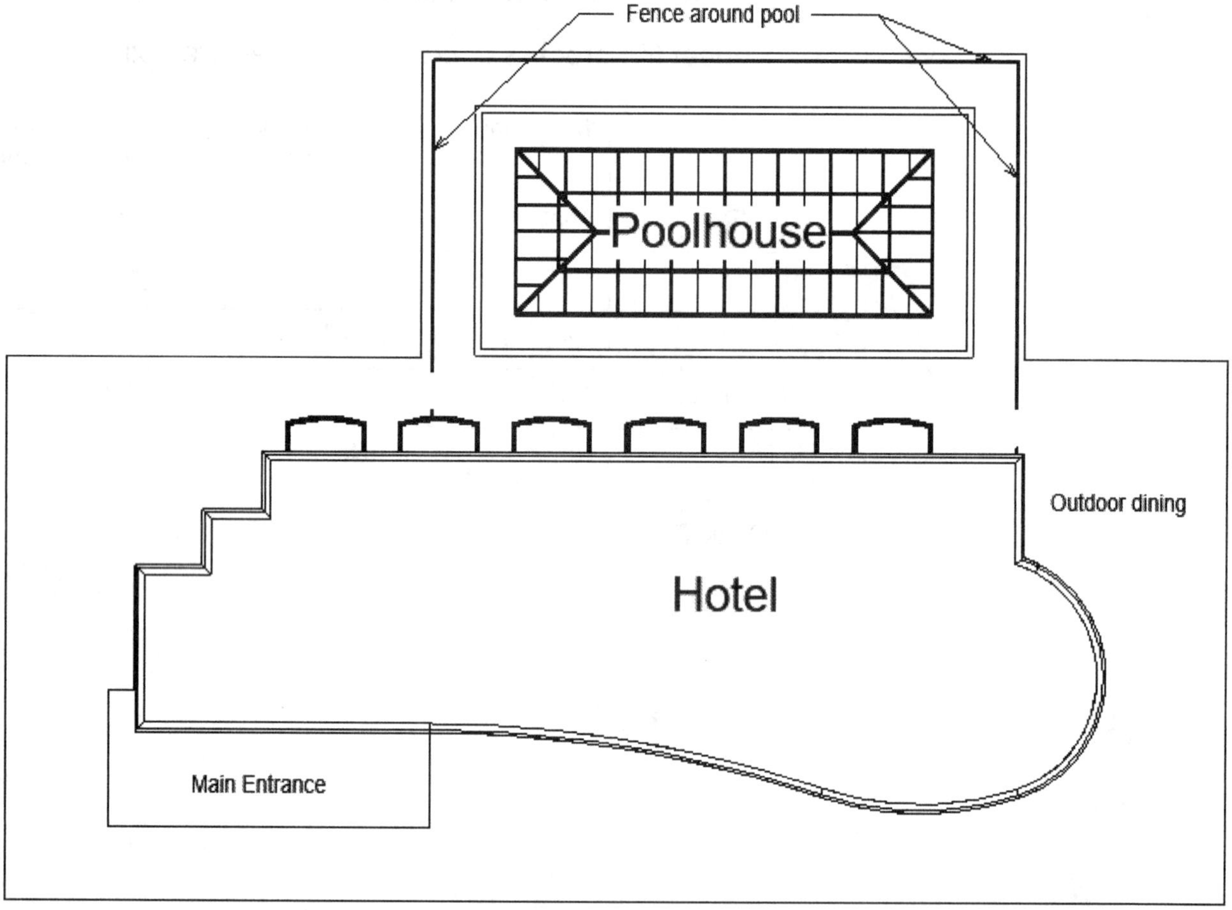

Figure 14–45

- To add the leaders to the Fence around the pool text, select the text and in the Modify | Text Notes tab> Leader panel, click (Add Left Side Straight Leader) and (Add Right Side Straight Leader). Then modify the Drag controls as needed.

Task 1 - Create Text with a List.

- Note: In this task, you are placing the text directly on the sheet. Check your office standards, as using a Legend view for general notes might be preferred.

1. Create a new sheet using the D-sized title block and name it **A1.0 - Site Plan**.
2. Add the **Floor Plans: Site** view to the sheet, as shown in Figure 14–46. The added text displays at the correct size for the sheet.

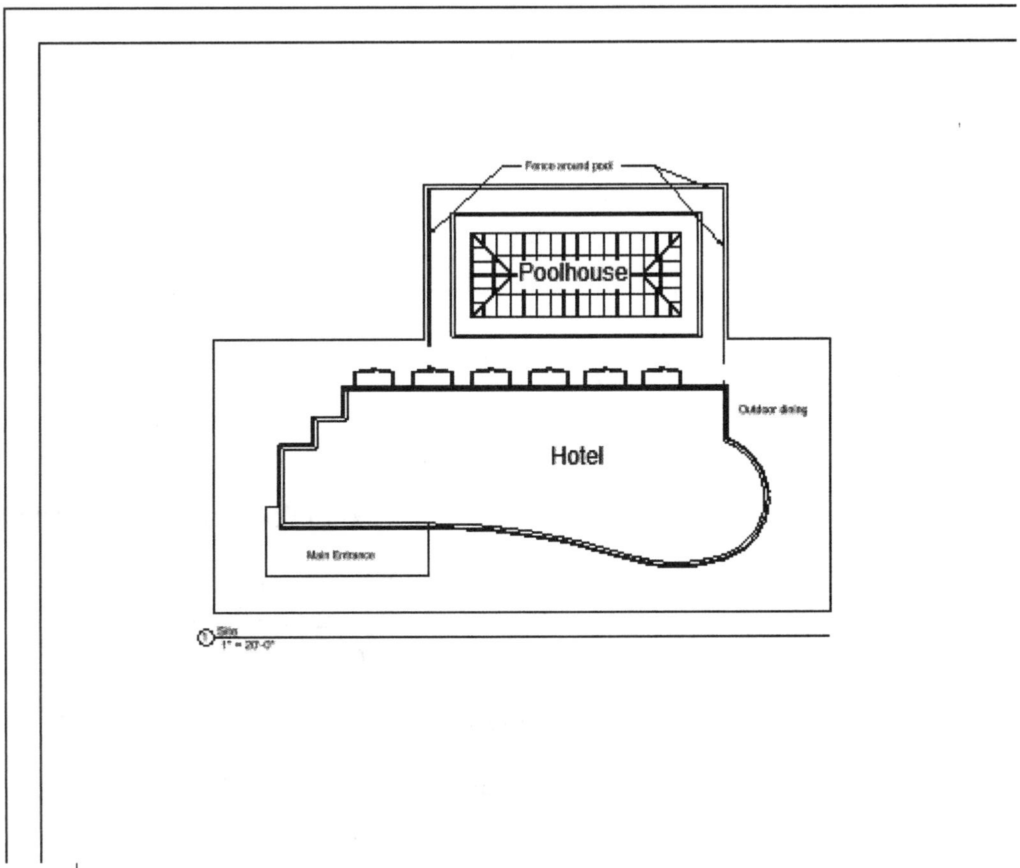

Figure 14–46

3. In a text editor (such as Word or Notepad), navigate to the practice files folder and open either **General Notes.docx** or **General Notes.txt**.
4. Copy the entire contents of the file to the clipboard.
5. In Autodesk Revit, start the **Text** command.

6. Verify that no leader is selected, set the text type to **1/8" Arial Narrow** and draw a text box similar to the one shown in Figure 14–47.

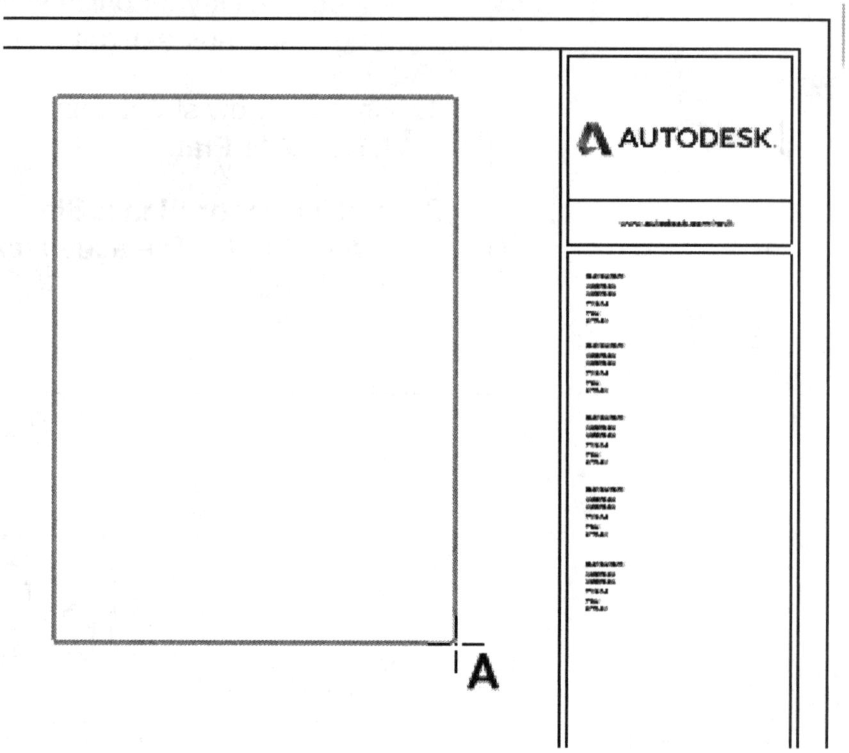

Figure 14–47

7. In the Edit Text dialog box>Clipboard panel, click (Paste).
8. Remain in Edit Text mode and zoom in on the text box. Note that there are numbered and lettered lists in the text, but the formatting is not quite correct.
9. Select all of the text and, in the *Edit Text* tab> Paragraph panel, click (List: Numbers).
10. The paragraphs are recognized and numbered but some of the existing numbers are still there.

11. Select the lettered paragraphs that are shown highlighted in Figure 14–48. In the *Edit Text* tab> Paragraph panel, click (List: Lowercase letters). This changes that list to a lettered list.

12. Zoom in and remove the additional numbers, as shown in Figure 14–48.

If you copied the text from the .TXT file, then you might need to also increase the indent and change the list type.

1. When materials which are unsuitable for subgrade, or other roadway purposes, occur within the limits of street construction, the contractor shall be required to excavate such material below the grade shown on plans, and the areas so excavated shall be backfilled with approved suitable materials. The extent of undercutting and backfilling shall be determined by the Department of Public Works.
2. All rough grading must be completed to the right-of-way limits prior to the installation of curb and gutter.
3. Temporary drainage during construction to be provided by the Developer to relieve areas that may cause damage to roadways as directed by the Department of Public Works
4. All construction methods & materials shall conform with the current specifications and standards of the Department of Public Works, City of Chesapeake, Virginia (DPW) except where otherwise noted. DPW's construction standards are set forth in their Public Facilities Manual, Volume II. A copy of which must be purchased from DPW by the Contractor and kept at the job site at all times. References to VDOT shall mean the current standards and/or specification of the Virginia Department of Transportation.
5. This plan does not guarantee the existence, non-existence, size, type, location alignment or depth of any or all underground utilities or other facilities. Where surface features (manholes, catch basins, valves, etc.) are unavailable or inconclusive, information shown may be from utility owner's records and/or electronic line tracing, the reliability of which is uncertain. The contractor shall perform whatever test excavation other investigation is necessary to verify tie-in inverts, locations and clearances, and shall report immediately any discrepancies. Utility companies shall be notified 48 hours in advance of any excavation in the proximity of their utilities. The contractor shall be responsible for repairing at his expense any existing utilities damaged during construction.
6. Elevations as shown hereon are in feet and are based on National Gedetric vertical datum of 1929.
7. Existing trees that are designated to be retained after construction shall be protected during construction in the following ways, and as per Virginia Erosion and Sediment Control Standard Specifications 1.85.
   a. Prior to any clearing, grading or construction, protective barriers shall be placed around all trees to be retained on the site to prevent the destruction or damage of trees. These will be located in a circular pattern with a radius equal to the length of the widest or longest ranch. Material will not be stockpiled within this defined area and other equipment are to be excluded to avoid soil compaction. The only exception to this requirement will be those specifically allowed by these standards and specifications.
   b. Boards or wires of non-protective nature will not be nailed or attached to trees during building operations.
   c. Heavy equipment operations will be cautioned to avoid damage to existing tree trunks, and roots during land leveling operations. Feeder roots should not be cut in an area equal to twice the tree circumference (measured 4-1/2' above ground in inches). Expressed in feet. (Example - circumference of ten inches would have a "no cut" zone of twenty feet in all directions from the tree). This should apply to ditching for all utilities services, if feasible.
   d. All tree limbs damaged during building or leveling, or removed for any other reason, will be sawed flush to tree trunk.
   e. All roots severed or severally damaged during building or land leveling shall be trimmed to remove damaged or splintered area. Exposed roots should be covered and moistened immediately after exposure.
8. All drainage structures inverts to be shaped in accordance with Chesapeake Standard IS-1
9. Before any work of any nature is started within the limits of City streets right-of-way, a permit must be obtained from the Department of Public Works, Chesapeake.
10. All power poles, mailboxes and fences are to be relocated as required.
11. Adjacent property owners shall be notified 30 days prior t

Figure 14–48

13. At the beginning of the list, add the text **General Notes**. Make it bold and underlined, as shown in Figure 14–49.

General Notes

1. When materials which are unsuitable for subgrade, or other roadway purposes, occur within the limits of street construction, the contractor shall be required to excavate such material below the grade shown on plans, and the areas so excavated shall be backfilled with approved suitable materials. The extent of undercutting and backfilling shall be determined by the Department of Public Works.
2. All rough grading must be completed to the right-of-way limits prior to the installation of curb and gutter.
3. Temporary drainage during construction to be provided by the Developer to relieve areas that may cause damage to roadways as directed by the Department of Public Works
4. All construction methods & materials shall conform with the current specifications and standards of the Department of Public Works, City of Chesapeake, Virginia (DPW) except where otherwise noted. DPW's construction standards are set forth in their Public Facilities Manual, Volume II. A copy of which must be purchased from DPW by the Contractor and kept at the job site at all times. References to VDOT shall mean the current standards and/or specification of the Virginia Department of Transportation.

Figure 14–49

14. Click outside the text box and use the controls if required to relocate or resize the text note.

15. Zoom out to see the full sheet.

16. Save the project.

14.3 Adding Detail Lines and Symbols

While annotating views for construction documents, you might need to add detail lines and symbols to clarify the design intent or show information, such as the life safety plan exit information, as shown in Figure 14–50.

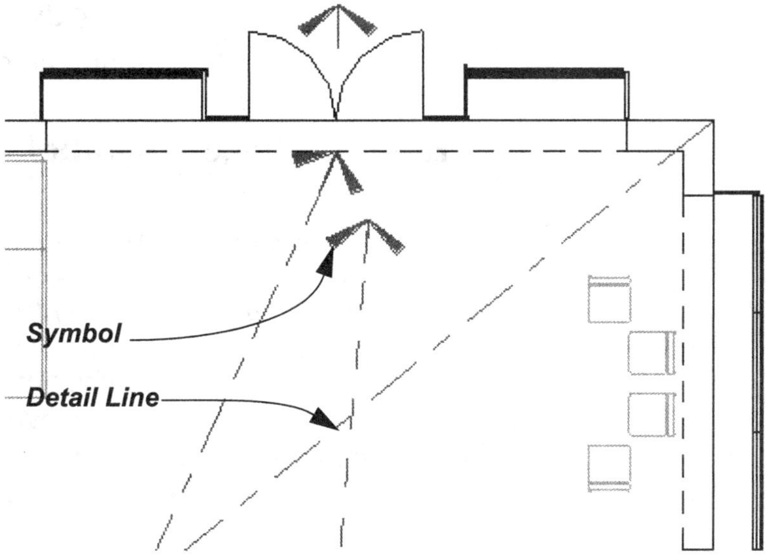

Figure 14–50

- Detail lines and symbols are view-specific, which means that they only display in the view in which they were created.

How To: Draw Detail Lines

1. In the *Annotation* tab>Detail panel, click (Detail Line).
2. In the *Modify | Place Detail Lines* tab>Line Style panel, select the type of line you want to use, as shown in Figure 14–51.

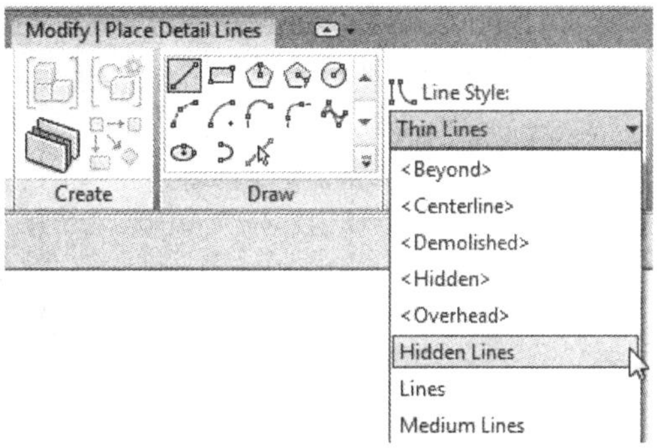

Figure 14–51

3. Use the tools in the Draw panel to create the detail lines.

Using Symbols

Symbols are 2D elements that only display in one view, while components can be in 3D and display in many views.

Many of the annotations used in working drawings are frequently repeated. Several of them have been saved as symbols in the Autodesk Revit software, such as the North Arrow, Center Line, and Graphic Scale annotations as shown in Figure 14–52.

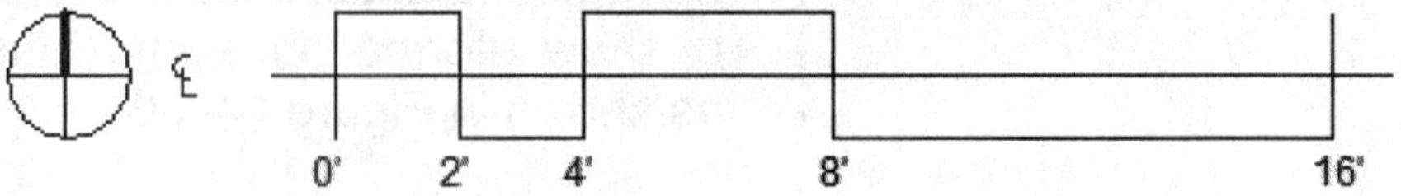

Figure 14–52

- You can also create or load custom annotation symbols.

How To: Place a Symbol

1. In the *Annotate* tab>Symbol panel, click (Symbol).
2. In the Type Selector, select the symbol you want to use.
3. In the *Modify | Place Symbol* tab>Mode panel, click (Load Family) if you want to load other symbols.
4. In the Options Bar, as shown in Figure 14–53, set the *Number of Leaders* and select **Rotate after placement** if you want to rotate the symbol as you insert it.

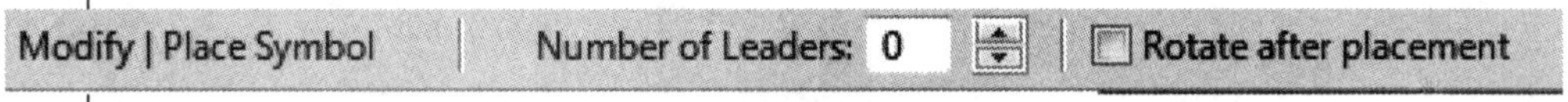

Figure 14–53

5. Place the symbol in the view. Rotate it if you selected the **Rotate after placement** option. If you specified leaders, use the controls to move them into place.

- In the *Annotate* tab>Symbol panel, click (Stair Path) to label the slope direction and walk line of a stair, as shown in Figure 14–54.

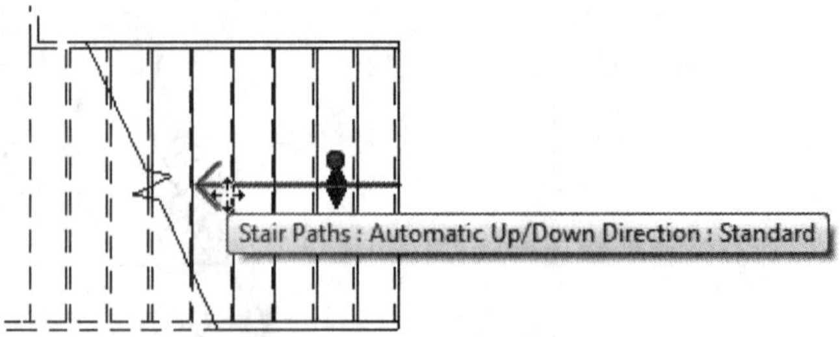

Figure 14–54

- For information about adding tags to dependent views see, *Appendix B.10 Annotating Dependent Views*.

Practice 14c Add Detail Lines and Symbols

Practice Objectives

- Add detail lines.
- Add symbols.

10 In this practice, you will modify a site plan by adding detail lines to layout the utilities. You will also add symbols for a power pole and north arrow, as shown in Figure 14–55.

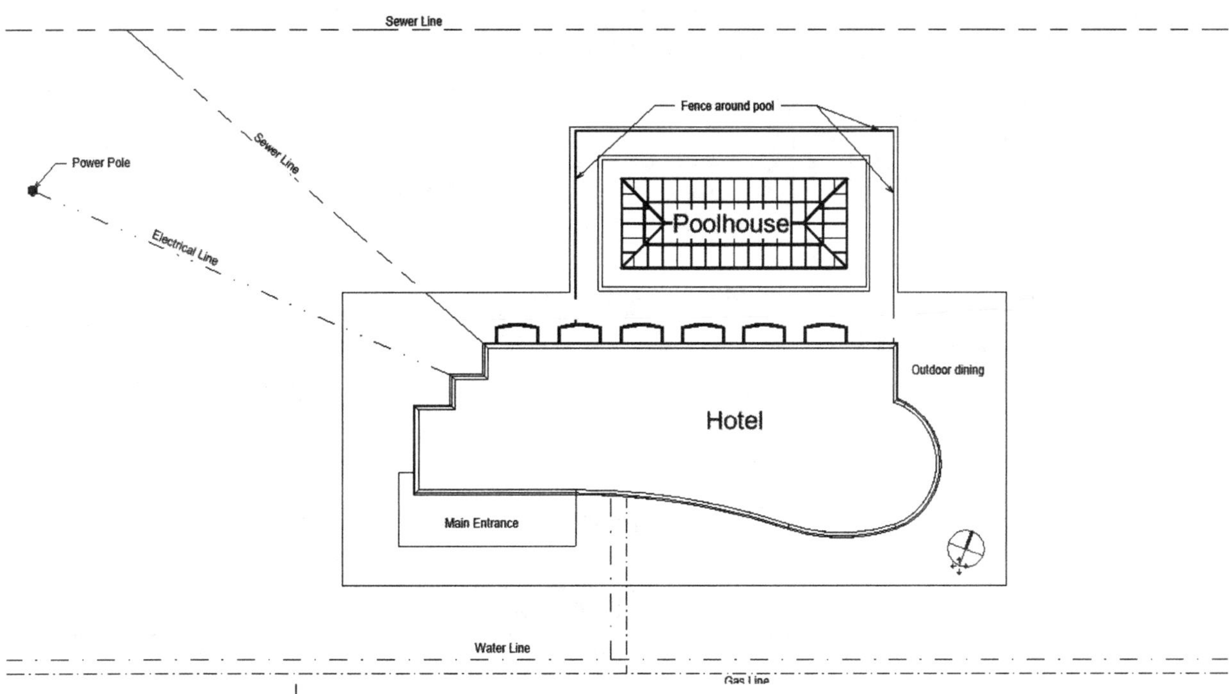

Figure 14–55

Task 1 - Create a Utilities Plan using Detail Lines.

1. Open the project **Modern-Hotel-Symbols.rvt**.
2. Open the **Floor Plans: Site** view.
3. In the *Annotate* tab>Detail panel, click  (Detail Line).
4. In the *Modify | Place Detail Lines* tab>Line Style panel, set the *Line Style:* to **Sewer Line**.
5. In the Options Bar, clear the **Chain** option.
6. Draw a horizontal line above the building, and another diagonal line from that line to the building, as shown in Figure 14–55.

7. Change the *Line Style* and add **Electric Lines, Water Lines,** and **Gas Lines**, as shown in Figure 14–56.

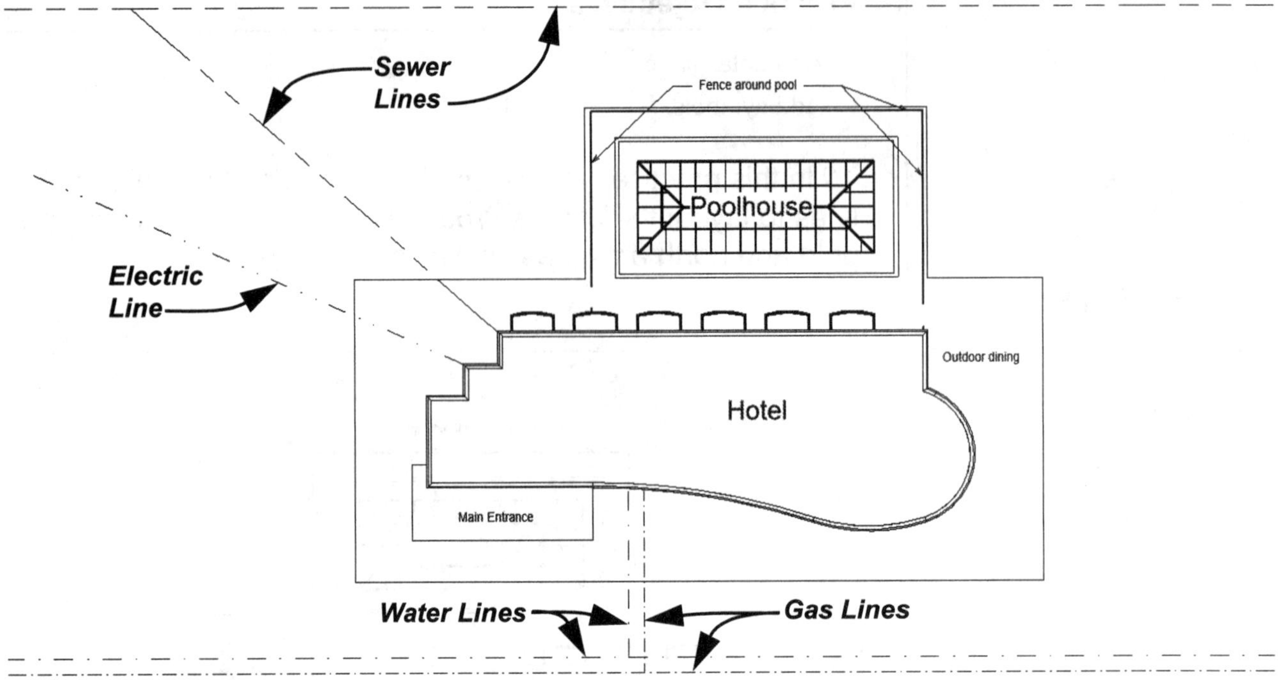

Figure 14–56

8. Add text to label them as needed.
9. Save the project.

Task 2 - Add Symbols

1. In the *Annotate* tab>Symbol panel, click  (Symbol).
2. In the *Modify | Place Symbol* tab>Mode panel, click  (Load Family).
3. In the *Practice Library* folder of your practice files folder, select **Power Pole Symbol.rfa** and click **Open**.

4. Add a power pole at the end of the Electrical Line, as shown in Figure 14–57.

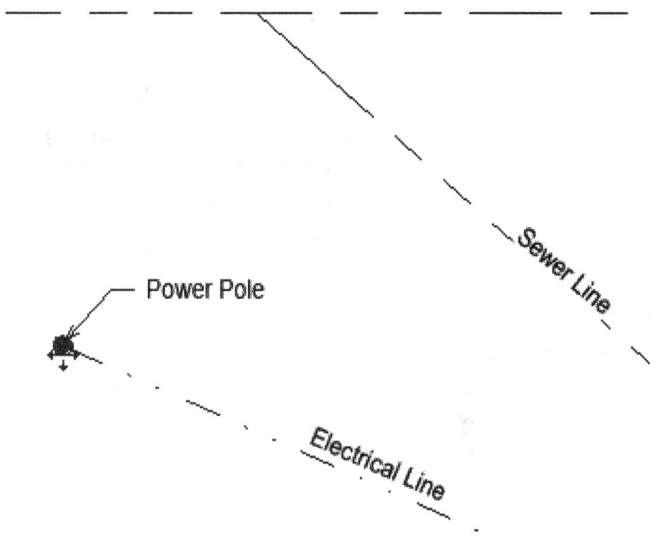

Figure 14–57

5. While still in the **Symbol** command, in the Type Selector, select **North Arrow 2** and place a north arrow below the hotel.

6. Rotate the North Arrow 20°, as shown in Figure 14–58.

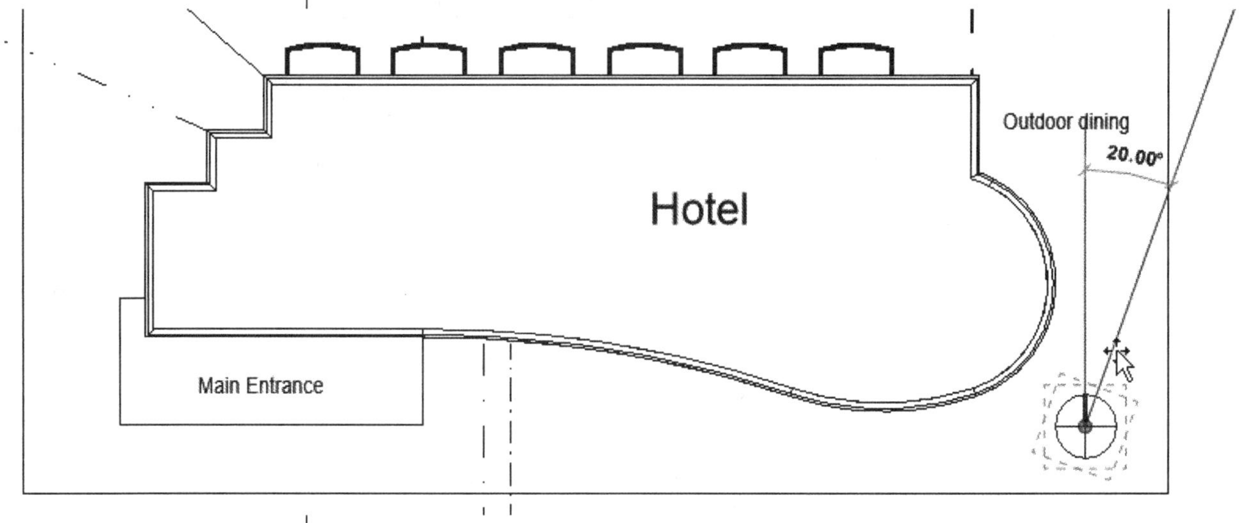

Figure 14–58

7. Save the project.

14.4 Creating Legends

A legend is a separate view that can be placed on multiple sheets. Legends can be used to hold installation notes that need to be placed on a sheet with each floor plan, key plans, or any 2D items that need to be repeated. You can also create and list the symbols that are used in your project, and provide explanatory notes next to the, as shown in Figure 14–59. Additionally, legends can provide a list of materials, or elevations of window types used in the project.

The elements in this figure are inserted using the ***Symbol*** *command rather that the* ***Legend Component*** *or* ***Detail Component*** *commands.*

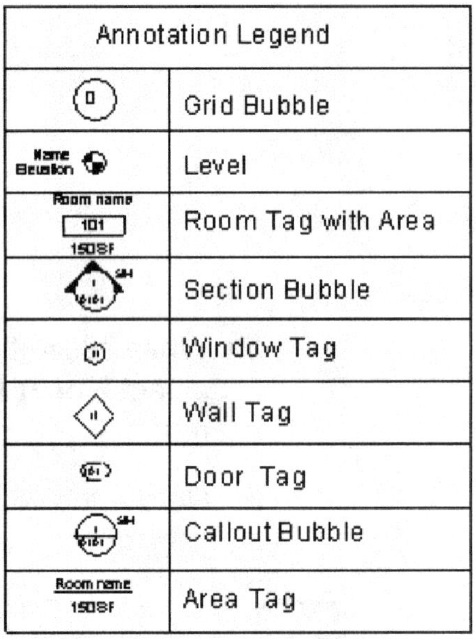

Figure 14–59

- You use (Detail Lines) and (Text) to create the table and explanatory notes. Once you have a legend view, you can use commands, such as (Legend Component), (Detail Component), and (Symbol), to place elements in the view.
- Unlike other views, legend views can be attached to more than one sheet.
- You can set a legend's scale in the View Status Bar.
- Elements in legends can be dimensioned.

How To: Create a Legend

1. In the *View* tab>Create panel, expand (Legends) and click (Legend) or in the Project Browser, right-click on the *Legends* area title and select **New Legend**.
2. In the New Legend View dialog box, enter a name and select a scale for the legend, as shown in Figure 14–60, and click **OK**.

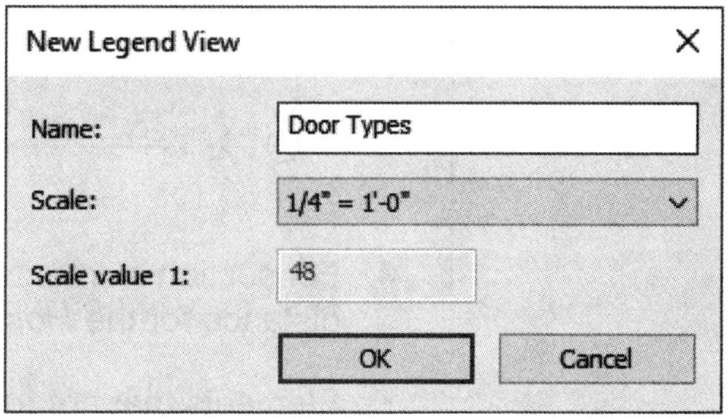

Figure 14–60

3. Place the components in the view first, and then sketch the outline of the table when you know the sizes. Use **Ref Planes** to line up the components.

How To: Use Legend Components

1. In the *Annotate* tab>Detail panel, expand (Component) and click (Legend Component).
2. In the Options Bar, select the *Family* type that you want to use, as shown in Figure 14–61.
   - This list contains all of the elements in a project that can be used in a legend. For example, you might want to display the elevation of all door types used in the project.

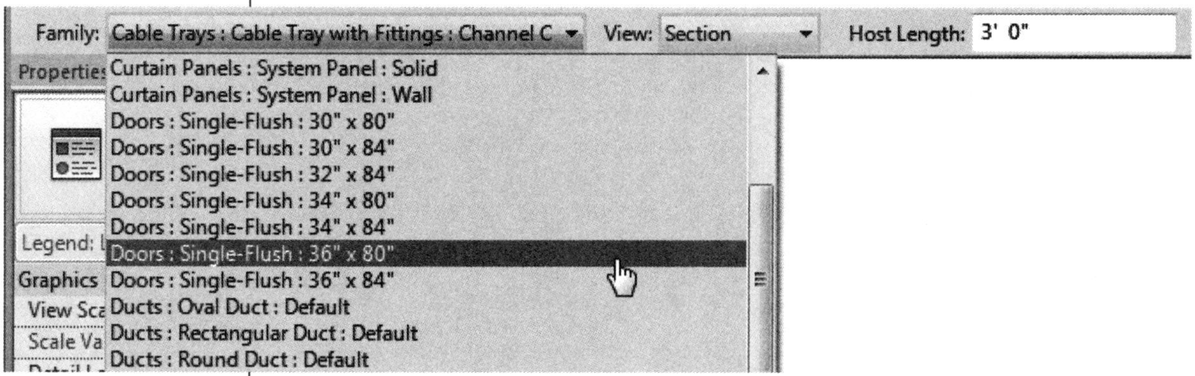

Figure 14–61

3. Select the *View* of the element that you want to use. For example, you might want to display the section of the floors or roofs, and the front elevation of the doors (as shown in Figure 14–62) and windows.

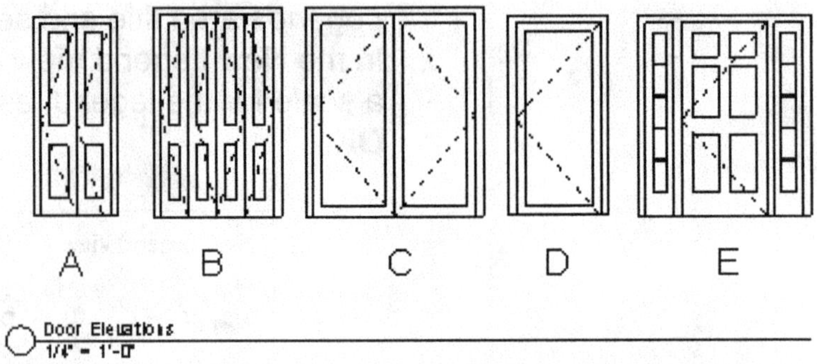

Figure 14–62

4. For section elements (such as walls, floors, and roofs), type a distance for the *Host Length*.

- Elements that are full size, such as planting components or doors, come in at their full size.
- Legends are views that can be placed on multiple sheets. You can use Copy to the Clipboard and Paste to copy legends from sheet to sheet.

Practice 14d Create Legends

Practice Objective

- Create legends using legend components and text.

In this practice, you will create door and window legends (as shown in Figure 14–63), by creating legend views, adding legend components, and labeling the door and window types with text.

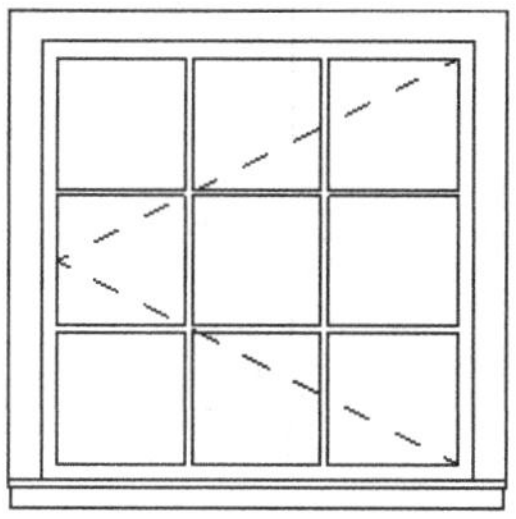

13

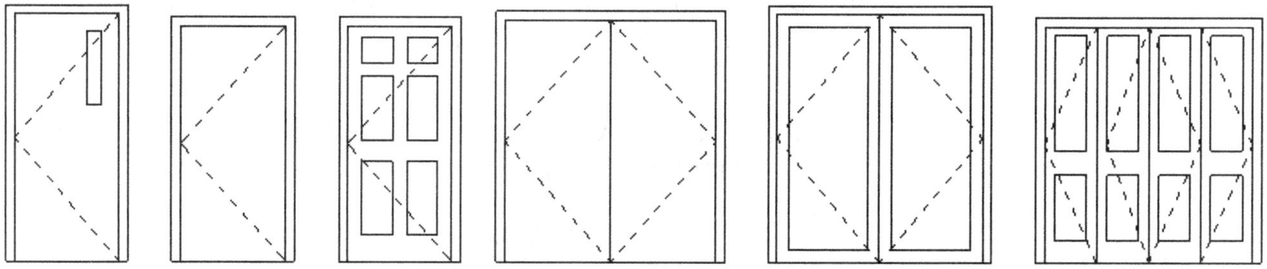

A B C D E F

Figure 14–63

Task 1 - Add window and door legends.

1. Open the project **Modern-Hotel-Legends.rvt**.
2. In the *View* tab>Create panel, expand (Legends) and click (Legend) to create a new legend view.
3. Name it **Window Elevations** and set the *Scale* to **1/4"=1'-0"**.
4. In the *Annotate* tab>Detail panel, expand (Component) and click (Legend Component).

5. In the Options Bar, set *Family* to **Windows : Casement 3 x 3 with Trim: 48" x 48"** and *View* to **Elevation: Front**. Place the component in the view. The window displays, as shown in Figure 14–64.

6. In the *Annotate* tab>Text panel, click (Text).

7. In the Type Selector, select **Text: 1/8" Arial Narrow** and add the window number 13 under the window, as shown in Figure 14–64.

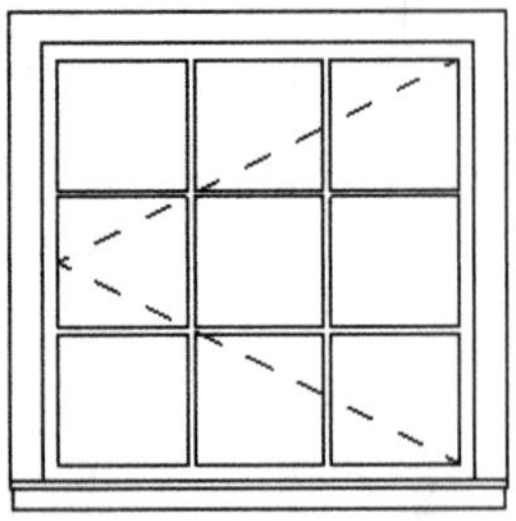

13

Figure 14–64

8. Create another legend view. Name it **Door Elevations** and set the *Scale* to **1/4"=1'-0"**.

9. In the Legend view, click (Legend Component) and add the elevations of the doors used in the project.

10. Label the doors as shown in Figure 14–65.

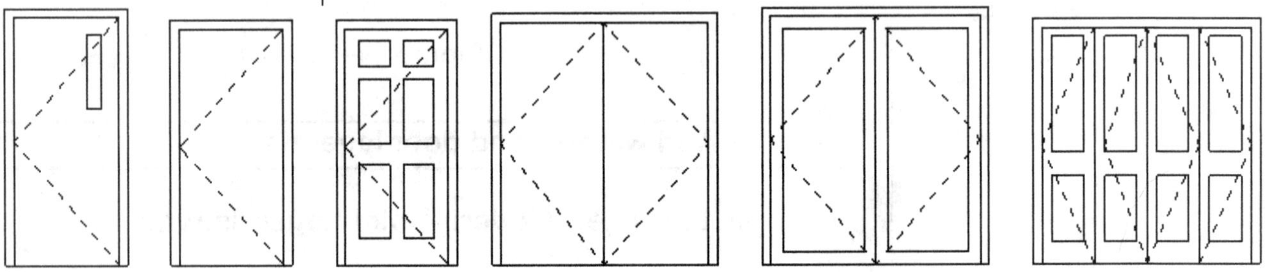

A B C D E F

Figure 14–65

11. Save the project.

Chapter Review Questions

1. When a wall is moved (as shown in Figure 14–66), how do you update the dimension?

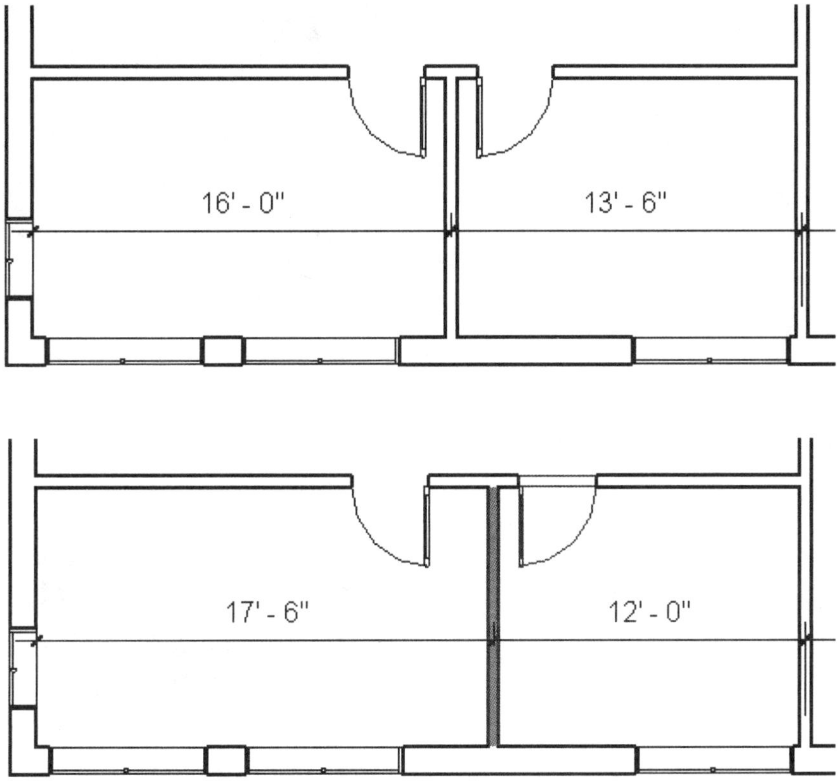

Figure 14–66

   a. Edit the dimension and move it over.
   b. Select the dimension and then click **Update** in the Options Bar.
   c. The dimension automatically updates.
   d. Delete the existing dimension and add a new one.

2. How do you create new text styles?
   a. Using the **Text Styles** command.
   b. Duplicate an existing type.
   c. They must be included in a template.
   d. Using the **Format Styles** command.

3. When you edit text, how many leaders can be added using the leader tools shown in Figure 14–67?

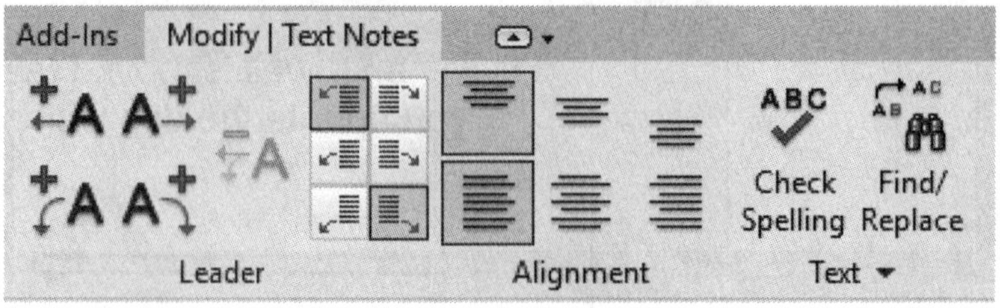

Figure 14–67

   a. One
   b. One on each end of the text.
   c. As many as you want at each end of the text.

4. Detail Lines created in one view also display in the related view.
   a. True
   b. False

5. Which of the following describes the difference between a symbol and a component?
   a. Symbols are 3D and only display in one view. Components are 2D and display in many views.
   b. Symbols are 2D and only display in one view. Components are 3D and display in many views.
   c. Symbols are 2D and display in many views. Components are 3D and only display in one view.
   d. Symbols are 3D and display in many views. Components are 2D and only display in one view.

6. When creating a Legend, which of the following elements cannot be added?
   a. Legend Components
   b. Tags
   c. Rooms
   d. Symbols

Command Summary

Button	Command	Location
Dimensions and Text		
	**Aligned (Dimension)**	• **Ribbon:** *Annotate* tab>Dimension panel or *Modify* tab>Measure panel, expanded drop-down list • **Quick Access Toolbar** • **Shortcut:** DI
	**Angular (Dimension)**	• **Ribbon:** *Annotate* tab>Dimension panel or *Modify* tab>Measure panel, expanded drop-down list
	**Arc Length (Dimension)**	• **Ribbon:** *Annotate* tab>Dimension panel or *Modify* tab>Measure panel, expanded drop-down list
	**Diameter (Dimension)**	• **Ribbon:** *Annotate* tab>Dimension panel or *Modify* tab>Measure panel, expanded drop-down list
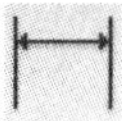	**Linear (Dimension)**	• **Ribbon:** *Annotate* tab>Dimension panel or *Modify* tab>Measure panel, expanded drop-down list
	**Radial (Dimension)**	• **Ribbon:** *Annotate* tab>Dimension panel or *Modify* tab>Measure panel, expanded drop-down list
	**Text**	• **Ribbon:** *Annotate* tab>Text panel • **Shortcut:** TX
Detail Lines and Symbols		
	**Detail Line**	• **Ribbon:** *Annotate* tab>Detail panel • **Shortcut:** DL
	**Stair Path**	• **Ribbon:** *Annotate* tab>Symbol panel
	**Symbol**	• **Ribbon:** *Annotate* tab>Symbol panel
Legends		
	**Legend (View)**	• **Ribbon:** *View* tab>Create panel> expand Legends
	**Legend Component**	• **Ribbon:** *Annotate* tab>Detail panel> expand Component

Adding Tags and Schedules

Adding tags to your views helps you to identify elements such as doors, windows, or walls in the model.Tags are 2D annotation families with labels that extract information about the elements being tagged from its properties. Tags are typically added when you insert an element, but can also be added at any point of the design process. The information captured in the elements in a project is used to populate schedules, which can be added to sheets to complete the construction documents.

Learning Objectives in this Chapter

- Add tags to elements in 2D and 3D views to prepare the views to be placed on sheets.
- Load tags that are required for projects.
- Modify schedule content including the instance and type properties of related elements.
- Add schedules to sheets as part of the construction documents.

15.1 Adding Tags

Tags identify elements that are listed in schedules. Door and window tags are inserted automatically if you use the **Tag on Placement** option when inserting the door or window or other elements. You can also add them later to specific views as required. Many other types of tags are available in the Autodesk® Revit® software, such as wall tags and furniture tags, as shown in Figure 15–1.

Additional tags are stored in the Library in the Annotations folder.

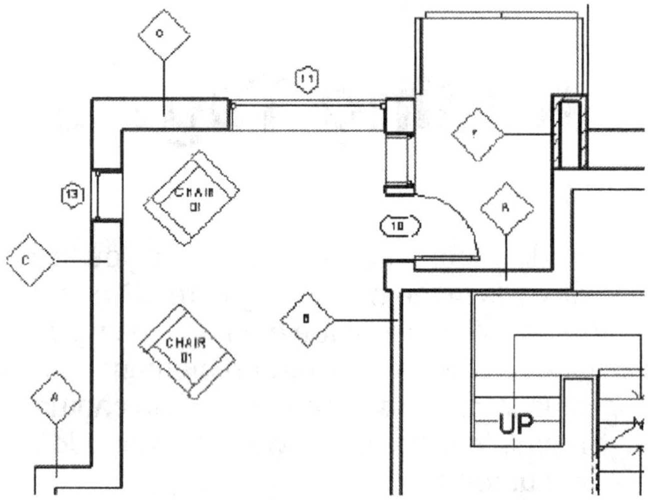

Figure 15–1

- The **Tag by Category** command works for most elements, except for a few that have separate commands.
- Tags can be letters, numbers, or a combination of the two.

You can place three types of tags, as follows:

- (Tag by Category): Tags according to the category of the element. It places door tags on doors and wall tags on walls.
- (Multi-Category): Tags elements belonging to multiple categories. The tags display information from parameters that they have in common.
- (Material): Tags that display the type of material. They are typically used in detailing.

How To: Add Tags

1. In the *Annotate* tab>Tag panel, click (Tag by Category), (Multi-Category), or (Material Tag) depending on the type of tag you want to place.

2. In the Options Bar, set the options as required, as shown in Figure 15–2.

Figure 15–2

3. Select the element you want to tag. If a tag for the selected element is not loaded, you are prompted to load it from the Library.

Tag Options

- You can set tag options for leaders and tag rotation, as shown in Figure 15–3. You can also press <Spacebar> to toggle the orientation while placing or modifying the tag.

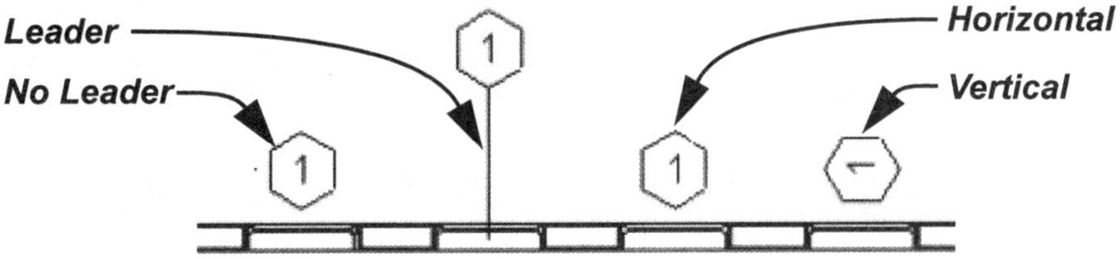

Figure 15–3

- Leaders can have an **Attached End** or a **Free End**, as shown in Figure 15–4. The attached end must be connected to the element being tagged. A free end has an additional drag control where the leader touches the element.

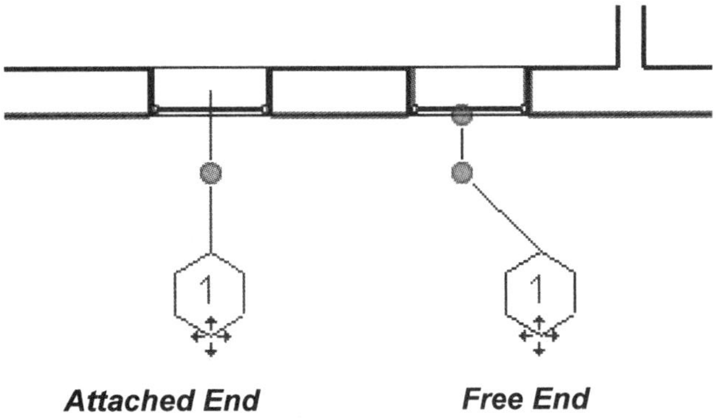

Figure 15–4

- If you change between **Attached End** and **Free End**, the tag does not move and the leader does not change location.

- The **Length** option specifies the length of the leader in plotting units. It is grayed out if **Leader** is not selected or if a **Free End** leader is defined.

- If a tag is not loaded a warning box opens as shown in Figure 15–5. Click **Yes** to open the Load Family dialog box in which you can select the appropriate tag.

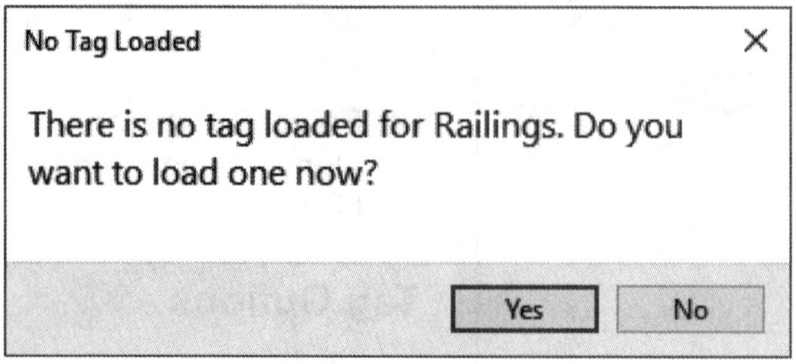

Figure 15–5

- Tags can be pinned to they stay in place if you move the element that is tagged. This is primarily used when tags have leaders, as shown in Figure 15–6.

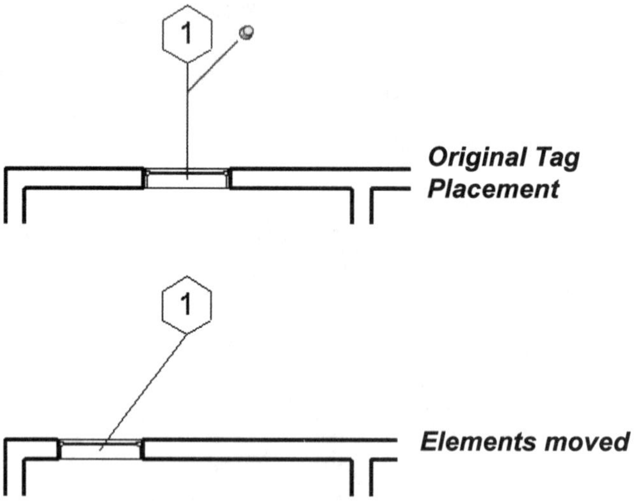

Figure 15–6

Room Tags

If tags were not added to room when they were created or wish to add room tags to another view, you must to use a specific command. In the *Architecture* tab>Room & Area panel, click

 (Tag Room) or in the *Annotate* tab>Tag panel, click

 (Room Tag) or type **RT**.

- You can change the name or number by clicking on the tag text to edit it, as shown in Figure 15–7.

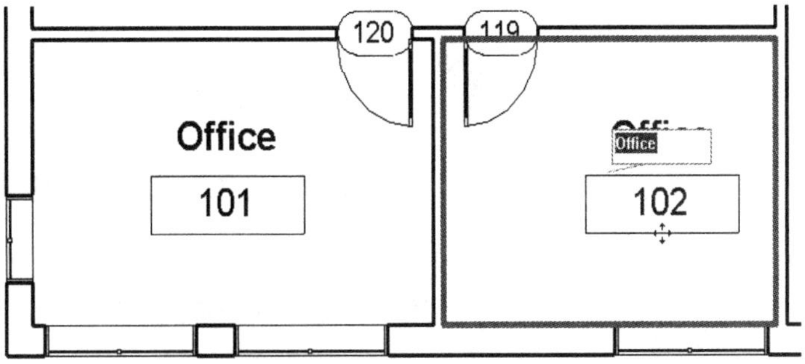

Figure 15–7

How To: Add Multiple Tags

1. In the *Annotate* tab>Tag panel, click (Tag All).
2. In the Tag All Not Tagged dialog box (shown in Figure 15–8), select the checkbox beside one or more categories to tag. Selecting the checkbox beside the Category title selects all of the tags.

To tag only some elements, select them before starting this command. In the Tag All Not Tagged dialog box, select ***Only selected objects in current view****.*

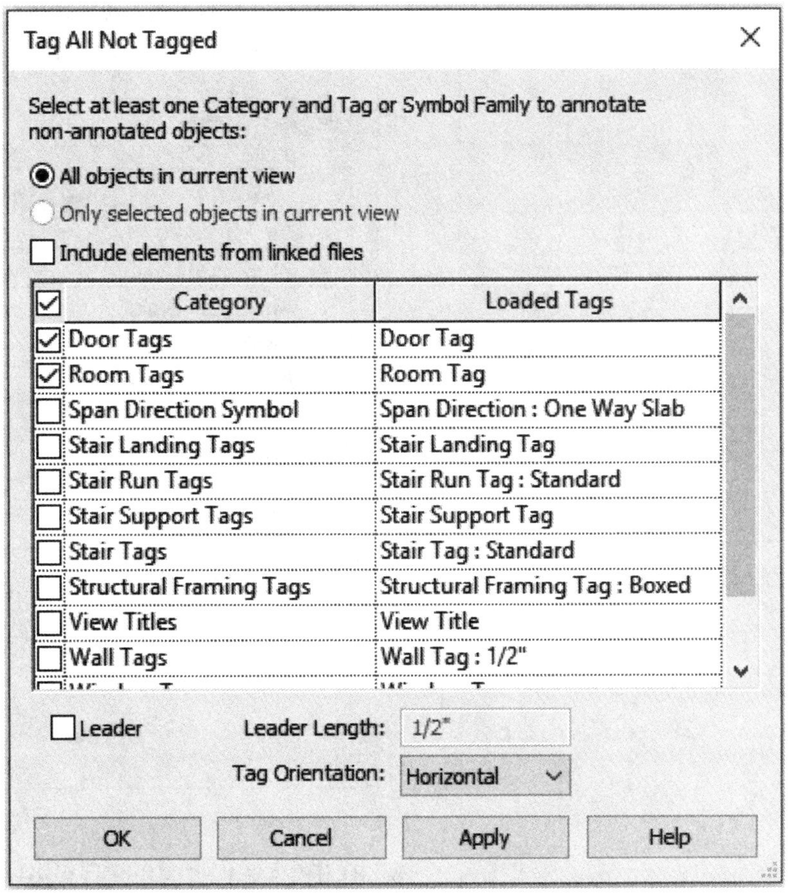

Figure 15–8

3. Set the *Leader* and *Tag Orientation* as required.
4. Click **Apply** to apply the tags and stay in the dialog box. Click **OK** to apply the tags and close the dialog box.

- When you select a tag, the properties of that tag display. To display the properties of the tagged element, in the *Modify* | *<contextual>* tab>Host panel, click (Select Host).
- Rooms can be tagged using **Tag all Not Tagged**.

How To: Load Tags

1. In the *Annotate* tab, expand the Tag panel and click (Loaded Tags And Symbols) or, when a Tag command is active, in the Options Bar click **Tags...**
2. In the Loaded Tags And Symbols dialog box (shown in Figure 15–9), click **Load Family...**.

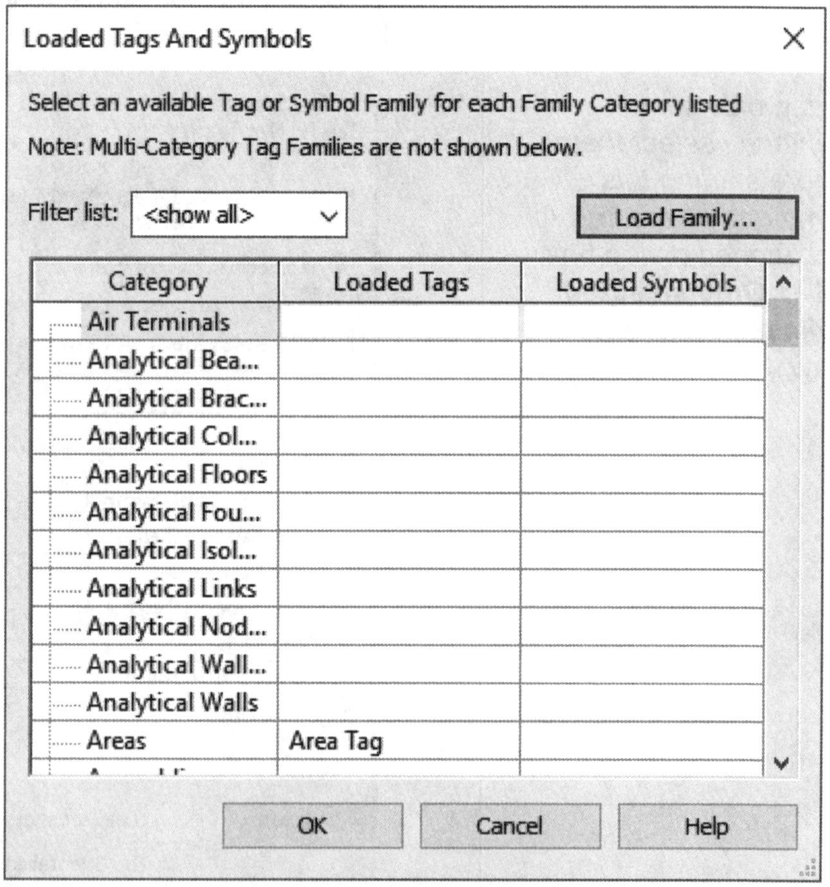

Figure 15–9

3. In the Load Family dialog box, navigate to the appropriate *Annotations* folder, select the tag(s) required and click **Open**.
4. The tag is added to the category in the dialog box. Click **OK**.

Instance vs.Type Based Tags

Doors are tagged in a numbered sequence, with each instance of the door having a separate tag number. Other elements (such as windows and walls) are tagged by type, as shown in Figure 15–10. Changing the information in one tag changes all instances of that element.

*An additional window tag (**Window Tag-Number.rfa**) is stored in the Annotations> Architectural folder in the Library. It tags windows using sequential numbers.*

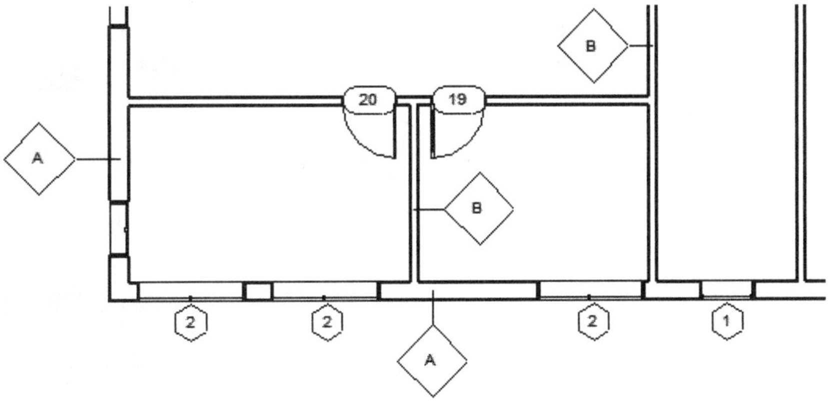

Figure 15–10

- To modify the number of an instance tag (such as a door or room), double-click directly on the number in the tag and modify it, or, you can modify the *Mark* property, as shown in Figure 15–11. Only that one instance updates.

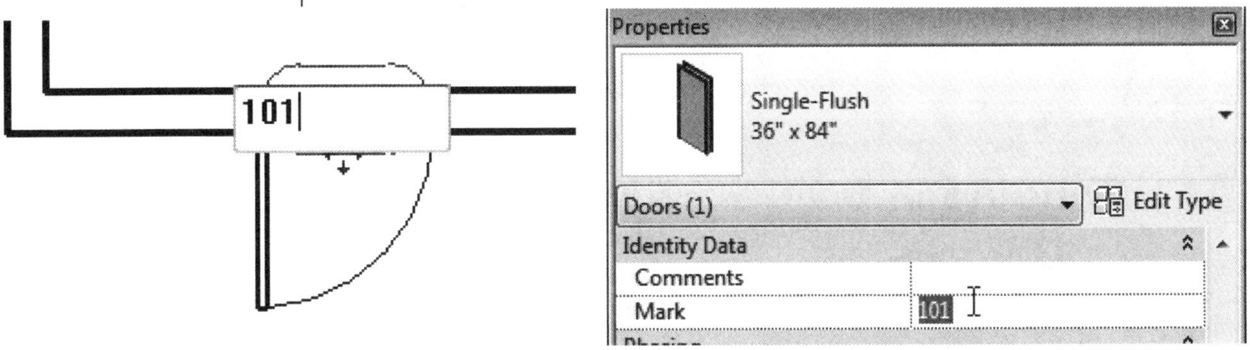

Figure 15–11

- To modify the number of a type tag, you can either double-click directly on the number in the tag and modify it, or select the element and, in Properties, click (Edit Type). In the Type Properties dialog box, in the *Identity Data* area, modify the *Type Mark*, as shown in Figure 15–12. All instances of this element then update.

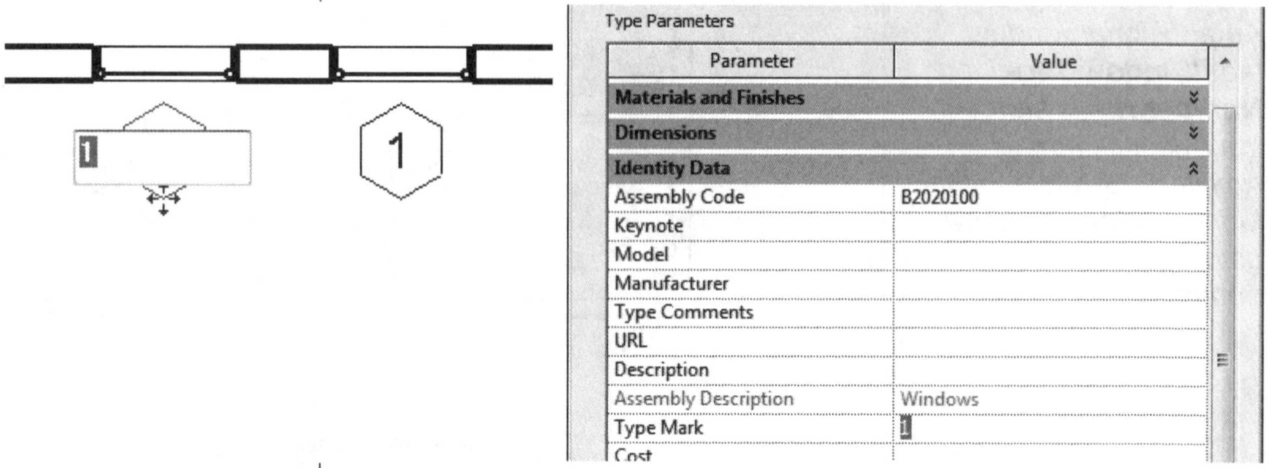

Figure 15–12

- When you change a type tag, an alert box opens to warn you that changing a type parameter affects other elements. If you want this tag to modify all other elements of this type, click **Yes**.

- If a type tag displays with a question mark, it means that no Type Mark has been assigned yet.

Tagging in 3D Views

You can add tags to isometric 3D views, as shown in Figure 15–13, as long as the views are locked first.

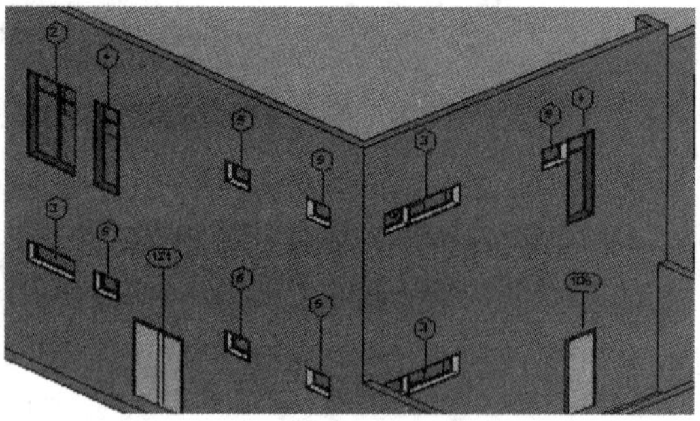

Figure 15–13

- Dimensions can be added to isometric 3D views whether they are locked or not. Proceed with caution when selecting the items to dimension to ensure that the witness lines and text orient as intended.

- Locked views can be used with perspective views. This enables you to create the view as you want it and then save it from being modified.

How To: Lock a 3D View

1. Open a 3D view and set it up as you want it to display.
2. In the View Control Bar, expand (Unlocked 3D View) and click (Save Orientation and Lock View).

- If you are using the default 3D view and it has not been saved, you are prompted to name and save the view first.
- You can modify the orientation of the view, expand (Locked 3D View) and click (Unlock View). This also removes any tags you have applied.
- To return to the previous locked view, expand (Unlocked 3D View) and click (Restore Orientation and Lock View).

Hint: Stair and Railing Tags

Tag by Category can be used to tag the overall stair, stair runs, landings, and railings, as shown in Figure 15–14. An additional type of tag, **Stair Tread/Riser Number**, creates a sequence of numbers for each tread or riser.

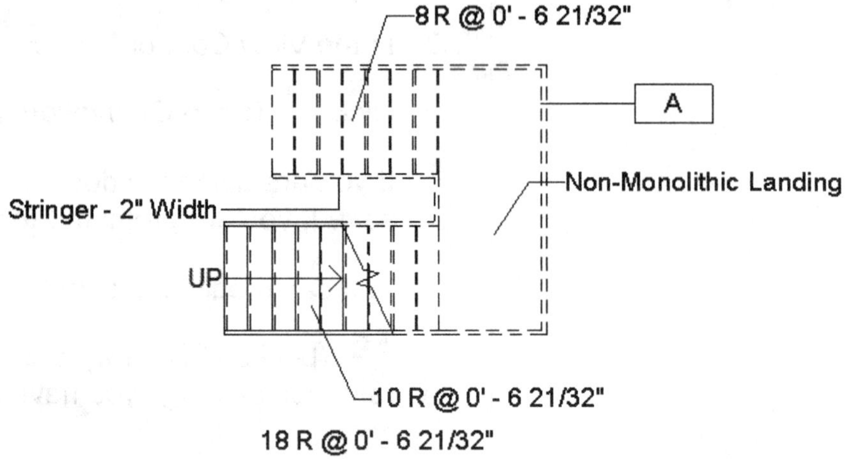

Figure 15–14

How To: Add Tread/Riser Number Tags to Stairs

1. Open a plan, elevation, or section view.
2. In the *Annotate* tab>Tag panel, click (Stair Tread/Riser Number).
3. In Properties setup the *Tag Type*, *Display Rule* and other parameters. These remain active for the project.
4. Select a reference line of a stair to place the numbers, as shown in Figure 15–15.

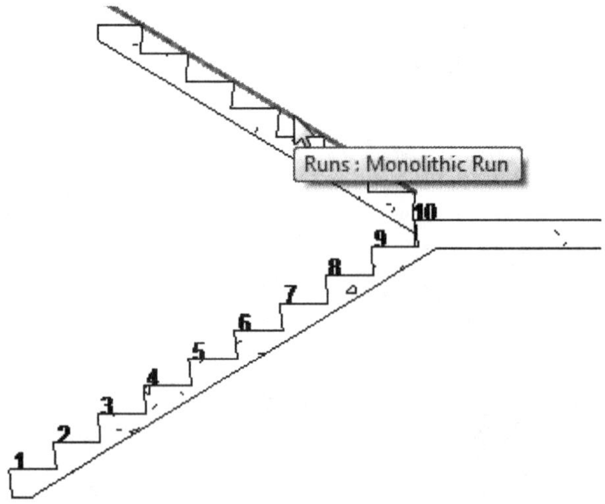

Figure 15–15

5. Continue selecting runs as required.

Practice 15a Add Tags

Practice Objectives

- Add tags to a model.
- Use the Tag All Not Tagged dialog box.
- Set the Type Mark parameter for tags.
- Add Room Tags.

In this practice, you will add wall tags in a floor plan and modify the Type Mark numbers for the walls. You will also tag all of the walls using the Tag All Not Tagged dialog box (as shown in Figure 15–16), and tag the room elements in a separate view.

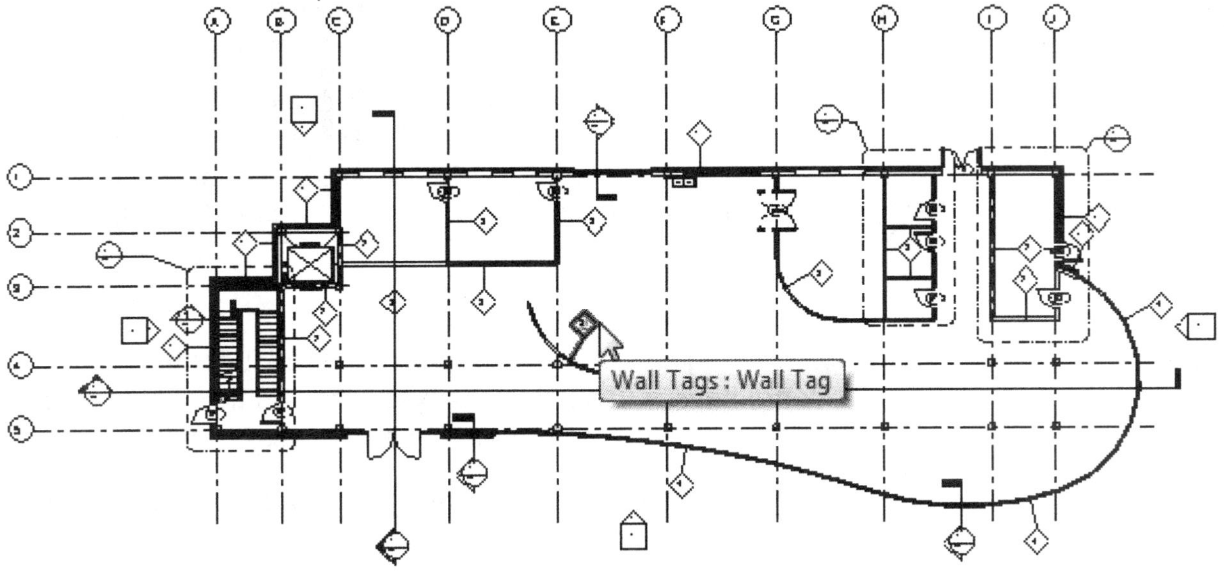

Figure 15–16

Task 1 - Add tags to a floor plan.

1. Open the project **Modern-Hotel-Tags.rvt**.

2. Open the **Floor Plans: Floor 1** view, zoom into the elevator and stair area near the left side of the building.

3. In the *Annotate* tab>Tag panel, click (Tag by Category). In the Options Bar, select **Leader** and verify that **Attached End** is selected.

4. Select the exterior wall, as shown in Figure 15–17.

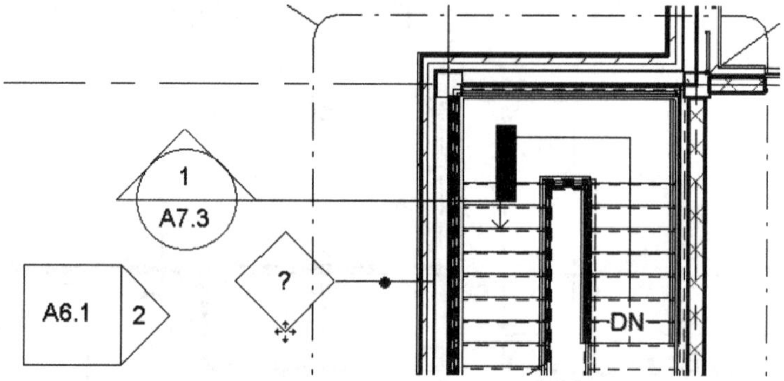

Figure 15–17

5. The tag comes in with a question mark because the wall does not have a *Type Mark* set yet. Click on the **?** in the tag and change the tag number to **1** and press <Enter>.

6. When alerted that you are changing a type parameter, click **Yes** to continue.

7. You are still in the **Tag** command. Add a tag to another exterior wall. This time, the tag number 1 comes in automatically as it is the same wall type as the first one.

8. Click (Modify).

9. Select the masonry wall dividing the stairs from the lobby.

10. In Properties, click (Edit Type).

11. In the Type Properties dialog box, in *Identity Data* area, set *Type Mark* to **2**, as shown in Figure 15–18. Click **OK**.

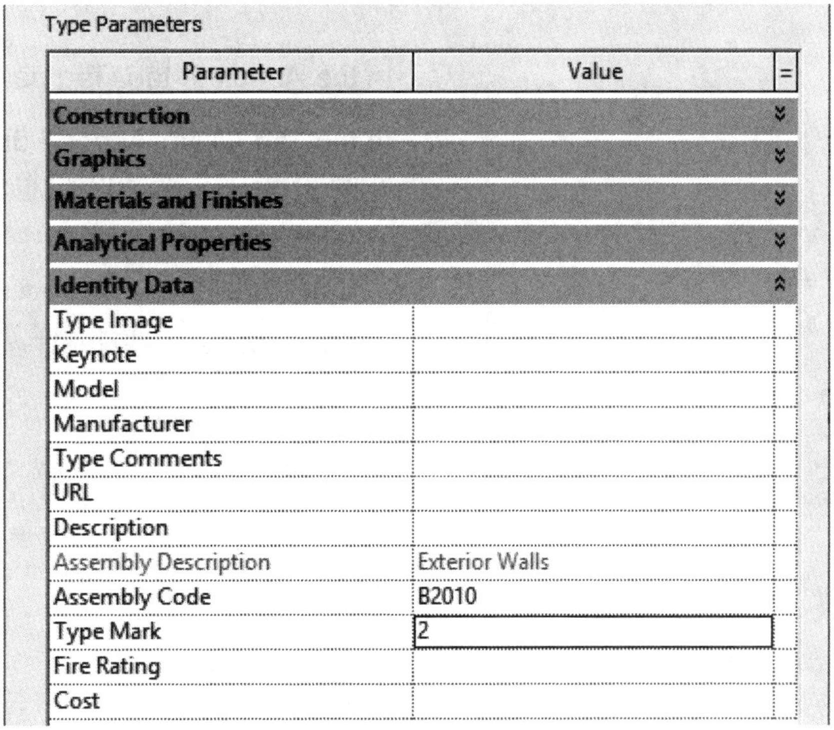

Figure 15–18

12. Select one of the interior partitions and set the *Type Mark* to **3**.

13. Use  (Tag By Category) to tag one of each of the wall types. The Type Mark displays as set in the Type Properties.

14. Zoom out to display the entire floor plan.

15. Save the project.

Task 2 - Tag all the rest of the walls and modify tag locations.

1. In the *Annotate* tab>Tag panel, click  (Tag All).
2. In the Tag All Not Tagged dialog box, select **Wall Tags** and select **Leader**, as shown in Figure 15–19.

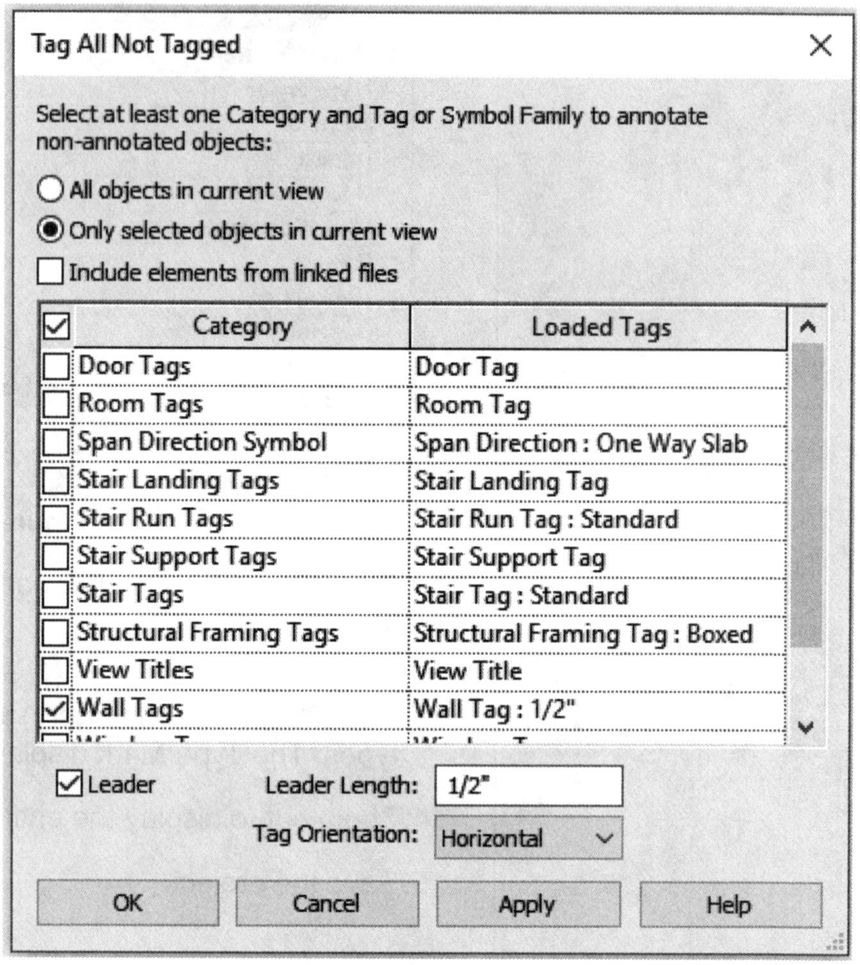

Figure 15–19

3. Click **OK** to add wall tags where they have not already been added.

4. Many of the tags overlap other annotation objects. Use the controls to move the tags and/or leaders to a more visible location, as shown in Figure 15–20.

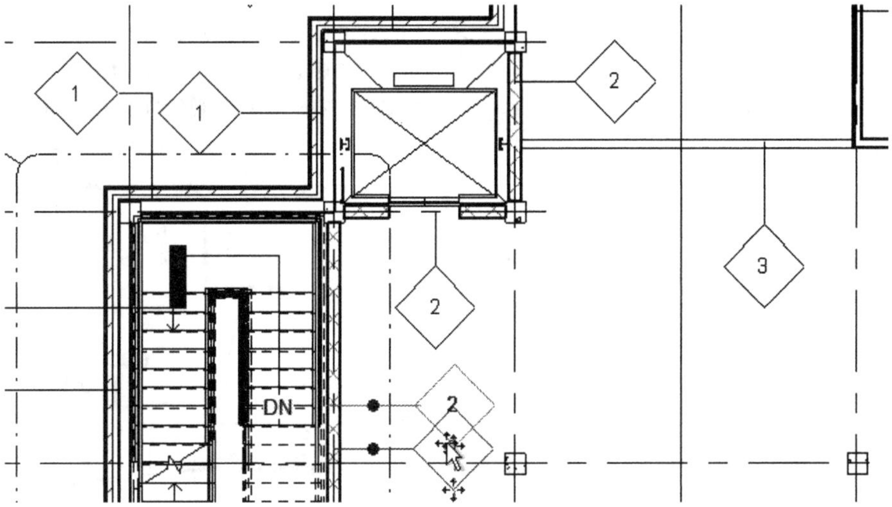

Figure 15–20

- Update the tag for the main curtain wall to type number **4**.
- If you want to have one tag pointing to two different walls, move the tag over top of another tag until they blend together, as shown in Figure 15–21. Then, modify the leader as required.

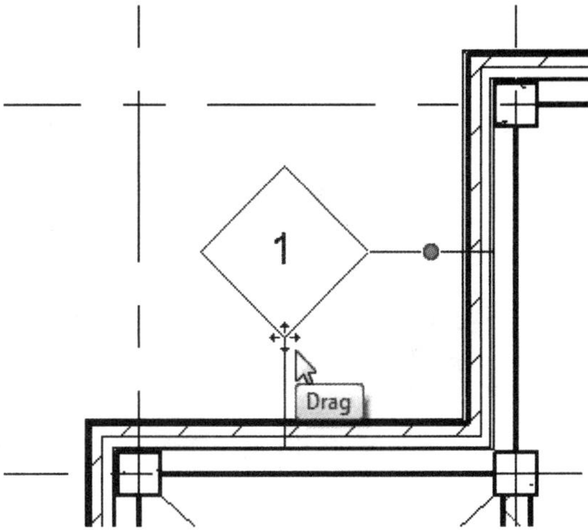

Figure 15–21

- Delete the wall tags that identify the storefront (inset) curtain walls along the back of the building and at the entrance.
- Delete any other wall tags you do not need to fully annotate the floor plan.

5. Save the project.

Task 3 - Add Room Tags.

1. Open the **Floor Plans: Floor 1 - Furniture Plan** view.
2. Hover the cursor over the open area inside the front door until you see the room element, as shown in Figure 15–22. The room elements do not display in this view but are available.

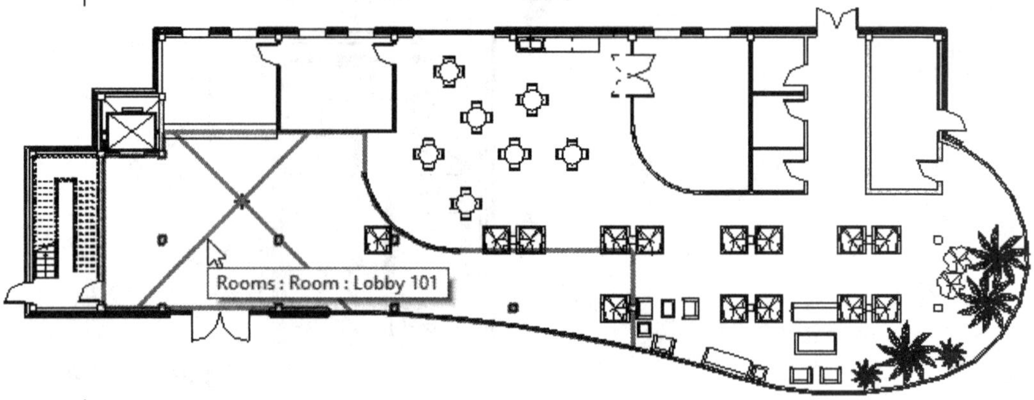

Figure 15–22

3. In the *Annotate* tab>Tab panel, click (Tag by Category). Note that you cannot select the room elements.
4. In the *Annotate* tab>Tag panel, click (Tag Room). The room elements display. Place tags in one or two rooms, as shown in Figure 15–23.

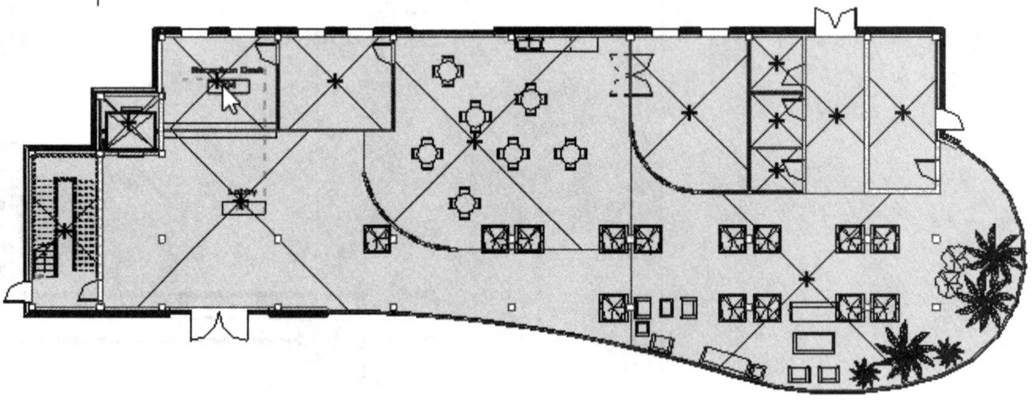

Figure 15–23

5. Click **Modify**.
6. In the *Annotate* tab>Tag panel, click (Tag All).
7. In the Tag All Not Tagged dialog box, select **Room Tags: Room Tag** and click **OK**. Room tags are added to all of the rooms in the view.

8. Zoom in on the stair on the left and move the tag outside the wall. It is no longer connected to the room element, as shown in Figure 15–24.

9. Read the warning information and click **OK** to close the dialog box.

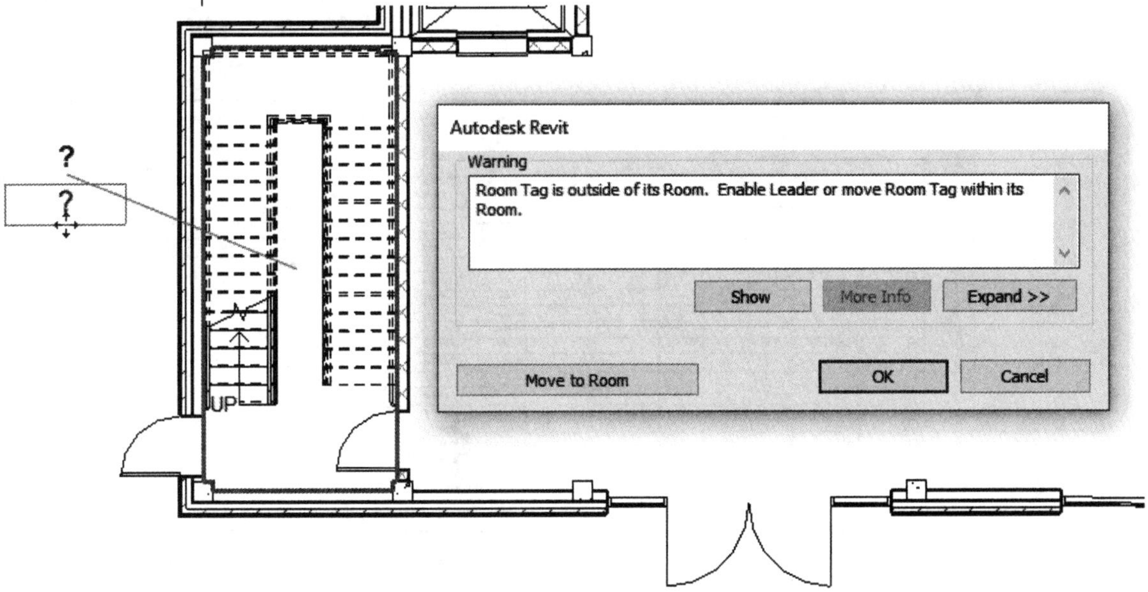

Figure 15–24

10. The tag is still selected, in the Options Bar select **Leader**. The room tag is now connected to the room element and displays the information as shown in Figure 15–25.

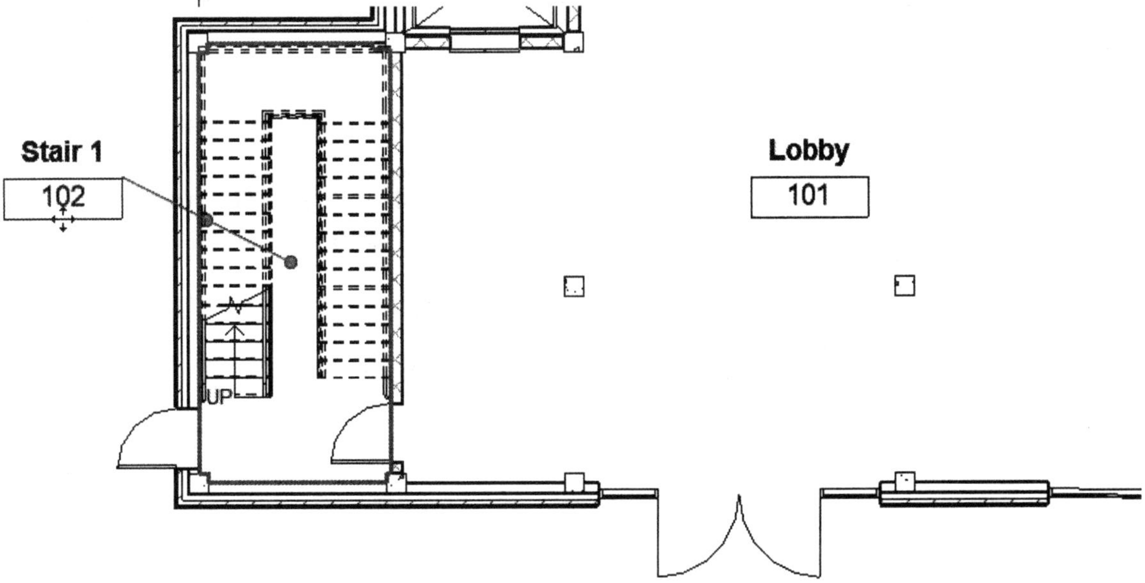

Figure 15–25

11. Save the project.

15.2 Working with Schedules

Schedules extract information from a project and display it in table form. Each schedule is stored as a separate view and can be placed on sheets, as shown in Figure 15–26. Any changes you make to the project elements that affect the schedules are automatically updated in both views and sheets.

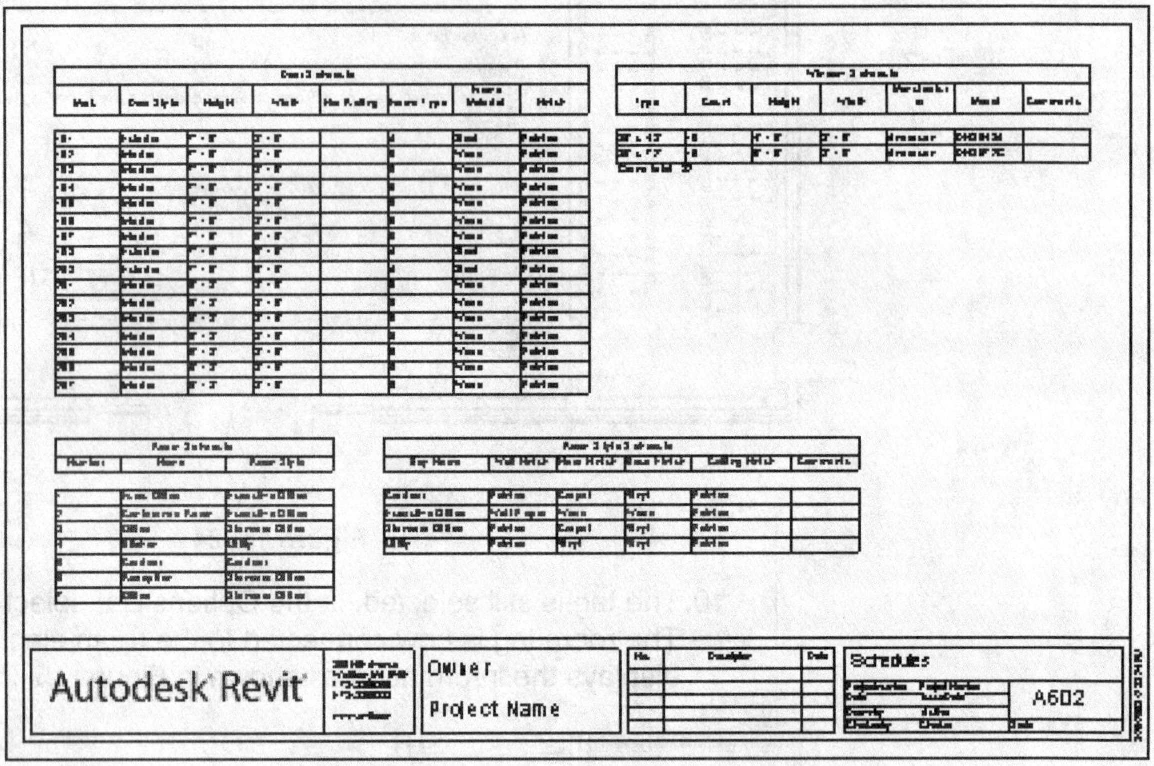

Figure 15–26

- The Architectural Template (**Default.rte**) does not include any schedules. The **Construction-Default.rte**, **Residential-Default.rte**, and **Commercial-Default.rte** template files do include useful schedules.

How To: Work with Schedules

1. In the Project Browser, expand the *Schedules/Quantities* area, as shown in Figure 15–27, and double-click on the schedule you want to open.

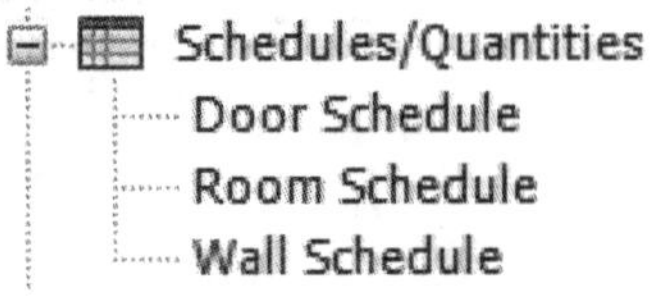

Figure 15–27

2. Schedules are automatically filled out with the information stored in the instance and type parameters of related elements that are added to the model.
3. Fill out additional information in either the schedule or Properties.
4. Drag and drop the schedule onto a sheet.

- You can zoom in to read small text in schedule views. Hold down the <Ctrl> key and scroll using the mouse wheel or press **<Ctrl> <+>** to zoom in or **<Ctrl> <->** to zoom out.

Modifying Schedules

Information in schedules is bi-directional:

- Make changes to elements and the schedule automatically updates.

- Make changes to information in the schedule cells and the elements automatically update.

How To: Modify Schedule Cells

If you change a Type Property in the schedule, it applies to all elements of that type. If you change an Instance Property, it only applies to that one element.

1. Open the schedule view.
2. Select the cell you want to change. Some cells have drop-down lists, as shown in Figure 15–28. Others have edit fields.

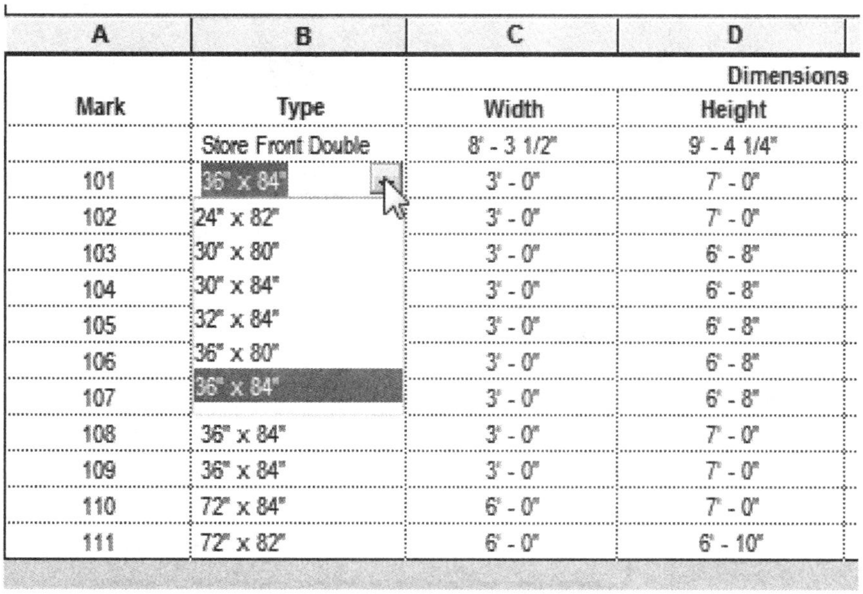

Figure 15–28

3. Add the new information. The change is reflected in the schedule, on the sheet, and in the elements of the project.

- If you change a Type Property, an alert box opens, as shown in Figure 15–29.

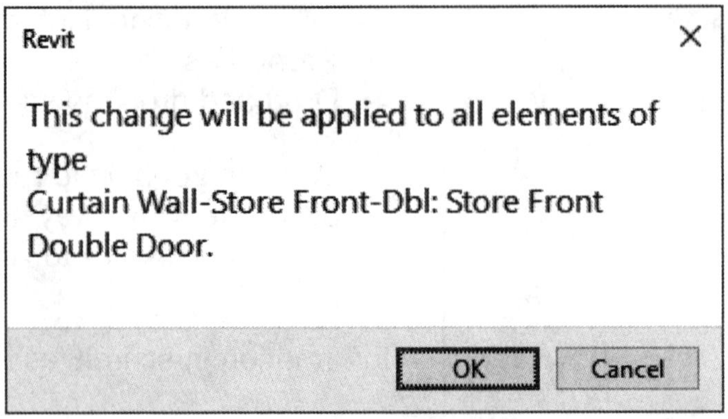

Figure 15–29

- When you select an element in a schedule, in the *Modify Schedule/Quantities* tab>Element panel, you can click  (Highlight in Model). This opens a close-up view of the element with the Show Element(s) in View dialog box, as shown in Figure 15–30. Click **Show** to display more views of the element. Click **Close** to finish the command.

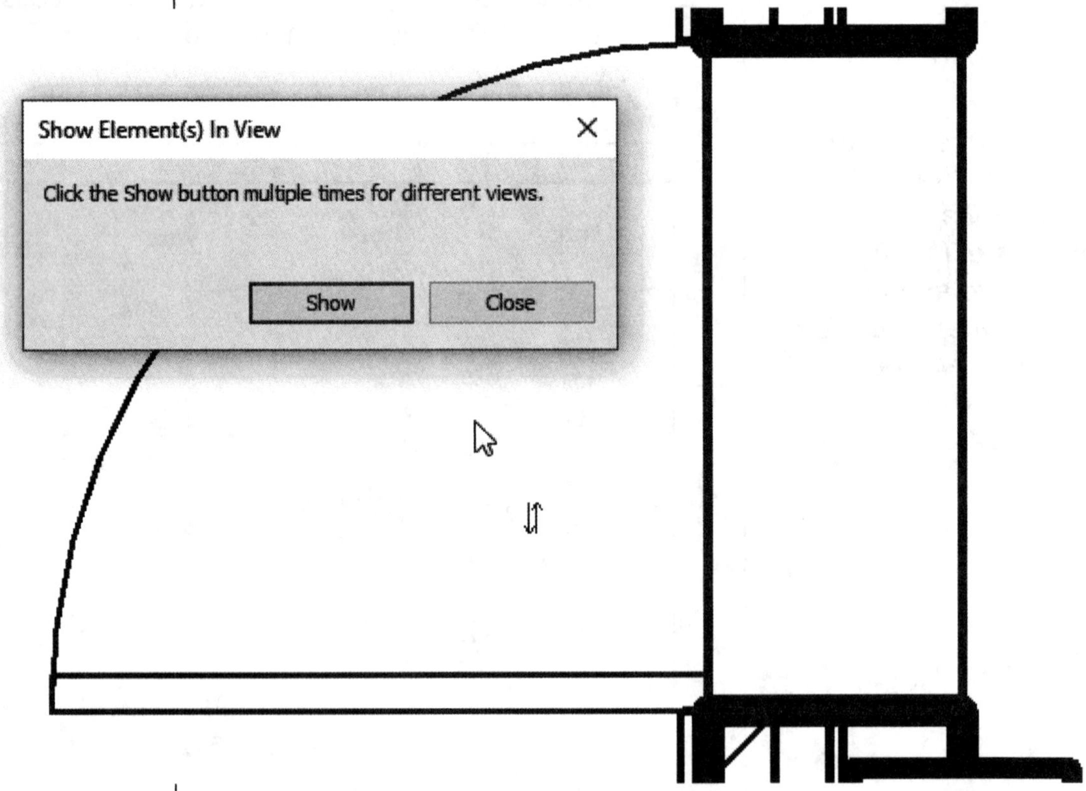

Figure 15–30

Hint: Customizing Schedules

Schedules are typically included in project templates, which are setup by the BIM Manager or other advanced users. They can be complex to create as there are many options.

- For information about creating basic schedules, see *Appendix B.12 Creating Building Component Schedules*.
- For information on using schedules data outside of Autodesk Revit see, *Appendix B.11 Importing and Exporting Schedules*.
- For more information about creating schedules, refer to the ASCENT guide *Autodesk Revit: BIM Management: Template and Family Creation*.

Modifying a Schedule on a Sheet

Once you have placed a schedule on a sheet, you can manipulate it to fit the information into the available space. Select the schedule to display the controls that enable you to modify it, as shown in Figure 15–31.

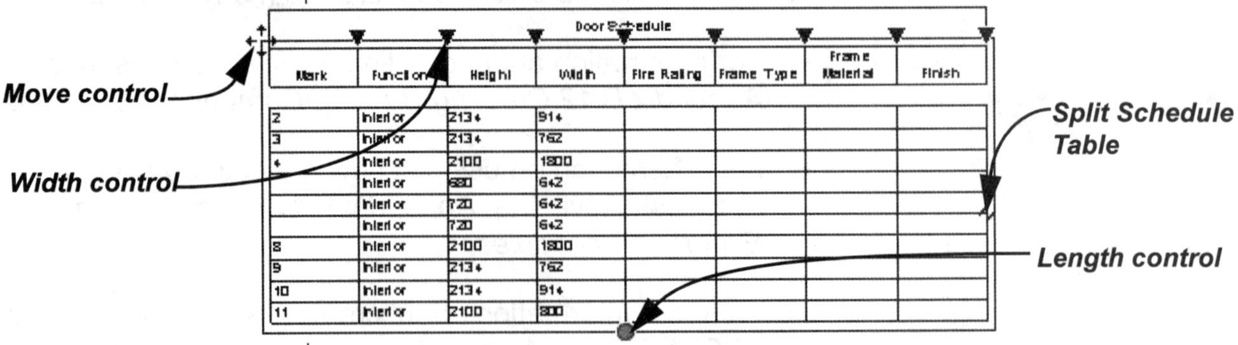

Figure 15–31

- The blue triangles modify the width of each column.
- The break mark splits the schedule into two parts.
- In a split schedule, you can use the arrows in the upper left corner to move that portion of the schedule table. The control at the bottom of the first table changes the length of the table and impacts any connected splits, as shown in Figure 15–32.

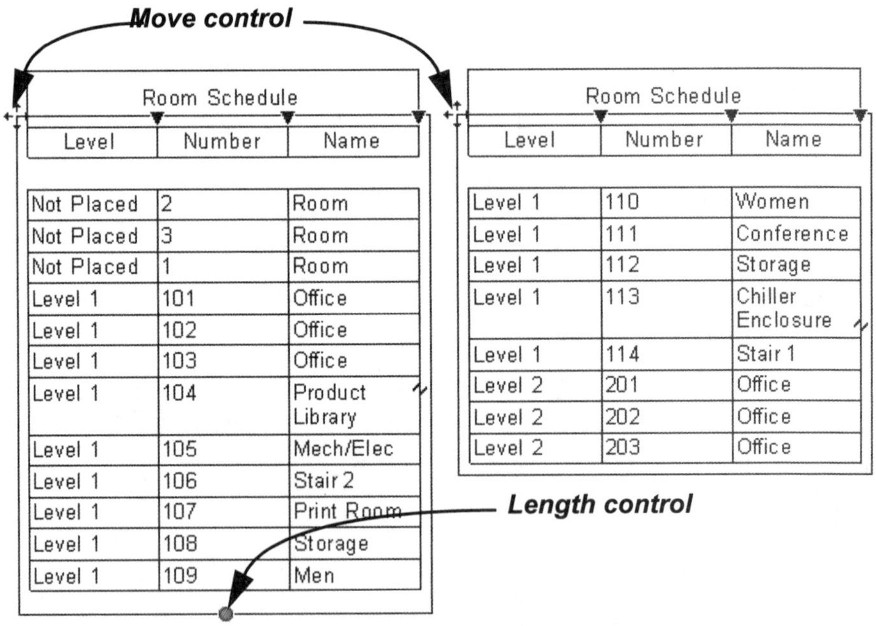

Figure 15–32

- To unsplit a schedule, drag the Move control from the side of the schedule that you want to unsplit back to the original column.

Practice 15b Work with Schedules

Practice Objectives

- Update schedule information.
- Add a schedule to a sheet.

In this practice, you will add information to a door schedule and to elements that are connected to the schedule. You will then place the schedule on a sheet, as shown in Figure 15–33.

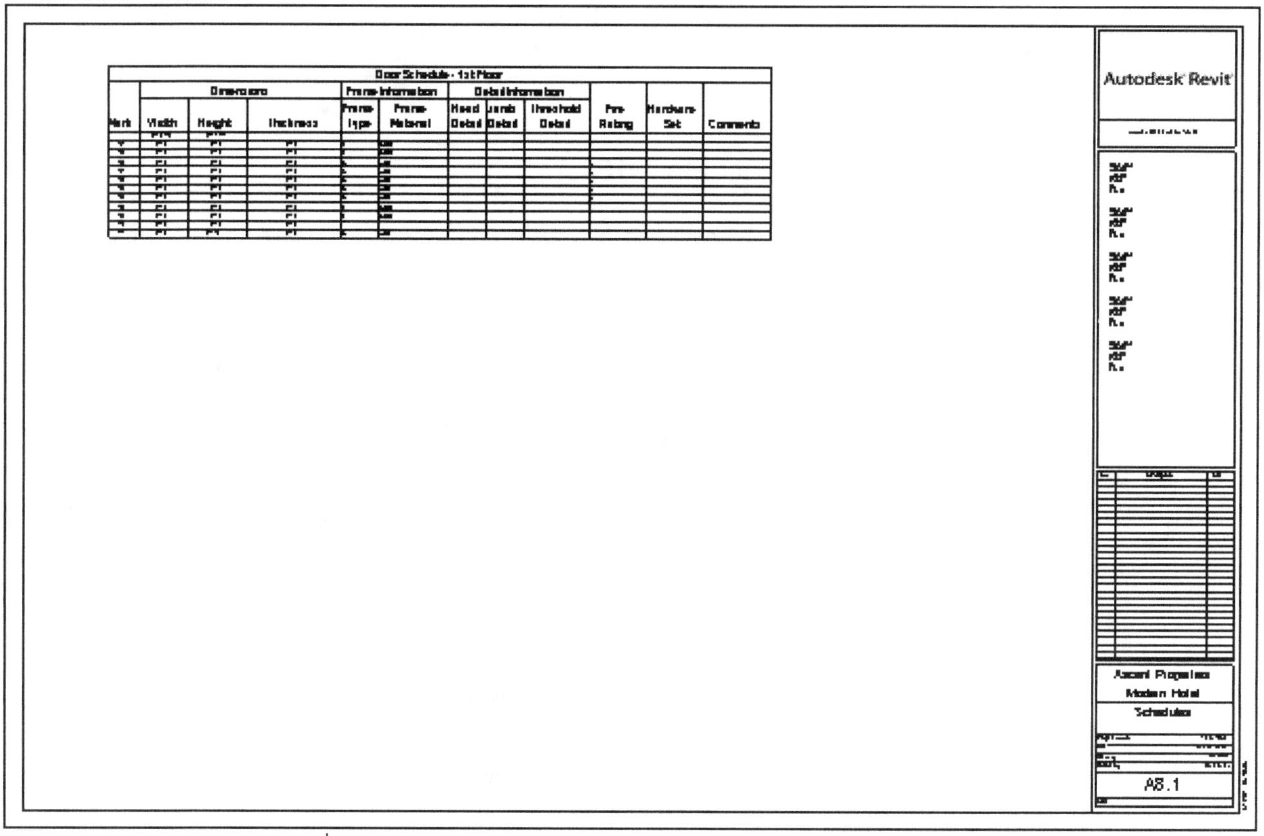

Figure 15–33

Task 1 - Fill in schedules.

1. Open the project **Modern-Hotel-Schedules.rvt**.
2. Open the **Floor Plans: Floor 1** view.
3. In the Project Browser, expand *Schedules/Quantities*. Four schedules have been added to this project.

4. Double-click on **Door Schedule - 1st Floor** to open it. The existing doors in the project are already populated with some of the basic information included with the door, as shown in Figure 15–34.

<Door Schedule - 1st Floor>

A	B	C	D	E	F	G	H	I	J
	Dimensions			Frame Information		Detail Information			
Mark	Width	Height	Thickness	Frame Type	Frame Material	Head Detail	Jamb Detail	Threshold Detail	Fire Rating
101	3' - 0"	7' - 0"	0' - 2"						A
102	3' - 0"	7' - 0"	0' - 2"						A
103	3' - 0"	6' - 8"	0' - 2"						B
104	3' - 0"	6' - 8"	0' - 2"						B
105	3' - 0"	6' - 8"	0' - 2"						B
106	3' - 0"	6' - 8"	0' - 2"						B
107	3' - 0"	6' - 8"	0' - 2"						B
108	3' - 0"	7' - 0"	0' - 2"						A
109	3' - 0"	7' - 0"	0' - 2"						A
110	6' - 0"	7' - 0"	0' - 2"						D
111	6' - 0"	6' - 6"	0' - 2"						

Figure 15–34

5. Select Mark **101**.

6. In the *Modify Schedules/Quantities* tab>Element panel, click (Highlight in Model).

7. In the Show Element(s) In View dialog box click **Show** until you see a plan view of the door, as shown in Figure 15–35. Then, click **Close**.

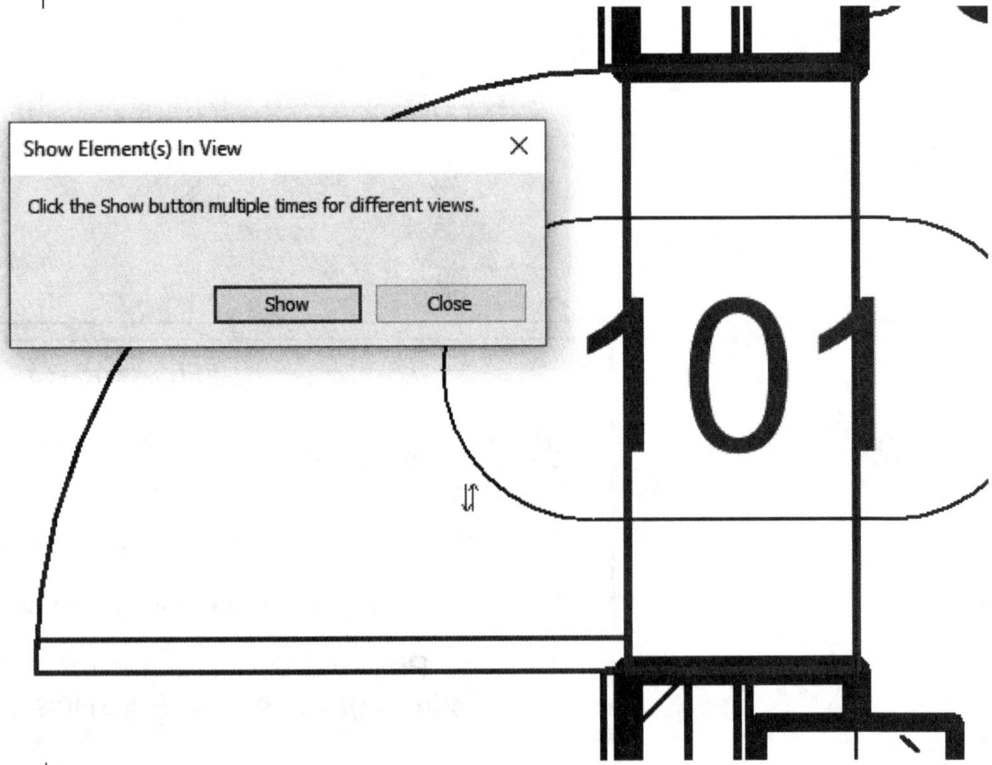

Figure 15–35

8. The door is still selected. In Properties, set the following:

   - *Frame Type:* **A**
   - *Frame Material:* **Steel**
   - *Finish:* **Coated**

9. Click (Edit Type).

10. In the Type Properties dialog box, in the *Identity Data* area, set the *Fire Rating* to **A**.

11. Click **OK** to finish.

12. Click on the *Door Schedule - 1st Floor* tab to open the view.

13. Note that the *Frame Type* and *Frame Material* display for one door and the matching exterior doors also have a fire rating.

14. Use the drop-down list and change the options for the matching doors, as shown in Figure 15–36.

<Door Sch

A	B	C	D	E	F
	Dimensions			Frame Information	
Mark	Width	Height	Thickness	Frame Type	Frame Material
101	3' - 0"	7' - 0"	0' - 2"	A	Steel
102	3' - 0"	7' - 0"	0' - 2"	A	Steel
103	3' - 0"	6' - 8"	0' - 2"		Steel
104	[illegible]	[illegible]	[illegible]		

Figure 15–36

15. In the Door Schedule view, specify the *Fire Rating* for some other doors in the schedule. When you change the fire rating, you are prompted to change all elements of that type. Click **OK**.

16. Open the **Floor Plans: Floor 1** view and zoom out if required.

17. Select the door to the office, then right-click and select **Select All Instances>In Entire Project**.

18. Look at the Status Bar beside (Filter) and note that more doors have been selected than are in the current view.

No visual changes to the door display because these are just text properties.

19. In Properties, set the *Construction and Materials* and the *Finishes* parameters as follows:
   - *Frame Type:* **B**
   - *Frame Material:* **Wood**
   - *Finish:* **Clear-coat**

20. Press <Esc> to clear the selection when you are finished.

21. Switch back to the schedule view to see the additions. Not all of the doors are showing because the schedule has been limited to the 1st floor doors.

22. Save the project.

Task 2 - Add schedules to a sheet.

1. In the Project Browser, open the sheet **A8.1 - Schedules**.

2. Drag and drop the **Door Schedule - 1st Floor** view onto the sheet, as shown in Figure 15–37.

Door Schedule - 1st Floor

Mark	Dimensions			Frame Information		Detail Information			Fire Rating	Hardware Set	Comments
	Width	Height	Thickness	Frame Type	Frame Material	Head Detail	Jamb Detail	Threshold Detail			
101	3' - 0"	7' - 0"	0' - 2"	A	Steel				A		
102	3' - 0"	7' - 0"	0' - 2"	A	Steel				A		
103	3' - 0"	6' - 8"	0' - 2"	B	Wood				B		
104	3' - 0"	6' - 8"	0' - 2"	B	Wood				B		
105	3' - 0"	6' - 8"	0' - 2"	B	Wood				B		
106	3' - 0"	6' - 8"	0' - 2"	B	Wood				B		
107	3' - 0"	6' - 8"	0' - 2"	B	Wood				B		
108	3' - 0"	7' - 0"	0' - 2"	A	Steel				A		
109	3' - 0"	7' - 0"	0' - 2"	A	Steel				A		
110	6' - 0"	7' - 0"	0' - 2"						D		
111	6' - 0"	6' - 10"	0' - 2"	B	Wood						

Figure 15–37

- Note that your schedule might look different than the one shown in Figure 15–37.

3. Zoom in and use the arrows at the top to modify the width of the columns so that the titles display correctly.

4. Click in empty space on the sheet to finish placing the schedule.

5. Switch back to the **Floor Plans: Floor 1** view and select the double-swing door at the kitchen.

6. In the Type Selector, change the size to **72" x 82"**. In Properties, add a Frame Type, Frame Material, and Finish.

7. Return to the sheet **A8.1 - Schedules**. The information is automatically populated, as shown in Figure 15–38.

Door					
	Dimensions			Frame Informa	
Mark	Width	Height	Thickness	Frame Type	Frar Mate
101	3'-0"	7'-0"	0'-2"	A	Steel
102	3'-0"	7'-0"	0'-2"	A	Steel
103	3'-0"	6'-8"	0'-2"	B	Wood
104	3'-0"	6'-8"	0'-2"	B	Wood
105	3'-0"	6'-8"	0'-2"	B	Wood
106	3'-0"	6'-8"	0'-2"	B	Wood
107	3'-0"	6'-8"	0'-2"	B	Wood
108	3'-0"	7'-0"	0'-2"	A	Steel
109	3'-0"	7'-0"	0'-2"	A	Steel
110	6'-0"	7'-0"	0'-2"		
111	6'-0"	6'-10"	0'-2"	B	Wood

Figure 15–38

8. Return to the 3D view and save the project.

Chapter Review Questions

1. Which of the following elements cannot be tagged using **Tag by Category**?
   a. Rooms
   b. Floors
   c. Walls
   d. Doors
2. What happens when you delete a door in an Autodesk Revit model, as shown in Figure 15–39?

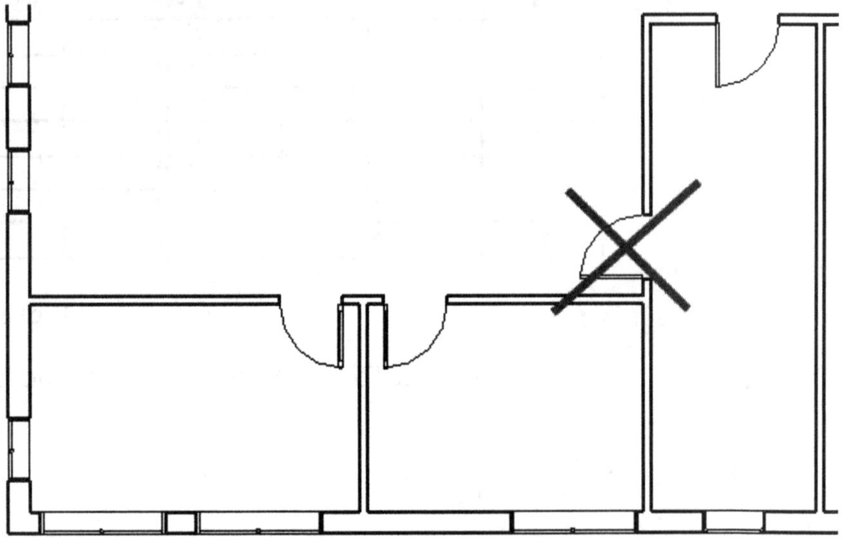

Figure 15–39

   a. You must delete the door on the sheet.
   b. You must delete the door from the schedule.
   c. The door is removed from the model, but not from the schedule.
   d. The door is removed from the model and the schedule.
3. In a schedule, if you change type information (such as a Type Mark) all instances of that type update with the new information.
   a. True
   b. False

Command Summary

Button	Command	Location
	**Material Tag**	• **Ribbon:** *Annotate* tab>Tag panel
	**Multi-Category**	• **Ribbon:** *Annotate* tab>Tag panel
	**Stair Tread/ Riser Number**	• **Ribbon:** *Annotate* tab>Tag panel
	**Tag All Not Tagged**	• **Ribbon:** *Annotate* tab>Tag panel
	**Tag by Category**	• **Ribbon:** *Annotate* tab>Tag panel • **Shortcut:** TG
	**Tag Room (Room Tag)**	• **Ribbon:** *Architecture* tab>Room & Area panel • Ribbon: *Annotate* tab>Tag panel • **Shortcut:** RT

Creating Details

Creating details is a critical part of the design process, as it is the step where you specify the exact information that is required to build a construction project. The elements that you can add to a model include detail components, detail lines, text, tags, symbols, and filled regions for patterning. Details can be created from views in the model, but you can also add 2D details in separate views.

Learning Objectives in this Chapter

- Create drafting views where you can add 2D details.
- Add detail components that show the typical elements in a detail.
- Annotate details using detail lines, text, tags, symbols, and patterns that define materials.

16.1 Setting Up Detail Views

Most of the work you do in the Autodesk® Revit® software is exclusively with *smart* elements that interconnect and work together in the model. However, the software does not automatically display how elements should be built to fit together. For this, you need to create detail drawings, as shown in Figure 16–1.

Details are created either in 2D drafting views, or in callouts from plan, elevation, or section views.

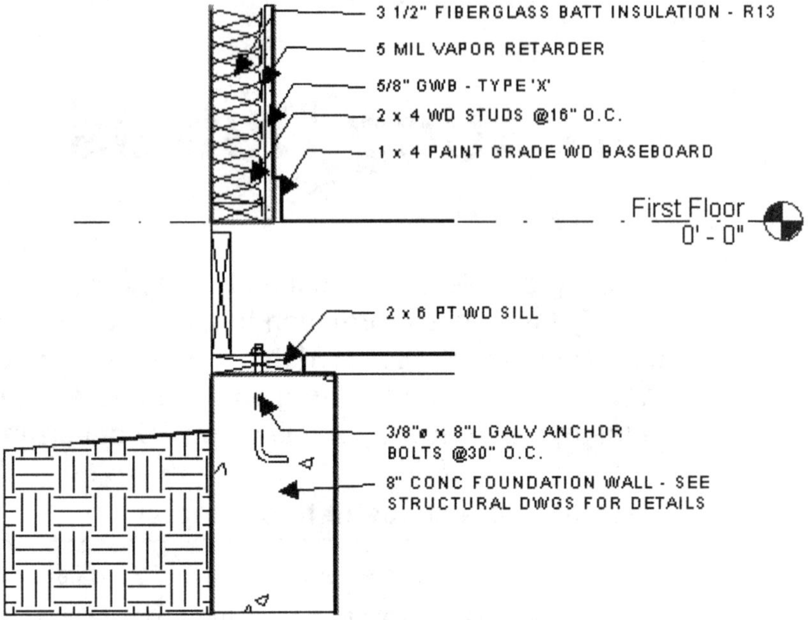

Figure 16–1

How To: Create a Drafting View

1. In the *View* tab>Create panel, click (Drafting View).
2. In the New Drafting View dialog box, enter a *Name* and set a *Scale*, as shown in Figure 16–2.

Drafting views are listed in their own section in the Project Browser.

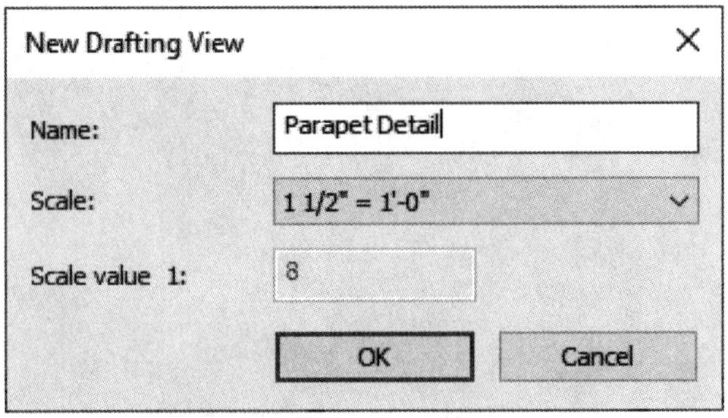

Figure 16–2

3. Click **OK**. A blank view is created with space in which you can sketch the detail.

How To: Create a Detail View from Model Elements

Callouts also have a Detail View Type that can be used in the same way.

1. Start the **Section** or **Callout** command.
2. In the Type Selector, select the **Detail View: Detail** type.
    - The marker indicates that it is a detail, as shown for a section in Figure 16–3.

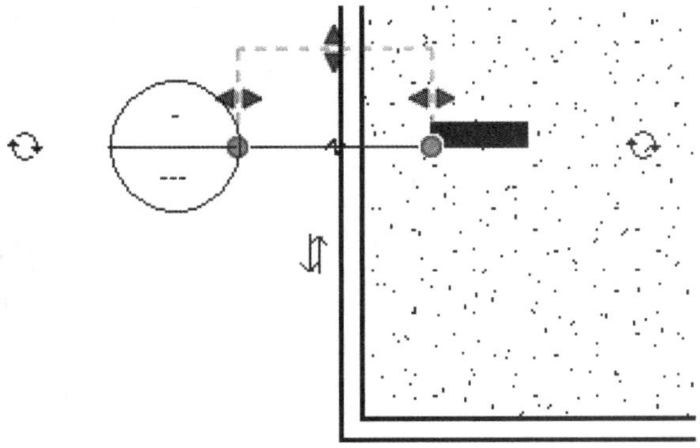

Figure 16–3

3. Place the section or a callout of the area you want to use for the detail.
4. Open the new detail. Use the tools to sketch on top of or add to the building elements.

- In this type of detail view when the building elements change, the detail changes as well, as shown in Figure 16–4.

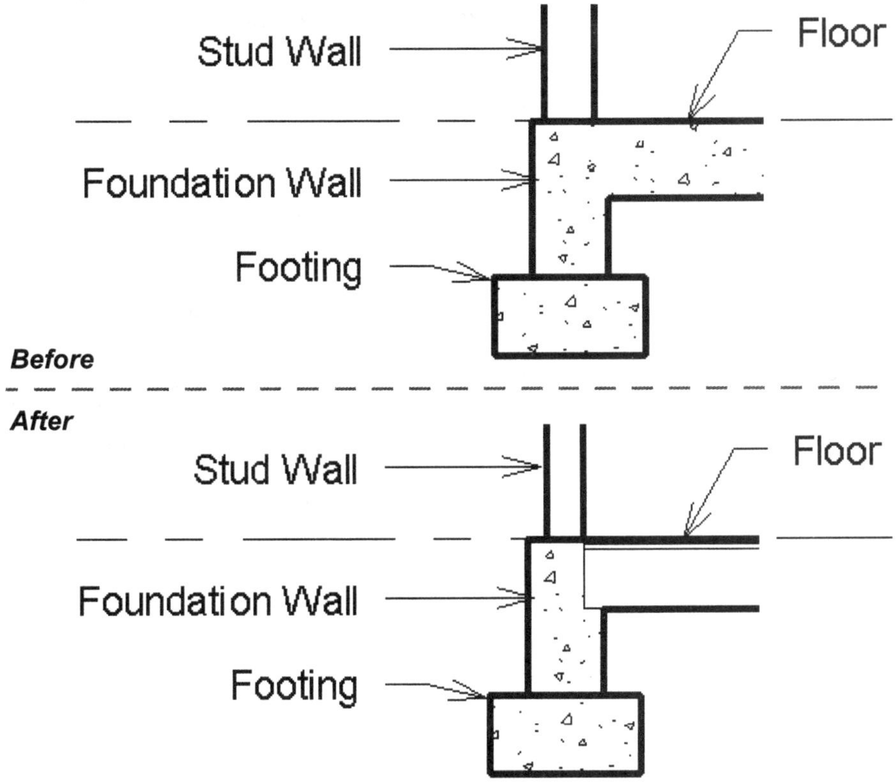

Figure 16–4

- You can create detail elements on top of the model and then toggle the model off so that it does not show in the detail view. In Properties, in the *Graphics* area, change *Display Model* to **Do not display**. You can also set the model to **Halftone**, as shown in Figure 16–5.

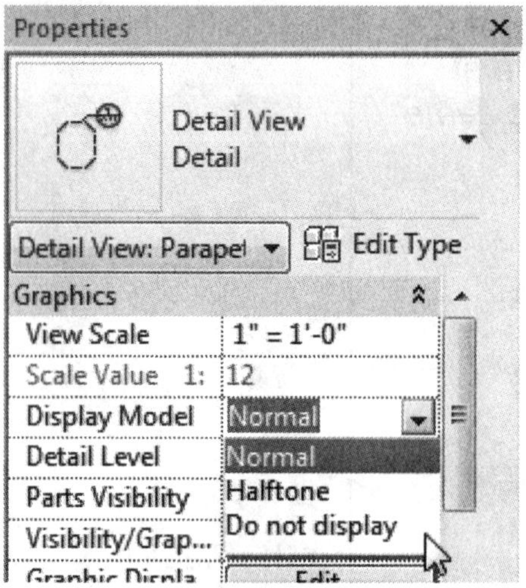

Figure 16–5

Referencing a Drafting View

Once you have created a drafting view, you can reference it in another view (such as a callout, elevation, or section view), as shown in Figure 16–6. For example, in a section view, you might want to reference an existing roof detail. You can reference drafting views, sections, elevations, and callouts.

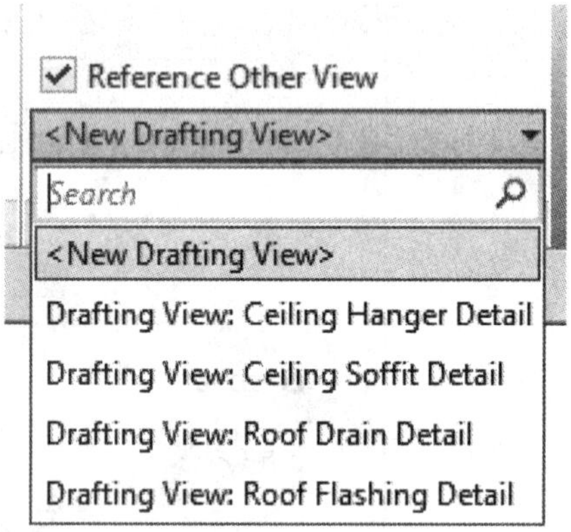

Figure 16–6

- You can use the search feature to limit the information displayed.

How To: Reference a Drafting View

1. Open the view in which you want to place the reference.
2. Start the **Section, Callout,** or **Elevation** command.
3. In the *Modify* | *<contextual>* tab>Reference panel select **Reference Other View**.
4. In the drop-down list, select **<New Drafting View>** or an existing drafting view.
5. Place the view marker.
6. When you place the associated drafting view on a sheet, the marker in this view updates with the appropriate information.

- If you select **<New Drafting View>** from the drop-down list, a new view is created in the *Drafting Views (Detail)* area in the Project Browser. You can rename it as required. The new view does not include any model elements.
- When you create a detail based on a section, elevation, or callout, you do not need to link it to a drafting view.
- You can change a referenced view to a different referenced view. Select the view marker and in the ribbon, select the new view from the list.

Saving Drafting Views

To create a library of standard details, save the non-model specific drafting views to your server. They can then be imported into a project and modified to suit. They are saved as .RVT files.

Drafting views can be saved in two ways:

- Save an individual drafting view to a new file.
- Save all of the drafting views as a group in one new file.

How To: Save One Drafting View to a File

1. In the Project Browser, right-click on the drafting view you want to save and select **Save to New File...**, as shown in Figure 16–7.

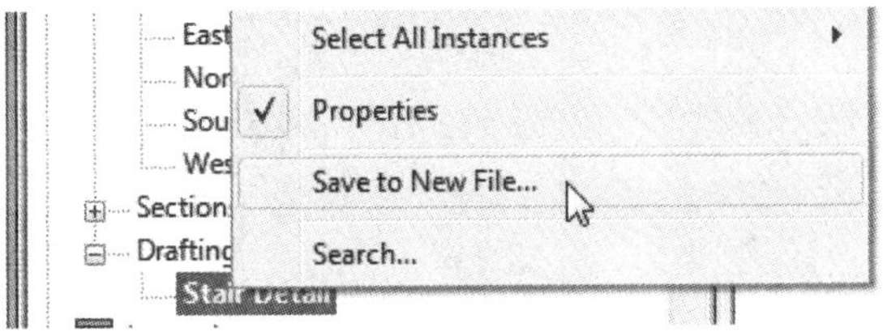

Figure 16–7

2. In the Save As dialog box, specify a name and location for the file and click **Save**.

How To: Save a Group of Drafting Views to a File

You can save sheets, drafting views, model views (floor plans), schedules, and reports.

1. In the *File* tab, expand (Save As), expand (Library) and then click (View).
2. In the Save Views dialog box, in the *Views:* pane, expand the list and select **Show drafting views only**.
3. Select the drafting views that you want to save, as shown in Figure 16–8.

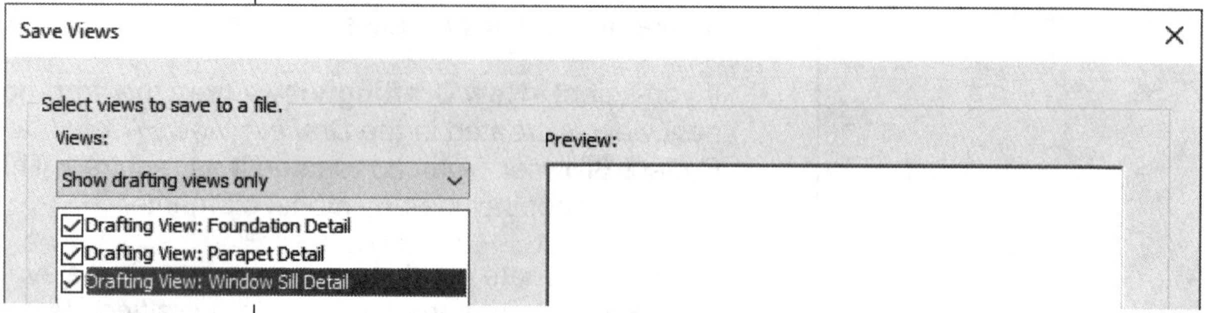

Figure 16–8

4. Click **OK**.
5. In the Save As dialog box, specify a name and location for the file and click **Save**.

How To: Use a Saved Drafting View in another Project

1. Open the project to which you want to add the drafting view.
2. In the *Insert* tab>Import panel, expand (Insert from File) and click (Insert Views from File).
3. In the Open dialog box, select the project in which you saved the detail and click **Open**.
4. In the Insert Views dialog box, limit the types of views to **Show drafting views only**, as shown in Figure 16–9.

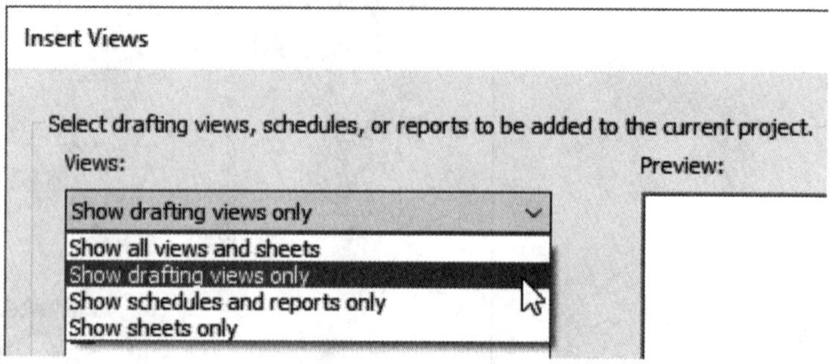

Figure 16–9

5. Select the view(s) that you want to insert and click **OK**.

Hint: Importing Details from Other CAD Software

You might already have a set of standard details created in a different CAD program, such as the AutoCAD® software. You can reuse the details in the Autodesk Revit software by importing them into a temporary project. Once you have imported the detail, it helps to clean it up and save it as a view before bringing it into your active project.

1. In a new project, create a drafting view and make it active.
2. In the *Insert* tab>Import panel, click (Import CAD).
3. In the Import CAD dialog box, select the file to import. Most of the default values are what you need. You might want to change the *Layer/Level colors* to **Black and White**.
4. Click **Open**.

- If you want to modify the detail, select the imported data. In the *Modify | [filename]* tab>Import Instance panel, expand (Explode) and click (Partial Explode) or (Full Explode). Click (Delete Layers) before you explode the detail. A full explode greatly increases the file size.
- Modify the detail using tools in the Modify panel. Change all the text and line styles to Autodesk Revit specific elements.

16.2 Adding Detail Components

Autodesk Revit elements, such as the casework section shown in Figure 16–10, typically require additional information to ensure that they are constructed correctly. To create details such as the one shown in Figure 16–11, you add detail components, detail lines, and various annotation elements.

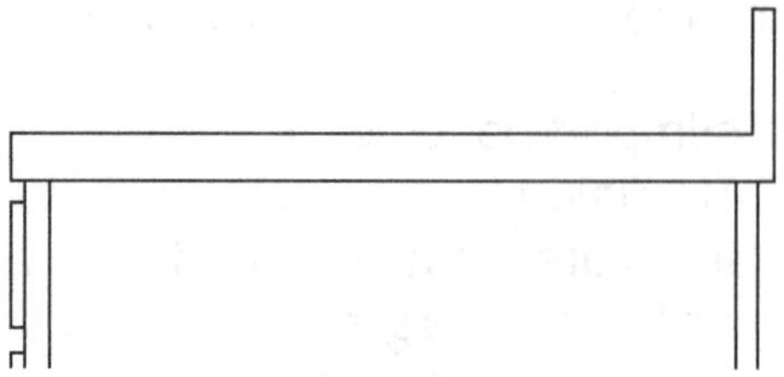

Section

Figure 16–10

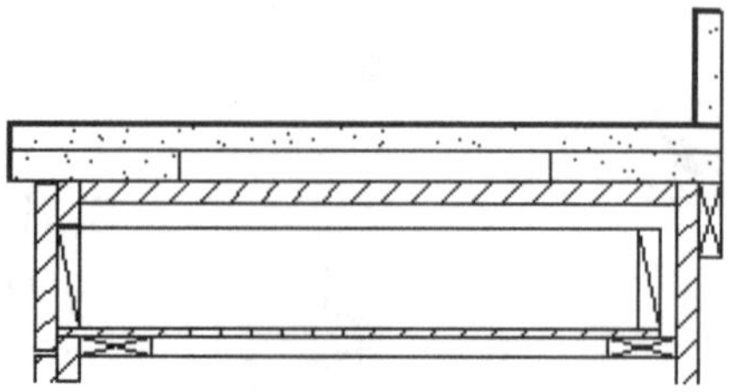

Detail Built on Section

Figure 16–11

- Detail elements are not directly connected to the model, even if model elements display in the view.

Detail Components

Detail components are families made of 2D and annotation elements. Over 500 detail components organized by CSI format are found in the *Detail Items* folder of the library, as shown in Figure 16–12.

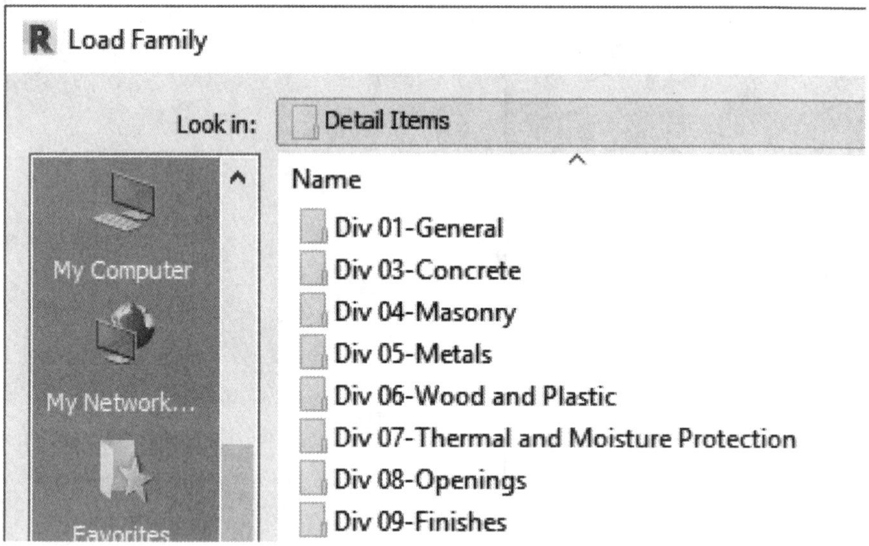

Figure 16–12

How To: Add a Detail Component

1. In the *Annotate* tab>Detail panel, expand  (Component) and click  (Detail Component).
2. In the Type Selector, select the detail component type. You can load additional types from the Library.
3. Many detail components can be rotated as you insert them by pressing <Spacebar>. Alternatively, select **Rotate after placement** in the Options Bar, as shown in Figure 16–13.

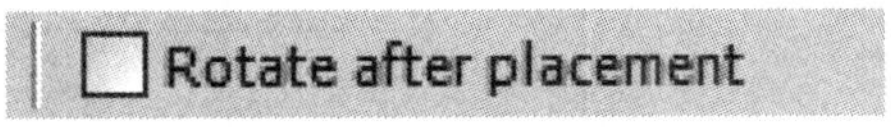

Figure 16–13

4. Place the component in the view.

Adding Break Lines

The Break Line is a detail component found in the *Detail Items\ Div 01-General* folder. It consists of a rectangular area (shown highlighted in Figure 16–14) which is used to block out elements behind it. You can modify the size of the area that is covered and change the size of the cut line using the controls.

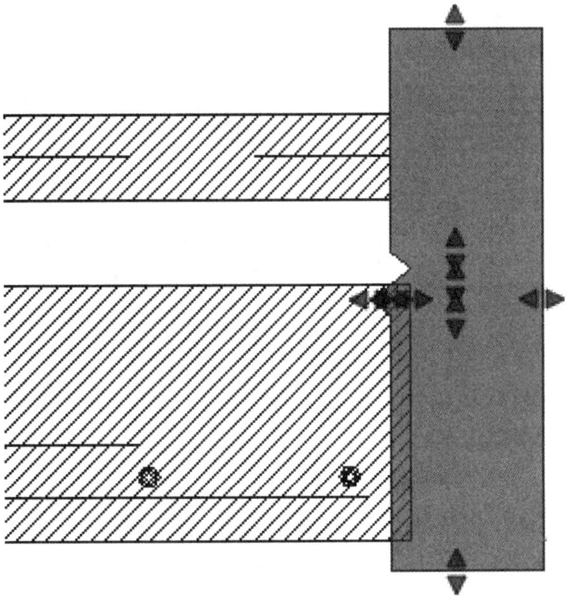

Figure 16–14

Hint: Working with the Draw Order of Details

When you select detail elements in a view, you can change the draw order of the elements in the *Modify | Detail Items* tab> Arrange panel. You can bring elements in front of other elements or place them behind elements, as shown in Figure 16–15.

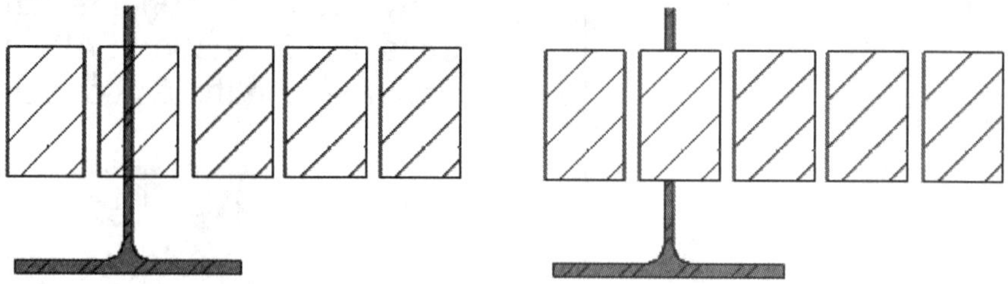

Draw order: front ***Draw order: back***

Figure 16–15

- **(Bring to Front):** Places element in front of all other elements.
- **(Send to Back):** Places element behind all other elements.
- **(Bring Forward):** Moves element one step to the front.
- **(Send Backward):** Moves element one step to the back.
- You can select multiple detail elements and change the draw order of all of them in one step. They keep the relative order of the original selection.

Repeating Details

Instead of having to insert a component multiple times (such as with a brick or concrete block), you can use (Repeating Detail Component) and create a string of components, as shown in Figure 16–16.

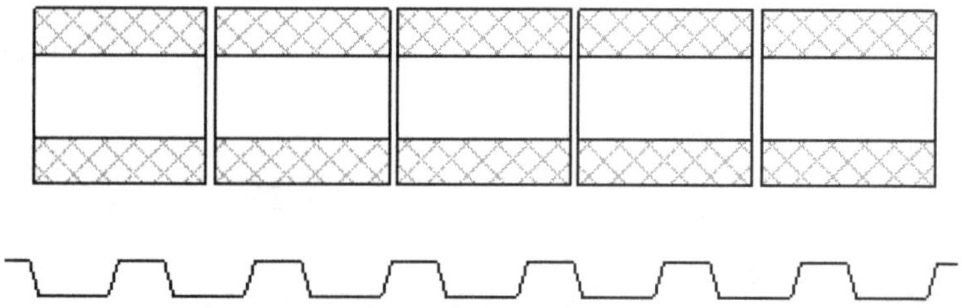

Figure 16–16

How To: Insert a Repeating Detail Component

1. In the *Annotate* tab>Detail panel, expand (Component) and click (Repeating Detail Component).
2. In the Type Selector, select the detail you want to use.
3. In the Draw panel, click (Line) or (Pick Lines).
4. In the Options Bar, type a value for the *Offset*, if required.
5. The components repeat as required to fit the length of the sketched or selected line, as shown in Figure 16–17. You can lock the components to the line.

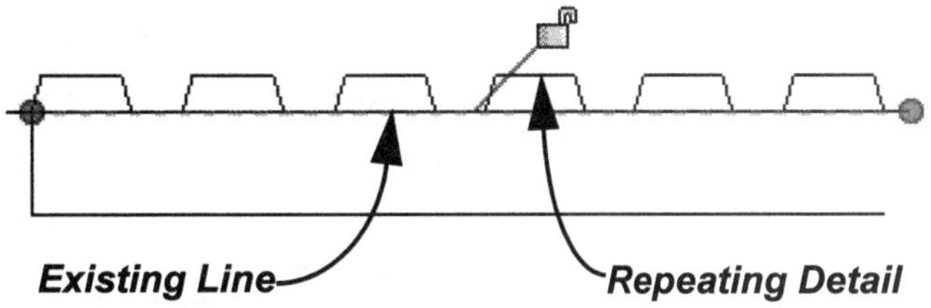

Figure 16–17

- For information on customizing repeating details, see *Appendix B.13 Creating a Repeating Detail*.

Hint: (Insulation)

Adding batt insulation is similar to adding a repeating detail component, but instead of a series of bricks or other elements, it creates the linear batting pattern, shown in Figure 16–18.

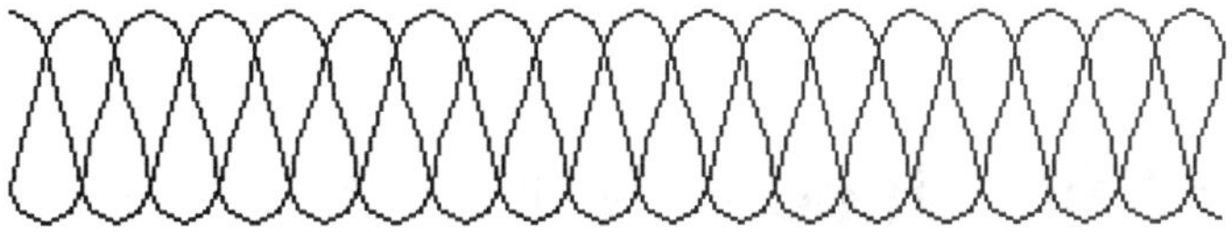

Figure 16–18

Before you place the insulation in the view, specify the *Width* and other options in the Options Bar, as shown in Figure 16–19.

Figure 16–19

16.3 Annotating Details

After you have added components and sketched detail lines, you need to add annotations to the detail view. You can place text notes and dimensions as shown in Figure 16–20, as well as symbols and tags. Filled regions are used to add hatching or poche.

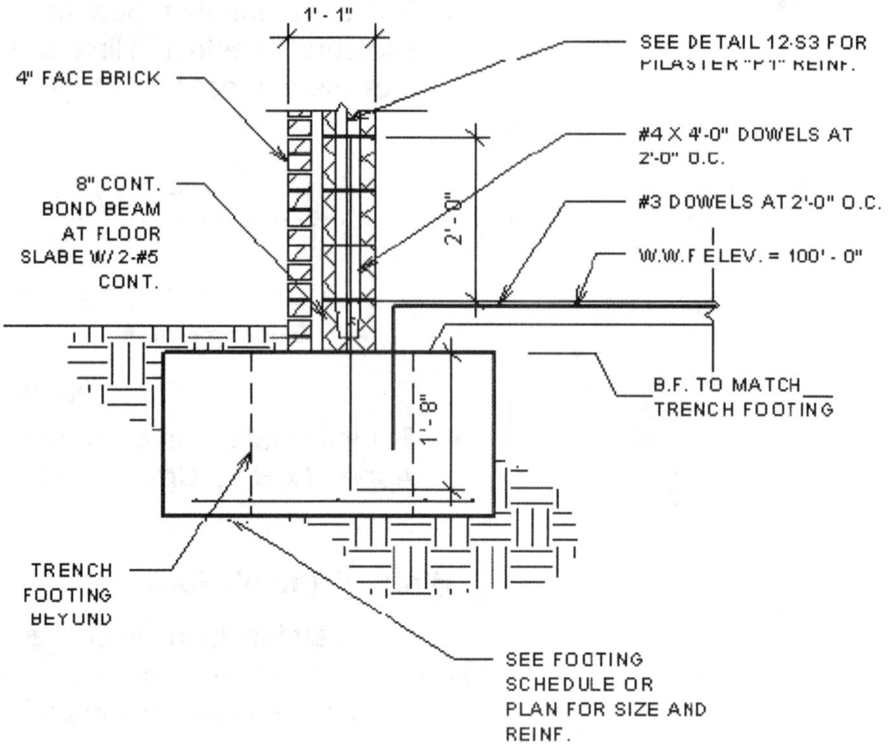

Figure 16–20

Creating Filled Regions

Many elements include material information that displays in plan and section views, while other elements need such details to be added. For example, the concrete wall shown in Figure 16–21 includes material information, while the earth to the left of the wall needs to be added using the **Filled Region** command.

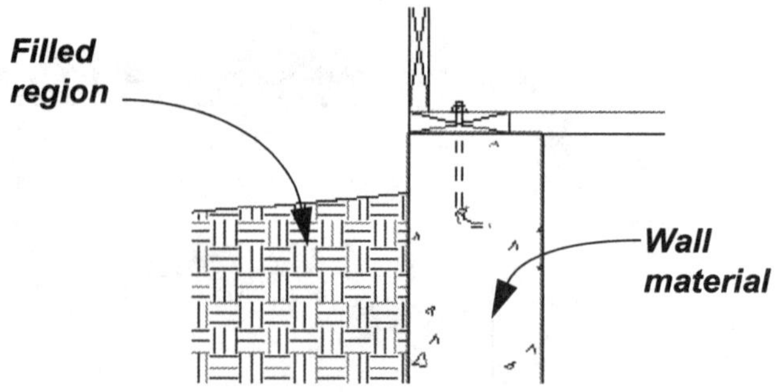

Figure 16–21

The patterns used in details are *drafting patterns*. They are scaled to the view scale and update if you modify it. You can also add full-size *model patterns*, such as a Flemish Bond brick pattern, to the surface of some elements.

How To: Add a Filled Region

1. In the *Annotate* tab>Detail panel, expand (Region) and click (Filled Region).
2. Create a closed boundary using the Draw tools.
3. In the Line Style panel, select the line style for the outside edge of the boundary. If you do not want the boundary to display, select the <Invisible lines> style.
4. In the Type Selector, select the fill type, as shown in Figure 16–22.

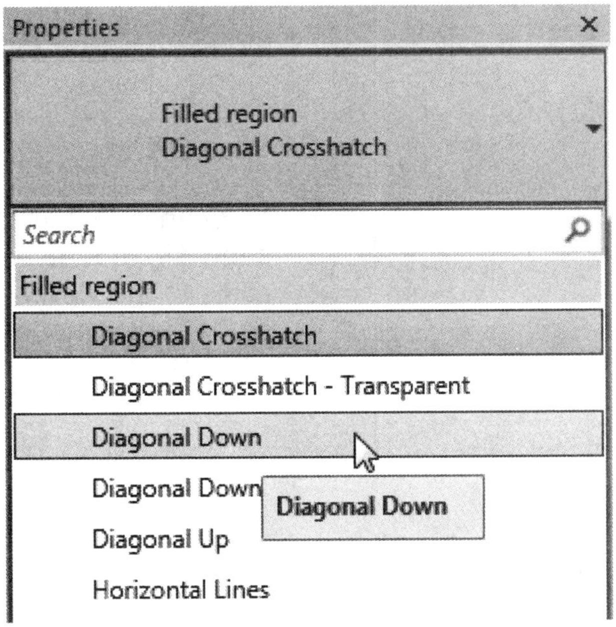

Figure 16–22

5. Click (Finish Edit Mode).

- You can modify a region by changing the fill type in the Type Selector or by editing the sketch.
- Double-click on the edge of the filled region to edit the sketch.

  If you have the Selection option set to (Select elements by face) you can select the pattern.

Hint: Creating a Filled Region Pattern Type

You can create a custom pattern by duplicating and editing an existing pattern type.

1. Select an existing region or create a boundary.
2. In Properties, click (Edit Type).
3. In the Type Properties dialog box, click **Duplicate** and name the new pattern.
4. Select the *Foreground/ Background Fill Pattern* and *Color* and specify the *Line Weight* and *Masking*, as shown in Figure 16–23.

Graphics	
Foreground Fill Pattern	Wood 3 [Drafting]
Foreground Pattern Color	Black
Background Fill Pattern	
Background Pattern Color	Black
Line Weight	1
Masking	☑

Figure 16–23

5. Click **OK**.

- You can select from two types of Fill Patterns: **Drafting**, as shown in Figure 16–24, and **Model**. Drafting fill patterns scale to the view scale factor. Model fill patterns display full scale on the model.

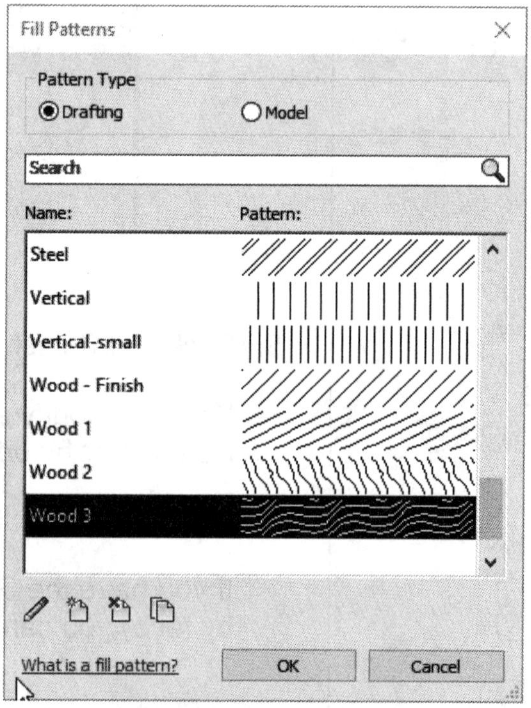

Figure 16–24

Adding Detail Tags

*The **Detail Item Tag.rfa** tag is located in the Annotations folder in the Library.*

Besides adding text to a detail, you can tag detail components using (Tag By Category). The tag name is set in the Type Parameters for that component, as shown in Figure 16–25. This means that if you have more than one copy of the component in your project, you do not have to rename it each time you place its tag.

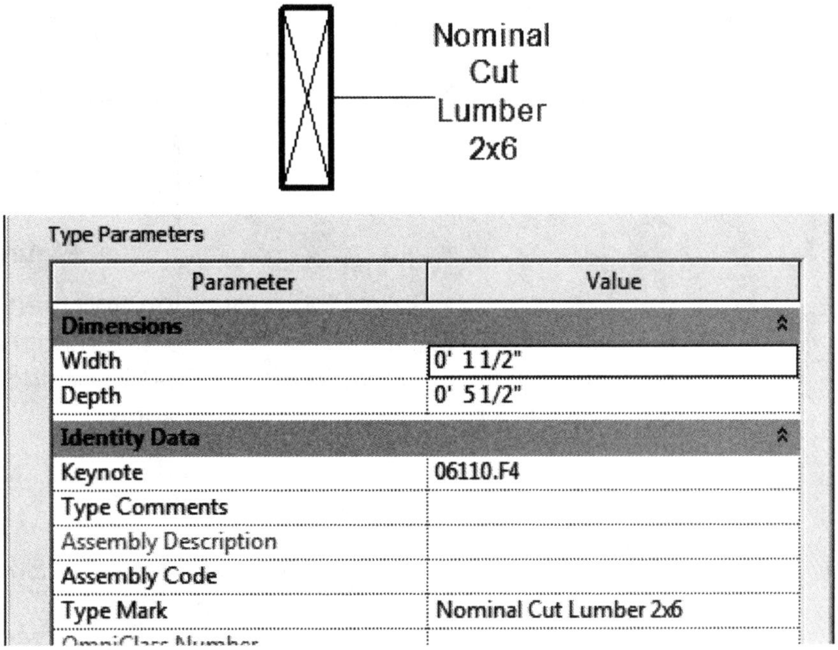

Parameter	Value
Dimensions	
Width	0' 1 1/2"
Depth	0' 5 1/2"
Identity Data	
Keynote	06110.F4
Type Comments	
Assembly Description	
Assembly Code	
Type Mark	Nominal Cut Lumber 2x6

Figure 16–25

- For more information on annotating using keynotes see, *Appendix B.14 Keynoting and Keynote Legends.*

Hint: Multiple Dimension Options

If you are creating details that show one element with multiple dimension values, as shown in Figure 16–26, you can easily modify the dimension text.

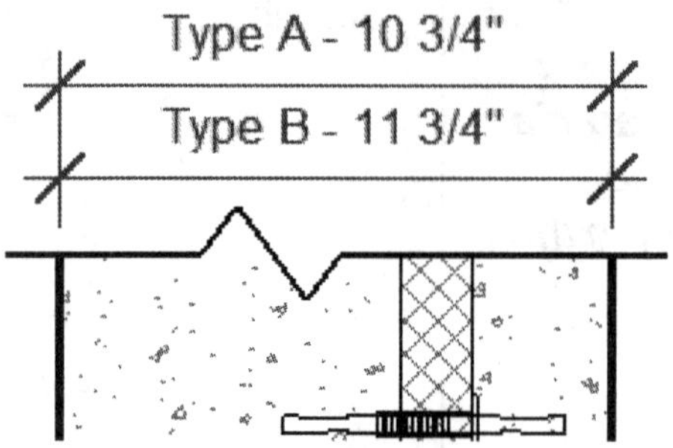

Figure 16–26

Select the dimension and then the dimension text. The Dimension Text dialog box opens. You can replace the text, as shown in Figure 16–27, or add text fields above or below, as well as a prefix or suffix.

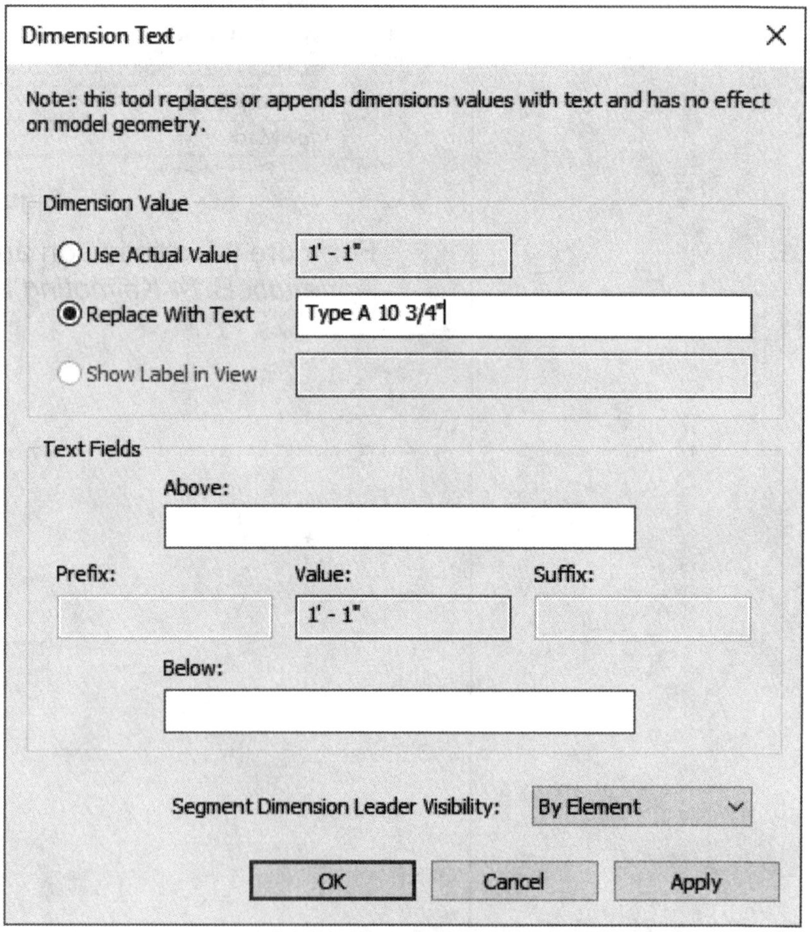

Figure 16–27

- This also works with Equality Text Labels.

Practice 16a

Create a Detail Based on a Section Callout

Practice Objectives

- Create a detail based on a section.
- Add filled regions, detail components, and annotations.

In this practice, you will create a detail based on a callout of a wall section. You will add repeating detail components, break lines, and detail lines, and add annotation to complete the detail, as shown in Figure 16–28.

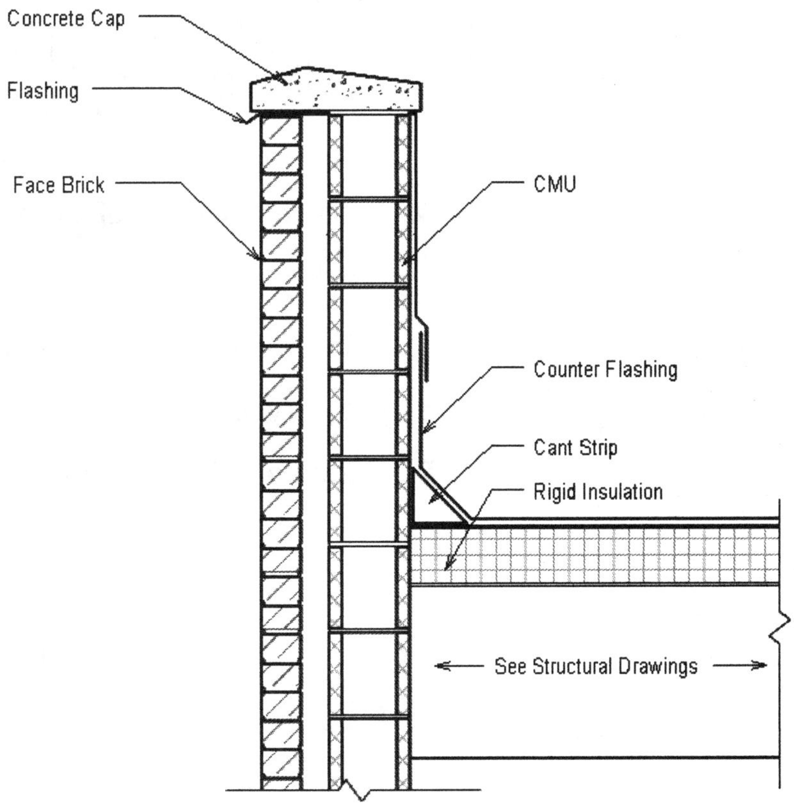

Figure 16–28

Task 1 - Create a callout of a wall section.

1. Open the file **Modern-Hotel-Detailing.rvt**.
2. Open the **Floor Plans: Floor 1** view.

3. Double-click on the wall section head shown in Figure 16–29. This guarantees that you open the right section.

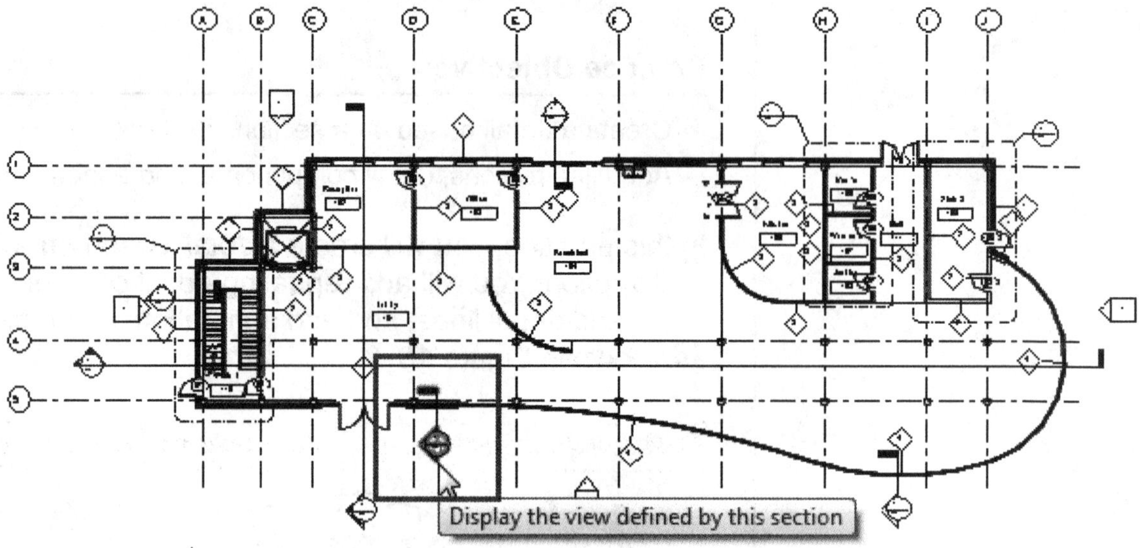

Figure 16–29

4. Zoom in to the top of the wall showing the parapet and the roof.

5. In the *View* tab>Create panel, click (Callout).

6. In the Type Selector, select **Detail View: Detail**.

7. Create a callout as shown in Figure 16–30.

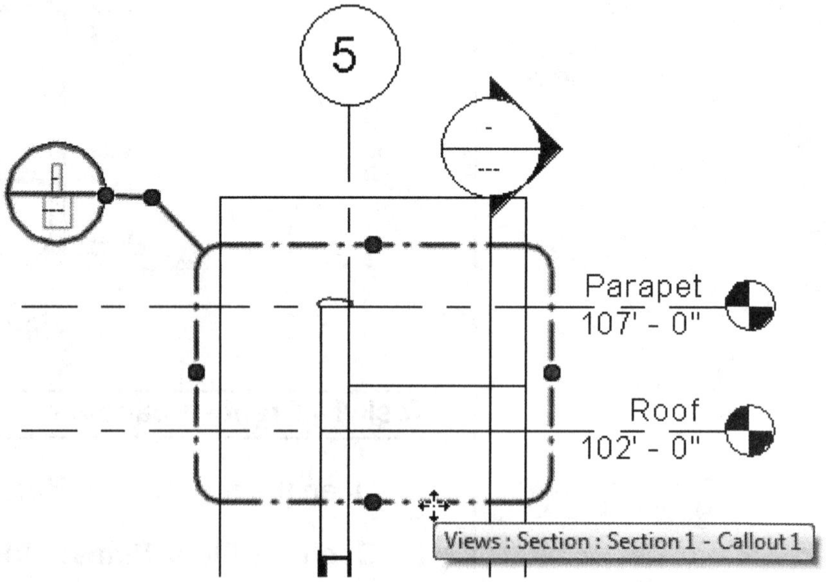

Figure 16–30

8. Double-click on the callout bubble to open the callout view.

9. In the View Control Bar, set the following parameters:
   - *Scale*: **1"=1'-0"**
   - *Detail Level*: (Fine)

10. Hide the levels, grids, and section markers (if displayed).

11. Toggle off the Crop Region.

12. In the Project Browser, in the *Detail Views (Detail)* node, rename the view to **Parapet Detail**.

13. Save the project.

Task 2 - Add repeating detail components and break lines.

1. In the *Annotate* tab>Detail panel, expand (Component) and click (Repeating Detail Component).

2. In the Type Selector, set the type to **Repeating Detail: Brick**.

3. Draw the brick line from the top of the parapet cap down, as shown in Figure 16–31.

Drawing from the top down insures that "mortar" is between the cap and the brick. This is how the detail elements were created.

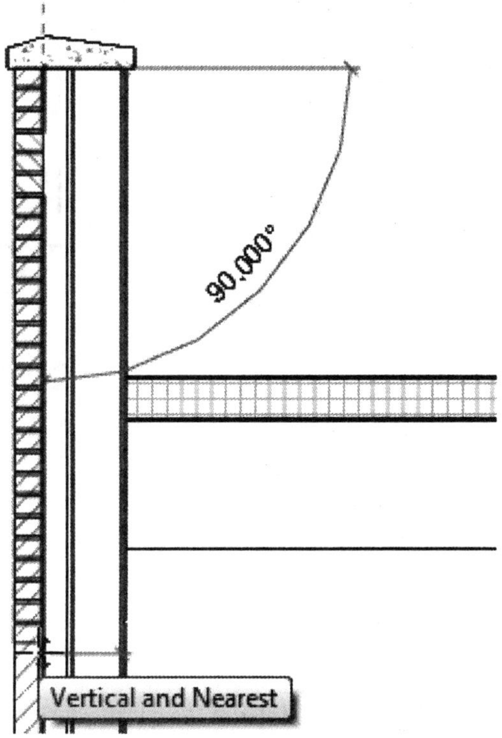

Figure 16–31

4. In the Type Selector, select **Repeating Detail: CMU**. Draw over the other side of the wall.

The Autodesk Revit software lists the last tool you used at the top of the drop-down list.

5. In the *Annotate* tab>Detail panel, expand (Repeating Detail Component) and click (Detail Component).
6. In the *Modify | Place Detail Component* tab>Mode panel, click (Load Family).
7. In the Load Family dialog box, navigate to the *Detail Items> Div 01-General* folder, select **Break Line.rfa**, and then click **Open**.
8. Add break lines to the bottom and right side of the detail. Press <Spacebar> to rotate the Break Line as required and use the controls to modify the size and depth, as shown in Figure 16–32.

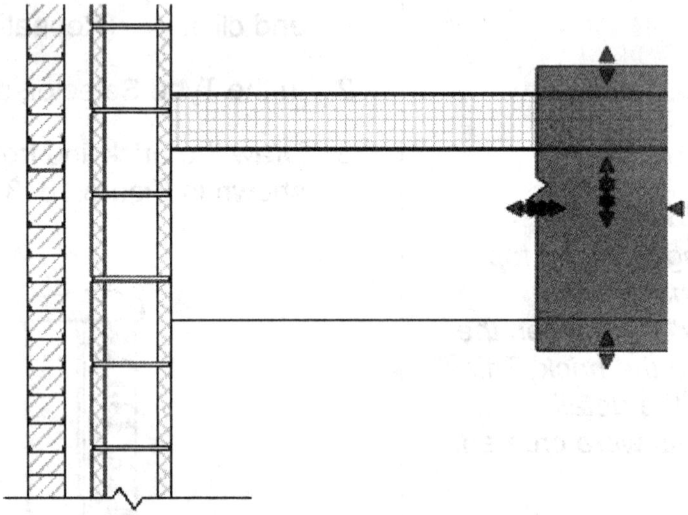

Figure 16–32

9. Save the project.

Task 3 - Draw flashing using detail lines.

1. In the *Annotate* tab>Detail panel, click (Detail Line).
2. In the *Modify | Place Detail Lines* tab>Line Style panel, verify that **Wide Lines** is selected.
3. Draw flashing similar to that shown in Figure 16–33.

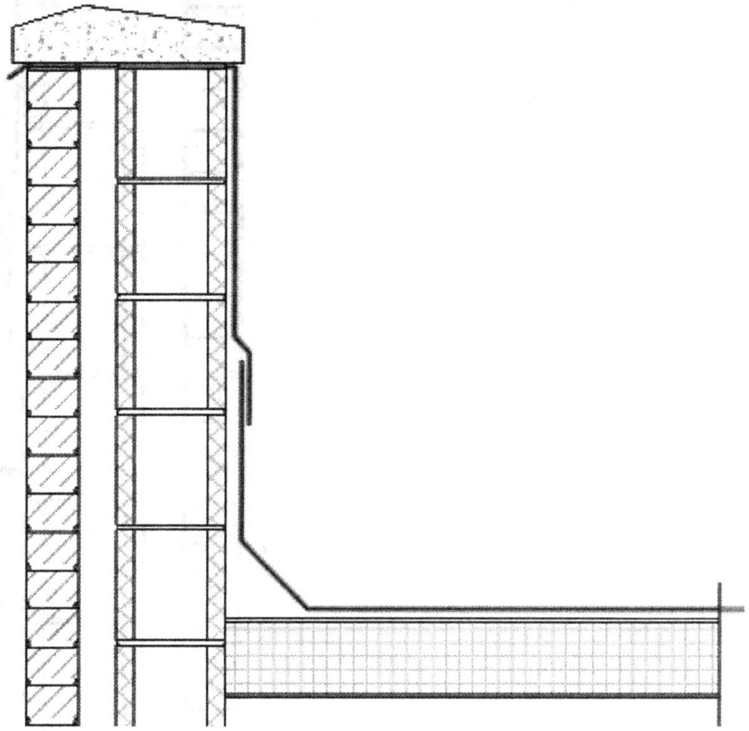

Figure 16–33

4. Using Detail Lines, add a cant strip under the flashing.
5. Save the project

Task 4 - Annotate the detail.

1. In the Quick Access Toolbar or on the *Annotate* tab>Text panel, click A (Text).
2. In the *Modify | Place Text* tab>Format panel, select A (Two-Segments).

3. Add the text and leaders shown in Figure 16–34. Use Alignments to place the leader points and text.

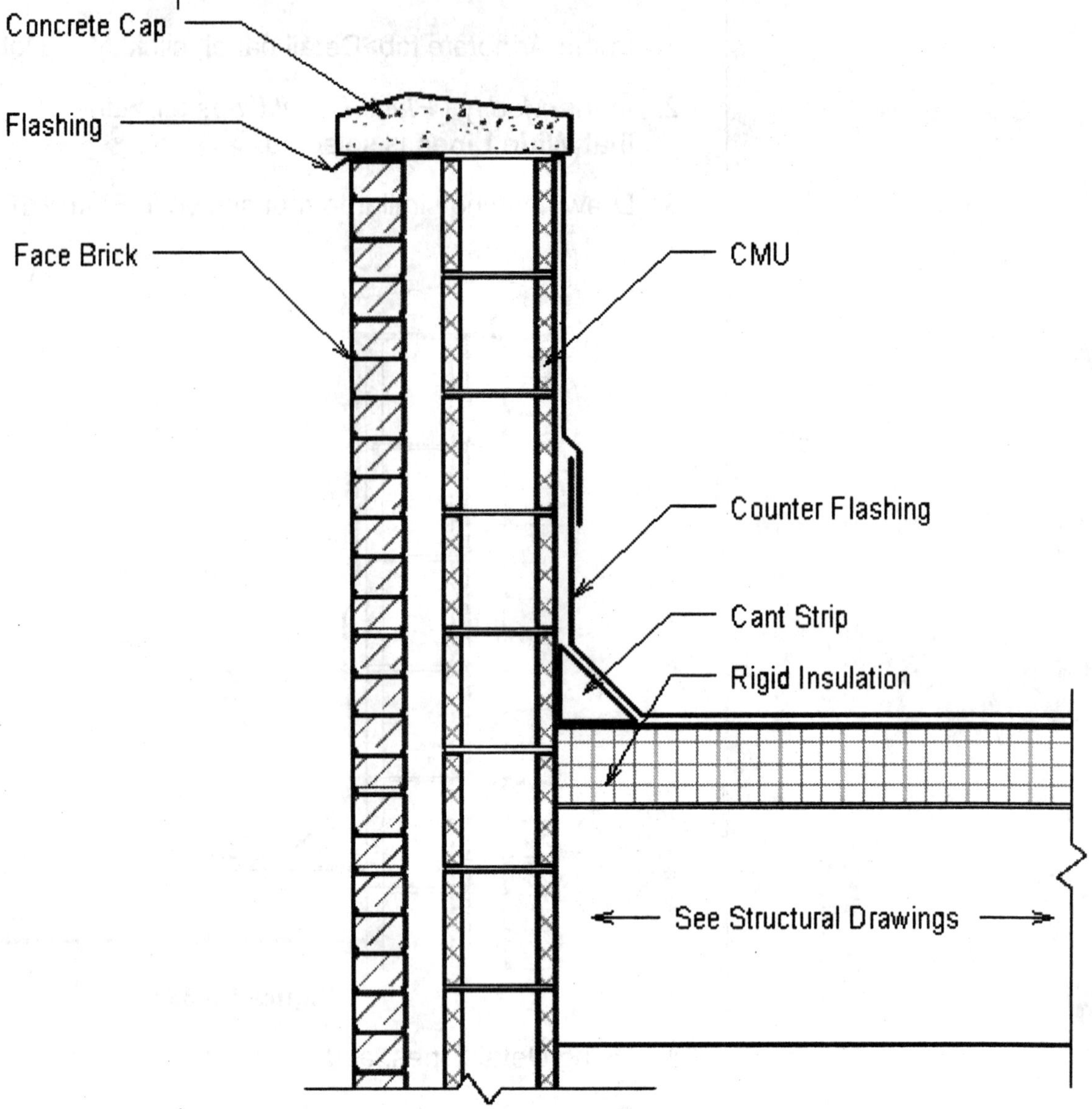

Figure 16–34

4. Save the project.

At this point, you have a hybrid between detail items and model items. You can continue to add detail items to replace the roofing. You can also add structural elements if you have time.

Practice 16b Create a Detail in a Detail View

Practice Objective

- Create and annotate details.

In this practice, you will create a footing detail in a drafting view. You will add detail components, lines, and annotations well as filled regions. You will place the view on a sheet (as shown in Figure 16–35), and place a callout in another view that references this view.

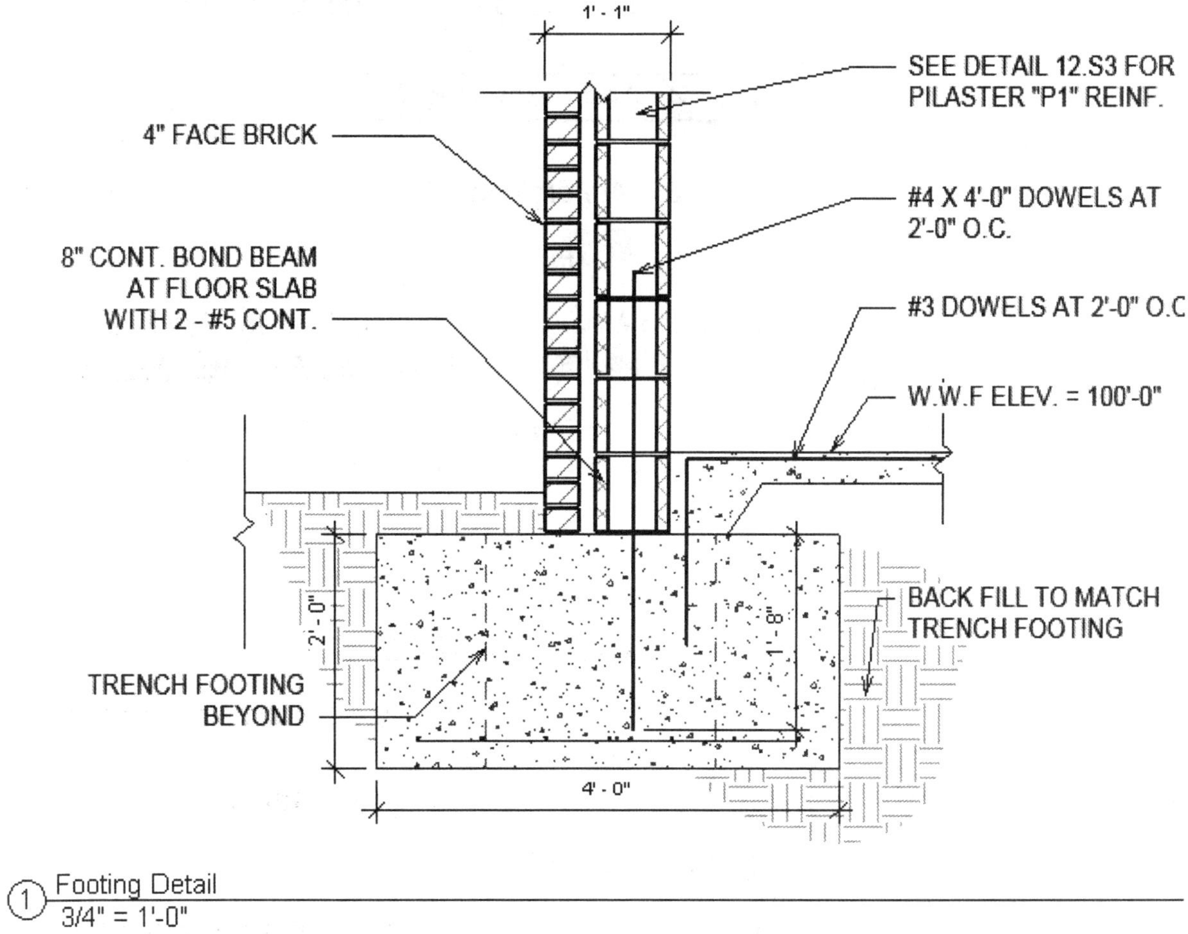

Figure 16–35

- This practice is designed with minimal direction so you can apply what you have learned.

Task 1 - Create a Detail.

1. Open the file **Modern-Hotel-Detailing.rvt**.
2. Create a drafting view named **Footing Detail** at a scale of **3/4" = 1'-0"**.
3. Use detail lines and detail components to add the footing, walls, floor, and rebar, as shown in Figure 16–35.
    - Use **Line Styles** to show the different weight and patterns (such as **Wide Line** and **Hidden Line**).
4. Add dimensions and text notes, as shown in Figure 16–35.

Task 2 - Add Filled Regions

1. In the *Annotate* tab>Detail panel, expand (Region) and click (Filled Region).
2. In the *Modify | Create Filled Region Boundary* tab>Line Style panel, select the Line Style **Medium Lines.**
3. Using the draw tools, sketch a boundary around the floor slab, as shown in Figure 16–36.

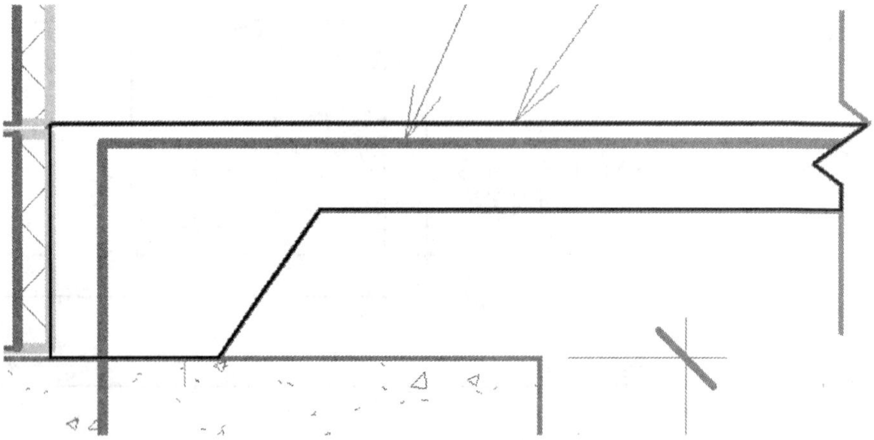

Figure 16–36

4. In the Type Selector, select **Filled region: Concrete**.
5. Click (Finish).

6. Add a filled region to the footing using the same **Concrete** pattern.

7. Create the curved filled regions shown in Figure 16–37, using the Line Style **<Invisible lines>** to sketch the boundary. Set the Filled Region type to **Earth**.

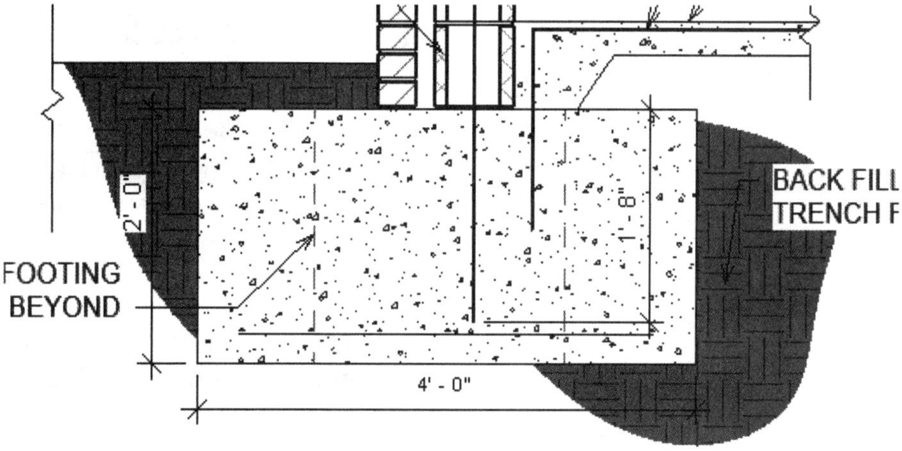

Figure 16–37

- The curved lines are made with splines.

8. The patterns might cover over some elements. Select the filled region and in the *Modify | Detail Items* tab>Arrange panel, click  (Send to Back).

9. Make any necessary adjustments to the annotation locations.

10. Save the project.

Task 3 - Add the detail to a sheet and connect it to a detail callout.

---

1. Create a new sheet named **A9.1 - Detail** and drag and drop the footing detail to this sheet.

2. Open the **Sections (Wall Section): Section 1** view.

3. Start the **Callout** command and select the **Detail View: Detail** type.

4. In the *Modify | Callout* tab>Reference panel, select **Reference Other View** and in the drop-down list, select **Drafting View: Footing Detail**, as shown in Figure 16–38.

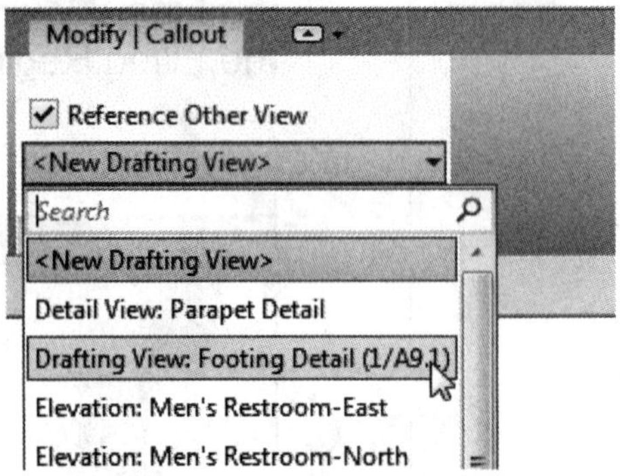

Figure 16–38

5. Draw the callout around the footing area. The correct detail is referenced, as shown in Figure 16–39.

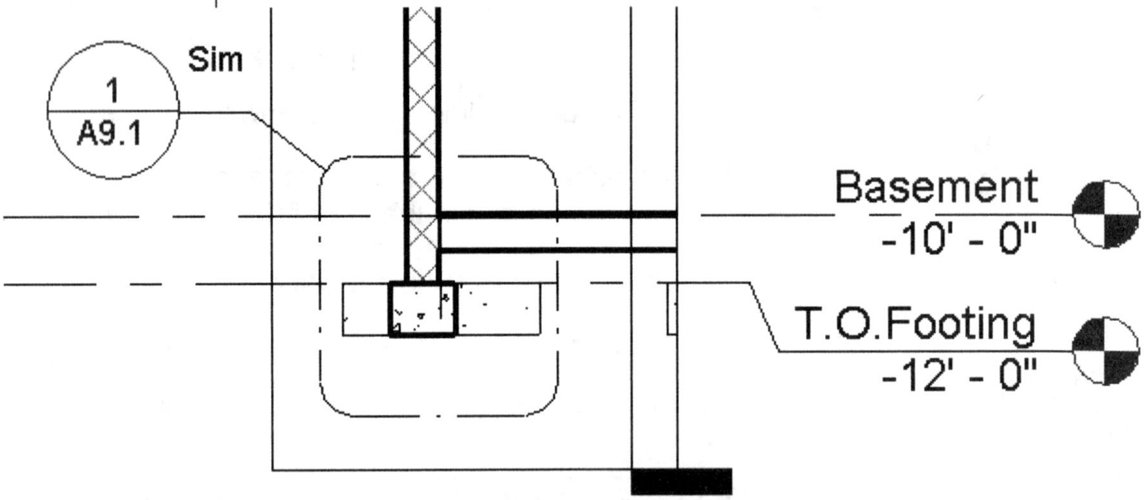

Figure 16–39

6. Save the project.

Chapter Review Questions

1. Which of the following are ways in which you can create a detail? (Select all that apply.)
   a. Make a callout of a section and sketch over it.
   b. Draw all of the elements from scratch.
   c. Import a CAD detail and modify or sketch over it.
   d. Insert an existing drafting view from another file.
2. In which type of view (access shown in Figure 16–40) can you NOT add detail lines?

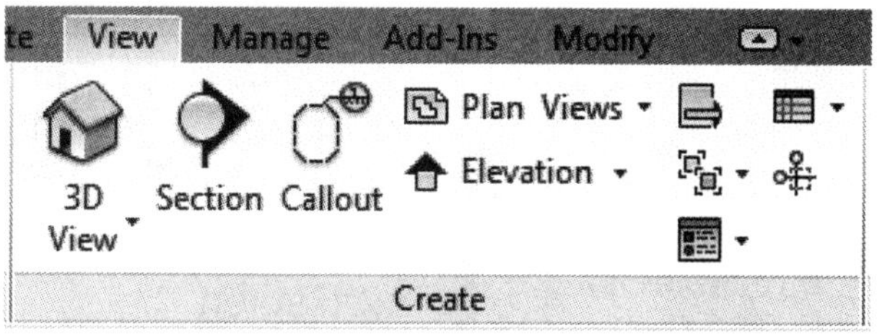

Figure 16–40

   a. Plans
   b. Elevations
   c. 3D views
   d. Legends
3. How are detail components different from building components?
   a. There is no difference.
   b. Detail components are made of 2D lines and annotation only.
   c. Detail components are made of building elements, but only display in detail views.
   d. Detail components are made of 2D and 3D elements.
4. When you sketch detail lines they are...
   a. Always the same width.
   b. Vary in width according to the view.
   c. Display in all views associated with the detail.
   d. Display only in the view in which they were created.

5. Which command do you use to add a pattern (such as concrete or earth as shown in Figure 16–41) to part of a detail?

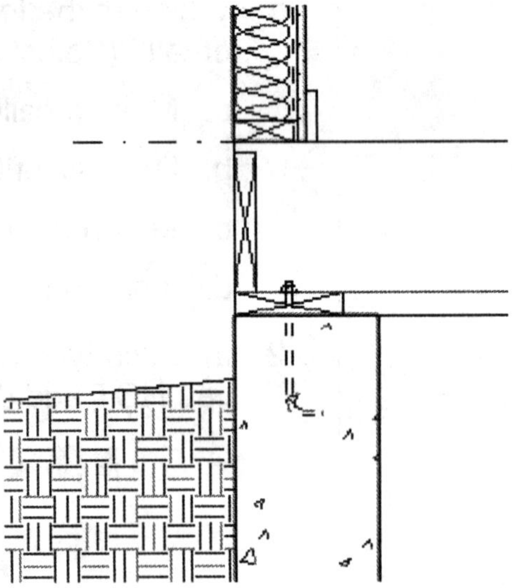

Figure 16–41

   a. Region
   b. Filled Region
   c. Masking Region
   d. Pattern Region

Command Summary

Button	Command	Location
CAD Import Tools		
	Delete Layers	• **Ribbon:** *Modify | <imported filename>* tab>Import Instance panel
	Full Explode	• **Ribbon:** *Modify | <imported filename>* tab>Import Instance panel> expand Explode
	Import CAD	• **Ribbon:** *Insert* tab>Import panel
	Partial Explode	• **Ribbon:** *Modify | <imported filename>* tab>Import Instance panel> expand Explode
Detail Tools		
	Detail Component	• **Ribbon:** *Annotate* tab>Detail panel> expand Component
	Detail Line	• **Ribbon:** *Annotate* tab>Detail panel
	Insulation	• **Ribbon:** *Annotate* tab>Detail panel
	Filled Region	• **Ribbon:** *Annotate* tab>Detail panel
	Repeating Detail Component	• **Ribbon:** *Annotate* tab>Detail panel> expand Component
View Tools		
	Bring Forward	• **Ribbon:** *Modify | Detail Items* tab> Arrange panel
	Bring to Front	• **Ribbon:** *Modify | Detail Items* tab> Arrange panel
	Drafting View	• **Ribbon:** *View* tab>Create panel
	Insert from File: Insert Views from File	• **Ribbon:** *Insert* tab>Import panel> expand Insert from File
	Send Backward	• **Ribbon:** *Modify | Detail Items* tab> Arrange panel
	Send to Back	• **Ribbon:** *Modify | Detail Items* tab> Arrange panel

Introduction to Worksets

Worksharing is a workflow used in the Autodesk® Revit® software when multiple people are working on a single project model. The model is broken up into worksets. Individuals open and work on in local files that are synchronized to a central file upon saving.

For more information about establishing and using Worksets, refer to the *Autodesk Revit Collaboration Tools* guide.

Learning Objectives in this Appendix

- Review worksharing principles.
- Open a local file to make changes to your part of a project.
- Synchronize your local file with the central file, which contains changes from all the local files.

A.1 Introduction to Worksets

When a project becomes too big for one person, it needs to be subdivided so that a team of people can work on it. Since Autodesk Revit projects include the entire building model in one file, the file needs to be separated into logical components, as shown in Figure A–1, without losing the connection to the whole. This process is called *worksharing* and the main components are worksets.

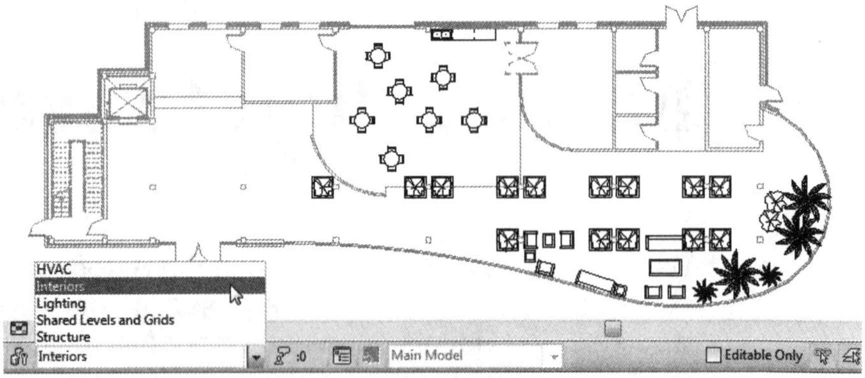

Figure A–1

When worksets are established in a project, there is one **central file** and as many **local files** as required for each person on the team to have a file, as shown in Figure A–2.

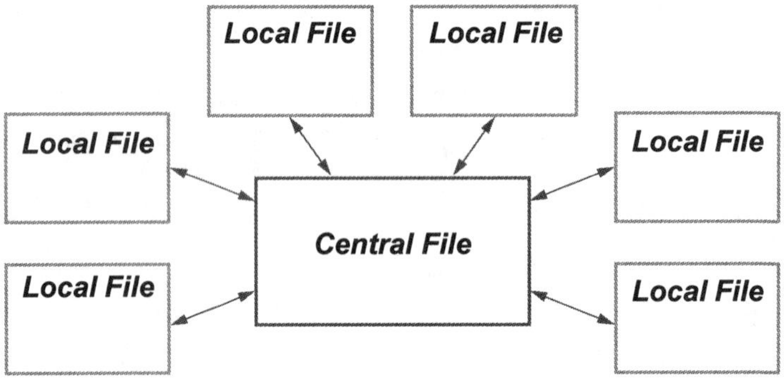

Figure A–2

- The **central file** is created by the BIM Manager, Project Manager, or Project Lead and is stored on a server, enabling multiple users to access it.

- A **local file** is a copy of the central file that is stored on your computer.

- All local files are saved back to the central file, and updates to the central file are sent out to the local files. This way, all changes remain in one file, while the project, model, views, and sheets are automatically updated.

How To: Create a Local File

1. In the *File* tab or Quick Access Toolbar, click  (Open). In the Open dialog box, navigate to the central file server location, and select the central file. Do not work in this file. Select **Create New Local**, as shown in Figure A–3.
2. Verify that this option is selected, and click **Open**.

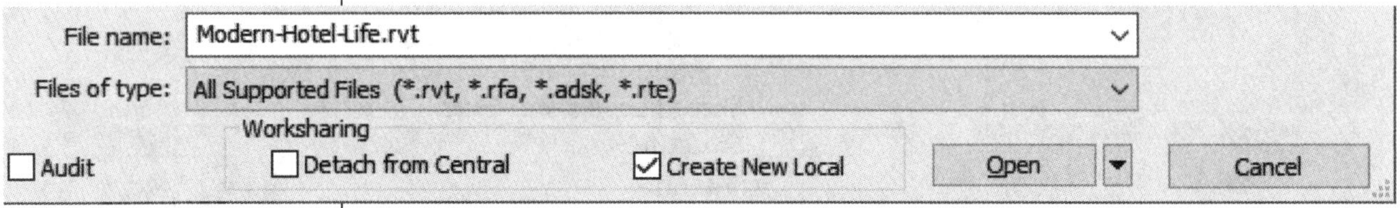

Figure A–3

User Names can be assigned in Options.

3. A copy of the project is created. It is named the same as the central file, but with your *User Name* added to the end.

- If you are working with a recently used central file, it may display in the Home Screen with the icon shown in Figure A–4. Clicking this file automatically creates a local copy of the model. The first time you use this option, a warning displays, as shown in Figure A–5.

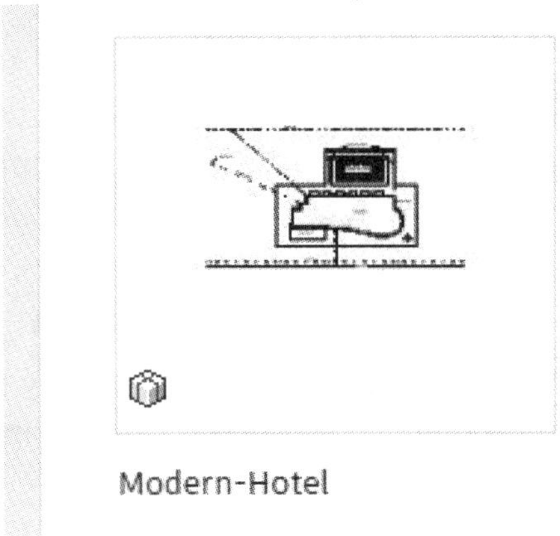

Figure A–4

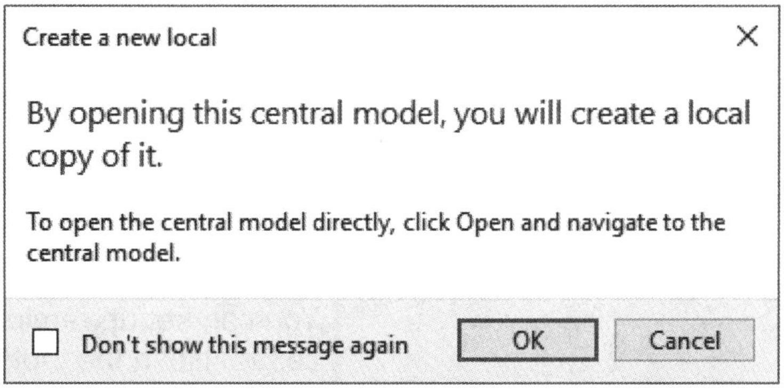

Figure A–5

4. You can save the file using the default name, or use  (Save As) and name the file according to your office's standard. It should include *Local* in the name to indicate that it is saved on your local computer, or that you are the only one working with that version of the file.

- Delete any old local files to ensure that you are working on the latest version.

How To: Work in a Workset-Related File

1. Open your local file.
2. In the Status Bar, expand the Active Workset drop-down list and select a workset, as shown in Figure A–6. By setting the active workset, other people can work in the project but cannot edit elements that you add to the workset.

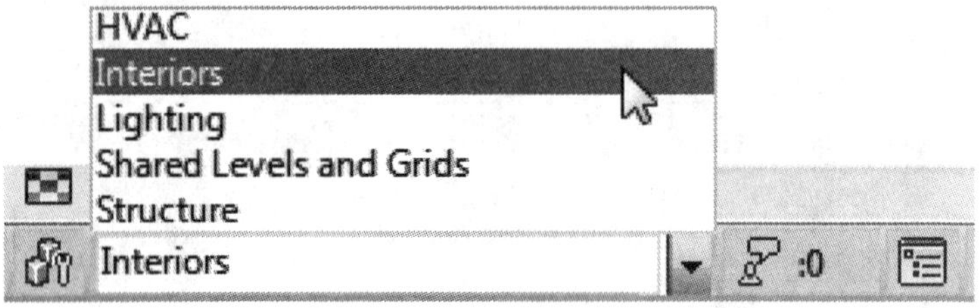

Figure A–6

3. Work on the project as required.

Saving Workset-Related Files

When you are using a workset-related file, you need to save the file locally and centrally.

- Save the local file frequently (every 15-30 minutes). In the Quick Access Toolbar, click (Save) to save the local file just as you would any other project.
- Synchronize the local file with the central file periodically (every hour or two) or after you have made major changes to the project.

Hint: Set up Notifications to Save and Synchronize

You can set up reminders to save and synchronize files to the central file in the Options dialog box, on the *General* pane, as shown in Figure A–7.

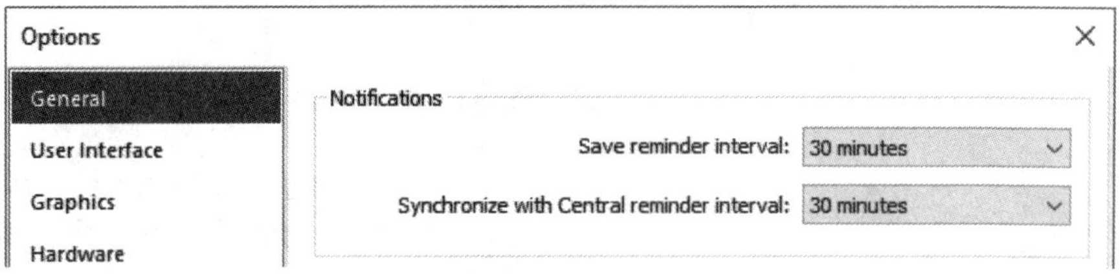

Figure A–7

Synchronizing to the Central File

There are two methods for synchronizing to the central file. They are located in the Quick Access Toolbar or the *Collaborate* tab> Synchronize panel.

Click (Synchronize Now) to update the central file and then the local file with any changes to the central file since the last synchronization. This does not prompt you for any thing. It automatically relinquishes elements borrowed from a workset used by another person, but retains worksets used by the current person.

Click (Synchronize and Modify Settings) to open the Synchronize with Central dialog box, as shown in Figure A–8, where you can set the location of the central file, add comments, save the file locally before and after synchronization, and set the options for relinquishing worksets and elements.

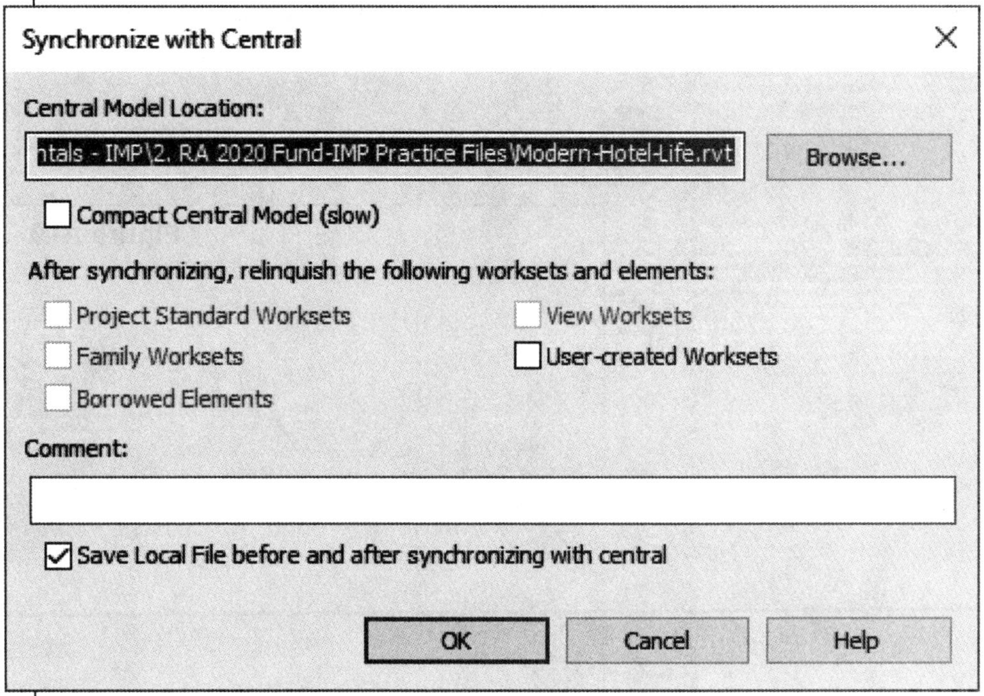

Figure A–8

- Ensure that **Save Local file before and after synchronizing with central** is checked before clicking **OK**. Changes from the central file might have been copied into your file.
- When you close a local file without saving to the central file, you are prompted with options, as shown in Figure A–9.

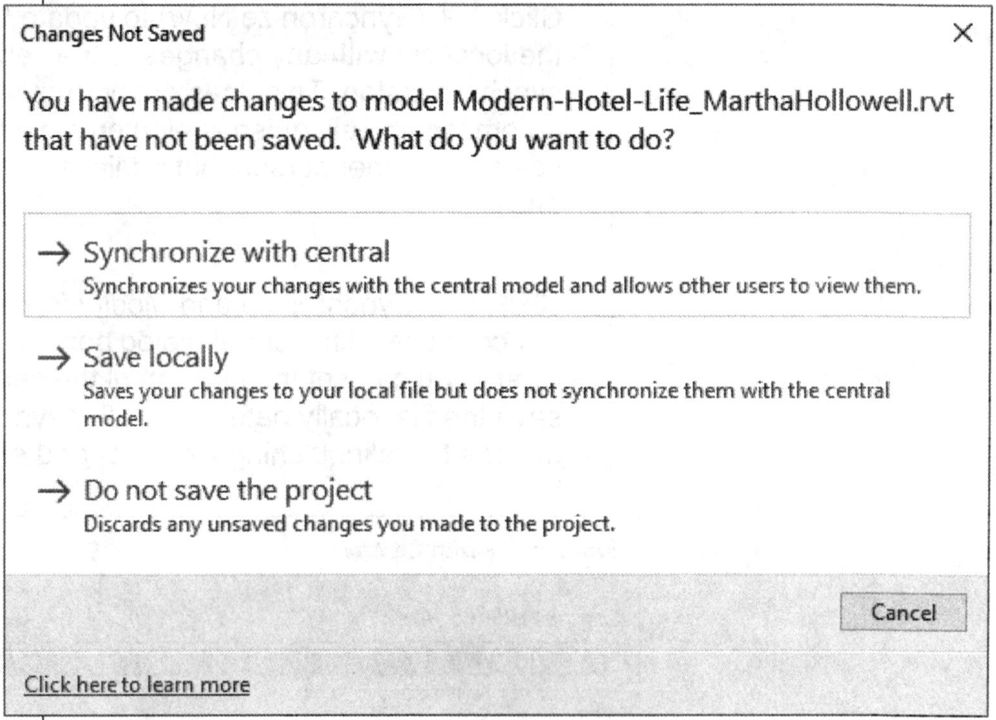

Figure A–9

Command Summary

Button	Command	Location
	**Save**	• **Quick Access Toolbar** • **File tab:** Save • **Shortcut:** <Ctrl>+<S>
	**Synchronize and Modify Settings**	• **Quick Access Toolbar** • **Ribbon:** *Collaborate* tab> Synchronize panel>expand Synchronize with Central
	**Synchronize Now**	• **Quick Access Toolbar** • **Ribbon:** *Collaborate* tab> Synchronize panel>expand Synchronize with Central

Additional Tools

There are many other tools available in the Autodesk® Revit® software that you can use when creating and using models. This appendix provides details about several tools and commands that are related to those covered in this guide.

Learning Objectives in this Appendix

- Save and use selection sets of multiple building elements.
- Edit wall joins.
- Add wall sweeps and reveals as well as roof fascias, gutters, and floor slab edges.
- Create a Curtain Wall type with an equally spaced grid pattern.
- Clarify views using Split Face, Paint, Linework, and Cut Profiles.
- Add dormers to roofs.
- Use guide grids to help place views on sheets.
- Add revision clouds, tags, and information.
- Use Path of Travel to analyze travel distances between points in the model.
- Annotate dependent views with matchlines and view references.
- Import and export schedules.
- Create basic building component schedules.
- Create repeating detail types.
- Place keynotes in a detail and add keynote legends that describe the full content of the keynotes.

B.1 Reusing Selection Sets

When multiple elements types are selected you can save the selection set so that it can be reused. For example, a structural column and an architectural column need to move together. Instead of picking each element, create a selection set that you can quickly access as shown in Figure B–1. You can also edit selection sets to add or remove elements from the set.

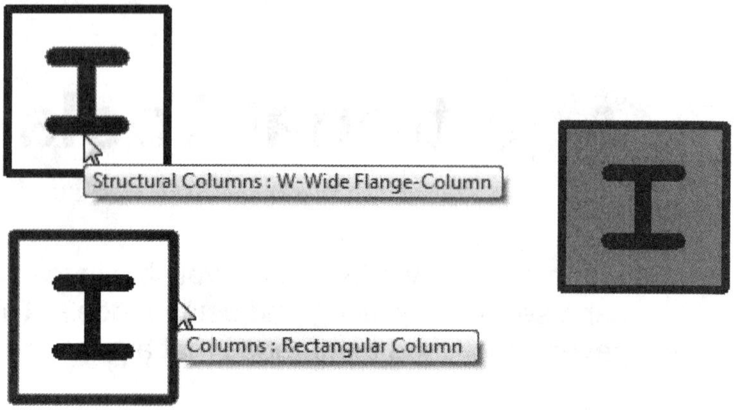

Figure B–1

- Selection sets are a filter of specific elements rather than types of elements.

How To: Save Selection Sets

1. Select the elements that you want to include in the selection set.
2. In the *Modify* | *Multi-Select* tab>Selection panel, click  (Save).
3. In the Save Selection dialog box, type a name for the set as shown in Figure B–2, and click **OK**.

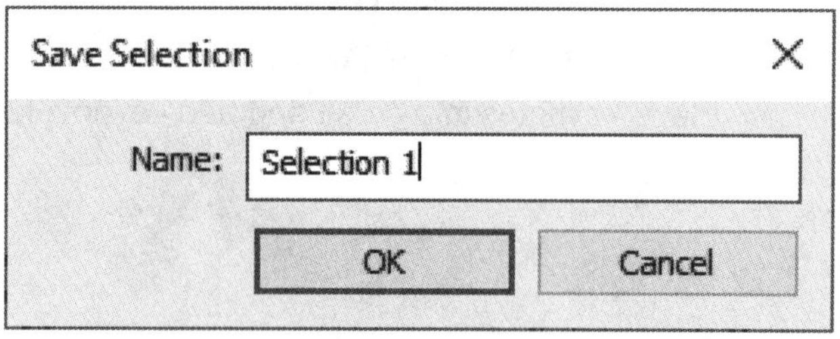

Figure B–2

How To: Retrieve Selection Sets

1. Select any other elements you might want to use. In the *Modify | Multi-Select* tab>Selection panel, click (Load). Alternatively, without any other selection, in the *Manage* tab>Selection panel, click (Load).
2. In the Retrieve Filters dialog box (shown in Figure B–3), select the set that you want to use and click **OK**.

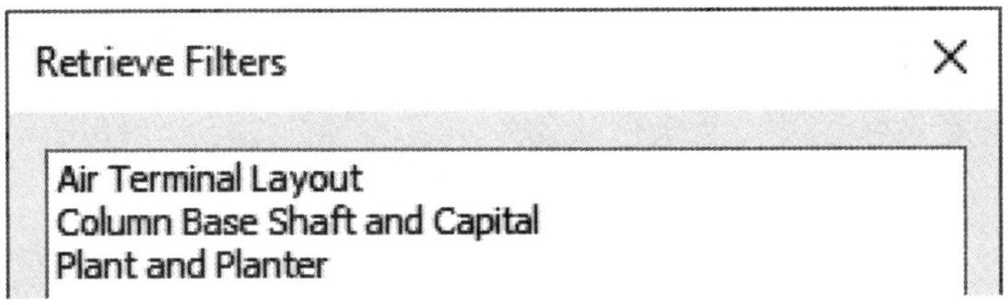

Figure B–3

3. The elements are selected and you can continue to select other elements or use the selection.

How To: Edit Selection Sets

1. If elements are selected, in the *Modify | Multi-Select* tab>Selection panel, click (Edit). Alternatively, without any selection, in the *Manage* tab>Selection panel, click (Edit).

Rule-based Filters are not selection sets but apply to categories of elements, such as the Interior filter shown in Figure B–4.

2. In the Edit Filters dialog box (shown in Figure B–4), in the **Selection Filters** node, select the set that you want to edit and click **Edit....**

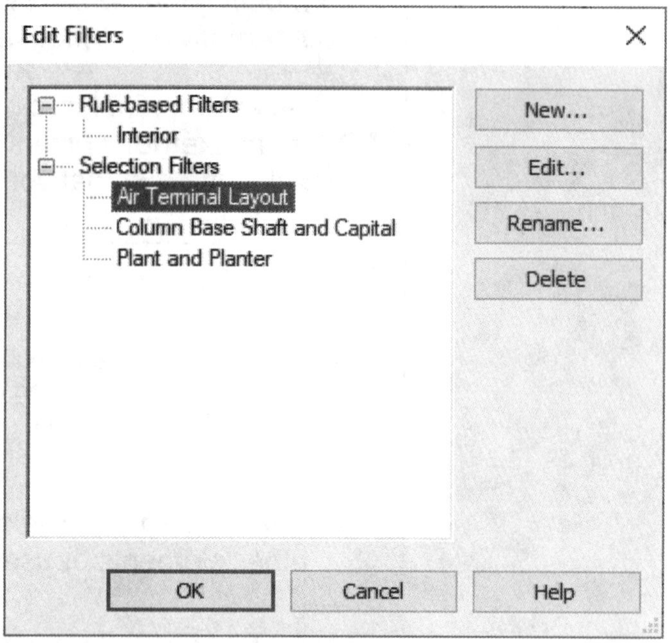

Figure B–4

- If you want to modify the name of the Filter, click **Rename....**

3. The selection set elements remain black while the rest of the elements are grayed out. The *Edit Selection Set* contextual tab displays as well, as shown in Figure B–5.

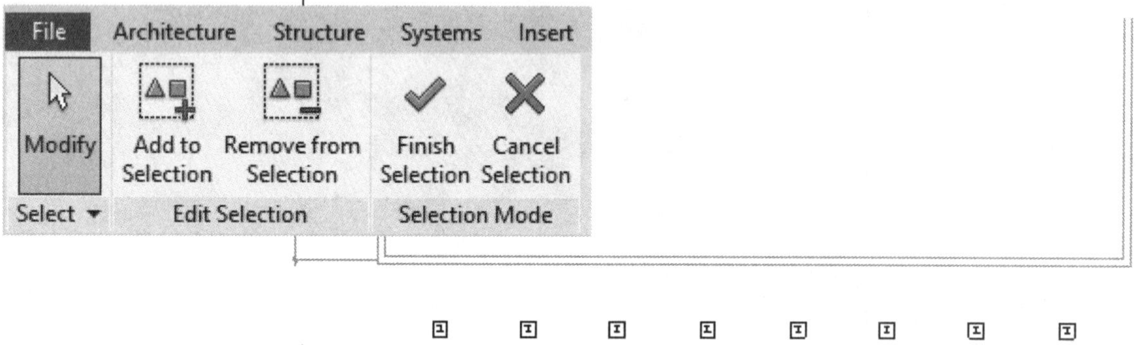

Figure B–5

4. Use  (Add to Selection) to select additional elements for the set and  (Remove from Selection) to delete elements from the set.
5. When you have finished editing, click  (Finish Selection).

- In the Filters dialog box, click **OK** to finish.

B.2 Editing Wall Joins

Use **Edit Wall Joins** to modify the configuration of the intersections, as shown in Figure B–6. Do not use this command if you have complex wall joins; instead, modify the length of the wall in relation to the adjoining walls.

Figure B–6

How To: Modify the Configuration of a Wall Join

1. In the *Modify* tab>Geometry panel, click  (Wall Joins).
2. Click on the wall join that you want to edit. There is a square box around the join. Hold <Ctrl> to select multiple joins.
3. In the Options Bar, the configuration options display, as shown in Figure B–7. Select the required option.

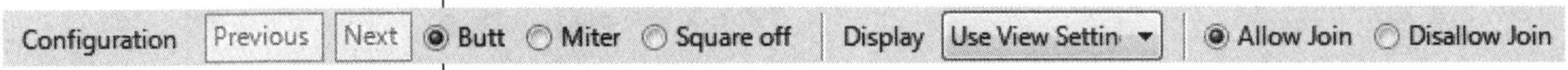

Figure B–7

- Select from three configurations: **Butt**, **Miter**, and **Square off**, as shown in Figure B–8.

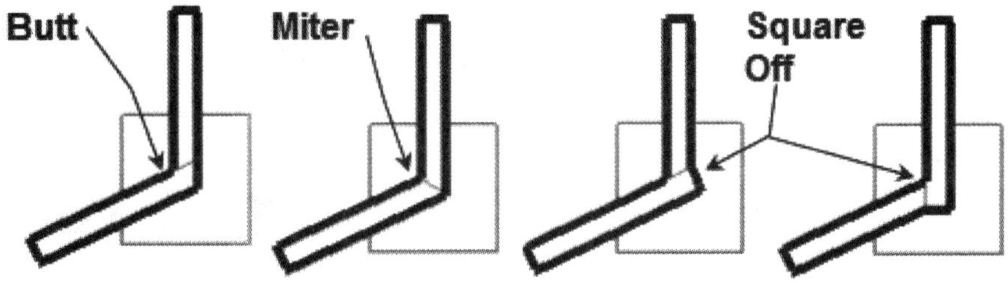

Figure B–8

- Click **Previous** and **Next** to toggle the butt or squared-off corner configurations through the various intersection options.
- **Allow Join** automatically cleans up the join while **Disallow Join** breaks the connection.

4. The **Wall Joins** command remains active until you select another command.

How To: Modify Display Options of Wall Joins

1. In the *Modify* tab>Geometry panel, click (Wall Joins).
2. Click on the wall join that you want to edit.
   - To modify multiple joins at the same time, draw a window around several wall intersections (as shown in Figure B–9), or hold <Ctrl> and pick additional intersections. A square box displays around each join.

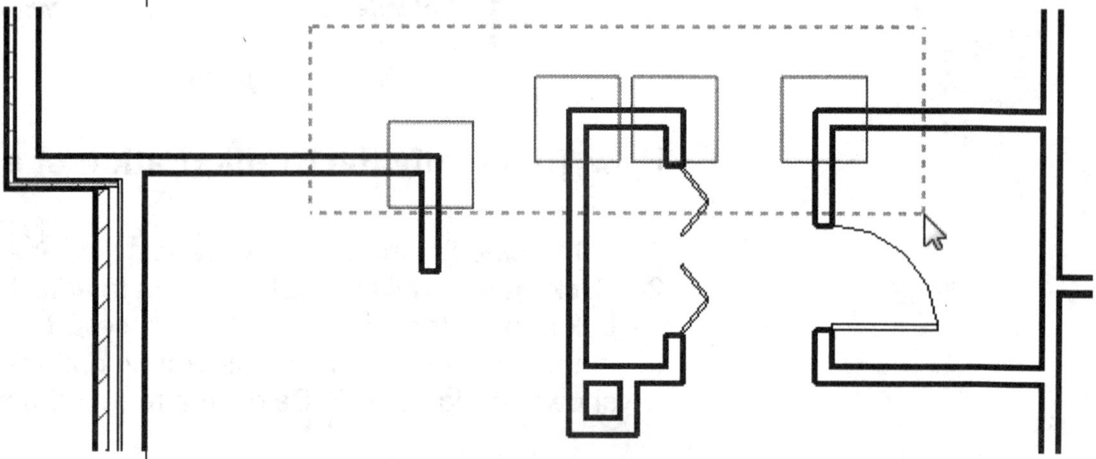

Figure B–9

- The *Display* controls whether or not wall joins are displayed. The options are **Use View Settings** (set up in View Properties), **Clean Join**, and **Don't Clean Join**, as shown in Figure B–10.

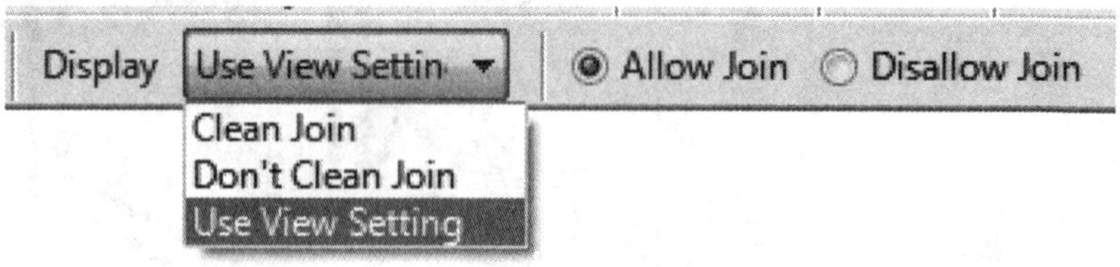

Figure B–10

3. If you select the end of a wall that is not joined to another wall, you can change the option to **Allow Join** in the Options Bar, as shown in Figure B–11. Reselect the wall join to make the configurations available.

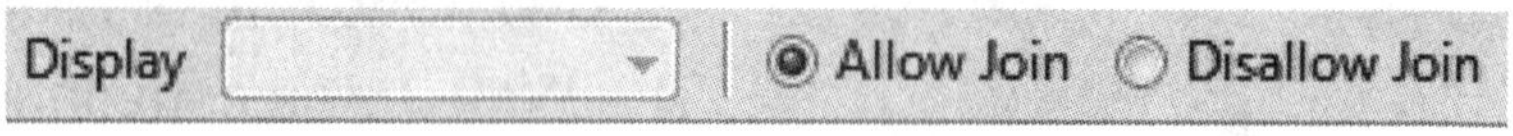

Figure B–11

B.3 Wall Sweeps and Reveals

The process of creating reveals, gutters, and floor slab edges, etc. is similar.

The Autodesk Revit software includes a series of commands that enable you to modify walls, roofs, and floors by sweeping a profile along an element. For example, you can quickly add a gutter along the full length of a roof, or a curb at the edge of a floor used as a balcony, as shown in Figure B–12. The element modified by the sweep is called the host. Therefore, all of these operations are known as host sweeps.

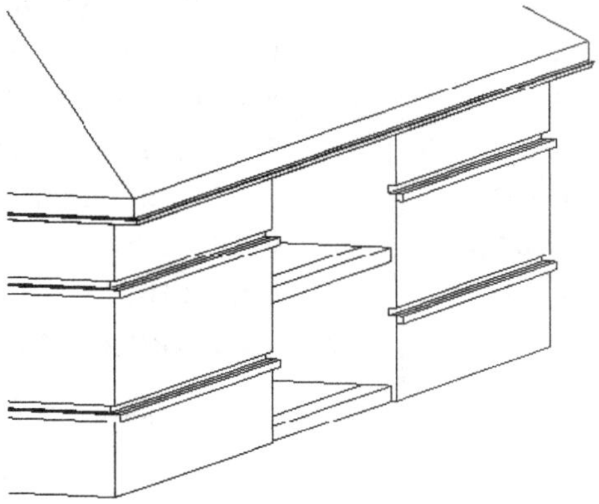

Figure B–12

- The software comes with a few standard profiles for the sweeps. You can also create your own custom profiles.
- Open a 3D view if you are working with walls. You can be in a plan or elevation view for working with roof and floor sweeps.
- There are specific commands to create wall sweeps and reveals, roof fascias and gutters, and floor slab edges. These are located by expanding the associated command in the *Architecture* tab>Build panel, as shown in Figure B–13. For walls and floors, they are also located in the *Structure* tab> Structure.

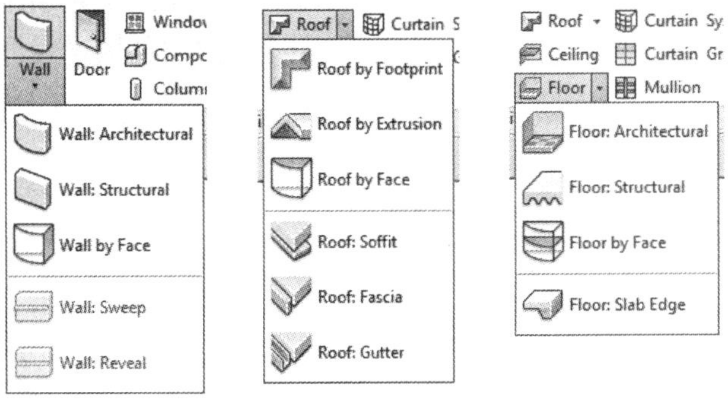

Figure B–13

- Wall Sweeps and Wall Reveals can only be applied in elevation, section, or 3D views.

How To: Use the Wall Sweep Command

1. Open an elevation or 3D view.
2. In the *Architecture* tab>Build panel, expand (Wall) and click (Wall Sweep).
3. In Properties, select a Wall Sweep type. (The Wall Sweep type needs to be set up before you start the command.)
4. In the *Modify | Place Wall Sweep* tab>Placement panel, click either (Horizontal) or (Vertical). (This is only for walls.)
5. Move the cursor over the element where you want to add the sweep and click to place it.
6. If you are doing horizontal sweeps, continue selecting elements. The sweep is placed at the same height as the first element.
7. To change sweep styles or the height, in the Placement panel, click (Restart Wall Sweep), or return to the **Modify** command to finish.

To specify a precise location for the sweep element, select it after you have created it and modify the dimensions as required.

How To: Set Up Sweep Profiles

1. In the *Insert* tab>Load from Library panel, click (Load Family).
2. In the Load Family dialog box, select the profile you want to use (in the *Profiles* folder) or select a custom profile.
3. Start the related host sweep command. For example, if you are working with a gutter, click (Roof: Gutter), or if you are working with a wall reveal, click (Wall: Reveal).
4. In Properties, select a Sweep type and click (Edit Type).
5. In the Type Properties dialog box, click **Duplicate...**.
6. Enter a new name for the type.

7. In the Type Properties dialog box, under *Construction*, select the *Profile*. You can also apply *Constraints* (for Wall Reveals and Wall Sweeps), *Materials and Finishes*, and *Identity Data*, as shown in Figure B–14.

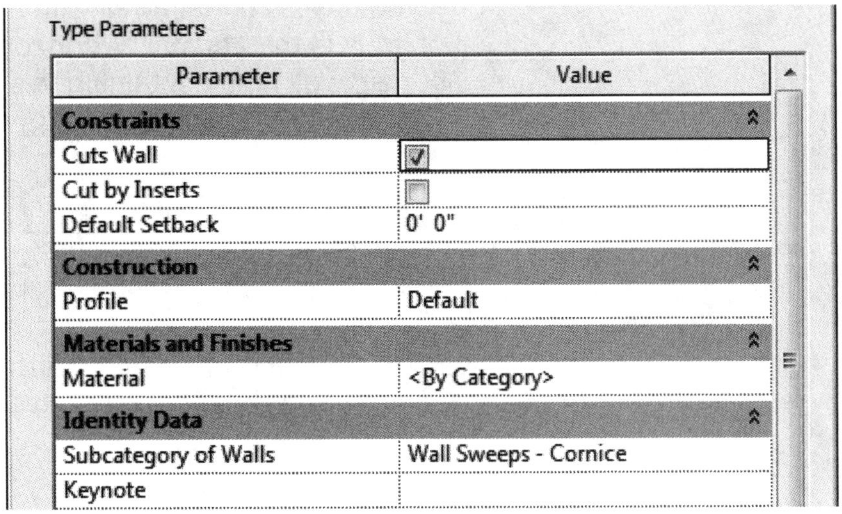
Type Parameters

Parameter	Value
Constraints	
Cuts Wall	☑
Cut by Inserts	☐
Default Setback	0' 0"
Construction	
Profile	Default
Materials and Finishes	
Material	<By Category>
Identity Data	
Subcategory of Walls	Wall Sweeps - Cornice
Keynote	

Figure B–14

8. Click **OK** to close the dialog box. The new type is set to be current.

Constraints

Constraints give you more control over how the sweep works.

Cuts Wall	If selected, cuts the geometry out of the host wall where it overlaps. Toggling this off might increase the performance if the project contains a large amount of sweeps.
Cut by Inserts	If selected, when doors or windows are inserted into a wall with a wall sweep, the insert cuts the sweep.
Default Setback	Specify the distance that the sweep is set back from interacting wall inserts.

B.4 Creating Curtain Wall Types with Automatic Grids

If you have a curtain wall with a fixed distance or a fixed number of grids in the vertical or horizontal direction, you can create a curtain wall type containing this information, as shown in Figure B–15. The automatic grid lines can also be set to an angle.

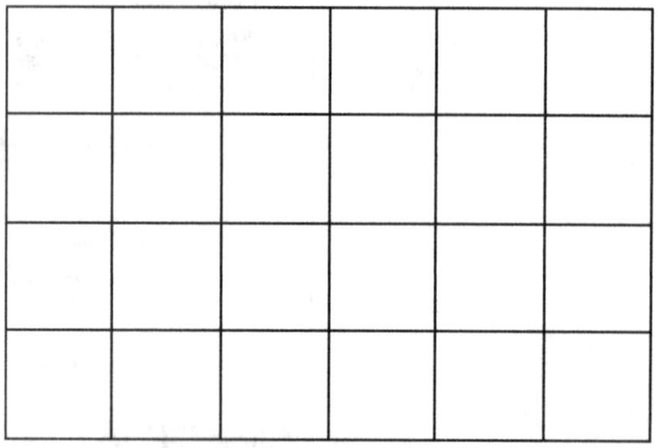

Figure B–15

How To: Create a Curtain Wall with Automatic Grids

1. In the *Architecture* tab>Build panel, click (Wall).
2. In the Type Selector, select a curtain wall similar to the one you want to create.
3. In Properties, click (Edit Type).
4. In the Type Properties dialog box, click **Duplicate...** to create a copy of the existing family type.
5. In the Name dialog box, give the curtain wall a name that describes its purpose, as shown in Figure B–16.
6. The new name automatically includes the family name, such as **Curtain Wall**. Therefore, you do not have to include the family name.

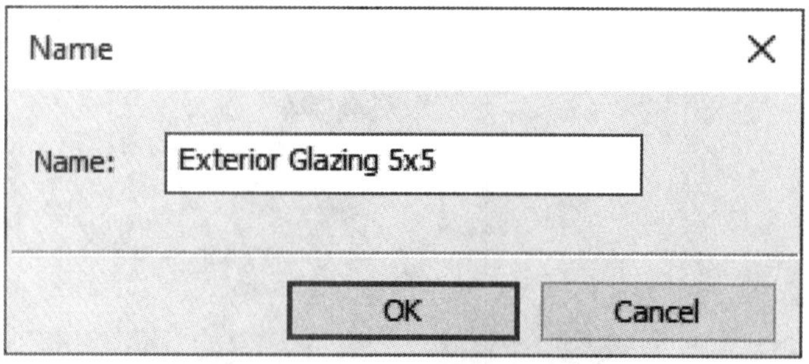

Figure B–16

Type Parameters apply to all instances of that type inserted into the Autodesk Revit software. This is true for all families (e.g., walls, doors, windows, etc.). Changing a Type Parameter changes all instances of that type in the project.

7. In the Type Properties dialog box, enter information for the *Construction*, *Vertical* and *Horizontal Grid Pattern*, and *Vertical* and *Horizontal Mullions* parameters, as shown in Figure B–17.

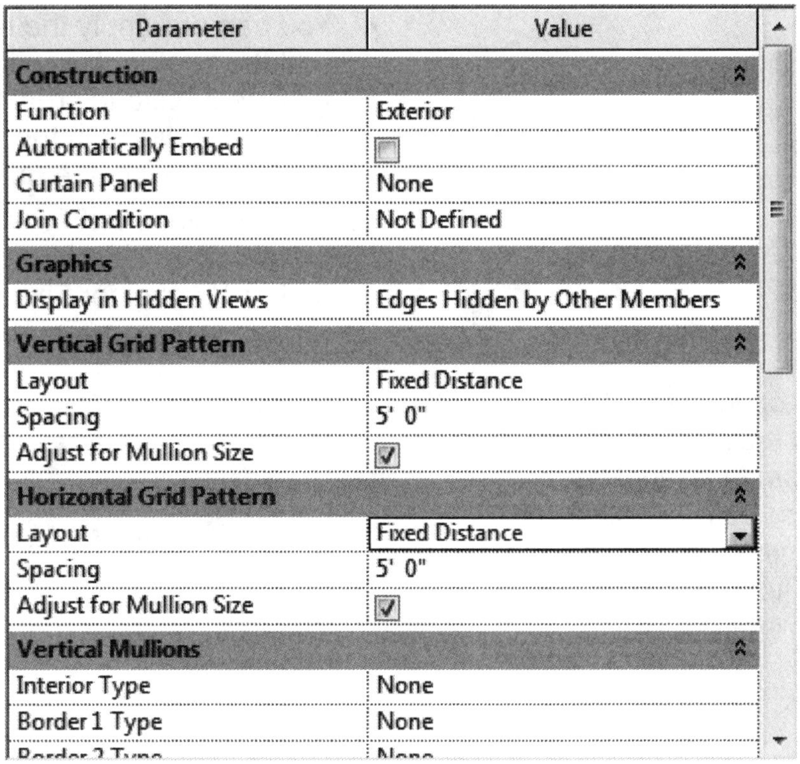

Figure B–17

- Enable the *Automatically Embed* parameter if you want to use the curtain wall as a storefront.
- Set the *Curtain Panel* to the primary type you plan to use. You can modify the panels once they are in the project.
- The Grid Patterns can be set to the following:

Fixed Distance	Grids are placed a specified distance apart. Specify the size in the **Spacing** option.
Fixed Number	Grids are divided across a wall based on a specified number. The *Number* of grid lines is specified in the Instance Parameters.
Maximum Spacing	Grids are spaced evenly with the greatest distance between them specified in the **Spacing** option.
None	No grids are specified.

- The **Adjust for Mullion Size** parameter ensures that panels inserted between grid lines are equal in size. This is very important if you use a different size of mullion on the borders from the ones on the interior separations.

- Mullions can be specified in the Type Parameters for Interior and Border mullions. The vertical **Border 1** type is applied to the left of the curtain wall and **Border 2** is applied to the right. The horizontal **Border 1** type is at the bottom and **Border 2** is at the top.
- You can pre-apply the mullions to the grid in the type or add them later. If you are planning to use the curtain wall type as a base to create a more complex curtain wall, do not add mullions in the type because doing so makes it difficult to select the grid lines to modify them.

8. Click **OK** to close the Type Properties dialog box.
9. In Properties, set the *Vertical* and *Horizontal Grid Pattern* (including *Number* for Fixed Number, *Justification*, *Angle*, and *Offset*), as shown in Figure B–18.

The options in Properties are Instance Parameters applied to the selected instance of the type inserted into the Autodesk Revit software.

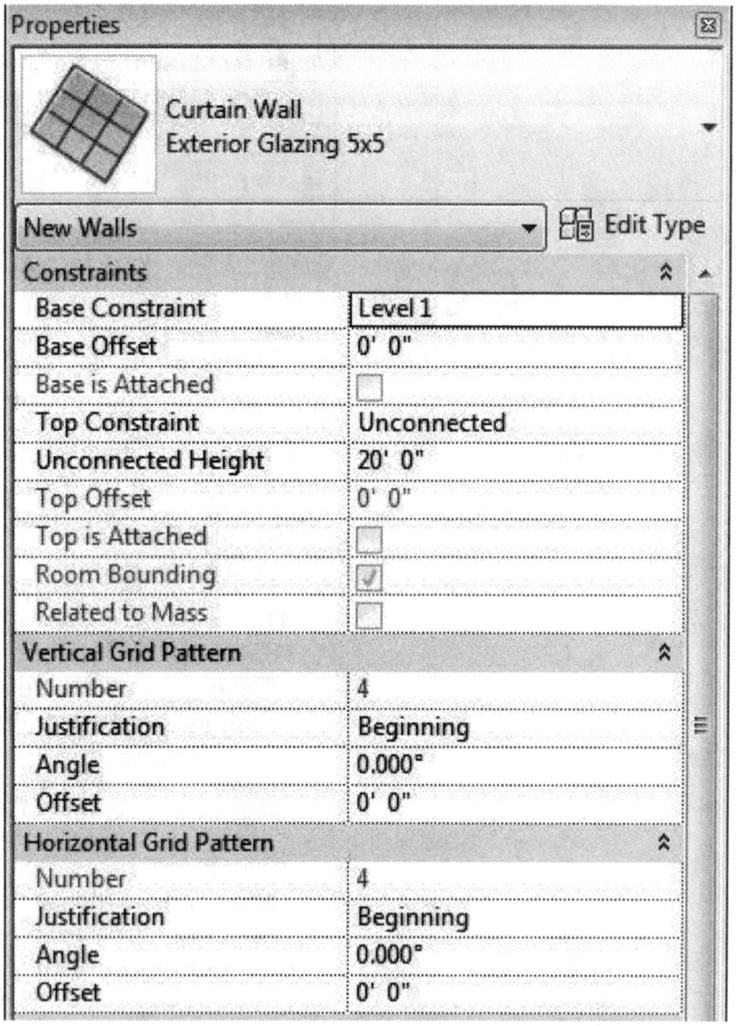

Figure B–18

B.5 Enhancing Views

When you start detailing views (such as elevations and sections), several tools can help clarify what you are trying to show. **Split Face** divides an elevation face into smaller separate faces. You can then use **Paint** to apply different materials to the faces, as shown in Figure B–19. **Linework** enables you to change the lineweight or line style of lines in a view to emphasize various components. In plan views and sections, you can use **Cut Profile** to enhance the views.

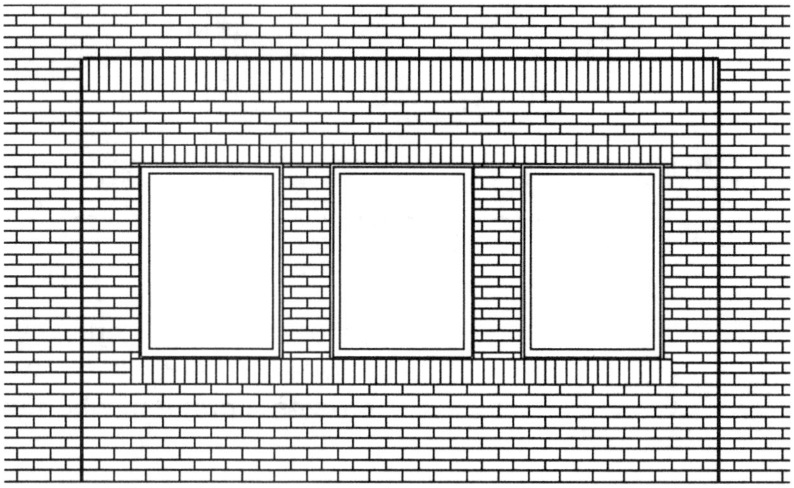

Figure B–19

- The changes made with **Split Face** and **Paint** are displayed in elevations and 3D views.
- Changes made using **Linework** are view-specific, applying only in the view in which they are made.
- Additional options for modifying the look of a view are found in the Graphic Display Options dialog box (In the View Control Bar, expand **Visual Styles** and select **Graphic Display Options...**). These include *Sketchy Lines* and *Depth Cueing* as well as other options for setting up views for rendering.

Splitting Faces

You can split a face into separate surfaces so you can apply different materials to each part. A sketch defines the split, which must be a closed shape completely inside the face, or an open shape that touches the face edges, as shown in Figure B–20. Windows are cut out of faces automatically.

Figure B–20

- Before you start working with split faces, ensure the walls are mitered. By default, the walls are butted to each other. This creates a problem when you select faces.

How To: Create a Split Face

1. Switch to an elevation view (a 3D view works as well).
2. In the *Modify* tab>Geometry panel, click (Split Face).
3. Select the edge of the face that you want to modify. Use <Tab> as required to toggle through the available faces.
4. In the *Modify | Split Face>Create Boundary* tab>Draw panel, use the sketch tools to create a sketch as required to define the split.
5. Click (Finish Edit Mode).

*If you have **Select elements by face** toggled on you can click directly on the face.*

- To save time, use a wall style that includes the primary material you want to use on the split face. For example, if you are working with brick, set the wall to a type that has a brick face. This way, you can work with the brick courses when you are creating the split face.

- When using a material, such as brick, you can snap to the pattern and even lock the split lines to the pattern as shown in Figure B–21.

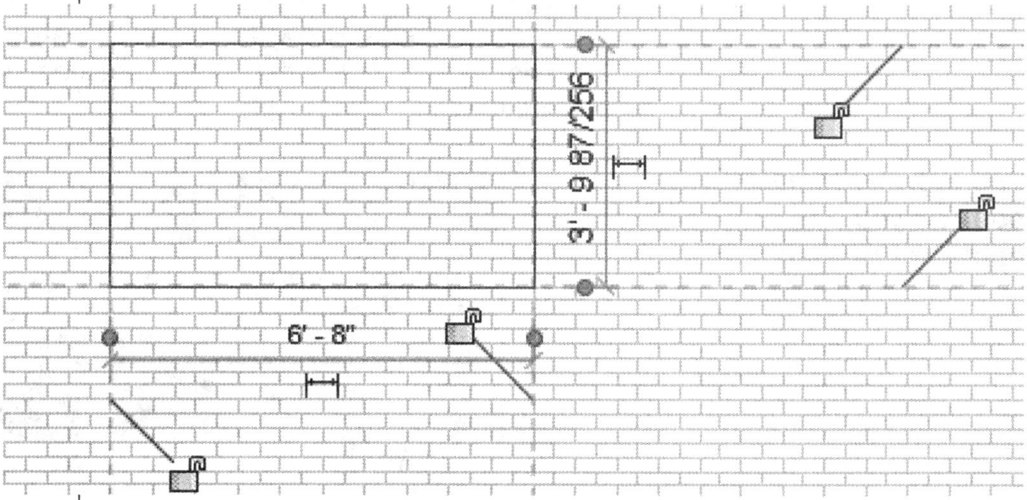

Figure B–21

You can double-click on the edge of the split face lines to switch to Edit Boundary mode. If you double-click on the face (with **Select elements by face** toggled on) it switches to Edit Profile mode, which impacts the entire wall, not just the split face boundary.

Applying Materials

Once you have a face split into sections, you can apply different materials to each part. For example, you might want a soldier course under each window on a brick wall. First, you would create the split face and then apply the new material using **Paint**, as shown in Figure B–22.

Figure B–22

How To: Apply Material with Paint

1. In the *Modify* tab>Geometry panel, click (Paint) or type **PT**.
2. In the Material Browser, select a material. You can run a search or filter the list using specific types of materials, as shown in Figure B–23.

The browser remains open as you are applying the paint.

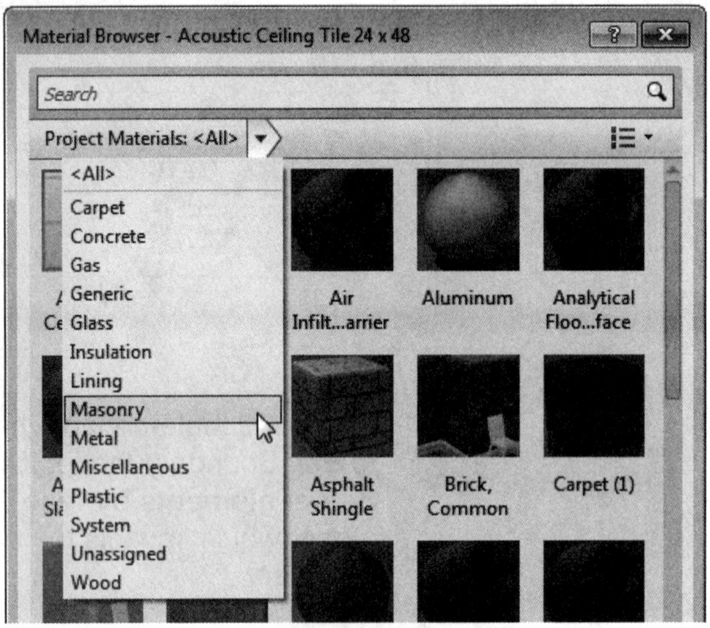

Figure B–23

3. Move the cursor over the face you want to paint. It should highlight. Click on the face to apply the material.
4. Continue selecting materials and painting other faces as required.
5. In the Material Browser, click **Done** to finish the command.

- Some material patterns display as shaded when you zoom out. Zoom in to display the pattern. Other material patterns only display when you are in the (Realistic) Visual Style.
- To change the material applied to a face, in the *Modify* tab> Geometry panel, expand (Paint) and click (Remove Paint). Select the face(s) from which you want to remove the material.
- If you paint the top of a wall, you can modify the location of the pattern using **Move**, **Rotate**, and **Align**, as well as dragging the pattern. Adjusting Linework

To emphasize a particular line or change the look of a line in elevations and other views, modify the lines with the **Linework** command. Changes made to lines with the **Linework** command are view-specific, applying only to the view in which you make them, as shown in Figure B–24.

- The **Linework** command can be used on project edges of model elements, cut edges of model elements, edges in imported CAD files, and edges in linked Autodesk Revit models.

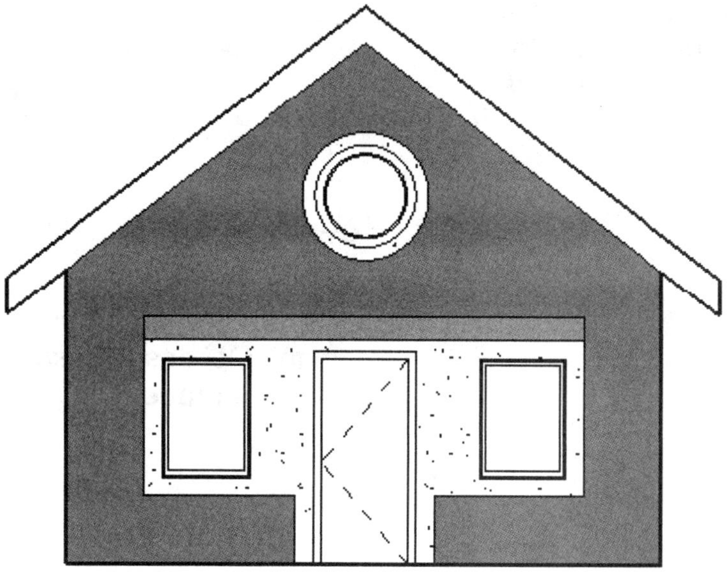

Figure B–24

How To: Adjust Linework

1. In the *Modify* tab>View panel, click  (Linework) or type the shortcut **LW**.
2. In the *Modify | Linework* tab>Line Style panel, select the line style you want to use from the list.
3. Move the cursor and highlight the line you want to change. You can use <Tab> to toggle through the lines as required.
4. Click on the line to change it to the new line style.
5. Click on other lines as required or return to the **Modify** command to finish.

- If the line is too long or short, you can modify the length using the controls at the end of the line

Editing Plan and Section Profiles

*If you are working on a compound face (such as a wall with several layers of information), change the Detail Level to **Medium** or **Fine** to display the fill patterns.*

In plan and section details, you might need to modify portions of the cut to show the specific intersection of two faces, as shown in Figure B–25. This can be done using **Cut Profile**. The cut profile changes the shape of the elements at their cut plane, but does not modify their 3D information. The cut is only displayed in the view in which it is sketched.

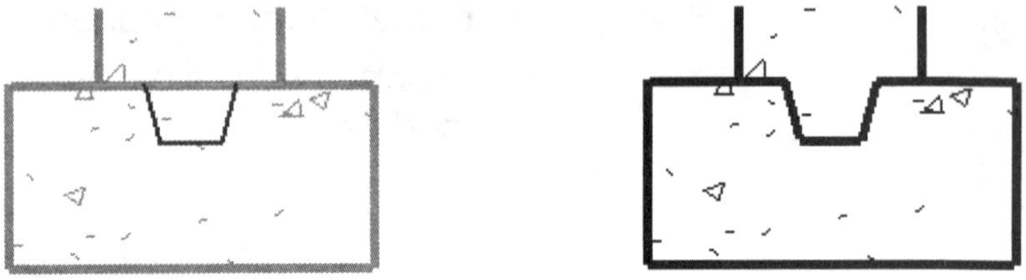

Figure B–25

- You can modify the cut of walls, floors, and roofs.

How To: Use Cut Profile

1. In the *View* tab>Graphics panel, click (Cut Profile).
2. In the Options Bar, select to edit the **Face** or the **Boundary between faces**, as shown in Figure B–26.

Figure B–26

3. Select the face or boundary that you want to edit.
4. In the *Modify | Create Cut Profile Sketch* tab>Draw panel, use the sketch tools to sketch a new profile, as shown in Figure B–27.

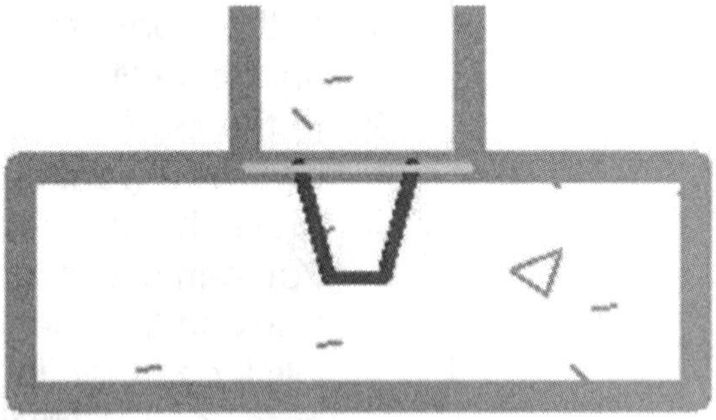

Figure B–27

5. Click (Finish Edit Mode).

- If a warning box opens, verify that the lines start and end on the same boundary line and that they do not make a closed loop or cross over each other.

B.6 Creating Dormers

You can add two types of dormers to a project. One type of dormer cuts through the roof, as shown in Figure B–28. This dormer type has walls supporting a separate roof. You create the supporting walls and dormer roof, and then cut a hole in the roof.

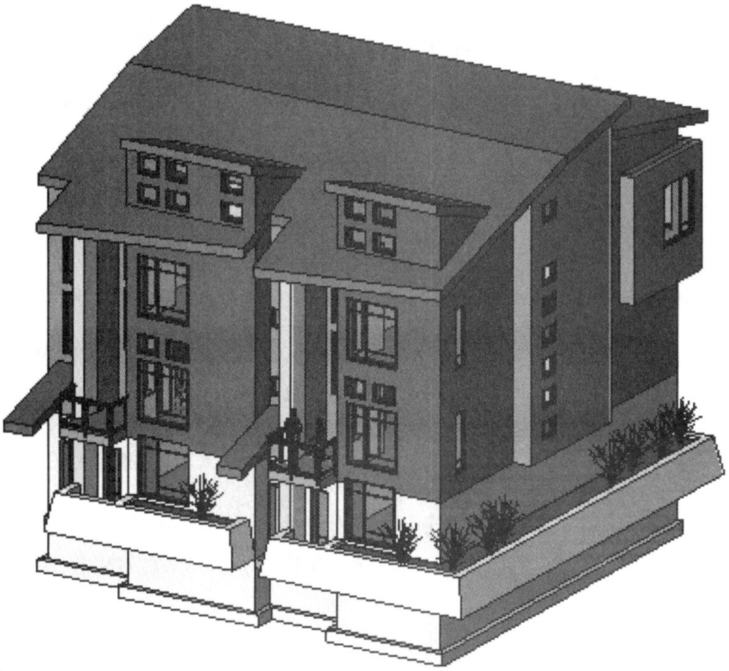

Figure B–28

The other type of dormers are part of the roof, as shown in Figure B–29. This is created by sketching the roof, modifying it, and adding slope arrows to define the additional peak.

Figure B–29

- The dormer must be added to a plane that defines a slope.

How To: Add a Dormer with Supporting Walls to a Roof

1. Draw the main roof. When it is placed correctly, create a secondary dormer roof and supporting walls, as shown in Figure B–30.

Figure B–30

2. Move the new dormer (walls and roof) into position as required.
3. In the *Modify* tab>Geometry panel, use (Join Geometry and (Join/Unjoin Roof) to connect the dormer walls/roof to the existing roof.
4. In the *Architecture* tab>Opening panel, click (Dormer Opening).
5. In a roof plan view, select the main roof (the one to be cut).
6. In the *Modify* | *Edit Sketch* tab>Pick panel, click (Pick Roof/Wall Edges) and select the opening to be cut.

- The dormer opening sketch does not need to be closed.
- Clean up the roofs and roof edges as required using tools such as **Join**, **Attach Top/Base**, etc.

How To: Add A Dormer Using Slope Arrows to a Roof

1. Draw a roof. When it is placed, select the roof. In the *Modify* | *Roofs* tab>Mode panel, click (Edit Footprint) to edit the roof sketch.

2. In the *Modify | Roofs>Edit Footprint* tab>Modify panel, click (Split Element) to split the edge of the roof between the two points where you want the dormer to be located. Do not delete the inner segment. You can use dynamic dimensions to help locate the points to split.

3. In the Selection panel, click (Modify) and select the new segment between the split points. In the Options Bar, clear the **Defines Slope** option for this segment.

4. In the Draw panel, click (Slope Arrow).
5. Draw a slope arrow from one end of the segment to the midpoint. Then sketch a second slope arrow from the other end to the midpoint, as shown in Figure B–31.

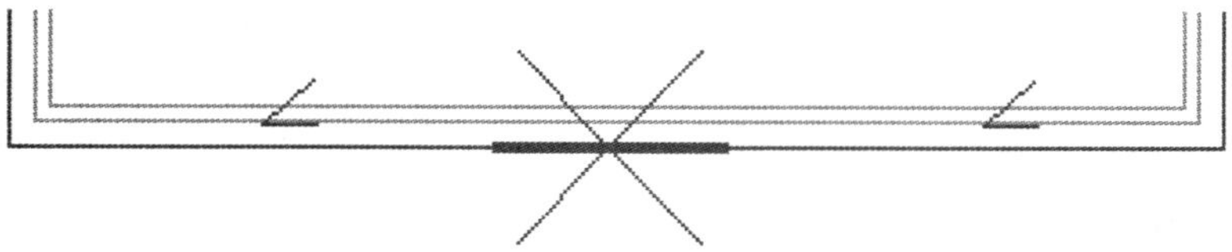

Figure B–31

6. Select the slope arrows. In Properties, specify the **Height at the Tail** or **Slope** and type the required properties.

7. In the Mode panel, click (Finish Edit Mode).
8. View the roof in a 3D view to verify the results, as shown in Figure B–32.

Figure B–32

B.7 Working with Guide Grids on Sheets

When moving a view to a guide grid, only orthogonal datum elements (levels and grids) and reference planes snap to the guide grid.

You can use a guide grid to help you place views on a sheet, as shown in Figure B–33. Guide grids can be set up per sheet. You can also create different types with various grid spacings.

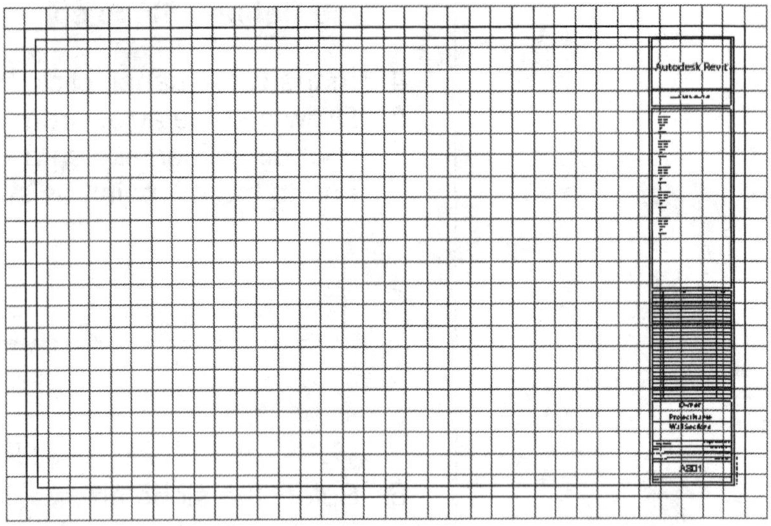

Figure B–33

- You can move guide grids and resize them using controls.

How To: Add A Guide Grid

1. When a sheet is open, in the *View* tab>Sheet Composition panel, click (Guide Grid).

2. In the Assign Guide Grid dialog box, select from existing guide grids (as shown in Figure B–34), or create a new one and give it a name.

Figure B–34

3. The guide grid displays using the specified sizing.

How To: Modify Guide Grid Sizing

1. If you create a new guide grid you need to update it to the correct size in Properties. Select the edge of the guide grid.
2. In Properties, set the *Guide Spacing*, as shown in Figure B–35.

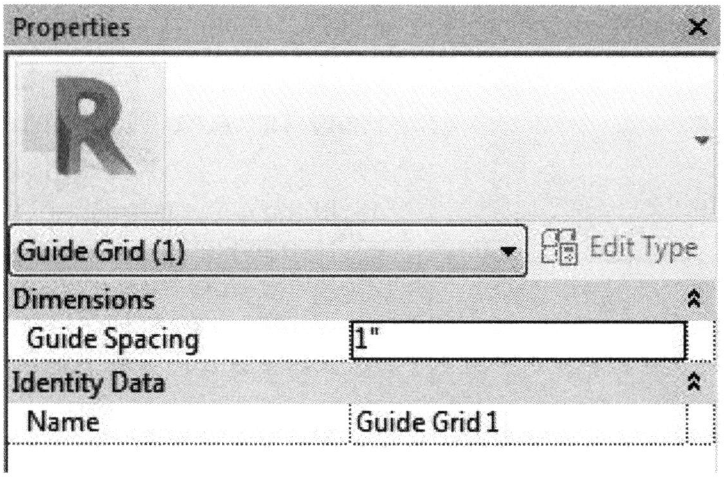

Figure B–35

B.8 Revision Tracking

When a set of working drawings has been put into production, you need to show where changes are made. Typically, these are shown on sheets using revision clouds and tags along with a revision schedule in the title block, as shown in Figure B–36. The revision information is setup in the Sheet Issues/Revisions dialog box.

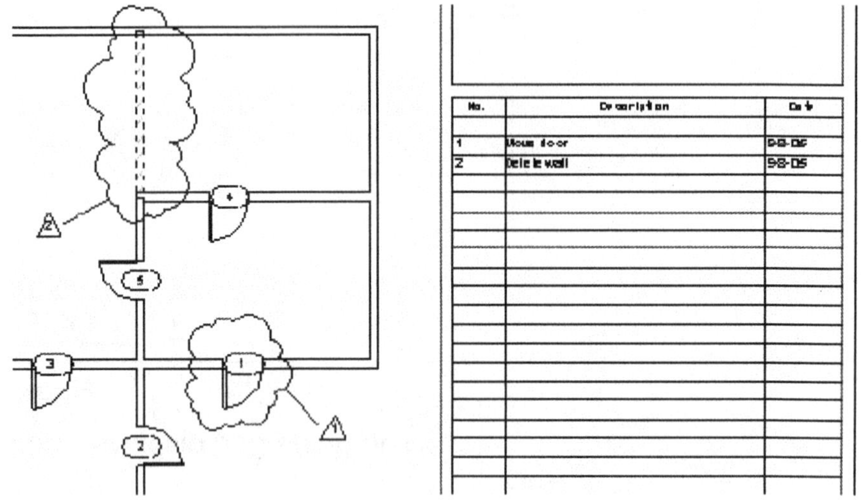

Figure B–36

- More than one revision cloud can be associated with a revision number.

- The title blocks that come with the Autodesk Revit software already have a revision schedule inserted into the title area. It is recommended that you also add a revision schedule to your company title block.

How To: Add Revision Information to the Project

1. In the *View* tab>Sheet Composition panel, click (Sheet Issues/Revisions).
2. In the Sheet Issues/Revisions dialog box, set the type of *Numbering* you want to use.
3. Click **Add** to add a new revision.

4. Specify the *Date* and *Description* for the revision, as shown in Figure B–37.

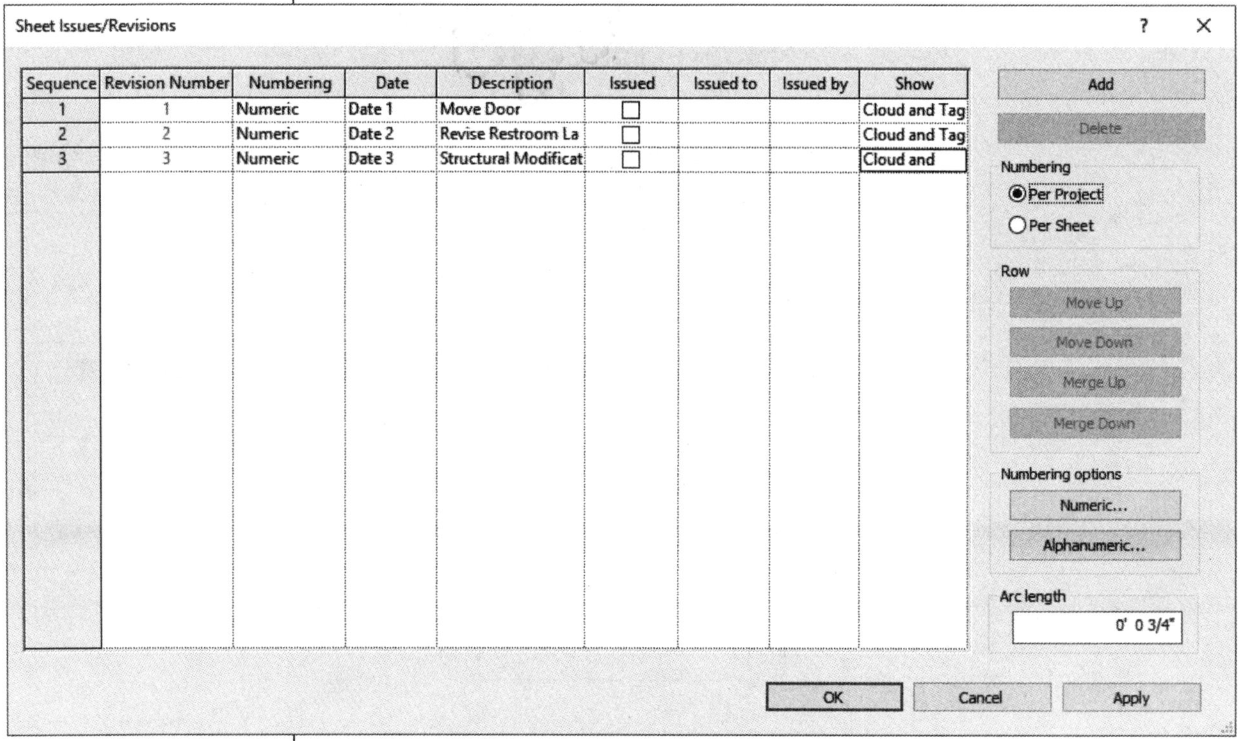

Figure B–37

- Do not modify the *Issued*, *Issued by*, or *Issued to* columns. You should wait to issue revisions until you are ready to print the sheets.

5. Click **OK** when you have finished adding revisions.
   - To remove a revision, select its *Sequence* number and click **Delete**.

Revision Options

- *Numbering:* specify **Per Project** (the numbering sequence is used throughout the project) or **Per Sheet** (the number sequence is per sheet).

- *Row*: To reorganize the revisions, select a row and click **Move Up** and **Move Down**, or use **Merge Up** and **Merge Down** to combine the revisions into one.

- *Numbering Options:* Click **Numeric...** or **Alphanumeric...** to bring up the Customize Numbering Options dialog box where you can specify the numbers or letters used in the sequence as well as any prefix or suffix, as shown for the *Alphanumeric* tab in Figure B–38.

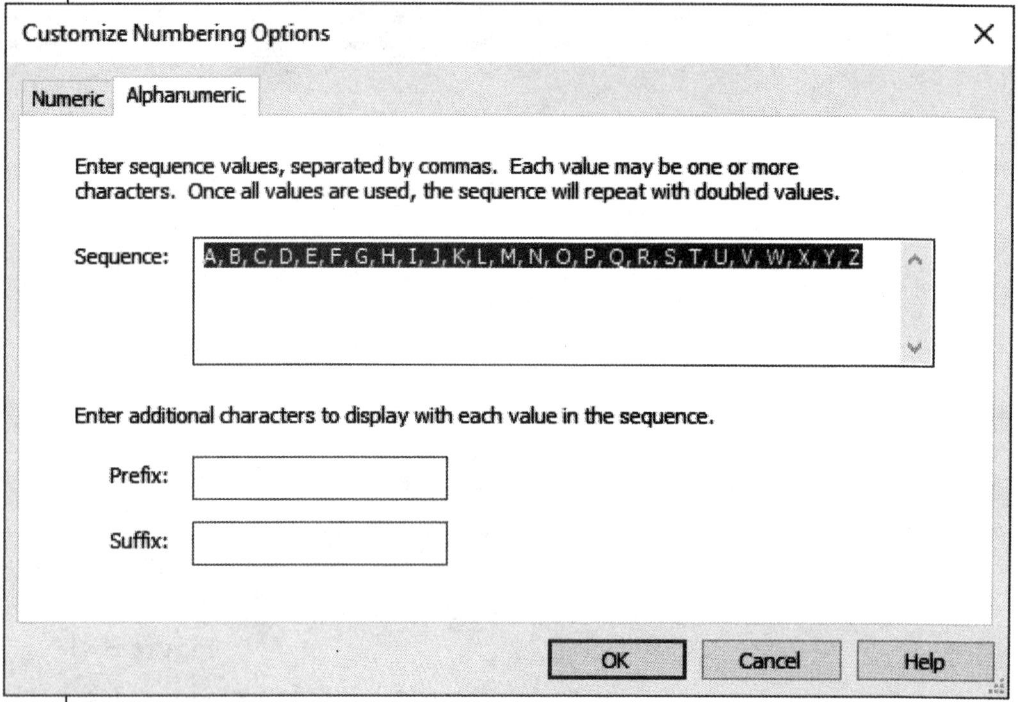

Figure B–38

- *Arc length:* Specify the length of the arcs that form the revision cloud. It is an annotation element and is scaled according to the view scale.

How To: Add Revision Clouds and Tag

1. In the *Annotate* tab>Detail panel, click (Revision Cloud).
2. In the *Modify | Create Revision Cloud Sketch* tab>Draw panel, use the draw tools to create the cloud.
3. Click (Finish Edit Mode).

If the revision table has not be set up, you can do this at a later date.

4. In the Options Bar or Properties, expand the Revision drop-down list and select from the Revision list, as shown in Figure B–39.

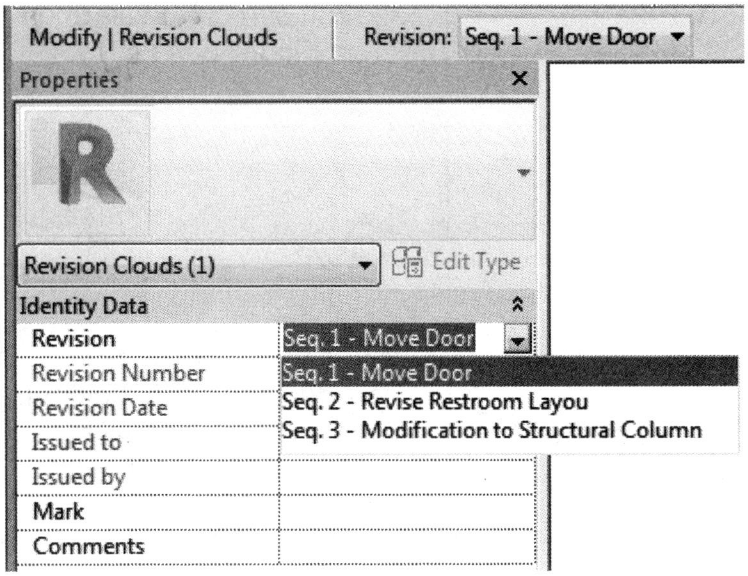

Figure B–39

5. In the *Annotate* tab>Tag panel, click (Tag By Category).
6. Select the revision cloud to tag. A tooltip containing the revision number and revision from the cloud properties displays when you hover the cursor over the revision cloud, as shown in Figure B–40.

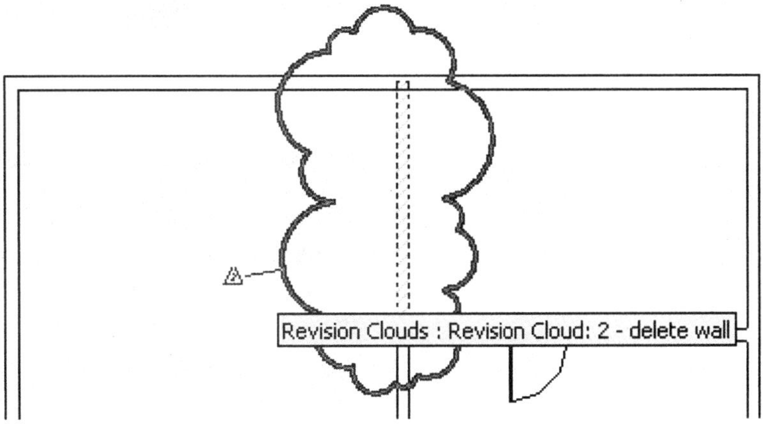

Figure B–40

- If the revision cloud tag is not loaded, load **Revision Tag.rfa** from the *Annotations* folder in the Library.
- The *Revision Number* and *Date* are automatically assigned according to the specifications in the revision table.

- Double-click on the edge of revision cloud to switch to the Edit Sketch mode and modify the size or location of the revision cloud arcs.

- You can create an open cloud (e.g., as a tree line), as shown in Figure B–41.

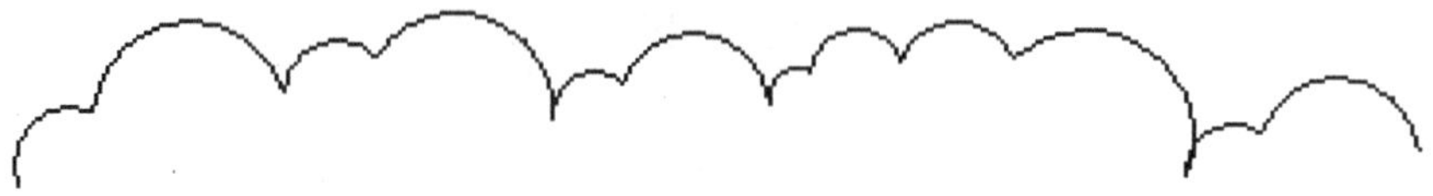

Figure B–41

Issuing Revisions

When you have completed the revisions and are ready to submit new documents to the field, you should first lock the revision for the record. This is called issuing the revision. An issued revision is noted in the tooltip of a revision cloud, as shown in Figure B–42.

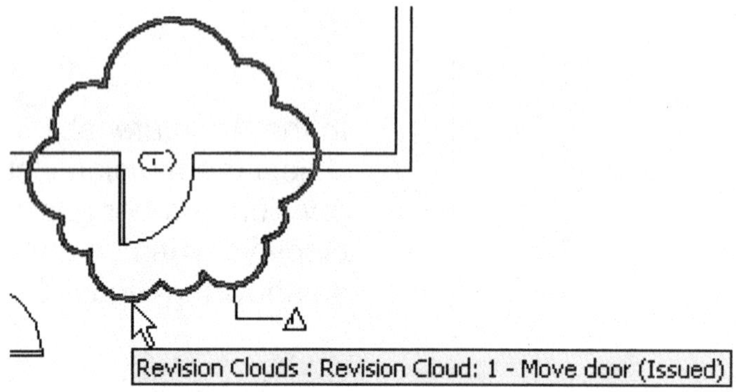

Figure B–42

How To: Issue Revisions

1. In the Sheet Issues/Revisions dialog box, in the row for the revision that you are issuing, type a name in the *Issued to* and *Issued by* fields, as required.
2. In the same row, select **Issued**.
3. Continue issuing any other revisions, as required.
4. Click **OK** to finish.

- Once **Issued** is selected, you cannot modify that revision in the Revisions dialog box or by moving the revision cloud(s). The tooltip on the cloud(s) note that it is **Issued**.

- You can unlock the revision by clearing the **Issued** option. Unlocking enables you to modify the revision after it has been locked.

B.9 Route Analysis

A typical part of a building design includes life safety diagrams that point out how people get out of a building. Codes frequently require specific distances to exits and so it is important to be able to record that information in the building model. The Path of Travel tool analyzes these distances between two points specified in plans, as shown in Figure B–43.

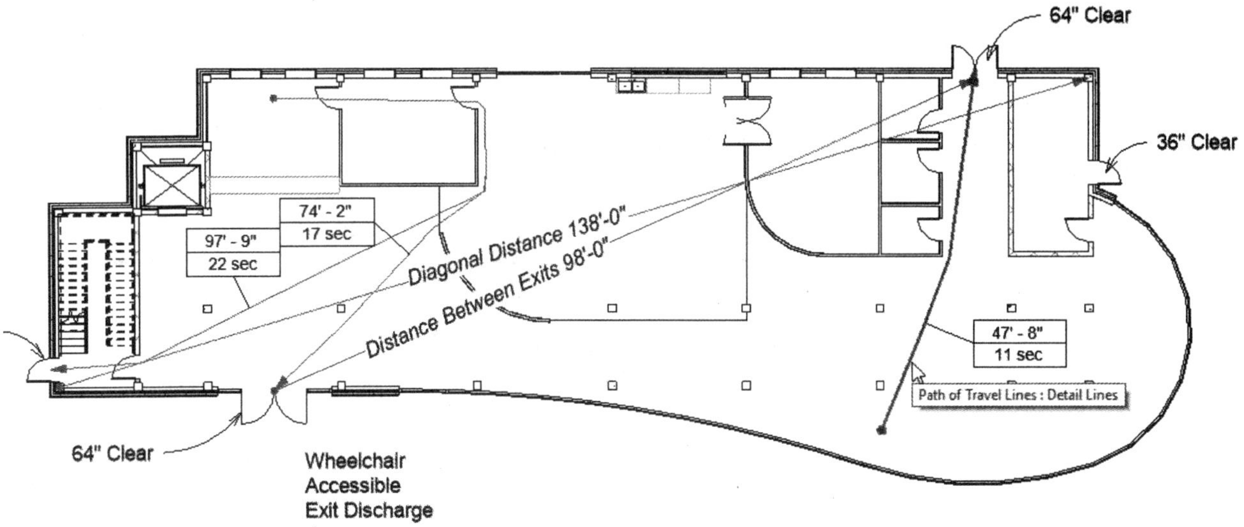

Figure B–43

- Path of Travel lines can be tagged and information included in schedules.

How To: Use Path of Travel Lines

1. In the *Analyze* tab> Route Analysis panel, click (Path of Travel).
2. Select the first point for the line of travel.
3. Select the second point for the line of travel.
4. Depending upon the Route Analysis Settings, the route is calculated.
5. Tag the travel lines as needed.

- Load the Path of Travel tag from the Revit Library in the *Annotations* folder.

Route Analysis Settings

You can specify categories of elements that impact the analysis and placement of travel lines. For example, in Figure B–24, only the door category is ignored in calculating the route, while, in Figure B–25, all categories are ignored, so you can calculate the distances between exits and the building diagonal.

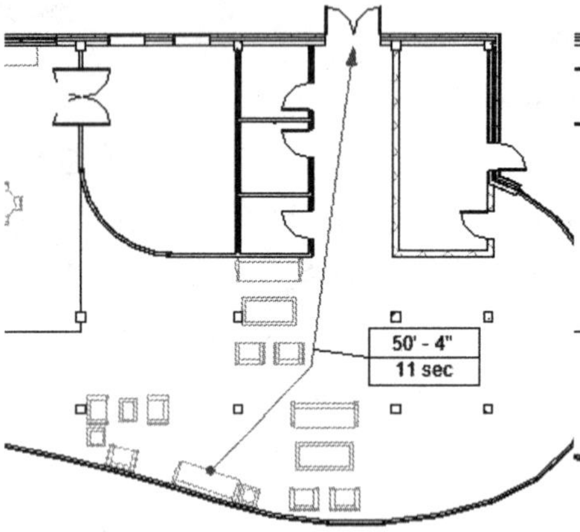

Figure B–44

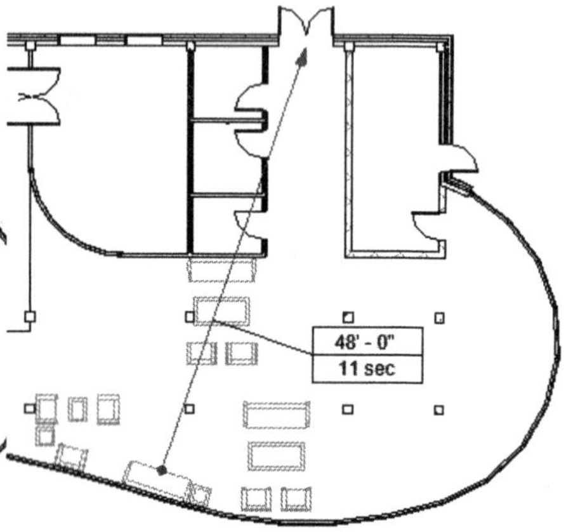

Figure B–45

- In the *Analyze* tab> Route Analysis panel title, click (Route Analysis Settings). In the Route Analysis Settings dialog box (as shown in Figure B–46), select the model categories you want to include or exclude.

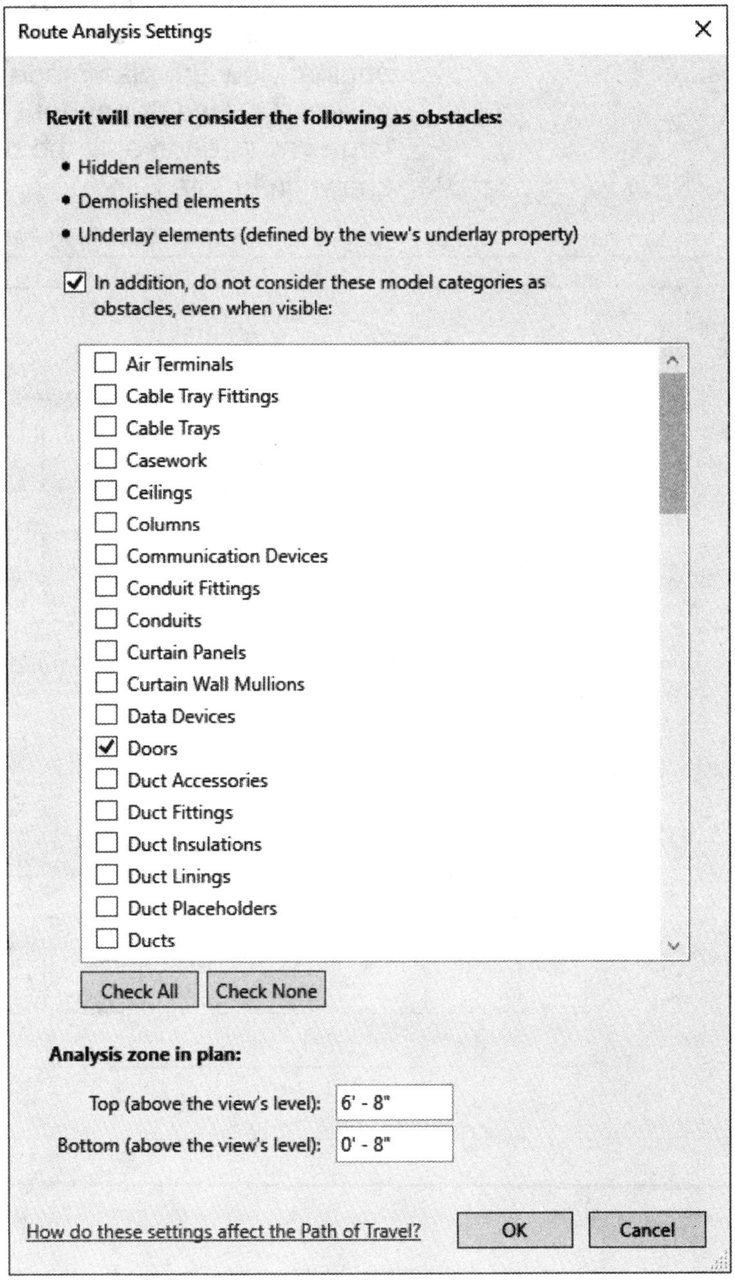

Figure B–46

B.10 Annotating Dependent Views

The **Duplicate as a Dependent** command creates a copy of the view and links it to the selected view. Changes made to the original view are also made in the dependent view and vice-versa. Use dependent views when the building model is so large you need to split the building up on separate sheets, as shown in Figure B–47.

Figure B–47

- Using one overall view with several dependent views makes it easier to see changes, such as *to the scale* or *detail level.*

- Dependent views display in the Project Browser under the top-level view, as shown in Figure B–48.

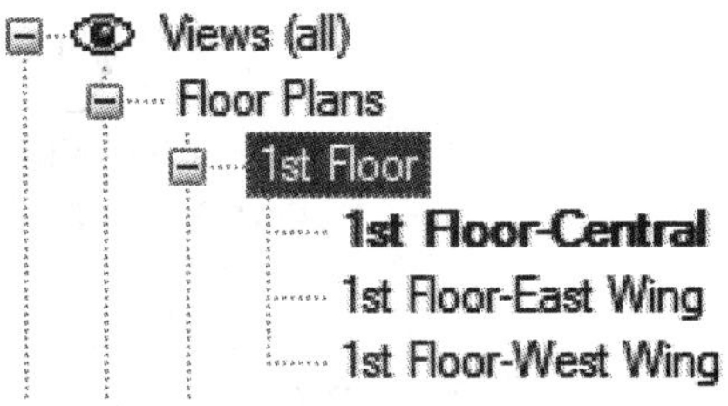

Figure B–48

How To: Duplicate Dependent Views

1. Select the view you want to use as the top-level view.
2. Right-click and select **Duplicate View>Duplicate as a Dependent**.
3. Rename the dependent views as required.
4. Modify the crop region of the dependent view to show the specified portion of the model.

- If you want to separate a dependent view from the original view, right-click on the dependent view and select **Convert to independent view**.

Annotating Views

To clarify and annotate dependent views, use **Matchlines** and **View References**, as shown in Figure B–49.

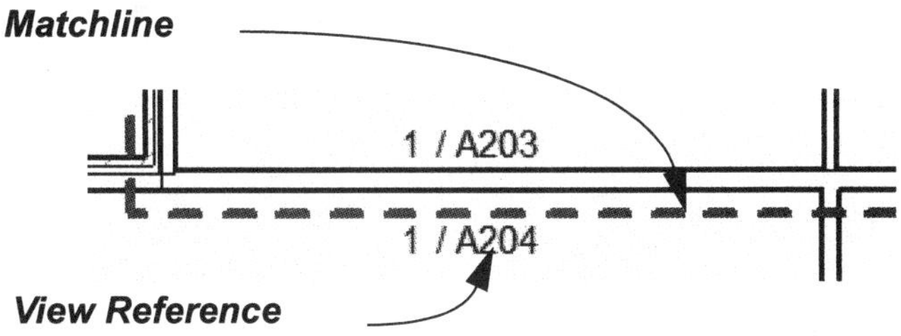

Figure B–49

- Sketch Matchlines in the primary view to specify where dependent views separate. They display in all related views and extend through all levels of the project by default.
- View References are special tags that display the sheet location of the dependent views.

How To: Add Matchlines

1. In the *View* tab>Sheet Composition panel, click (Matchline).
2. In the Draw panel, click (Line) and sketch the location of the matchline.
3. In the Matchline panel, click (Finish Edit Mode) when you are finished.

- To modify an existing matchline, select it and click (Edit Sketch) in the *Modify | Matchline* tab>Mode panel.
- To modify the color and linetype of Matchlines, in the *Manage* tab>Settings panel, click (Object Styles). In the Object Styles dialog box that opens, in the *Annotation Objects* tab, you can make changes to Matchline properties.

How To: Add View References

1. In the *View* tab>Sheet Composition panel or *Annotate* tab> Tag panel, click (View Reference).
2. In the *Modify | View Reference* tab>View Reference panel specify the *View Type* and *Target View*, as shown in Figure B–50.

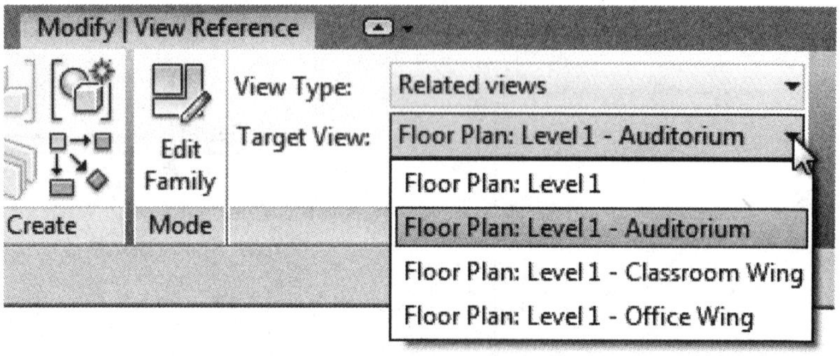

Figure B–50

3. Place the tag on the side of the matchline that corresponds to the target view.
4. Select another target view from the list and place the tag on the other side of the matchline.

5. The tags display as empty dashes until the views are placed onto sheets. They then update to include the detail and sheet number, as shown in Figure B–51.

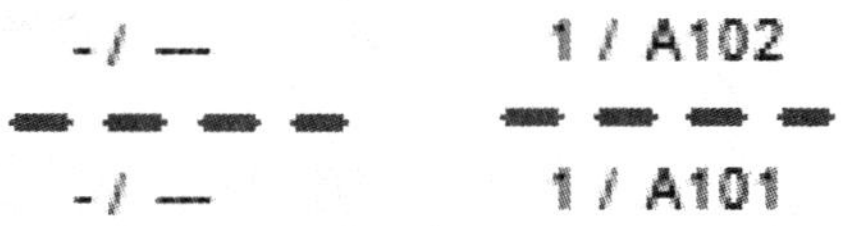

Figure B–51

- Double-click on the view reference to open the associated view.

- If only a label named **REF** displays when you place a view reference, it means you need to load and update the tag. The **View Reference.rfa** tag is located in the *Annotations* folder. Once you have the tag loaded, in the Type Selector, select one of the view references and, in Properties, click (Edit Type). Select the **View Reference** tag in the drop-down list, as shown in Figure B–52, and click **OK** to close the dialog box. The new tag displays.

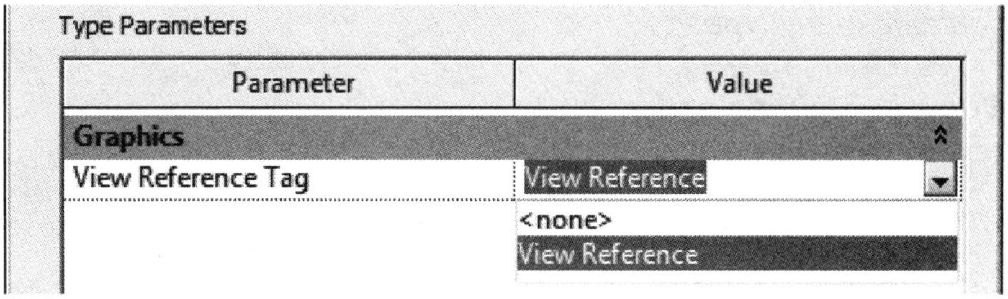

Figure B–52

B.11 Importing and Exporting Schedules

Schedules are views and can be copied into your project from other projects. Only the formatting information is copied; the information about individually scheduled items is not included. That information is automatically added by the project the schedule is copied into. You can also export the schedule information to be used in spreadsheets.

How To: Import Schedules

1. In the *Insert* tab>Import panel, expand (Insert from File) and click (Insert Views from File).
2. In the Open dialog box, locate the project file containing the schedule you want to use.
3. Select the schedules you want to import, as shown in Figure B–53.

If the referenced project contains many types of views, change Views: to ***Show schedules and reports only****.*

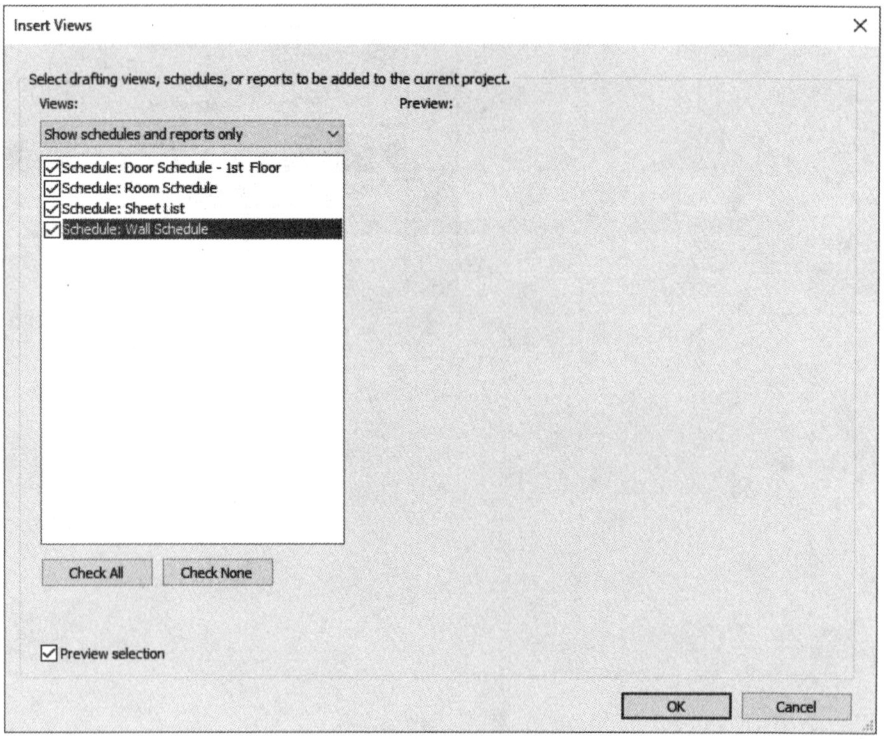

Figure B–53

4. Click **OK**.

How To: Export Schedule Information

1. Switch to the schedule view that you want to export.
2. In the File tab, click (Export)> (Reports)> (Schedule).
3. Select a location and name for the text file in the Export Schedule dialog box and click **Save**.
4. In the Export Schedule dialog box, set the options in the *Schedule appearance* and *Output options* areas that best suit your spreadsheet software, as shown in Figure B–54.

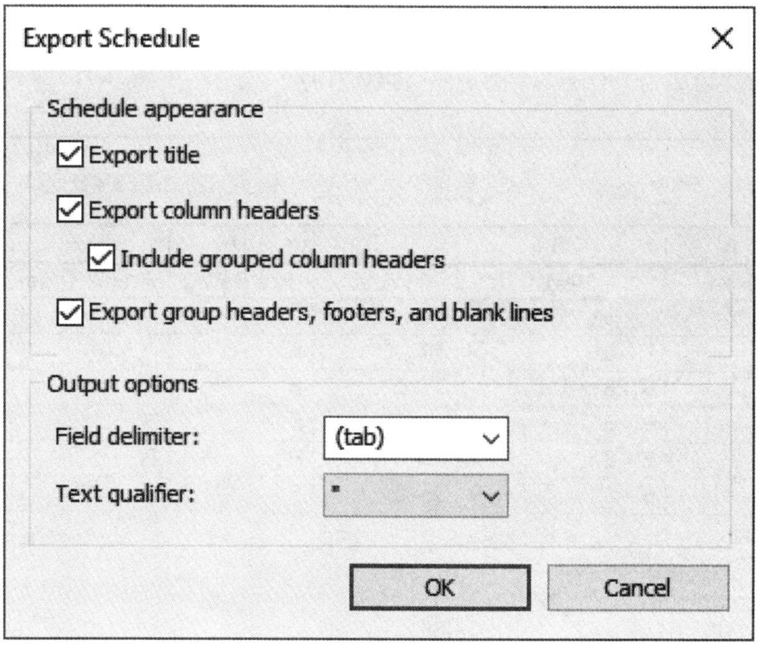

Figure B–54

5. Click **OK**. A new text file is created that you can open in a spreadsheet, as shown in Figure B–55.

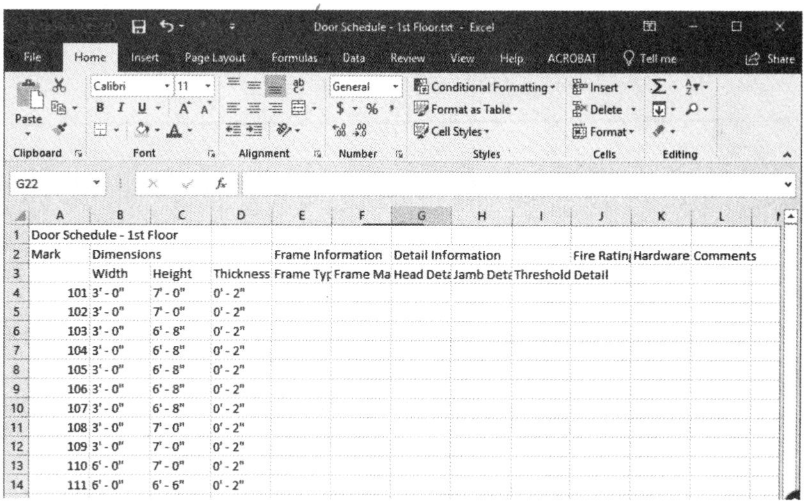

Figure B–55

B.12 Creating Building Component Schedules

A Building Component schedule is a table view of the type and instance parameters of a specific element. You can specify the parameters (fields) you want to include in the schedule. All of the parameters found in the type of element you are scheduling are available to use. For example, a door schedule (as shown in Figure B–56) can include instance parameters that are automatically filled in (such as the **Height** and **Width**) and type parameters that might need to have the information assigned in the schedule or element type (such as the **Fire Rating** and **Frame**).

<Door Schedule>

A	B	C	D	E	F	G	H
Mark	Height	Width	Fire Rating	Frame Type	Frame Material	Finish	Function
2	7' - 0"	10' - 0"	A	A	Steel	Brushed	Exterior
3	6' - 8"	3' - 0"	B	B	Wood	Paint	Interior
4	6' - 8"	3' - 0"	B	B	Wood	Paint	Interior
5	6' - 8"	3' - 0"	B	B	Wood	Paint	Interior
6	6' - 8"	3' - 0"	B	B	Wood	Paint	Interior

Figure B–56

How To: Create a Building Component Schedule

1. In the *View* tab>Create panel, expand (Schedules) and click (Schedule/Quantities) or in the Project Browser, right-click on the Schedule/Quantities node and select **New Schedule/Quantities**.
2. In the New Schedule dialog box, select the type of schedule you want to create from the *Category* list, as shown in Figure B–57.

In the Filter list drop-down list, you can specify the discipline(s) to show only the categories that you want to display.

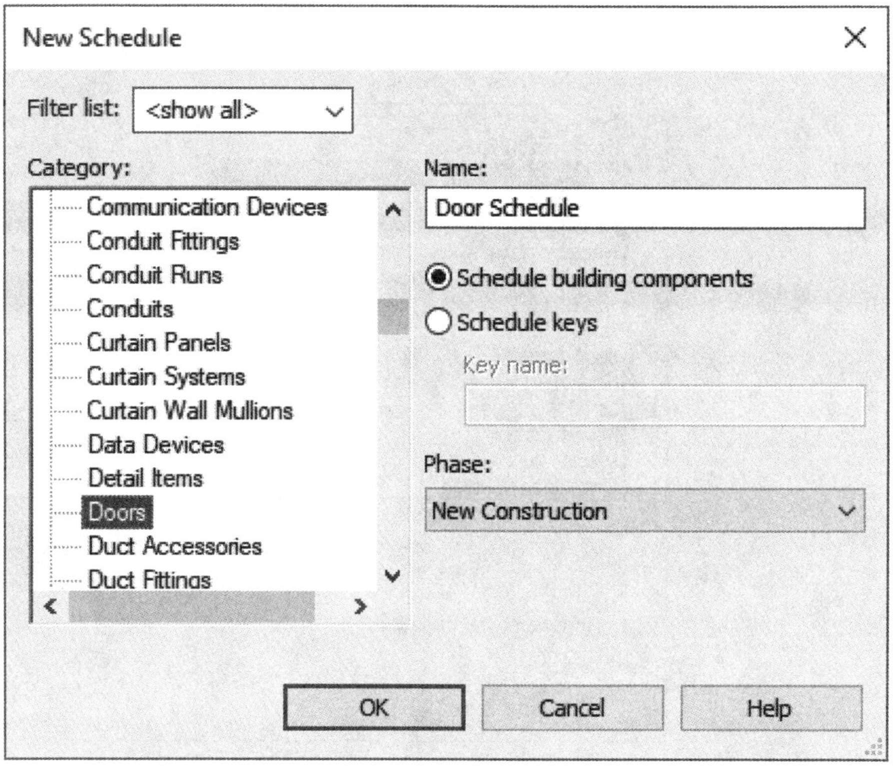

Figure B–57

3. Type a new *Name*, if the default does not suit.
4. Select **Schedule building components.**
5. Specify the *Phase* as required.
6. Click **OK**.
7. Fill out the information in the Schedule Properties dialog box. This includes the information in the *Fields*, *Filter*, *Sorting/Grouping*, *Formatting*, and *Appearance* tabs.
8. Once you have entering the schedule properties, click **OK**. A schedule report is created in its own view.

Schedule Properties – Fields Tab

In the *Fields* tab, you can select from a list of available fields and organize them in the order in which you want them to display in the schedule, as shown in Figure B–58.

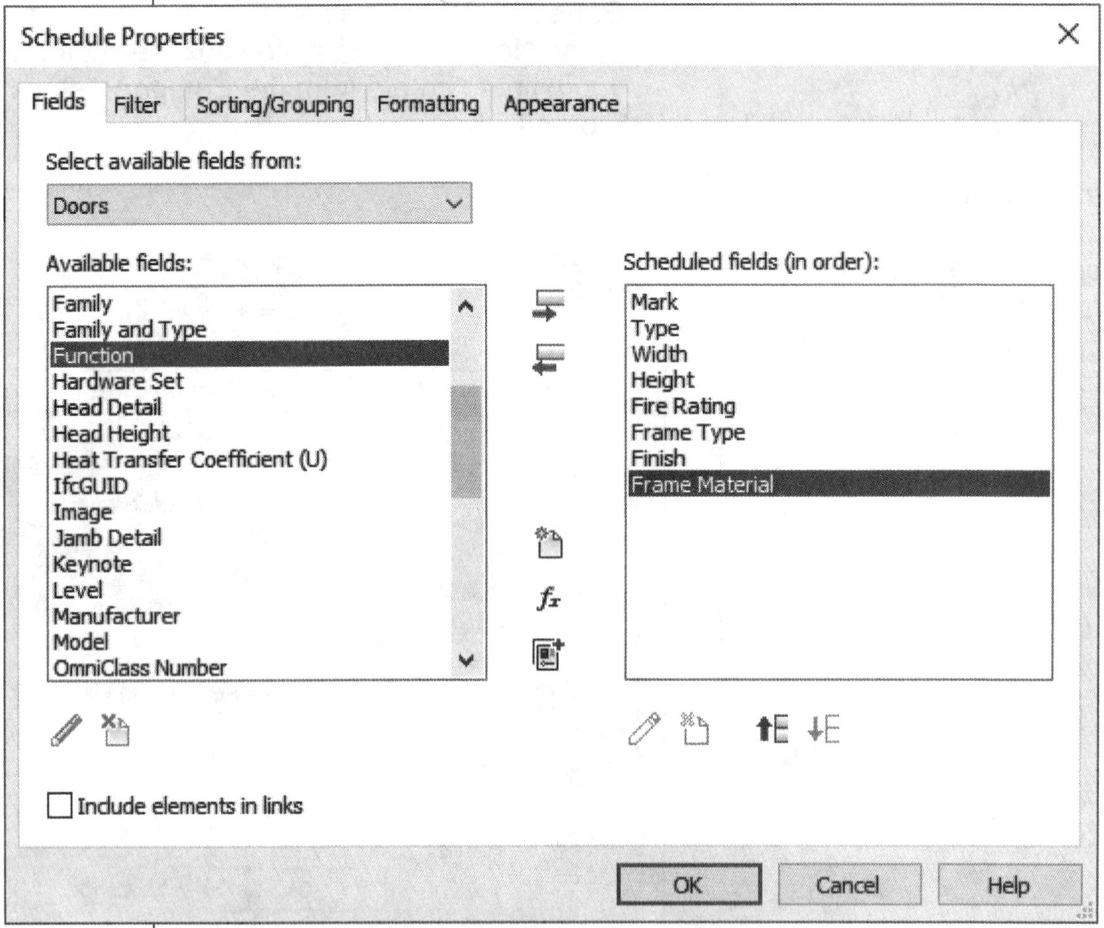

Figure B–58

How To: Fill out the Fields Tab

You can also double-click on a field to move it from the Available fields to the Scheduled fields area.

1. In the *Available fields* area, select one or more fields you want to add to the schedule and click (Add parameter(s)). The field(s) are placed in the *Scheduled fields (in order)* area.
2. Continue adding fields, as required.
   - Click (Remove parameter(s)) to move a field from the *Scheduled fields* area back to the *Available fields* area.
   - Use (Move parameter up) and (Move parameter down) to change the order of the scheduled fields.

Other Fields Tab Options

Select available fields from	Enables you to select additional category fields for the specified schedule. The available list of fields depends on the original category of the schedule. Typically, they include room information.
Include elements in links	Includes elements that are in files linked to the current project, so that their elements can be included in the schedule.
(New parameter)	Adds a new field according to your specification. New fields can be placed by instance or by type.
fx **(Add Calculated parameter)**	Enables you to create a field that uses a formula based on other fields.
(Combine parameters)	Enables you to combine two or more parameters in one column.You can put any fields together even if they are used in another column.
(Edit parameter)	Enables you to edit custom fields. This is grayed out if you select a standard field.
(Delete parameter)	Deletes selected custom fields. This is grayed out if you select a standard field.

Schedule Properties – Filter Tab

In the *Filter* tab, you can set up filters so that only elements meeting specific criteria are included in the schedule. For example, you might only want to show information for one level, as shown in Figure B–59. You can create filters for up to eight values. All values must be satisfied for the elements to display.

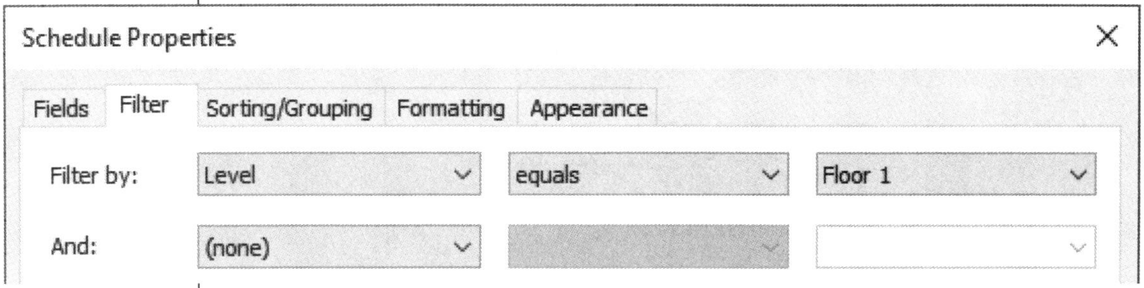

Figure B–59

- The parameter you want to use as a filter must be included in the schedule. You can hide the parameter once you have completed the schedule, if required.

Filter by	Specifies the field to filter. Not all fields are available to be filtered.
Condition	Specifies the condition that must be met. This includes options such as **equal**, **not equal**, **greater than**, and **less than**.
Value	Specifies the value of the element to be filtered. You can select from a drop-down list of appropriate values. For example, if you set ***Filter By*** to **Level**, it displays the list of levels in the project.

Schedule Properties – Sorting/Grouping Tab

In the *Sorting/Grouping* tab, you can set how you want the information to be sorted, as shown in Figure B–60. For example, you can sort by **Mark** (number) and then **Type**.

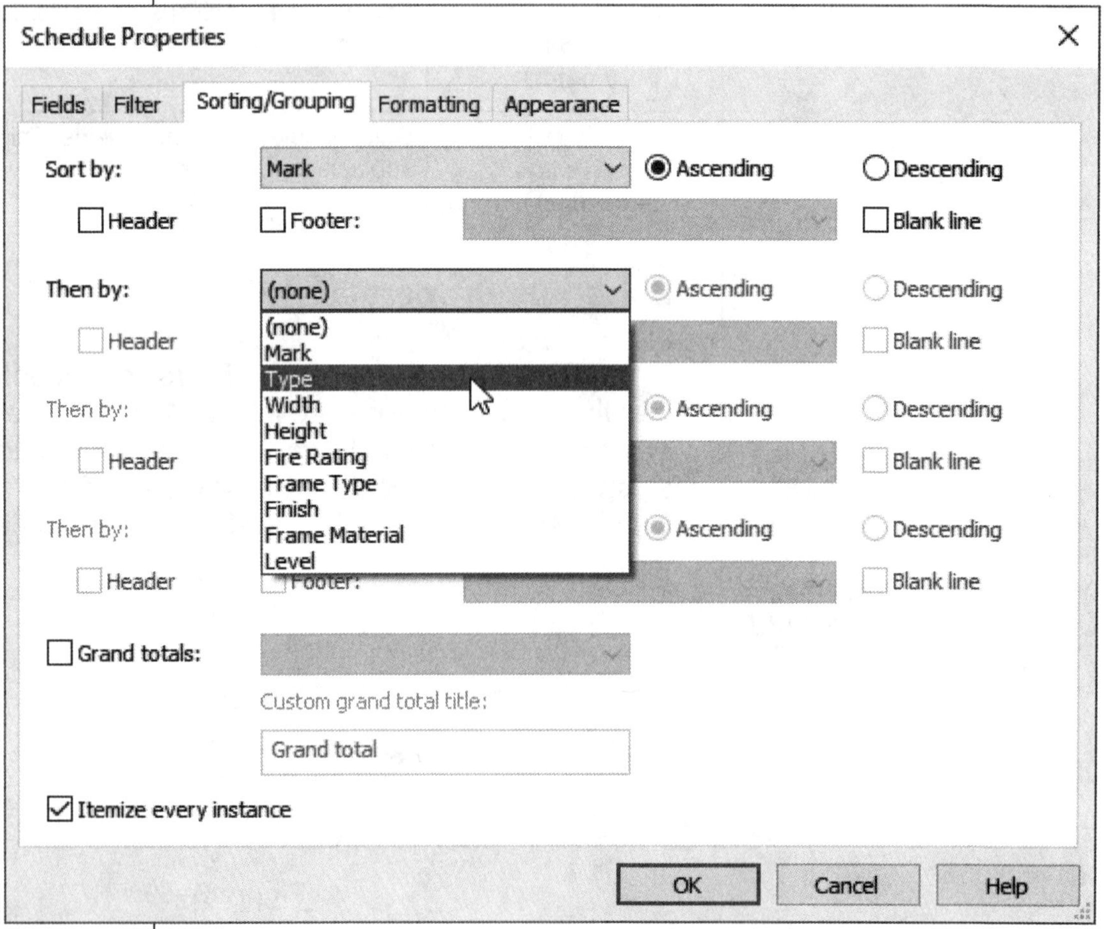

Figure B–60

Sort by	Enables you to select the field(s) you want to sort by. You can select up to four levels of sorting.
Ascending/ Descending	Sorts fields in **Ascending** or **Descending** order.
Header/ Footer	Enables you to group similar information and separate it by a **Header** with a title and/or a **Footer** with quantity information.
Blank line	Adds a blank line between groups.
Grand totals	Selects which totals to display for the entire schedule. You can specify a name to display in the schedule for the Grand total.
Itemize every instance	If selected, displays each instance of the element in the schedule. If not selected, displays only one instance of each type, as shown below.

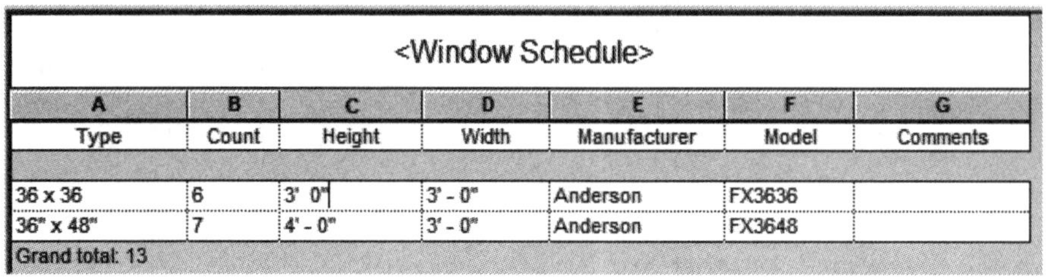

<Window Schedule>

A	B	C	D	E	F	G
Type	Count	Height	Width	Manufacturer	Model	Comments
36 x 36	6	3' 0"	3' - 0"	Anderson	FX3636	
36" x 48"	7	4' - 0"	3' - 0"	Anderson	FX3648	
Grand total: 13						

Schedule Properties – Formatting Tab

In the *Formatting* tab, you can control how the headers of each field display, as shown in Figure B–61.

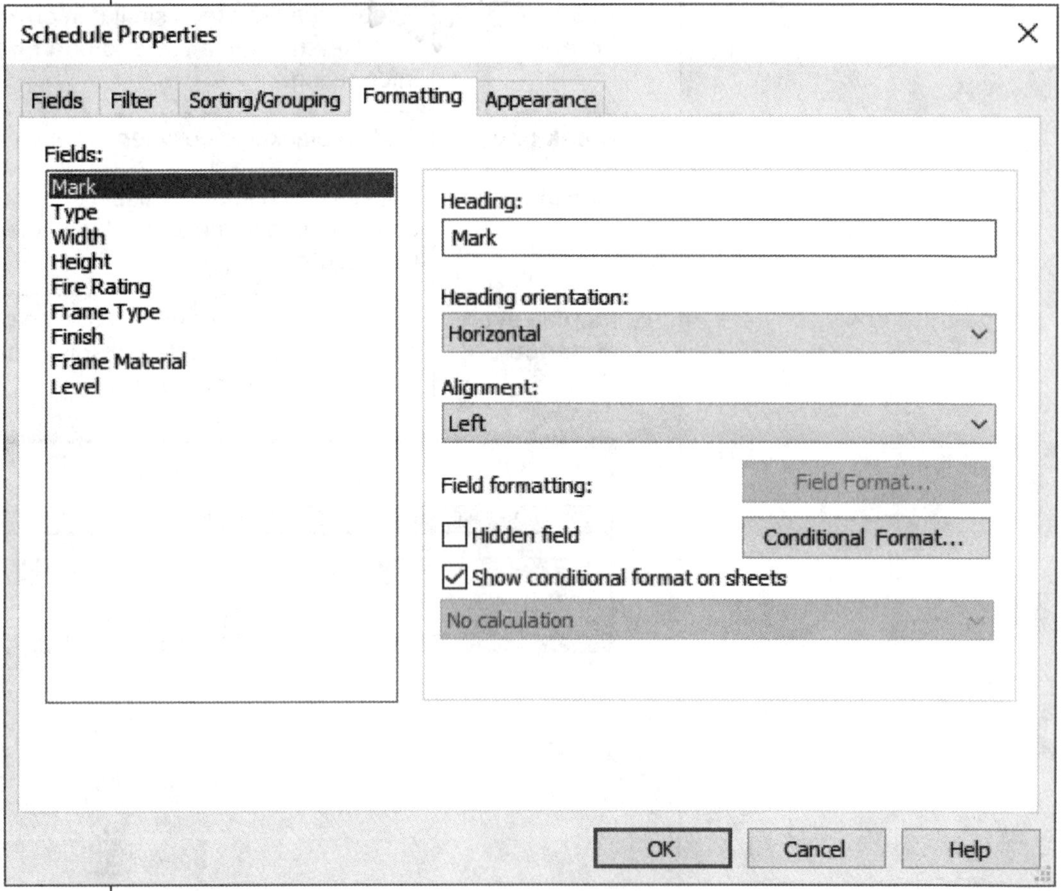

Figure B–61

Fields	Enables you to select the field for which you want to modify the formatting.
Heading	Enables you to change the heading of the field if you want it to be different from the field name. For example, you might want to replace **Mark** (a generic name) with the more specific **Door Number** in a door schedule.
Heading orientation	Enables you to set the heading on sheets to **Horizontal** or **Vertical**. This does not impact the schedule view.
Alignment	Aligns the text in rows under the heading to be **Left**, **Right**, or **Center**.
Field Format...	Sets the units format for the length, area, volume, angle, or number field. By default, this is set to use the project settings.
Conditional Format...	Sets up the schedule to display visual feedback based on the conditions listed.
Hidden field	Enables you to hide a field. For example, you might want to use a field for sorting purposes, but not have it display in the schedule. You can also modify this option in the schedule view later.
Show conditional format on sheets	Select if you want the color code set up in the Conditional Format dialog box to display on sheets.
Calculation options	Select the type of calculation you want to use. All values in a field are: • **Standard** - Calculated separately. • **Calculate totals** - Added together. • **Calculate minimum** - Reviewed and only the smallest amount is displayed. • **Calculate maximum** - Reviewed and only the largest amount is displayed. • **Calculate minimum and maximum** - Reviewed and both the smallest and largest amounts are displayed. • This is often used with rebar sets.

Schedule Properties – Appearance Tab

In the *Appearance* tab, you can set the text style and grid options for a schedule, as shown in Figure B–62.

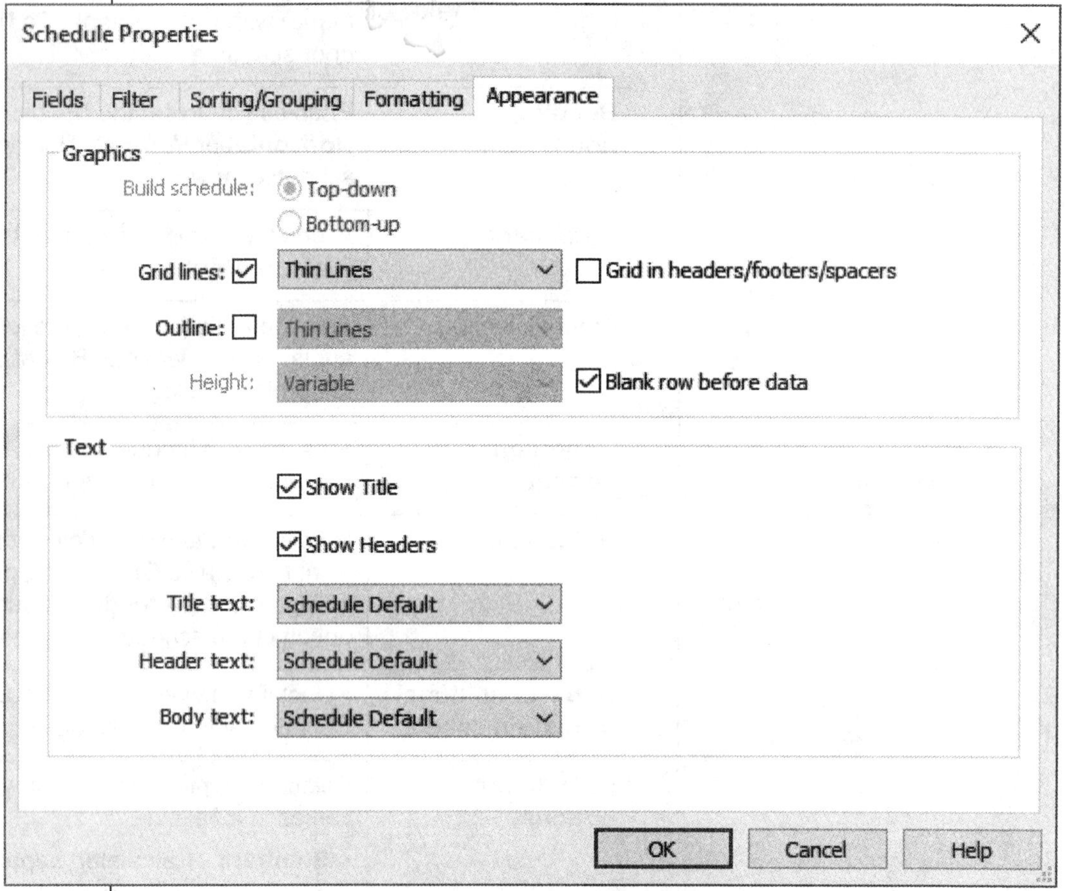

Figure B–62

Grid lines	Displays lines between each instance listed and around the outside of the schedule. Select the style of lines from the drop-down list; this controls all lines for the schedule, unless modified.
Grid in headers/ footers/spacers	Extends the vertical grid lines between the columns.
Outline	Specify a different line type for the outline of the schedule.
Blank row before data	Select this option if you want a blank row to be displayed before the data begins in the schedule.
Show Title/Show Headers	Select these options to include the text in the schedule.
Title text/Header text/Body Text	Select the text style for the title, header, and body text.

Schedule Properties

Schedule views have properties including the *View Name*, *Phases* and methods of returning to the Schedule Properties dialog box as shown in Figure B–63. In the *Other* area, select the button next to the tab that you want to open in the Schedule Properties dialog box. In the dialog box, you can switch from tab to tab and make any required changes to the overall schedule.

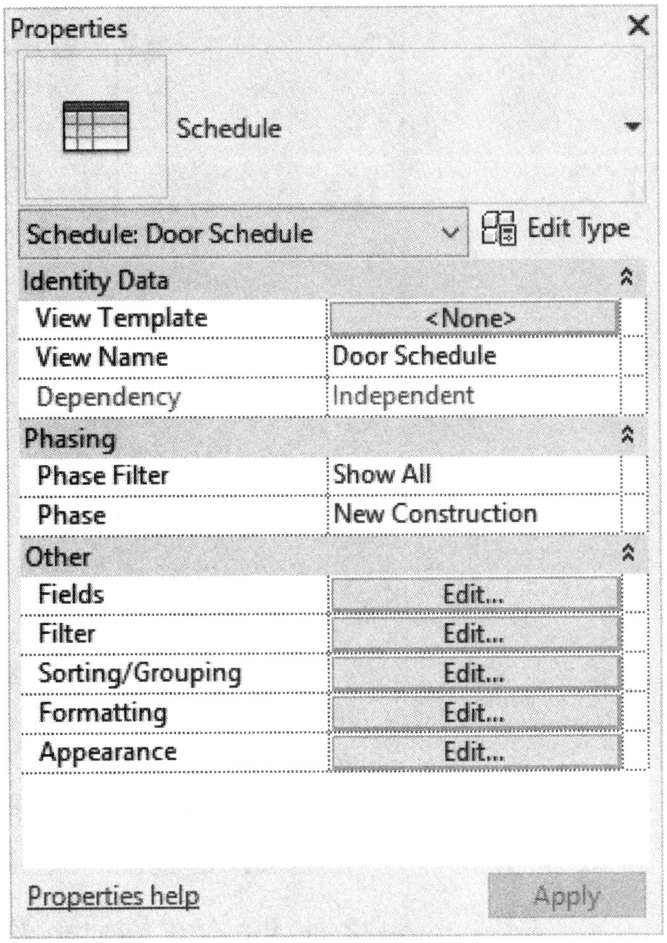

Figure B–63

B.13 Creating a Repeating Detail

Repeating detail components are very useful when working on complex details, such as those that include a brick wall. You can also create a repeating detail using any detail component, such as the glass block shown in Figure B–64.

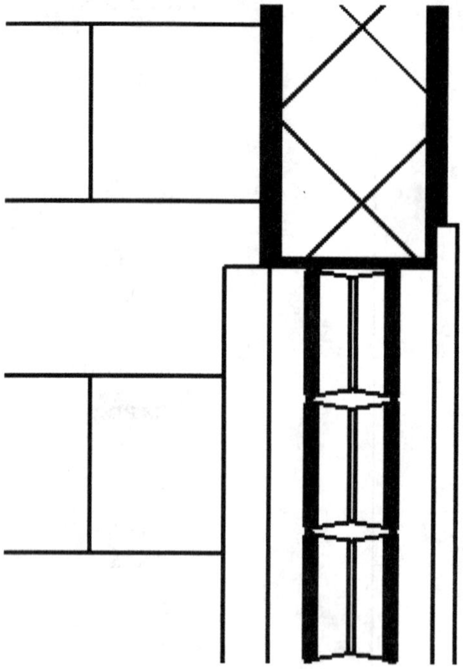

Figure B–64

How To: Create a Repeating Detail

1. Load the detail component you want to use.
2. In the *Annotate* tab>Detail panel, expand (Component) and click (Repeating Detail Component).
3. In Properties, click (Edit Type).
4. In the Type Properties dialog box, click **Duplicate....** Enter a name.
5. Set the *Detail* parameter. This is the component name.

6. Fill out the rest of the parameters, as shown in Figure B–65.

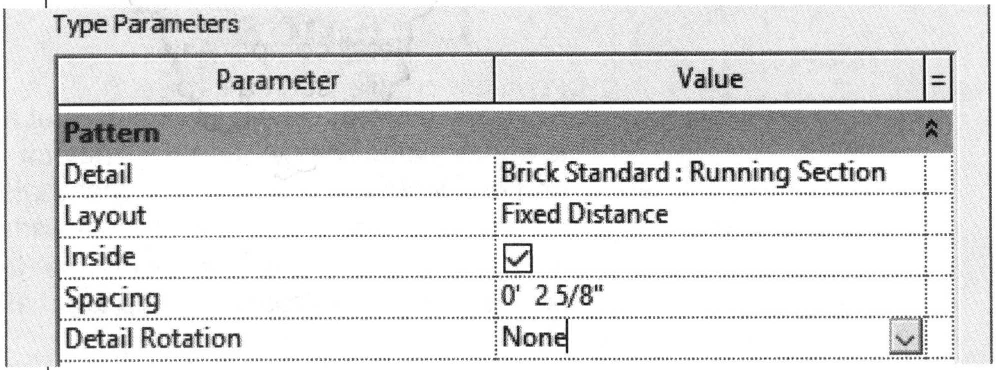

Figure B–65

7. Set the *Layout* to **Fill Available Space**, **Fixed Distance**, **Fixed Number**, or **Maximum Spacing**. Select **Inside** if you want all components to be within the specified distance or line. Leaving this option clear causes the first component to start before the first point.
8. Set the *Spacing* between components if you are using **Fixed Distance** or **Maximum Spacing**.
9. Set the *Detail Rotation* as required, and close the dialog box.

B.14 Keynoting and Keynote Legends

Keynotes are special kinds of tags that apply specific numbering to various elements in a detail. They can be used on all model and detail elements, as well as materials.Using keynotes requires less room on a view than standard text notes, as shown in Figure B–66. The full explanation of the note is shown in a corresponding *keynote legend* placed elsewhere in the sheet or sheet set.

By default, the Autodesk Revit software uses the CSI master format system of keynote designations.

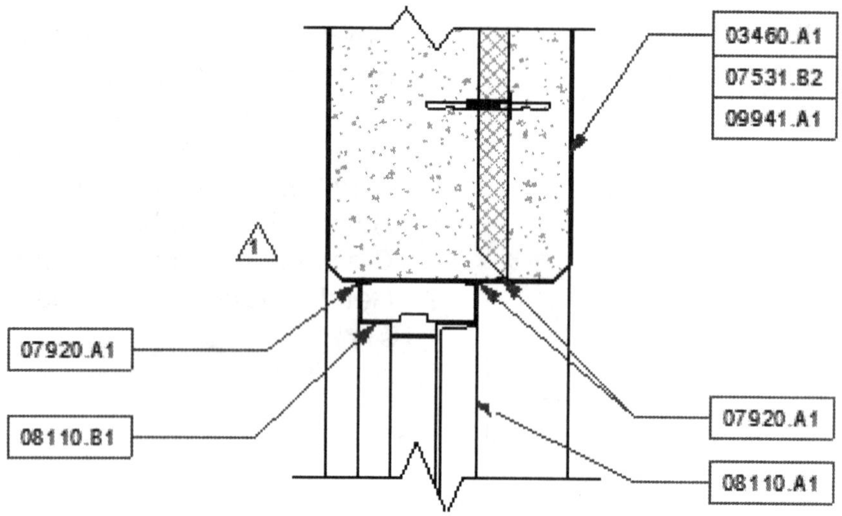

Figure B–66

- Keynote tags are found in the Library in the *Annotations* folder and must be loaded into a project before you can apply them.

There are three types of keynote tags:

- **Element:** Used to tag elements, such as a door, wall, or detail components.
- **Material:** Used for the material assigned to a component or applied onto a surface.
- **User:** A keynote that must first be developed in a keynote table.

How To: Place a Keynote

1. In the *Annotate* tab>Tag panel, expand (Keynote) and click (Element Keynote), (Material Keynote), or (User Keynote).
2. Move the cursor over the element you want to keynote and select it.
3. If an element has keynote information assigned to it, the keynote is automatically applied. If it is not assigned, the Keynotes dialog box opens, as shown in Figure B–67.

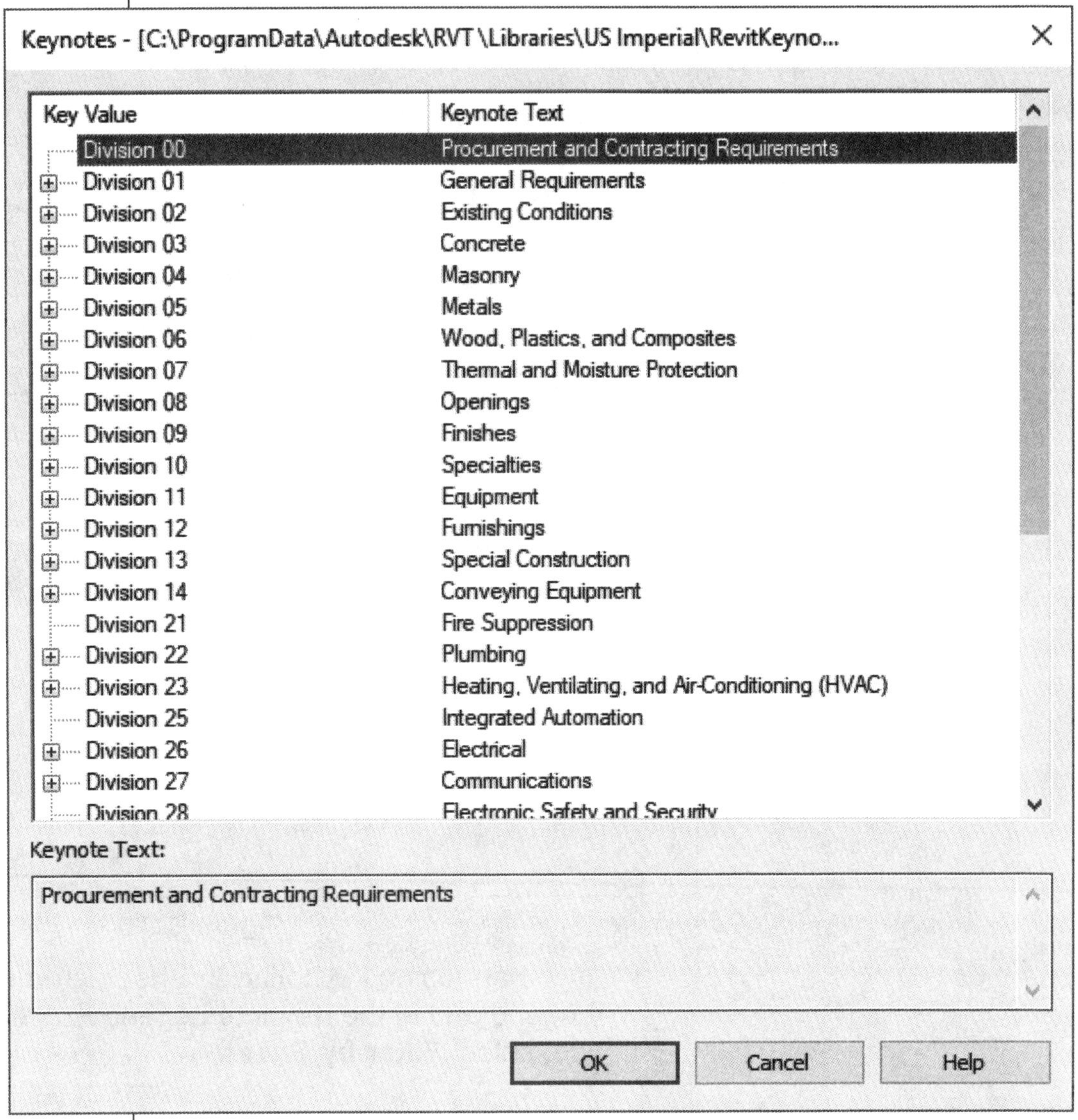

Figure B–67

4. Select the keynote you need from the list of divisions and click **OK**.

The keynote remembers the leader settings from the last time it was used.

- The options for keynotes are the same as for other tags, including orientation and leaders, as shown in Figure B–68.

Figure B–68

Hint: Setting the Keynote Numbering Method

Keynotes can be listed by the full keynote number or by sheet, as shown in Figure B–69. Only one method can be used at a time in a project, but you can change between the two methods at any time in the project.

1. In the *Annotate* tab>Tag panel, expand (Keynote) and click (Keynoting Settings).

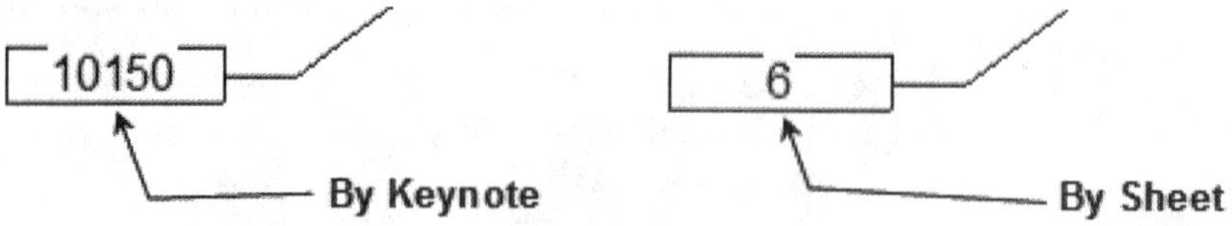

Figure B–69

2. In the Keynoting Settings dialog box, specify the *Keynote Table* information and the *Numbering Method*, as shown in Figure B–70.

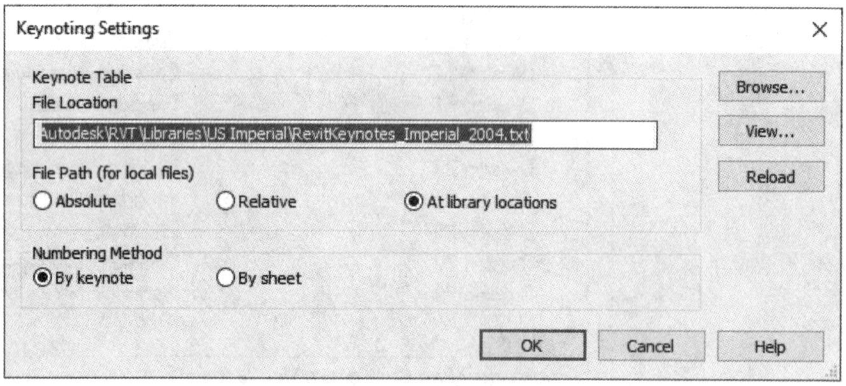

Figure B–70

- If you are using keynoting by sheet, create the Keynote Legend and in the Keynote Legend Properties, in the *Filter* tab, select **Filter by Sheet.**

- Keynotes are stored in a keynote table (a text file), as shown in Figure B–71. Any updates made to the keynote table are reflected in the project after it is closed and then re-opened.

RevitKeynotes_Imperial - Notepad

File Edit Format View Help

```
01000    Division 01 - General Requirements
02000    Division 02 - Sitework
03000    Division 03 - Concrete
04000    Division 04 - Masonry
05000    Division 05 - Metals
06000    Division 06 - Wood and Plastics
07000    Division 07 - Thermal and Moisture
08000    Division 08 - Doors and Windows
09000    Division 09 - Finishes
10000    Division 10 - Specialties
11000    Division 11 - Equipment
12000    Division 12 - Furnishings
13000    Division 13 - Special Construction
14000    Division 14 - Conveying
```

Figure B–71

Keynote Legends

A keynote legend is different from a standard legend.

A keynote legend is a table containing the information stored in the keynote that is placed on a sheet, as shown in Figure B–72. In the Autodesk Revit software, it is created in a similar way to schedules.

Keynote Legend	
Key Value	**Keynote Text**
04050	Basic Masonry Materials and Methods
05050	Basic Metal Materials and Methods
05100	Structural Metal Framing
08110.G1	2 3/4" Single Rabbet HM Door Frame
08210	Wood Doors
10150	Compartments and Cubicals
12400	Furnishings and Accessories

Figure B–72

How To: Create a Keynote Legend

1. In the *View* tab>Create panel, expand (Legends) and click (Keynote Legend).
2. Type a name in the New Keynote Legend dialog box and click **OK**.

3. The Keynote Legend Properties dialog box typically only displays two scheduled fields, which are already set up for you, as shown in Figure B–73.

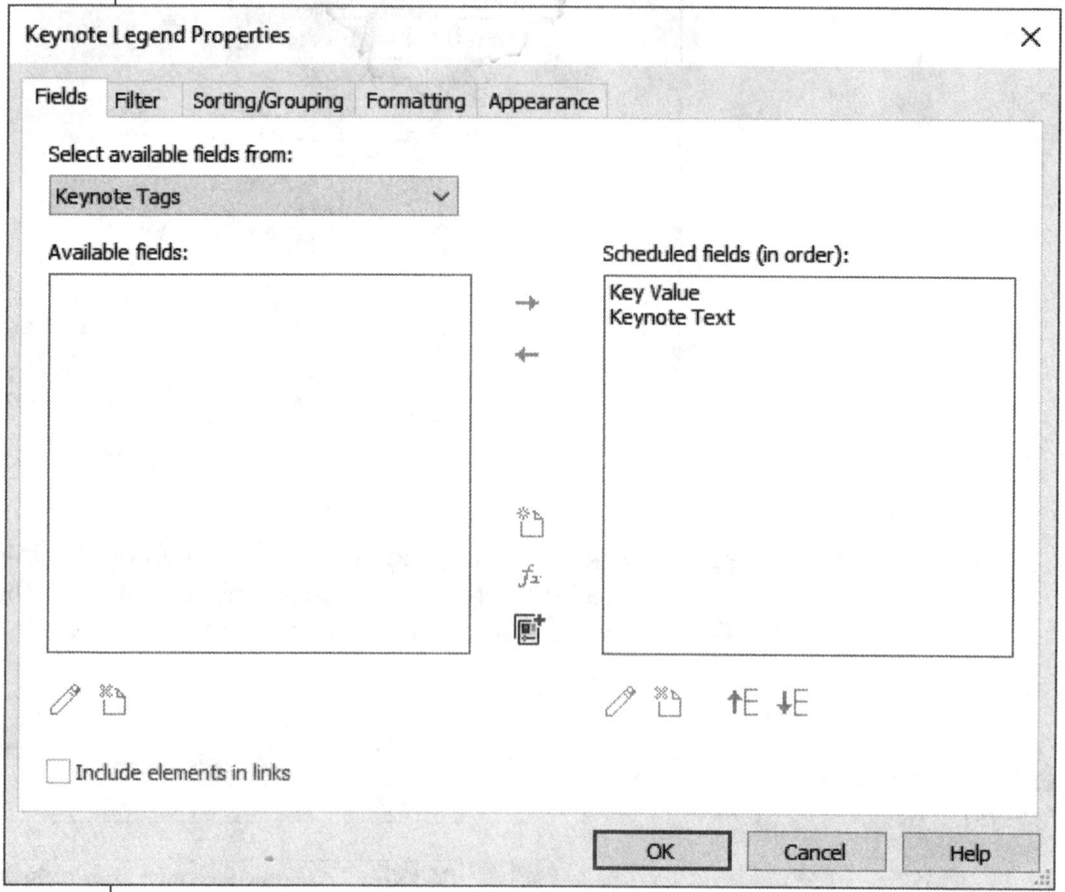

Figure B–73

4. In the other tabs, set up the format of the table as required.
5. Click **OK** to create the keynote legend.
6. When you are ready to place a keynote legend, drag it from the Project Browser onto the sheet. You can manipulate it in the same way, similar to modifying other schedules.

- As you add keynotes to the project, they are added to the keynote legend, as shown in Figure B–74.

Keynote Legend	
Key Value	Keynote Text
04 21 00.A	Standard Brick - 3/8" Joint
04 21 00.A	Roman Brick - 3/8" Joint
04 21 00.A	Triple Brick - 1/2" Joint
05 12 00.A	L9x4x0.625

Keynote Legend	
Key Value	Keynote Text
04 21 00.A	Standard Brick - 3/8" Joint
04 21 00.A	Roman Brick - 3/8" Joint
04 21 00.A	Triple Brick - 1/2" Joint
05 12 00.A	L9x4x0.625
06 01 10.A	1x8R
09 30 13.A	Ceramic Tile

Figure B–74

Command Summary

Button	Command	Location
Analysis		
	Path of Travel	• **Ribbon:** *Analyze* tab>Route Analysis panel
Annotations		
	Matchline	• **Ribbon:** *View* tab>Sheet Composition panel
	View Reference	• **Ribbon:** *View* tab>Sheet Composition panel or *Annotate* tab>Tag panel
Curtain Walls		
	Edit Type	• **Properties** (with a Curtain Wall type selected)
Details		
	Edit Type	• **Properties** (with a Repeating Detail element selected)
Dormers		
	Dormer	• **Ribbon:** *Architecture* tab>Opening panel
Revisions		
	Revision Cloud	• **Ribbon:** *Annotate* tab>Detail panel
	Sheet Issues/ Revisions	• **Ribbon:** *Manage* tab>Settings panel> expand Additional Settings
Schedules		
	Insert Views from File	• **Ribbon**: *Insert* tab>expand **Insert from File**
n/a	**Schedule (Export)**	• **File tab:** expand Export> Reports>Schedule
	Schedule/ Quantities	• **Ribbon:** *View* tab>Create panel> expand Schedules • **Project Browser:** right-click on Schedule/Quantities node> New Schedule/Quantities...
Selection Sets		
	Edit Selection	• **Ribbon:** *Modify* | *Multi-Select* tab> Selection panel
	Load Selection	• **Ribbon:** *Modify* | *Multi-Select* tab> Selection panel

	**Save Selection**	• **Ribbon:** *Modify* | *Multi-Select* tab>Selection panel
	**Add to Selection**	• **Ribbon:** *Edit Selection Set* tab>Edit Selection panel
	**Remove from Selection**	• **Ribbon:** *Edit Selection Set* tab>Edit Selection panel
Sweeps and Reveals		
	**Floor: Slab Edge**	• **Ribbon:** *Architecture* tab>Build panel or *Structure* tab>Structure panel> expand Floor
	**Roof: Fascia**	• **Ribbon:** *Architecture* tab>Build panel> expand Roof
	**Roof: Gutter**	• **Ribbon:** *Architecture* tab>Build panel> expand Roof
	**Wall: Reveal**	• **Ribbon:** *Architecture* tab>Build panel or *Structure* tab>Structure panel> expand Wall
	**Wall: Sweep**	• **Ribbon:** *Architecture* tab>Build panel or *Structure* tab>Structure panel> expand Wall
Views		
	**Cut Profile**	• **Ribbon:** *View* tab>Graphics panel
	**Insert Views from File**	• **Ribbon:** *Insert* tab>Import panel> expand Insert from File
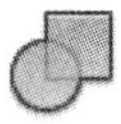	**Join Geometry**	• **Ribbon:** *Modify* tab>Geometry panel> expand Join
	**Line Styles**	• **Ribbon:** *Manage* tab>Settings panel> expand Additional Settings
	**Linework**	• **Ribbon:** *Modify* tab>View panel • **Shortcut:** LW
	**Paint**	• **Ribbon:** *Modify* tab>Geometry panel
	**Pick New Host**	• **Ribbon:** *Modify* | *varies* tab>Host panel
	**Split Face**	• **Ribbon:** *Modify* tab>Geometry panel
	**Unjoin Geometry**	• **Ribbon:** *Modify* tab>Geometry panel> expand Join
	**Wall Joins**	• **Ribbon:** *Modify* tab>Geometry panel

Certification Exam Objectives

The following table will help you to locate the exam objectives in the chapters of the Autodesk® Revit® 2020 Architecture guides to help you prepare for the Autodesk Revit Architecture Certified Professional exam.

Exam Topic	Exam Objective	Learning Guide	Chapter & Section(s)
	Copy and monitor elements in a linked file	• Revit Collaboration Tools	• 2.3
	Use worksharing	• Revit Collaboration Tools	• 4.1, 4.2, 4.3
	Import DWG and image files	• Revit Fundamentals for Architecture	• 3.1
		• Revit Collaboration Tools	• 3.1, 3.2, 3.3
	Use Worksharing Visualization	• Revit Collaboration Tools	• 4.4
	Assess review warnings in Revit	• Revit Fundamentals for Architecture	• 12.1

Exam Topic	Exam Objective	Learning Guide	Chapter & Section(s)
Documentation			
	Create and modify filled regions	• Revit Fundamentals for Architecture	• 16.3
	Place detail components and repeating details	• Revit Fundamentals for Architecture	• 16.2
	Tag elements (doors, windows, etc.) by category	• Revit Fundamentals for Architecture	• 15.1
	Use dimension strings	• Revit Fundamentals for Architecture	• 14.1
	Set the colors used in a color scheme legend	• Revit Architecture: Conceptual Design and Visualization	• 2.3
	Work with phases	• Revit Collaboration Tools	• 1.1
Elements and Families			
	Change elements within a curtain wall (grids, panels, mullions	• Revit Fundamentals for Architecture	• 6.2, 6.3, 6.4
	Create compound walls	• Revit BIM Management	• 3.1
	Create a stacked wall	• Revit BIM Management	• 3.3
	Differentiate system and component families	• Revit BIM Management	• 3.1 • 4.1
	Work with family parameters	• Revit BIM Management	• 4.2
	Create a new family type	• Revit Fundamentals for Architecture	• 5.3
		• Revit BIM Management	• 4.4
	Use family creation procedures	• Revit BIM Management	• 4.1 to 4.4

Exam Topic	Exam Objective	Learning Guide	Chapter & Section(s)
Modeling			
	Create a building pad	• Revit Architecture: Site and Site Designer	• 1.2
	Define floor for a mass	• Revit Architecture: Conceptual Design and Visualization	• 1.7
	Create a stair with a landing	• Revit Fundamentals for Architecture	• 12.1
	Create elements such as floors, ceilings, or roofs	• Revit Fundamentals for Architecture	• 9.1 • 10.1 • 11.2, 11.4
	Generate a toposurface	• Revit Architecture: Site and Site Designer	• 1.1
	Model railings	• Revit Fundamentals for Architecture	• 12.3
	Edit a model element's material (door, window, furniture)	• Revit Fundamentals for Architecture	• 5.3 • B.4
	Change a generic floor / ceiling / roof to a specific type	• Revit Fundamentals for Architecture	• 9.1 • 10.1 • 11.2
	Attach walls to a roof or ceiling	• Revit Fundamentals for Architecture	• 11.2
	Edit room-aware families	• Revit BIM Management	• 5.1
Views			
	Define element properties in a schedule	• Revit Fundamentals for Architecture	• 15.3
	Control visibility	• Revit Fundamentals for Architecture	• 7.1
	Use levels	• Revit Fundamentals for Architecture	• 3.3
	Create a duplicate view for a plan, section, elevation, drafting view, etc.	• Revit Fundamentals for Architecture	• 7.2
	Create and manage legends	• Revit Fundamentals for Architecture	• 14.4
	Manage view position on sheets	• Revit Fundamentals for Architecture	• 13.2
	Organize and sort items in a schedule	• Revit Fundamentals for Architecture	• B.12
		• Revit BIM Management	• 2.2

Index

S

T